WILEY

IFRS

Practical Implementation Guide and Workbook

THIRD EDITION

WILEY

IFRS

Practical Implementation Guide and Workbook

THIRD EDITION

Abbas Ali Mirza   Graham J. Holt

JOHN WILEY & SONS, INC.

Contents

FOREWORD

TO THE FIRST EDITION

by the Chairman of IASB

I and my fellow Board members at the International Accounting Standards Board (IASB) are committed to developing high quality, understandable, and enforceable global accounting standards that meet the demands for comparable and transparent information in the world's capital markets. Recently we completed a work program to develop and issue a stable platform of such standards. Those standards, the International Financial Reporting Standards (IFRS), are now being implemented in a large number of countries around the world. This is a major achievement on the road towards the global acceptance of a single set of accounting standards.

The responsibility for achieving high quality financial reporting, however, does not rest solely with IASB. Our role is limited to providing the set of standards that entities should apply to achieve high quality, comparable, and transparent financial reporting. For IFRS to be properly understood, implemented, and applied in practice, education and training of all relevant parties—including financial statement preparers, auditors, regulators, financial analysts, and other users of financial statements as well as accounting students—is essential.

This book should be a helpful tool in this regard. The approach of the book is to discuss core concepts and other key elements of the standards and to provide training material in the form of worked case studies and questions to support successful learning of the material. Consequently, the book should be useful for students who prepare for professional exams and for financial statement preparers, auditors, regulators, financial analysts, and other users of financial statements who in their work need to be familiar with the standards. The book should help practitioners and students alike understand, implement, and apply the key elements of the standards.

Sir David Tweedie
Chairman of IASB
December 2005

FOREWORD
TO THE FIRST EDITION
by the Secretary General of IOSCO

In recent years much has been written about International Financial Reporting Standards (IFRS) so it is opportune that a publication such as this would be released at this time particularly since this initiative helps to bring such clarity and focus to the debate.

Globalization is taking place at an ever more rapid pace. As cross-border financial activity increases, capital markets become more dependent on each other. As financial markets become ever more interdependent, there is a greater need for the development of internationally recognized and accepted standards dealing with capital market regulation.

The development of IFRS can be seen within this broader framework. They represent an especially useful instrument designed to promote a stable and more secure international regulatory environment. At the same time, IFRS deliver on accounting and disclosure objectives as well as the pursuit of improved transparency of global financial reporting.

For the International Organization of Securities Commissions (IOSCO), the development and subsequent progress of IFRS represents a priority outcome. The organization has been a key stakeholder with an active involvement in the process of setting the standards and in continually assessing their quality.

This involvement reflects a long history of commitment by IOSCO to efforts aimed at strengthening the integrity of international markets through the promotion of high quality accounting standards, including rigorous application and enforcement.

At the same time, there is an obligation of international standard setters to be responsive to concerns over the application and interpretation of the standards. This is a key complement to the success of IFRS and one which we take seriously.

Ultimately, accounting standards setting is a continuous process that must respond to changes and developments in the markets and the information needs of investors. Indeed, it has always been the case that effective financial reporting is fundamental to investor confidence as well as good corporate governance.

In the long term, the adoption of IFRS in many countries and their use in numerous cross-border transactions will help to bring about these high quality global accounting standards by providing transparent and comparable information in financial reports.

Although as an international standards setter IOSCO is not in position to endorse external publications, we have always recognized that by helping to promote clear information about the IFRS, publications such as this one serve a particularly useful function both as an educational opportunity and also to encourage confidence in these standards. On that basis it is most welcome.

Philippe Richard
IOSCO Secretary General
March 2006

PREFACE

Achieving consistency in financial reporting worldwide is the need of the hour, especially if meaningful comparisons are to be made of financial information emanating from different countries using accounting standards that, until recently, were vastly different from each other. Thus, there has arisen the urgent need for promulgation of a common set of global accounting standards or, in other words, global convergence into a common language of accounting for the financial world. International Financial Reporting Standards (IFRS), the standards promulgated by the International Accounting Standards Board (IASB), previously known as International Accounting Standards (IAS) that were issued by the International Accounting Standards Committee (IASC), the IASB's predecessor body, appear to be emerging as the global accounting standards and, according to some, could even qualify for the coveted title of "the Esperanto of accounting."

This is a challenging and exciting time to be writing a book on IFRS. Challenging, because it is indeed a daunting task to publish a book on a body of knowledge such as IFRS. This is also an exciting time to be writing a book on a subject of global importance such as IFRS, since the IASB standards are rapidly being adopted in a large number of countries all around the world. The FASB is working with the IASB to align their standards, which may mean that eventually the USA will adopt IFRS.

Whether you are an accountant, auditor, investor, banker, regulator, or financial analyst, understanding and appreciating the fundamental principles and requirements of IFRS has become more important than ever before. In this new financial world, knowledge of the fundamental principles of IFRS is essential to meet the growing demands of a changing regulatory and market environment. Cognizant of that, we embarked on this book project to help users and preparers of IFRS financial statements alike.

We have written this book with the end user in mind, which should make it user-friendly. For instance, if you are an accountant or an auditor working in a country that has adopted IFRS, you are now faced with the challenges of being able to apply these standards and to read and understand financial statements prepared in accordance with them. This book will help you to do that. We believe that this book's real strength lies in the fact that it explains the IASB standards in a lucid manner so even first-time adopters of IFRS can understand the subject. The book illustrates the practical application of the IASB standards, using easy-to-apply illustrations and simple examples. It goes a step futher and provides copious learning aids in the form of case studies (with worked solutions), multiple-choice questions (with answers), and practical insights. We hope its simple, step-by-step approach will guide you in the application of IFRS.

In general, the structure and contents of the book are consistent with the order and scope of each standard; each chapter discusses a specific IFRS, and the chapters are ordered consistent with the numbering of the IFRS currently in effect. This structure allows you to use the book as a handbook, side by side with the bound volume of standards issued by IASB. The only exception is the chapter on IAS 39, which is located immediately after the chapter on IAS 32 in this book, since both standards address the same topic: the accounting for financial instruments. Also, the chapters dealing with IAS precede the chapters dealing with IFRS.

We hope that this book will greatly facilitate learning and will also help readers to understand the technical complexities of the standards. Although a great deal of effort has gone into writing this book, we sincerely believe that there is always scope for improvement. *Any suggestions and comments for future editions are therefore encouraged.* We humbly submit that any views expressed in this publication are ours alone and do not necessarily represent those of the firms or organizations we are part of.

Finally, we wish all our readers a very educating journey through the book.

Abbas Ali Mirza
Graham Holt
March 2011

ACKNOWLEDGMENTS

This book would not have seen the light of the day without the help of so many wonderful people around the globe who have helped us to put it together. This IFRS workbook project was conceived and conceptualized way back in 1998, but due to certain unanticipated issues that surfaced later, the project was dropped, only to be revived in 2005. We would be remiss in our duties if we did not thank the editors at John Wiley & Sons, Inc., USA, who had implicit faith in our abilities and greatly helped us in giving shape to this creative endeavor. In particular, we wish to place on record our sincere appreciation of the help provided to us by the following individuals of John Wiley & Sons: David Pugh, for his patronage of this book project; John DeRemigis, for his stewardship of this book project from its incubation stages in 1998 to its completion in 2011 and for his perseverance for these many years; Judy Howarth and Brandon Dust, for their able guidance and patience; Natasha Andrews-Noel and Pam Reh and their editorial staff, for their creative and valuable editorial comments and assistance; and the staff of the marketing department for their outstanding marketing plans and ideas.

We also wish to place on record our sincere appreciation of the untiring efforts of Ms. Liesel Knorr, the current president of the German Accounting Standards Board and formerly technical director of the International Accounting Standards Committee (IASC), the predecessor body to the IASB, for her thorough technical review of the entire manuscript. Her invaluable comments have all been taken into account in writing this book.

We are also grateful to all our friends and colleagues who helped us during the preparation of this book.

Abbas Ali Mirza wishes to place on record his sincere gratitude for all the constructive suggestions offered to him by his friends and family in conceptualizing the idea of such a workbook on IFRS during its formative stages. Furthermore, for their unstinting support, creative ideas, and invaluable contributions, he also wishes to thank his peers and mentors, in particular: Omar Fahoum, chairman and managing partner, Deloitte & Touche (M.E.); and all his partners and colleagues from Deloitte & Touche (M.E.), including but not limited to Joe El Fadl, Graham Lucas, Anis Sadek, Saba Sindaha, Cynthia Corby, Akbar Ahmed, Clovis Karam, Samir Madbak, Mutasem Dajani, Wissam Moukahal, Padmanabha Acharya, Ganesh Vishnampettai and Anish Mehta and Jude Rodrigues for their support and inspiration for the project, and his long-time friend, Graham Martins, managing partner, Pannell Kerr Forster (PKF), United Arab Emirates, for his guidance and support.

Graham Holt wishes to thank everyone who has directly and indirectly helped him in preparing this book, and his wife Joanne for her love and support.

ABOUT THE AUTHORS

Abbas Ali Mirza is a partner at Deloitte & Touche (M.E.) based in Dubai and handles audits as partner in charge of major international clients (including SEC clients) and large business groups of the firm. At Deloitte he is also responsible for regional functions, such as technical consultation on complex accounting issues. He is the designated "IFRS Leader" for Deloitte, Middle East, and has been featured for several years now on Deloitte's IFRS global public Web site www.iasplus.com in the SPOTLIGHT on Deloitte IFRS Leaders' section.

Abbas Ali Mirza has had a distinguished career in accounting, auditing, taxation, and business consulting and has worked for international audit and consulting firms in the United States of America, the Middle East, and India. He is a frequent principal/keynote speaker at major global conferences on International Financial Reporting Standards (IFRS) and has chaired world-class events on accounting, such as the World Accounting Summit held in Dubai since its inception in 2005 for seven years now. He has coauthored another book on IFRS published by John Wiley & Sons, Inc., *Wiley: IFRS Interpretations and Application*, for ten years since the book was first published in 1997. He holds or has held many important positions of repute in the accounting business and profession globally including

- 21st Session Chairman, United Nations' Intergovernmental Working Group of Experts on International Standards on Accounting & Reporting (ISAR), to which position he was elected at the UNCTAD in Geneva in November 2004
- Formerly member of the Developing Nations Permanent Task of the International Federation of Accountants (IFAC), later renamed IFAC's Developing Nations Committee
- Formerly member of the Accounting Standards Committee, Securities and Exchange Board of India (SEBI), India
- Chairman of Auditors' Group, Dubai Chamber of Commerce and Industry (DCCI)
- Chairman of the Dubai Chapter of Institute of Chartered Accountants of India for three terms
- Board Member and former President of the Indian Business and Professional Council of Dubai

Graham Holt qualified as a Chartered Accountant (Institute of Chartered Accountants in England & Wales) with Price Waterhouse and is a fellow of the Association of Chartered Certified Accountants (ACCA). He holds B.Com and MA Econ qualifications also. As a current ACCA examiner, he has been prominent in the development of their IFRS stream and their examination structure. He is an Executive Head of the Division of Accounting and Finance at the Manchester Metropolitan University Business School. Graham has given lectures on IFRS throughout the world and has many publications in the subject area. He has also been involved in running training courses on IFRS.

Chapter 1

INTRODUCTION TO INTERNATIONAL FINANCIAL REPORTING STANDARDS

INTRODUCTION

Need for a Common Set of Accounting and Financial Reporting Standards

As the oft quoted verse from the world-renowned works of Shakespeare (*Romeo and Juliet*) goes: "What's in a name? That which we call a rose by any other name would smell as sweet." One wonders if the same can be said of financial statements prepared in different jurisdictions of the world. Not too far in the distant past, countries and economic regional blocs, such as Europe, would not be swayed by the thought of converging to a single set of global accounting standards and, due to nationalistic approaches to accounting standard setting, a financial statement issued in Japan (under the Japanese accounting standards) was vastly different in terms of accounting treatments and disclosures compared to a financial statement issued in other major parts of the world, say, in Germany where German accounting standards were used. In other words, the "name" that was given to the set of accounting standards used in the preparation of financial statements did matter for several countries since their national standard setters strongly believed that their own (national) accounting standards were suitable for their needs and were compatible to other globally preferred accounting standards.

However, due to the advent of globalization, the falling of the erstwhile insurmountable trade barriers between nations, and more recently the much-awaited response to the global financial crisis, together with calls by world leaders, things have changed dramatically in terms of the preferred set of standards of accounting globally. The accounting and financial world is now seriously considering the notion of using a single set of accounting and financial reporting standards that would be used by most, if not all, the nations around the globe, it appears that in all likelihood the name of that set of global accounting standards may be the International Financial Reporting Standards (IFRS®).

With this transformation of our world into a "flat world" (as some claim) the magical phenomenon of globalization has led to the emergence of a "global village" that we all live in now. The robust waves of globalization surging through the world seem to have transformed businesses across the globe as well as the manner in which they deal with each other across boundaries. If therefore, as the old adage goes, "accounting is the language of business," then businesses around

1

the world cannot afford to be speaking in different languages to each other while exchanging and sharing financial results of their international business activities with each other, and also while reporting the results of business and trade to their international stakeholders. As one school of thought believes, since business enterprises around the world are so highly globalized now and need to speak to each other in a common language of business, there is a real need for adopting a single set of accounting standards to unify the accounting world under one canvas and more importantly, solve the problem of diversity of accounting practices across borders.

Historically, countries around the world have had their own national accounting standards (which some countries have treasured for whatever reason, most likely due to the pride of national sovereignty). However, with such a compulsion to be part of the globalization movement, wherein businesses across national boundaries are realizing that it is an astute business strategy to embrace the world as their workplace and marketplace, having different rules (standards) of accounting for the purposes of reporting financial results would not help them at all (rather, it would serve as an impediment to smooth flows of information), and therefore, businesses have realized that they need to talk to each other in a common language. Thus, there is an urgent need for a common set of global, or even universal, accounting and financial reporting standards that are understood, used, and interpreted by different people around the world in the same manner.

The adoption of accounting standards that require high-quality, transparent, and comparable information is welcomed by investors, creditors, financial analysts, and other users of financial statements. Without a common set of accounting and financial reporting standards, it is difficult to compare financial information prepared by entities located in different parts of the world. In an increasingly global economy, the use of a single set of high-quality accounting standards facilitates investment and other economic decisions across borders, increases market efficiency, and reduces the cost of raising capital. International Financial Reporting Standards (IFRS) are increasingly becoming the set of globally accepted accounting standards that meet the needs of the world's increasingly integrated global capital markets.

What Are IFRS?

IFRS is a set of standards promulgated by the International Accounting Standards Board (IASB), an international standard-setting body based in London, United Kingdom. The IASB places emphasis on developing standards based on sound, clearly-stated principles, on which interpretations may be required (sometimes referred to as **principles-based standards**). This contrasts with sets of standards, like US GAAP, the national accounting standards of the United States, which contain significantly more application guidance. These standards are sometimes referred to as **rules-based standards,** but that is really a misnomer as US standards also are based on principles—they just contain more application guidance (or "rules"). IFRS also generally do not provide "bright lines" in distinguishing between circumstances in which different accounting requirements are specified. This reduces the chances of 'structuring' transactions to achieve particular accounting effects.

According to one school of thought, since IFRS are primarily "principles-based" standards, the IFRS-approach to standard setting focuses more on the business or the economic purpose of a transaction and the underlying rights and obligations and therefore, instead of providing prescriptive rules (or guidance), IFRS promulgates Standards that lay down guidance in the form of "principles."

This significant difference in approach to standard setting between IFRS and US GAAP is responsible for the limited number of pages that the IFRS Standards are spread over compared to US GAAP (US GAAP extends to over 20,000 pages of accounting literature as opposed to IFRS which presently is covered in approximately 2,000 to 3,000 pages).

WORLDWIDE ADOPTION OF IFRS

International Financial Reporting Standards (IFRS), which were initially called International Accounting Standards (IAS), are gaining acceptance worldwide. This section discusses the extent to which IFRS are recognized around the world and includes a brief overview of the history and key elements of the international standard-setting process. In the last few years, the international accounting standard-setting process has been able to claim a number of successes in achieving greater recognition and use of IFRS.

A major breakthrough came in 2002 when the European Union (EU) adopted legislation that required listed companies in Europe to apply IFRS in their consolidated financial statements. The legislation came into effect in 2005 and applies to more than 8,000 companies in 30 countries, including France, Germany, Italy, Spain, and the United Kingdom. The adoption of IFRS in Europe means that IFRS have replaced national accounting standards and requirements as the basis for preparing and presenting group financial statements for listed companies in Europe.

Outside Europe, many other countries also have been moving to IFRS. By 2005, IFRS had become mandatory in many countries in Africa, Asia, and Latin America. In addition, countries such as Australia, Hong Kong, New Zealand, Philippines, and Singapore have adopted national accounting standards that mirror IFRS. According to estimates, currently more than 100 countries require or permit IFRS in preparing and presenting financial statements, and many other countries are expected to adopt or apply IFRS in the coming years. In the period 2011–2012 several major players such as Canada and India are expected to adopt IFRS.

The adoption of standards that require high-quality, transparent, and comparable information is welcomed by investors, creditors, financial analysts, and other users of financial statements. Without common standards, it is difficult to compare financial information prepared by entities located in different parts of the world. In an increasingly global economy, the use of a single set of high-quality accounting standards facilitates investment and other economic decisions across borders, increases market efficiency, and reduces the cost of raising capital. IFRS are increasingly becoming the set of globally accepted accounting standards that meet the needs of the world's increasingly integrated global capital markets.

REMAINING EXCEPTIONS

Measured in terms of the size of the capital markets, the most significant remaining exception to the global recognition of IFRS is the United States. In the US domestic entities continue to follow US GAAP (Generally Accepted Accounting Principles). However, IFRS are being considered for adoption in the United States as well.

The International Accounting Standards Board (IASB), the body responsible for setting IFRS, works closely with the national accounting standard-setting body in the US Financial Accounting Standards Board (FASB), to converge (that is, narrow the differences between) US GAAP and IFRS.

In the United States, the domestic securities regulator (Securities and Exchange Commission, SEC) has dropped its prior requirement for non-US companies that raise capital in US markets to prepare a reconciliation of their IFRS financial statements to US GAAP. This means that non-US companies (foreign private issuers, FPIs) raising capital in US markets no longer are required to reconcile their IFRS financial statement to US GAAP beginning with financial years ending after November 15, 2007. With this important SEC initiative IFRS have already made major inroads into the US capital markets.

The SEC is currently considering whether to permit US companies to use IFRS instead of US GAAP in preparing their financial statements. This is in response to the recognition that the world's rapidly integrating capital markets would benefit from having a set of globally accepted accounting and financial reporting standards and that IFRS have become the primary contender for that title. Additionally, many question why US companies should continue to be required to use US GAAP when non-US companies are permitted to raise capital in US markets without reconciling their IFRS financial statements to US GAAP.

The SEC has announced a Work Plan whereby it will assess and confirm by 2011 whether or not it would recommend that the United States should abandon US GAAP and adopt IFRS, and if they do decide to adopt IFRS, when that would finally happen. The possible timescale for adoption of IFRS according to the initial SEC announcement through a SEC Roadmap (which approach was later modified and replaced with the SEC Work Plan) has been extended and is now expected to be around 2014.

On June 2, 2010, the IASB and the US Financial Accounting Standards Board (FASB), jointly referred to as the Boards, announced a modified strategy for the convergence of IFRS and US GAAP. The Boards first entered into a Memorandum of Understanding (MOU), which was updated in 2008, and a very aggressive work plan was agreed upon in order to complete the MOU projects by 2011. On June 24, 2010, the IASB issued a revised work plan for those MOU and non-MOU projects affected by the joint modified strategy announcement by the Boards, confirming their goal to complete several of these projects by June 2011 while extending the timeline for other nonurgent projects.

THE INTERNATIONAL ACCOUNTING STANDARDS COMMITTEE

From 1973 until 2001, the body in charge of setting the international standards was the International Accounting Standards Committee (IASC). The principal significance of IASC was to encourage national accounting standard setters around the world to improve and harmonize national accounting standards. Its objectives, as stated in its Constitution, were to

- Formulate and publish in the public interest accounting standards to be observed in the presentation of financial statements and to promote their worldwide acceptance and observance
- Work generally for the improvement and harmonization of regulations, accounting standards, and procedures relating to the presentation of financial statements

IASC and the Accounting Profession

IASC always had a special relationship with the international accounting profession. IASC was created in 1973 by agreement between the professional accountancy bodies in nine countries, and, from 1982, its membership consisted of all those professional accountancy bodies that were members of the International Federation of Accountants (IFAC), that is, professional accountancy bodies in more than 100 countries. As part of their membership in IASC, professional accountancy bodies worldwide committed themselves to use their best endeavors to persuade governments, standard-setting bodies, securities regulators, and the business community that published financial statements should comply with IAS.

IASC Board

The members of IASC (i.e., professional accountancy bodies around the world) delegated the responsibility for all IASC activities, including all standard-setting activities, to the IASC Board. The Board consisted of 13 country delegations representing members of IASC and up to four other organizations appointed by the Board. The Board, which usually met four times per year, was supported by a small secretariat located in London, United Kingdom.

The Initial Set of Standards Issued by IASC

In its early years, IASC focused its efforts on developing a set of basic accounting standards. These standards usually were worded broadly and contained several alternative treatments to accommodate the existence of different accounting practices around the world. Later these standards came to be criticized for being too broad and having too many options.

Improvements and Comparability Project

Beginning in 1987, IASC initiated work to improve its standards, reduce the number of choices, and specify preferred accounting treatments in order to allow greater comparability in financial statements. This work took on further importance as securities regulators worldwide started to take an active interest in the international accounting standard-setting process.

Core Standards Work Program

During the 1990s, IASC worked increasingly closely with the International Organization of Securities Commissions (IOSCO) on defining its agenda. In 1993, the Technical Committee of IOSCO held out on the possibility of IOSCO endorsement of IASC Standards for cross-border listing and capital-raising purposes around the world and identified a list of core standards that

IASC would need to complete in order to gain such an endorsement. In response, IASC in 1995 announced that it had agreed on a work plan to develop the comprehensive set of core standards sought after by IOSCO. This effort became known as the Core Standards Work Program.

After three years of intense work to develop and publish standards that met IOSCO's criteria, IASC completed the Core Standards Work Program in 1998. In 2000, the Technical Committee of IOSCO recommended that securities regulators worldwide permit foreign issuers to use IASC Standards for cross-border offering and listing purposes, subject to certain supplemental treatments.

International Accounting Standards and SIC Interpretations

During its existence, IASC issued 41 numbered Standards, known as International Accounting Standards (IAS), as well as a *Framework for the Preparation and Presentation of Financial Statements*. While some of the Standards issued by the IASC have been withdrawn, many are still in force. In addition, some of the Interpretations issued by the IASC's interpretive body, the Standing Interpretations Committee (SIC), are still in force.

List of IAS Still in Force for 2009 Financial Statements

IAS 1, *Presentation of Financial Statements*
IAS 2, *Inventories*
IAS 7, *Statement of Cash Flows*
IAS 8, *Accounting Policies, Changes in Accounting Estimates and Errors*
IAS 10, *Events After the Reporting Period*
IAS 11, *Construction Contracts*
IAS 12, *Income Taxes*
IAS 16, *Property, Plant, and Equipment*
IAS 17, *Leases*
IAS 18, *Revenue*
IAS 19, *Employee Benefits*
IAS 20, *Accounting for Government Grants and Disclosure of Government Assistance*
IAS 21, *The Effects of Changes in Foreign Exchange Rates*
IAS 23, *Borrowing Costs*
IAS 24, *Related-Party Disclosures*
IAS 26, *Accounting and Reporting by Retirement Benefit Plans*
IAS 27, *Consolidated and Separate Financial Statements*
IAS 28, *Investments in Associates*
IAS 29, *Financial Reporting in Hyperinflationary Economies*
IAS 31, *Interests in Joint Ventures*
IAS 32, *Financial Instruments: Presentation*
IAS 33, *Earnings Per Share*
IAS 34, *Interim Financial Reporting*
IAS 36, *Impairment of Assets*
IAS 37, *Provisions, Contingent Liabilities, and Contingent Assets*
IAS 38, *Intangible Assets*
IAS 39, *Financial Instruments: Recognition and Measurement*
IAS 40, *Investment Property*
IAS 41, *Agriculture*

List of SIC Interpretations Still in Force for 2009 Financial Statements

SIC 7, *Introduction of the Euro*
SIC 10, *Government Assistance—No Specific Relation to Operating Activities*
SIC 12, *Consolidation—Special-Purpose Entities*
SIC 13, *Jointly Controlled Entities—Nonmonetary Contributions by Venturers*
SIC 15, *Operating Leases—Incentives*
SIC 21, *Income Taxes—Recovery of Revalued Nondepreciable Assets*
SIC 25, *Income Taxes—Changes in the Tax Status of an Entity or Its Shareholders*
SIC 27, *Evaluating the Substance of Transactions Involving the Legal Form of a Lease*

SIC 29, *Service Concession Arrangements: Disclosures*

SIC 31, *Revenue—Barter Transactions Involving Advertising Services*

SIC 32, *Intangible Assets—Web Site Costs*

THE INTERNATIONAL ACCOUNTING STANDARDS BOARD

In 2001, fundamental changes were made to strengthen the independence, legitimacy, and quality of the international accounting standard-setting process. In particular, the IASC Board was replaced by the International Accounting Standards Board (IASB) as the body in charge of setting the international standards.

Key Differences between IASC and IASB

The IASB differs from the IASC Board, its predecessor body, in several key areas:

- Unlike the IASC Board, the IASB does not have a special relationship with the international accounting profession. Instead, IASB is governed by a group of Trustees of diverse geographic and functional backgrounds who are independent of the accounting profession.
- Unlike the members of the IASC Board, members of the IASB are individuals who are appointed based on technical skill and background experience rather than as representatives of specific national accountancy bodies or other organizations.
- Unlike the IASC Board, which only met about four times a year, the IASB Board usually meets each month. Moreover, the number of technical and commercial staff working for IASB has increased significantly as compared with IASC. (Similar to IASC, the headquarters of the IASB is located in London, United Kingdom.)

The interpretive body of the IASC (SIC) was replaced in 2002 by the International Financial Reporting Interpretations Committee (IFRIC). The latest name of this interpretive arm of the IASB is IFRS Interpretations Committee (which until March 31, 2010 was named International Financial Reporting Interpretations Committee (IFRIC)).

The name of the organization that comprises both the IASB and its Trustees is the IFRS Foundation (which until March 31, 2010, was named International Accounting Standards Committee Foundation). The objectives of the IFRS Foundation, as stated in its Constitution, are

1. To develop, in the public interest, a single set of high-quality, understandable, and enforceable global accepted financial reporting standards based on clearly articulated principles that require high-quality, transparent, and comparable information in financial statements and other financial reporting to help investors and other participants in the various capital markets of the world and other users of the information to make economic decisions.
2. To promote the use and rigorous application of those standards.
3. In fulfilling the objectives associated with 1. and 2., to take account of, as appropriate, the needs of a range of sizes and types of entities in diverse economic settings.
4. To promote and facilitate adoption of IFRS through convergence of national accounting standards and IFRS.

At its first meeting in 2001, IASB adopted all outstanding IAS issued by the IASC as its own Standards. Those IAS continue to be in force to the extent that they are not amended or withdrawn by the IASB. New Standards issued by IASB are known as IFRS. When referring collectively to IFRS, that term includes both IAS and IFRS.

List of IFRS Issued by the IASB to December 31, 2009

IFRS 1, *First-Time Adoption of International Financial Reporting Standards*

IFRS 2, *Share-Based Payment*

IFRS 3, *Business Combinations*

IFRS 4, *Insurance Contracts*

IFRS 5, *Noncurrent Assets Held for Sale and Discontinued Operations*

IFRS 6, *Exploration for and Evaluation of Mineral Resources*

IFRS 7, *Financial Instruments: Disclosures*

IFRS 8, *Operating Segments*
IFRS 9, *Financial Instruments*
IFRS for SMEs*

* NOTE: In July 2009 the IASB promulgated the much-awaited "IFRS for Small and Medium-Sized Enterprises (SMEs)." It provides standards applicable to private entities (that are not publicly accountable as defined in this standard).

One of the initial projects undertaken by IASB was to identify opportunities to improve the existing set of Standards by adding guidance and eliminating inconsistencies and choices. The improved Standards, adopted in 2003, formed part of IASB's stable platform of Standards for use in 2005 when a significant number of countries around the world moved from national accounting requirements to IFRS, such as all the countries in the European Union.

STRUCTURE AND GOVERNANCE

Diagram of the Current IASB Structure

IFRS Foundation and the Trustees:

The governance of the IFRS Foundation rests on the shoulders of the Trustees of the IFRS Foundation (the "IFRS Foundation Trustees" or, simply, the "Trustees"). The Trustees comprise 22 individuals that are chosen from around the world. In order to ensure a broad international representation it is required that

- Six Trustees are appointed from North America
- Six from Europe
- Six from Asia/Oceanic region
- One from Africa
- One from South America
- Two from any part of the world, subject to maintaining overall geographical balance

The Trustees are independent of the standard-setting activities (which is the primary responsibility of the Board members of the IASB). The Trustees, on the other hand, are responsible for broad strategic issues, such as

- Appointing the members of IASB, the IFRS Interpretations Committee, and the IFRS Advisory Council
- Approving the budget of the IFRS Foundation and determining the basis of funding it
- Reviewing the strategy of the IFRS Foundation and the IASB and its effectiveness, including consideration, but not determination, of the IASB's agenda (which if allowed may impair the Trustees' independence of the standard-setting process)
- Establishing and amending operating procedures, consultative arrangements, and "due process" for the IASB, the IFRS Interpretations Committee, and the IFRS Advisory Council
- Approving amendments to the Constitution after consulting the IFRS Advisory Council and following the required "due process"
- Fostering and reviewing the development of the educational programs and materials that are consistent with the objectives of the IFRS Foundation
- Generally, exercising all powers of the IFRS Foundation except those expressly reserved for IASB, the IFRS Interpretations Committee, and the IFRS Advisory Council

Monitoring Board

In order to enhance public accountability of the IFRS Foundation, while maintaining the operational independence of the IFRS Foundation and the IASB, the Monitoring Board, a new body, was created in 2009. The Monitoring Board comprises capital market authorities (e.g. representatives of institutions such as the IOSCO, the US SEC, and the European Commission) and its responsibilities include participating in the appointment of the Trustees of the IFRS Foundation, advising the Trustees in the fulfillment of their responsibilities, and holding meetings with the Trustees to discuss matters referred by the Monitoring Board to the IFRS Foundation or the IASB.

The Board

The Board is responsible for all standard-setting activities, including the development and adoption of IFRS. The Board members are from around the world and are selected by the Trustees based on technical skills and relevant business and market experience. The Board, which usually meets once a month, has currently 15 full-time members. The Board members are from a mix of backgrounds, including auditors, preparers of financial statements, users of financial statements, and academics. According to the IFRS Constitution, the Board shall comprise 14 members, increasing to 16 members at a date no later than July 1, 2012.

IFRS Advisory Council

The Trustees appoint the members of the **IFRS Advisory Council** (which until March 2010 was named the Standards Advisory Council, SAC). The primary responsibility of the IFRS Advisory Council is to provide advice to the IASB on agenda decisions and priorities in the IASB's work. The IFRS Advisory Council provides a forum for organizations and individuals with an interest in international financial reporting. It encompasses diverse geographical and professional backgrounds.

The IFRS Advisory Council shall comprise 40 members approximately. Members are appointed for a three-year renewable term. Currently the membership of the IFRS Advisory Council includes chief financial and accounting officers from some of the world's largest corporations and international organizations, leading financial analysts and academics, regulators, accounting standard setters, and partners from leading accounting firms.

IFRS Interpretations Committee

IASB's interpretive body, IFRS Interpretations Committee (which until March 2010 was named International Financial Reporting Interpretations Committee, IFRIC), is the IASB's interpretive body and is in charge of developing interpretive guidance on accounting issues that are not specifically dealt with in IFRS or that are likely to receive divergent or unacceptable interpretations in the absence of authoritative guidance. The Trustees select members of the IFRS Interpretations Committee keeping in mind personal attributes such as technical expertise and diversity of international business and market experience in the practical application of IFRS and analysis of financial statements prepared in accordance with IFRS.

The IFRS Interpretations Committee is comprised of 14 voting members. The Trustees, if they deem fit, may also appoint nonvoting observers representing regulatory bodies, who shall have the right to attend and speak at the meetings of the IFRS Interpretations Committee. A member of the IASB, the Director of Technical Activities, or another senior member of the IASB staff, or another appropriately qualified individual, is appointed by the Trustees to chair the IFRS Interpretations Committee. The IFRS Interpretations Committee meets as and when required, and ten voting members present in person or by telecommunication constitute a quorum. Meetings of the IFRS Interpretations Committee (and the IASB) are open to the public but certain discussions may be held in private at the discretion of the IFRS Interpretations Committee. It is important to note that an IFRS Interpretations Committee interpretation requires the IASB's approval before its final issuance.

List of IFRIC Interpretations issued up to December 31, 2009

IFRIC 1, *Changes in Existing Decommissioning, Restoration, and Similar Liabilities*
IFRIC 2, *Members' Shares in Cooperative Entities and Similar Instruments*
IFRIC 3, *Emission Rights* (withdrawn)
IFRIC 4, *Determining Whether an Arrangement Contains a Lease*
IFRIC 5, *Rights to Interests Arising from Decommissioning, Restoration, and Environmental Rehabilitation Funds*
IFRIC 6, *Liabilities Arising from Participating in a Specific Market—Waste Electrical and Electronic Equipment*
IFRIC 7, *Applying the Restatement Approach under IAS 29, "Financial Reporting in Hyperinflationary Economies"*
IFRIC 8, *Scope of IFRS 2* (withdrawn)
IFRIC 9, *Reassessment of Embedded Derivatives*
IFRIC 10, *Interim Financial Reporting and Impairment*
IFRIC 11, *IFRS 2—Group and Treasury Share Transactions* (withdrawn)
IFRIC 12, *Service Concession Arrangements*
IFRIC 13, *Customer Loyalty Programs*
IFRIC 14, *IAS 19—The Limit on a Defined Benefit Asset, Minimum Funding Requirements, and Their Interaction*
IFRIC 15, *Agreements for the Construction of Real Estate*
IFRIC 16, *Hedges of a Net Investment in a Foreign Operation*
IFRIC 17, *Distribution of Noncash Assets to Owners*
IFRIC 18, *Transfer of Assets from Customers*
IFRIC 19, *Extinguishing Financial Liabilities with Equity Instruments*

Standard-Setting Due Process

As part of its due process in developing new or revised Standards, the Board publishes an Exposure Draft of the proposed Standard for public comment in order to obtain the views of all interested parties. It also publishes a "Basis for Conclusions" to its Exposure Drafts and Standards to explain how it reached its conclusions and to give background information. When one or more Board members disagree with a Standard, the Board publishes those dissenting opinions with the Standard. To obtain advice on major projects, the Board often forms advisory committees or other specialist groups and may also hold public hearings and conduct field tests on proposed Standards.

THE WAY FORWARD

IFRS are clearly emerging as a global financial reporting benchmark and most countries have already started using them as their benchmark standards for listed companies. With the recent issuance of "IFRS for SMEs," a stand-alone set of standards for private entities that do not have public accountability, the global reach of the IASB is further enhanced. However, if these international standards are not applied uniformly across the world due to interpretational differences, then their effectiveness as a common medium of international financial reporting will be in question; especially if different entities within the region apply them differently based on their interpretation of the standards, it would make global comparison of published financial statements of entities using IFRS difficult. Debate still rages amongst accountants and auditors globally on many burning and contentious accounting issues that need a common stand based on proper interpretation of these standards.

According to one school of thought, IFRS are fast emerging as the much-awaited answer to the "billion dollar question" on the minds of accountants, financial professionals, financial institutions, and regulators, that is: *Which set of accounting standards would solve the conundrum of diversity in accounting practices worldwide by qualifying as a single or a common set of standards for the world of accounting to follow and rely upon?*

Undoubtedly, for years US GAAP was leading this much-talked-about international race to qualify as the most acceptable set of accounting standards worldwide. However, due to several reasons, including the highly publicized corporate debacles such as that at Enron in the United States, the global preference (or choice) of most countries internationally has now clearly tilted in favor of IFRS as the most acceptable set of international accounting and financial reporting standards worldwide.

With the current acceptance of IFRS in over 100 countries (and with several more expected to adopt IFRS in the coming years) one can probably argue that IFRS could possibly qualify as an "Esperanto of international accounting" ("Esperanto" referring to the well-known "universal language"). However, some still believe that the race for global acceptance of IFRS is not over yet. While more than 100 countries have adopted IFRS as their national accounting standards, there are some very important jurisdictions in the financial world (such as the United States) which have not yet fully accepted IFRS for financial reporting of their domestic companies. Therefore, unless the United States, the largest economic superpower of the world for years now, accepts IFRS as their national GAAP (replacing US GAAP) it may be difficult to call IFRS the world's standards.

There is however a good possibility of the US SEC's accepting IFRS ultimately. Judging from the amazing turnaround in the attitude of the US Securities and Exchange Commission, which has already allowed use of IFRS by foreign private issuers for filings on US stock exchanges, one may expect, that is if the SEC's Work Plan to convergence with IFRS goes through successfully without any glitches, that by the year 2014 (unless the date of convergence is extended further for whatever reason), the world of accounting may be rejoicing and celebrating under a strong common banner of a global set of accounting and financial reporting standards, namely, the IFRS. However, some may believe that the idea of a single set of standards for the world may be wishful thinking, especially since the US SEC's Road Map was amended and was replaced with the SEC's Work Plan. But as things stand presently it may be expected that there is a strong possibility of allowing the use of IFRS in the United States in some form or another.

Chapter 2

IASB FRAMEWORK

INTRODUCTION

The *Framework for the Preparation and Presentation of Financial Statements* (the "*Framework*") sets out the concepts that underlie the preparation and presentation of financial statements, that is, the objectives, assumptions, characteristics, definitions, and criteria that govern financial reporting. Therefore, the *Framework* is often referred to as the "conceptual framework." The *Framework* deals with

1. The objective of financial statements
2. Underlying assumptions
3. The qualitative characteristics that determine the usefulness of information in financial statements
4. The definition, recognition, and measurement of the elements from which financial statements are constructed
5. Concepts of capital and capital maintenance

The *Framework* does not have the force of a Standard. Instead, its purposes include, first, to assist and guide the International Accounting Standards Board (IASB) as it develops new or revised Standards and, second, to assist preparers of financial statements in applying Standards and in dealing with topics that are not addressed by a Standard. Thus, in case of a conflict between the *Framework* and a specific Standard, the Standard prevails over the *Framework*.

PRACTICAL INSIGHT

In the absence of a Standard or an Interpretation that specifically applies to a transaction, other event, or condition, IAS 8, *Accounting Policies, Changes in Accounting Estimates and Errors,* requires management to use its judgment in developing and applying an accounting policy that results in information that is relevant and reliable. In making that judgment, management is required to refer to, and consider the applicability of, in descending order: (a) the requirements and guidance in Standards and Interpretations dealing with similar and related issues; and (b) the definitions, recognition criteria, and measurement concepts for assets, liabilities, income,

---

and expenses in the *Framework*. Thus, the *Framework* serves as a guide for preparers to resolve accounting issues in the absence of more specific requirements.

OBJECTIVE OF FINANCIAL STATEMENTS

The objective of financial statements is to provide information about the financial position, performance, and changes in financial position of an entity that is useful to a wide range of users in making economic decisions (e.g., whether to sell or hold an investment in the entity). Users include present and potential investors, employees, lenders, suppliers and other trade creditors, customers, governments and their agencies, and the public. Because investors are providers of risk capital, it is presumed that financial statements that meet their needs will also meet most of the needs of other users.

UNDERLYING ASSUMPTIONS

Normally, two assumptions underlying the preparation and presentation of financial statements are the accrual basis and going concern.

Accrual Basis

When financial statements are prepared on the *accrual basis of accounting*, the effects of transactions and other events are recognized when they occur (and not as cash or its equivalent is received or paid), and they are recorded in the accounting records and reported in the financial statements of the periods to which they relate.

The accrual basis assumption is also addressed in IAS 1, *Presentation of Financial Statements*, which clarifies that when the accrual basis of accounting is used, items are recognized as assets, liabilities, equity, income, and expenses (the elements of financial statements) when they satisfy the definitions and recognition criteria for those elements in the *Framework*.

Going Concern

When financial statements are prepared on a *going concern* basis, it is assumed that the entity has neither the intention nor the need to liquidate or curtail materially the scale of its operations, but will continue in operation for the foreseeable future. If this assumption is not valid, the financial statements may need to be prepared on a different basis and, if so, the basis used is disclosed.

The going concern assumption is also addressed in IAS 1, which requires management to make an assessment of an entity's ability to continue as a going concern when preparing financial statements.

QUALITATIVE CHARACTERISTICS OF FINANCIAL STATEMENTS

Qualitative characteristics are the attributes that make the information provided in financial statements useful to users. According to the *Framework*, the four principal qualitative characteristics are

1. Understandability
2. Relevance
3. Reliability
4. Comparability

Understandability

"Understandability" refers to information being readily understandable by users who have a reasonable knowledge of business and economic activities, accounting, and a willingness to study the information with reasonable diligence.

Relevance

"Relevance" refers to information being relevant to the decision-making needs of users. Information has the quality of relevance when it influences the economic decisions of users by helping them evaluate past, present, or future events or confirming, or correcting, their past evaluations. The concept of relevance is closely related to the concept of *materiality*. The *Framework* describes materiality as a threshold or cutoff point for information whose omission or misstatement could influence the economic decisions of users taken on the basis of the financial statements.

The concept of materiality is further addressed in IAS 1, which specifies that each material class of similar items shall be presented separately in the financial statements and that items of a dissimilar nature or function shall be presented separately unless they are immaterial. Under the concept of materiality, a specific disclosure requirement in a Standard or an Interpretation need not be met if the information is not material.

Reliability

"Reliability" refers to information being free from material error and bias and can be depended on by users to represent faithfully that which it either purports to represent or could reasonably be expected to represent. According to the *Framework,* to be reliable, information must

- Be free from material error
- Be neutral, that is, free from bias
- Represent faithfully the transactions and other events it either purports to represent or could reasonably be expected to represent (*representational faithfulness*). If information is to represent faithfully the transactions and other events that it purports to represent, the *Framework* specifies that they need to be accounted for and presented in accordance with their substance and economic reality even if their legal form is different (*substance over form*)
- Be complete within the bounds of materiality and cost

Related to the concept of reliability is *prudence,* whereby preparers of financial statements should include a degree of caution in exercising judgments needed in making estimates, such that assets or income are not overstated and liabilities or expenses are not understated. However, the exercise of prudence does not justify the deliberate understatement of assets or income, or the deliberate overstatement of liabilities or expenses, because the financial statements would not be neutral and, therefore, not reliable.

Comparability

"Comparability" refers to information being comparable through time and across entities. To achieve comparability, like transactions and events should be accounted for similarly by an entity throughout an entity, over time for that entity, and by different entities.

Consistency of presentation is also addressed in IAS 1. It specifies that the presentation and classification of items in the financial statements, as a general rule, shall be retained from one period to the next, with specified exceptions.

Constraints

In practice, there is often a trade-off between different qualitative characteristics of information. In these situations, an appropriate balance among the characteristics must be achieved in order to meet the objective of financial statements.

Examples

Examples of trade-offs between qualitative characteristics of information follow:

- There is a trade-off between reporting relevant information in a timely manner and taking time to ensure that the information is reliable. If information is not reported in a timely manner, it may lose its relevance. Therefore, entities need to balance relevance and reliability in determining when to provide information.
- There is a trade-off between benefit and cost in preparing and reporting information. In principle, the benefits derived from the information by users should exceed the cost for the preparer of providing it.

- There is a trade-off between providing information that is relevant, but is subject to measurement uncertainty (e.g., the fair value of a financial instrument), and providing information that is reliable but not necessarily relevant (e.g., the historical cost of a financial instrument).

ELEMENTS OF FINANCIAL STATEMENTS

The *Framework* describes the elements of financial statements as broad classes of financial effects of transactions and other events. The elements of financial statements are

- **Assets.** An asset is a resource controlled by the entity as a result of past events and from which future economic benefits are expected to flow to the entity.
- **Liabilities.** A liability is a present obligation of the entity arising from past events, the settlement of which is expected to result in an outflow from the entity of resources embodying economic benefits.
- **Equity.** Equity is the residual interest in the assets of the entity after deducting all of its liabilities.
- **Income.** Income is increases in economic benefits during the accounting period in the form of inflows or enhancements of assets or decreases of liabilities that result in increases in equity, other than those relating to contributions from equity participants.
- **Expenses.** Expenses are decreases in economic benefits during the accounting period in the form of outflows or depletions of assets or incurrences of liabilities that result in decreases in equity, other than those relating to distributions to equity participants.

According to the *Framework*, an item that meets the definition of an element should be recognized (i.e., incorporated in the financial statements) if

1. It is probable that any future economic benefit associated with the item will flow to or from the entity.
2. The item has a cost or value that can be measured with reliability.

The *Framework* notes that the most common measurement basis in financial statements is historical cost, but that other measurement bases are also used, such as current cost, realizable or settlement value, and present value.

CONCEPTS OF CAPITAL AND CAPITAL MAINTENANCE

The *Framework* distinguishes between a financial concept of capital and a physical concept of capital. Most entities use a financial concept of capital, under which capital is defined in monetary terms as the net assets or equity of the entity. Under a physical concept of capital, capital is instead defined in terms of physical productive capacity of the entity.

Under the financial capital maintenance concept, a profit is earned if the financial amount of the net assets at the end of the period exceeds the financial amount of the net assets at the beginning of the period, after excluding any distributions to, and contributions from, owners during the period. Under the physical capital maintenance concept, a profit is instead earned if the physical productive capacity (or operating capability) of the entity (or the resources or funds needed to achieve that capacity) at the end of the period exceeds the physical productive capacity at the beginning of the period, after excluding any distributions to, and contributions from, owners during the period.

FUTURE DEVELOPMENTS

In October 2004 IASB added a project to its agenda to develop a new framework. This project is conducted jointly with the US Financial Accounting Standards Board (FASB). The objective is to develop a common conceptual framework that brings together and improves upon the existing frameworks of IASB and FASB.

This IASB project is being addressed in the following eight Phases:

Phase A: Objectives and Qualitative Characteristics
Phase B: Elements and Recognition

Phase C: Measurement
Phase D: Reporting Entity
Phase E: Presentation and Disclosure
Phase F: Purpose and Status of Framework
Phase G: Applicability to Not-for-Profit Entities
Phase H: Other issues, if necessary

A brief overview of the status of the various Phases (mentioned previously) is set out below:

Phase A—A Discussion Paper (DP) was issued in 2006 and an Exposure Draft (ED) was issued in May 2008 and the final Phase A chapters of Framework are expected in third quarter of 2010.
Phase C—Round tables have been held on Phase C in 2007 with a DP and an ED planned for 2011.
Phase D—A DP was issued in 2008 and an ED was issued in March 2010 with Final Phase D chapters planned for the fourth quarter of 2010.
Phases B, E, F, G, H: Timing is not yet determined by the IASB.

Bird's-Eye View of the Exposure Draft Issued in March 2010

On March 11, 2010, the IASB published an Exposure Draft (ED), "Conceptual Framework for Financial Reporting—The Reporting Entity." As part of Phase A, "Objectives and Qualitative Characteristics" of the Conceptual Framework Project, IASB tentatively decided that the objective of the "general-purpose financial reporting" is to provide financial information about the "reporting entity" that is useful to present and potential stakeholders (investors, lenders, and other creditors).

The ED provides a definition of a "reporting entity" and specifies three features of a reporting entity:

- Economic activities are being conducted, have been conducted, or will be conducted
- The economic activities can be objectively distinguished from those of other entities and from the economic environment in which the entity exists
- Financial information about the economic activities has the potential to be useful to existing and potential stakeholders (investors, lenders, and other creditors)

The ED reiterates that the existence of a legal structure does not determine the existence of a "reporting entity." In other words, it focuses on economic activities as opposed to a legal entity. This approach would suggest that even a portion of a legal entity (such as a branch or a division) may represent a "reporting entity" if its economic activities can be distinguished objectively from the rest of the entity.

The ED also deals with the much-debated subject of "control" and suggests that the identification of "control" is the principal means of determining which entities should be reported as a single unit in consolidated financial statements. The ED also broadly defines **"control"** and suggests that **"an entity controls another entity when it has the power to direct the activities of that other entity to generate benefits (or limit losses to) itself."** Detailed definition and guidance on this subject will be finalized at the standard level as part of the "consolidation project" which is expected to be completed towards the end of 2010.

The ED acknowledges that other types of financial statements may also provide useful information and in this context the ED elaborates upon the concept of "combined financial statements" and recognizes that two or more "commonly controlled entities" may be combined and their "combined financial statements" may provide useful information.

To stay current in this area, readers should monitor development on this project.

MULTIPLE-CHOICE QUESTIONS

1. What is the authoritative status of the *Framework*?

(a) It has the highest level of authority. In case of a conflict between the *Framework* and a Standard or Interpretation, the *Framework* overrides the Standard or Interpretation.

(b) If there is a Standard or Interpretation that specifically applies to a transaction, it overrides the *Framework*. In the absence of a Standard or an Interpretation that specifically applies, the *Framework* should be followed.

(c) If there is a Standard or Interpretation that specifically applies to a transaction, it overrides the *Framework*. In the absence of a Standard or an Interpretation that specifically applies to a transaction, management should consider the applicability of the *Framework* in developing and applying an accounting policy that results in information that is relevant and reliable.

(d) The *Framework* applies only when IASB develops new or revised Standards. An entity is never required to consider the *Framework*.

2. What is the objective of financial statements according to the *Framework*?

(a) To provide information about the financial position, performance, and changes in the financial position of an entity that is useful to a wide range of users in making economic decisions.

(b) To prepare and present a balance sheet, an income statement, a cash flow statement, and a statement of changes in equity.

(c) To prepare and present comparable, relevant, reliable, and understandable information to investors and creditors.

(d) To prepare financial statements in accordance with all applicable Standards and Interpretations.

3. Which of the following are underlying assumptions of financial statements?

(a) Relevance and reliability.

(b) Financial capital maintenance and physical capital maintenance.

(c) Accrual basis and going concern.

(d) Prudence and conservatism.

4. What are qualitative characteristics of financial statements according to the *Framework*?

(a) Qualitative characteristics are the attributes that make the information provided in financial statements useful to users.

(b) Qualitative characteristics are broad classes of financial effects of transactions and other events.

(c) Qualitative characteristics are nonquantitative aspects of an entity's position and performance and changes in financial position.

(d) Qualitative characteristics measure the extent to which an entity has complied with all relevant Standards and Interpretations.

5. Which of the following is **not** a qualitative characteristic of financial statements according to the *Framework*?

(a) Materiality.

(b) Understandability.

(c) Comparability.

(d) Relevance.

6. When should an item that meets the definition of an element be recognized, according to the *Framework*?

(a) When it is probable that any future economic benefit associated with the item will flow to or from the entity.

(b) When the element has a cost or value that can be measured with reliability.

(c) When the entity obtains control of the rights or obligations associated with the item.

(d) When it is probable that any future economic benefit associated with the item will flow to or from the entity and the item has a cost or value that can be measured with reliability.

Chapter 3

PRESENTATION OF FINANCIAL STATEMENTS (IAS 1)

INTRODUCTION

IAS 1 provides guidelines on the presentation of the "general-purpose financial statements," thereby ensuring comparability both with the entity's financial statements of previous periods and with those of other entities. It provides overall requirements for the presentation of financial statements, guidance on their structure, and the minimum requirements for their content. It also prescribes the components of the financial statements that together would be considered a complete set of financial statements.

SCOPE

The requirements of IAS 1 are to be applied to all "general-purpose financial statements" that have been prepared and presented in accordance with International Financial Reporting Standards (IFRS). "General-purpose financial statements" are those intended to meet the needs of users who are not in a position to demand reports that are tailored according to their information needs. IAS 1 is not applicable to condensed interim financial statements prepared according to IAS 34. Modification of the presentation requirements of the Standard may be required by nonprofit entities and those entities whose share capital is not equity.

DEFINITIONS OF KEY TERMS

Impracticable. Applying a requirement becomes impracticable when the entity cannot apply a requirement despite all reasonable efforts to do so.

International Financial Reporting Standards (IFRS). Standards and interpretations adopted by the International Accounting Standards Board (IASB). They include

1. International Financial Reporting Standards
2. International Accounting Standards
3. Interpretations originated by the IFRS Interpretations Committee, (until March 31, 2010, named International Financial Reporting Interpretations Committee [IFRIC]) or the former Standing Interpretations Committee (SIC)

Material. An item is deemed to be material if its omission or misstatement would influence the economic decisions of a user taken on the basis of the financial statements. Materiality is determined based on the item's nature, size, and/or the surrounding circumstances.

Notes to financial statements. A collection of information providing descriptions and disaggregated information relating to items included in the financial statements (i.e., statement of financial position, statement of comprehensive income, statement of changes in equity, and statement of cash flows), as well as those that do not appear in the financial statements but are disclosed due to requirements of IFRS.

Other comprehensive income comprises items of income and expenses (including reclassification adjustments) that are not recognized in profit or loss, as required or permitted by other IFRS.

Owners are holders of instruments classified as equity.

Profit or loss is the total of income less expenses, excluding the components of other comprehensive income.

Total comprehensive income is the change in equity during a period resulting from transactions and other events, other than those changes resulting from transactions with owners in their capacity as owners.

PRACTICAL INSIGHT

"Materiality" as a concept has been the subject of debate for years, yet there are no clear-cut parameters to compute materiality. What would normally be expected to influence one person's viewpoint may not necessarily influence another person's economic decisions based on the financial statements. Furthermore, materiality is not only "quantitative" (i.e., measured in terms of numbers) but also "qualitative" (because it depends not only on the "size" of the item but also on the "nature" of the item). For instance, in some cases, transactions with "related parties" (as defined under IAS 24), although not material when the size of the transactions is considered, may be considered "material" because they are with related parties (this is where the "qualitative" aspect of the definition of the term "material" comes into play). Materiality is therefore a very subjective concept.

PURPOSE OF FINANCIAL STATEMENTS

Financial statements provide stakeholders with information about the entity's financial position, financial performance, and cash flows by providing information about its assets, liabilities, equity, income and expenses, other changes in equity, and cash flows.

Components of a Complete Set of Financial Statements

The components of a complete set of financial statements comprise

- A statement of financial position as at the end of the period.
- A statement of comprehensive income for the period (presented as either a single statement or an income statement with a statement of recognized gains and losses).
- A statement of changes in equity for the period.
- A statement of cash flows for the period.
- Notes, comprising a summary of significant accounting policies and other explanatory information.
- A statement of financial position as at the beginning of the earliest comparative period when an entity applies an accounting policy retrospectively or makes a retrospective restatement of items in its financial statements.

While the Standard clarifies that an entity may use titles for statements other than those used in this Standard, it stresses that an entity shall present with equal prominence all of the components of financial statements in a complete set of financial statements.

OVERALL CONSIDERATIONS

Fair Presentation and Compliance with IFRS

"Fair presentation" implies that the financial statements "present fairly" (or alternatively, in some jurisdictions [countries], present a "true and fair" view) of the financial position, financial performance, and cash flows of an entity.

"Fair presentation" requires *faithful representation* of the effects of transactions and other events and conditions in accordance with the definitions and recognition criteria for assets, liabilities, income, and expenses laid down in the IASB's *Framework.* The application of IFRS, with additional disclosure where required, is expected to result in financial statements that achieve a "fair presentation."

Under IAS 1, entities are required to make an *explicit statement of compliance with IFRS* in their notes if their financial statements comply with IFRS.

By disclosure of the accounting policies used or notes or explanatory material, an entity cannot correct inappropriate accounting policies.

PRACTICAL INSIGHT

In practice, some entities believe that even if an inappropriate accounting policy was used in presenting the financial statements (say, use of "cash basis" as opposed to the "accrual basis" to account for certain expenses), as long as it is disclosed by the entity in notes to the financial statements, the problem would be rectified. Recognizing this tendency, IAS 1 categorically prohibits such shortcut methods from being employed by entities presenting financial statements under IFRS.

In *extremely rare circumstances,* if management believes that compliance with a particular requirement of the IFRS will be so misleading that it would conflict with the objectives of the financial statements as laid down in the IASB's *Framework,* then the entity is allowed to depart from that requirement (of the IFRS), provided the relevant regulatory framework does not prohibit such a departure. This is referred to as "true and fair override" in some jurisdictions. In such circumstances, it is incumbent upon the entity that departs from a requirement of IFRS to disclose

1. That management has concluded that the financial statements present fairly the entity's financial position, financial performance, and cash flows
2. That it has complied with all applicable Standards and Interpretations except that it has departed from a particular requirement to achieve fair presentation
3. The title of the Standard or the Interpretation from which the entity has departed, the nature of the departure, including the treatment that the Standard or Interpretation would require, the reason why that treatment would be misleading in the circumstances that it would conflict with the objective of the financial statements set out in the *Framework,* and the treatment adopted
4. The financial impact on each item in the financial statements of such a departure for each period presented

Furthermore, in the extremely rare circumstances when management concludes that compliance with the requirements in a Standard or Interpretation would be so misleading that it would conflict with the IASB's *Framework* but where the relevant regulatory framework prohibits such departure, the entity shall, to the maximum extent possible, reduce the perceived misleading aspects of compliance by disclosing: the title of the Standard or Interpretation in question, the nature of the requirement, and the reason why management has concluded that complying with that requirement is so misleading that it conflicts with the IASB's *Framework,* and for each period presented, the adjustments to each item in the financial statements that management has concluded would be necessary to achieve a fair presentation.

Going Concern

Financial statements should be prepared on a going concern basis unless management intends to liquidate the entity or cease trading or has no realistic option but to do so. When upon assessment it becomes evident that there are material uncertainties regarding the ability of the business to continue as a going concern, those uncertainties should be disclosed. In the event that the financial statements are not prepared on a going concern basis, that fact should be disclosed, together with the basis on which they are prepared, along with the reason for such a decision. In making the assessment about the going concern assumption, management takes into account all available information about the future, which is at least 12 months from the balance sheet date.

CASE STUDY 1

Facts

XYZ Inc. is a manufacturer of televisions. The domestic market for electronic goods is currently not doing well, and therefore many entities in this business are switching to exports. As per the audited financial statements for the year ended December 31, 20XX, the entity had net losses of $2 million. At December 31, 20XX, its current assets aggregate to $20 million and the current liabilities aggregate to $25 million. Due to expected favorable changes in the government policies for the electronics industry, the entity is projecting profits in the coming years. Furthermore, the shareholders of the entity have arranged alternative additional sources of finance for its expansion plans and to support its working needs in the next 12 months.

Required

Should XYZ Inc. prepare its financial statements under the going concern assumption?

Solution

The two factors that raise doubts about the entity's ability to continue as a going concern are

1. The net loss for the year of $2 million
2. At the balance sheet date, the working capital deficiency (current liabilities of $25 million) exceeds its current assets (of $20 million) by $5 million

However, there are two mitigating factors:

1. The shareholders' ability to arrange funding for the entity's expansion and working capital needs
2. Projected future profitability due to expected favorable changes in government policies for the industry the entity is operating within

Based on these sets of factors—both negative and positive (mitigating) factors—it may be possible for the management of the entity to argue that the going concern assumption is appropriate and that any other basis of preparation of financial statements would be unreasonable at the moment. However, if matters deteriorate further instead of improving, then in the future another detailed assessment would be needed to ascertain whether the going concern assumption is still valid.

Accrual Basis of Accounting

Excluding the cash flow statement, all other financial statements must be prepared on an accrual basis, whereby assets and liabilities are recognized when they are receivable or payable rather than when actually received or paid.

Consistency of Presentation

Entities are required to retain their presentation and classification of items in successive periods unless an alternative would be more appropriate or if so required by a Standard.

Materiality and Aggregation

Each material class of similar items shall be presented separately in the financial statements. Material items that are dissimilar in nature or function should be separately disclosed.

Offsetting

Assets and liabilities, income and expenses cannot be offset against each other unless required or permitted by a Standard or an Interpretation. Measuring assets net of allowances, for instance, presenting receivables net of allowance for doubtful debts, is not offsetting. Furthermore, there are transactions other than those that an entity undertakes in the ordinary course of business that do not generate "revenue" (as defined under IAS 18); instead they are incidental to the main revenue-generating activities. The results of these transactions are presented, when this presentation reflects the substance of the transaction or event, by netting any income with related expenses arising on the same transactions. For instance, gains or losses on disposal of noncurrent assets are reported by deducting from the proceeds on disposal the carrying amount of the assets and related selling expenses.

Comparative Information

Comparative information (including narrative disclosures) relating to the previous period should be reported alongside current period disclosure, unless otherwise required.

In case there is a change in the presentation or classification of items in the financial statements, the comparative information needs to be appropriately reclassified, unless it is impracticable to do so.

STRUCTURE AND CONTENT

Identification of the Financial Statements

Financial statements should be clearly identified from other information in the same published document (such as an annual report). Furthermore, the name of the entity, the period covered, presentation currency, and so on also must be displayed prominently.

Reporting Period

Financial statements should be presented at least annually. In all other cases, that is, when a period shorter or longer than one year is used, the reason for using a different period and lack of total comparability with the previous period's information must be disclosed.

Statement of Financial Position

Current and noncurrent assets and liabilities should be classified separately on the face of the statement of financial position except in circumstances when a liquidity-based presentation provides more reliable and relevant information.

Current assets. A current asset is one that is likely to be realized within the normal operating cycle or 12 months after the reporting period, held for trading purposes, or is cash or a cash equivalent. All other assets are noncurrent.

Current liabilities. A current liability is one that is likely to be settled within the normal operating cycle or 12 months after the reporting period, held for trading purposes, or there is no unconditional right to defer settlement for at least 12 months after the balance sheet date. All other liabilities are noncurrent.

The *minimum line items* that should be included in the statement of financial position are

1. Property, plant, and equipment
2. Investment property
3. Intangible assets
4. Financial assets (excluding amounts shown under 5, 8, and 9)
5. Investments accounted for using the equity method
6. Biological assets
7. Inventories
8. Trade and other receivables
9. Cash and cash equivalents
10. Trade and other payables
11. Provisions

12. Financial liabilities (excluding amounts shown under 10 and 11)
13. Liabilities and assets for current tax
14. Deferred tax liabilities and deferred tax assets
15. Minority interest, presented within equity
16. Issued capital and reserves attributable to equity holders of the parent

Deferred tax assets (liabilities) cannot be classified as current assets (liabilities). Additional line items are disclosed only if disclosure is relevant for further insight. Subclassifications of line items are required to be disclosed in either the statement of financial position or the notes. Other such disclosures include

- Numbers of shares authorized, issued and fully paid, and issued but not fully paid
- Par value
- Reconciliation of shares outstanding at the beginning and the end of the period
- Description of rights, preferences, and restrictions
- Treasury shares, including shares held by subsidiaries and associates
- Shares reserved for issuance under options and contracts
- Description of the nature and purpose of each reserve within owners' equity
- Nature and purpose of each reserve

Equivalent information would be disclosed by entities without share capital.

EXTRACTS FROM PUBLISHED FINANCIAL STATEMENTS

BARLOWORLD, Annual Report 2009
Company Balance Sheet
at September 30

	Notes	*2009 Rm*	*2008 Rm*	*2007 Rm*
Assets				
Noncurrent assets		**14,097**	9,142	9,889
Property, plant, and equipment	2	**449**	267	132
Intangible assets	3	**22**	23	24
Long-term financial assets	4	**13,561**	8,837	9,731
Deferred taxation assets	5	**65**	15	2
Current assets		**4**	42	155
Trade and other receivables	6	**4**	42	45
Cash and cash equivalents	7			6
Assets classified as held for sale	8			104
Total assets		**14,101**	9,184	10,044
Equity and liabilities				
Capital and reserves				
Share capital and premium	9	**49**	40	11
Other reserves	11	**160**	149	15
Retained income	11	**8,232**	4,117	6,762
Interest of shareholders of Barloworld Limited		**8,441**	4,306	6,788
Noncurrent liabilities		**3,582**	2,783	1,617
Interest-bearing	10	**3,578**	2,775	1,576
Provisions	12	**3**	8	41
Other noninterest-bearing	13	**1**		
Current liabilities		**2,078**	2,095	1,639
Trade and other payables		**54**	51	96
Provisions	12	**2**	8	17
Amounts due to bankers and short-term loans	14	**2,022**	2,036	1,526
Total equity and liabilities		**14,101**	9,184	10,044

Statement of Comprehensive Income

IAS 1 offers the choice of presenting all items of income and expense recognized in the period: *either* in a single statement of comprehensive income, *or* in two statements; that is, a statement displaying components of profit or loss, together with another statement beginning with profit or loss and displaying components of "other comprehensive income."

The standard prescribes, as a minimum, the following line items to be presented in a statement of comprehensive income:

- Revenue, finance costs, share of profit or loss from associates and joint ventures accounted for using the equity method, tax expense, amounts required to be disclosed under IFRS 5 relating to "discontinued operations"
- Profit or loss for the reporting period
- Each component of other comprehensive income classified by nature
- Share of other comprehensive income of associates and joint ventures accounted for using the equity method
- Total comprehensive income

Profit or loss for the reporting period as well as total comprehensive income for the period attributable to noncontrolling interests and owners of the parent are required to be disclosed separately.

Since the Standard prescribes minimum line item disclosure, an entity is permitted to present additional line items, headings, and subtotals in the statement of comprehensive income and the separate income statement (if the entity opts to present this statement). Such additional disclosures are allowed when such presentation is relevant to an understanding of the entity's financial performance.

ILLUSTRATION 1

(Single statement approach)

Statement of Comprehensive Income

	20X9	20X8
Revenue	780,000	710,000
Expenses	(500,000)	(550,000)
Profit before tax	280,000	160,000
Income tax expense	(50,000)	(30,000)
Profit for the year from continuing operations	**230,000**	**130,000**
Loss for the year from discontinued operations	(61,000)	--
Profit for the year	**169,000**	**130,000**
Other comprehensive income:		
Exchange differences on translating foreign operations	10,000	20,000
Available-for-sale financial assets	4,800	7,000
Cash flow hedges	2,400	4,400
Gains on property revaluation	16,000	14,000
Actuarial (losses)/gains on defined benefit pension plans	(1,334)	2,666
Share of other comprehensive income of associates	800	(1,400)
Income tax relating to components of other comprehensive income	(8,000)	(7,800)
Other comprehensive income for the year, net of tax	24,666	38,866
Total comprehensive income for the year	**193,666**	**168,866**
Profit attributable to:		
Owners of the parent	152,542	117,780
Minority interest	16,458	12,220
	169,000	**130,000**
Total comprehensive income attributable to:		
Owners of the parent	173,208	150,246
Minority interest	20,458	18,620
	193,666	**168,866**

ILLUSTRATION 2

Two statements approach:

1) Income statement

	20X9	20X8
Revenue	780,000	710,000
Expenses	(500,000)	(550,000)
Profit before tax	280,000	160,000
Income tax expense	(50,000)	(30,000)
Profit for the year from continuing operations	**230,000**	**130,000**
Loss for the year from discontinued operations	(61,000)	--
Profit for the year	**169,000**	**130,000**
Profit attributable to:		
Owners of the parent	152,542	117,780
Noncontrolling interest	16,458	12,220
	169,000	130,000

2) Statement of comprehensive income

	20X9	20X8
Profit for the year	169,000	130,000
Other comprehensive income:		
Exchange differences on translating foreign operations	10,000	20,000
Available-for-sale financial assets	4,800	7,000
Cash flow hedges		
Gains on property revaluation	16,000	14,000
Actuarial (losses)/gains on defined benefit pension plans	(1,334)	2,666
Share of other comprehensive income of associates	800	(1,400)
Income tax relating to components of other comprehensive income	(8,000)	(7,800)
Other comprehensive income for the year, net of tax	24,666	38,866
Total comprehensive income for the year	**193,666**	**168,866**
Total comprehensive income attributable to:		
Owners of the parent	173,208	150,246
Noncontrolling interest	20,458	18,620
	193,666	168,866

Profit or Loss for the Period

An entity shall recognize all items of income and expense in a period in profit or loss unless an IFRS requires or permits otherwise.

An entity shall present an analysis of expenses recognized in profit or loss using a classification based on either their nature or their function within the entity, whichever provides information that is reliable and more relevant.

ILLUSTRATION 3

An example of a classification using the **"nature of expense"** method is as follows:

Revenue	x
Other income	x
Changes in inventories of finished goods and work in progress	x
Raw materials and consumables used	x
Employee benefits expenses	x
Depreciation and amortization expense	x
Other expenses	x
Total expenses	(x)
Profits before tax	x

ILLUSTRATION 4

An example of a classification using the **"function of expense"** method is as follows:

Revenue	x
Costs of sales	(x)
Gross profits	x
Other income	x
Distribution costs	(x)
Administrative expenses	(x)
Other expenses	(x)
Profits before tax	x

An entity classifying expenses by the "function of expense" method shall disclose additional information on the nature of expenses, including depreciation and amortization expense and employee benefits expense.

Material income and expense should be disclosed separately with their nature and amount. (Examples of circumstances that give rise to separate disclosure of material income and expenses are: write-down of inventories to their net realizable value or property, plant, and equipment to their recoverable amount, as well as reversals of such write-downs).

Statement of Changes in Equity

The entity is required to present a statement of changes in equity, showing in the statement:

1. Total comprehensive income for the period, presenting separately total amount attributable to the owners of the parent and to the noncontrolling interests (NCI)
2. For each component of equity, the effects of retrospective application or retrospective restatement recognized in accordance with IAS 8
3. For each component of equity a reconciliation between the carrying amount at the beginning and the end of the period, separately disclosing changes resulting from

   a. Profit or loss for the period
   b. Each item of other comprehensive income
   c. Transactions with owners in their capacity as owners, showing separately

   - Contributions by and distributions to owners
   - Changes in ownership interests in subsidiaries that do not result in a loss of control

The amount of total dividends recognized as distributions to owners during the period and the related amount per share should be disclosed in either the statement of changes in equity or in the notes.

Statements of Cash Flows

The statement of cash flows serves as a basis for evaluating the entity's ability to generate cash and cash equivalents and the needs to utilize these cash flows. Requirements of cash flow statement presentation have been elaborated upon in IAS 7, *Statement of Cash Flows*.

EXTRACTS FROM PUBLISHED FINANCIAL STATEMENTS

BARLOWORLD LIMITED, Annual Report, 2009

Consolidated cash flow statement
for the year ended September 30

	Notes	2009 Rm	2008 Rm	2007 Rm
Cash flows from operating activities				
Cash receipts from customers		45,525	46,589	49,697
Cash paid to employees and suppliers		(41,056)	(42,855)	(43,858)

	Notes	2009 Rm	2008 Rm	2007 Rm
Cash generated from operations	A	**4,469**	3,734	5,839
Finance costs		**(994)**	(980)	(902)
Realized fair value adjustments on financial instruments		**(180)**	(157)	(16)
Dividends received from investments and associates		**14**	26	41
Interest received		**146**	188	338
Taxation paid	B	**(603)**	(830)	(1,412)
Cash flow from operations		**2,852**	1,981	3,888
Dividends paid (including minority shareholders)		**(434)**	(622)	(2,629)
Cash retained from operating activities		**2,418**	1,359	1,259
Cash flows from investing activities				
Acquisition of subsidiaries, investments and intangibles	C	**219**	(996)	(349)
Proceeds on disposal of subsidiaries, investments and intangibles	D	**7**	1,098	1,432
Net investment in fleet leasing and rental assets	E	**(707)**	(1,904)	(2,283)
Acquisition of other property, plant and equipment		**(910)**	(973)	(1,485)
Replacement capital expenditure		**(522)**	(305)	(451)
Expansion capital expenditure		**(388)**	(668)	(1,034)
Proceeds on disposal of property, plant and equipment		**180**	169	121
Proceeds on sale of leasing assets				1,684
Net cash used in investing activities		**(1,211)**	(2,606)	(880)
Net cash inflow/(outflow) before financing activities		**1,207**	(1,247)	379
Cash flows from financing activities				
Proceeds on share issue		**12**	23	139
Pension fund payment			(759)	
Proceeds from long-term borrowings		**4,379**	3,298	1,376
Repayment of long-term borrowings		**(4,328)**	(1,285)	(3,207)
(Decrease)/increase in short-term interest-bearing liabilities		**(710)**	70	704
Net cash (used in)/from financing activities		**(647)**	1,347	(988)
Net increase/(decrease) in cash and cash equivalents		**560**	100	(609)
Cash and cash equivalents at beginning of year		**1,238**	1,201	2,134
Cash and cash equivalents held for sale at beginning of year		**31**		
Effect of foreign exchange rate movement on cash balance		**(57)**	54	(6)
Effect of cash balances classified as held for sale		**(145)**	(31)	
Effect of unbundling of Coatings on cash balance			(86)	
Effect of unbundling Pretoria Portland Cement on cash balance				(318)
Cash and cash equivalents at end of year		**1,627**	1,238	1,201
Cash balances not available for use due to reserving restrictions		**360**	292	235

Notes

The notes should disclose the basis of preparation of financial statements, significant accounting policies, information required by IFRS but not disclosed in the statements, and additional information not presented in the statements but required for further comprehension. Notes should be systematically presented, and each item in the statements should be cross-referenced to the relevant note.

Disclosure of significant accounting policies. The summary of significant accounting policies in the notes should include the measurement bases used in the financial statements, and all other accounting policies required for further understanding. Furthermore, it should include significant judgments made by management while applying the accounting policies.

Key sources of estimation uncertainty. The notes should contain key assumptions concerning the future as well as other key sources of estimation that will pose a significant risk of causing a material adjustment to the carrying amounts of assets and liabilities within the next financial period. In such a case, the notes should include details, nature, and carrying amount of those assets and liabilities.

Other Disclosures Required by IAS 1

An entity shall disclose in the notes

1. The amount of dividends proposed or declared before the financial statements were authorized for issue but not recognized as a distribution to equity holders during the period, and the related amount per share
2. The amount of cumulative preference dividends not recognized

Furthermore, an entity should disclose the following items, if not disclosed elsewhere in information published with the financial statements:

1. The domicile and legal form of the entity, its country of incorporation, and the address of its registered office (or principal place of business, if different from the registered office)
2. A description of the nature of the entity's operations and its principal activities
3. The name of the parent and the ultimate parent of the group

"Capital Disclosures" (amendment to IAS 1, effective January 1, 2007)

As part of its project to develop IFRS 7, *Financial Instruments: Disclosures,* the IASB also amended IAS 1 to add requirements for disclosures of

- The entity's objectives, policies, and processes for managing "capital"
- Quantitative data about what the entity regards as "capital"
- Whether the entity has complied with any capital requirements and if it has not complied, the consequences of such noncompliance

These disclosure requirements apply to all entities, *effective for annual periods beginning on or after January 1, 2007,* with earlier application encouraged.

IFRS does not define the term "capital" and therefore with this new disclosure requirement any ambiguity or controversy with respect to the interpretation of such an important aspect of the financial position of an entity should be put to rest. For example, in certain jurisdictions, it is a common practice to show as part of "equity," subordinated loans from owners that are in the nature of "equity" and have distinct features of "equity" (i.e., they are noninterest-bearing and have no repayment terms specified and thus are long-term in nature) and thus could be considered "residual interest." In such jurisdictions, usually companies do not infuse huge amounts of share capital; instead, they manage the business using long-term and medium-term loans from their owners/ shareholders that are in the nature of "equity." Financial institutions therefore treat such owner/shareholder loans on par with share capital for the purpose of satisfying their lending norms and thus provide funds and other banking facilities to such companies in these jurisdictions on the strength of both share capital and such loans from the owners/shareholders. In such circumstances it is therefore obvious that these entities intend to treat as "capital" both "share capital" and even such owner/shareholder loans as their "true" capital. With such practices prevalent in many jurisdictions around the world, IAS 1 makes it incumbent upon an entity to clearly define and disclose what the entity regards as "capital" for the purposes of running its business and for obtaining financing. In other words, IAS 1 requires disclosure of what an entity's objectives, policies, and processes are for managing "capital" and quantitative data about what the entity regards as "capital."

Furthermore, in case there are any capital requirements that an entity has to comply with (say, "minimum capital" as per the corporate law governing the jurisdiction where the entity is incorporated), then IAS 1 also requires disclosure of whether the entity has in fact complied with those capital requirements. In the event the entity has not complied with such capital requirements, IAS 1 further requires disclosures of consequences of such noncompliance.

ILLUSTRATION 5

Illustrative capital disclosures under IAS 1

1. XYZ company's objectives in managing its capital are

    a. To ensure that the entity's ability to continue as a going concern is safeguarded so that it can continue to meet its financial obligations as and when they fall due and by protecting its ability to provide returns to its shareholders and other stakeholders.

    b. To provide adequate returns to the shareholders by operating the business at predetermined optimal levels, by ensuring the present revenue stream from operations is maintained at least at the current levels and by effectively collecting its receivables as agreed with debtors while extending credit.

2. Based on the financial covenants imposed on ABC Inc. by the international consortium of bankers from whom the entity has obtained working capital loans and other indirect banking facilities (L/C and L/G facilities), the entity maintains, at all times during the year, a debt/equity ratio of at least 1 to 3. For the purposes of computing debt/equity ratio the banks have agreed to include in "equity" the following:

    a. Share capital
    b. Share premium
    c. Retained earning
    d. Shareholders' loans in the nature of equity (including subordinated loans)
    e. Statutory reserve (as per local commercial company law)
    f. Revaluation reserve

OTHER AMENDMENTS TO IAS 1

IAS 1 (revised 2007), Effective for Annual Periods Beginning on or after January 1, 2009

In September 2007 the IASB issued a revised IAS 1 and they made many changes to the terminology including changes to the titles of individual financial statements. For instance, the title "balance sheet" will in the future be referred to as a "statement of financial position." The most significant changes are set out here:

-   There is a new requirement to include a "statement of financial position" at the beginning of the earliest comparative period presented whenever an entity applies a change in accounting policy retrospectively, or makes a retrospective restatement of items in its financial statements, or when it reclassifies items in the financial statements
-   All items of income and expense (including those accounted for directly in equity) must, after the revisions become effective, be presented either in a single statement (a "statement of comprehensive income") **or** in two statements (with a separate "income statement" and "statement of comprehensive income")
-   Entities are no longer permitted to present items of "other comprehensive income" (e.g., gains or losses on revaluation of property, plant, and equipment) separately in the "statement of changes in equity" ("such nonowner movements must now be presented in a statement of comprehensive income")
-   Entities are no longer permitted to present transactions with owners in their capacity as owners in the notes to the financial statements (since now the "statement of changes in equity" must be presented as a separate financial statement)
-   New detailed requirements have been added regarding the presentation of items of "other comprehensive income"

IAS 1 (revised 2008), Effective January 1, 2009, Disclosures about Puttable Shares and Obligations Arising Only on Liquidation

In February 2008 the IASB published an amendment to IAS 1 that requires the following additional disclosures if an entity has a "puttable instrument" that is presented as equity:

-   Summary quantitative data about the amount classified as equity
-   The entity's objectives, policies, and processes for managing its obligation to repurchase or redeem the instruments when required to do so by the instrument holders, including any changes from the previous period
-   The expected cash outflow on redemption or repurchase of that class of financial instruments
-   Information about how the expected cash outflow on redemption or repurchase was determined

If an instrument is reclassified into and out of each category (financial liabilities or equity) the amount, timing, and reason for that reclassification must be disclosed. If an entity is a limited-life entity, disclosure is also required regarding the length of its life.

Changes to IAS 1 Made by the IASB's Annual "Improvements to IFRS" Projects

Annual improvements to IFRS 2008. In May 2008 the IASB published the amendments to 20 IFRS (including IAS 1) resulting from its Annual Improvements Project, which is designed to make nonurgent but necessary minor amendments to IFRS. Through the "Improvements to IFRS 2008" issuance the IASB made an amendment to IAS 1 (2007), effective for periods beginning on or after January 1, 2009, whereby it clarified that financial instruments classified as held for trading in accordance with IAS 39 are not always required to be presented as current liabilities or current assets.

Annual improvements to IFRS 2009 In April 2009 the IASB issued "Improvements to IFRS 2009" (second in the series of omnibus amendments by the IASB which are meant to make nonurgent but necessary minor changes to several IFRS), which incorporated amendments to 12 IFRS, including IAS 1. Through this amendment to IAS 1, which is effective for periods beginning on or after January 1, 2010 (with earlier application permitted), the definition of "current liability" has been amended. Under the earlier definition, if the counterparty could require settlement in the form of equity instruments at any time, a liability would be classified as current, even if the entity could not be required to settle in cash or other assets within 12 months. With this revision, a liability is now classified as current or noncurrent based on requirements to transfer cash or other assets, and the effect of conversion options is ignored. In other words, the potential settlement of a liability by the issuance of equity is not relevant to its classification as current or noncurrent. This amendment permits a liability to be classified as a "noncurrent liability" (provided the entity has an unconditional right to defer settlement by transfer of cash or other assets for at least 12 months after the reporting period) even if the entity could be required by the counterparty to settle in shares at any time.

Annual improvements to IFRS 2010. In May 2010 the IASB issued "Improvements to IFRS 2010" incorporating amendments to seven IFRS, including IAS 1. This is the third in the series of omnibus amendments by the IASB as part of its drive to make nonurgent and minor (but required) changes to several IFRS. Through this amendment to IAS 1, which is effective for periods beginning on or after January 1, 2011 (with earlier application permitted), the IASB clarified that an entity may present the analysis of other comprehensive income by item either in the statement of changes in equity or in the notes to the financial statements.

MULTIPLE-CHOICE QUESTIONS

1. Which of the following reports is **not** a component of the financial statements according to IAS 1?

    (a) Statement of financial position.
    (b) Statement of changes in equity.
    (c) Director's report.
    (d) Notes to the financial statements.

2. XYZ Inc. decided to extend its reporting period from a year (12-month period) to a 15-month period. Which of the following is not required under IAS 1 in case of change in reporting period?

    (a) XYZ Inc. should disclose the reason for using a longer period than a period of 12 months.
    (b) XYZ Inc. should change the reporting period only if other similar entities in the geographical area in which it generally operates have done so in the current year; otherwise its financial statements would not be comparable to others.
    (c) XYZ Inc. should disclose that comparative amounts used in the financial statements are not entirely comparable.

3. Which of the following is **not** specifically a required disclosure of IAS 1?

    (a) Name of the reporting entity or other means of identification, and any change in that information from the previous year.
    (b) Names of major/significant shareholders of the entity.
    (c) Level of rounding used in presenting the financial statements.
    (d) Whether the financial statements cover the individual entity or a group of entities.

4. Which one of the following is not required to be presented as minimum information on the face of the balance sheet, according to IAS 1?

    (a) Investment property.
    (b) Investments accounted for under the equity method.
    (c) Biological assets.
    (d) Contingent liability.

5. When an entity opts to present the income statement classifying expenses by function, which of the following is not required to be disclosed as "additional information"?

    (a) Depreciation expense.
    (b) Employee benefits expense.
    (c) Director's remuneration.
    (d) Amortization expense.

Chapter 4

INVENTORIES (IAS 2)

BACKGROUND AND INTRODUCTION

The Standard prescribes the accounting treatment for inventories. The main issue with respect to accounting for inventory is the amount of cost to be recognized as an asset. In addition, the Standard provides guidance on the determination of the cost and subsequent recognition of expense (including write-down of inventory to its net realizable value). The Standard also provides guidance on the cost flow assumptions ("cost formulas") that are to be used in assigning costs to inventories.

SCOPE

This Standard applies to all inventories other than

- Work in progress under construction contracts and directly related service contracts (IAS 11, *Construction Contracts*)
- Financial instruments
- Biological assets related to agricultural activity and agricultural produce at the point of harvest (under IAS 41, *Agriculture*)

This Standard does *not* apply to the *measurement* of inventories held by

- Producers of agriculture and forest products, agricultural produce after harvest, and minerals and minerals products, to the extent that they are measured at net realizable value in accordance with best practices within those industries. *When such inventories are measured at net realizable value, changes in that value are recognized in the profit or loss in the period of change.*
- Commodity brokers-traders who measure their inventories at fair value less cost to sell. When such inventories are measured at fair value less cost to sell, the changes in fair value less costs to sell are recognized as profit or loss in the period of change.

PRACTICAL INSIGHT

Although inventories referred to in the previous section (where biological assets are discussed) are excluded from *all* requirements of this Standard, the inventories referred to in the section following it, are excluded *only* from *measurement requirements* of this Standard (IAS 2). In other words, all requirements of this Standard, except the requirements relating to "measurement," apply. Therefore, the principles of measurement of inventories under IAS 2 (i.e., lower of cost or net realizable value) do not apply to the inventories discussed there.

DEFINITIONS OF KEY TERMS

Inventory. An asset that is

1. Held for sale in the normal course of business
2. In the process of production for such sale
3. In the form of materials or supplies to be used in the production process or in the rendering of services

Net realizable value. The estimated selling price in the normal course of business less estimated cost to complete and estimated cost to make a sale.

Fair value. The amount at which an asset could be exchanged, or a liability settled, between knowledgeable, willing parties in an arm's-length transaction.

MEASUREMENT OF INVENTORIES

In general, inventories are valued at the *"lower of cost and net realizable value."* There are, however, two exceptions to this principle of measuring inventories; they are clearly explained in the Standard (these are covered in an earlier section of this chapter).

COST OF INVENTORIES

The cost of inventories comprises all

1. Costs of purchase
2. Costs of conversion
3. "Other costs" incurred in bringing the inventories to their present location and condition

Costs of Purchase

The costs of purchase constitute all of

- The purchase price
- Import duties
- Transportation costs
- Handling costs directly pertaining to the acquisition of the goods

Trade discounts and rebates are deducted when arriving at the cost of purchase of inventory.

Costs of Conversion of Inventory

Costs of conversion of inventory includes costs directly attributable to the units of production, for example, direct labor. The conversion costs could also include variable and fixed manufacturing overhead incurred in converting raw materials into finished goods. *Fixed overhead costs* are those costs that remain constant irrespective of the units of production. The best example would be the depreciation of factory building and equipment. *Variable costs* are those costs that vary directly with the volume of production, such as indirect material and labor costs. The allocation of overhead to the cost of conversion is based on the "normal capacity" of the facility. *Normal capacity* is the production that is normally achieved on average over a number of periods, taking into account the loss of capacity that may result. Costs that could not be reasonably allocated to the cost of inventory should be expensed as they are incurred. When the production process leads to "joint products" or "by-products," then the cost of conversion of each product should be ascertained based on some rational and consistent basis, such as the "relative sales value" method.

Other Costs in Valuing Inventories

Other costs in valuing inventories include those costs that are incurred in bringing the inventories to their present location and condition. An example of such "other costs" is costs of designing products for specific customer needs.

Excluded Costs from Inventory Valuation

Certain costs are not included in valuing inventory. They are recognized as expenses during the period they are incurred.

Examples of such costs are

1. Abnormal amounts of wasted materials, labor, or other production costs
2. Storage costs unless they are essential to the production process
3. Administrative overheads that do not contribute to bringing inventories to their present location and condition
4. Selling costs

Inventory Purchased on Deferred Settlement Terms

When inventories are purchased on deferred settlement terms, such arrangements in reality contain a financing element. That portion of the price that can be attributable to extended settlement terms, the difference between the purchase price for normal credit terms and the amount paid, is recognized as interest expense over the period of the financing arrangement.

Inventories of Service Providers

Inventories of service providers are measured at costs of their production. These costs consist primarily of labor and other costs of personnel directly used in providing the service, including cost of supervisory personnel, and attributable overheads. *The costs of inventories of service providers should not include profit margins or nonattributable overheads that are generally used in prices quoted by service providers to their customers.*

CASE STUDY 1

Facts

Brilliant Trading Inc. purchases motorcycles from various countries and exports them to Europe. Brilliant Trading has incurred these expenses during 2009:

1. Cost of purchases (based on vendors' invoices)
2. Trade discounts on purchases
3. Import duties
4. Freight and insurance on purchases
5. Other handling costs relating to imports
6. Salaries of accounting department
7. Brokerage commission payable to indenting agents for arranging imports
8. Sales commission payable to sales agents
9. After-sales warranty costs

Required

Brilliant Trading Inc. is seeking your advice on which costs are permitted under IAS 2 to be included in cost of inventory.

Solution

Items 1, 2, 3, 4, 5, and 7 are permitted to be included in cost of inventory under IAS 2. Salaries of accounting department, sales commission, and after-sales warranty costs are not considered cost of inventory under IAS 2 and thus are not allowed to be included in cost of inventory.

TECHNIQUES FOR MEASUREMENT OF COSTS

Techniques for measurement of costs such as the standard cost method and the retail method may be used if results more or less equal actual costs. The standard cost method takes into account normal levels of material, labor, efficiency, and capacity utilization. The retail method is often used by entities in the retail industry for which large numbers of inventory items have similar gross profit margins. The cost is determined by subtracting the percentage gross margin from the sales value. The percentage used takes into account inventory that has been marked down to market value (if market is lower than cost).

COST FORMULAS

In cases of inventories that are not ordinarily interchangeable and goods or services produced and segregated for specific projects, costs shall be assigned using the *specific identification* of their individual costs.

In all other cases, the cost of inventories should be measured using *either* of the following:

- The *FIFO* (first-in, first-out) method.
- The weighted-average cost method.

The FIFO method assumes that the inventories that are purchased first are sold first, with the ending or remaining items in the inventory being valued based on prices of most recent purchases. However, using the weighted-average cost method, the cost of each item is determined from the weighted-average of the cost of similar items at the beginning of a period and the cost of items purchased or produced during the period.

Inventories having a similar nature and use to the entity should be valued using the same cost formula. However, in case of inventories with different nature or use, different cost formulas may be justified.

CASE STUDY 2

First-in, First-out (FIFO) Method

Facts

XYZ Inc. is a newly established international trading company. It commenced its operation in 2009. XYZ imports goods from China and sells in the local market. It uses the FIFO method to value its inventory. Listed next are the purchases and sales made by the entity during the year 2009:

Purchases

January 2009	10,000 units	@ $ 25 each
March 2009	15,000 units	@ $ 30 each
September 2009	20,000 units	@ $ 35 each

Sales

May 2009	15,000 units
November 2009	20,000 units

Required

Based on the FIFO cost flow assumption, compute the value of inventory at May 31, 2009, September 30, 2009, and December 31, 2009.

Solution

(a) January 2009 Purchase + 10,000 units @ $25 = $ 250,000
    March 2009 Purchase + 15,000 units @ $30 = $_450,000
    Total $_700,000

(b) May 2009 Sales (15,000 units) – 10,000 units @ $25 = $ (250,000)
    – 5,000 units @ $30 = $_(150,000)
    $_(400,000)

(c) **Inventory valued on FIFO basis at May 31, 2009:**

    10,000 units @ $30 = $_300,000

(d) September 2009 Purchase + 20,000 units @ $35 = $_700,000

(e) **Inventory valued on FIFO basis at September 30, 2009:**

    10,000 units @ $30 = $ 300,000
    20,000 units @ $35 = $_700,000
    $1,000,000

(f) November 2009 Sales (20,000 units) – 10,000 units @ $30 = $ (300,000)
    – 10,000 units @ $35 = $_(350,000)
    $_(650,000)

(g) **Inventory valued on FIFO basis at December 31,2009:**

    10,000 units @ $35 = $_350,000

CASE STUDY 3

Weighted-Average Cost Method

Facts

Vigilant LLC, a newly incorporated company, uses the latest version of a software package (EXODUS) to cost and value its inventory. The software uses the weighted-average cost method to value inventory. The following are the purchases and sales made by Vigilant LLC during 2009 (as a newly set up company, Vigilant LLC has no beginning inventory):

Purchases
January 100 units @ $250 per unit
March 150 units @ $300 per unit
September 200 units @ $350 per unit

Sales
March 150 units
December 170 units

Required

Vigilant LLC has approached you to compute the value of its inventory and the cost per unit of the inventory at March 31, 2009; September 30, 2009; and December 31, 2009; under the weighted-average cost method.

Solution

Month	Purchases/Sales/Balance			Rate per unit	Amount	Weighted-average cost per unit	Valuation date
Jan 15	Purchases	100	units	$250	$25,000		
Jan 31	Balance	100	units				
Mar 10	Purchases	150	units	$300	$45,000		
Mar 10	Balance	250	units	$280	$70,000		
Mar 15	Sales	(150)	units	$280	$(42,000)		
Mar 31	Balance	100	units		$28,000	$280.00	March 31, 2009
Sep 25	Purchases	200	units	$350	$70,000		
Sep 30	Balance	300	units		$98,000	$326.667	September 30, 2009
Dec 15	Sales	(170)	units	$326.667	$(55,533)		
Dec 31	Balance	130	units		$42,467	$326.667	December 31, 2009

NET REALIZABLE VALUE

Inventories are written down to net realizable value (NRV) on the basis that assets should not be carried in excess of amounts likely to be realized from their sale or use. Write-down of inventories becomes necessary for several reasons; for example, inventories may be damaged or become obsolete or their selling prices may have declined after year-end (or period-end).

Inventories are usually written down to their NRV on an item-by-item basis, but in certain conditions, also by a group of similar or related items. It is, however, not appropriate to mark down inventories by classification of inventories, such as finished goods, or all inventories in a geographical segment or industry.

NRV estimates are based on the most reliable evidence of the inventories' realizable amounts. They take into account price fluctuations or costs directly related to events after the period-end, confirming conditions that exist at the period-end. Estimates of NRV also take into account the reason or purpose for which inventories are held. For instance, NRV of a quantity of inventory being held to satisfy firm sales contracts or service contracts are based on contract prices.

Inventories of raw materials and other supplies held for use in the production of inventories are not written down below cost if the finished goods in which they will be used are expected to be sold at or above cost. However, when a decrease in the price of raw materials indicates that the cost of the finished goods exceeds net realizable value, the materials are written down to NRV. In such cases, the replacement cost of the raw materials may be the best available measure of their NRV.

NRV is assessed in each successive period. If changes in economic circumstances warrant, earlier write-downs are reversed to make the new carrying amount equal to the lower of cost and the revised NRV.

CASE STUDY 4

Facts

Moonstruck Enterprises Inc. is a retailer of Italian furniture and has five major product lines: sofas, dining tables, beds, closets, and lounge chairs. At December 31, 200X, quantity on hand, cost per unit, and net realizable value (NRV) per unit of the product lines are as follows:

Product line	Quantity on hand	Cost per unit ($)	NRV per unit ($)
Sofas	100	1,000	1,020
Dining tables	200	500	450
Beds	300	1,500	1,600
Closets	400	750	770
Lounge chairs	500	250	200

Required

Compute the valuation of the inventory of Moonstruck Enterprises at December 31, 200X, under IAS 2 using the "lower of cost and NRV" principle.

Solution

Product line	Quantity on hand	Cost per unit ($)	Inventory at cost ($)	NRV per unit ($)	Lower of cost and NRV ($)
Sofas	100	1,000	100,000	1,020	100,000
Dining tables	200	500	100,000	450	90,000
Beds	300	1,500	450,000	1,600	450,000
Closets	400	750	300,000	770	300,000
Lounge chairs	500	250	125,000	200	100,000
			$1,075,000		$1,040,000

RECOGNITION OF EXPENSE

When inventory is sold, the carrying amount of inventory should be recognized as an expense when the related revenue is recognized. Moreover, the amount of any inventory written down to net realizable value is recognized as an expense. The amount of any reversal of a write-down of inventory should be a reduction to the amount written off in the period it was reversed.

DISCLOSURE

The financial statements should disclose

- Accounting policies adopted for measuring inventories and the cost flow assumption (i.e., cost formula) used
- Total carrying amount as well as amounts classified as appropriate to the entity
- Carrying amount of any inventories carried at fair value less costs to sell
- Amount of inventory recognized as expense during the period
- Amount of any write-down of inventories recognized as an expense in the period
- Amount of any reversal of a write-down to net realizable value and the circumstances that led to such reversal
- Circumstances requiring a reversal of the write-down
- Carrying amount of inventories pledged as security for liabilities

EXTRACTS FROM PUBLISHED FINANCIAL STATEMENTS

LECTRA, Annual Report, 2009

(in thousands of euros)	2009	2008
Raw materials	18,424	25,416
Finished goods and works-in-progress (1)	10,186	13,609
Inventories, gross value	**28,610**	**39,025**
Raw materials	(5,251)	(5,313)
Finished goods and works-in-progress (1)	(4,911)	(5,098)
Write-downs	**(10,162)**	**(10,411)**
Raw materials	13,173	20,103
Finished goods and works-in-progress (1)	5,275	8,511
Inventories, net value	**18,448**	**28,614**

Notes to Financial Statements

Accounting Policies

Inventories

Inventories of raw materials are valued at the lower of purchase cost (based on weighted-average cost, including related costs) and their net realizable value. Finished goods and works-in-progress are valued at the lower of standard industrial cost (adjusted at year-end on an actual cost basis) and their net realizable value.

Net realizable value is the estimated selling price in the normal course of business, less the estimated cost of completion or upgrading of the product and unavoidable selling costs.

Inventory cost does not include interest expense.

Note 7. Inventories

1. Including demonstration and second-hand equipment.

€2,063,000 of inventory fully written down were scrapped in the course of 2009 (€2,540,000 in 2008), thereby diminishing the gross value and write-downs by the same amount.

Progress made in the utilization of the new production and inventory management software programs since their deployment on January 1, 2007, and since the deployment of modules of these software programs dedicated to the subsidiaries, resulted in a sharp reduction in Group inventories in 2009.

Inventory write-downs charged for the year amounted to €3,275,000 (€3,652,000 in 2008). Reversals of previous write-downs relating to sales transactions amounted to €1,542,000 (€818,000 in 2008), booked against the charges for the period.

NESTLE, Annual Report, 2009

Notes to Financial Statements

Accounting Policies

Inventories

Raw materials and purchased finished goods are valued at purchase cost. Work-in-progress and manufactured finished goods are valued at production cost. Production cost includes direct production costs and an appropriate proportion of production overheads and factory depreciation.

Raw material inventories and purchased finished goods are accounted for using the FIFO (first-in, first-out) method. The weighted-average cost method is used for other inventories.

An allowance is established when the net realizable value of any inventory item is lower than the value calculated above.

BARLOWORLD, Annual Report, 2009

Notes to the Consolidated Annual Financial Statements for the Year Ended September 30

Inventories

(In euros millions)	*2009*	*2008*	*2007*
Raw materials and components			116
Work-in-progress	295	291	321
Finished goods	3,318	3,939	2,740
Merchandise	3,054	3,219	2,647
Consumable stores	21	26	17
Other inventories	49	20	28
Total inventories	**6,737**	**7,495**	**5,869**
Per business segment:			
Continuing operations			
Equipment	4,296	4,955	3,184
Automotive	1,695	1,870	1,711
Handling	738	769	602
Logistics	5	7	5
Corporate	3	11	5
Total continuing operations	**6,737**	**7,612**	**5,507**
Discontinued operations			
Coating			362
Scientific			231
Total discontinued operations			593
Total group	**6,737**	**7,612**	**6,100**
Amounts classified as held for sale		(117)	(231)
Total per balance sheet	**6,737**	**7,495**	**5,869**
The value of inventories has been determined on the following bases:			
First-in, first-out and specific identification	6,381	7,081	5,394
Weighted-average	356	414	475
	6,737	7,495	5,869
Inventory pledged as security for liabilities	109	170	29
The secured liabilities are included under trade and other payables (note 18)			
Amount of write-down of inventory to net realizable value and losses of inventory	22	13	5
Amount of reversals of inventory previously written down	7	5	1
Amounts removed during the year from cash flow hedge reserve and included in the initial cost of inventory	(55)	(2)	2

MULTIPLE-CHOICE QUESTIONS

1. Inventory should be stated at
   (a) Lower of cost and fair value.
   (b) Lower of cost and net realizable value.
   (c) Lower of cost and nominal value.
   (d) Lower of cost and net selling price.
   (e) Choices b and d.
   (f) Choices a and c.
   (g) Choices a, b, and d.

2. Which of the following costs of conversion **cannot** be included in cost of inventory?
   (a) Cost of direct labor.
   (b) Factory rent and utilities.
   (c) Salaries of sales staff (sales department shares the building with factory supervisor).
   (d) Factory overheads based on normal capacity.

3. Inventories are assets
   (a) Used in the production or supply of goods and services for administrative purposes.
   (b) Held for sale in the ordinary course of business.
   (c) Held for long-term capital appreciation.
   (d) In the process of production for such sale.
   (e) In the form of materials or supplies to be consumed in the production process or the rendering of services.
   (f) Choices b and d.
   (g) Choices b, d, and e.

4. The cost of inventory should **not** include
   (a) Purchase price.
   (b) Import duties and other taxes.
   (c) Abnormal amounts of wasted materials.
   (d) Administrative overhead.
   (e) Fixed and variable production overhead.
   (f) Selling costs.
   (g) Choices c, d, and f.

5. ABC LLC manufactures and sells paper envelopes. The stock of envelopes was included in the closing inventory as of December 31, 2009, at a cost of $50 each per pack. During the final audit, the auditors noted that the subsequent sale price for the inventory at January 15, 2010, was $40 each per pack. Furthermore, inquiry reveals that during the physical stock take, a water leakage has created damages to the paper and the glue. Accordingly, in the following week, ABC LLC spent a total of $15 per pack for repairing and reapplying glue to the envelopes. The net realizable value and inventory write-down (loss) amount to
   (a) $40 and $10 respectively.
   (b) $45 and $10 respectively.
   (c) $25 and $25 respectively.
   (d) $35 and $25 respectively.
   (e) $30 and $15 respectively.

Chapter 5

STATEMENT OF CASH FLOWS (IAS 7)

BACKGROUND AND INTRODUCTION

IAS 1, *Presentation of Financial Statements,* makes it incumbent upon entities preparing financial statements under International Financial Reporting Standards (IFRS) to present a statement of cash flows as an integral part of the financial statements. IAS 7, *Statement of Cash Flows,* lays down rules regarding statement of cash flows preparation and reporting. The statement of cash flows provides information about an entity's cash receipts and cash payments (i.e., cash flows) for the period for which the financial statements are presented.

The statement of cash flows replaced the "fund flow statement," which most accounting standards around the world (including the then International Accounting Standards) previously required to be presented as an integral part of the financial statements. The *fund flow statement* reported the movements or changes in funds. Certain standards interpreted the term "funds" as "net liquid funds;" most others, however, interpreted "funds" as "working capital." Most standard setters revised their standards in favor of the statement of cash flows, probably due to the ambiguity in the interpretation of the concept of "funds" coupled with the growing importance of the concept of "cash generated by operations." With the change in requirements, whereby an entity is required to report a statement of cash flows (in lieu of a funds flow statement) as an integral part of its financial statements, the emphasis has clearly shifted globally from reporting movements in funds (say, working capital) to cash inflows and cash outflows (i.e., cash receipts and cash payments) for the period for which the financial statements are presented.

SCOPE

All entities, regardless of the nature of their activities, should prepare a statement of cash flows in accordance with the requirements of IAS 7. The statement of cash flows should be presented as an integral part of the financial statements for each period for which the financial statements are presented. Recognizing that no matter how diverse the principal revenue-generating activities of the entities are, their needs for cash to pay their obligations (liabilities) and to produce returns for the shareholders is the same, the statement of cash flows has been made mandatory for all entities.

> **DEFINITIONS OF KEY TERMS**
> **(in accordance with IAS 7, paragraph 6)**
>
> **Cash.** Comprises cash on hand and demand deposits with banks.
> **Cash equivalents.** Short-term, highly liquid investments that are readily convertible into known amounts of cash and that are subject to an insignificant amount of risk of changes in value.
> **Operating activities.** Principal revenue-producing activities of the entity and other activities that are not investing or financing activities.
> **Investing activities.** Activities of the entity that relate to acquisition and disposal of long-lived assets and other noncurrent assets (including investments) other than those included in cash equivalents.
> **Financing activities.** Activities that result in changes in the size and composition of the equity capital and borrowings of an entity.

BENEFITS OF PRESENTING A STATEMENT OF CASH FLOWS

When presented along with the other components of financial statements (namely, a statement of financial position, a statement of comprehensive income, and a statement of changes of equity), a statement of cash flows provides this additional information to users of financial statements:

1. A better insight into the financial structure of an entity, including its liquidity and solvency, and its ability to affect the amounts and timing of cash flows in order to adapt to changing circumstances and opportunities.
2. Enhanced information for the purposes of evaluation of changes in assets, liabilities, and equity of an entity.

Furthermore, a statement of cash flows also

3. Enhances the comparability of reporting operating performance by different entities because it eliminates the effects of using different accounting treatments for similar transactions.
4. Serves as an indicator of the amount, timing, and certainty of future cash flows.

CASH AND CASH EQUIVALENTS

True Significance of the Term "Cash Equivalents"

Cash equivalents are held by the entity for meeting short-term commitments. The true meaning of cash equivalents can be best understood by analyzing the definition given by the Standard. According to the definition, cash equivalents are required to possess these two attributes:

1. They should be "short term" in nature; that is, they are held for meeting short-term cash commitments. In other words, an investment normally qualifies as a cash equivalent only if it has a short maturity, say, three months or less, from the date of acquisition.

   Example

   A time deposit with a bank (or a fixed deposit, as it is referred to in some countries) with an original maturity of six months would **not** qualify as a cash equivalent.

2. They should be "highly liquid investments" that are "readily convertible to known amounts of cash and are subject to an insignificant risk of changes in value."

   Example

   Investments in equity shares of another entity would **not** qualify as cash equivalents because they are subject to risk of changes in values that could be "significant" depending on how their market values fluctuate in reacting to economic conditions or other factors. However, investments in redeemable preference shares acquired within a short period of their maturity and with a specified redemption date qualify as cash equivalents.

Bank Borrowings as Cash Equivalents

Amounts due to a bank are generally considered to be financing activities. However, in certain countries, bank overdrafts that are repayable on demand and form an integral part of an entity's cash management may be included as a component of cash equivalents. In order for a bank overdraft to be thus included in cash equivalents (in other words, *offset* other cash equivalents being a negative cash equivalent), an important characteristic of such banking arrangements is that the bank balance should fluctuate from being positive to overdrawn (i.e., negative) during the period/ year for which the cash flow statement is being prepared.

PRACTICAL INSIGHT

In certain countries, banks offer to their long-standing customers a service (sometimes referred to as bounce protection) wherein the banks cover up to a certain amount of overdrawn balance in a customer's current account with the bank by way of an accommodation to the customer. This is a temporary accommodation, and the bank's customer whose account is overdrawn is usually allowed a limit for this facility. Some banks charge the customer a fee for this kind of a service.

Let us examine how this operates in practice. Say an entity issues checks to its creditors in the expectation that collections from checks deposited with the bank would clear in time and be enough to cover the funds needed to pay the checks issued to its creditors. For reasons beyond the control of the entity, the checks deposited are not cleared in time. The bank has to step in temporarily and cover its customer by honoring the checks issued to its creditors. The bounce protection arrangement thus is invoked. In such cases, it would be appropriate to view such a bank arrangement as an integral part of the entity's cash management; because the account with the bank may fluctuate from positive to overdrawn from time to time, such a bank overdraft would qualify as a component of cash equivalents.

Regular bank overdrafts that are part of the funded facilities negotiated with banks by entities on a periodic basis (whereby the banks lend funds to the entities based on criteria such as predetermined working capital requirements or a percentage of the net book value of trade receivables) would not meet the criteria of cash equivalents and therefore are considered financing activities for the purposes of the cash flow statement.

Movements in Cash Equivalents

Movements within or between the items of cash equivalents are excluded from cash flows for the purposes of the preparation of the statement of cash flows, as they are part of the cash management of the entity as opposed to its operating, financing, and investing activities.

CASE STUDY 1

Facts

XYZ Inc., as part of its cash management activities, invested $10 million in redeemable preference shares (within three months from the date of their redemption). To do so, XYZ instructed its bank to use a maturing time deposit (a two-month fixed deposit) with the bank.

Required

Determine how XYZ Inc. would treat, in its statement of cash flows, the cash outflows resulting from the investment of funds in redeemable preferred shares and the cash inflows resulting from the withdrawal of funds from the bank by using a maturing time deposit.

Solution

These would not be considered either as a cash inflow or a cash outflow for the purposes of the statement of cash flows of XYZ Inc. because both activities are part of the entity's cash management and comprised movements between components of cash equivalents.

PRESENTATION OF THE STATEMENT OF CASH FLOWS

IAS 7 requires that a statement of cash flows should be classified into four components: (1) operating activities, (2) investing activities, (3) financing activities, and (4) cash and cash equivalents. In other words, the statement of cash flows provides information about an entity's cash receipts and cash payments (i.e., cash flows) for the period categorized under three headings (1) operating activities, (2) investing activities, and (3) financing activities—along with changes in cash and cash equivalents. Such classification of information provided by the statement of cash flows allows users of financial statements to assess the impact of those activities on the financial position of the entity and the amount of cash and cash equivalents.

Due care must be taken to include transactions under the appropriate category. Whatever classification chosen has to be applied in a consistent manner from year to year.

Example

If "interest received" is presented as a cash flow from investing activities in year 1, the same classification should be followed from year to year, even though IAS 7 allows "interest received" to be presented either as a cash flow from operating activities or as cash flow from investing activities.

A single transaction may include cash flows that are classified partly as one type of activity and partly as another category.

Example

Cash payment made toward repayment of a bank loan has two components: the repayment of the principal portion of the loan, which is classified as a financing activity, and repayment of the interest, which is classified as an operating activity.

OPERATING ACTIVITIES

Cash flows from operating activities are mainly derived from principal revenue-generating activities of the entity. This is a critical indicator of the financial strength of an entity because it is an important source of internal finance. Financial statement users usually look at cash flows from operating activities as a gauge of an entity's ability to maintain its operating capability and support other activities, such as servicing debt and repaying of borrowings, paying dividends to shareholders, and making investments without recourse to external funding.

Common examples of cash flows from operating activities are

Cash Inflows

1. Cash collections from customers from sale of goods and the rendering of services
2. Cash receipts from "other revenues," such as royalties, fees, and commissions
3. Cash refunds of income taxes unless they can be specifically identified with financing or investing activities

Cash Outflows

1. Cash payments to suppliers of goods and services
2. Cash payments to or on behalf of employees
3. Cash payment of income taxes unless they can be specifically identified with financing or investing activities

In addition, other examples are operating cash flows from contracts held for trading or dealing (futures and options) and, in the case of insurance entities, cash receipts and payments for premiums and claims, annuities, and policy benefits. Furthermore, cash flows that do not meet the criteria of investing or financing activities also are classified as cash flows from operating activities.

INVESTING ACTIVITIES

Investing activities include the purchase and disposal of property, plant, and equipment and other long-term assets, such as investment property. They also include purchase and sale of debt and equity and debt instruments of other entities that are not considered cash equivalents or held for dealing or trading purposes. Investing activities also include cash advances and collections on loans made to other entities. This, however, does not include loans and advances made by banks and other financial institutions to their customers that would be classified as "operating activities" as they are cash flows from these entities' principal revenue-producing activities.

Common examples of cash flows relating to investing activities are

Cash Inflows

1. Proceeds from disposal of property, plant, and equipment
2. Proceeds from disposal of debt instruments of other entities
3. Proceeds from the sale of equity instruments of other entities

Cash Outflows

1. Purchase of property, plant, and equipment
2. Acquisition of debt instruments of other entities
3. Purchase of equity instruments of other entities (unless held for trading purposes or considered to be cash equivalents)

FINANCING ACTIVITIES

Financing activities include obtaining resources from and returning resources to the owners. Also included in this category is obtaining resources through borrowings (short-term or long-term) and repayments of the amounts borrowed.

Common examples of cash flows relating to financing activities are

Cash Inflows

1. Proceeds from issuance of share capital
2. Proceeds from issuing debt instruments (debentures)
3. Proceeds from bank borrowings

Cash Outflows

1. Payment of dividends to shareholders
2. Repayment of principal portion of debt, including finance lease obligations
3. Repayment of bank borrowings

NONCASH TRANSACTIONS

IAS 7 requires that noncash investing and financing activities should be excluded from the statement of cash flows and reported "elsewhere" in the financial statements, where all relevant information about these activities is disclosed. This requirement is interpreted as the necessity to disclose noncash activities in the footnotes to financial statements instead of including them in the statement of cash flows.

Common examples of noncash activities are

1. Conversion of debt (convertible debentures) to equity
2. Issuance of share capital to acquire property, plant, and equipment

CASE STUDY 2

Facts

On January 1, 2009, Dramatic Inc. issued convertible bonds with conversion to take place on or before the expiry of two years from the date of issuance of the debt. On December 15, 2010, the board of directors of Dramatic Inc. decided to convert the bonds at year-end and issue equity shares.

Required

How would Dramatic Inc. treat this transaction in its cash flow preparation?

Solution

On conversion of the bonds into equity, it would appear that two types of cash flows have occurred: a cash inflow resulting from increase of share capital and a cash outflow due to repayment of debt. However, these are noncash activities, and no cash flows have occurred. The Standard mandates that such noncash activities be disclosed in the footnotes to the financial statements.

DIRECT VERSUS INDIRECT METHOD

Financial statement preparers have a choice between the direct and the indirect method in presenting the operating activities section of the statement of cash flows. IAS 7 recommends the direct method of presenting net cash from operating activities. In practice, however, preparers of financial statements prefer to present the statement of cash flows under the indirect method rather than the recommended direct method (possibly due to the ease of preparation).

The *direct method* presents the items that affected cash flow and the amounts of those cash flows. Entities using the direct method normally report these major classes of cash receipts and cash payments:

1. Cash collections from customers
2. Interest and dividends received (alternatively, IAS 7 permits interest received and dividends received to be classified as investing cash flows rather than as operating cash flows because they are returns on investments)
3. Cash paid toward operating expenses including salaries to employees, and so on
4. Payments to suppliers
5. Interest paid (alternatively, IAS 7 permits interest paid to be classified as a financing cash flow, because this is the cost of obtaining financing)
6. Income taxes paid

Example

Statement of Cash Flows—Direct Method (Operating Activities Section)

Cash flows from operating activities:		
Cash collections from customers	$900,000	
Cash dividends received	100,000	
Cash paid to employees	(300,000)	
Cash paid to suppliers	(200,000)	
Cash paid for other operating expenses	(150,000)	
Income taxes paid	(100,000)	
Interest paid	(150,000)	
Net cash flows from operating activities		$100,000

CASE STUDY 3

Facts

XYZ Inc. is preparing its statement of cash flows under the direct method and has provided this information:

Net credit sales	$5,000,000
Accounts receivable, end of the year	1,500,000
Accounts receivable, beginning of the year	2,500,000
Purchases (on account)	4,000,000
Trade payable, end of the year	1,900,000
Trade payable, beginning of the year	2,000,000
Operating expenses	3,000,000
Accrued expenses, beginning of the year	500,000
Accrued expenses, end of the year	400,000
Depreciation on property, plant, and equipment	600,000

Required

For the purposes of the statement of cash flows under the direct method, you are required to compute the cash collections from customers, payments to suppliers, and cash paid for operating expenses.

Solution

1. Cash collections from customers

Net sales	$5,000,000
Add: Accounts receivables, beginning of the year	2,500,000
	7,500,000
Less: Accounts receivables, end of the year	(1,500,000)
Cash collections from customers	$6,000,000

2. Cash paid to suppliers

Purchases	$4,000,000
Add: Accounts payable, end of the year	1,900,000
	5,900,000
Less: Accounts payable, beginning of the year	(2,000,000)
Payments to suppliers	$3,900,000

3. Cash paid for operating expenses

Operating expenses	$3,000,000
Add: Accrued expenses, beginning of the year	500,000
	3,500,000
Less: Accrued expenses, end of year	(400,000)
Less: Depreciation on property, plant, and equipment	(600,000)
Cash paid toward operating expenses	$2,500,000

The *indirect method* is the more popular of the two methods despite the recommendation by IAS 7 to present the cash flows from operating activities under the direct method. A possible reason for this could be that the indirect method is easier to use than the direct method because it derives net cash flows from operating activities from the net operating results for the year as reported in the income statement. Under the indirect method, the first item presented is the net income (or loss) for the year as reported in the income statement. Noncash items of revenue and expense are added or deducted to arrive at net cash provided by operating activities. For instance, depreciation on property, plant, and equipment is added back because these expenses reduce (increase) net income (loss) for the year without affecting cash from operating activities. Similarly, gain on sale of property, plant, and equipment is deducted from net income for the year because it does not affect cash flow from operating activities. Changes in inventory, accounts receivable, and other operating assets and liabilities are used to convert the accrual-basis net income (loss) for the year to arrive at cash flows from operating activities.

CASE STUDY 4

Facts

Excellent Inc. has provided the following information and requests you to prepare the operating activities of the statement of cash flows under the indirect method:

Net income before taxes	$400,000
Depreciation on property, plant, and equipment	200,000
Loss on sale of building	100,000
Interest expense	150,000
Interest payable, beginning of the year	100,000
Interest payable, end of the year	50,000
Income taxes paid	100,000
Accounts receivable, beginning of the year	500,000
Accounts receivable, end of the year	850,000
Inventory, beginning of the year	500,000
Inventory, end of the year	400,000
Accounts payable, beginning of the year	200,000
Accounts payable, end of the year	500,000

Required

Please prepare the operating activities section of the statement of cash flows using the indirect method.

Solution

Statement of Cash Flows—Indirect Method (Operating Activities Section)

Cash flows from operating activities:		
Net income before income taxes	$400,000	
Adjustments for:		
Depreciation on property, plant, and equipment	200,000	
Loss on sale of building	100,000	
Interest expense	150,000	
	850,000	
Increase in accounts receivable	(350,000)	
Decrease in inventories	100,000	
Increase in accounts payable	300,000	
Cash generated from operations	900,000	
Interest paid	(200,000)	
Income taxes paid	(100,000)	
Net cash flows from operating activities		$600,000

REPORTING CASH FLOWS ON A GROSS BASIS VERSUS A NET BASIS

Financial Institutions

IAS 7 permits financial institutions to report cash flows arising from certain activities on a net basis. These activities, and the related conditions under which net reporting would be acceptable, are set out below:

1. Cash receipts and payments on behalf of customers when the cash flows reflect the activities of the customers rather than those of the bank; for example, the acceptance and repayment of demand deposits
2. Cash flows relating to deposits with fixed maturity dates
3. Placements and withdrawals of deposits from other financial institutions
4. Cash advances and loans to bank customers and repayments thereon

Entities other than Financial Institutions

In the case of cash flows of entities other than financial institutions, the preference is clearly for the "gross" cash receipts and cash payments. This way the cash inflows and cash outflows are each separately presented instead of being presented as net amounts. Doing this gives the users of financial statements more meaningful information. To understand this better, let us look at an example: Reporting the net change in long-term loans payable would not reveal the cash inflows and the cash outflows relating to the loans and may obscure the true financing activities of the entity. Thus, when cash inflows from the proceeds of the loans and cash outflows from repayment of the loans are disclosed separately, users of financial statements will get a better understanding of the financing activities of the entity. IAS 7 specifies *two exceptions* in cases of entities other than financial institutions where netting of cash flows is permitted.

1. Items with quick turnovers, large amounts, and short maturities may be presented as net cash flows.
2. Cash receipts and payments on behalf of customers reflecting the activities of the customers rather than those of the entities. These flows may also be reported on a net rather than a gross basis.

FOREIGN CURRENCY CASH FLOWS

1. Cash flows arising from transactions in a foreign currency shall be recorded in an entity's functional currency by using the rate of exchange between the functional currency and the foreign currency on the date of the cash flow.
2. Foreign subsidiaries must prepare separate statements of cash flows and translate the statements to the functional currency at the exchange rate prevailing on the date of cash flow.

REPORTING FUTURES, FORWARD CONTRACTS, OPTIONS, AND SWAPS

IAS 7 recognizes that cash flows from futures contracts, forward contracts, option contracts, and swap contracts are normally classified as investing activities, except under the following two circumstances:

1. When such contracts are held for dealing or trading purposes and thus represent operating activities.
2. When the payments or receipts are considered by the entities as financing activities and are reported accordingly.

When a contract is accounted for as a hedge of an identifiable position, the cash flows of the contract are classified in the same manner as the cash flows of the position being hedged.

RECONCILIATION OF CASH AND CASH EQUIVALENTS

IAS 7 makes it incumbent upon an entity to disclose the components of cash and cash equivalents and also to present a reconciliation of the difference, if any, between the amounts reported in the statement of cash flows and equivalent items reported in the balance sheet.

ACQUISITIONS AND DISPOSALS OF SUBSIDIARIES AND OTHER BUSINESS UNITS

IAS 7 recognizes that an entity may acquire or dispose subsidiaries or other business units during the year and thus requires that the aggregate cash flows from acquisitions and from disposals of subsidiaries or other business units should be presented separately as part of the investing activities section of the statement of cash flows. IAS 7 has also prescribed these disclosures in respect to both acquisitions and disposals:

1. The total consideration included
2. The portion thereof discharged by cash and cash equivalents
3. The amount of cash and cash equivalents in the subsidiary or business unit acquired or disposed
4. The amount of assets and liabilities (other than cash and cash equivalents) acquired or disposed, summarized by major category

OTHER DISCLOSURES REQUIRED AND RECOMMENDED BY IAS 7

Certain unique additional disclosures are prescribed by IAS 7 because such information may enable users of financial statements to gain better insight into the liquidity or solvency of an enterprise. These additional disclosures follow:

1. **Required disclosure.** Amount of *significant* cash and cash equivalent balances held by an entity that are not available for use by the group *should be disclosed* along with a commentary by management.

PRACTICAL INSIGHT

The term used is "significant," which has not been defined in IAS 7. This may cause interpretational problems while applying this provision of IAS 7 in practice.

---

2. **Recommended disclosures.** Entities are *encouraged* to make these disclosures, together with a commentary by management:

   a. Amount of undrawn borrowing facilities, indicating restrictions on their use, if any
   b. In the case of investments in joint ventures, which are accounted for using proportionate consolidation, the aggregate amount of cash flows from operating, investing, and financing activities that are attributable to the investment in the joint venture
   c. Aggregate amount of cash flows that are attributable to the increase in operating capacity separately from those cash flows that are required to maintain operating capacity
   d. Amount of cash flows segregated by reported industry and geographical segments

---

PRACTICAL INSIGHT

These "recommended" disclosures are unique to IAS 7. Such disclosures are not required under other accounting standards (not even under US generally accepted accounting principles). They are useful in enabling the users of financial statements to understand the enterprise's financial position better.

COMPREHENSIVE CASE STUDY

This case study shows the preparation of the cash flow statement under IAS 7 under the direct and indirect methods.

Facts

Financial information for Tremendous Enterprises Inc. for the year ended December 31, 2009, follows:

TREMENDOUS ENTERPRISES INC.
BALANCE SHEETS
As of December 31, 2009, and 2008

	2009	*2008*
Assets		
Cash and cash equivalents	$ 4,500	$ 1,500
Trade receivables	7,500	3,750
Inventory	3,000	2,250
Intangible asset, net	1,500	2,250
Due from associates	28,500	28,500
Property, plant, and equipment, cost	18,000	33,750
Accumulated depreciation	(7,500)	(9,000)
Property, plant, and equipment, net	10,500	24,750
Total assets	$55,500	$63,000
Liabilities		
Accounts payable	$ 7,500	$18,750
Income taxes payable	3,000	1,500
Deferred taxes payable	4,500	3,000
Total liabilities	15,000	23,250
Shareholders' equity		
Share capital	9,750	9,750
Retained earnings	30,750	30,000
Total shareholders' equity	40,500	39,750
Total liabilities and shareholders' equity	$55,500	$63,000

TREMENDOUS ENTERPRISES INC.
STATEMENT OF INCOME
For the Year Ended December 31, 2009

Sales	$45,000
Cost of sales	(15,000)
Gross operating income	30,000
Administrative and selling expenses	(3,000)
Interest expenses	(3,000)
Depreciation of property, plant, and equipment	(3,000)
Amortization of intangible asset	(750)
Investment income	4,500
Net income before taxation	24,750
Taxes on income	(6,000)
Net income	$18,750

Additional Information

This additional information is relevant to the preparation of the statement of cash flows:

1. All sales made by Tremendous Enterprises Inc. ("company") are credit sales. All purchases are on account.
2. Interest expense for the year 2009 was $3,000, which was fully paid during the year.
3. The company pays salaries and other employee dues before the end of each month. All administration and selling expenses incurred were paid before December 31, 2005.
4. Investment income comprised dividend income from investments in shares of blue chip companies. This was received before December 31, 2009.
5. Equipment with a net book value of $11,250 and original cost of $15,750 was sold for $11,250.
6. The company declared and paid dividends of $18,000 to its shareholders during 2005.
7. Income tax expense for the year 2009 was $6,000, against which the company paid $3,000 during 2009 as an estimate.

Required

Using all the given financial information for Tremendous Enterprises Inc., prepare the statement of cash flows according to the requirements of IAS 7 under both the direct and the indirect methods.

Solution

a. A worksheet can be prepared analyzing the changes in the balance sheet figures as the first step to the preparation of the statement of cash flows.

Cash Flow Worksheet Analyzing Changes in Balance Sheet Figures (all figures in US dollars)

	2009	2008	Change	Cash flow effect operating	Cash flow effect investing	Cash flow effect financing	Cash and equivalents
Cash and equivalents	4,500	1,500	3,000				3,000
Trade receivables	7,500	3,750	3,750	(3,750)			
Inventory	3,000	2,250	750	(750)			
Intangible asset	1,500	2,250	(750)	750			
Due from associates	28,500	28,500	--				
Property, plant, and	10,500	24,750	(14,250)	3,000	11,250		
equipment	55,500	63,000	(7,500)				
Accounts payable	7,500	18,750	(11,250)	(11,250)			
Income taxes payable	3,000	1,500	1,500	1,500			
Deferred taxes payable	4,500	3,000	1,500	1,500			
Share capital	9,750	9,750	--				
Retained earnings	30,750	30,000	750	14,250	4,500	(18,000)	--
	55,500	63,000	(7,500)	5,250	15,750	(18,000)	3,000
				A	B	C	A+B+C

b.   Direct Method

TREMENDOUS ENTERPRISES INC.
STATEMENT OF CASH FLOWS
For the Year Ended December 31, 2009

Cash flows from operating activities:

Cash receipts from customers	$ 41,250	
Cash paid to suppliers and employees	(30,000)	
Cash provided by operations	11,250	
Interest paid	(3,000)	
Income taxes paid	(3,000)	
Net cash flows from operating activities		$ 5,250

Cash flows from investing activities:

Proceeds from the sale of equipment	11,250	
Dividends received	4,500	
Cash flows from investing activities		15,750

Cash flows from financing activities:

Dividends paid	(18,000)	
Cash flows used in financing activities		(18,000)
Net increase in cash and cash equivalents		3,000
Cash and cash equivalents, beginning of year		1,500
Cash and cash equivalents, end of year		$ 4,500

Details of the computations of amounts shown in the statement of cash flows follow:

Cash received from customers during the year

Credit sales	45,000	
Plus: Accounts receivable, beginning of year	3,750	
Less: Accounts receivable, end of year	(7,500)	
Cash collections from customers during the year		$ 41,250

Cash paid to suppliers and employees

Cost of sales	15,000	
Less: Inventory, beginning of year	(2,250)	
Plus: Inventory, end of year	3,000	
Plus: Accounts payable, beginning of year	18,750	
Less: Accounts payable, end of year	(7,500)	
Plus: Administrative and selling expenses paid	3,000	
Cash paid to suppliers and employees during the year		$ 30,000
Interest paid **equals** interest expense charged to the income statement (per additional information)		$ 3,000

Income taxes paid during the year

Tax expense during the year (comprising current and deferred portions)	6,000	
Plus: Income taxes payable, beginning of year	1,500	
Plus: Deferred taxes payable, beginning of year	3,000	
Less: Income taxes payable, end of year	(3,000)	
Less: Deferred taxes payable, end of year	(4,500)	
Cash paid toward income taxes		$ 3,000
Proceeds from sale of equipment (per additional information)		$ 11,250
Dividends received during 2005 (per additional information)		$ 4,500
Dividends paid during 2005 (per additional information)		$ 18,000

c.   Indirect Method

TREMENDOUS ENTERPRISES INC.
STATEMENT OF CASH FLOWS
For the Year Ended December 31, 2009

Cash flows from operating activities:

Net income before taxation	$ 24,750
Adjustments for:	
Depreciation of property, plant, and equipment	3,000
Amortization of intangible assets	750
Investment income	(4,500)
Interest expense	3,000
Operating income before changes in operating assets and liabilities	27,000

Increase in accounts receivable	(3,750)	
Increase in inventories	(750)	
Decrease in accounts payable	(11,250)	
Cash provided by operations	11,250	
Interest paid	(3,000)	
Income taxes paid	(3,000)	
Net cash from operating activities		5,250
Cash flows from investing activities:		
Proceeds from sale of equipment	11,250	
Dividends received	4,500	
Cash from investing activities		15,750
Cash flows from financing activities:		
Dividends paid	(18,000)	
Cash used in financing activities		(18,000)
Net increase in cash and cash equivalents		3,000
Cash and cash equivalents, beginning of year		1,500
Cash and cash equivalents, end of year		$ 4,500

EXTRACTS FROM PUBLISHED FINANCIAL STATEMENTS

BARLOWORLD
Consolidated Cash Flow Statement
For the Year Ended September 30

	2009 *Rm*	2008 *Rm*	2007 *Rm*
Cash flows from operating activities			
Cash receipts from customers	**45,525**	46,589	49,697
Cash paid to employees and suppliers	**(41,056)**	(42,855)	(43,858)
Cash generated from operations	**4,469**	3,734	5,839
Finance costs	**(994)**	(980)	(16)
Realized fair value adjustments on financial instruments	**(180)**	(157)	41
Dividends received from investments and associates	**14**	26	338
Interest received	**146**	188	(1,412)
Taxation paid	**(603)**	(830)	--
Cash flow from Operations	**2,852**	1,981	3,888
Dividends paid (including minority shareholders)	**(434)**	(622)	(2,629)
Cash retained from operating activities	**2,418**	1,359	1,259
Cash flows from investing activities			
Acquisition of subsidiaries, investments, and intangibles	**219**	(996)	(349)
Proceeds on disposal of subsidiaries, investments and intangibles	**7**	1,098	1,432
Net investment in fleet leasing and rental assets	**(707)**	(1,904)	(2,283)
Acquisition of other property, plant, and equipment	**(910)**	(973)	(1,485)
Replacement capital expenditure	**(522)**	(305)	(451)
Expansion capital expenditure	**(388)**	(668)	(1,034)
Proceeds on disposal of property, plant, and equipment	**180**	169	121
Proceeds on sale of leasing assets			1,684
Net cash used in investing activities	**(1,211)**	(2,606)	(880)
Net cash inflow/(outflow) before financing activities	**1,207**	(1,247)	379
Cash flows from financing activities			
Proceeds on share issue	**12**	23	139
Pension fund payment		(759)	
Proceeds from long-term borrowings	**4,379**	3,298	1,376
Repayment of long-term borrowings	**(4,328)**	(1,285)	(3,207)
(Decrease)/increase in short-term interest-bearing liabilities	**(710)**	70	704
Net cash (used in)/from financing activities	**(647)**	1,347	(988)
Net increase/(decrease) in cash and cash equivalents	**560**	100	(609)
Cash and cash equivalents at beginning of year	**1,238**	1,201	2,134
Cash and cash equivalents held for sale at beginning of year	**31**		
Effect of foreign exchange rate movement on cash balance	**(57)**	54	(6)
Effect of cash balances classified as held for sale	**(145)**	(31)	
Effect of unbundling of Coatings on cash balance		(86)	
Effect of unbundling Pretoria Portland Cement on cash balance			(318)
Cash and cash equivalents at end of year	**1,627**	1,238	1,201
Cash balances not available for use due to reserving restrictions	**360**	292	235

CONSOLIDATED BALANCE SHEET

at September 30	Notes	*2009* *Rm*	2008 *Rm*	2007 *Rm*
Assets				
Noncurrent assets		**12,582**	13,269	12,019
Property, plant and equipment	2	**7,854**	8,056	6,847
Goodwill	3	**2,319**	2,421	2,046
Intangible assets	4	**280**	205	274
Investment in associates and joint ventures	5	**731**	1,095	928
Finance lease receivables	6	**463**	436	619
Long-term financial assets	7	**279**	568	686
Deferred taxation assets	8	**656**	488	619
Current assets		**17,513**	20,688	18,636
Vehicle rental fleet	2	**1,692**	1,934	3,902
Inventories	9	**6,737**	7,495	5,869
Trade and other receivables	10	**4,747**	6,854	6,185
Taxation		**53**	11	32
Cash and cash equivalents	11	**1,627**	1,238	1,201
Assets classified as held for sale	12	**2,657**	3,156	1,447
Total assets		**30,095**	33,957	30,655
Equity and liabilities				
Capital and reserves				
Share capital and premium	13	**252**	242	223
Other reserves	14	**2,688**	3,745	2,584
Retained income	14	**8,913**	8,861	8,334
Interest of shareholders of Barloworld Limited		**11,853**	12,848	11,141
Minority interest	14	**217**	185	80
Interest of all shareholders		**12,070**	13,033	11,221
Noncurrent liabilities		**6,486**	6,252	6,638
Interest-bearing	15	**5,278**	5,022	4,379
Deferred taxation liabilities	8	**249**	266	610
Provisions	16	**185**	325	344
Other non-interest-bearing	17	**774**	639	1,305
Current liabilities		**11,539**	14,672	12,796
Trade and other payables	18	**5,775**	7,335	6,854
Provisions	16	**580**	731	600
Taxation		**108**	344	445
Amounts due to bankers and short-term loans	19	**3,567**	4,266	4,687
Liabilities directly associated with assets classified as held for sale	12	**1,509**	1,996	210
Total equity and liabilities		**30,095**	33,957	30,655

Notes to the Consolidated Cash Flow Statement
For the Year Ended September 30

	2009 Rm	2008 Rm	2007 Rm
A. Cash generated from operations is calculated as follows:			
Profit before taxation—continuing operations	1,026	1,860	2,031
(Loss)/profit before taxation—discontinued operation	(182)	(335)	1,932
Adjustment for:			
Depreciation	2,145	2,121	1,961
Amortization of intangible assets	65	57	70
Profit on disposal of plant and equipment including rental assets	(258)	(142)	(44)
Profit on disposal of properties	--	(30)	(45)
Profit on disposal of subsidiaries and investments	--	--	65
Dividends received	(14)	(26)	(2)
Interest received	(146)	(188)	(338)
Finance costs	994	980	902
Fair value adjustments on financial instruments	202	83	(300)
(Reversal of) /impairment losses	(4)	382	323
Realization of translation reserve on disposal of offshore subsidiaries	--	--	(197)
BEE IFRS 2 charge	6	337	--
Noncash movement in provisions	(223)	155	--
Other noncash flow items	(14)	27	12
Operating cash flows before movements in working capital	3,587	5,281	6,370
Continuing operations	3,403	4,914	3,970
Discontinued operations	184	367	2,400
Decrease/(increase) in working capital	882	(1,547)	(531)
Decrease/(increase) in inventories	522	(1,265)	(1,113)
Decrease/(increase) in receivables	2,195	(887)	(860)
(Decrease)/increase in payables	(1,835)	605	1,442
Cash generated from operations	4,469	3,734	5,839
B. Taxation paid is reconciled to the amounts disclosed in the income statement as follows:			
Amounts unpaid less overpaid at beginning of year	(325)	(430)	(688)
Per the income statement (excluding deferred taxation)	(362)	(756)	(1,376)
Adjustment in respect of subsidiaries acquired and sold including translation adjustments	31	(3)	7
Effect of unbundling	--	34	215
Amounts unpaid less overpaid at end of year	53	325	430
Cash amounts paid	(1,007)	(975)	(874)
C. Acquisition of subsidiaries, investments, and intangibles:			
Inventories acquired		335	
Receivables acquired		327	
Payables, taxation, and deferred taxation acquired		(526)	
Borrowing net of cash		(256)	
Property, plant, and equipment, noncurrent assets, goodwill and minority shareholders		5,532	
Total net assets acquired		412	
Less: Existing share of net assets of associates before acquisition		(234)	
Net assets acquired		178	
Goodwill arising on acquisitions		566	
Total purchase consideration		744	
Less: Noncash purchase consideration		(33)	
Net cash cost of subsidiaries acquired		711	
Investments and intangible assets acquired	(219)	285	349
Cash amounts paid to acquire subsidiaries, investment, and intangibles	(219)	996	349
Bank balances and cash in subsidiaries acquired		98	

		2009	2008	2007
		Rm	*Rm*	*Rm*
D.	**Proceeds on disposal of subsidiaries, investments, and intangibles:**			
	Inventories disposed	96	271	932
	Finance lease receivables disposed	--	259	676
	Receivables disposed	52	298	(670)
	Payables, taxation, and deferred taxation balances disposed	(31)	(209)	50
	Borrowings net of cash	(117)	(189)	--
	Property, plant, and equipment, noncurrent assets, goodwill, and intangibles	4	322	501
	Net assets disposed	4	752	1,489
	Less: Noncash consideration on deconsolidation of subsidiary	(2)	(26)	--
	Total net assets disposed	2	726	1,489
	Profit/(loss) on disposal	--	370	(69)
	Net cash proceeds on disposal of subsidiaries	2	1,096	1,420
	Proceeds on disposal of investments and intangibles	5	2	12
	Cash proceeds on disposal of subsidiaries, investments, and intangibles	7	1,098	1,432
E.	**Net investment in fleet leasing and rental assets:**			
	Net investment in fleet leasing and equipment rental assets	(642)	(1,155)	(1,310)
	Additions to fleet leasing and equipment rental assets	(2,213)	(2,983)	(2,314)
	Less: Proceeds on disposal of fleet leasing and equipment rental assets	1,571	1,828	1,004
	Net investment in leasing receivables	(139)	(13)	(46)
	Net investment in car rental vehicles	74	(736)	(927)
	Additions to vehicle rental fleet during the year	(3,387)	(4,515)	(3,741)
	Less: Proceeds on disposal of vehicle rental fleet	3,461	3,779	2,814
	Net investment in fleet leasing and rental assets	(707)	(1,904)	(2,283)

MULTIPLE-CHOICE QUESTIONS

1. An entity purchases a building and the seller accepts payment partly in equity shares and partly in debentures of the entity. This transaction should be treated in the statement of cash flows as follows:

(a) The purchase of the building should be investing cash outflow and the issuance of shares and the debentures financing cash outflows.

(b) The purchase of the building should be investing cash outflow and the issuance of debentures as financing cash outflows while the issuance of shares as investing cash outflow.

(c) This does not belong in a cash flow statement and should be disclosed only in the footnotes to the financial statements.

(d) Ignore the transaction totally since it is a noncash transaction. No mention is required in either the cash flow statement or anywhere else in the financial statements.

2. An entity (other than a financial institution) receives dividends from its investment in shares. How should it disclose the dividends received in the statement of cash flows prepared under IAS 7?

(a) Operating cash inflow.

(b) Either as operating cash inflow or as investing cash inflow.

(c) Either as operating cash inflow or as financing cash inflow.

(d) As an adjustment in the "operating activities" section of the cash flow because it is included in the net income for the year and as a cash inflow in the "financing activities" section of the cash flow statement.

3. How should gain on the sale of an office building owned by the entity be presented in a statement of cash flows?

(a) As an inflow in the "investing activities" section of the cash flow because it pertains to a long-term asset.

(b) As an inflow in the "financing activities" section of the statement of cash flows because the building was constructed with a long-term loan from a bank that needs to be repaid from the sale proceeds.

(c) As an adjustment to the net income in the "operating activities" section of the

statement of cash flows prepared under the indirect method.

(d) Added to the sale proceeds and presented in the "investing activities" section of the statement of cash flows.

4. How should an unrealized gain on foreign currency translation be presented in a statement of cash flows?

(a) As an inflow in the "financing activities" section of the statement of cash flows because it arises from a foreign currency translation.

(b) It should be ignored for the purposes of the statement of cash flows as it is an unrealized gain.

(c) It should be ignored for the purposes of the statement of cash flows as it is an unrealized gain but it should be disclosed in the footnotes to the financial statements by way of abundant precaution.

(d) As an adjustment to the net income in the "operating activities" section of the statement of cash flows.

5. How should repayment of a long-term loan comprising repayment of the principal amount and interest due to date on the loan be treated in a statement of cash flows?

(a) The repayment of the principal portion of the loan is a cash flow belonging in the "investing activities" section; the interest payment belongs either in the "operating activities" section or the "financing activities" section.

(b) The repayment of the principal portion of the loan is a cash flow belonging in the "investing activities" section; the interest payment belongs either in the "operating activities" section or the "investing activities" section.

(c) The repayment of the principal portion of the loan is a cash flow belonging in the "investing activities" section; the interest payment belongs in the "operating activities" section (because IAS 7 does not permit any alternatives in case of interest payments).

(d) The repayment of the principal portion of the loan is a cash flow belonging in the "investing activities" section; the interest payment should be netted against interest received on bank deposits, and the net amount of interest should be disclosed in the "operating activities" section.

Chapter 6

ACCOUNTING POLICIES, CHANGES IN ACCOUNTING ESTIMATES AND ERRORS (IAS 8)

BACKGROUND AND INTRODUCTION

"Comparability" is one of the four qualitative attributes (or characteristics) of financial statements according to the International Accounting Standards Board (IASB) *Framework*. For users of financial statements, it is important to be able to compare not only the financial statements of an entity from one period to another but also the financial statements of different entities. Such information is needed in order to make relative comparisons of financial performance and financial position and changes in financial position.

IAS 8 prescribes criteria for selecting and changing accounting policies and the disclosures thereof and also sets out the requirements and disclosures for changes in accounting estimates and corrections of errors. In doing so it purports to achieve these objectives:

- To enhance the relevance and reliability of an entity's financial statements
- To ensure the comparability of the financial statements of an entity over time as well as with financial statements of other entities

DEFINITIONS OF KEY TERMS
(in accordance with IAS 8)

Accounting policies. The specific principles, bases, conventions, rules, and practices applied by an entity in preparing and presenting financial statements.

Change in accounting estimate. An adjustment of the carrying amount of an asset or a liability, or the amount of periodic consumption of an asset, that results from the assessment of the present status of, and expected future benefits and obligations associated with, assets and liabilities. Changes in accounting estimates result from new information or new developments and, accordingly, are *not* corrections of errors.

Prior period errors. Omissions from, and misstatements in, financial statements for one or more prior periods arising from a failure to use, or misuse of, reliable information that was

59

available at the time *and* could reasonably be expected to have been obtained and taken into account in the preparation and presentation of financial statements.

ACCOUNTING POLICIES

Accounting policies are essential for a proper understanding of the information contained in the financial statements prepared by the management of an entity. An entity should clearly outline all significant accounting policies it has used in preparing the financial statements. This is because under International Financial Reporting Standards (IFRS) alternative treatments are possible, making it all the more important for an entity to clearly state which accounting policy it has used in the preparation of the financial statements. For instance, under IAS 2 an entity has the choice of the weighted-average method or the first-in, first-out (FIFO) method in valuing its inventory. Unless the entity discloses which method of inventory valuation it has used in the preparation of its financial statements, users of these financial statements would not be able to use the financial statements properly to make relative comparisons with other entities.

SELECTION AND APPLICATION OF ACCOUNTING POLICIES

When a Standard or Interpretation specifically applies to a transaction, other event, or condition, the accounting policy applied to that item shall be determined by applying that Standard or Interpretation and considering the relevant Implementation Guidance issued by the IASB for the Standard or Interpretation.

If the extant IASB Standards or Interpretations do not address a specific transaction, other event, or condition, management shall develop and apply a policy that is relevant to the decision-making needs of the users of financial statements and that is reliable as well. In this context, "reliable" means to

- Represent faithfully the financial position, financial performance, and cash flows
- Reflect the economic substance of transactions, other events, and conditions
- Be neutral
- Be prudent
- Be complete in all material respects

In making these judgments, the management of an entity should apply the following sources in *descending order:*

- The requirements and guidance in Standards and Interpretations dealing with similar and related issues
- The definitions, recognition criteria, and measurement concepts for assets, liabilities, income, and expenses as outlined in the IASB's *Framework*

The Standard notes that IFRS are sometimes accompanied by guidance notes that assist entities in applying their requirements. Each guidance note states whether or not it is an integral part of the IFRS. A guidance note that is an integral part of the IFRS is mandatory; a guidance note that is not an integral part of the IFRS is not mandatory but may be useful when applying the IFRS.

Furthermore, in making the judgment, the management of an entity may also consider the most recent pronouncements of other standard-setting bodies that use a similar conceptual framework to develop standards, other accounting literature, and accepted industry practices, to the extent that these do not conflict with the sources of primary reference (i.e., the IASB Standards and Interpretations and its *Framework*).

Standards are normally published in advance of the required implementation date. In the intervening period, where a new/revised Standard that is relevant to an entity has been issued but is not yet effective, the entity discloses this fact. It also provides the known or reasonably estimable information relevant to assessing the impact that the application of the Standard might have on the entity's financial statements in the period of initial recognition.

When an entity applies an accounting Standard or Interpretation for the first time it applies the specific transitional provisions, if any, of that Standard or Interpretation. For example, a new standard may specify that it should only be applied prospectively and, if so, the entity does not make prior period adjustments for the effect of the change.

PRACTICAL INSIGHT

According to IAS 8, when an entity's management is faced with a situation of interpretation of the IASB Standards on a matter that is not expressly covered by the existing IASB Standards or Interpretations, then it should look at the IASB's *Framework* for answers. While doing so it should also research recent pronouncements of other standard setters to the extent that these do not conflict with the IASB Standards or Interpretations or its *Framework*.

For example, compare Standards issued to date by the IASB to US generally accepted accounting principles (GAAP), which address not only general accounting standards but are replete with industry-specific rules and guidance. US GAAP contains accounting pronouncements and guidelines for industries ranging from oil and gas to real estate; the IASB Standards are geared toward general accounting standards and not so much industry-specific guidance, although some of the recently promulgated IASB Standards seek to address industry-specific standards as well. To date, the only industries that are covered by the IASB Standards are the insurance and the extractive industries. Thus, according to IAS 8, if an entity's management is seeking answers to accounting matters or issues relating to a specific industry that the IASB Standards have not yet addressed, then guidance under US GAAP (or other national standards that provide such guidance) may be consulted, keeping in mind that the guidance to be applied must not conflict with the primary source of reference (i.e., the IASB Standards and Interpretations or the IASB's *Framework*).

CONSISTENCY OF ACCOUNTING POLICIES

Once selected, accounting policies must be applied consistently for similar transactions, other events, and conditions unless a Standard or Interpretation specifically otherwise requires or permits categorization of items for which different policies may be appropriate.

If a Standard or Interpretation requires or permits such categorization, an appropriate accounting policy shall be selected and applied consistently to each category.

FACTORS GOVERNING CHANGES IN ACCOUNTING POLICIES

Once selected, an accounting policy may be changed only if the change

- Is required by a Standard or an Interpretation.
- Results in financial statements providing reliable and more relevant information.

PRACTICAL INSIGHT

In the year in which an entity changes its accounting system from manual to computerized, it may be required to switch from the first-in, first-out (FIFO) method (which it used while valuing inventory manually) to the weighted-average method. This change may be essential because the computerized system, which is tailor-made for the industry to which the entity belongs, is capable of valuing inventories under the weighted-average method only and is not equipped to value inventories under the FIFO method, because industry best practice dictates that only weighted-average is appropriate for the industry to which the entity belongs. Under these circumstances, this change in method of valuing inventories from the FIFO to the weighted-average method is probably justified because it results in financial statements providing reliable and more relevant information (and is comparable to other entities within the industry to which the entity belongs).

These items are **not** considered changes in accounting policies:

- The application of an accounting policy for transactions, other events, or conditions that differ in substance from those previously occurring
- The application of a new accounting policy for transactions, other events, or conditions, that did not occur previously or were immaterial

APPLYING CHANGES IN ACCOUNTING POLICIES

A change in accounting policy required by a Standard or Interpretation shall be applied in accordance with the transitional provisions therein. If a Standard or Interpretation contains no transitional provisions or if an accounting policy is changed **voluntarily,** the change shall be applied *retrospectively.* That is to say, the new policy is applied to transactions, other events, and conditions as if the policy had always been applied.

The practical impact of this is that corresponding amounts (or "comparatives") presented in financial statements must be restated as if the new policy had always been applied. The impact of the new policy on the retained earnings prior to the earliest period presented should be adjusted against the opening balance of retained earnings.

CASE STUDY 1

Facts

1. All Change Co. Inc. changed its accounting policy in 20X9 with respect to the valuation of inventories. Up to 20X8, inventories were valued using a weighted-average cost (WAC) method. In 20X9 the method was changed to first-in, first-out (FIFO), as it was considered to more accurately reflect the usage and flow of inventories in the economic cycle. The impact on inventory valuation was determined to be

At December 31, 20X7:	an increase of $10,000
At December 31, 20X8:	an increase of $15,000
At December 31, 20X9:	an increase of $20,000

2. The statements of comprehensive income prior to adjustment are

	20X9	20X8
Revenue	$250,000	$200,000
Cost of sales	100,000	80,000
Gross profit	150,000	120,000
Administration costs	60,000	50,000
Selling and distribution costs	25,000	15,000
Net profit	$ 65,000	$ 55,000

Required

Present the change in accounting policy in the Statement of Comprehensive Income and the Statement of Changes in Equity in accordance with the requirements of IAS 8.

Solution

The statements of comprehensive income after adjustment would be

ALL CHANGE CO. INC.
STATEMENT OF COMPREHENSIVE INCOME
For the Year Ended December 31, 20X9

	20X9	20X8 (restated)
Revenue	$250,000	$200,000
Cost of sales	95,000	75,000
Gross profit	155,000	125,000
Administration costs	60,000	50,000
Selling and distribution costs	25,000	15,000
Net profit	70,000	60,000

Explanation

In each year, Cost of Sales will be reduced by $5,000, the net impact on the opening and closing inventories of change in accounting policy.

The impact on the "retained earnings" included in the "statement of changes in equity" would be as follows (the shaded figures represent the situation if there had been no change in accounting policy):

ALL CHANGE CO, INC.
STATEMENT OF CHANGES IN EQUITY (Retained earnings columns only)
For the Year Ended December 31, 20X9

	Retained earnings	*Retained earnings*
At January 1, 20X8, as originally stated (say)	$300,000	$300,000
Change in accounting policy for valuation of inventory	10,000	
At January 1, 20X8, as restated	310,000	
Net profit for the year as restated	60,000	55,000
At December 31, 20X8	370,000	355,000
Net profit for the year	70,000	65,000
At December 31, 20X9	$440,000	$420,000

Explanation

The cumulative impact at December 31, 20X8, is an increase in retained earnings of $15,000 and at December 31, 20X9, of $20,000.

LIMITATIONS OF RETROSPECTIVE APPLICATION

Retrospective application of a change in accounting policy need not be made if it is *impracticable* to determine either the period-specific effects or the cumulative effect of the change. "Impracticable" is very strictly defined in the Standard in order to preclude simplistic statements used to avoid restating earlier periods.

Applying a requirement of a Standard or Interpretation is "impracticable" when the entity cannot apply it after making every effort to do so. For a particular prior period, it is "impracticable" to apply a change in an accounting policy if

- The effects of the retrospective application are not determinable
- The retrospective application requires assumptions about what management's intentions would have been at the time
- The retrospective application requires significant estimates of amounts, and it is impossible to distinguish objectively, from other information, information about those estimates that

  - Provides evidence of circumstances that existed at that time
  - Would have been available at that time

The standard includes guidance for determining circumstances in which it is impracticable to apply a new policy retrospectively or to restate retrospectively for the correction of errors. IAS 8 does not permit the use of hindsight when retrospectively applying an accounting policy or correcting prior period errors.

Where it is impracticable to determine the period-specific effects of the change on comparative information for one or more prior periods presented, the retrospective application or restatement is applied retrospectively only to the extent that it is practicable. The retrospective application or restatement is applied to adjust assets and liabilities at the beginning of the earliest period presented for which retrospective application is practicable, and a corresponding adjustment is made to the opening balance of each affected component of equity for that period. In simple terms the entity should go back as far as it can.

Where it is impracticable to determine the cumulative effect, at the beginning of the current period, of the retrospective application or restatement, the entity adjusts the comparative information to apply the retrospective application or restatement prospectively from the earliest date possible.

DISCLOSURES WITH RESPECT TO CHANGES IN ACCOUNTING POLICIES

When initial application of a Standard or Interpretation has an effect on current or prior periods, or would have an effect but it is impracticable to determine, or might have an effect, an entity shall disclose

- The title of the Standard or Interpretation.
- If applicable, that the change is made in accordance with the transitional provisions.
- The nature of the change.
- If applicable, a description of the transitional provisions.
- If applicable, the transitional provisions that might have an effect on future periods.
- For current and each prior period presented to the extent practicable, the amount of the adjustment for each financial statement line item.
- The amount of the adjustment relating to periods before those presented.
- If retrospective application is impracticable, the circumstances making it impracticable and the date from which the accounting policy has been applied.

Similar disclosures are required for *voluntary changes in accounting policies* with the addition that a description must be provided of the reason for the new policy providing reliable and more relevant information.

In addition to the foregoing, disclosures *are required* regarding *Standards or Interpretations that have been issued but are not yet effective.* Such disclosures comprise the fact that certain Standards or Interpretations have been issued (at the date of authorization of the financial statements) but were not effective **and** also include known or reasonably estimable information relevant to assessing the possible impact of the new Standard or Interpretation.

CHANGES IN ACCOUNTING ESTIMATES

Many items in the financial statements cannot be measured with accuracy and are thus estimated. This is due to uncertainties inherent in business activities. Accounting, the language of business, has to translate these uncertainties into figures that are then reported in the financial statements. Thus accounting estimates are a very important part of the process of financial reporting. Common examples of accounting estimates include

- Bad debts
- Inventory obsolescence
- Useful lives of property, plant, and equipment
- Fair values of financial assets or financial liabilities
- Provision for warranty obligations

Accounting estimates may change as circumstances change or experience grows. Thus a change in estimate does not warrant restating the financial statements of a prior period because it is not a correction of an error.

CASE STUDY 2

Facts

Accurate Inc. was incorporated on January 1, 20X7, and follows IFRS in preparing its financial statements. In preparing its financial statements for financial year ending December 31, 20X9, Accurate Inc. used these useful lives for its property, plant, and equipment:

    Buildings: 15 years
    Plant and machinery: 10 years
    Furniture and fixtures: 7 years

On January 1, 20X0, the entity decides to review the useful lives of the property, plant, and equipment. For this purpose it hired external valuation experts. These independent experts certified the *remaining* useful lives of the property, plant, and equipment of Accurate Inc. at the beginning of 20X0 as

Buildings: 10 years
Plant and machinery: 7 years
Furniture and fixtures: 5 years

Accurate Inc. uses the straight-line method of depreciation. The original cost of the various components of property, plant, and equipment were

Buildings: $15,000,000
Plant and machinery: $10,000,000
Furniture and fixtures: $3,500,000

Required

Compute the impact on the statement of comprehensive income for the year ending December 31, 20X0, if Accurate Inc. decides to change the useful lives of the property, plant, and equipment in compliance with the recommendations of external valuation experts. Assume that there were no salvage values for the three components of the property, plant, and equipment either initially or at the time the useful lives were revisited and revised.

Solution

1. The annual depreciation charges prior to the change in estimate were

Buildings: $15,000,000/15	=	$1,000,000
Plant and machinery: $10,000,000/10	=	$1,000,000
Furniture and fixtures: $3,500,000/7	=	$ 500,000
Total	=	$2,500,000 (A)

2. The revised annual depreciation for the year ending December 31, 20X0, would be

Buildings: [$15,000,000 – ($1,000,000 × 3)]/10	=	$1,200,000
Plant and machinery: [$10,000,000 – ($1,000,000 × 3)]/7	=	$1,000,000
Furniture and fixtures: [$3,500,000 – ($500,000 × 3)]/5	=	$ 400,000
Total	=	$2,600,000 (B)

3. The impact on Statement of Comprehensive Income for the year ending December 31, 20X0

=	(B) – (A)
=	$2,600,000 – $2,500,000
=	$100,000

Occasionally it may be difficult to distinguish between changes in measurement bases (i.e., accounting policies) and changes in estimate. In such cases, the change is treated as a change in estimate.

Changes in accounting estimates are to be adjusted prospectively in the period in which the estimate is amended and, if relevant, to *future periods* if they are also affected.

CASE STUDY 3

Facts

On January 1, 20X5, Robust Inc. purchased heavy-duty equipment for $400,000. On the date of installation, it was estimated that the machine has a useful life of ten years and a residual value of $40,000. Accordingly the annual depreciation worked out to $36,000 = [($400,000 – $40,000)/10].

On January 1, 20X9, after four years of using the equipment, the company decided to review the useful life of the equipment and its residual value. Technical experts were consulted. According to them, the remaining useful life of the equipment at January 1, 20X9, was seven years and its residual value was $46,000.

Required

Compute the revised annual depreciation for the year 20X9 and *future years*.

Solution

The revised annual depreciation based on the remaining useful life and *revised* residual value will be computed based on this formula:

Revised annual depreciation = (Net book value at January 1, 20X9 – revised residual value)/remaining useful life

Net book value at January 1, 20X9:

= $400,000 – ($36,000 × 4 years)

= $256,000

Revised annual depreciation for 20X9 and future years:

= ($256,000 – $46,000)/7 = $30,000

Disclosures with Respect to Changes in Accounting Estimates

An entity should disclose amounts and nature of changes in accounting estimates. In addition, it should also disclose changes relating to future periods, unless impracticable. The definition of "impracticable," which has been explained for the purposes of "changes in accounting policy," applies in the case of "changes in accounting estimates" as well.

CORRECTION OF PRIOR PERIOD ERRORS

Errors can arise in recognition, measurement, presentation, or disclosure of items in financial statements. If financial statements contain either material errors or intentional immaterial errors that achieve a particular presentation, then they do not comply with IFRS. Misstatements or omissions are "material" if they could, either individually or cumulatively, influence the decisions of users of financial statements.

Discovery of material errors relating to prior periods shall be corrected by restating comparative figures in the financial statements for the year in which the error is discovered, unless it is "impracticable" to do so. Again, the strict definition of "impracticable" (as explained previously) applies.

Disclosures in Respect of Correction of Prior Period Errors

With respect to the correction of prior period errors, IAS 8, paragraph 49, requires disclosure of

- The nature of the prior-period error.
- For each period presented, to the extent practicable, the amount of the correction:
  - For each financial statement line item affected.
  - For entities to which IAS 33 applies, for basic and diluted earnings per share.
- The amount of the correction at the beginning of the earliest prior period presented.
- If retrospective restatement is "impracticable" for a particular prior period, the circumstances that led to the existence of that condition and a description of how and from when the error has been corrected.

*Once disclosed, these disclosures are **not** to be repeated in financial statements of subsequent periods.*

CASE STUDY 4

In its 20X9 annual accounts, Joke included the corrected 20X8 consolidated cash flow figures as the comparative numbers to the 20X9 consolidated cash flow statement. The 20X9 accounts did not include any reference to the fact that the comparative numbers accompanying the 20X8 cash flow statement had been corrected. Joke had issued a communication to the market about the changes.

Required

Discuss the implications of the above events.

Solution

The changes to the comparative figures were material errors and should have been adjusted in accordance with IAS 8, paragraph 42, and supported by the relevant disclosures which would have included disclosure of the nature of the prior period errors. Even if the corrections to the 20X8 cash flow statement had been adequately communicated to the market through an announcement, further disclosures were necessary in the 20X9 accounts.

IAS 1, paragraphs 14 and 15, state that in virtually all circumstances a fair presentation is achieved by compliance with applicable IFRS. The fact that relevant information has already been communicated to the market does not release Joke from the obligation to apply IFRS when preparing its annual accounts. A press announcement cannot stand in the place of information that is required to be disclosed, and audited, within a set of annual financial statements.

CASE STUDY 5

Facts

1. The internal auditor of Vigilant Inc. noticed in 20X9 that in 20X8 the entity had omitted to record in its books of accounts an amortization expense amounting to $30,000 relating to an intangible asset.
2. An extract from the statement of comprehensive income for the years ended December 31, 20X8 and 20X9, *before correction of the error* follows:

	20X9	*20X8*
Gross profit	$300,000	$345,000
General and administrative expenses	(90,000)	(90,000)
Selling and distribution expenses	(30,000)	(30,000)
Amortization	(30,000)	XXXX
Net income before income taxes	150,000	225,000
Income taxes	(30,000)	(45,000)
Net profit	$120,000	$180,000

3. The "retained earnings" of Vigilant Inc. for 20X8 and 20X9 *before correction of the error* are

	20X9	*20X8*
Retained earnings, beginning of the year	$225,000	$ 45,000
Retained earnings, ending of the year	$375,000	$225,000

4. Vigilant Inc.'s income tax rate was 20% for both years.

Required

Present the accounting treatment prescribed by IAS 8 for the correction of the errors.

Solution

As an illustration of the accounting treatment and presentation of financial statements in accordance with IAS 8, a condensed version of Vigilant Inc.'s Statement of Comprehensive Income and Statement of Changes in Equity follows:

VIGILANT INC.
STATEMENT OF COMPREHENSIVE INCOME
For the Year Ended December 31, 20X9

	20X9	*20X8 restated*
Gross profit	$300,000	$345,000
General and Administrative expenses and Selling and Distribution expenses including amortization (see Explanation below)	(150,000)	(150,000)
Net income before income taxes	150,000	195,000
Income taxes	(30,000)	(39,000)
Net profit	$120,000	$156,000

VIGILANT INC.
STATEMENT OF CHANGES IN EQUITY (RETAINED EARNINGS COLUMNS ONLY)
For the Year Ended December 31, 20X9

	20X9	20X8 restated
Retained earnings, beginning, as reported previously	$225,000	$45,000
Correction of error, net of income taxes of $6,000 (see Explanation below)	(24,000)	--
Retained earnings, beginning, as restated	201,000	45,000
Net profit	120,000	156,000
Retained earnings, ending	$321,000	$201,000

VIGILANT INC.
For the Year Ended December 31, 20X9

Notes to the Financial Statements (Extract)

Note XX: The company omitted to record an amortization charge in the amount of $30,000 in 20X8. The financial statements for 20X8 have been restated to correct this error.

Explanation

According to the IAS 8, the amount of correction of an error that relates to prior periods should be reported by adjusting the opening balance of retained earnings. Comparative information should be restated unless it is "impracticable" to do so. The steps in preparing the revised financial statements and related disclosures are

1. As presented in the Statement of Changes in Equity (retained earnings columns only), the opening retained earnings were adjusted by $24,000, which represented the amount of error, $30,000, net of income tax effect of $6,000.
2. The comparative amounts in the Statement of Comprehensive Income were restated as

General and Administrative and Selling and Distribution expenses, including depreciation, before correction	$120,000
Amount of correction	30,000
As restated	**$150,000**
Income taxes before correction	$ 45,000
Amount of correction	(6,000)
As restated	**$ 39,000**

EXTRACTS FROM PUBLISHED FINANCIAL STATEMENTS

J. SAINSBURY PLC Financial Statements to March 21, 2009

2. Accounting policies

(a) Statement of compliance

The Group's financial statements have been prepared in accordance with International Financial Reporting Standards ("IFRS") as adopted by the European Union and International Financial Reporting Interpretations Committee ("IFRICs") interpretations and with those parts of the Companies Act 1985 applicable to companies reporting under IFRS. The Company's financial statements have been prepared on the same basis and as permitted by Section 230(3) of the Companies Act 1985; no income statement is presented for the Company.

(b) Basis of preparation

The financial statements are presented in sterling, rounded to the nearest million (£m) unless otherwise stated. They have been prepared under the historical cost convention, except for derivative financial instruments, investment properties and available-for-sale financial assets that have been measured at fair value.

The preparation of financial statements in conformity with IFRS requires the use of judgments, estimates and assumptions that affect the reported amounts of assets and liabilities at the date of the financial statements and the reported amounts of revenues and expenses during the reporting period. The estimates and associated assumptions are based on historical experience and various other factors that are believed to be reasonable under the circumstances, the results of which form the basis of making the judgments about carrying values of assets and liabilities that are not readily apparent from other sources. Actual results may differ from these estimates. The areas involving a higher degree of judgment or complexity, or areas where assumptions and estimates are significant to the financial statements are disclosed in note 2c.

New Standards, interpretation and amendments to published standards

Effective for the Group in these financial statements:

- IFRIC 12, *Service Concession Arrangements*

  The above interpretation to published standards has had no material impact on the results or the financial position of the Group for the 52 weeks to March 21, 2009.

Effective for the Group for the financial year beginning March 22, 2009:

- Revised IAS 1, *Presentation of Financial Statements,* amendments to IAS 1 relating to the disclosure of puttable instruments and obligations arising on liquidation
- Revised IAS 27, *Consolidated and Separate Financial Statements* relating to the cost of an investment on first-time adoption
- Amendments to IAS 32, *Financial Instruments: Presentation* relating to puttable instruments and obligations arising on liquidation
- Amendment to IFRS 2, *Share-Based Payment*
- Amendment to IFRS 7, *Financial Instruments: Disclosures*
- IFRS 8, *Operating Segments*
- IFRIC 13, *Customer Loyalty Programs*
- IFRIC 14, *IAS 19—The Limit on a Defined Benefit Asset, Minimum Funding Requirements and Their Interaction*

MULTIPLE-CHOICE QUESTIONS

1. XYZ Inc. changes its method of valuation of inventories from weighted-average method to first-in, first-out (FIFO) method. XYZ Inc. should account for this change as
    (a) A change in estimate and account for it prospectively.
    (b) A change in accounting policy and account for it prospectively.
    (c) A change in accounting policy and account for it retrospectively.
    (d) Account for it as a correction of an error and account for it retrospectively.

2. Change in accounting policy does **not** include
    (a) Change in useful life from ten years to seven years.
    (b) Change of method of valuation of inventory from FIFO to weighted-average.
    (c) Change of method of valuation of inventory from weighted-average to FIFO.
    (d) Change from the practice (convention) of paying as Christmas bonus one month's salary to staff before the end of the year to the new practice of paying one-half month's salary only.

3. When a public shareholding company changes an accounting policy voluntarily, it has to
    (a) Inform shareholders prior to taking the decision.
    (b) Account for it retrospectively.
    (c) Treat the effect of the change as an extraordinary item.
    (d) Treat it prospectively and adjust the effect of the change in the current period and future periods.

4. When it is difficult to distinguish between a change of estimate and a change in accounting policy, then an entity should
    (a) Treat the entire change as a change in estimate with appropriate disclosure.
    (b) Apportion, on a reasonable basis, the relative amounts of change in estimate and the change in accounting policy and treat each one accordingly.
    (c) Treat the entire change as a change in accounting policy.
    (d) Since this change is a mixture of two types of changes, it is best if it is ignored in the year of the change; the entity should then wait for the following year to see how the change develops and then treat it accordingly.

5. When an independent valuation expert advises an entity that the salvage value of its plant and machinery had drastically changed and thus the change is material, the entity should

    (a) Retrospectively change the depreciation charge based on the revised salvage value.
    (b) Change the depreciation charge and treat it as a correction of an error.
    (c) Change the annual depreciation for the current year and future years.
    (d) Ignore the effect of the change on annual depreciation, because changes in salvage values would normally affect the future only since these are expected to be recovered in future.

6. An entity wishes to accelerate its depreciation policy because of changes in the useful life of the asset. How should the change be dealt with?
    (a) By retrospective restatement.
    (b) By retrospective application.
    (c) By prospective application.
    (d) By disclosure of an error.

7. In determining which accounting policy is suitable for the preparation of the financial statements, an entity should look to
    (a) IFRS only.
    (b) IFRICs only.
    (c) The *Framework* only.
    (d) IFRS, IFRICs and the *Framework*.

8. Where it is impracticable to determine the period-specific effects of the change on comparative information for one or more prior periods presented, the retrospective application or restatement is applied
    (a) Retrospectively only to the extent that it is practicable.
    (b) Prospectively only to the extent that it is practicable.
    (c) Retrospectively to the extent that estimates can be made.
    (d) Prospectively to the extent estimates can be made.

9. Applying a requirement of a Standard or Interpretation is "impracticable" when the entity cannot apply it after making every effort to do so. Which of the following is not included in the definition of "impracticable"?
    (a) The effects of the retrospective application are not determinable.
    (b) The retrospective application requires assumptions about what management's intentions would have been at the time.
    (c) The retrospective application requires significant estimates of amounts.
    (d) The entity would find the determination of the effects to be immaterial.

10. Standards are normally published in advance of the required implementation date. In the intervening period, where a new/revised standard that is relevant to an entity has been issued but is not yet effective, the entity should

(a) Disclose this fact together with the impact.
(b) Not disclose any information.
(c) Only apply the standard at the implementation date.
(d) Only disclose the fact that the standard has been issued.

Chapter 7

EVENTS AFTER THE REPORTING PERIOD (IAS 10)

BACKGROUND AND INTRODUCTION

The end of the reporting period is the pivotal date at which the financial position of an entity is determined and reported. Thus, events that occur up to that date are critical in arriving at an entity's financial results and the financial position. However, sometimes events occurring after the reporting period may provide additional information about events that occurred before and up to the end of the reporting period. This information may have an impact on the financial results and the financial position of the entity. It is imperative that those post-reporting period events up to a certain "cut-off date" (discussed later and referred to as the authorization date) be taken into account in preparing the financial statements for the year ended and at the end of the reporting period.

Additionally, certain events that occur after the end of the reporting period might not affect the figures reported in the financial statements but may warrant disclosure in footnotes to the financial statements. Informing users of financial statements about such post–reporting period events through footnote disclosures helps them make informed decisions with respect to the entity, keeping in mind the impact these post–reporting period events may have on the financial position of the entity at the end of the reporting period.

SCOPE

IAS 10, *Events after the Reporting Period,* provides guidance on accounting and disclosure of events after the reporting period. For the purposes of this Standard, post–reporting period events are categorized into "adjusting" and "nonadjusting" events. The issue addressed by the Standard, IAS 10, is to what extent anything that happens during the period when the financial statements are being prepared should be reflected in those financial statements. The Standard distinguishes between events that provide information about the state of the entity at the end of the reporting period and those that concern the next financial period. A secondary issue is the cutoff point beyond which the financial statements are considered to be finalized.

DEFINITIONS OF KEY TERMS

Events after the reporting period. Those post–reporting period events, both favorable and unfavorable that occur between the end of the reporting period and the date when the financial statements are authorized for issue.

Adjusting events after the reporting period. Those post–reporting period events that provide evidence of conditions that existed at the end of the reporting period.

Nonadjusting events after the reporting period. Those post–reporting period events that are indicative of conditions that arose after the reporting period.

AUTHORIZATION DATE

The authorization date is the date when the financial statements could be considered legally authorized for issuance. The determination of the authorization date is critical to the concept of events after the reporting period. The authorization date serves as the cutoff point after the end of the reporting period up to which the post–reporting period events are to be examined in order to ascertain whether such events qualify for the treatment prescribed by IAS 10. This Standard explains the concept through the use of examples.

The general principles that need to be considered in determining the "authorization date" of the financial statements are set out next.

- When an entity is required to submit its financial statements to its shareholders for approval after they have already been issued, the authorization date in this case would mean the date of original issuance and not the date when these are approved by the shareholders.
- When an entity is required to issue its financial statements to a supervisory board made up wholly of nonexecutives, "authorization date" would mean the date on which management authorizes them for issue to the supervisory board.

CASE STUDY 1

Facts

The preparation of the financial statements of Excellent Corp. for the accounting period ended December 31, 2009, was completed by the management on March 15, 2010. The draft financial statements were considered at the meeting of the board of directors held on March 20, 2010, on which date the board approved them and authorized them for issuance. The annual general meeting (AGM) was held on April 10, 2010, after allowing for printing and the requisite notice period mandated by the corporate statute. At the AGM the shareholders approved the financial statements. The approved financial statements were filed by the corporation with the Company Law Board (the statutory body of the country that regulates corporations) on April 20, 2010.

Required

Given these facts, what is the "authorization date" in terms of IAS 10?

Solution

The date of authorization of the financial statements of Excellent Corp. for the year ended December 31, 2009, is March 20, 2010, the date when the board approved them and authorized them for issue (and not the date they were approved in the AGM by the shareholders). Thus, all post–reporting period events between December 31, 2009, and March 20, 2010, need to be considered by Excellent Corp. for the purposes of evaluating whether they are to be accounted for or reported under IAS 10.

CASE STUDY 2

Suppose in the above-cited case, the management of Excellent Corp. was required to issue the financial statements to a supervisory board (consisting solely of nonexecutives including representatives of a trade union). The management of Excellent Corp. had issued the draft financial statements to the supervisory board on March 16, 2010. The supervisory board approved them on March 17, 2010, and the shareholders approved them in the AGM held on April 10, 2010. The approved financial statements were filed with the Company Law Board on April 20, 2010.

Required

Would the new facts have any effect on the date of authorization?

Solution

In this case, the date of authorization of financial statements would be March 16, 2010, the date the draft financial statements were issued to the supervisory board. Thus, all post–reporting period events between December 31, 2009, and March 16, 2010, need to be considered by Excellent Corp. for the purposes of evaluating whether they are to be accounted for or reported under IAS 10.

ADJUSTING AND NONADJUSTING EVENTS (AFTER THE REPORTING PERIOD)

Two kinds of events after the end of the reporting period are distinguished by the Standard. These are, respectively, "adjusting events after the reporting period" and "nonadjusting events after the reporting period." Adjusting events are those post–reporting period events that provide evidence of conditions that actually existed at the end of the reporting period, albeit they were not known at the time. Financial statements should be adjusted to reflect adjusting events after the end of the reporting period.

Typical examples of *adjusting events* are

- The bankruptcy of a customer after the reporting period usually suggests a loss of trade receivable at the end of the reporting period.
- The sale of inventory at a price substantially lower than its cost after the reporting period confirms its net realizable value at the end of the reporting period.
- The sale of property, plant, and equipment for a net selling price that is lower than the carrying amount is indicative of an impairment before the end of the reporting period.
- The determination of an incentive or bonus payment after the reporting period when an entity has a constructive obligation at the end of the reporting period.
- A deterioration in the financial position (recurring losses) and operating results (working capital deficiencies) of an entity that has a bearing on the entity's continuance as a "going concern" in the foreseeable future.

CASE STUDY 3

Facts

During the year 2009, Taj Corp. was sued by a competitor for $15 million for infringement of a trademark. Based on the advice of the company's legal counsel, Taj Corp. accrued the sum of $10 million as a provision in its financial statements for the year ended December 31, 2009. Subsequent to the end of the reporting period, on February 15, 2010, the Supreme Court of the country decided in favor of the party alleging infringement of the trademark and ordered the defendant (Taj Corp.) to pay the aggrieved party a sum of $14 million. The financial statements were prepared by the company's management on January 31, 2010, and approved by the board on February 20, 2010.

Required

Should Taj Corp. adjust its financial statements for the year ended December 31, 2009?

Solution

Taj Corp. should adjust the provision upward by $4 million to reflect the award decreed by the Supreme Court (assumed to be the final appellate authority on the matter in this example) to be paid by Taj Corp. to its competitor.

Had the judgment of the Supreme Court been delivered on February 25, 2010, or later, this post–reporting period event would have occurred after the cut-off point (i.e., the date the financial statements were authorized for original issuance). If so, adjustment of financial statements would not have been required.

CASE STUDY 4

Facts

Shiny Corp. carries its inventory at the lower of cost and net realizable value. At December 31, 2009, the cost of inventory, determined under the first-in, first-out (FIFO) method, as reported in its financial statements for the year then ended, was $10 million. Due to severe recession and other negative economic trends in the market, the inventory could not be sold during the entire month of January 2010. On February 10, 2010, Shiny Corp. entered into an agreement to sell the entire inventory to a competitor for $6 million.

Required

Presuming the financial statements were authorized for issuance on February 15, 2010, should Shiny Corp. recognize a write-down of $4 million in the financial statements for the year ended December 31, 2009?

Solution

Yes, Shiny Corp. should recognize a write-down of $4 million in the financial statements for the year ended December 31, 2009.

Examples of nonadjusting events include:

- Declaration of an equity dividend
- Decline in the market value of an investment after the reporting period
- Entering into major purchase commitments in the form of issuing guarantees after the reporting period
- Classification of assets as held for sale under IFRS 5 and the purchase, disposal, or expropriation of assets after the reporting period
- Commencing a lawsuit relating to events that occurred after the reporting period

CASE STUDY 5

Facts

The statutory audit of ABC Inc. for the year ended June 30, 2009, was completed on August 30, 2009. The financial statements were signed by the managing director on September 8, 2009, and approved by the shareholders on October 10, 2009. The following three post–reporting period events have occurred:

1. On July 15, 2009, a customer owing $900,000 to ABC Inc. filed for bankruptcy. The financial statements include an allowance for doubtful debts pertaining to this customer of only $50,000.
2. ABC Inc.'s issued capital comprised 100,000 equity shares. The company announced a bonus issue of 25,000 shares on August 1, 2009.
3. Specialized equipment costing $545,000 purchased on March 1, 2009, was destroyed by fire on June 13, 2009. On June 30, 2009, ABC Inc. has booked a receivable of $400,000 from the insurance company pertaining to this claim. After the insurance company completed its investigation, it was discovered that the fire took place due to negligence of the machine operator. As a result, the insurer's liability was zero on this claim by ABC Inc.

Required

How should ABC Inc. account for these three post–reporting period events?

Solution

1. ABC Inc. should increase its allowance for doubtful debts to $900,000 because the customer's bankruptcy is indicative of a financial condition that existed at the end of the reporting period. This is an "adjusting event."
2. IAS 33, *Earnings Per Share*, requires a disclosure of transactions as "stock splits" or "rights issue," which are of significant importance after the reporting period. This is a nonadjusting event, and only disclosure is needed.

3. This is an adjusting event because it relates to an asset that was recognized at the end of the reporting period. However, as the insurance company's liability is zero, ABC Inc. must adjust its receivable on the claim to zero.

DIVIDENDS PROPOSED OR DECLARED AFTER THE BALANCE SHEET DATE

Dividends on equity shares proposed or declared after the reporting period should not be recognized as a liability at the end of the reporting period. Such declaration is a nonadjusting subsequent event and footnote disclosure is required, unless immaterial.

GOING CONCERN CONSIDERATIONS

Deterioration in an entity's financial position after the reporting period could cast substantial doubts about an entity's ability to continue as a going concern. IAS 10 requires that an entity should not prepare its financial statements on a going concern basis if management determines after the reporting period either that it intends to liquidate the entity or cease trading, or that it has no realistic alternative but to do so. IAS 10 notes that disclosures prescribed by IAS 1 under such circumstances should also be complied with.

DISCLOSURE REQUIREMENTS

IAS 10 requires these three disclosures:

1. The date when the financial statements were authorized for issue and who gave that authorization. If the entity's owners have the power to amend the financial statements after issuance, this fact should be disclosed.
2. If information is received after the reporting period about conditions that existed at the end of the reporting period, disclosures that relate to those conditions should be updated in light of the new information.
3. Where nonadjusting events after the reporting period are of such significance that nondisclosure would affect the ability of the users of financial statements to make proper evaluations and decisions, disclosure should be made for each such significant category of nonadjusting event regarding the nature of the event and an estimate of its financial effect or a statement that such an estimate cannot be made.

EXTRACTS FROM PUBLISHED FINANCIAL STATEMENTS

BARLOWORLD

Notes to the Consolidated Annual Financial Statements for the Year Ended September 30

28. Dividends

	2009 *Rm*	2008 *Rm*	2007 *Rm*
Ordinary shares			
Final dividend No. 160 paid on January 19, 2009: 150 cents per share (2008: No. 158 – 200 cents per share; 2007: No. 155 – 450 cents per share)	312	409	911
Special dividend paid on April 2, 2007: 500 cents per share			1,017
Interim dividend No 161 paid on June 8, 2009: 40 cents per share (2008: No. 159 – 100 cents per share; 2007: No. 157 – 175 cents per share)	84	205	357
Paid to Barloworld Limited shareholders	396	614	2,285
Paid to minorities	38	8	344
	434	622	2,629

On November 16, 2009, the directors declared dividend No. 162 of 70 cents per share.

An estimated dividend liability of R157 million and an estimated STC liability of R11 million have not been included in these financial statements.

In compliance with the requirements of the JSE Limited, the following dates are applicable:

Date declared	Monday	November 16, 2009
Last day to trade cum dividend	Friday	January 8, 2010
Shares trade ex dividend	Monday	January 11, 2010
Record date	Friday	January 15, 2010
Payment date	Monday	January 18, 2010

Share certificates may not be dematerialized or rematerialized between Monday, January 11, 2010, and Friday, January 15, 2010, both days inclusive.

Analysis of dividends declared in respect of current year's earnings:

| | Cents | Cents | Cents |
Ordinary dividends per share	*2009*	*2008*	*2007*
Interim dividend	40	100	175
Final dividend	70	150	200
	110	250	375

6% cumulative nonredeemable preference shares

Preference dividends totaling R67 000 were declared on each of the following dates:

- April 28, 2009 (paid on May 25, 2009)
- November 14, 2008 (paid on November 24, 2008)
- April 25, 2008 (paid on May 26, 2008)
- October 10, 2007 (paid on November 5, 2007)
- April 26, 2007 (paid on May 28, 2007)
- September 29, 2006 (paid on October 30, 2006)

MULTIPLE-CHOICE QUESTIONS

1. ABC Ltd. decided to operate a new amusement park that will cost $1 million to build in the year 2009. Its financial year-end is December 31, 2009. ABC Ltd. has applied for a letter of guarantee for $700,000. The letter of guarantee was issued on March 31, 2010. The audited financial statements have been authorized to be issued on April 18, 2010. The adjustment required to be made to the financial statement for the year ended December 31, 2009, should be

(a) Booking a $700,000 long-term payable.

(b) Disclosing $700,000 as a contingent liability in 2009 financial statement.

(c) Increasing the contingency reserve by $700,000.

(d) Do nothing.

2. A new drug named "EEE" was introduced by Genius Inc. onto the market on December 1, 2009. Genius Inc.'s financial year ends on December 31, 2009. It was the only company that was permitted to manufacture this patented drug. The drug is used by patients suffering from an irregular heartbeat. On March 31, 2010, after the drug was introduced, more than 1,000 patients died. After a series of investigations, authorities discovered that when this drug was simultaneously used with "BBB," a drug used to regulate hypertension, the patient's blood would clot and the patient suffered a stroke. A lawsuit for $100,000,000 has been filed against Genius Inc. The financial statements were authorized for issuance on April 30, 2010. Which of the following options is the appropriate accounting treatment for this post–reporting period event under IAS 10?

(a) The entity should provide $100,000,000 because this is an "adjusting event" and the financial statements were authorized to be issued after the accident.

(b) The entity should disclose $100,000,000 as a contingent liability because it is an "adjusting event."

(c) The entity should disclose $100,000,000 as a "contingent liability" because it is a present obligation with an improbable outflow.

(d) Assuming the probability of the lawsuit being decided against Genius Inc. is remote, the entity should disclose it in the footnotes, because it is a nonadjusting material event.

3. At the balance sheet date, December 31, 2009, ABC Inc. carried a receivable from XYZ, a major customer, at $10 million. The "authorization date" of the financial statements is on February 16, 2006. XYZ declared bankruptcy on Valentine's Day (February 14, 2010). ABC Inc. will

(a) Disclose the fact that XYZ has declared bankruptcy in the footnotes.

(b) Make a provision for this post–reporting period event in its financial statements (as opposed to disclosure in footnotes).

(c) Ignore the event and wait for the outcome of the bankruptcy because the event took place after the year-end.

(d) Reverse the sale pertaining to this receivable in the comparatives for the prior period and treat this as an "error" under IAS 8.

4. Excellent Inc. built a new factory building during 2005 at a cost of $20 million. At December 31, 2009, the net book value of the building was $19 million. Subsequent to year-end, on March 15, 2010, the building was destroyed by fire and the claim against the insurance company proved futile because the cause of the fire was negligence on the part of the caretaker of the building. If the date of authorization of the financial statements for the year ended December 31, 2009, was March 31, 2010, Excellent Inc. should

(a) Write off the net book value to its scrap value because the insurance claim would not fetch any compensation.

(b) Make a provision for one-half of the net book value of the building.

(c) Make a provision for three-fourths of the net book value of the building based on prudence.

(d) Disclose this nonadjusting event in the footnotes.

5. International Inc. deals extensively with foreign entities, and its financial statements reflect these foreign currency transactions. Subsequent to the balance sheet date, and before the "date of authorization" of the issuance of the financial statements, there were abnormal fluctuations in foreign currency rates. International Inc. should

(a) Adjust the foreign exchange year-end balances to reflect the abnormal adverse fluctuations in foreign exchange rates.

(b) Adjust the foreign exchange year-end balances to reflect all the abnormal fluctuations in foreign exchange rates (and not just adverse movements).

(c) Disclose the post–balance sheet event in footnotes as a nonadjusting event.

(d) Ignore the post–balance sheet event.

Chapter 8

CONSTRUCTION CONTRACTS (IAS 11)

BACKGROUND AND INTRODUCTION

The objective of IAS 11, *Construction Contracts,* is to prescribe the criteria for the accounting of revenue and costs in relation to construction contracts. Due to the nature of such contracts—the commencement and completion dates are usually well separated, often crossing reporting period ends—the Standard focuses on the allocation of revenue and costs to those reporting periods in which the construction contract is executed.

The Standard shall be applied in accounting for construction contracts in the financial statements of *contractors*. Construction contracts also include contracts for services that are directly related to the construction of an asset, such as project management or design.

DEFINITIONS OF KEY TERMS
(in accordance with IAS 11)

Construction contract. A contract specifically negotiated for the construction of an asset or combination of assets that are closely interrelated or interdependent in terms of their design, technology, function, or ultimate use, or purpose.

Fixed-price contract. A construction contract in which the contractor agrees to a fixed price.

Cost-plus contract. A construction contract in which the contractor is reimbursed for allowable or defined costs plus a percentage of such costs or a fixed fee.

Variation. An instruction by the customer for the change in the scope of the work to be performed in the contract.

Claim. An amount that the contractor seeks to collect from a customer or another party as reimbursement for costs not included in the contract price.

Incentive payments. Additional amounts paid to the contractor if specified performance standards are met or exceeded.

COMBINING AND SEGMENTING CONSTRUCTION CONTRACTS

The provisions of this Standard usually are applied to construction contracts separately. Sometimes, however, it is necessary to the Standard to separate parts of one contract or to consider a group of contracts as one. The purpose is to properly reflect the substance of the transaction rather than the legal form.

Segmenting Contracts

When a contract covers the construction of a number of assets, the contract for construction of each asset shall be considered a separate contract when

1. Separate proposals have been submitted for each asset.
2. Each asset has been subject to separate negotiation and both contractor and customer were able to accept or reject that part of the contract relating to each asset.
3. The costs and revenues of each asset are separately identifiable.

CASE STUDY 1

Facts

XYZ, Inc. is negotiating with the local government to build a new bridge after demolishing the existing bridge in downtown near the city center. At the initial meeting, it was indicated that the government would not be willing to pay for both components of the contract an amount exceeding $100,000. The government representatives insisted that separate proposals would need to be submitted and negotiated and that the contractor should maintain separate records for each component of the contract and upon request furnish details of the contract costs incurred to date by component. After submission of the separate proposals, it was agreed that the split of the contract price of $100,000 would be in the ratio of 70% for construction of the new bridge and 30% for demolishing the existing bridge.

Required

Evaluate in light of the provisions of IAS 11 whether the contract for the construction of the new bridge and the contract for demolishing the existing bridge should be segmented and treated as separate contracts or be combined and treated as a single contract.

Solution

The two contracts should be *segmented* and treated as *separate contracts* because

- Separate proposals were submitted for the two contracts.
- The two contracts were negotiated separately.
- Costs and revenues of each contract can be identified separately.

Combining Contracts

A group of contracts, each with a single or even with different customers, shall be treated as a *single contract* when

1. The group of contracts is negotiated as one single package.
2. The contracts are so closely interrelated that they are effectively (i.e., *in substance*) part of one project with one overall profit margin.
3. The contracts are performed either concurrently or in continuous sequence.

CASE STUDY 2

Facts

Universal Builders Inc. is well known for its expertise in building flyovers and maintaining these structures. Impressed with Universal's track record, the local municipal authorities have invited them to submit a tender for a two-year contract to build a super flyover in the heart of the city (the largest in the region) and another tender for maintenance of the flyover for ten years after completion of the construction.

Required

Evaluate whether these two contracts should be segmented or combined into one contract for the purposes of IAS 11.

Solution

The two contracts should be *combined* and treated as a *single contract* because

- The two contracts are very closely related to each other and, in fact, are part of a single contract with an overall profit margin.
- The contracts have been negotiated as a single package.
- The contracts are performed in a continuous sequence.

Sometimes a contract may provide for the construction of an additional asset at the option of the customer or may be amended to include the construction of an additional asset. Under such circumstances, the additional asset shall be treated as a separate contract when it differs significantly from the asset(s) covered by the original contract *or* when the price is negotiated without regard to the original contract price.

CONTRACT REVENUE

Contract revenue shall comprise the *initial price agreed* in the contract together with *variations, claims, and incentives* to the extent that it is probable that they will result in revenue *and* they are capable of being *reliably measured*.

Variations, Claims, and Incentives

Over time, the contract value may need to be amended either upward or downward. There can be a significant degree of uncertainty and, therefore, changes in the estimation when assessing the contract value and hence revenue to be recognized in financial statements. In all cases, the amount must be *reliably measurable* and *realization is probable*. For example

- It should be probable that a customer will approve *variations*.
- Negotiations should be sufficiently advanced with respect to *claims*.
- A contract should be at a sufficiently advanced stage to make it probable that *incentive* milestones will be achieved.

CONTRACT COSTS

Contract costs shall consist of

1. Costs that *relate directly* to the specific contract.
2. Costs that are *attributable* to contract activity in general and can be allocated to contracts.
3. Such *other costs* as are specifically chargeable under the terms of the contract.

Common examples of costs that are considered related directly to specific contracts are

- Site labor costs, including site supervisions
- Materials used in construction
- Depreciation of machinery, plant, and equipment used in construction
- Cost of hiring plant (if not owned by the contractor)
- Cost of moving plant to and from contract site
- Design and technical assistance costs directly related to the contract
- Cost of rectification and guarantee work, including warranty costs
- Claims from third parties

These costs may be *reduced by* any *incidental income* resulting from sale of surplus material and the disposal of equipment at the end of the contract.

Costs that may be attributable to contract activity in general and can be allocated to specific contracts are insurance, construction overhead, and the like. General contract activity costs must be allocated on a systematic and rational basis assuming a "normal" level of construction activity.

Costs that may be specifically charged to the customer under the terms of the contract include percentage of general and administrative overheads or development costs that the customer has specifically agreed to reimburse under the terms of the contract.

Costs that cannot be attributed to contract activity or cannot be allocated to a contract are excluded from costs of construction contract. Examples of such costs are

- Selling and marketing costs
- General and administrative costs for which the reimbursement is not specified in the contract
- Research and development costs for which reimbursement is not specified in the contract
- Depreciation on idle plant and equipment whose use cannot be attributable to any construction contract

A matter of debate in this area is costs incurred in securing a contract, such as travel, promotion, and meeting costs, and the like. Usually only those costs incurred after winning the contract are included as contract costs. However, the Standard states that if such "precontract" costs are reliably measurable and it is probable that the contract will be secured, then such costs are included as part of the overall contract cost. In practice, if the contract has been secured by the time the financial statements are authorized for issue, then the condition of probability of securing the contract is satisfied and the costs can be included. However, it should be noted that once such "precontract" costs have been expensed, they cannot be reinstated once the contract is secured.

RECOGNITION OF CONTRACT REVENUE AND EXPENSES

Contract revenue and contract costs should be recognized in the income statement when the *outcome* of the contract can be *estimated reliably.*

The revenue and costs should be recognized by reference to the *stage of completion* at the end of the reporting period.

When it is likely that contract costs will exceed contract revenue, then the entire *loss* must be recognized in the income statement immediately, regardless of the stage of completion.

The percentage of completion of a contract at any reporting date is estimated on a cumulative basis. Therefore, *changes in estimates* are automatically accounted for in the period in which the change occurs and in future periods, which is in accordance with IAS 8, *Accounting Policies, Changes in Accounting Estimates, and Errors.*

FIXED-PRICE CONTRACT

With respect to a fixed-price contract, the outcome can be estimated reliably when

- Total contract revenue can be measured reliably
- It is probable that the economic benefit of the contract will flow to the entity
- Both the costs to complete the contract and the stage of completion can be reliably estimated
- The costs attributable to the contract can be clearly identified and measured

COST-PLUS CONTRACT

With respect to a cost-plus contract, the outcome can be reliably estimated when

- It is probable that the economic benefit of the contract will flow to the entity.
- The costs attributable to the contract, whether specifically reimbursable or not, can be clearly identified and measured.

PERCENTAGE-OF-COMPLETION METHOD

The recognition of revenues and expenses by references to the stages of completion of a contract is referred to as the *percentage of completion method*. The manner in which this method works is simple: The contract revenues are matched with the contract costs incurred in reaching the stage of completion. Such comparison results in the reporting of revenue, expenses, and profit that can be attributed to the proportion of the work completed.

IAS 11 recognizes only the percentage-of-completion method of recognition for revenues and expenses. The "completed-contract method" whereby no contract revenues or profits are recognized until the contracts are completed or are substantially complete is not permitted under IAS 11.

The *stage of completion* of a contract can be estimated by a variety of means. Depending on the nature of the contract, an entity may employ the method that measures reliably the work performed. These include

- The proportion that costs incurred to date bear to expected total costs required to complete the contract.
- Certification or surveys of work performed.
- Completion of physical proportion of the contract work.

Very often, and as a matter of prudence, unless a contract is sufficiently far advanced, revenue is recognized only to the extent of costs incurred (i.e., zero profit is recognized). How far is "sufficiently far advanced" is a matter of judgment. Many entities state that a contract should be at least 50% complete; others, 75%; some, much lower percentages. Clearly hindsight can be very beneficial. If the contract is complete by the time the financial statements are authorized for issue, it is a much simpler task to estimate the actual stage of completion at the end of the reporting period. For other cases, a robust estimating system with a proven track record of no significant inaccuracies is a must if an entity wishes to reliably estimate final outcome when the percentage complete is low at the time of estimation.

CASE STUDY 3

Facts

Miracle Construct Inc. is executing a gigantic project of constructing the tallest building in the country. The project is expected to take three years to complete.

The company has signed a fixed-price contract of $12,000,000 for the construction of this prestigious tower.

The details of the costs incurred to date in the first year are

Site labor costs	$1,000,000
Cost of construction material	3,000,000
Depreciation of special plant and equipment used in contracting to build the tallest building	500,000
Marketing and selling costs to get the tallest building in the country the right exposure	1,000,000
Total	$5,500,000
Total contract cost estimated to complete	$5,500,000

Required

Calculate the percentage of completion and the amounts of revenue, costs, and profits to be recognized under IAS 11.

Solution

1. Contract cost incurred to date

Site labor cost	$ 1,000,000
Material cost	3,000,000
Depreciation of special plant and equipment	500,000
	$ 4,500,000

NOTE: IAS 11 does not allow "marketing and selling costs" to be considered contract costs.

2.	Cost to complete	=	$5,500,000
3.	Percentage of completion	=	4,500,000/(4,500,000 + 5,500,000)
		=	4,500,000/10,000,000
		=	45%

4. Revenue, costs, and profits to be recognized in the first year:

Revenue	=	12,000,000 × 0.45 = $5,400,000
Costs	=	10,000,000 × 0.45 = $4,500,000
Profit	=	$900,000

In all cases, care must be taken in estimating percentage complete to exclude costs that relate to *future activity*, such as materials delivered to site. Such costs are recognized as an asset, provided it is probable that they will be recovered. Such costs represent amounts incurred on behalf of the customer and are thus amounts due from a customer. These costs are often classified as "contract work in progress."

PRACTICAL INSIGHT

In order to take advantage of bulk or volume discounts on purchase of construction materials, such as steel or cement, contractors sometimes buy significant quantities of those items and stock them at a site where a big construction contract is in progress. The costs of such materials are future costs because these are not meant for immediate consumption at the site where they are stored. Such costs qualify for the treatment explained previously in case of future costs. At year-end they may need to be estimated in order to report them on the balance sheet as "contract work in progress."

It should be borne in mind that the billing schedule, and even the realization of interim invoices for such advance deliveries, need not bear any relation to the level of revenue that should be recognized in the income statement. Similarly, invoices received from, and payments made to, subcontractors in advance of the work actually being performed also need to be excluded.

A more reliable method is the independent certification or survey of the value of work done as of the reporting date and then ensuring that all costs relating to such work have been fully recognized.

IFRIC 12

In certain countries construction or maintenance of infrastructure for public services (roads, bridges, water distribution facilities) is contracted out to private sector operators. The private sector operators are usually paid for their services over the term of the arrangements. Such arrangements are often described as "build-operate-transfer" ("BOT") or "rehabilitate-operate-transfer" or a "public-to-private service concession arrangement."

During November 2006, the IASB issued IFRIC 12, *Service Concession Arrangements*, which is effective for annual periods beginning on or after January 1, 2008. This IFRIC provides guidance on the accounting by private sector operators for "public-to-private" service concession arrangements. It should be noted that this Interpretation does not specify the accounting by grantors of the concessions.

This Interpretation sets out general principles for recognizing and measuring the obligations and related rights in service concession arrangements (disclosure requirements about service concession arrangements are detailed in SIC-29).

This IFRIC addresses the following issues, and the consensus views on these issues are

1. Treatment of the operator's rights over the infrastructure—IFRIC 12 categorically states that the operator's right over the infrastructure shall not be recognized as property, plant, and equipment of the operator since the service arrangement does not convey the right to control the use of the public service infrastructure to the operator.

2. Recognition and measurement of arrangement consideration—If the operator constructs or upgrades infrastructure (i.e., provides construction or upgrade services) used in providing a public service or operates and maintains it for a specified period of time, then the operator shall recognize and measure revenue in accordance with IASs 11 and 18 for the services it performs.

3. Construction or upgrade services—The operator shall account for revenue and costs relating to construction or upgrade services in accordance with IAS 11.

4. Consideration given by the grantor to the operator—If the operator renders construction or upgrade services, the consideration received or receivable by the operator shall be recognized at its fair value. The consideration may be rights to a financial asset or an intangible asset.

5. Recognizing a "financial asset"—The operator shall recognize a financial asset to the extent that it has an unconditional contractual right to receive cash or any other financial asset from or at the direction of the grantor for the construction services. Usually, the grantor has little, if any, discretion to avoid payment, because the agreement is enforceable by law (please refer to chapters on financial instruments for detailed discussion on financial assets).

6. Recognizing an "intangible asset"—The operator shall recognize an intangible asset to the extent that it receives a right or a license to charge users of the public service (for a detailed discussion on intangible assets please refer to the chapter on "intangible assets"). A right to charge users of the public service is not an unconditional right to receive cash because the amounts are contingent and depend on the extent that the public uses the service. The operator shall account separately for the construction services paid partly by a financial asset and partly by an intangible asset. The consideration received or receivable for both components shall be recognized initially at the fair value of the consideration received or receivable.

IFRIC 15

Agreements for the construction of real estate may relate to residential, commercial, or industrial developments. Construction often spans more than one accounting period, may take place on land the buyer owns or leases before construction begins, and agreements may require progress payments. The objectives of IFRIC 15 are to clarify the definition of a construction contract and the articulation between IAS 11 and IAS 18 and to provide guidance on how to account for revenue when the agreement for the construction of real estate falls within the scope of IAS 18.

IFRIC 15 addresses the accounting for revenue and associated expenses by entities that undertake the construction of real estate directly or through subcontractors. It clarifies how these revenues and expenses should be recognized if an agreement between a developer and a buyer is reached before the construction of the real estate is completed. It is common practice for real estate developers to market their developments well before the start of any construction, and this activity continues throughout the construction period. Some real estate developers recognize revenue from these arrangements as construction progresses by reference to the stage of completion of the development, while others recognize revenue only when the completed unit is handed over to the buyer. Also, this Interpretation provides guidance on how to determine whether an agreement is within the scope of IAS 11 or IAS 18.

There are three different revenue recognition approaches within existing standards that could potentially be applied to real estate marketed prior to the completing of construction.

It could be accounted for as

- A construction contract in accordance with IAS 11.
- The rendering of services in accordance with IAS 18.
- The sale of goods in accordance with IAS 18.

IFRIC 15 states where the agreement allows the buyer to specify major structural elements of design before or during construction, then the agreement should be considered to be a construction contract.

When construction takes place independently of the agreement and the buyer only has a limited ability to influence designs, the agreement should be considered to be in accordance with IAS 18.

Agreement for the Rendering of Services or Sale of Goods (IAS 18)

Where the agreement falls within the scope of IAS 18 and the entity is not required to acquire and supply construction materials, the agreement is for the rendering of services. The entity is responsible only for assembling materials supplied by others (i.e., it has no inventory risk for the construction materials) and therefore the constructor is rendering a service.

Revenue is recognized by reference to the stage of completion of the transaction using the percentage-of-completion method. As stated in IAS 18, paragraph 21, the requirements of IAS 11 are generally applicable to the recognition of revenue and the associated expenses for such a transaction.

When an agreement involves the provision of construction materials and labor and it does not fall to be accounted for as a construction contract under IAS 11, it will be an agreement for the sale of goods under IAS 18. The applicable recognition criteria are those set out in IAS 18, paragraph 14. Revenue can only be recognized when the entity has transferred control and significant risks and rewards of ownership of the goods to the buyer, and the interpretation distinguishes between circumstances in which these criteria are met:

1. At a single point in time, for example at completion or upon delivery. Revenue is recognized when the significant risks and rewards of ownership are transferred to the buyer and all the criteria are met in accordance with IAS 18, paragraph 14.
2. Continuously as construction progresses. It is noted in the interpretation that agreements with continuous transfer might not be encountered frequently. However, one example of a situation that would constitute a continuous transfer is if the agreement is terminated before construction is complete, the buyer retains the work in progress, and the entity has the right to be paid for the work to date. When the criteria are met continuously, revenue is recognized by reference to the stage of completion of the transaction using the percentage-of-completion method. As stated in IAS 18, paragraph 21, the requirements of IAS 11 are generally applicable to the recognition of revenue and the associated expenses for such a transaction.

This interpretation supersedes the current guidance for real estate in the Appendix to IAS 18. It is applicable retrospectively for annual periods beginning on or after January 1, 2009.

DISCLOSURES

An entity shall disclose the following six items:

1. The amount of contract revenue recognized as revenue in the period
2. The methods used to determine the contract revenue recognized in the period
3. The methods used to determine the stage of completion of contracts in progress at the balance sheet date
4. For contracts in progress at the balance sheet date

   a. The aggregate amount of costs incurred, and recognized profits less recognized losses, to date
   b. Advances received
   c. Retentions

5. The gross amount due from customers for contract work as an asset
6. The gross amount due to customers for contract work as a liability

The gross amount due from customers for contract work is the net amount of costs incurred plus recognized profits, less the sum of recognized losses and progress billings for contracts in progress for which costs incurred plus recognized profits, less recognized losses exceeds progress billings.

The gross amount due to customers for contract work is the net amount of costs incurred plus recognized profits, less the sum of recognized losses and progress billings for contracts in progress for which progress billings exceed incurred plus recognized profits, less recognized losses.

EXTRACTS FROM PUBLISHED FINANCIAL STATEMENTS

HOLCIM, Annual Report, 2009

Notes to the Consolidated Financial Statement

34 Construction contracts

Million CHF	*2009*	*2008*
Contract revenue recognized during the year	**1,487**	**1,691**
Contract costs incurred and recognized profits (less recognized losses) to date	3,127	2,550
Progress billings to date	(3,151)	(2,578)
Due to contract customers at the end of the reporting period	**(24)**	**(28)**
Of which:		
Due from customers for contract work	26	37
Due to customers for contract work	(50)	(65)

CASE STUDY 4

Facts

In year 1, Slow Build Inc. was invited to tender for the construction of a residential block and connected shopping arcade with common plaza and garden and play areas. Tenders were required to detail the costs of each element separately, but it was clear that only one contractor would win the entire contract due to the interrelated aspects of the development.

During year 1, Slow Build Inc. management traveled to the United States to visit three possible designers in order to obtain their preliminary design proposals, of which only one would be selected. The cost of the visit was $20,000. Later in year 1, having selected one designer, Slow Build Inc. returned to the United States to clarify design details and request construction of a scale model in order to make a presentation of the tender to the ultimate customer. The cost of the second trip was $15,000.

During year 2, but before its year 1 financial statements were authorized for issue, Slow Build Inc. was notified that it had been awarded the contract. However, the contract was not signed until after the year 1 financial statements were issued.

The contract was for a total price of $16 million, comprising $9 million for the residential block, $5 million for the shopping arcade, and $2 million for the common plaza, garden, and play area. A mobilization advance of $1 million would be paid at the outset, $1 million was payable at the end of year 2, $5 million at the end of year 3, and $8 million was payable at the end of year 4, at which point the development would be complete and $1 million was to be held back as a retention for one year.

Slow Build Inc. initially estimated that the total cost of the project would be $12 million, of which $7 million would be for the residential block, $4 million for the shopping arcade, and $1 million for the plaza, gardens, and play area. Included in this cost is $1 million of plant acquired specifically for the project that could not be used subsequently. The estimated residual value of this plant at the end of the contract was $100,000. Also included in the overall cost was 30 months of depreciation on general plant and equipment already owned by Slow Build Inc. at $50,000 per month. The on-site accounts staff cost included in the estimate was $5,000 per month. Their role was to maintain and record time cards of workers and receive and issue materials.

Costs incurred at each year-end were

	Year 2	*Year 3*	*Year 4*	*Total*
Residential block	$1,000,000	$3,000,000	$3,000,000	$7,000,000
Shopping arcade	500,000	1,800,000	1,700,000	4,000,000
Plaza, gardens, & play area	--	200,000	800,000	1,000,000
Total	$1,500,000	$5,000,000	$5,500,000	$12,000,000

The costs at the end of year 2 include $250,000 of materials delivered to the site for use in year 3.

The $200,000 in year 3 for the plaza, gardens, and play area was an advance to subcontractors who would mobilize in year 4.

During year 3, due to a fire at the neighboring plot, the police cordoned off the whole area for a month while investigations were conducted. During this time all plant and equipment remained idle on site. However, work continued in Slow Build Inc.'s workshop and yard.

During year 3, the customer requested a variation in the contract with a value of $1 million and a cost of $750,000. However, the variation was not approved by the customer until after Slow Build Inc.'s year 3 financial statements were authorized for issue. Slow Build Inc. incurred the extra costs for the variation in year 3.

Required

Provide Slow Build Inc.'s statement of comprehensive income and the amounts that should be presented in the statement of financial position for each of the years 1, 2, 3, and 4.

Solution

Statement of comprehensive income	Year 1	Year 2	Year 3	Year 4
	$'000	$'000	$'000	$'000
Contract revenue	15	1,250	8,266	7,469
Contract costs	(35)	(1,250)	(6,250)	(5,100)
Gross (loss)/profit	(20)	--	2,016	2,369

The percentage completion based on the proportion that costs incurred at each year-end bear to the estimated total costs are

	Note	Year 1 $'000	Year 2 $'000	Year 3 $'000	Year 4 $'000	Total $'000
Estimated costs	(a)		1,500	5,500	5,000	12,000
Precontract costs	(b)	15	0			15
Materials at site	(c)		(250)	250		--
Idle plant depreciation	(d)			(50)		(50)
Costs of variation	(e)			750		750
Subcontractor advance	(f)			(200)	200	
Residual value of plant					(100)	(100)
Total costs		15	1,250	6,250	5,100	12,615
Percentage complete		0.125	10.62	59.57	100.00	
Memorandum		15/11,915	1,265/11,915	7,515/12,615		

Year 1:

Note (a): The customer has made it clear that, despite separate tenders being required for each part of the development, only one contractor would get the contract and the development was heavily interdependent. Consequently, the contract should be treated as one, and not segmented.

Note (b): The second trip to the designers can be reasonably identified as being specifically incurred to secure the contract. It was probable that Slow Build Inc. would secure the contract, as it had been so notified, even though the contract was not secured until after the year 1 financial statements were authorized for issue. Accordingly $15,000 can be included in the contract cost. The cost of the initial trip of $20,000 was more exploratory in nature and thus cannot be included. As Slow Build Inc. can reasonably expect to recover the costs of the second trip, but as the contract was not sufficiently far advanced to reasonably forecast the outcome (0.125% complete), no profit is accrued. Revenue of $15,000 can be accrued in year 1, and the total trip expenses are charged to the income statement.

The percentage complete is based on the contract cost of $12 million less the expected residual value of the plant specifically acquired for the contract.

Year 2:

Note (c): At the end of year 2, materials were only delivered to site. Therefore, they are excluded from the percentage complete calculation. However, in the opinion of management, the contract still remained sufficiently incomplete to recognize profit, but the costs could be reasonably assumed to be recoverable and revenue is accrued equal to cost.

The percentage complete is based on the contract cost of $12 million less the expected residual value of the plant specifically acquired for the contract.

Year 3:

Note (c): The materials delivered to site in year 2 were used in year 3 and are included in contract costs.

Note (d): Depreciation on idle plant for one month is deducted as the delay was not part of the construction activity.

Note (e): The costs of the variation are included as the costs were incurred. However, as the variation was not approved by the customer until after the year 3 financial statements were authorized for issue, the percentage complete is still applied to the initial contract price of $12,000,000. In the opinion of management, the contract is sufficiently far advanced to deem the final outcome reasonably certain, so 59.57% ($7,148,000) of the contract price is recognized as revenue. Therefore, $7,148,000 less cumulative revenue to year 2 of $1,265,000, or $5,883,000, is recognized in year 3.

Note (f): The subcontractor advance is deducted from the cost, as it is an advance for work to be executed in year 4.

The percentage complete is based on the contract cost of $12 million less the expected residual value of the plant specifically acquired for the contract plus the cost of variation. This is applied to the initial contract value of $16 million, as the variation is not approved.

Year 4:

In year 4 the contract is complete and the full contract revenue of $17 million (including the approved variation), less revenue recognized in earlier years, is taken to the income statement.

Overall, the contract has revenue of $17 million and costs of $12.615 million, earning a profit of $4,385,000 ($2,016,000 + $2,369,000). The loss in year 1 arises solely from the initial business trip, which is not a contract cost.

Statement of financial position

	Year 1	Year 2	Year 3	Year 4
Cumulative progress billings		$2,000,000	$7,000,000	$16,000,000
Variation				1,000,000
Total cumulative billings		2,000,000	7,000,000	17,000,000
Cumulative revenue recognized	$15,000	1,265,000	9,531,000	17,000,000
Disclosed as due from customers	15,000		2,531,000	
Disclosed as due to customers		735,000		
Disclosed as debtors (retention)				1,000,000
Contracts in progress				
Costs incurred	15,000	1,265,000	7,515,000	n/a
Recognized profits	--	--	2,016,000	n/a

MULTIPLE-CHOICE QUESTIONS

1. Lazy Builders Inc. has incurred the following contract costs in the first year on a two-year fixed price contract for $4.0 million to construct a bridge:

- Material cost = $2 million
- Other contract costs (including site labor costs) = $1 million
- Cost to complete = $2 million

How much profit or loss should Lazy Inc. recognize in the first year of the three-year construction contract?

(a) Loss of $0.5 million prorated over two years.
(b) Loss of $1.0 million (expensed immediately).
(c) No profit or loss in the first year and deferring it to second year.
(d) Since 60% is the percentage of completion, recognize 60% of loss (i.e., $0.6 million).

2. Brilliant Inc. is constructing a skyscraper in the heart of town and has signed a fixed-price two-year contract for $21.0 million with the local authorities. It has incurred the following cost relating to the contract by the end of first year:

- Material cost = $5 million
- Labor cost = $2 million
- Construction overhead = $2 million
- Marketing costs = $0.5 million
- Depreciation of idle plant and equipment = $0.5 million

At the end of the first year, it has estimated cost to complete the contract = $9 million. What profit or loss from the contract should Brilliant Inc. recognize at the end of the first year?

(a) $1.5 million (9/18 × 3.0)
(b) $1.0 million (9/18 × 2.0)
(c) $1.05 million (10/19 × 2.0)
(d) $1.28 million (9.5/18.5 × 2.5)

3. Mediocre Inc. has entered into a very profitable fixed-price contract for constructing a high-rise building over a period of three years. It incurs the following costs relating to the contract during the first year:

- Cost of material = $2.5 million
- Site labor costs = $2.0 million
- Agreed administrative costs as per contract to be reimbursed by the customer = $1 million
- Depreciation of the plant used for the construction = $0.5 million
- Marketing costs for selling apartments when they are ready = $1.0 million

Total estimated cost of the project = $18 million.

The percentage of completion of this contract at the year-end is

(a) 50% (= 6.0/18.0)
(b) 27% (= 4.5/16.5)
(c) 25% (= 4.5/18.0)
(d) 39% (= 7.0/18)

4. A construction company is in the middle of a two-year construction contract when it receives a letter from the customer extending the contract by a year and requiring the construction company to increase its output in proportion of the number of years of the new contract to the previous contract period. This is allowed in recognizing additional revenue according to IAS 11 if

(a) Negotiations have reached an advanced stage and it is probable that the customer will accept the claim.
(b) The contract is sufficiently advanced and it is probable that the specified performance standards will be exceeded or met.
(c) It is probable that the customer will approve the variation and the amount of revenue arising from the variation, and the amount of revenue can be reliably measured.
(d) It is probable that the customer will approve the variation and the amount of revenue arising from the variation, whether the amount of revenue can be reliably measured or not.

5. A construction company signed a contract to build a theater over a period of two years, and with this contract also signed a maintenance contract for five years. Both the contracts are negotiated as a single package and are closely interrelated to each other. The two contracts should be

(a) Combined and treated as a single contract.
(b) Segmented and considered two separate contracts.
(c) Recognized under the completed-contract method.
(d) Treated differently—the building contract under the completed-contract method and maintenance contract under the percentage-of-completion method.

Chapter 9

INCOME TAXES (IAS 12)

BACKGROUND AND INTRODUCTION

The Standard Applies to the Accounting for Income Taxes

IAS 12 uses a liability method and adopts a statement of financial position approach. Instead of accounting for the timing differences between the accounting and tax consequences of revenue and expenses, it accounts for the temporary differences between the accounting and tax bases of assets and liabilities. The Accounting Standard adopts a full-provision statement of financial position approach to accounting for tax.

It is assumed that the recovery of all assets and the settlement of all liabilities have tax consequences and that these consequences can be estimated reliably and are unavoidable.

The main reason why deferred tax has to be provided for is that International Financial Reporting Standards (IFRS) recognition criteria are different from those that are normally set out in tax law. Thus there will be income and expenditure in financial statements that will not be allowed for taxation purposes in many jurisdictions.

A deferred tax liability or asset is recognized for future tax consequences of past transactions. There are some exemptions to this general rule.

DEFINITIONS OF KEY TERMS

Tax base. Value that the Standard assumes that each asset and liability has for tax purposes.

Temporary differences. Differences between the carrying amount of an asset and liability and its tax base.

The belief is that an entity will settle its liabilities and recover its assets eventually over time and at that point the tax consequences will crystallize. For example, if a machine has a carrying value in the financial statements of $5 million and its tax value is $2 million, then there is a taxable temporary difference of $3 million.

The tax base of a liability is normally its carrying amount less amounts that will be deductible for tax in the future. The tax base of an asset is the amount that will be deductible for tax purposes against future profits generated by the asset.

The Standard sets out two kinds of temporary differences: a *taxable temporary difference* and a *deductible temporary difference*.

A taxable temporary difference results in the payment of tax when the carrying amount of the asset or liability is settled.

In simple terms, this means that a deferred tax liability will arise when the carrying value of the asset is greater than its tax base or when the carrying value of the liability is less than its tax base.

Deductible temporary differences are differences that result in amounts being deductible in determining taxable profit or loss in future periods when the carrying value of the asset or liability is recovered or settled. When the carrying value of the liability is greater than its tax base or when the carrying value of the asset is less than its tax base, a deferred tax asset may arise.

This means, for example, that when an accrued liability is paid in future periods, part or all of that payment may become allowable for tax purposes.

CASE STUDY 1

Facts

An entity has the following assets and liabilities recorded in its statement of financial position at December 31, 20X9:

	Carrying value $ million
Property	10
Plant and equipment	5
Inventory	4
Trade receivables	3
Trade payables	6
Cash	2

The value for tax purposes of property and for plant and equipment are $7 million and $4 million respectively. The entity has made a provision for inventory obsolescence of $2 million, which is not allowable for tax purposes until the inventory is sold. Further, an impairment charge against trade receivables of $1 million has been made. This charge does not relate to any specific trade receivable but to the entity's assessment of the overall collectability of the amount. This charge will not be allowed in the current year for tax purposes but will be allowed in the future. Income tax paid is at 30%.

Required

Calculate the deferred tax provision at December 31, 20X9.

Solution

	Carrying value $m	Tax base $m	Temporary difference $m
Property	10	7	3
Plant and equipment	5	4	1
Inventory	4	6	(2)
Trade receivables	3	4	(1)
Trade payables	6	6	--
Cash	2	2	--
			1

The deferred tax provision will be $1 million × 30%, or $300,000.

Because the provision against inventory and the impairment charge are not currently allowed, the tax base will be higher than the carrying value by the respective amounts.

Every asset or liability is assumed to have a tax base. Normally this tax base will be the amount that is allowed for tax purposes.

Some items of income and expenditure may not be taxable or tax deductible, and they will never enter into the computation of taxable profit. These items sometimes are called permanent differences.

Generally speaking, these items will have the same tax base as their carrying amount; that is, no temporary difference will arise.

For example, if an entity has on its statement of financial position interest receivable of $2 million that is not taxable, then its tax base will be the same as its carrying value, or $2 million. There is no temporary difference in this case. Therefore, no deferred taxation will arise.

CASE STUDY 2

Facts

An entity acquired plant and equipment for $1 million on January 1, 20X9. The asset is depreciated at 25% a year on the straight-line basis, and local tax legislation permits the management to depreciate the asset at 30% a year for tax purposes.

Required

Calculate any deferred tax liability that might arise on the plant and equipment at December 31, 20X9, assuming a tax rate of 30%.

Solution

$15,000 (30% of the temporary difference of $50,000). The carrying value of the plant and equipment is $750,000 and the tax written down value will be $700,000, thus giving a taxable temporary difference of $50,000.

CURRENT TAX LIABILITIES AND ASSETS

The Standard also deals with current tax liabilities and current tax assets.

An entity should recognize a liability in the statement of financial position in respect of its current tax expense both for the current and prior years to the extent that it is not yet paid.

ACCOUNTING FOR DEFERRED TAX

To account for deferred tax under IAS 12, first prepare a statement of financial position that shows all the assets and liabilities in the accounting statement of financial position and their tax base.

Also show any other items that may not have been recognized as assets or liabilities in the accounting statement of financial position but that may have a tax base. Then take the difference between these values and the accounting values, and calculate the deferred tax based on these differences.

Most taxable differences arise because of differences in the timing of the recognition of the transaction for accounting and tax purposes.

Examples

1. Accumulated depreciation that differs from accumulated tax depreciation
2. Employee expenditure recognized when incurred for accounting purposes and when paid for tax purposes
3. Costs of research and development, which may be expensed in one period for accounting purposes but allowed for tax purposes in later periods

Often where assets and liabilities are valued at fair value for accounting purposes, there is no equivalent measurement for tax purposes. For example, property, plant, and equipment may be revalued to fair value, but there may be no adjustment to the tax value for this increase or decrease. Similarly, assets and liabilities can be revalued on a business acquisition, but for tax purposes, again, there may be no adjustment to the value.

Summary of Accounting for Deferred Tax

The process of accounting for deferred tax is shown in the following seven steps:

1. Determine the tax base of the assets and liabilities in the statement of financial position.

2. Compare the carrying amounts in the statement of financial position with the tax base. Any differences will normally affect the deferred taxation calculation.
3. Identify the temporary differences that have not been recognized due to exceptions in IAS 12.
4. Apply the tax rates to the temporary differences.
5. Determine the movement between opening and closing deferred tax balances.
6. Decide whether the offset of deferred tax assets and liabilities between different companies is acceptable in the consolidated financial statements.
7. Recognize the net change in deferred taxation.

CASE STUDY 3

Facts

An entity has revalued its property and has recognized the increase in the revaluation reserve in its financial statements. The carrying value of the property was $8 million and the revalued amount was $10 million. Tax base of the property was $6 million. In this country, the tax rate applicable to profits is 35% and the tax rate applicable to profits made on the sale of property is 30%.

Required

If the revaluation took place at the entity's year-end of December 31, 20X9, calculate the deferred tax liability on the property as of that date.

Solution

$1.2 million. The carrying value after revaluation is $10 million, the tax base is $6 million, and the rate of tax applicable to the sale of property is 30%; therefore, the answer is $10 million minus $6 million multiplied by 30%, or $1.2 million.

CASE STUDY 4

Facts

An entity has spent $600,000 in developing a new product. These costs meet the definition of an intangible asset under IAS 38 and have been recognized in the statement of financial position. Local tax legislation allows these costs to be deducted for tax purposes when they are incurred. Therefore, they have been recognized as an expense for tax purposes. At the year-end the intangible asset is deemed to be impaired by $50,000.

Required

Calculate the tax base of the intangible asset at the accounting year-end.

Solution

Zero, because the tax authority has already allowed the intangible asset costs to be deducted for tax purposes.

CONSOLIDATED FINANCIAL STATEMENTS

Temporary differences can also arise from adjustments on consolidation.

The tax base of an item is often determined by the value in the entity accounts, that is, for example, the subsidiary's accounts.

Deferred tax is determined on the basis of the consolidated financial statements and not the individual entity accounts.

Therefore, the carrying value of an item in the consolidated accounts can be different from the carrying value in the individual entity accounts, thus giving rise to a temporary difference.

An example is the consolidation adjustment that is required to eliminate unrealized profits and losses on intergroup transfer of inventory. Such an adjustment will give rise to a temporary difference, which will reverse when the inventory is sold outside the group.

IAS 12 does not specifically address how intergroup profits and losses should be measured for tax purposes. It says that the expected manner of recovery or settlement of tax should be taken into account.

CASE STUDY 5

Facts

A subsidiary sold goods costing $10 million to its parent for $11 million, and all of these goods are still held in inventory at the year-end. Assume a tax rate of 30%.

Required

Explain the deferred tax implications.

Solution

The unrealized profit of $1 million will have to be eliminated from the consolidated statement of comprehensive income and from the consolidated statement of financial position in group inventory. The sale of the inventory is a taxable event, and it causes a change in the tax base of the inventory. The carrying amount in the consolidated financial statements of the inventory will be $10 million, but the tax base is $11 million. This gives rise to a deferred tax asset of $1 million at the tax rate of 30%, which is $300,000 (assuming that both the parent and subsidiary are resident in the same tax jurisdiction).

CASE STUDY 6

Facts

An entity has acquired a subsidiary on January 1, 20X9. Goodwill of $2 million has arisen on the purchase of this subsidiary. The subsidiary has deductible temporary differences of $1 million and it is probable that future taxable profits are going to be available for the offset of this deductible temporary difference. The tax rate during 20X4 is 30%. The deductible temporary difference has not been taken into account in calculating goodwill.

Required

What is the figure for goodwill that should be recognized in the consolidated statement of financial position of the parent?

Solution

$1.7 million. A deferred tax asset of $1 million × 30%, or $300,000, should be recognized because it is stated that future taxable profits will be available for offset. Thus at the time of acquisition there is an additional deferred tax asset that has not as yet been taken into account. The result of this will be to reduce goodwill from $2 million to $1.7 million.

TEMPORARY DIFFERENCES NOT RECOGNIZED FOR DEFERRED TAX

There are some temporary differences that are not recognized for deferred tax purposes. These arise

1. From goodwill
2. From the initial recognition of certain assets and liabilities
3. From investments when certain conditions apply

The IAS does not allow a deferred tax liability for goodwill on initial recognition or where any reduction in the value of goodwill is not allowed for tax purposes. Because goodwill is the residual amount after recognizing assets and liabilities at fair value, recognizing a deferred tax liability in respect of goodwill would simply increase the value of goodwill; therefore, the recognition of a deferred tax liability in this regard is not allowed. Deferred tax liabilities for goodwill could be recognized to the extent that they do not arise from initial recognition.

CASE STUDY 7

Facts

An entity has acquired a subsidiary, and goodwill arising on the transaction amounts to $20 million. Goodwill is not allowable for tax purposes in the entity's jurisdiction. Tax rate for the entity is 30% and the subsidiary is 60%-owned.

Required

Calculate the deferred tax liability relating to goodwill and explain whether a taxable temporary difference would arise if goodwill was allowable for tax purposes on an amortized basis.

Solution

Zero. A deferred tax liability should not be recognized for any taxable temporary difference, which arises on the initial recognition of goodwill. Where goodwill is deductible for tax purposes on an amortized basis, a taxable temporary difference will arise in future years being the difference between the carrying value in the entity's accounts and the tax base.

The second temporary difference not recognized is on the initial recognition of certain assets and liabilities, which are not fully deductible or liable for tax purposes. For example, if the cost of an asset is not deductible for tax purposes then this has a tax base of nil.

Generally speaking this gives rise to a taxable temporary difference. However, the Standard does not allow an entity to recognize any deferred tax that occurs as a result of this initial recognition. Thus no deferred tax liability or asset is recognized where the carrying value of the item on initial recognition differs from its initial tax base. An example of this is a nontaxable government grant that is related to the acquisition of an asset. Note, however, that if the initial recognition occurs on a business combination, or an accounting or taxable profit or loss arises, then deferred tax should be recognized.

CASE STUDY 8

Facts

An entity purchases plant and equipment for $2 million. In the tax jurisdiction, there are no tax allowances available for the depreciation of this asset; neither are any profits or losses on disposal taken into account for taxation purposes. The entity depreciates the asset at 25% per annum. Taxation is 30%.

Required

Explain the deferred tax position of the plant and equipment on initial recognition and at the first year-end after initial recognition.

Solution

The asset would have a tax base of zero on initial recognition, and this would normally give rise to a deferred tax liability of $2 million @ 30%, or $600,000. This would mean that an immediate tax expense has arisen before the asset was used. IAS 12 prohibits the recognition of this expense. This could be classified as a permanent difference.

At the date of the first accounts, the asset would have been depreciated by, say, 25% of $2 million, or $500,000. As the tax base is zero, this would normally cause a deferred tax liability of $1.5 million at 30%, or $450,000. However, this liability has arisen from the initial recognition of the asset and therefore is not provided for.

A further temporary difference not recognized relates to investments in subsidiaries, associates, and joint ventures. Normally deferred tax assets and liabilities should be recognized on these investments. Such temporary differences often will be as a result of the undistributed profits of such entities. However, where the parent or the investor can control the timing of the reversal of a taxable temporary difference and it is probable that the temporary difference will not reverse in the foreseeable future, then a deferred tax liability should not be recognized. This would be the case where the parent is able to control when and if the retained profits of the subsidiary are to be distributed.

Similarly, a deferred tax asset should not be recognized if the temporary difference is expected to continue into the foreseeable future and there are no taxable profits available against which the temporary difference can be offset.

In the case of a joint venture or an associate, normally a deferred tax liability would be recognized, because normally the investor cannot control the dividend policy. However, if there is an agreement between the parties that the profits will not be distributed, then a deferred tax liability would not be provided for.

DEFERRED TAX ASSETS

Deductible temporary differences give rise to deferred tax assets. Examples of this are tax losses carried forward or temporary differences arising on provisions that are not allowable for taxation until the future.

These deferred tax assets can be recognized if it is probable that the asset will be realized.

Realization of the asset will depend on whether there are sufficient taxable profits available in the future.

Sufficient taxable profits can arise from three different sources:

1. They can arise from existing taxable temporary differences. In principle, these differences should reverse in the same accounting period as the reversal of the deductible temporary difference or in the period in which a tax loss is expected to be used.
2. If there are insufficient taxable temporary differences, the entity may recognize the deferred tax asset where it feels that there will be future taxable profits, other than those arising from taxable temporary differences. These profits should relate to the same taxable authority and entity.
3. The entity may be able to prove that it can create tax planning opportunities whereby the deductible temporary differences can be utilized.

Wherever tax planning opportunities are considered, management must have the capability and ability to implement them.

Similarly, an entity can recognize a deferred tax asset arising from unused tax losses or credits when it is probable that future taxable profits will be available against which these can be offset. However, the existence of current tax losses is probably evidence that future taxable profit will not be available.

The evidence to suggest that future taxable profits are available must be relevant and reliable. For example, the existence of signed sales contracts and a good profit history may provide such evidence. The period for which these tax losses can be carried forward under the tax regulations must be taken into account also.

PRACTICAL INSIGHT

Isotis SA, a Swiss entity, disclosed in its financial statements that it has available tax losses of €92 million. Of that amount, €49 million relates to Dutch companies and €43 million to Swiss companies. The Dutch losses can be carried forward indefinitely, but the Swiss losses are available for only seven years. The entity feels that it is unlikely to utilize all the losses and, therefore, does not recognize a deferred tax asset.

Where an entity has not been able to recognize a deferred tax asset because of insufficient evidence concerning future taxable profit, it should review the situation at each subsequent statement of financial position date to see whether some or all of the unrecognized asset can be recognized.

CASE STUDY 9

Facts

As a consequence of the reorganization, and a change in government legislation, the tax authorities have allowed a revaluation of the noncurrent assets of Josey for tax purposes to market value at December 31, 20X9. There has been no change in the carrying values of the noncurrent assets in the financial statements.

The tax base and the carrying values after the revaluation are as follows:

	Carrying amount at December 31, 20X9 $m	*Tax base at December 31, 20X9 after revaluation $m*	*Tax base at December 31, 20X9 before revaluation $m*
PPE	2.5	3.25	2.4
Vehicles	1.5	1.75	1.4

Other taxable temporary differences amounted to $1.25 million at December 31, 20X9. Assume income tax is paid at 30%. The deferred tax provision at December 31, 20X9, had been calculated using the tax values before revaluation.

Required

Show the impact on the financial statements of the above.

Solution

The differences between IFRS carrying amounts for the noncurrent assets and tax bases will represent temporary differences. The general principle in IAS 12, *Income Taxes*, is that deferred tax liabilities should be recognized for all taxable temporary differences. A deferred tax asset should be recognized for deductible temporary differences, unused tax losses and unused tax credits to the extent that it is probable that taxable profit will be available against which the deductible temporary differences can be utilized.

A deferred tax asset cannot be recognized where it arises from negative goodwill or the initial recognition of an asset/liability other than in a business combination. The carrying amount of deferred tax assets should be reviewed at each statement of financial position date and reduced to the extent that it is no longer probable that sufficient taxable profit will be available to allow the benefit of part or all of that deferred tax asset to be utilized. Any such reduction should be subsequently reversed to the extent that it becomes probable that sufficient taxable profit will be available.

The recognition of deferred tax assets will result in the recognition of income. This amount cannot be reported in equity, as IAS 12 only allows deferred tax to be recognized in equity if the corresponding entry is recognized in equity as well. This is not the case in this situation, as the revaluation was not recognized for IFRS purposes.

	Carrying amount $m	*Tax base $m*	*Temporary difference $m*
Property	2.5	3.25	0.75
Vehicles	1.5	1.75	0.25
Other taxable temporary differences			(1.25)
			0.75

The deferred tax asset would be $0.75 million × 30% (i.e., $0.225 million subject to there being sufficient taxable profit).

The deferred tax provision relating to these assets would have been

Property	2.5	2.4	0.1
Vehicles	1.5	1.4	**0.1**
			0.2
Other taxable temporary differences			**1.25**
			1.45

$1.45 million at 30%(i.e., $0.435 million)

The impact on the statement of comprehensive income would be significant, as the deferred tax provision of $0.435 million would be released and a deferred tax asset of $0.225 million credited to it.

TAX RATES

The tax rates that should be used to calculate deferred tax are the ones that are expected to apply in the period when the asset is realized or the liability settled. The best estimate of this tax rate is the rate that has been enacted or substantially enacted by the end of the reporting period.

The tax rate that should be used should be that which was applicable to the particular tax that has been levied. For example, if tax is going to be levied on a gain on a particular asset, then the rate of tax relating to those types of gain should be used in order to calculate the deferred taxation amount.

DISCOUNTING

Deferred tax assets and liabilities should not be discounted. The reason for this is generally because it is difficult to accurately predict the timing of the reversal of each temporary difference.

CASE STUDY 10

Facts

An entity operates in a jurisdiction where the tax rate is 30% for retained profits and 40% for distributed profits. Management has declared a dividend of $10 million, which is payable after the year-end. A liability has not been recognized in the financial statements at the year-end. The taxable profit before tax of the entity was $100 million.

Required

Calculate the current income tax expense for the entity for the current year.

Solution

$30 million (30% of $100 million). The tax rate that should be applied should be that relating to retained profits.

CURRENT AND DEFERRED TAX RECOGNITION

Current and deferred tax should both be recognized as income or expense and included in the net profit or loss for the period.

However, to the extent that the tax arises from a transaction or event that is recognized outside profit or loss, either in other comprehensive income or directly in equity, then the tax that relates to these items should also be recognized in other comprehensive income or directly in equity. For example, a change in the carrying amount of property due to a revaluation may lead to tax consequences, which will be recognized in other comprehensive income.

Any tax arising from a business combination should be recognized as an identifiable asset or liability at the date of acquisition.

Current tax assets and current tax liabilities should be offset in the statement of financial position only if the enterprise has the legal right and the intention to settle these on a net basis and they are levied by the same taxation authority.

The tax expense relating to profit or loss for the period should be presented on the face of the statement of comprehensive income, and the principal elements of the expense should also be disclosed.

> **PRACTICAL INSIGHT**
>
> Rockwood International A/S, a Danish entity, discloses that in its financial statements within deferred tax assets, a setoff of €63 million has taken place; within deferred tax liabilities, a set-off of €37 million has occurred. There are certain conditions set out in IAS 12 as to the situations where setoffs of deferred tax assets and liabilities can occur.

DIVIDENDS

There are certain tax consequences of dividends. In some countries, income taxes are payable at different rates if part of the net profit is paid out as dividend.

IAS 12 requires disclosure of the potential tax consequences of the payment of dividends.

The Effect of Share-Based Payment Transactions

In some jurisdictions, tax relief is given on share-based payment transactions. A deductible temporary difference may arise between the carrying amount, which will be zero and its tax base which will be the tax relief in future periods. A deferred tax asset may therefore be recognized.

CASE STUDY 11

Facts

A parent has recognized in its own financial statements a dividend receivable of $500,000 from an 80%-owned subsidiary. The dividend is not taxable in the country in which the entity operates.

Required

Calculate the temporary difference arising from the recognition of the dividend receivable in the accounts of the parent.

Solution

Zero. There is no temporary difference arising in respect of the dividend, as the carrying amount of $500,000 is the same as the tax base.

DISCLOSURE: KEY ELEMENTS

For disclosure, requirements to the Standard are quite extensive. For example:

1. IAS 12 requires an explanation of the relationship between tax expense and accounting profit.
2. The basis on which the tax rate has been computed should be disclosed, as well as an explanation of any changes in the applicable tax rate.
3. The aggregate current and deferred tax that relates to items that are recognized directly in equity and **the amount of income tax relating to each component of other comprehensive income** should be disclosed.
4. The aggregate amount of temporary differences associated with companies for which no deferred tax liabilities have been recognized should be disclosed.
5. The net deferred tax balances of the current and the previous period should be analyzed by types of temporary difference and types of unused tax loss and unused tax credits.

IAS 12 sets out many other disclosure requirements.

REVISION OF IAS 12

The IASB is to attempt to resolve problems in practice under IAS 12, *Income Tax*, without changing the fundamental approach and ostensibly without increasing divergence from US GAAP.

The IFRIC and IASB staffs have dealt with many issues on IAS 12, which seems to indicate that it is a standard that is difficult to apply. Income tax is also frequently identified as a source of significant reconciling items for US-listed foreign registrants applying IFRS.

The project originally started as a convergence project with US GAAP. The Exposure Draft of an IFRS to replace IAS 12 was issued in March 2009. However, the IASB has decided to consider a fundamental review of the accounting for income tax and has changed the project objective in order to resolve problems in practice under IAS 12.

In March 2010, the Board decided that the scope of the project should be to consider the following practice issues:

1. Uncertain tax positions, but only after the revision of IAS 37 is finalized
2. Deferred tax on property remeasurement at fair value

The Board also decided to introduce the following proposals that were generally supported by respondents to the Exposure Draft issued in March 2009:

1. The introduction of an initial step to consider whether the recovery of an asset or settlement of a liability will affect taxable profit
2. The recognition of a deferred tax asset in full and an offsetting valuation allowance to the extent necessary
3. Guidance on assessing the need for a valuation allowance
4. Guidance on substantive enactment
5. The allocation of current and deferred taxes within a group that files a consolidated tax return

The Board also indicated that it would explore the possibility of resolving the issue of the tax effect of dividends by certain entities such as real estate investment trusts and cooperative societies.

In September 2010, the IASB published an Exposure Draft, *Deferred Tax: Recovery of Underlying Assets.* This proposes an exception to the normal rule in IAS 12 that measurement of deferred tax in respect of an asset depends on the asset's expected manner of recovery. The proposal introduces a rebuttable presumption that certain assets measured at fair value are recovered entirely by sale. The rebuttable presumption applies to the deferred tax liabilities or assets that arise from investment properties, property, plant, and equipment or intangible assets that are measured on an ongoing basis using the fair value model or revaluation model. The presumption could be rebutted only when there is clear evidence that the underlying asset's economic benefits will be consumed by the entity throughout the asset's economic life.

CASE STUDY 12

Facts

Statement of Financial Position at January 1, 20X9

	Local GAAP $m
Property, plant, and equipment	7,000
Goodwill	3,000
Intangible assets	2,000
Financial assets	6,000
Total noncurrent assets	18,000
Trade and other receivables	7,000
Other receivables	1,600
Cash and cash equivalents	700
Total current assets	9,300
Total assets	27,300
Issued capital	6,000
Revaluation reserve	1,500
Retained earnings	6,130
Total equity	13,630

Interest-bearing loans	8,000
Trade and other payables	4,000
Employee benefits	1,000
Current tax liability	70
Deferred tax liability	600
Total liabilities	13,670
Total equity and liabilities	27,300

1. Tax bases of the above assets and liabilities are the same as their carrying amounts except for

	Tax base $m
Property, plant, and equipment	1,400
Trade receivables	7,500
Interest-bearing loans	8,500
Financial assets	7,000

- The intangible assets are development costs that are allowed for tax purposes when the cost is incurred. The costs were incurred in 20X7.
- Included in trade and other payables is an accrual for compensation to be paid to employees. It is allowed for taxation when the payment is made and totals $200 million.

2. During 20X8, a building was revalued. At January 1, 20X9, there was $1500 million remaining in the revaluation reserve in respect of this building.
3. The following adjustments to the financial statements will have to be made to comply with IFRS 1, *First-Time Adoption of IFRS,* on January 1, 20X9:

- Intangible assets of $400 million do not qualify for recognition under IFRS 1.
- The financial assets are all classified as at fair value through profit or loss and their fair value is $6,500 million, which is to be included in the IFRS accounts.
- A pension liability of $50 million is to be recognized under IFRS 1 that was not recognized under local generally accepted accounting principles (GAAP). The tax base of the liability is zero.

4. The entity is likely to be very profitable in the future.

Required

Calculate the deferred tax provision at January 1, 20X9, showing the amount of the adjustment required to the deferred tax provision and any amounts to be charged to revaluation reserve. (Assume a tax rate of 30%.)

Solution

	Local GAAP $m	Adjustment $m	Tax base $m	Temporary differences $m
Property, plant, and equipment	7,000		1,400	5,600
Goodwill	3,000		NR	--
Intangible assets	2,000	(400)	--	1,600
Financial assets	6,000	500	7,000	(500)
Total noncurrent assets	18,000	100	8,400	
Trade and other receivables	7,000		7,500	(500)
Other receivables	1,600		1,600	--
Cash and cash equivalents	700		700	--
Total current assets	9,300		9,800	--
Total assets	27,300	100	18,200	6,200
Interest-bearing loans	8,000		8,500	500
Trade and other payables	4,000		3,800	(200)
Employee benefits	1,000	50	1,000	(50)
Current tax liability	70		70	--
Deferred tax liability	600		600	--
Total liabilities	13,670	50	13,970	250
	6,000			

Issued capital			--
Revaluation reserve	1,500	(50)	
Retained earnings	6,130	(400)	
		500	
Total equity	13,630	50	6,450

CASE STUDY 13

Facts

East is a private entity, and it has recently acquired two 100% owned subsidiaries, West and North. West and North are themselves private entities. East has a business plan whereby in a few years it is going to acquire a stock exchange listing for its shares and capital. East acquired West on July 1, 20X9. When East acquired West, it had unused tax losses. On July 1, 20X9, it seemed that West would have sufficient taxable profit in the future to realize the deferred tax asset created by these losses. However, subsequent events have shown that the future taxable profit will not be sufficient to realize all of the unused tax losses.

West has made a general impairment charge of $4 million against its total accounts receivable. West gets tax relief on impairment of specific accounts receivable. Because of the current economic situation, West feels that impairment charges will increase in the future.

West has investments that are valued at fair value in the statement of financial position and any gain or loss is taken to the statement of comprehensive income. The gains and losses become taxable when the investments are sold.

East acquired North on July 1, 20X9, for $10 million, when the fair value of the net assets was $8 million. The tax base of the net assets acquired was $7 million. Any impairment loss on goodwill is not allowed as a deduction in determining taxable profit.

During the current year, North has sold goods to East of $10 million. North has made a profit of 20% on the selling price on the transaction. East has $5 million worth of these goods recorded in its statement of financial position at the current year-end.

The directors of East have decided that during the period up to the date they intend to list the shares of the entity, they will realize the earnings of the subsidiary, North, through dividend payments. Tax is payable on any remittance of dividends to the holding entity. In the current year no dividends have been declared or paid.

Taxation is payable for listed entities at 40% and for private entities at 35% in the jurisdiction.

Required

Prepare a memorandum that sets out the deferred tax implications of the above information for the East Group.

Solution

The creation of a group through the purchase of subsidiaries during the period has a major impact on the deferred taxation charge. Deferred taxation is looked at from the point of view of the group as a whole. Individual companies may not have sufficient future taxable profits to offset any unused tax losses, but in the group situation, a deferred tax asset may be recognized if there are sufficient taxable profits within the group.

Differences arise between the fair values of the net assets being recognized and their tax bases. In the case of the acquisition of North, deferred taxation will be calculated on the basis of the difference between the fair value of the net assets of $8 million and the tax base of $7 million, giving taxable temporary differences of $1 million.

No provision is required for deferred taxation regarding the temporary difference arising on the recognition of non-tax-deductible goodwill of $2 million, but goodwill will increase by the deferred tax arising on the acquisition of North.

East is hoping to achieve a stock exchange listing of its shares in the near future. This may affect the tax rate used to calculate deferred tax. The current tax rate for private companies is 35%; for public companies, it is 40%. Therefore, a decision will have to be made as to whether the temporary differences are going to reverse at the higher tax rate; if so, deferred tax will be provided for at this rate.

In the case of West, the entity has investments that are stated at fair value in the statement of financial position. The gains and losses are taxed when the investments are sold; therefore, a temporary difference will arise, as the tax treatment is different from the accounting treatment. The tax base is not adjusted for any surplus on the investments. Therefore, the difference between the carrying amount of the investments and the tax base will give rise to a deferred tax liability. The resultant deferred tax expense will be charged against the statement of comprehensive income, not equity, as the surplus on the investments has already gone to the statement of comprehensive income.

In the case of the impairment of trade receivables, because the tax relief is available only on the specific impairment of an account, a deductible temporary difference arises that represents the difference between the carrying amount of the trade receivables and their tax base, which in this case will be zero. It appears that the impairment loss is likely to increase in the future. Therefore, it is unlikely that the temporary difference will actually reverse soon. It does not affect the fact that a provision for deferred tax ought to be made. A deferred tax asset will arise at the value of the difference between the tax base and carrying value of the trade receivables at the tax rate applicable for the East Group of companies. This is subject to the general rule in IAS 12 that there will be sufficient taxable profits available in the future against which this deductible temporary difference can be offset.

East has unused tax losses brought forward. These can create a deferred taxed asset. However, deferred tax assets should be recognized only to the extent that they can be recovered in the future. Thus the deferred tax assets must be capable of being realized. If a deferred tax asset can be realized, then it can be recognized for that amount. Generally speaking, the future realization of the deferred tax asset is dependent on the existence of sufficient taxable profit of the appropriate type being available in the future. The appropriate type would normally be taxable operating profit or taxable gain. In general, suitable taxable profits will be created only in the same taxable entity and will be assessed by the same taxation authority as the income. It is possible that tax planning opportunities may be available to the group in order that these unrelieved tax losses may be utilized. Tax planning opportunities should be considered only in determining the extent to which a deferred tax asset will be realized. They should never be used to reduce a deferred tax liability. Any asset recognized as a result of implementing a tax planning strategy should be reduced by the costs of implementing it. In this case, any deferred tax asset arising should be recognized together with the corresponding adjustment to goodwill.

Intergroup profits are eliminated on consolidation. Therefore, $1 million should be taken from the value of inventory in the group statement of financial position at year-end. However, because an equivalent adjustment has not been made for tax purposes, a temporary difference will arise between the carrying amount of the inventory in the group accounts and its value in East's statement of financial position. The tax base of the inventory will be $5 million and the carrying value will be $4 million, giving rise to a temporary difference of $1 million.

Temporary differences can arise between the carrying amount of the parent's investment in a subsidiary and its tax base. Often this difference is caused by the undistributed earnings in the subsidiary. This temporary difference can be different from the one that arises in the separate financial statements of the parent, where the parent carries its investment at cost less impairment or at a revalued amount. IAS 12 requires recognition of all taxable temporary differences associated with the parent's investments in its subsidiaries, except when the parent can actually control the timing of the reversal of the temporary difference and it is probable that the temporary difference will not reverse in the near future. The provision is required if the parent entity cannot control the timing of the remittance of undistributed profits or it is probable a remittance will take place in the near future.

The parent, East, appears to be recovering the carrying value of its investment in North through the payment of dividends. The method of recovering the value of the investment in the subsidiary is obviously under control of the parent entity. Because the payment of dividends is under the control of East, IAS 12 would not require the recognition of a deferred tax liability in respect of the undistributed profits of North.

CASE STUDY 14

Facts

In accordance with national regulation, Frontier applied IFRS recognition and measurement principles in its interim consolidated financial statements for the first six months of 20X9 and local GAAP for presentation and disclosure. Frontier develops and sells software.

Since 20X4, Frontier has incurred substantial annual losses except for 20X7 and 20X8, when it made a small profit before tax. In those two years, most of the profit consisted of income recognized on revaluation of a deferred tax asset. Frontier announced early in 20X9 that it anticipated substantial growth and profit. Later in the year, Frontier announced that the expected profit would not be achieved and that, instead, a substantial loss would be incurred. Frontier had a history of reporting significant negative variances from its anticipated results.

Frontier's recognized deferred tax assets have been increasing year on year.

Frontier's deferred tax assets consist primarily of unused tax losses that can be carried forward but against which there are virtually no taxable temporary differences to offset.

Required

Discuss whether Frontier should be recognizing deferred tax assets.

Solution

The recognition of deferred tax assets on losses carried forward is not in accordance with IAS 12. Frontier is not able to provide convincing evidence to ensure that it would be able to generate sufficient taxable profits against which the unused tax losses could be offset. Frontier does not have sufficient taxable temporary differences against which the unused tax losses can be offset. Frontier's activities have generated either significant losses or very minimal profits; they have never produced significant pretax profits. The decision is based mainly on the following:

1. History of Frontier's pretax profits
2. Previously published budget expectations and realized results in the past
3. Frontier's expectations for the next few years

Historically, substantial negative variances arose between budgeted and realized results. Also, in 20X9, Frontier had announced that it would not achieve the expected profit, but rather would record a substantial loss. The losses are not of a type that could clearly be attributed to external events that might not be expected to recur.

SICs

SIC 21, *Income Taxes—Recovery of Revalued Nondepreciable Assets,* deals with the situation where a nondepreciable asset (land) is carried at revaluation. The carrying amount of such an asset is considered not to be recovered through usage. Therefore, SIC 21 says that the deferred tax liability or asset arising from revaluation is measured based on the tax consequences of the sale of the asset rather than through use. This may result in the use of the tax rate, which relates to capital profits rather than the rate applicable to earnings.

SIC 25, *Income Taxes—Changes in the Tax Status of an Entity or Its Shareholders,* states that a change in tax status does not give rise to increases or decreases in the pretax amounts recognized directly in equity. Therefore, SIC 25 concludes that the current and deferred tax consequences of the change in tax status should be included in net profit or loss for the period. If a transaction or event does result in a direct credit or charge to equity, for example on the revaluation of PPE under IAS 16, the tax consequence would still be recognized in equity.

EXTRACTS FROM PUBLISHED FINANCIAL STATEMENTS

J. SAINSBURY PLC Financial Statements to March 21, 2009

Deferred taxation

The movements in deferred income tax assets and liabilities during the financial year, prior to the offsetting of the balances within the same tax jurisdiction, are shown below.

Group	Accelerated tax depreciation £m	Fair value gains £m	Other property £m	Other £m	Total £m
Deferred income tax liabilities					
At March 23, 2008	(165)	(30)	(68)	(39)	(302)
Credit/(charge) to statement of comprehensive income	27	--	(25)	12	14
Credit to equity	--	4	--	--	4
At March 21, 2009	**(138)**	**(26)**	**(93)**	**(27)**	**(284)**
At March 25, 2007	(200)	(29)	(72)	(39)	(340)
Credit/(charge) to statement of comprehensive income	28	--	(2)	(2)	24
Charge to equity	--	(3)	--	--	(3)
Rate change adjustment to statement of comprehensive income	7	--	6	2	15
Rate change adjustment to equity	--	2	--	--	2
At March 22, 2008	(165)	(30)	(68)	(39)	(302)

	Provisions £m	Retirement benefit obligations £m	Share-based payment £m	Capital losses1 £m	Tax losses £m	Total £m
Deferred income tax assets						
At March 23, 2008	11	(129)	31	68	--	(19)
(Charge)/credit to statement of comprehensive income	(8)	(37)	(4)	4	--	(45)
Credit to equity	--	253	--	--	--	253
At March 21, 2009	**3**	**87**	**27**	**72**	**--**	**189**
At March 25, 2007	14	48	30	72	8	172
(Charge)/credit to statement of comprehensive income	(3)	(26)	9	2	--	(18)
Charge to equity	--	(161)	(19)	--	(8)	(188)
Prior year adjustment to equity	--	--	13	--	--	13
Rate change adjustment to statement of comprehensive income	--	--	(1)	(6)	--	(7)
Rate change adjustment to equity	--	10	(1)	--	--	9
At March 22, 2008	11	(129)	31	68	--	(19)

Net deferred income tax liability
At March 21, 2009   **(95)**
At March 22, 2008   (321)

[1] *In prior years, the deferred tax liability in relation to other property was offset by the deferred tax asset on capital losses. This year the balances have been disclosed separately, with the prior year values reclassified for comparative purposes.*

Company	Other property1 £m	Total £m
Deferred income tax liabilities		
At March 23, 2008	(65)	(65)
Charge to statement of comprehensive income	--	--
At March 21, 2009	**(65)**	**(65)**
At March 25, 2007	(70)	(70)
Charge to statement of comprehensive income	--	--
Rate change adjustment to statement of comprehensive income	5	5
At March 22, 2008	(65)	(65)

[1] *In prior years, the deferred tax liability in relation to other property was offset by the deferred tax asset on capital losses. This year the balances have been disclosed separately, with the prior year values.*

STANDARD CHARTERED PLC—Annual Report, 2009

Taxation

Deferred tax is provided in full, using the liability method, on temporary differences arising between the tax bases of assets and liabilities and their carrying amounts in the consolidated financial statements. Deferred income tax is determined using tax rates (and laws) that have been enacted or substantially enacted as at the statement of financial position date, and that are expected to apply when the related deferred income tax asset is realized or the deferred income tax liability is settled.

Deferred tax assets are recognized where it is probable that future taxable profit will be available against which the temporary differences can be utilized.

Income tax payable on profits is based on the applicable tax law in each jurisdiction and is recognized as an expense in the period in which profits arise. The tax effects of income tax losses available for carry-forward are recognized as an asset when it is probable that future taxable profits will be available against which these losses can be utilized.

Current and deferred tax relating to items which are charged or credited directly to equity, is credited or charged directly to equity and is subsequently recognized in the statement of comprehensive income together with the current or deferred gain or loss.

Source: Standard Chartered PLC annual report 2009. © Standard Chartered PLC

MULTIPLE-CHOICE QUESTIONS

1. A subsidiary has sold goods costing $1.2 million to its parent for $1.4 million. All of the inventory is held by the parent at year-end. The subsidiary is 80% owned, and the parent and subsidiary operate in different tax jurisdictions. The parent pays taxation at 30%, and the subsidiary pays taxation at 30%. Calculate any deferred tax asset that arises on the sale of the inventory from the subsidiary entity to the parent.

    (a) $ 60,000
    (b) $ 200,000
    (c) $ 48,000
    (d) $ 80,000

2. An entity issued a convertible bond on January 1, 20X4 that matures in five years. The bond can be converted into ordinary shares at any time. The entity has calculated that the liability and equity components of the bond are $3 million for the liability component and $1 million for the equity component, giving a total amount of the bond of $4 million. The interest rate on the bond is 6%, and local tax legislation allows a tax deduction for the interest paid in cash. Calculate the deferred tax liability arising on the bond at the year ending December 31, 20X4. The local tax rate is 30%.

    (a) $1.2 million.
    (b) $900,000
    (c) $300,000
    (d) $4 million.

3. An entity is undertaking a reorganization. Under the plan, part of the entity's business will be demerged and will be transferred to a separate entity, Entity Z. This also will involve a transfer of part of the pension obligation to Entity Z. Because of this, Entity Z will have a deductible temporary difference at its year-end of December 31, 20X4. It is anticipated that Entity Z will be loss-making for the first four years of its existence, but thereafter it will become a profitable entity. The future forecasted profit is based on estimates of sales to intergroup companies. Should Entity Z recognize the deductible temporary difference as a deferred tax asset?

    (a) The entity should recognize a deferred tax asset.
    (b) Management should not recognize a deferred tax asset, as future profitability is not certain.
    (c) The entity should recognize a deferred tax asset if the authenticity of the budgeted profits can be verified.
    (d) The entity should recognize a deferred tax asset if the intergroup profit in the budgeted profit is eliminated.

4. An entity has revalued its property and has recognized the increase in the revaluation reserve in its financial statements. The carrying value of the property was $8 million, and the revalued amount was $10 million. Tax base of the property was $6 million. In the country, the tax rate applicable to profits is 35% and the tax rate applicable to profits made on the sale of property is 30%. Where will the tax liability be recognized and at what amount?

    (a) In the statement of comprehensive income at $600,000.
    (b) In equity at $1.2 million.
    (c) In the statement of recognized income and expense at $1.4 million.
    (d) In retained earnings at $700,000.

5. The current liabilities of an entity include fines and penalties for environmental damage. The fines and penalties are stated at $10 million. The fines and penalties are not deductible for tax purposes. What is the tax base of the fines and penalties?

    (a) $10 million.
    (b) $3 million.
    (c) $13 million.
    (d) Zero.

6. An entity acquired plant and equipment for $2 million on January 1, 20X9. The asset is depreciated at 25% a year on the straight-line basis, and local tax legislation permits the management to depreciate the asset at 30% a year for tax purposes. Calculate any deferred tax liability which might arise on the plant and equipment at December 31, 20X9, assuming a tax rate of 30%.

    (a) $ 500,000
    (b) $ 600,000
    (c) $ 30,000
    (d) $ 25,000

7. An entity has spent $10 million in developing a new product. These costs meet the definition of an intangible asset under IAS 38 and have been recognized in the statement of financial position. Local tax legislation allows these costs to be deducted for tax purposes when they are incurred and, therefore, they have been recognized as an expense for tax purposes. At the year-end the intangible asset is deemed to be impaired by $3 million. What is the tax base of the intangible asset at the accounting year-end?

    (a) $10 million.
    (b) $3 million.
    (c) $7 million.
    (d) Zero

8. Which of the following examples would not give rise to a temporary difference?

    (a) Revenue from installment sales recognized under the installment method for taxation.
    (b) Recognition of goodwill in a business combination.

(c) Depreciation used for accounting purposes whilst an accelerated method is used for tax purposes.

(d) Warranty costs recognized for accounting purposes but not recognized for tax purposes until paid.

9. Entity X is involved in a business acquisition on January 1, 20X9. At the date of acquisition the deferred tax assets were $300,000. On January 1, 20X9, the directors considered that realization of the deferred tax assets were not probable. What effect would this decision have on the allocation of the purchase price?

(a) The unrecognized deferred tax would be allocated to goodwill, which would increase by $300,000.

(b) The value of goodwill would decrease by $300,000.

(c) There would be no effect on goodwill.

(d) Negative goodwill of $300,000 would arise.

10. An entity has calculated its deferred tax provision as $7 million. It feels that if discounting is taken into account, the provision would only need to be $5 million. The provision does not take into account a dividend receivable, which has been recognized in its own financial statements for $1.5 million from an 80%-owned subsidiary. The dividend is not taxable in the country in which the entity operates. The tax rate is 30%. What is the deferred tax provision in the financial statements of the entity?

(a) $5 million.

(b) $7 million.

(c) $5.45 million.

(d) $7.45 million.

11. An entity has the following assets and liabilities recorded in its statement of financial position at December 31, 20X9: property, plant, and equipment has a carrying value of $15 million; inventory has a carrying value of $7 million; trade receivables has a carrying value of $6.5 million; trade payables has a carrying value of $4 million; and cash has a carrying value of $2.5 million. The value for tax purposes of property, plant, and equipment is $12 million. The entity has made a provision for inventory obsolescence of $1.5 million, which is not allowable for tax purposes until the inventory is sold. A general impairment charge against trade receivables of $1 million has been made. This charge will not be allowed in the current year for tax purposes but will be in the future. The tax bases of current liabilities and cash are the same as their carrying amounts. Income tax paid is at 30%. Calculate the deferred tax provision at December 31, 20X9.

(a) $1.8 million.

(b) $1.65 million.

(c) $1.05 million.

(d) $150,000

12. An entity has acquired a subsidiary on July 1, 20X9. Goodwill of $24 million has arisen on the purchase of this subsidiary. This subsidiary has deductible temporary differences of $10 million and it is probable that future taxable profits are going to be available for the offset of this deductible temporary difference. The tax rate during 20X9 is 30%. The deductible temporary difference has not been taken into account in calculating goodwill. What is the figure for goodwill that should be recognized in the consolidated statement of financial position of the holding company?

(a) $21 million.

(b) $14 million.

(c) $10 million.

(d) $24 million.

Chapter 10

PROPERTY, PLANT, AND EQUIPMENT (IAS 16)

BACKGROUND AND INTRODUCTION

This Standard prescribes rules regarding the recognition, measurement, and disclosures relating to property, plant, and equipment (often referred to as fixed assets) that would enable users of financial statements to understand the extent of an entity's investment in such assets and the movements therein.

The principal issues involved relate to the recognition of items of property, plant, and equipment, determining their costs, and assessing the depreciation and impairment losses that need to be recognized.

SCOPE

The requirements of IAS 16 are applied to accounting for all property, plant, and equipment unless another Standard permits otherwise, *except* for

- Property, plant, and equipment classified as held for sale in accordance with IFRS 5
- Biological assets relating to agricultural activity under IAS 41
- Mineral rights, mineral reserves, and similar nonregenerative resources

DEFINITIONS OF KEY TERMS
(in accordance with IAS 16)

Property, plant, and equipment. Tangible assets that are held for use in production or supply of goods and services, for rental to others, or for administrative purposes *and* are expected to be used during more than one period.

Cost. The amount paid or fair value of other consideration given to acquire or construct an asset.

Useful life. The period over which an asset is expected to be utilized or the number of production units expected to be obtained from the use of the asset.

Residual value (of an asset). The estimated amount, less estimated disposal costs that could be currently realized from the asset's disposal if the asset were already of an age and condition expected at the end of its useful life.

Depreciable amount. The cost of an asset less its residual value.

Depreciation. The systematic allocation of the depreciable amount of an asset over its expected useful life.

Fair value. The amount for which an asset could be exchanged between knowledgeable willing parties in an arm's-length transaction.

RECOGNITION OF AN ASSET

Criteria for Recognition

An item of property, plant, and equipment should be recognized as an asset *if and only if* it is probable that future economic benefits associated with the asset will flow to the entity *and* the cost of the item can be measured reliably.

Any expenditure incurred that meets these recognition criteria must be accounted for as an asset. The Standard makes reference to individually insignificant items that can be aggregated. However, very often, in practice, entities adopt an accounting policy to expense items that are below a predetermined *de minimis* level in order to avoid undue cost in maintaining the relevant records, which includes tracking the whereabouts of the asset. The definition and recognition criteria can also be applied to spare parts, although these are often carried as inventory and expensed as and when utilized. However, major spare parts are usually recognized as property, plant, and equipment.

For many years the issue of replacement of part of an asset ("subsequent costs"), often involving significant expenditure, was a difficult matter to address; merely adding the cost of the replacement part to the cost of the original asset posed certain logical flaws vis-à-vis the preexisting and the replaced, part. This was particularly the case when the replaced part was not separately identified in the overall cost of the original asset. This problem also existed for major inspection costs, such as those for ships and aircraft, which were usually required to retain sea- or airworthiness. The matter was further exacerbated by an additional recognition criterion that subsequent costs should add to the utility or useful life of the asset; in some circumstances, this criterion resulted in day-to-day repairs being capitalized. This issue was partly addressed by an interpretation of the Standing Interpretations Committee (SIC) that permitted adding major overhaul or inspection costs to the original asset if an amount representing the major overhaul or inspection component of the original cost of the asset was separately identified on initial recognition and was separately depreciated, and thereby could be written out of the asset records.

The current Standard applies the two basic recognition criteria referred to previously, to *all* expenditures (and dispenses with the increased utility or increased useful life criteria). If the two basic criteria are satisfied, then the cost should be recognized as an asset. If the cost of the replaced asset was not separately identifiable, then the cost of the replacement can be used as an indication of the cost of the replaced item, which should be removed from the asset record.

CASE STUDY 1

This case study is concerned with subsequent costs.

Facts

Road Truckers Inc. has acquired a heavy road transporter at a cost of $100,000 (with no breakdown of the component parts). The estimated useful life is ten years. At the end of the sixth year, the power train requires replacement, as further maintenance is uneconomical due to the off-road time required. The remainder of the vehicle is perfectly roadworthy and is expected to last for the next four years. The cost of a new power train is $45,000.

Required

Can the cost of the new power train be recognized as an asset, and, if so, what treatment should be used?

Solution

The new power train will produce economic benefits to Road Truckers Inc., and the cost is measurable. Hence the item should be recognized as an asset. The original invoice for the transporter did not specify the cost of the power train; however, the cost of the replacement—$45,000—can be used as an indication (usually by discounting) of the likely cost, six years previously. If an appropriate discount rate is 5% per annum, $45,000 discounted back six years amounts to $33,500 [$45,000/(1.05)]^6, which would be written out of the asset records. The cost of the new power train, $45,000, would be added to the asset record, resulting in a new asset cost of $111,500 ($100,000 − $33,500 + $45,000).

Measurement at Recognition

An item of property, plant, and equipment that satisfies the recognition criteria should be recognized initially at its cost. The Standard specifies that cost comprises

- Purchase price, including import duties, nonrefundable purchase taxes, less trade discounts and rebates
- Costs directly attributable to bringing the asset to the location and condition necessary for it to be used in a manner intended by the entity
- Initial estimates of dismantling, removing, and site restoration if the entity has an obligation that it incurs on acquisition of the asset or as a result of using the asset other than to produce inventories

Examples of directly attributable costs include

- Employee benefits of those involved in the construction or acquisition of an asset
- Cost of site preparation
- Initial delivery and handling costs
- Installation and assembly costs
- Costs of testing, less the net proceeds from the sale of any product arising from test production
- Borrowing costs to the extent permitted by IAS 23, *Borrowing Costs*
- Professional fees

Examples of costs that are *not* directly attributable costs and therefore must be expensed in the income statement include

- Costs of opening a new facility (often referred to as preoperative expenses)
- Costs of introducing a new product or service
- Advertising and promotional costs
- Costs of conducting business in a new location or with a new class of customer
- Training costs
- Administration and other general overheads
- Costs incurred while an asset, capable of being used as intended, is yet to be brought into use, is left idle, or is operating at below full capacity
- Initial operating losses
- Costs of relocating or reorganizing part or all of an entity's operations

CASE STUDY 2

This case study is concerned with directly attributable costs.

Facts

Extravagant Inc. is installing a new plant at its production facility. It has incurred these costs:

1.	Cost of the plant (cost per supplier's invoice plus taxes)	$2,500,000
2.	Initial delivery and handling costs	$200,000
3.	Cost of site preparation	$600,000
4.	Consultants used for advice on the acquisition of the plant	$700,000
5.	Interest charges paid to supplier of plant for deferred credit	$200,000

| 6. | Estimated dismantling costs to be incurred after 7 years | $300,000 |
| 7. | Operating losses before commercial production | $400,000 |

Required

Please advise Extravagant Inc. on the costs that can be capitalized in accordance with IAS 16.

Solution

According to IAS 16, these costs can be capitalized:

1.	Cost of the plant	$2,500,000
2.	Initial delivery and handling costs	200,000
3.	Cost of site preparation	600,000
4.	Consultants' fees	700,000
5.	Estimated dismantling costs to be incurred after 7 years	300,000
		$4,300,000

Interest charges paid on "deferred credit terms" (see discussion under the "Measurement of Cost" section) to the supplier of the plant (*not* a qualifying asset) of $200,000 and operating losses before commercial production amounting to $400,000 are not regarded as directly attributable costs and thus cannot be capitalized. They should be written off to the income statement in the period they are incurred.

Measurement of Cost

The cost of an asset is measured at the cash price equivalent at the date of acquisition. If payment is "deferred" beyond normal credit terms, then the difference between the cash price and the total price is recognized as a finance cost and treated accordingly.

If an asset is acquired in exchange for another asset, then the acquired asset is measured at its fair value unless the exchange lacks commercial substance or the fair value cannot be reliably measured, in which case the acquired asset should be measured at the carrying amount of the asset given up, where carrying amount is equal to cost less accumulated depreciation and impairment losses. For impairment losses, reference should be made to IAS 36. In this context, any compensation received for impairment or loss of an asset shall be included in the income statement.

Measurement After Recognition

After initial recognition of an item of property, plant, and equipment, the asset should be measured using either the cost model or the revaluation model. Once selected, the policy shall apply to an entire class of property, plant, and equipment. This means that an entity cannot "cherry-pick" those assets to measure at cost or at revaluation, which would result in like assets having different measurement bases.

The cost model requires an asset, after initial recognition, to be carried at cost less accumulated depreciation and impairment losses.

The revaluation model requires an asset, after initial recognition, to be measured at a revalued amount, which is its fair value less subsequent depreciation and impairment losses. In this case, fair value must be reliably measurable. Revaluations must be made with sufficient regularity to ensure that the carrying amount is not materially different from fair value. However, if an asset is revalued, then the entire class of asset must be revalued, again to avoid "cherry-picking" and a mixture of valuation bases.

When an asset is revalued, any increase in carrying amount should be recognized in other comprehensive income and accumulated in equity under the heading of revaluation surplus. Any reduction in value arising from a revaluation should first be recognized in other comprehensive income to the extent of any credit balance existing in the revaluation surplus *relating to the same asset*.

The revaluation reserve may be released to retained earnings in one of two ways:

1. When the asset is disposed of or otherwise derecognized, the surplus can be transferred to retained earnings.
2. The difference between the depreciation charged on the revalued amount and that based on cost can be transferred from the revaluation reserve to retained earnings. Under no circumstances can the revaluation surplus be credited back to the profit or loss.

Example of Treatment of Revaluation

Value Assets Inc. has an item of plant with an initial cost of $100,000. At the date of revaluation, accumulated depreciation amounted to $55,000. The fair value of the asset, by reference to transactions in similar assets, is assessed to be $65,000. The entries to be passed would be

Accumulated depreciation	55,000	
Asset cost		55,000
Being elimination of accumulated depreciation against the cost of the asset		
Asset cost	20,000	
Other comprehensive income		20,000
Being uplift of net asset value to fair value		

The net result is that the asset has a carrying amount of $65,000: $100,000 – $55,000 + $20,000.

DEPRECIATION

Each part of an item of property, plant, and equipment with a cost that is significant in relation to the whole shall be depreciated separately, and such depreciation charge shall be charged to the income statement unless it is included in the cost of producing another asset.

Depreciation shall be applied to the depreciable amount of an asset on a systematic basis over its expected useful life. Expected *useful* life is the period used, *not* the asset's *economic* life, which could be appreciably longer.

The depreciable amount takes account of the expected residual value of the assets. Both the useful life and the residual value shall be reviewed annually and the estimates revised as necessary in accordance with IAS 8.

Depreciation still needs to be charged even if the fair value of an asset exceeds its residual value. The rationale for this is the definition of residual value, detailed previously. Residual value is the estimated amount, less estimated disposal costs, that could be currently realized from the asset's disposal if the asset were *already of an age and condition expected at the end of its useful life*. This definition precludes the effect of inflation and, in all likelihood, will be less than fair value.

Depreciation commences when an asset is in the location and condition that enables it to be used in the manner intended by management. Depreciation shall cease at the earlier of its derecognition (sale or scrapping) or its reclassification as "held for sale" (see IFRS 5). Temporary idle activity does not preclude depreciating the asset, as future economic benefits are consumed not only through usage but also through wear and tear and obsolescence. Useful life therefore needs to be carefully determined based on use, maintenance programs, expected capacity, expected output, expected wear and tear, technical or commercial innovations, and legal limits.

Example of a Change in Useful Life and Residual Value

Mind Changing Inc. owns an asset with an original cost of $200,000. On acquisition, management determined that the useful life was ten years and the residual value would be $20,000. The asset is now eight years old, and during this time there have been no revisions to the assessed residual value. At the end of year 8, management has reviewed the useful life and residual value and has determined that the useful life can be extended to 12 years in view of the maintenance program adopted by the company. As a result, the residual value will reduce to $10,000. These changes in estimates would be effected in this way:

The asset has a carrying amount of $56,000 at the end of year 8: $200,000 (cost) less $144,000 (accumulated depreciation). Accumulated depreciation is calculated as

Depreciable amount equals cost less residual value = $200,000 – $20,000 = $180,000.

Annual depreciation = depreciable amount divided by useful life = $180,000/10 = $18,000.

Accumulated depreciation = $18,000 × no. of years (8) = $144,000.

Revision of the useful life to 12 years results in a remaining useful life of 4 years (12 – 8). The revised depreciable amount is $46,000: carrying amount of $56,000 – the revised residual amount of $10,000. Thus depreciation should be charged in future at $11,500 per annum ($46,000 divided by 4 years).

DERECOGNITION

The carrying amount of an item of property, plant, and equipment shall be derecognized on disposal or when no future economic benefit is expected from its use or disposal. Any gain on disposal is the difference between the net disposal proceeds and the carrying amount of the asset. Gains on disposal shall *not* be classified in the income statement as revenue.

In May 2008 the IASB's omnibus standard under annual improvements process was published, which intended to deal with nonurgent, minor amendments to several IFRS including IAS 16. The standard captioned *Improvements to IFRSs 2008* amended IAS 16 and added provisions relating to sale of assets held previously for rental to others. According to this amendment an entity, in the course of ordinary activities that routinely sells items of property, plant, and equipment which it previously held for rental to others, should transfer such assets at their carrying amount when they cease to be rented and are held for sale. Furthermore, the amendment clarified that the proceeds from the sale of such assets should be recognized as revenue in accordance with IAS 18.

PRACTICAL INSIGHT

Car rental companies in their normal course of business rent cars to their customers and regularly purchase fleets of cars which are then disposed of on an ongoing basis over a period of time, say every three years, so that customers of the rental car companies are regularly serviced by renting newer models. Therefore, at periodic intervals cars that are disposed of are then replaced with new vehicles that are placed in service for rental to their customers.

Prior to this amendment to IAS 16 there might have been some disparity in accounting treatment of cars held for sale (which would be classified as "inventory") but, which were previously held for rental to others (when they were treated as "property, plant, and equipment") however, now, with this clear cut guidance available in the standard with respect to treatment of assets held for sale which were previously held for rental to others there should be no confusion in the manner in which such assets are carried in the books and therefore should help in standardizing the accounting treatment in such situations.

IFRIC INTERPRETATION 1

This interpretation applies to changes in the measurement of any existing decommissioning, restoration, or similar liability that is both

1. Recognized as part of the cost of an item of property, plant, and equipment in accordance with IAS 16.
2. Recognized as a liability in accordance with IAS 37.

While the guidance in this Interpretation relating to the recognition of the liability in accordance with IAS 37 has been dealt with and explained in the relevant chapter of this book (Chapter 30), the guidance with respect to changes in the measurement of the cost of an item of property, plant, and equipment under IAS 16 is explained in this chapter.

According to the IFRIC 1 "consensus," changes in the measurement of an existing decommissioning, restoration, and similar liability that result from changes in the estimated timing or amount of the outflow of resources, or a change in the discount rate, shall be accounted differently based on whether the related asset is measured under IAS 16 using the "cost model" or the "revaluation model."

1. If the related asset is measured using the "cost model" (under IAS 16) then changes in the liability shall be added to, or deducted from, the cost of the related asset in the current period; the amount deducted from the cost of the asset shall not exceed its carrying amount and if the adjustment results in an addition to the cost of the related asset the entity shall consider whether there is an indication of "impairment" in accordance with IAS 36.

2. If, on the other hand, the related asset is measured using the "revaluation model" (under IAS 16) then changes in the liability affect the "revaluation surplus" or "deficit" previously recognized on that asset, as set out in the following two steps:

   a. A decrease in the liability shall be credited directly to "revaluation surplus" in equity, except when it reverses a revaluation deficit that was previously recognized in profit or loss, in which case it shall be recognized in profit or loss.

   b. An increase in the liability shall be recognized in profit or loss, except that it shall be debited to "revaluation surplus" in equity (to the extent of any credit balance existing in the "revaluation surplus" in respect of the asset). In the event that a decrease in liability exceeds the carrying amount that would have been recognized had the asset been carried under the "cost model," the excess shall be recognized immediately in profit or loss.

   Further, a change in the liability is an indication that the asset may have to be revalued in order to ensure that the carrying amount remains closer to fair value at the balance sheet date. Any such revaluation shall be taken in determining the amounts to be taken to profit or loss and equity. (If a revaluation is necessary, all assets of that class shall be revalued together instead of piecemeal revaluations.)

   Lastly, as required by IAS 1, change in "revaluation surplus" resulting from a change in the liability shall be separately disclosed in the "statement of changes in equity."

The adjusted depreciated amount of the asset is depreciated over its useful life. Therefore, once the related asset has reached the end of its useful life, all later changes in liability shall be recognized in profit or loss as they occur. (This applies whether the "cost model" or the "revaluation model" is used.)

DISCLOSURE

Disclosures with respect to each class of property, plant, and equipment are extensive and comprise

- Measurement bases for determining gross carrying amounts
- Depreciation methods
- Useful lives or depreciation rates used
- Gross carrying amount and accumulated depreciation (aggregated with accumulated impairment losses) at the beginning and end of the period
- Additions
- Assets classified as held for sale
- Acquisitions through business combinations
- Increases and decreases arising from revaluations and from impairment losses and reversals thereof
- Depreciation
- Net exchange differences recognized under IAS 21
- Other changes
- Existence and amounts of restrictions on ownership title
- Assets pledged as security for liabilities
- Assets in the course of construction
- Contractual commitments for the acquisition of property, plant, and equipment
- Compensation for assets impaired, lost, or given up

If property, plant, and equipment are stated at revalued amounts, these items must be specified:

- The effective date of the valuation
- Whether an independent valuer was involved
- Methods and significant assumptions used in assessing fair values
- The extent to which fair values were measured by reference to observable prices in an active market, recent market transactions on an arm's-length basis, or were estimated using other techniques

- For each class of asset revalued, the carrying amount that would have been recognized if the class had not been revalued
- The revaluation surplus, indicating the change for the period and any restrictions on distributions to shareholders

EXTRACTS FROM PUBLISHED FINANCIAL STATEMENTS

HOLCIM, Annual Report, 2009

Notes to Financial Statements

13. Property, Plant, and Equipment

Property, plant, and equipment are valued at acquisition or construction cost less depreciation and impairment loss. Cost includes transfers from equity of any gains or losses on qualifying cash flow hedges. Depreciation is charged so as to write off the cost of property, plant, and equipment over their estimated useful lives, using the straight-line method, on the following bases:

Land	No depreciation except on land with raw material reserves
Building and installations	20 to 40 years
Machinery	10 to 30 years
Furniture, vehicles, and tools	3 to 10 years

Costs are only included in the asset's carrying amount when it is probable that economic benefits associated with the item will flow to the Group in future periods and the cost of the item can be measured reliably. Costs include the initial estimate of the costs of dismantling and removing the item and restoring the site on which it is located. All other repairs and maintenance expenses are charged to the income statement during the period in which they are incurred.

Mineral reserves, which are included in the class "land" of property, plant, and equipment, are valued at cost and are depreciated based on the physical unit-of-production method over their estimated commercial lives.

Costs incurred to gain access to mineral reserves are capitalized and depreciated over the life of the quarry, which is based on the estimated tons of raw material to be extracted from the reserves.

Interest cost on borrowings to finance construction projects which necessarily takes a substantial period of time to get ready for their intended use are capitalized during the period of time that is required to complete and prepare the asset for its intended use. All other borrowing costs are expensed in the period in which they are incurred.

Government grants received are deducted from property, plant, and equipment and reduce the depreciation charge accordingly.

Leases of property, plant, and equipment where the Group has substantially all the risks and rewards of ownership are classified as finance leases. Property, plant, and equipment acquired through a finance lease are capitalized at the date of the commencement of the lease term at the present value of the minimum future lease payments as determined at the inception of the lease. The corresponding lease obligations, excluding finance charges, are included in either current or long-term financial liabilities.

For sale-and-leaseback transactions, the book value of the related property, plant, or equipment remains unchanged. Proceeds from a sale are included as a financing liability and the financing costs are allocated over the term of the lease in such a manner that the costs are reported over the relevant periods.

BASF, Annual Report, 2009

Property, plant, and equipment are stated at acquisition or production cost less scheduled depreciation over their estimated useful lives. Low-value assets are fully written off in the year of acquisition and are shown as disposals. The revaluation method is not used.

The cost of self-constructed plants includes direct costs, appropriate allocations of material and manufacturing costs, and a share of the administrative costs associated with the construction of the plants. Borrowing costs that are incurred during the period of construction are capitalized. For companies in Germany, borrowing costs were capitalized at 4.5% whereas country-specific rates were used for Group companies outside Germany.

Expenses related to scheduled maintenance turnarounds of large-scale plants are capitalized as part of the asset and depreciated using the straight-line method over the period until the next planned turnaround. Both movable and immovable fixed assets are depreciated using the straight-line method. The weighted-average depreciation periods used were as follows:

Depreciation Periods in Years

	2009	2008
Buildings and structural installations	19	24
Machinery and technical equipment	11	11
Factory and office equipment and other facilities	7	7

Impairment losses are recorded whenever events or changes in circumstances indicate that the carrying amount of an asset may not be recoverable. The evaluation is based on the present value of the expected future cash flows. An impairment loss is recorded for the difference between the carrying amount and the value of discounted future cash flows.

Investment properties held to realize capital gains or rental income are immaterial. They are valued at the lower of acquisition cost less scheduled depreciation and fair value.

Property, Plant, and Equipment

Developments in 2009

In euro millions	Land, land rights, and buildings	Machinery and technical equipment	Miscellaneous equipment and fixtures	Advance payments and construction in progress	Total
Acquisition costs					
Balance as of January 1, 2009	7,470	36,979	2,817	1,881	49,147
Changes in scope of consolidation	(7)	(3)	1	--	(9)
Additions	633	1,653	172	1,668	4,126
Disposals	(167)	(746)	(115)	(26)	(1,054)
Transfers	163	1,123	75	(1,399)	(38)
Exchange differences	(21)	(173)	(14)	(21)	(229)
Balance as of December 31, 2009	8,071	38,833	2,936	2,103	51,943
Depreciation					
Balance as of January 1, 2009	4,427	27,357	2,325	6	34,115
Changes in scope of consolidation	(12)	(6)	--	--	(18)
Additions	281	2,142	183	8	2,614
Disposals	(128)	(695)	(105)	(1)	(929)
Transfers	(2)	27	(34)	--	(9)
Exchange differences	(5)	(100)	(10)	--	(115)
Balance as of December 31, 2009	4,561	28,725	2,359	13	36,658
Net book value as of December 31, 2009	3,510	10,108	577	2,090	16,285

The acquisition of Ciba and its purchase price allocation resulted in additions to fixed assets of €1,766 million in 2009. Furthermore, in 2009 we undertook, primarily, expansion projects at our Ludwigshafen site, particularly in the syngas facility, the construction of the plant to produce cyclododecanone as well as the capacity expansion of the Ecoflex/Ecovio plant and the connection to the propylene pipeline. Furthermore, there were investments made in the resins plant in Wyandotte, Michigan, and the expansion of the polyol plant in Geismar, Louisiana, the construction of the oleum/sulfuric acid plant and the expansion of the Deacon plant in Antwerp as well as the construction of the OPAL natural gas pipeline and the development of the natural gas fields in Norway.

Overall, €106 million in impairment losses were recognized. Impairment losses of €67 million in 2009 related to the restructuring of the acquired Ciba sites, were primarily reported as special charges in the Performance Products segment.

Additional impairment losses were reported under the Chemicals segment for restructuring at the sites in Feluy, Belgium; and Frankfurt, Germany; as well as under the Functional Solutions segment at the site in Nanjing, China.

MULTIPLE-CHOICE QUESTIONS

1. Healthy Inc. bought a private jet for the use of its top-ranking officials. The cost of the private jet is $15 million and can be depreciated either using a composite useful life or useful lives of its major components. It is expected to be used over a period of seven years. The engine of the jet has a useful life of five years. The private jet's tires are replaced every two years. The private jet will be depreciated using the straight-line method over

   (a) Seven years composite useful life.
   (b) Five years useful life of the engine, two years useful life of the tires, and seven years useful life applied to the balance cost of the jet.
   (c) Two years useful life based on conservatism (the lowest useful life of all the parts of the jet).
   (d) Five years useful life based on a simple average of the useful lives of all major components of the jet.

2. An entity imported machinery to install in its new factory premises before year-end. However, due to circumstances beyond its control, the machinery was delayed by a few months but reached the factory premises before year-end. While this was happening, the entity learned from the bank that it was being charged interest on the loan it had taken to fund the cost of the plant. What is the proper treatment of freight and interest expense under IAS 16?

   (a) Both expenses should be capitalized.
   (b) Interest may be capitalized but freight should be expensed.
   (c) Freight charges should be capitalized but interest cannot be capitalized under these circumstances.
   (d) Both expenses should be expensed.

3. XYZ Inc. owns a fleet of over 100 cars and 20 ships. It operates in a capital-intensive industry and thus has significant *other* property, plant, and equipment that it carries in its books. It decided to revalue its property, plant, and equipment. The company's accountant has suggested the alternatives that follow. Which one of the options should XYZ Inc. select in order to be in line with the provisions of IAS 16?

   (a) Revalue only one-half of each class of property, plant, and equipment, as that method is less cumbersome and easy compared to revaluing all assets together.
   (b) Revalue an entire class of property, plant, and equipment.
   (c) Revalue one ship at a time, as it is easier than revaluing all ships together.
   (d) Since assets are being revalued regularly, there is no need to depreciate.

4. An entity installed a new production facility and incurred a number of expenses at the point of installation. The entity's accountant is arguing that most expenses do not qualify for capitalization. Included in those expenses are initial operating losses. These should be

   (a) Deferred and amortized over a reasonable period of time.
   (b) Expensed and charged to the income statement.
   (c) Capitalized as part of the cost of the plant as a directly attributable cost.
   (d) Taken to retained earnings since it is unreasonable to present it as part of the current year's income statement.

5. IAS 16 requires that revaluation surplus resulting from initial revaluation of property, plant, and equipment should be treated in one of the following ways. Which of the four options mirrors the requirements of IAS 16?

   (a) Credited to retained earnings as this is an unrealized gain.
   (b) Released to the income statement an amount equal to the difference between the depreciation calculated on historical cost vis-à-vis revalued amount.
   (c) Deducted from current assets and added to the property, plant, and equipment.
   (d) Debited to the class of property, plant, and equipment that is being revalued and credited to other comprehensive income and accumulated in equity under the heading of revaluation surplus.

Chapter 11

LEASES (IAS 17)

BACKGROUND AND INTRODUCTION

This Standard prescribes the accounting treatment for leases in the financial statements of lessees and lessors.

SCOPE

This Standard shall be applied in accounting for leases other than

1. Leases to explore for or use nonregenerative resources such as oil, natural gas, and so forth
2. Licensing arrangements for motion pictures, video recordings, music, and so on

This Standard shall *not* be applied in the *measurement* of

- Property held by lessees that is an investment property (see IAS 40)
- Investment property provided by lessors under operating leases (see IAS 40)
- Biological assets held by lessees under finance leases (see IAS 41)
- Biological assets provided by lessors under operating leases (see IAS 41)

DEFINITIONS OF KEY TERMS
(in accordance with IAS 17)

Lease. An agreement whereby the lessor conveys to the lessee in return for payment the right to use an asset for an agreed period of time.

Finance lease. A lease that transfers substantially all the risks and rewards of ownership of an asset. Title need not necessarily be eventually transferred.

Operating lease. A lease that is not a finance lease.

Minimum lease payments. The payments over the lease term that are required to be made. For a lessee, this includes any amounts guaranteed to be paid; for a lessor, this includes any residual value guaranteed to the lessor.

The definition of a lease includes those contracts for hire of an asset that contain provisions for the hirer to acquire title to the asset upon fulfillment of agreed conditions—these are sometimes called hire purchase contracts.

PRACTICAL INSIGHT

RHI AG, an Austrian entity, states in its financial statements that the move to International Financial Reporting Standards (IFRS) has increased the opening book value of all its noncurrent assets by €69 million. It explains that, under Austrian generally accepted accounting principles (GAAP), the depreciation of noncurrent assets is influenced partly by tax considerations, while under IFRS, it is in line with expected useful lives.

Included in the above total are increases of €5 million resulting from the capitalization of finance leases under IAS 17, *Leases,* and decreases of €7 million unscheduled depreciation under IAS 36, *Impairment of Assets.*

CLASSIFICATION OF LEASES

The classification of a lease as either a finance lease or an operating lease is critical as significantly different accounting treatments are required for the different types of lease. The classification is based on the extent to which risks and rewards of ownership of the leased asset are transferred to the lessee or remain with the lessor. Risks include technological obsolescence, loss from idle capacity, and variations in return. Rewards include rights to sell the asset and gain from its capital value.

A lease is classified as a finance lease if it transfers substantially all the risks and rewards of ownership to the lessee. If it does not, then it is an operating lease. When classifying a lease, it is important to recognize the substance of the agreement and not just its legal form. The commercial reality is important. Conditions in the lease may indicate that an entity has only a limited exposure to the risks and benefits of the leased asset. However, the substance of the agreement may indicate otherwise. Situations that, individually or in combination, *would usually* lead to a lease being a finance lease include

- Transfer of ownership to the lessee by the end of the lease term.
- The lessee has the option to purchase the asset at a price that is expected to be lower than its fair value such that the option is likely to be exercised.
- The lease term is for a major part of the *economic* life of the asset, even if title to the asset is not transferred.
- The present value of the minimum lease payments is equal to substantially all of the fair value of the asset.
- The leased assets are of a specialized nature such that only the lessee can use them without significant modification.

Situations that, individually or in combination, *could* lead to a lease being a finance lease include

- If the lessee can cancel the lease, and the lessor's losses associated with cancellation are borne by the lessee.
- Gains or losses from changes in the fair value of the residual value of the asset accrue to the lessee.
- The lessee has the option to continue the lease for a secondary term at substantially below-market rent.

It is evident from these descriptions that a large degree of judgment has to be exercised in classifying leases; many lease agreements are likely to demonstrate only a few of the situations listed, some of which are more persuasive than others. In all cases, the substance of the transaction needs to be properly analyzed and understood. Emphasis is placed on the risks that the lessor retains more than the benefits of ownership of the asset. If there is little or no related risk, then the agreement is likely to be a finance lease. If the lessor suffers the risk associated with a movement in the market price of the asset or the use of the asset, then the lease is usually an operating lease.

The purpose of the lease arrangement may help the classification. If there is an option to cancel, and the lessee is likely to exercise such an option, then the lease is likely to be an operating lease.

Classifications of leases are to be made at *the inception* of the lease. The inception of a lease is the earlier of the agreement date and the date of the commitment by the parties to the principal provisions of the lease. If the lease terms are subsequently altered to such a degree that the lease would have had a different classification at its inception, a new lease is deemed to have been entered into. Changes in estimates such as the residual value of an asset are not deemed to be a change in classification.

IAS 17 was amended to delete guidance stating that a lease of land with an indefinite economic life is normally classified as an operating lease, unless at the end of the lease term, title is expected to pass to the lessee. Under the amendments, a land lease with a lease term of several decades or longer may be classified as a finance lease, even if at the end of the lease term title will not pass to the lessee, because in such arrangements substantially all risks and rewards are transferred to the lessee and the present value of the residual value of the leased asset is considered negligible. Also, when a lease includes both land and buildings elements, an entity should determine the classification of each element, taking account of the fact that land normally has an indefinite economic life. If as a result of the amendments, a lease is reclassified as a finance lease, then that reclassification should be effected retrospectively. If, however, information necessary to apply the amendments retrospectively is not available, then classification is determined based on the facts and circumstances at the adoption date of the amendments. The asset and liability relating to a land lease are recognized at their respective fair values, with any difference between those values being recognized in retained earnings. In classifying a lease of land and buildings, land and buildings elements would normally be separate. However, separate measurement of the land and buildings elements is not required if the amounts for land are immaterial or the lessee's interest in both land and buildings is classified as an investment property in accordance with IAS 40 and the fair value model is adopted. If title to the land is likely to pass at the end of the lease, it is likely that both leases will be finance leases.

Difficulties arise because the minimum lease payments need to be allocated between the land and the building element in proportion to their relative fair values of the leasehold interests at the beginning of the lease. If the allocation cannot be made reliably, then both leases are treated as finance leases or as operating leases, depending on which classification the arrangement more clearly follows.

PRACTICAL INSIGHT

SWISSCOM AG states in its financial statements that revised IAS 17 requires that the land and buildings elements of a lease of land and buildings should be considered separately for the classification of leases. The land element is classified normally as an operating lease unless title passes to the lessee at the end of the lease term. SWISSCOM discloses that it entered into sale and leaseback transactions, some of which are classified as finance leases with no distinction being made between the land and buildings elements. In accordance with revised IAS 17, those land elements classified as finance leases will be derecognized. Although there will be an effect on assets and liabilities, SWISSCOM says there will not be any material effect on operating income.

If the lessee is to classify the land and buildings as investment property under IAS 40 and the fair value model is adopted (the required model for operating leases under IAS 40), then separate measurement is *not* required. Under IAS 40, property held by a lessee under an operating lease can be classified as investment property and accounted for *as if it were a finance lease.*

CASE STUDY 1

Facts

An entity enters into a lease agreement on July 1, 20X8 that lasts for seven years. The asset's economic life is 7.5 years. The fair value of the asset is $5 million, and lease payments of $450,000 are payable every six months commencing January 1, 20X9. The present value of the minimum lease payments is $4.6 million. The lease payments were originally due to commence on July 1, 20X8, but the lessor has agreed to postpone the first payment until January 1, 20X9. The asset was received by the entity on July 1, 20X8.

Required

Describe how the lease agreement should be treated for the year ended January 31, 20X9.

Solution

The lease liability should be recognized when the asset is received by the entity and the lease agreement commences, which is July 1, 20X8. The lease is a finance lease because it is for substantially all of the asset's economic life and the present value of the minimum lease payments is substantially all (92%) of the fair value of the asset.

During the six-month period before the commencement of the lease payments, interest will be accrued on the lease liability using the interest rate implicit in the lease. In the period to January 31, 20X9, seven months of interest will be accrued. The cash payment on January 1, 20X9, will be apportioned as to the repayment of the lease liability and payment of accrued interest. The asset will be depreciated over the lease term (seven years) in accordance with the depreciation policy for "owned" assets.

LEASES IN THE FINANCIAL STATEMENTS OF LESSEES

Finance Leases

At the commencement of the lease term, a lessee shall recognize an asset and a liability at the fair value of the leased asset or, if lower, at the present value of the minimum lease payments. The appropriate discount rate in the present value calculation is the rate implicit in the finance lease— that rate which discounts the lease payments to the fair value of the asset plus any initial direct costs of the lessor.

The impact of this treatment is to reflect the economic substance of the transaction. The lessee has acquired an asset for the substantial part of its useful life and expects to obtain substantially all the benefits from its use. In other words, the lease arrangement is merely a financing vehicle for the acquisition of an asset.

Subsequent to initial recognition, the lease payments are apportioned between the repayment of the outstanding liability and the finance charge so as to reflect a constant periodic rate of interest on the liability. Methods of calculation vary and include sum of the digits, which is a rough approximation, and more complex amortization models.

The asset needs to be depreciated over its expected *useful* life under IAS 16, using rates for similar assets. However, if there is no reasonable certainty that ownership will transfer to the lessee, then the shorter of the lease term and the useful life should be used.

Disclosures for Finance Leases

The following disclosures for finance leases are required in addition to those required by the financial instruments standards:

- For each class of asset, the net carrying value at the end of the reporting period
- A reconciliation between the total of the minimum lease payments and their present value
- The total of the future minimum lease payments analyzed as to

  - Not later than one year
  - Later than one year but not later than five years
  - Later than five years

- Contingent rents
- Total future minimum lease payments expected to be received under noncancelable sub-leases
- A general description of the lessee's material leasing arrangements

Operating Leases

Lease payments under operating leases shall be recognized as an expense on a straight-line basis over the lease term unless another basis is more representative of the pattern of the user's benefit, even if the payments follow a different pattern.

It is important to recognize the impact of incentives in operating leases. Often incentives to enter into operating leases take the form of up-front payments, rent-free periods, and the like. These need to be appropriately recognized over the lease term *from its commencement*. Thus, a rent-free period does not mean that the lessee avoids a rent charge in its statement of comprehensive income. It has to apportion the rent for the entire lease over the entire period, resulting in a reduced annual charge.

CASE STUDY 2

Facts

Jay has entered into a lease of property whereby the title to the land does not pass to the entity at the end of the lease but the title to the building passes after 15 years. The lease commenced on July 1, 20X9, when the value of the land was $54 million and the building value was $18 million. Annual lease rentals paid in arrears commencing on June 30, 20X6, are $6 million for land and $2 million for buildings. The entity has allocated the rentals on the basis of their relative fair values at the start of the lease.

The payments under the lease terms are reduced after every six years, and the minimum lease term is 30 years. The net present value of the minimum lease payments at July 1, 20X9, was $40 million for land and $17 million for buildings. The buildings are written off on the straight-line basis over their useful life of 15 years. Assume an effective interest rate of 7%.

Required

Discuss how Jay should treat this lease under IAS 17.

Solution

IAS 17 requires the substance of the transaction to be reviewed and the extent to which the risks and rewards of ownership of the leased asset are transferred to be determined. If the risks and rewards of ownership are substantially transferred to the lessee, then the lease is a finance lease. The Standard requires the land and buildings elements to be considered separately. Normally a lease of land will be regarded as an operating lease unless the title passes to the lessee. In this case the title does not pass and the present value of the lease payments is only 74% of the fair value of the land, which does not constitute substantially all of the fair value of the leased asset, one of the criteria for the determination of a finance lease.

In the case of the buildings, the title passes after 15 years, and the lease runs for the whole of its economic life, which indicates a finance lease. The present value of the minimum lease payments is 94% of the fair value of the lease at its inception, an amount that indicates that the lessee is effectively purchasing the building. Thus it would appear to be a finance lease. Property, plant, and equipment would increase by $17 million with a corresponding increase in noncurrent liabilities. The noncurrent liability ($17 million) will be reduced by the payment on June 30, 20X0 ($2 million), and increased by the interest charge ($17 million × 0.07, or $1.2 million).

The land will not appear on the statement of financial position and the operating lease rentals will be charged to the statement of comprehensive income.

Disclosures for Operating Leases

In addition to the disclosures required by the financial instruments standards, these disclosures are required:

- Total future minimum lease payments under noncancelable operating leases for each of the following:
  - Not later than one year
  - Later than one year and not later than five years
  - Later than five years
- Total future minimum lease payments expected to be received under noncancelable subleases
- Lease and sublease payments and contingent rents recognized as an expense
- A general description of the significant leasing arrangements

CASE STUDY 3

Facts

An entity enters into a finance lease to lease a truck from another entity. The truck's fair value is $140,000. The lease rentals are payable monthly, and the lease term is five years. The present value of the minimum lease payments at the inception of the lease is $132,000 and the unguaranteed residual value of the truck is estimated at $20,000.

Required

At which amount will the lease liability be recorded in the financial accounts at the inception of the lease?

Solution

The lease asset and liability will be recorded at $132,000, which is the present value of the minimum lease payments. A lease liability should be recorded at the lower of the fair value of the leased asset and the present value of the minimum lease payment. The difference between the minimum lease payments and the fair value of $8,000 will represent the present value of the unguaranteed residual value ($20,000).

CASE STUDY 4

Facts

An entity leases an asset from another entity. The fair value of the asset is $100,000, and the lease rentals are $18,000, payable half yearly. The first payment is made on the delivery of the asset. The unguaranteed residual value of the asset after the three-year lease period is $4,000. The implicit interest rate in the lease is 9.3% (approximately), and the present value of the minimum lease payment is $96,936.

Required

Show how this lease would be accounted for in the accounts of the lessee.

Solution

The number of payments is six with a total value of $108,000. The use of the approximate implicit interest rate will give a rounding error.

Payment	$ Balance	$ Finance Charge	$ Payment	$ Lease Liability
1	96,936	0	(18,000)	78,936
2	78,936	3,670	(18,000)	64,606
3	64,606	3,004	(18,000)	49,610
4	49,610	2,306	(18,000)	33,916
5	33,916	1,577	(18,000)	17,493
6	17,493	507 (813 – 306)	(18,000)	0

There is a rounding error of $306, which would be taken off the last finance charge to be taken to the statement of comprehensive income.

LEASES IN THE FINANCIAL STATEMENTS OF LESSORS

Finance Leases

Lessors shall recognize assets held under finance leases as a receivable equal to the net investment in the lease. The net investment in the lease is the aggregate of the minimum lease payments and any unguaranteed residual value (the "gross investment") discounted at the rate implicit in the lease.

Due to the definition of the interest rate implicit in the lease—that rate which discounts the lease payments to the fair value of the asset plus the initial direct costs of the lessor—the initial direct costs of the lessor are automatically included in the receivable. The direct costs of the lessor are those costs directly attributable to negotiating and arranging a lease.

Subsequent to initial recognition, finance income is recognized based on a pattern reflecting a constant rate of return on the net investment in the lease. Receipts under the finance lease are apportioned to the gross investment, as a reduction in the debtor, and to the finance income element.

Lessors who are manufacturers or dealers should recognize profit on the transaction in the same way as for normal sales of the entity. Thus a finance lease will create a profit or loss from the sale of the asset at normal selling prices and a finance income over the lease term. If artificially low rates of interest are quoted, profit is calculated using market interest rates.

Disclosures for Finance Leases

In addition to the requirements of the financial instruments standards, these disclosures are required:

- A reconciliation between the gross carrying amount of the investment in the lease and the present value of the future minimum lease payments receivable
- The gross investment in the lease and the future minimum lease payments for each of the following:

  - Not later than one year
  - Later than one year but not later than five years
  - Later than five years

- Unearned finance income
- Unguaranteed residual value
- Doubtful recoverable lease payments
- Contingent rents recognized as income
- A general description of the significant leasing arrangements

Operating Leases

Lessors shall show assets subject to operating leases in the financial statement in accordance with the nature of the asset—motor vehicles, plant and equipment, and so on.

Lease income from operating leases shall be recognized in the statement of comprehensive income on a straight-line basis over the lease term unless another basis reflects better the nature of the benefit received. As mentioned earlier, any incentives should be considered.

Depreciation on the asset subject to a lease is recognized as an expense and should be determined in the same manner as similar assets of the lessor. Additionally, the lessor should apply the principles of IAS 16, 36, and 38 as appropriate.

Initial direct costs of negotiating and arranging the lease shall be added to the cost of the asset and expensed over the lease term in the same pattern as the income is recognized.

Disclosures for Operating Leases

In addition to the requirements of the financial instruments standards, these disclosures are required:

- The future minimum lease payments under noncancelable operating leases for each of the following:

- Not later than one year
- Later than one year but not later than five years
- Later than five years

- Contingent rents recognized as income
- A general description of the significant leasing arrangements

---

PRACTICAL INSIGHT

SIC 27, *Evaluating the Substance of Transactions Involving the Legal Form of a Lease,* considers whether an arrangement meets the definition of a lease under IAS 17, *Leases,* and, if not, how a company should account for a fee it may receive. Examples are given of indicators that demonstrate that it is inappropriate to grant immediate recognition of the entire fee as income.

Deutsche Post discloses that it leases to companies electronic sorting systems although it remains the beneficial and legal owner of all the assets and they remain available to Deutsche Post for its operating activities. The note in its 2002 financial statements refers to SIC 27 and discloses that the net present value benefit from the transactions has been recognized immediately, which results in income of €136 million and expenses of €40 million being recognized.

SALE AND LEASEBACK TRANSACTIONS AND OTHER TRANSACTIONS INVOLVING THE LEGAL FORM OF A LEASE

Very often entities enter into complex financing arrangements involving lease-like arrangements. Careful analysis of such arrangements needs to be undertaken to ensure that the substance of the transaction is properly reflected, not just the legal form.

A common financing transaction is a sale and leaseback whereby the owner of an asset sells it to a financier who then leases the asset back to the original owner. Analysis is required to determine if the leaseback is a finance or an operating lease. A finance lease results in the lessee *having to defer any profit on disposal over the lease term.* If the leaseback is an operating lease and the entire transaction is at fair value, gain or loss on disposal is recognized immediately.

Other more complex transactions need to be analyzed for their substance and often involve a series of transactions involving leases. On occasion, just tax benefits arise; sometimes there is no real transaction when the series of transactions is viewed in its entirety. In such cases the substance needs to be clearly reflected in the financial statements.

In the case of an operating lease, if the sale price is below fair value and the loss is compensated by future lease payments at below market price, then the loss should be deferred and amortized in proportion to the lease payments over the useful life of the asset.

If the loss is not compensated by future lease payments, it should be recognized immediately.

If the sale price is above fair value and the rentals are above the normal market rates, the excess over fair value should be deferred and amortized over the useful life of the asset.

PRACTICAL INSIGHT

KONINKLIJKE PHILIPS ELECTRONICS NV stated in its financial statements that gains arising on sale and leaseback transactions that are deferred under US generally accepted accounting principles (GAAP) will be released to equity as IAS 17, *Leases,* does not permit such deferral.

CASE STUDY 5

Facts

An entity sells a piece of a plant to a 100% owned subsidiary and leases it back over a period of four years. The remaining useful life of the plant is ten years. The selling price of the plant was 20% below its carrying and market value. The lease rentals were based on market rates. The entity has no right to buy the plant back.

Required

Discuss how this transaction should be dealt with in the entity's financial statements.

Solution

The lease will almost certainly be an operating lease, as the lease period is not for the majority of the plant's life and the rentals are based on market rates. However, the selling price was below the carrying and market value, and this loss has not been compensated by future rentals. Therefore, the loss should be recognized immediately.

The transaction will be eliminated on consolidation, but the individual entity accounts will recognize it. Also, the entities are related parties; therefore, the substance of the transaction will have to be carefully scrutinized. Although the entity has no right to reacquire the asset, it can exercise the right through its control of the 100% subsidiary. This control may change the designation of the lease.

CASE STUDY 6

Facts

An entity leases a motor vehicle over a period of five years. The economic life of the vehicle is estimated at seven years. The entity has the right to buy the vehicle at the end of the lease term for 50% of its market value plus a nominal payment of 0.5% of the market value at that date. This nominal payment is to cover the selling costs of the vehicle.

Required

How should the lease be classified in the financial statements of the entity?

Solution

The lease will be a finance lease as the entity is likely to buy the vehicle at the price stated because it will be sold at 50% of the market value of the vehicle plus a nominal charge. SIC 15, *Operating Lease— Incentives,* clarifies the recognition of incentives related to operating leases by both the lessee and lessor. Lease incentives should be considered an integral part of the consideration for the use of the leased asset. IAS 17 requires an entity to treat incentives as a reduction of lease income or lease expense. Incentives should be recognized by both the lessor and the lessee over the lease term, using a single amortization method applied to the net consideration.

CASE STUDY 7

Facts

The manufacturing property of the group, other than the head office, was held on an operating lease over eight years. On reorganization on December 31, 20X9, the lease has been renegotiated and is held for 12 years at a rent of $25 million per annum paid in arrears. The fair value of the property is $175 million and its remaining economic life is 13 years. The lease relates to the buildings and not the land. The factor to be used for an annuity at 10% for 12 years is 6.8137.

Required

Show the effect of the above in the financial statements.

Solution

Under IAS 17, *Leases*, operating lease payments should be recognized as an expense in profit or loss over the lease term on a straight-line basis, unless another systematic basis is more representative of the time pattern of the user's benefit. The provisions of the lease have changed significantly and would need to be reassessed. The lease term is now for the major part of the economic life of the assets, and at the inception of the lease, the present value of the minimum lease payments is substantially all of the fair value of the leased asset. (Fair value $175 million, NPV of lease payments $170.5 million) Even if title is not transferred at the end of the lease, the lease can still be a finance lease. Any change in the estimate of the length of life of a lease would not change its classification, but where the provisions of the lease have changed, reassessment of its classification takes place. Thus it would appear that the lease is now a finance lease, and it would be shown in the statement of financial position at the present value of the lease payments, as this is lower than the fair value.

IFRIC 4, *Determining Whether an Arrangement Contains a Lease,* deals with agreements that do not take the legal form of a lease but which give rights to use assets in return for payment. Such agreements would include outsourcing arrangements and telecommunication contracts. If the agreement conveys a right to control the use of the underlying asset, then it should be accounted for under IAS 17. This is the case if any of the following conditions are met:

- The purchaser in the arrangement has the ability or right to operate the asset or direct others to operate the asset.
- The purchaser has the ability or right to control physical access to the asset.
- There is only a remote possibility that parties other than the purchaser will take more than an insignificant amount of the output of the asset and the price that the purchaser will pay is neither fixed per unit of output nor equal to the current market price at the time of delivery.

SIC 27, *Evaluating the Substance of Transactions Involving the Legal Form of a Lease,* states that the accounting for arrangements between an enterprise and an investor should reflect the substance of the arrangement. All aspects of the arrangement should be evaluated to determine its substance, with weight given to those aspects and implications that have an economic effect.

When the overall economic effect cannot be understood without reference to the series of transactions as a whole, the series of transactions should be accounted for as one transaction.

CASE STUDY 8

Mercurex is purchasing vehicle parts from Sparecar. The contract is to last for three years and Sparecar is to design, develop, and manufacture the parts. Sparecar will construct machinery for this purpose but the machinery is so specific that it cannot be used on other contracts. Sparecar maintains the machinery but the know-how has been granted royalty-free to Mercurex. The price of each part includes a fixed price to cover the cost of the machinery. If Mercurex decides not to purchase a minimum number of parts to cover the cost of the machinery, then Mercurex has to repay Sparecar for the cost of the machinery including any interest incurred.

Mercurex can purchase the machinery at any time in order to safeguard against the cessation of production by Sparecar. The purchase price would be the cost of the machinery not yet recovered by Sparecar. The machinery has a life of three years and the parts are only sold to Mercurex who sets the levels of production for a period. Mercurex can perform a predelivery inspection on each part and can reject a defective part.

Required

How would the above be accounted for in the financial statements?

Solution

Entities often enter into agreements that do not take the legal form of a lease but still convey the right to use an asset in return for payment. IFRIC 4, *Determining Whether an Arrangement Contains a Lease,* provides guidance on when such arrangements are leases. If it is determined that the arrangement constitutes a lease, then it is accounted for under IAS 17, *Leases.* IFRIC 4 sets out when the assessment should be made and how to deal with the payments. Under IFRIC 4, a lease is based on the substance of the arrangement, which means assessing if

1. Fulfillment of the contract is dependent upon the use of a specified asset.
2. The contract conveys the right to use the asset. This means by operating the asset, controlling physical access, or if there is only a remote possibility that parties other than the purchaser will take more than a significant amount of the asset's output and the price the purchaser will pay is neither fixed per unit of output nor equal to the current market price.

In this case it seems that the contract contains a lease for the following reasons:

1. The completion of the contract depends upon the construction and use of a specific asset, which is the specialized machinery which is dedicated to the production of the parts and cannot be used for other production. All of the output is to be sold to Mercurex, who can inspect the parts and reject defective parts before delivery.
2. The contract allows Mercurex the right to use the asset because it controls the underlying use, as it is remote that any other party will receive any more than an insignificant amount of its production. The only customer is Mercurex, who sets the levels of production and has a purchase option at any time.
3. The price of the production is not fixed, as it is a "take or pay" contract, as Mercurex is committed to fully repay the cost of the machinery, nor is it equal to the current market price because the supply is not marked to market during the contract.
4. The payments for the lease are separable from any other elements in the contract (IFRIC 4) as Sparecar will recover the cost of the machinery through a fixed price per part over the life of the contract.

The contract contains a finance lease in the financial statements of Mercurex because of the specialized nature of the machinery and because the contract is for the life of the asset (three years). The payments under the contract will be separated between the lease element and the revenue for the sale of the parts. Sparecar will recognize a lease receivable equal to the net present value of the minimum lease payments. Sparecar does not normally sell machinery nor recognize revenue on the sale of machinery and, therefore, no gain or loss should be recognized and the initial carrying amount of the receivable will equal the production cost of the machinery (IAS 17). Lease payments will be split into interest income and receipt of the lease receivables.

THE FUTURE OF LEASE ACCOUNTING

The basic lease accounting model has not changed for many years and has been the subject of significant criticism. The major criticism is that the rules that determine lease classification may result in similar transactions being reported very differently, leading to lack of comparability and significant amounts of finance not being recognized. The FASB and IASB are working to develop a common standard for lease accounting and they expect to release an Exposure Draft shortly. For lessees, as outlined in their joint Discussion Paper and Exposure Draft (issued in March 2009 and August 2010 respectively), the Boards believe all lease contracts should be treated in a manner similar to the treatment of finance leases. A single conceptual model for the recognition and measurement of all lease contracts is proposed by removing the existing requirement for lessees to classify leases as finance or operating leases.

It is argued that the right obtained by the lessee in a lease contract is the right to use the leased asset during the lease term, and that this right meets the definition of an asset. Additionally, the lessee incurs an obligation to pay rentals in a lease contract, and that this obligation meets the definition of a liability.

A lessee would recognize in its statement of financial position, an asset representing its right to use the leased item for the lease term and a corresponding liability for its obligation to pay rentals. Under this approach, all leases would be accounted for in a similar manner and the classifications of finance and operating leases would be eliminated. The Boards believe the right-of-use model is the most consistent with their conceptual frameworks and increases the transparency of lease accounting. As leases are a form of financing, the obligations recognized under the right-of-use approach would be consistent with how businesses reflect other financing arrangements.

Leases initially would be measured at cost, which is the present value of the lease payments, including initial direct costs incurred by the lessee. Present values would be calculated using the lessee's incremental borrowing rate as the discount rate. If the rate implicit in the lease is readily determinable, this rate can be used. Lessees would not have to determine the lessor's implicit rate as in most cases it will be difficult to identify. The implicit rate is more likely to be identifiable in leases of plant and equipment, particularly when it also may be purchased outright. For other types of leases, including property leases with rents based on cost per square meter, the lessee rarely knows the implicit rate.

The lease asset will be subsequently measured at amortized cost. The expense recorded would be presented as depreciation expense rather than rent expense. The lessee's obligation would be also subsequently measured at amortized cost using the effective interest rate method under which payments would be allocated between principal and interest over the lease term. As a result the interest expense would be higher in the early years of a lease compared to the current straight-line treatment for rent expense.

The IASB and FASB found it difficult to agree upon a single lessor accounting model and decided that concerns about the application of each of the two approaches in certain fact patterns could only be addressed through a dual model.

- For leases where the lessor retains exposure to significant risks or benefits associated with the leased asset either during the term of the contract or subsequent to the term of the contract, the "performance obligation" approach would be followed. The lessor recognizes the underlying asset and a lease receivable, representing the right to receive rental payments from the lessee, with a corresponding performance obligation, representing the obligation to permit the lessee to use the leased asset.
- For all other leases, the "derecognition approach" would be followed. The lessor recognizes a receivable, representing the right to receive rental payments from the lessee and records revenue. In addition, a portion of the carrying value of the leased asset is viewed as having transferred to the lessee and is derecognized and recorded as cost of sales. Lessors under either approach would also need to estimate the lease term and contingent payments and true-up these estimates as facts and circumstances change.

EXTRACTS FROM PUBLISHED FINANCIAL STATEMENTS

STANDARD CHARTERED PLC–Annual Report, 2009

Leases

Where a Group company is the lessee

The leases entered into by the Group are primarily operating leases. The total payments made under operating leases are charged to the statement of comprehensive income on a straight-line basis over the period of the lease.

When an operating lease is terminated before the lease period has expired, any payment required to be made to the lessor by way of penalty is recognized as an expense in the period in which termination takes place.

Where the Group is a lessee under finance leases, the leased assets are capitalized and included in "Property, plant, and equipment" with a corresponding liability to the lessor recognized in "Other liabilities." Finance charges payable are recognized over the period of the lease based on the interest rate implicit in the lease to give a constant periodic rate of return.

Where a Group company is the lessor

When assets are leased to customers under finance leases, the present value of the lease payments is recognized as a receivable. The difference between the gross receivable and the present value of the receivable is recognized as unearned finance income. Lease income is recognized over the term of the lease using the net investment method (before tax), which reflects a constant periodic rate of return ignoring tax cash flows.

Assets leased to customers under operating leases are included within "Property, plant, and equipment" and depreciated over their useful lives. Rental income on these leased assets is recognized in the statement of comprehensive income on a straight-line basis unless another systematic basis is more representative.

Source: Standard Chartered PLC Annual Report 2009. © Standard Chartered PLC

J. SAINSBURY PLC Financial Statements to March 21, 2009

Leases are classified as finance leases when the terms of the lease transfer substantially all the risks and rewards of ownership to the Group. All other leases are classified as operating leases. For property leases, the land and building elements are treated separately to determine the appropriate lease classification.

Finance leases

Assets funded through finance leases are capitalized as property, plant, and equipment and depreciated over their estimated useful lives or the lease term, whichever is shorter. The amount capitalized is the lower of the fair value of the asset or the present value of the minimum lease payments during the lease term at the inception of the lease. The resulting lease obligations are included in liabilities.

Operating leases

Assets leased under operating leases are not recorded on the statement of financial position. Rental payments are charged directly to the statement of comprehensive income.

Lease incentives

Lease incentives primarily include up-front cash payments or rent-free periods. Lease incentives are capitalized and spread over the period of the lease term.

Leases with predetermined fixed rental increases

The Group has a number of leases with predetermined fixed rental increases. These rental increases are accounted for on a straight-line basis over the term of the lease.

Operating lease income

Operating lease income consists of rentals from subtenant agreements and is recognized as earned.

MULTIPLE-CHOICE QUESTIONS

1. The classification of a lease as either an operating or finance lease is based on
   (a) The length of the lease.
   (b) The transfer of the risks and rewards of ownership.
   (c) The minimum lease payments being at least 50% of the fair value.
   (d) The economic life of the asset.

2. The accounting concept that is principally used to classify leases into operating and finance is
   (a) Substance over form.
   (b) Prudence.
   (c) Neutrality.
   (d) Completeness.

3. Which of the following situations would *prima facie* lead to a lease being classified as an operating lease?
   (a) Transfer of ownership to the lessee at the end of the lease term.
   (b) Option to purchase at a value below the fair value of the asset.
   (c) The lease term is for a major part of the asset's life.
   (d) The present value of the minimum lease payments is 50% of the fair value of the asset.

4. The classification of a lease is normally carried out
   (a) At the end of the lease term.
   (b) After a "cooling off" period of one year.
   (c) At the inception of the lease.
   (d) When the entity deems it to be necessary.

5. Where there is a lease of land and buildings and the title to the land is to be transferred to the lessee at the end of the short lease, generally the lease is treated as if
   (a) The land is a finance lease; the building is a finance lease.
   (b) The land is a finance lease; the building is an operating lease.
   (c) The land is an operating lease; the building is a finance lease.
   (d) The land is an operating lease; the building is an operating lease.

6. The lease of land and buildings when split causes difficulty in the allocation of the minimum lease payments. In this case the minimum lease payments should be split
   (a) According to the relative fair value of the two elements.
   (b) By the entity based on the useful life of the two elements.
   (c) Using the sum of the digits method.
   (d) According to any fair method devised by the entity.

7. An entity classifies a lease of land and buildings as an investment property under IAS 40. The entity has adopted the fair value model. In this case
   (a) Separate measurement of the lease of land and buildings is compulsory.
   (b) Separate measurement of the lease of land and buildings is not required.
   (c) The lease is treated as an operating lease.
   (d) The lease cannot be treated as an operating lease.

8. Which is the correct accounting for a finance lease in the accounts of the lessee (assuming fair value is used)?

(a) Dr Asset account
    Cr Liability account } with fair value
    Dr Statement of comprehensive income with
    Cr Asset account } depreciation of asset
    Dr Statement of comprehensive income } finance charge for period
    Cr Liability account
    Dr Liability account } cash paid in period
    Cr Cash

(b) Dr Liability account
    Cr Asset account } with fair value
    Dr Statement of comprehensive income with
    Cr Asset account } depreciation of asset
    Dr Liability account
    Cr Statement of comprehensive income } finance charge for period
    Dr Liability account } cash paid in period
    Cr Cash

(c) Dr Asset account
    Cr Liability account } with fair value
    Dr Asset account with
    Cr Statement of comprehensive income } depreciation of asset
    Dr Liability account
    Cr Statement of comprehensive income } finance charge for period
    Dr Liability account } cash paid in period
    Cr Cash

(d) Dr Asset account
    Cr Liability account } with fair value
    Dr Statement of comprehensive income with
    Cr Asset account } depreciation of asset
    Dr Liability account
    Cr Statement of comprehensive income } finance charge for period
    Dr Liability account } cash paid in period
    Cr Cash

9. Which is the correct accounting treatment for an operating lease payment in the accounts of the lessee?

(a) Dr Cash
    Cr Operating lease rentals/statement of comprehensive income

(b) Dr Operating lease rentals/statement of comprehensive income
    Cr Cash

(c) Dr Asset account
   Cr Cash
(d) Dr Cash
   Cr Asset account

10. Which is the correct accounting treatment for a finance lease in the accounts of a lessor?

(a) Treat as a noncurrent asset equal to net investment in lease. Recognize all finance payments in statement of comprehensive income.

(b) Treat as a receivable equal to gross amount receivable on lease. Recognize finance payments in cash and by reducing debtor.

(c) Treat as a receivable equal to net investment in the lease. Recognize finance payment by reducing debtor and taking interest to statement of comprehensive income.

(d) Treat as a receivable equal to net investment in the lease. Recognize finance payments in cash and by reduction of debtor.

11. The profit on a finance lease transaction for lessors who are manufacturers or dealers should

(a) Not be recognized separately from finance income.

(b) Be recognized in the normal way on the transaction.

(c) Only be recognized at the end of the lease term.

(d) Be allocated on a straight-line basis over the life of the lease.

12. In the case of sale and leaseback transactions, if the sale is at below the fair value of the assets and the loss is compensated by future lease payments, then the loss is

(a) Recognized immediately in reserves.

(b) Deferred and amortized over the useful life of the asset.

(c) Deferred until the end of the lease term.

(d) Recognized immediately in the profit and loss.

13. Lessors should show assets that are out on operating leases and income from there as follows:

(a) The asset should be kept off the statement of financial position and the lease income should go to reserves.

(b) The asset should be kept off the statement of financial position and the lease income should go to the statement of comprehensive income.

(c) The asset should be shown in the statement of financial position according to its nature and the lease income should go to reserves.

(d) The asset should be shown in the statement of financial position according to its nature with the lease income going to the statement of comprehensive income.

14. The current accounting standard IAS 17, *Leases*, was criticized for not reflecting current practice. Why was there a need to look to change IAS 17?

(a) The FASB wanted change.

(b) To ensure comparability and bring leasing finance onto the statement of financial position.

(c) For legal reasons.

(d) Because of the recent credit crisis.

15. What is the fundamental principle that is driving the proposed leasing standard?

(a) All leases should be treated as if they were finance leases.

(b) All leases should be treated as if they were operating leases.

(c) All leases should be off statement of financial position.

(d) All leases should be treated as intangible assets.

16. On what basis would the lessee recognize a leasing asset in the statement of financial position?

(a) Ownership.

(b) Right to receive rental payments.

(c) Right to use the asset.

(d) On signing a contractual agreement.

Chapter 12

REVENUE (IAS 18)

BACKGROUND AND INTRODUCTION

The *Framework for the Preparation and Presentation of Financial Statements* defines "income" as "increases in economic benefits during the accounting period in the form of inflows or enhancements of assets or decreases of liabilities that result in increases in equity, other than those relating to contributions from equity participants." Income encompasses *both* revenue and gains.

"Revenue" should be distinguished from "gains." Revenue arises from an entity's ordinary activities. Gains, however, include such items as the profit on disposal of noncurrent assets, or on retranslating balances in foreign currencies, or fair value adjustments to financial and nonfinancial assets.

This Standard prescribes the requirements for the recognition of revenue in an entity's financial statements. Revenue can take various forms, such as sales of goods, provision of services, royalty fees, franchise fees, management fees, dividends, interest, subscriptions, and so on.

The principal issue in the recognition of revenue is its *timing*—at what point is it probable that future economic benefit will flow to the entity and can the benefit be measured reliably.

Some of the recent highly publicized financial scandals that caused turmoil in the financial world globally were allegedly the result of financial manipulations resulting from recognizing revenue based on inappropriate accounting policies. Such financial shenanigans resulting from the use of aggressive revenue recognition policies have drawn the attention of the accounting world to the importance of accounting for revenue.

It is absolutely critical that the point of recognition of revenue is properly determined. For instance, in the case of sale of goods, is revenue to be recognized on receipt of the customer order, on completion of production, on the date of shipment, or on delivery of goods to the customer? The decision as to when and how revenue should be recognized has a significant impact on the determination of "net income" for the year (i.e., the "bottom line"), and thus it is a very critical element in the entire process of the preparation of the financial statements.

SCOPE

The requirements of IAS 18 are to be applied in accounting for revenue arising from

- Sale of goods
- Rendering of services

- The use by others of the entity's assets thus yielding interest, royalties, or dividends

The Standard does not deal with revenue arising from the following items, as they are dealt with by other Standards:

- Leases (IAS 17)
- Dividends from investments accounted under the equity method (IAS 28)
- Insurance contracts (IFRS 4)
- Changes in fair values of financial instruments (IAS 39)
- Changes in the values of current assets
- Initial recognition and changes in value of biological assets (IAS 41)
- Initial recognition of agricultural produce (IAS 41)
- Extraction of minerals

DEFINITIONS OF KEY TERMS
(in accordance with IAS 18)

Revenue. The gross inflow of economic benefits *during a period* arising in the course of ordinary activities when those inflows result in increases in equity, other than increases relating to contributions from equity participants.

Fair value. The amount for which an asset can be exchanged, or a liability settled, between knowledgeable, willing parties in an arm's-length transaction.

PRACTICAL INSIGHT

"Revenue" refers only to those amounts received or receivable by an entity on its own account. Amounts received or receivable for the accounts of others are not classified as income as there is no increase in equity; such items are liabilities. Examples include sales taxes (amounts owed to the government), insurance premiums collected by an agent (revenue in this case would be the commission), and the like.

MEASUREMENT OF REVENUE

Revenue is to be measured at the fair value of the consideration received or receivable. In most cases, the value is easily determined by the sales contract after taking into account trade discounts or rebates.

CASE STUDY 1

Facts

Big Bulk has arrangements with its customers that, in any 12-month period ending March 31, if they purchase goods for a value of at least $1 million, they will receive a retrospective discount of 2%. Big Bulk's year-end is December 31, and it has made sales to a customer during the period April 1 to December 31 of $900,000.

Required

How much revenue should Big Bulk recognize?

Solution

Based on a prorated calculation, Big Bulk will make sales to its customers of $1.2 million ($900,000 × 12/9). Therefore, Big Bulk should accrue a retrospective rebate of 2% on $900,000 and recognize revenue of $882,000.

However, transactions can be more complex, for example, if longer-than-normal credit is offered at below-market rates of interest or if assets are exchanged. In both cases, the transaction needs to be carefully analyzed.

CASE STUDY 2

Facts

Nice Guy Inc. sells goods with a cost of $100,000 to Start-up Co. for $140,000 and a credit period of six months. Nice Guy Inc.'s normal cash price would have been $125,000 with a credit period of one month or with a $5,000 discount for cash on delivery.

Required

How should Nice Guy Inc. measure the income from the transaction?

Solution

Effectively, Nice Guy Inc. is financing Start-up Co. for a period of six months. The normal price would have been $120,000 ($125,000 – the cash discount of $5,000). Therefore, revenue should be accounted at an amount that discounts the actual sale amount of $140,000 back to $120,000.

The difference between the nominal amount of $140,000 and the discounted value would be recognized as interest income over the period of finance of six months.

The exchange of goods or services needs to be examined differently. If goods or services of similar nature and value are exchanged, essentially no transaction has occurred and no revenue is recognized.

If, however, goods or services of a dissimilar nature are exchanged, a revenue transaction is recognized at the fair value of the goods or services received. If such fair value is not readily determinable, revenue is recognized at the fair value of the goods given up or services provided. In both cases, revenue is adjusted for any cash or cash equivalents transferred.

SIC 31 deals with barter transactions involving advertising services. The Interpretation applies to the measurement of fair value of revenue from these barter transactions. It states that such revenue can be measured only by reference to nonbarter transactions that

- Involve advertising similar to the advertising in the barter transaction
- Occur frequently
- Represent a predominant number of transactions and amount when compared to nonbarter transactions to provide advertising that is similar to advertising in barter transactions
- Involve cash and/or another form of consideration (e.g., marketable securities) that has a reliably measurable fair value
- Do not involve the same counterpart as in the barter transaction

IDENTIFICATION OF A TRANSACTION

Usually when applying the recognition criteria of the Standard, one applies it to each transaction. However, occasions arise with more complex transactions when the criteria need to be applied to *components* of a transaction.

CASE STUDY 3

Facts

Full Service Co. sells some equipment, the cash price of which is $100,000, for $140,000 with a commitment to service the equipment for a period of two years, with no further charge.

Solution

Full Service Co. would recognize revenue on the sale of goods of $100,000. The balance of $40,000 would be recognized over two years as service revenue.

SALE OF GOODS

The Standard prescribes that revenue from the sale of goods should be recognized when *all* of the following criteria are satisfied:

- The significant risks and rewards of ownership of the goods have been transferred to the buyer.
- The seller retains neither continuing managerial involvement to the degree usually associated with ownership nor effective control over the goods sold.
- The amount of the revenue can be reliably measured.
- It is probable that economic benefits associated with the transaction will flow to the seller.
- The costs incurred or to be incurred in respect of the transaction can be measured reliably.

The transfer of "significant" risks and rewards is essential. For example, if goods are sold but the receivable will be collected only if the buyer is able to sell, then "significant" risks of ownership are retained by the original seller and no sale is recognized.

The point of time at which significant risks and rewards of ownership transfer to the buyer requires careful consideration involving examining the circumstances surrounding the transaction. Generally, the transfer of significant risks and rewards of ownership takes place when title passes to the buyer or the buyer receives possession of the goods. However, in some circumstances, the transfer of risks and rewards of ownership does not coincide with transfer of legal title or the passing of possession, as when a building that is still under construction is sold.

PRACTICAL INSIGHT

In the case of retail sales, wherein customers have a right to return the goods or right to seek a refund, the retention of risks and rewards is not considered that "significant" that revenue from the sale of goods is *not* recognized at the point when goods are sold to the customers. The risk not transferred is the risk of goods sold being returned by customers or the risk of customers seeking refunds. Revenue in such a situation is recognized at the time of sale provided the seller can reliably estimate future returns (based on some rational basis, such as past experience and other pertinent factors) and recognize a provision under IAS 37.

Furthermore, the *costs* incurred in respect of the transaction must be reliably measured.

CASE STUDY 4

Facts

Bespoke Inc. has manufactured a machine specifically to the design of its customer. The machine could not be used by any other party. Bespoke Inc. has never manufactured this type of machine before and expects a number of faults to materialize in its operation during its first year of use, which Bespoke Inc. is contractually bound to rectify at no further cost to the customer. The nature of these faults could well be significant. As of Bespoke Inc.'s year-end, the machine had been delivered and installed, the customer invoiced for $100,000 (the contract price), and the costs incurred by Bespoke Inc. up to that date amounted to $65,000.

Required

How should Bespoke Inc. recognize this transaction?

Solution

As Bespoke Inc. has not manufactured this type of machine earlier, it is not in a position to reliably measure the cost of rectification of any faults that may materialize. Consequently, the cost to Bespoke Inc. of the transaction cannot be reliably measured and no sale should be recognized.

Very often, contracts for the sale of goods can be *subject to conditions*, such as

- Subject to inspection and/or installation. If installation is a quick and simple process (i.e., it forms an insignificant part of the sales contract), revenue can be recognized on delivery.
- On approval with a right of return. The contract is recognized when goods are accepted or a period of right of return has lapsed.
- On consignment. The contract is recognized only when the consignee has sold the goods.
- Cash on delivery. The contract is recognized when cash is received.
- "Layaway" when goods are delivered on final installment. If history shows that full payment is normally received, revenue could be recognized when a significant deposit is received and the goods are on hand and ready for delivery. Otherwise revenue would be recognized only on delivery.

In other words, if the seller retains significant risks of ownership, the transaction is not regarded as a sale for the purposes of recognizing revenue. A seller may retain significant risks of ownership, which may be manifested in numerous ways. The next case study shows circumstances wherein the seller retains significant risks of ownership.

CASE STUDY 5

Which of the following situations signify that "risks and rewards" have **not** been transferred to the buyer?

1. XYZ Inc. sells goods to ABC Inc. In the sales contract, there is a clause that the seller has an obligation for unsatisfactory performance, which is not governed by normal warranty provisions.
2. Zeta Inc. shipped machinery to a destination specified by the buyer. A significant part of the transaction involves installation that has not yet been fulfilled by Zeta Inc.
3. The buyer has the right to cancel the purchase for a reason not specified in the contract of sale (duly signed by both parties) and the seller is uncertain about the outcome.

Solution

1. According to the clause in the sales contract, XYZ Inc. has an obligation beyond the normal warranty provision. Thus "risks and rewards of ownership" have not been transferred to the buyer on the date of the sale.
2. "Risks and rewards of ownership" have not been transferred to the buyer on the date of the delivery of the machinery because a significant part of the transaction (i.e., installation) is yet to be done.
3. "Risks and rewards of ownership" will not be transferred to the buyer due to the "unspecified uncertainty" arising from the terms of the contract of sale (duly signed by both parties), which allow the buyer to retain the right of cancellation of the sale due to which the seller is uncertain of the outcome.

A transaction is not deemed a sale until it is probable that the future economic benefits will flow to the entity. In some of the cases, the receipt of consideration may be doubtful. Until the uncertainty is removed, the sale should not be recognized.

PRACTICAL INSIGHT

When uncertainty arises about collectability of revenue booked in an earlier period, then the uncollectible amount is to be recognized as an expense as opposed to adjusting the revenue originally recognized in an earlier period.

Revenues recognized and the costs (expenses) associated with them should be matched and recognized simultaneously—this is essential because if costs cannot be measured reliably, then the related revenue should not be recognized. In such a situation, any consideration received from such transactions is booked as a liability.

RENDERING OF SERVICES

Revenue from the rendering of services can be recognized by reference to the stage of completion if the final outcome can be reliably estimated. This would be the case if

- The amount of revenue can be measured reliably.
- It is probable that economic benefits associated with the transaction will flow to the seller.
- The stage of completion can be measured reliably.
- The costs incurred and the cost to complete can be measured reliably.

This method of revenue recognition mirrors that prescribed by IAS 11 for construction contracts. The requirements laid down in that Standard are just as applicable for the rendering of services, such as robust budgeting and costing systems. The methodologies for estimating the proportion of service rendered, such as surveys, or the ratio of costs incurred to estimate total costs are also similar. Additionally, if the outcome cannot be reliably estimated, then revenue is recognized only to the extent that costs are recoverable.

Examples

- Installation fees are recognized over the period of installation by reference to the stage of completion.
- Subscriptions usually are recognized on a straight-line basis over the subscription period.
- Insurance agency commissions would be recognized on commencement of the insurance *unless* the agent is likely to have to provide further services, in which case a portion of the revenue would be deferred to cover the cost of providing that service.
- Fees from development of customized software are recognized by reference to stage of completion, including postdelivery support.
- Event admission fees are recognized when the event occurs. If subscription to a number of events is sold, the fee is allocated to each event.
- Tuition fees would be recognized over the period in which tuition is provided.
- Financial service fees depend on the services that are being rendered. Very often they are treated as an adjustment to the effective interest rate on the financial instrument that is being created. This would be the case for origination and commitment fees. Investment management fees would be recognized over the period of management.

INTEREST, ROYALTIES, AND DIVIDENDS

Revenue arising from the use by others of an entity's asset that yield interest, dividends, or royalties are recognized in this way:

- Interest is recognized using the "effective interest method."
- Royalties are recognized on an accruals basis in accordance with the royalty agreement.
- Dividends are recognized when the shareholder has a right to receive payment.

The cost of acquisition of debt instruments and shares needs to be examined carefully. Very often the cost includes accrued interest or shares may be *cum div* or with dividends. In this case, the subsequent receipt of interest or dividends will need to be allocated against the cost of the instrument rather than recognized as revenue. Similarly, receipt of dividends out of preacquisition reserves of subsidiary or associate would be treated as a reduction in the cost of the investment and not as revenue.

DISCLOSURES

The Standard requires the following disclosures:

- The accounting policies adopted for the recognition of revenue, including the methods for determining stage of completion for the rendering of services
- The amount of each significant category of revenue recognized during the period, including

  - Sale of goods
  - Rendering of services
  - Interest
  - Royalties
  - Dividends

- The amount of revenue recognized from the exchange of goods or services included in each category

IFRIC 12, *SERVICE CONCESSION ARRANGEMENTS*

A service concession arrangement is an arrangement whereby a government or other public-sector body contracts with a private operator to develop (or upgrade), operate, and maintain the grantor's infrastructure assets such as roads, bridges, tunnels, airports, energy distribution networks, prisons, or hospitals. The grantor controls or regulates what services the operator must provide using the assets, to whom, and at what price, and also controls any significant residual interest in the assets at the end of the term of the arrangement.

The objective of IFRIC 12 is to clarify how certain aspects of IFRS are to be applied to service concession arrangements. IFRIC 12 draws a distinction between two types of service concession arrangements. The first type is where the operator receives a financial asset, specifically an unconditional contractual right to receive a specified or determinable amount of cash or another financial asset from the government in return for constructing or upgrading a public-sector asset, and then operating and maintaining the asset for a specified period of time. This category includes guarantees by the government to pay for any shortfall between amounts received from users of the public service and specified or determinable amounts.

The second type is where the operator receives an intangible asset that is a right to charge for use of a public-sector asset that it constructs or upgrades and then must operate and maintain for a specified period of time. A right to charge users is not an unconditional right to receive cash, because the amounts are contingent on the extent to which the public uses the service.

IFRIC 12 allows for the possibility that both types of arrangement may exist within a single contract: to the extent that the government has given an unconditional guarantee of payment for the construction of the public-sector asset, the operator has a financial asset; to the extent that the operator has to rely on the public using the service in order to obtain payment, the operator has an intangible asset.

Financial Asset Model

The operator recognizes a financial asset to the extent that it has an unconditional contractual right to receive cash or another financial asset from or at the direction of the grantor for the construction services. The operator has an unconditional right to receive cash if the grantor contractually guarantees to pay the operator

1. Specified or determinable amounts
2. The shortfall, if any, between amounts received from users of the public service and specified or determinable amounts, even if payment is contingent on the operator ensuring that the infrastructure meets specified quality or efficiency requirements

The operator measures the financial asset at fair value.

Intangible Asset Model

The operator recognizes an intangible asset to the extent that it receives a right (a license) to charge users of the public service. A right to charge users of the public service is not an unconditional right to receive cash because the amounts are contingent on the extent that the public uses the service.

The operator measures the intangible asset at fair value.

Operating Revenue

The operator of a service concession arrangement recognizes and measures revenue in accordance with IAS 11 and 18 for the services it performs.

Accounting by the Government (Grantor)

IFRIC 12 does not address accounting for the government side of service concession arrangements. IFRIC 12 is effective for annual periods beginning on or after January 1, 2008.

IFRIC 13, *CUSTOMER LOYALTY PROGRAMS*

This Interpretation applies to customer loyalty award credits that

1. An entity grants to its customers as part of a sales transaction (i.e., a sale of goods, rendering of services, or use by a customer of entity assets).
2. Subject to meeting any further qualifying conditions, the customers can redeem in the future for free or discounted goods or services.

This Interpretation addresses accounting by the entity that grants award credits to its customers as incentive to buy their goods and services.

According to the consensus in IFRIC 13

- An entity shall apply IAS 18 and account for award credits as a separately identifiable component of the sales transaction(s) in which they are granted (the "initial sale").
- The fair value of the consideration received or receivable in respect of the initial sale shall be allocated between the award credits and the other components of the sale.
- The consideration allocated to the award credits shall be measured by reference to their fair value, (i.e., the amount for which the award credits could be sold separately).

Effective date: This IFRIC was issued in June 2007 and is effective for annual periods beginning on or after July 1, 2008. Earlier application is permitted.

CASE STUDY 6

Facts

Locond, an airline, operates a customer loyalty program in which members are granted "loyalty points" when they buy airline tickets. Members can redeem the points for air travel or other services with Locond or with its partner companies participating in the program, which include certain airline companies, credit card companies, hotel chains, and car rental companies. In its previous financial statements, the accounting treatment for these points had been as follows:

The estimated value of all the points outstanding was calculated as the estimated value of a point multiplied by the number of points granted, not yet redeemed.

The estimated value of a point was not the fair value but was an estimate based on the specific terms and conditions of the program.

The estimated value of all the points was recognized as a deduction against revenue (not as an expense) and recognized as a liability on the statement of financial position and described as deferred revenue.

The revenue for these points was recognized when the points were redeemed.

Up to March 31, 20X9, the value of a point had been calculated as a weighted-average of three components.

1. A component reflecting those points which were going to be redeemed with Locond: the value of this component was based on the discounted incremental cost of the passenger carried (e.g., catering, ticket issue costs, etc.).
2. A component reflecting those points which were going to be redeemed with a partner: the value of the component was based on the billing from Locond's partners in the program.
3. A component reflecting those points which were never going to be redeemed and to which no value was attributed.

The weighting of each component was based on Locond's historic data of how the points had been redeemed in practice.

Locond chose to apply IFRIC 13 as of April 1, 20X9. The main impact for Locond was that the points now had to be measured at their fair value.

Locond retained the same 3 components but changed the method used to measure the component reflecting those points which will be redeemed with Locond to fair value, the fair value being based on the "average" fare of Locond. The extra cost for fuel is excluded as the client usually pays for this extra charge.

Required

Discuss the above accounting treatment by Locond.

Solution

The accounting treatment adopted by Locond complies with the requirements of IFRIC 13, specifically, that the points were accounted for at their fair value.

Paragraph 6 of the IFRIC requires that the consideration allocated to the award credits be measured by reference to their fair value (i.e., the amount for which the award credits could be sold separately). Paragraph AG 2 clarifies that the fair value of the points should be reduced to take account of the proportion of awards that are not expected to be redeemed.

AMENDMENT TO IAS 18 ANNUAL IMPROVEMENTS 2009

Determining Whether an Entity Is Acting as a Principal or as an Agent

Paragraph 8 states that "in an agency relationship, the gross inflows of economic benefits include amounts collected on behalf of the principal and which do not result in increases in equity for the entity. The amounts collected on behalf of the principal are not revenue. Instead, revenue is the amount of commission."

Determining whether an entity is acting as a principal or an agent depends on facts and circumstances and requires judgment. An entity is acting as a principal when it has exposure to the significant risks and rewards associated with the sale of goods or the rendering of services. Features that, individually or in combination, may indicate that an entity is acting as a principal include

1. The entity has the primary responsibility for providing the goods or services desired by the customer or for fulfilling the order, for example by being responsible for the acceptability of the products or services ordered or purchased by the customer.
2. The entity has inventory risk before or after the customer order, during shipping or on return.
3. The entity has discretion in establishing prices directly or indirectly, such as by providing additional goods or services.
4. The entity has credit risk.

An entity is acting as an agent when it does not have exposure to the significant risks and rewards associated with the sale of goods or the rendering of services. One feature that may indicate that an entity is acting as an agent is that the amount the entity earns is predetermined, being either a fixed fee per transaction or a stated percentage of the amount billed to the customer.

The IASB and the FASB are undertaking a joint project to develop a revenue model that would apply to all industries and all types of revenue-generating transactions. This new standard will replace IAS 11, *Construction Contracts,* and IAS 18, *Revenue.* The IASB issued DP *Preliminary Views on Revenue Recognition in Contracts with Customers* in December 2008. The IASB issued ED/2010/6 *Revenue from Contracts with Customers* in June of 2010.

The two fundamental issues highlighted relate to the application of the guidance on "control" and "separation." As currently described in the ED, constituents believe the notion of control is not sufficiently clear to allow entities to determine when control has transferred to the customer and therefore when revenue should be recognized. The second fundamental issue relates to the identification of separate performance obligations within a contract. Many believe the guidance in the ED is impractical and may not result in useful information.

IFRIC 15, *AGREEMENTS FOR THE CONSTRUCTION OF REAL ESTATE*

Agreements for the construction of real estate are widespread and may relate to residential, commercial, or industrial developments. Construction often spans more than one accounting period, it may take place on land the buyer owns or leases before construction begins, and agreements may require progress payments. The objectives of the Interpretation are to clarify the definition of a construction contract and the articulation between IAS 11 and IAS 18 and to provide guidance on how to account for revenue when the agreement for the construction of real estate falls within the scope of IAS 18.

IFRIC 15 addresses the accounting for revenue and associated expenses by entities that undertake the construction of real estate directly or through subcontractors. It clarifies how these revenues and expenses should be recognized if an agreement between a developer and a buyer is reached before the construction of the real estate is completed.

It is common practice for real estate developers to market their developments well before the start of any construction, and this activity continues throughout the construction period. Some real estate developers recognize revenue from these arrangements as construction progresses by reference to the stage of completion of the development, while others recognize revenue only when the completed unit is handed over to the buyer.

Also, this interpretation provides guidance on how to determine whether an agreement is within the scope of IAS 11 or IAS 18.

There are three different revenue recognition approaches within existing standards that could potentially be applied to real estate marketed prior to the completing of construction.

It could be accounted for as any of the following three:

1. A construction contract in accordance with IAS 11.
2. The rendering of services in accordance with IAS 18.
3. The sale of goods in accordance with IAS 18.

The IFRIC states that where the agreement allows the buyer to specify major structural elements of design before or during construction, then the agreement should be considered to be a construction contract.

When construction takes place independently of the agreement and the buyer only has a limited ability to influence designs, the agreement should be considered to be in accordance with IAS 18.

Agreement for the Rendering of Services or Sale of Goods (IAS 18)

Where the agreement falls within the scope of IAS 18 and the entity is not required to acquire and supply construction materials, the agreement is for the rendering of services. The entity is responsible only for assembling materials supplied by others (i.e., it has no inventory risk for the construction materials) and therefore the constructor is rendering a service.

Revenue is recognized by reference to the stage of completion of the transaction using the percentage-of-completion method. As stated in IAS 18 paragraph 21, the requirements of IAS 11 are generally applicable to the recognition of revenue and the associated expenses for such a transaction.

When an agreement involves the provision of construction materials and labor and it does not fall to be accounted for as a construction contract under IAS 11, it will be an agreement for the sale of goods under IAS 18. The applicable recognition criteria are those set out in IAS 18, paragraph 14.

Revenue can only be recognized when the entity has transferred control and significant risks and rewards of ownership of the goods to the buyer, and the interpretation distinguishes between circumstances in which these two criteria are met:

1. At a single point in time, for example at completion or upon delivery. Revenue is recognized when the significant risks and rewards of ownership are transferred to the buyer and all the criteria are met in accordance with IAS 18, paragraph 14.
2. Continuously as construction progresses. It is noted in the Interpretation that agreements with continuous transfer might not be encountered frequently. However, one example of a situation, which would constitute a continuous transfer, is if the agreement is terminated before construction is complete. The buyer retains the work in progress and the entity has the right to be paid for the work to date. When the criteria are met continuously, revenue is recognized by reference to the stage of completion of the transaction using the percentage-of-completion method. As stated in IAS 18, paragraph 21, the requirements of IAS 11 are generally applicable to the recognition of revenue and the associated expenses for such a transaction.

This interpretation supersedes the current guidance for real estate in the Appendix to IAS 18. It is applicable retrospectively for annual periods beginning on or after January 1, 2009.

DISCLOSURES

When an entity recognizes revenue using the percentage-of-completion method for agreements that meet all the criteria in IAS 18 paragraph 14, continuously as construction progresses, the following three disclosures are required:

[IFRIC 15 paragraph 20]

> *1. How the entity determines which agreements meet all the criteria in IAS 18 continuously as construction progresses*
> *2. The amount of revenue arising from such arrangements in the period*
> *3. The methods used to determine the stage of completion of agreements in progress*

For any such agreements that are in progress at the reporting date, the aggregate amount of costs incurred and recognized profits (less recognized losses) to date, as well as the amount of advances received should be disclosed.

IFRIC 18, *TRANSFERS OF ASSETS FROM CUSTOMERS*

Sometimes an entity receives one or more noncash assets from its customers in return for goods or services that the entity agrees to provide to its customers using the asset(s) it receives. For example, a real estate developer (in this example, the customer) might construct an electricity substation and transfer that substation to an electricity network provider. The customer does that so that the persons to whom it will eventually sell the houses it is building will have a connection to an electricity network and will therefore be in a position to be supplied with electricity.

In some other cases, an entity will receive cash from its customers and will be required to use that cash to construct or acquire an asset that it will then use to provide goods or services to its customers. For example, an alternative arrangement to the one described in the real estate developer/electricity network provider example could be that the real estate developer asks the electricity network provider to build the substation and reimburses the network provider for that work.

IFRIC 18 provides guidance on the transfers of assets for entities that receive items of property, plant, and equipment (PPE). It addresses three issues: how to account for the transferred item, how to account for the credit side of the transfer transaction, and how to account for a transfer of cash that is used to construct or acquire an item of PPE in a transfer transaction.

IFRIC 18 explains that, if an entity receives an item of PPE in a transfer that falls within the scope of IFRIC 18, it should recognize that item as an asset if both the item meets the definition of an asset under the IASB's *Framework* and the recognition criteria for PPE are met. IFRIC 18 also explains that, when an entity first recognizes such an asset, it shall measure it at its fair value.

When an entity receives an asset in a transfer falling within the scope of IFRIC 18, it will do so in return for accepting some sort of obligation to provide goods or services. IFRIC 18 requires the fair value of the asset received to be credited to the statement of comprehensive income as revenue under IAS 18, *Revenue*.

When that revenue is recognized will depend on the exact obligation accepted and when that obligation is fulfilled. IFRIC 18 requires the entity that receives the asset to identify which services arise from the transfer transaction.

1. When only one service is identified, the entity recognizes revenue when that service is delivered in accordance with IAS 18, *Revenue*.
2. If more than one service is identified, the entity is required to allocate the fair value of the asset it receives to each of the identified services, and apply the recognition criteria of IAS 18 to each of those services.
3. When the service or one of those services is an ongoing type of service—such as ongoing access to a supply of goods or services—revenue is recognized based on the terms of the transfer transaction, although the period over which it is recognized shall not exceed the useful life of the transferred asset.

Sometimes an entity will receive a transfer in the form of cash from its customer that it must use to construct or acquire an asset that it will use to provide goods or services to its customer using that asset. The accounting for a cash transfer that IFRIC 18 requires is similar to the accounting for a noncash asset transfer as described previously. That is, the entity will recognize the item of PPE it constructs or acquires when the item of PPE meets the recognition requirements under IAS 16. The entity also recognizes revenue under IAS 18 when it has delivered the goods or services it has agreed to provide under the transfer transaction.

CASE STUDY 7

Facts

Locklomond plc designs and manages business solutions and IT infrastructures. Locklomond enters into contracts with both customers and suppliers. The supplier produces bug fixes and provides new releases and updates. Client complaints and requests are channeled through Locklomond's service department, which has a maintenance contract with the customer. The terms of the contract support accruals accounting by Locklomond.

Up to and including 20X8, Locklomond recognized revenue and related costs on standard software maintenance contracts when the customer was invoiced, which was at the beginning of the contract period. Midway through December 20X8, Locklomond acquired an entity, which recognized revenue derived from a similar type of maintenance contract as Locklomond on a straight-line basis over the term of the contract.

Locklomond considered both policies to comply with the requirements of IAS 18, paragraph 20, but on advice, and in response to analyst comment, it decided to adopt the practice of the entity for the group. Locklomond concluded that the two recognition methodologies did not, in substance, represent two different accounting policies and did not, therefore, consider adoption of the new practice to be a change in policy.

Locklomond presented the change as a change in accounting estimate as, in its view, its previous policy complied with the standard and did not breach any of its requirements. From 20X9, Locklomond recognized revenue and the related costs on a straight-line basis over the contract term, presenting the change as a change in an accounting estimate.

As a result, revenue and cost of sales were adjusted by $18 million and $12 million respectively in 20X9, reducing that year's profits by $6 million.

Required

Discuss the above accounting treatment.

Solution

The change in accounting treatment should have been presented as a correction of an error in accordance with IAS 8, as the previous policy applied was not in accordance with paragraph 20 of IAS 18, *Revenue*, which requires revenue arising from transactions involving the rendering of services to be recognized with reference to the stage of completion at the statement of financial position date.

The change in accounting treatment should not be accounted for as a change in estimate. According to IAS 8, paragraph 5, changes in an accounting estimate result from changes in circumstances, new information, or more experience, which was not the case in this instance.

IAS 18, paragraph 20, requires that revenue associated with the rendering of a service should be recognized by reference to the stage of completion of the transaction at the end of the reporting period, provided that the outcome of the transaction can be estimated reliably. IAS 18, paragraph 26, states that, when the outcome cannot be estimated reliably, revenue should be recognized only to the extent that expenses are recoverable.

Given that the maintenance contract with the customer involved the rendering of services over a period, the previous policy applied of recognizing revenue on invoice at the commencement of the contract did not comply with IAS 18. The subsequent change in policy to one which recognized revenue over the contract term, therefore, was the correction of an error rather than a change in estimate and should have been presented as such in accordance with IAS 8 and been effected retrospectively.

EXTRACTS FROM PUBLISHED FINANCIAL STATEMENTS

VODAPHONE PLC Annual Report, March 31, 2010

Revenue Recognition and Presentation

Arrangements with multiple deliverables

In revenue arrangements including more than one deliverable, the deliverables are assigned to one or more separate units of accounting and the arrangement consideration is allocated to each unit of accounting based on its relative fair value.

Determining the fair value of each deliverable can require complex estimates due to the nature of the goods and services provided. The Group generally determines the fair value of individual elements based on prices at which the deliverable is regularly sold on a stand-alone basis after considering volume discounts where appropriate.

Presentation: gross versus net

When deciding the most appropriate basis for presenting revenue or costs of revenue, both the legal form and substance of the agreement between the Group and its business partners are reviewed to determine each party's respective role in the transaction.

Where the Group's role in a transaction is that of principal, revenue is recognized on a gross basis. This requires revenue to comprise the gross value of the transaction billed to the customer, after trade discounts, with any related expenditure charged as an operating cost.

Where the Group's role in a transaction is that of an agent, revenue is recognized on a net basis with revenue representing the margin earned.

J. SAINSBURY PLC Financial Statements to March 21, 2009

Revenue

Revenue consists of sales through retail outlets and excludes Value Added Tax. Sales through retail outlets are shown net of the cost of Nectar reward points issued and redeemed, staff discounts, vouchers and sales made on an agency basis. Commission income is recognized in revenue based on the terms of the contract.

Revenue is recognized when the significant risks and rewards of products and services have been passed to the buyer and can be measured reliably.

Interest income is recognized in the income statement for all instruments measured at amortized cost using the effective interest method. This calculation takes into account interest received or paid, fees and commissions received or paid, that are integral to the yield as well as incremental transaction costs.

Fees and commissions earned by Sainsbury's Bank, that are not integral to the yield, are recognized in the income statement as the service is provided. Where there is a risk of potential claw back, an appropriate element of the insurance commission receivable is deferred and amortized over the expected average life of the underlying loan.

UNILEVER Annual Report, 2009

Revenue recognition

Turnover comprises sales of goods and services after deduction of discounts and sales taxes. It does not include sales between group companies. Discounts given by Unilever include rebates, price reductions and incentives given to customers, promotional couponing and trade communication costs.

Turnover is recognized when the risks and rewards of the underlying products and services have been substantially transferred to the customer. Revenue from services is recognized as the services are performed. Interest income is recognized as interest accrues using the effective interest method.

MULTIPLE-CHOICE QUESTIONS

1. "Bill and hold" sales, in which delivery is delayed at the buyer's request but the buyer assumes title and accepts invoicing, should be recognized when
  (a) The buyer makes an order.
  (b) The seller starts manufacturing the goods.
  (c) The title has been transferred but the goods are kept on the seller's premises.
  (d) It is probable that the delivery will be made, payment terms have been established, and the buyer has acknowledged the delivery instructions.

2. ABC Inc. is a large manufacturer of machines. XYZ Ltd., a major customer of ABC Inc., has placed an order for a special machine for which it has given a deposit of €112,500 to ABC Inc. The parties have agreed on a price for the machine of €150,000. As per the terms of the sales agreement, it is an FOB (free on board) contract and the title passes to the buyer when goods are loaded onto the ship at the port. When should the revenue be recognized by ABC Inc.?
  (a) When the customer orders the machine.
  (b) When the deposit is received.
  (c) When the machine is loaded on the port.
  (d) When the machine has been received by the customer.

3. Revenue from an artistic performance is recognized once
  (a) The audience registers for the event online.
  (b) The tickets for the concert are sold.
  (c) Cash has been received from the ticket sales.
  (d) The event takes place.

4. X Ltd., a large manufacturer of cosmetics, sells merchandise to Y Ltd., a retailer, which in turn sells the goods to the public at large through its chain of retail outlets. Y Ltd. purchases merchandise from X Ltd. under a consignment contract. When should revenue from the sale of merchandise to Y Ltd. be recognized by X Ltd.?
  (a) When goods are delivered to Y Ltd.
  (b) When goods are sold by Y Ltd.
  (c) It will depend on the terms of delivery of the merchandise by X Ltd. to Y Ltd. (i.e., CIF [cost, insurance, and freight] or FOB).
  (d) It will depend on the terms of payment between Y Ltd. and X Ltd. (i.e., cash or credit).

5. M Ltd, a new company manufacturing and selling consumable products, has come out with an offer to refund the cost of purchase within one month of sale if the customer is not satisfied with the product. When should M Ltd. recognize the revenue?
  (a) When goods are sold to the customers.
  (b) After one month of sale.
  (c) Only if goods are not returned by the customers after the period of one month.
  (d) At the time of sale along with an offset to revenue of the liability of the same amount for the possibility of the return.

6. Micrium, a computer chip manufacturing company, sells its products to its distributors for onward sales to the ultimate customers. Due to frequent fluctuations in the market prices for these goods, Micrium has a "price protection" clause in the distributor agreement that entitles it to raise additional billings in case of upward price movement. Another clause in the distributor's agreement is that Micrium can at any time reduce its inventory by buying back goods at the cost at which it sold the goods to the distributor. Distributors pay for the goods within 60 days from the sale of goods to them. When should Micrium recognize revenue on sale of goods to the distributors?
  (a) When the goods are sold to the distributors.
  (b) When the distributors pay to Micrium the cost of the goods (i.e., after 60 days of the sale of goods to the distributors).
  (c) When goods are sold to the distributor provided estimated additional revenue is also booked under the "protection clause" based on past experience.
  (d) When the distributor sells goods to the ultimate customers and there is no uncertainty with respect to the "price protection" clause or the buyback of goods.

7. Company XYZ Inc. manufacturers and sells standard machinery. One of the conditions in the sale contract is that installation of machinery will be undertaken by XYZ Inc. During December 2005, XYZ received a special onetime contract from ABC Ltd. to manufacture, install, and maintain customized machinery. It is the first time XYZ Inc. will be producing this kind of machinery, and it is expecting numerous changes that would need to be made to the machine after the installation is completed, which one period is described in the contract of sale as the "maintenance period." The total cost of making the changes during the maintenance period cannot be reasonably estimated at the time of the installation. When should the revenue from sale of this special machine be recognized?
  (a) When the machinery is produced.
  (b) When the machinery is produced and delivered.
  (c) When the installation is complete.

    (d) When the maintenance period as per the contract of sale expires.

8.   According to the consensus in IFRIC 13, an entity shall apply IAS 18 and account for award credits as a separately identifiable component of the sales transaction in which they are granted. The consideration allocated to the award credits shall be measured by reference to their
    (a) Cost.
    (b) Replacement value.
    (c) Fair value.
    (d) Net realizable value.

9.   IFRIC 18 provides guidance on the transfers of assets for entities that receive items of PPE. It addresses three issues. Which of the following issues does it not address?
    (a) How to account for the transferred item.
    (b) How to derecognize the item.
    (c) How to account for the credit side of the transfer transaction.
    (d) How to account for a transfer of cash that is used to construct or acquire an item of PPE.

10. An entity is acting as a principal when it has exposure to the significant risks and rewards associated with the sale of goods or the rendering of services. Which of the following features indicates that an entity is not acting as a principal?
    (a) The entity has the primary responsibility for providing the goods or services desired by the customer or for fulfilling the order, for example by being responsible for the acceptability of the products or services ordered or purchased by the customer.
    (b) The entity has inventory risk before or after the customer order, during shipping or on return.
    (c) The entity has discretion in establishing prices directly or indirectly, such as by providing additional goods or services.
    (d) The entity does not have the credit risk.

Chapter 13

EMPLOYEE BENEFITS (IAS 19)

SCOPE

This Standard sets out the accounting and disclosure by employers for employee benefits.
The Standard identifies four main categories of employee benefit:

1. Short-term employee benefits, such as wages, salaries, vocational holiday benefit, sick pay, profit sharing, or bonus plans paid within 12 months of the end of the period, and nonmonetary benefits, such as medical care and so on, for current employees.
2. Postemployment benefits, such as pensions, postemployment medical benefits, and postemployment life insurance.
3. Termination benefits, such as severance pay.
4. Other long-term employee benefits including long service leave or sabbatical leave.

Postemployment benefits are categorized as either defined contribution plans or defined benefit plans.

The distinction between short-term and long-term employee benefits is that short-term employee benefits are those that are due to be settled within 12 months of the end of the period in which the employee renders the related service. The Standard achieves this by using in IAS 19 the term "due to be settled" in the definition of short-term employee benefits rather than the term "fall due" and by using the term "are not due to be settled" in the definition of other long-term employee benefits rather than the term "do not fall due."

CASE STUDY 1

The salaried employees of A are entitled to 25 days paid leave each year. The entitlement accrues evenly over the year and unused leave may be carried forward for one year. The holiday year is the same as the financial year. At April 30, 20X0, A has 1800 salaried employees and the average unused holiday entitlement is four days per employee. 10% of employees leave without taking their entitlement and there is no cash payment when an employee leaves in respect of holiday entitlement. There are 260 working days in the year and the total annual salary cost is $29 million. No adjustment has been made in the financial statements for the above and there was no opening accrual required for holiday entitlement.

Required

What would be the accrual in the financial statements for holiday pay entitlement?

Solution

An accrual should be made under IAS 19:

1,800 employees × 4 days × 90%= 6,480 days
Number of working days = 260 days × 1,800 = 468,000
Accrual is 6,480/468,000 × $29 million = $401,538

DEFINITIONS OF KEY TERMS
(in accordance with IAS 19)

Multiemployer plan. Either a defined contribution or a defined benefit plan that pools the assets contributed by various companies that are not under common control and uses those assets to provide benefits to employees of more than one entity.

Present value of a defined benefit obligation. The present value before deducting any plan assets or any expected payments required to settle the obligation that has occurred as a result of the service of employees in the current and previous periods.

Current service cost. The increase in the present value of the defined benefit obligation that occurs as a result of employee service in the current period.

Interest cost. The increase in the period in the present value of the defined benefit obligation that arises because the benefits payable are one year closer to the settlement of the scheme.

Plan assets. Those assets held by the employee benefit fund, including any qualifying insurance policies.

Return on plan assets. The interest, dividends, and any other income that is derived from the plan assets together with any realized or unrealized gains or losses on those assets less the cost of administering the plan and any tax payable by the plan.

Actuarial gains and losses. Experience adjustments and the effects of any changes in actuarial assumptions. Experience adjustments are differences between the previous actuarial assumptions and what has actually happened.

Past service cost. The increased present value of a defined benefit obligation for employee service in previous periods that has arisen because of the introduction of changes to the benefits payable to employees. Past service costs may be positive or negative depending on whether the benefits are improved or reduced.

DEFINED CONTRIBUTION PLANS AND DEFINED BENEFIT PLANS—CLASSIFICATION

In defined contribution plans, an entity pays a fixed contribution into a separate entity (fund) and will have no legal or constructive obligation to pay further contributions if the fund does not have sufficient assets to pay employee benefits relating to employee service in the current and prior periods. An entity should recognize contributions to a defined contribution plan where an employee has rendered service in exchange for those contributions.

All other postemployment benefit plans are classified as defined benefit plans. Defined benefit plans can be unfunded, partly funded, or wholly funded.

DEFINED BENEFIT PLANS

IAS 19 requires an entity to account not only for its legal obligation to defined benefit plans but also for any constructive obligation that arises.

In accounting for defined benefit plans, an entity should determine the present value of any defined benefit obligation and the fair value of any plan assets with such regularity that the amount shown in the financial statements does not differ materially from the amounts that would be determined at the end of the reporting period.

Defined benefit plans should use the projected unit credit method to measure their obligations and costs.

DEFINED CONTRIBUTION PLANS

Under a defined contribution plan, payments or benefits provided to employees may be simply a distribution of total fund assets or a third party—for example, an insurance entity—may assume the obligation to provide the agreed level of payments or benefits to the employees. The employer is not required to make up any shortfall in the fund's assets.

CONTRASTING DEFINED BENEFIT AND DEFINED CONTRIBUTION

Under the defined benefits scheme, the benefits payable to the employees are not based solely on the amount of the contributions, as in a defined contribution scheme; rather, they are determined by the terms of the defined benefit plan.

This means that the risks remain with the employer, and the employer's obligation is to provide the agreed amount of benefits to current and former employees. The benefits normally are based on such factors as age, length of service, and compensation.

The employer retains the investment and actual risks of the plan. The accounting for defined benefit plans is more complex than defined contributions plans.

CASE STUDY 2

Facts

According to the pension plan of an entity, the employees and entity contribute 5% of the employee's salary to the plan, and the employee is guaranteed a return of the contributions plus 3% a year by the employer.

Required

What classification would be given to the above pension scheme?

Solution

It is a defined benefit plan, as the employer has guaranteed a fixed rate of return and therefore carries the risk.

ACCOUNTING FOR DEFINED CONTRIBUTION SCHEMES

The accounting for a defined contribution scheme is fairly simple because the employer's obligation for each period is determined by the amount that had to be contributed to the scheme for that period.

Contributions can be based on a formula that uses employee compensation as the basis for its calculation.

There are no actuarial assumptions required to measure the obligation or expense, and there are no actuarial gains or losses.

The employer recognizes the contribution payable at the end of each period based on employee service during that period. This amount is reduced by any payments made to employees in the period.

If the employer has made payments in excess of the required amount, this excess is treated as a prepayment to the extent that the excess will lead to reduction in future contributions or refund of cash.

ACCOUNTING FOR DEFINED BENEFIT PLANS

The obligation of an employer under a defined benefit plan is to provide an agreed amount of benefits to current and former employees in the future. Benefits may be in the form of cash payments or could be in-kind in terms of medical or other benefits.

Normally benefits will be based on age, length of service, and wage and salary levels. Pensions and other long-term benefits plans are basically measured in the same way. Actuarial gains and losses of long-term benefits plans other than pensions are reported immediately in net income.

The defined benefit plan can be unfunded, partially funded, or wholly funded by the employer. The employer contributes to a separate entity or fund that is legally separate from the reporting entity.

This fund then pays the benefits. The payment of benefits depends on the fund's financial position and the performance of its investments.

However, the payment of benefits will also depend on the employer's ability to pay and to make good any shortfall in the fund. The employer is essentially guaranteeing the fund's investment and actuarial risk.

Accounting for defined benefit plans is more complex because actuarial assumptions are needed to determine the obligation and the expenses. Often the actual results differ from those determined under the actuarial valuation method. The difference between these results creates actuarial gains and losses.

Discounting is used because the obligations often will be settled several years after the employee gives the service. Usually actuaries are employed to calculate the defined benefit obligation and also the current and past service costs.

KEY INFORMATION: DEFINED BENEFIT PLANS

The entity must determine certain key information for each material employee benefit plan. This information is required:

- A reliable estimate is required of the amount of the benefit that the employees have earned in the current and prior period for service rendered.
- That benefit must be discounted using the projected unit credit method in order to determine the present value of the defined benefit obligation and the current service cost.
- The fair value of any plan assets should be determined.
- The total amount of actuarial gains and losses and the amount of those actuarial gains and losses that are to be recognized must be calculated.
- The past service costs should be determined in cases in which there has been a change or an introduction of a plan.
- The resulting gain or loss should be calculated in cases in which a plan has been curtailed, changed, or settled.

The entity must account not only for its legal obligation but also for any constructive obligation that arises from any informal practices. For example, the situation could arise wherein the entity has no realistic alternative but to pay employee benefits even though the formal terms of a defined benefit plan may permit an entity to terminate its obligation under the plan.

CASE STUDY 3

Facts

A director of an entity receives a retirement benefit of 10% of his final salary per annum for his contractual period of three years. The director does not contribute to the scheme. His anticipated salary over the three years is Year 1 $100,000, Year 2 $120,000, and Year 3 $144,000. Assume a discount rate of 5%.

Required

Calculate the current service cost, the pension liability, and the interest cost for the three years.

Solution

Year	Salary	Current service cost	Discounted current service cost	Interest cost (5% × liability)	Liability brought forward	Liability at year-end
1	$ 100,000	$ 14,400	$13,061	$ --	$ --	$ 13,061
2	120,000	14,400	13,714	653	13,061	27,428
3	144,000	14,400	14,400	1,372	27,428	43,200
Total		43,200	41,175	2,025		

STATEMENT OF FINANCIAL POSITION

The amount recognized in the statement of financial position could be either an asset or a liability calculated at the statement of financial position date.

The amount recognized will be

- The present value of the defined benefit obligation, plus
- Any actuarial gains less losses not yet recognized because the gains and losses fall outside the limits of the corridor, minus
- Any past service cost not yet recognized, and minus
- The fair value of the plan assets at the statement of financial position date.

If the result of the preceding calculation is a positive amount, then a liability is incurred, and it is recorded in full in the statement of financial position.

Any negative amount is an asset that is subject to a recoverability test. The asset recognized is the lesser of the negative amount calculated above or the net total of

- Any unrecognized net actuarial losses and past service costs
- The present value of any benefits available in the form of refunds or reductions in future employer contributions to the plan

CASE STUDY 4

Facts

An entity has these balances relating to its defined benefit plan:

- Present value of the obligation: $33 million
- Fair value of plan assets: $37 million
- Actuarial losses: $3 million unrecognized
- Past service cost: $2 million unrecognized
- Present value of available future refunds and reduction in future contributions: $1 million

Required

Calculate the value that will be given to the net plan asset under IAS 19.

Solution

The negative amount (asset) determined under the Standard will be $33 million minus $37 million, minus $3 million, minus $2 million, which equals negative $9 million. The limit under IAS 19 is computed in this way: unrecognized actuarial losses of $3 million plus unrecognized past service cost of $2 million, plus the present value of available future refunds and reductions in future contributions of $1 million, which equals $6 million. The entity recognizes an asset of $6 million and discloses the fact that the limit has reduced the carrying amount of the asset by $3 million.

Any element of the asset that is not recognized in the statement of financial position must be disclosed. It is often difficult to determine the benefits available in the form of refunds or reductions in future employer contributions.

The control of pension and benefit plans is often dependent on national laws and regulations, which are unlikely to allow refunds to employers of overfunded amounts. The trustees of the pension plan are also unlikely to allow the management of an entity to reduce the contributions to a plan up to the limit of any overfunded amount.

PRACTICAL INSIGHT

Océ, NV, a Dutch entity, accounted for pension liabilities in accordance with IAS 19 for the first time in its accounts. The entity says that the adoption of IAS 19 results in more transparent reporting and reduces volatility of pension costs. A note discloses that comparative figures relating to pension disclosures are not available and that the effect of adopting IAS 19 is to increase the provision for pensions by €260 million and decrease net assets by €175 million.

STATEMENT OF COMPREHENSIVE INCOME

The amount of the expense or income for a particular period is determined by a number of factors. The pension expense is the net of these items:

1. Current service cost
2. Interest cost
3. The expected return on any plan assets and on any reimbursement rights
4. Actuarial gains and losses to the extent recognized
5. Past service cost to the extent that the Standard requires the entity to recognize it
6. The effect of any curtailments or settlements

MEASURING THE DEFINED BENEFIT OBLIGATION

The entity should use the projected unit credit method to determine the present value of its defined benefit obligation, the related current service cost, and past service cost.

This method looks at each period of service, which creates an additional increment of benefit entitlement. The method then measures each unit of benefit entitlement separately to build up the final obligation. The whole of the postemployment benefit obligation is discounted. The use of this method involves a number of actuarial assumptions. These assumptions are the entity's best estimate of the variables that will determine the final cost of the postemployment benefits provided. These variables include assumptions about mortality rates, change in retirement age, and financial assumptions, such as discount rates and benefit levels.

Any assumptions should be compatible, unbiased, and neither imprudent nor excessively conservative. The Standard provides guidance on certain key assumptions.

PLAN ASSETS

Plan assets are measured at fair value. Fair value is normally market value where available or an estimated value where it is not.

Fair value can be determined by discounting future expected cash flows using a discount rate that reflects risk and the maturity or expected disposal date of those assets. Plan assets specifically exclude:

1. Unpaid contributions due from the employer
2. Nontransferable financial instruments issued by the entity and held by the fund
3. Nonqualifying insurance policies

IAS 19's definition of "return on plan assets" was amended to clarify that the deduction of plan administration costs is appropriate only to the extent that they are not reflected in the measurement of the defined benefit obligation. In other words, the costs of administering the plan may be either recognized in the rate of return on plan assets or included in the actuarial assumptions used to measure the defined benefit obligation.

PENSION ASSETS AND LIABILITIES

Often an entity may have a number of employment benefit plans. Plan assets and plan liabilities from the different plans are normally presented separately in the statement of financial position.

The offsetting of assets and liabilities is permitted only where there is a legally enforceable right to use the surplus in one plan to settle the obligation in another. The employer also must intend to settle the obligations on a net basis or to realize the surplus in one plan and settle the obligation in another plan simultaneously.

Because of these requirements, it is unlikely that the offsetting of assets and liabilities will occur.

If an entity acquires another entity, then the purchaser recognizes the assets and liabilities arising from the acquiree's postemployment benefits at the present value of the defined benefit obligation less the fair value of any plan assets. At the acquisition date, the present value of the obligation includes

1. Actuarial gains and losses that arose before the acquisition date, whether inside or outside the 10% corridor
2. Past service costs that arise from benefit changes before the acquisition date
3. Amounts that had arisen under the transitional provisions that the acquiree had not recognized

When an entity first adopts this Standard, the entity will apply IAS 8, *Accounting Policies, Changes in Accounting Estimates, and Errors*. IAS 19 sets out the transitional arrangements in paragraphs 153 to 156.

CURTAILMENTS AND SETTLEMENTS

A curtailment occurs when an entity either reduces the number of employees covered by the plan or amends the terms of a defined benefit plan. An amendment would normally be such that a material element of future service by current employees will no longer qualify for benefits or will qualify for a reduction in benefits.

Curtailments are likely to have a significant impact on the entity's financial statements and often are linked to restructuring or reorganization. They should be recognized in the financial statements at the same time as the restructuring.

An entity settles its obligations when it enters into a transaction that eliminates a future legal and constructive obligation for part or all of the benefits provided under a defined benefit plan.

Settlements are usually lump-sum cash payments made to or on behalf of plan participants in exchange for the right to receive specified future benefits. A settlement occurs together with a curtailment if a plan is terminated such that the obligation is settled and the plan ceases to exist.

The plan does not cease to exist if the plan is replaced by a new plan that offers benefits that are in substance identical. If the entity acquires an insurance policy to fund some or all of the employee benefits, the acquisition of such a policy is not a settlement if the entity retains a legal or constructive obligation to pay further amounts if the insurance policy does not pay the employee benefits.

Where a curtailment relates to only some employees covered by the plan, the obligation is only partly settled, and any gain or loss calculated should include a proportionate share of the previously unrecognized past service cost and actuarial gains and losses.

The settlement gain and loss is based on

1. Any resultant change in defined benefit obligation
2. Any resultant change in the fair value of the plan assets
3. Any related actuarial gains and losses and past service cost that have not been recognized previously

Before determining the effect of a curtailment, the entity shall remeasure the obligation and plan assets using current actuarial assumptions.

IAS 19 was amended to clarify that a curtailment is considered to have occurred to the extent that benefit promises are impacted by future salary increases and a reduction in the present value of a defined benefit obligation results in a negative past service cost.

CASE STUDY 5

Facts

An entity closes down its subsidiary, and the employees of that subsidiary will earn no further pension benefits. The entity has a defined benefit obligation with a net present value of $20 million. The plan assets have a fair value of $16 million, and there are net cumulative and unrecognized actuarial gains of $8 million. The entity had adopted IAS 19 two years previously, and it has decided to recognize the increased liability of $10 million over a five-year period from that date. The curtailment reduces the net present value of the obligation by $2 million to $18 million.

Required

Calculate the curtailment gain and the net liability recognized in the statement of financial position after the curtailment.

Solution

	Before curtailment $m	Gain on curtailment $m	After curtailment $m
NPV of obligation	20	2	18
Fair value of plan assets	(16)	--	(16)
	4	(2)	2
Unrecognized actuarial gains	8	(0.8)	7.2
Unrecognized transitional amount (3/5 of 10)	(6)	0.6	(5.4)
Net liability in statement of financial position	6	(2.2)	3.8

ACTUARIAL GAINS AND LOSSES—DEFINED BENEFIT PLANS

An entity can recognize actuarial gains and losses in the following ways.

An entity should recognize a portion of its actuarial gains and losses as income or expense if the net cumulative unrecognized actuarial gains and losses at the end of the previous reporting period (i.e., at the beginning of the current financial year) exceeds the greater of

1. 10% of the present value of the defined benefit obligation at the beginning of the year
2. 10% of the fair value of the plan assets at the same date

These limits should be calculated and applied separately for each defined plan. The excess determined by this method is then divided by the expected average remaining lives of the employees in the plan.

An entity can adopt any other systematic method that results in a faster recognition of actuarial gains and losses, provided that the same basis is applied to both gains and losses and that the basis is applied consistently from period to period.

Entities have the option of recognizing actuarial gains and losses in full in the period in which they occur or in the statement of other comprehensive income. This must be done for all defined benefit plans and for all of its actuarial gains and losses.

CASE STUDY 6

Facts

An entity has a defined benefit pension plan. As of January 1, 20X9, these values relate to the pension scheme:

- Fair value of plan assets: $50 million
- Present value of defined benefit obligation: $45 million
- Cumulative unrecognized actuarial gains: $8 million
- Average remaining working lives of employees: 20 years

At the end of the period at December 31, 20X9, the fair value of the plan assets has risen by $5 million. The present value of the defined benefit obligation has risen by $3 million. The actuarial gain is $10 million, and the average remaining working lives of the employees is 20 years. The entity wishes to know the difference between the corridor approach and the full recognition of actuarial gains and losses.

Required

Show how the actuarial gain or loss for the period ending December 31, 20X9, could be recognized in the financial statements.

Solution

Corridor Approach

The entity must recognize the portion of the net actuarial gain or loss in excess of 10% of the greater of defined benefit obligation or the fair value of the plan assets at the beginning of the year.

Unrecognized actuarial gain at the beginning of the year was $8 million. The limit of the corridor is 10% of $50 million, or $5 million. The difference is $3 million, which divided by 20 years is $0.15 million.

Full Recognition Approach

Under this approach, the full amount of the actuarial gains ($10 million) will be recognized in the statement of recognized income and expense.

PRACTICAL INSIGHT
Georg Fisher AG, a Swiss entity, discloses in its accounts that under IAS 19, unrecognized actuarial losses amounted to 163 million Swiss francs, but these reduce to 60 million Swiss Francs when calculated in accordance with Swiss law. This difference is due to the fact that future salary and pension increases are excluded from the calculation under Swiss law but not under IAS 19.

IFRIC 14, *IAS 19—THE LIMIT ON A DEFINED BENEFIT ASSET, MINIMUM FUNDING REQUIREMENTS, AND THEIR INTERACTION*

In July 2007 the IASB issued IFRIC 14, which applies to all postemployment defined benefits and other long-term employee defined benefits. This Interpretation addresses three issues.

1. When should refunds or reductions in future contributions be regarded as available in accordance with paragraph 58 of IAS 19?

   According to the consensus, an entity shall determine the availability of a refund or a reduction in future contributions in accordance with the terms and conditions of the plan and any statutory requirements in the jurisdiction of the plan.

2. How might a minimum funding requirement affect the availability of reductions in future contributions?

   According to the consensus, an entity shall analyze any minimum funding requirement at a given date into contributions that are required to cover (a) any existing shortfall for past service on the minimum funding basis and (b) the future accrual of benefits.

3. When can a minimum funding requirement give rise to a liability?

   According to the consensus, if an entity has an obligation under a minimum funding requirement to pay contributions to cover an existing shortfall on the minimum funding basis in respect of services already received, the entity shall determine whether the contributions payable will be available as a refund or reduction in future contributions after they are paid into the plan. To the extent that the contributions payable will not be available after they are paid into the plan, the entity shall recognize a liability when the obligation arises. An entity shall apply paragraph 58A of IAS 19 before determining the liability in accordance with paragraph 24.

Effective date: Annual periods beginning on or after January 1, 2008. Earlier application is encouraged.

The IASB issued an amendment to IFRIC 14, *IAS 19—The Limit on a Defined Benefit Asset, Minimum Funding Requirements and Their Interaction.* The amendment, issued on November 26, 2009, removes an unintended consequence of IFRIC 14 related to voluntary pension prepayments when there is a minimum funding requirement. This amendment will affect a relatively small number of companies as mentioned above. Companies that have a defined benefit pension plan that is subject to a minimum funding requirement under local legislation and have prepaid (or expect to prepay) the minimum funding requirement in respect of future employee service, leading to a pension surplus, will be affected.

DISCLOSURE

The elements of the pension expense can be either segregated and presented as current service cost, interest cost, and return of plan assets or presented as a single amount within the statement of comprehensive income.

Sufficient disclosure is required to provide an understanding of the significance of the entity's employee benefit plans.

The pension disclosures are set out in paragraphs 120 to 143 of the Standard; they are extensive and quite detailed. Items that require disclosure are the accounting policy for recognizing actuarial gains and losses, description of the plan, components of the total expense in the statement of comprehensive income, principal actuarial assumptions used, reconciliation of the net liability for assets recognized in the statement of financial position from one year to the next, the funded status of the plan, the fair value of the plan assets for each category of the entity's own financial instruments, any property occupied or other assets used by the reporting entity, and disclosures about related-party transactions and contingencies.

On April 29, 2010, the IASB published for public comment an Exposure Draft (ED) of proposed amendments to IAS 19, *Employee Benefits*. The proposals would amend the accounting for defined benefit plans through which some employers provide long-term employee benefits, such as pensions and postemployment medical care. In defined benefit plans, employers bear the risk of increases in costs and of possible poor investment performance. The ED proposes improvements to the recognition, presentation, and disclosure of defined benefit plans. The ED does not address measurement of defined benefit plans or the accounting for contribution-based benefit promises.

Proposed amendments:

1. Immediate recognition of all estimated changes in the cost of providing defined benefits and all changes in the value of plan assets. This would eliminate the various methods currently in IAS 19, including the "corridor" method that allows deferral of some of those gains or losses.
2. A new presentation approach that would clearly distinguish between different types of gains and losses arising from defined benefit plans. The effect is to remove from IAS 19 the option for entities to recognize in profit or loss all changes in defined benefit obligations and in the fair value of plan assets.
3. Improved disclosures about matters such as the following four:

   a. The characteristics of the company's defined benefit plans
   b. The amounts recognized in the financial statements
   c. Risks arising from defined benefit plans
   d. Participation in multiemployer plans

The IASB revisited the ED in September 2010 in order to publish a final standard in March 2011. The amendments relating to termination benefits will be published with amendments arising from the ED to create a comprehensive package of amendments to the standard.

CASE STUDY 6

An entity has created a voluntary fund to provide retirement benefits for its employees who have more than seven years service and have a permanent contract with the entity. The entity has a history of paying benefits to its employees, which are adjusted for inflation. The entity has signed a contract with a pension fund to establish a fund for the employees. Contributions are paid by the entity and if the fund does not have enough assets to pay the pensions, the entity increases its contributions.

Required

Should the entity account for the fund as a defined benefit or defined contribution scheme?

Solution

The entity has a constructive obligation or possibly a legal obligation to pay contributions to the scheme. Informal practices can give rise to a constructive obligation where the entity has no realistic alternative but to pay employee benefits. IAS 19 explains that an entity should account not only for its legal obligation but also its constructive obligation. Therefore the fund should be accounted for as a defined benefit scheme.

CASE STUDY 7

Facts

This information related to a defined benefit plan for the year ended December 31, 20X9:

1. Current service cost of providing benefits for the year to December 31, 20X9: $30 million
2. Average remaining working life of employees: 10 years
3. Benefits paid to retired employees in the year: $31 million
4. Contributions paid to the fund: $21 million
5. Present value of obligation to provide benefits: $2,200 million at January 1, 20X9, and $2,500 million at December 31, 20X9
6. Fair value of plan assets: $2,100 million at January 1, 20X9, and $2,400 million at December 31, 20X9
7. Net cumulative unrecognized gains at January 1, 20X9: $252 million
8. Past service cost: $115 million. All of these benefits have vested.
9. Discount rates and expected rates of return on plan assets:

	January 1, 20X9	*January 1, 20X0*
Discount rate	5%	6%
Expected rate of return on plan assets	7%	8%

The entity wishes to use the corridor approach to recognizing actuarial gains and losses.

Required

Show the amounts that will be recognized in the statement of financial position and statement of comprehensive income for the year ended December 31, 20X9, under IAS 19, *Employee Benefits,* and the movement in the net liability in the statement of financial position.

Solution

	at December 31, 20X9 *$m*
Amounts recognized in statement of financial position:	
Present value of the obligation	2,500
Fair value of plan assets	(2,400)
	100
Unrecognized actuarial gains	336
Liability recognized in statement of financial position	436

	at December 31, 20X9
	$m
Expense recognized in statement of comprehensive income for year ended December 31, 20X9:	
Current service cost	30
Interest cost	110
Expected return on assets	(147)
Past service cost	115
Actuarial gain recognized	(3)
Expense in statement of comprehensive income	105

	$m
Movement in net liability in statement of financial position:	
Opening net liability (2,200 – 2,100 + 252)	352
Expense	105
Contributions	(21)
Closing liability	436

	$m
Changes in the present value of obligation and fair value of plan assets:	
Present value of obligation January 1, 20X9	2,200
Interest cost (5% of 2,200)	110
Current service cost	30
Past service cost	115
Benefits paid	(31)
Actuarial loss on obligation (balance)	76
Present value of obligation December 31, 20X9	2,500

	$m
Fair value of plan assets January 1, 20X9	2,100
Expected return on plan assets (7% of 2100)	147
Contributions	21
Benefits paid	(31)
Actuarial gain on plan assets (balance)	163
Fair value of plan assets December 31, 20X9	2,400

Using the Corridor Approach

	$m
Limits of corridor:	
Net cumulative unrecognized actuarial gains at January 1, 20X9	252
Limits of corridor (greater of 10% of 2200 [present value of obligation] and 2100 [fair value of plan assets] at January 1, 20X9)	(220)
Excess	32

Average remaining working lives of employees is ten years. Therefore, the actuarial gain to be recognized in the statement of comprehensive income is $32 million divided by 10, or $3.2 million.

	$m
Actuarial gains and losses recognized in statement of financial position	
Balance at January 1, 20X9	252
Actuarial loss on obligation	(76)
Actuarial gain—plan assets	163
	339
Actuarial gain to statement of comprehensive income	(3)
Unrecognized actuarial gain	336

EXTRACTS FROM PUBLISHED FINANCIAL STATEMENTS

J. SAINSBURY PLC Financial Statements to March 21, 2009

Employee costs

	2009 £m	2008 £m
Employee costs for the Group during the year amounted to:		
Wages and salaries, including bonus and termination benefits	1,758	1,682
Social security costs	121	116
Pension costs—defined contribution schemes	31	28
Pension costs—defined benefit schemes (note 31)	53	78
Share-based payments expense (note 32)	40	53
	2,003	1,957

	Number 000's	Number 000's
The average number of employees, including Directors, during the year were:		
Full-time	49.7	48.8
Part-time	98.8	99.1
	148.5	147.9
Full-time equivalent	97.3	96.6

All employees were employed in the United Kingdom for the periods presented.

Pensions

The Group operates various defined benefit and defined contribution pension schemes for its employees. A defined benefit scheme is a pension plan that defines an amount of pension benefit that an employee will receive on retirement. A defined contribution scheme is a pension plan under which the Group pays fixed contributions into a separate entity.

In respect of defined benefit pension schemes, the pension scheme surplus or deficit recognized in the statement of financial position represents the difference between the fair value of the plan assets and the present value of the defined benefit obligation at the statement of financial position date. The defined benefit obligation is actuarially calculated on an annual basis using the projected unit credit method. Plan assets are recorded at fair value.

STANDARD CHARTERED PLC Annual Report, 2009

Employee benefits

Pension obligations

The Group operates a number of pension and other postretirement benefit plans around the world, including defined contribution plans and defined benefit plans.

For defined contribution plans, the Group pays contributions to publicly or privately administered pension plans on a mandatory, contractual, or voluntary basis, and such amounts are charged to operating expenses. The Group has no further payment obligations once the contributions have been paid.

For funded defined benefit plans, the liability recognized in the statement of financial position is the present value of the defined benefit obligation at the statement of financial position date less the fair value of plan assets. For unfunded defined benefit plans the liability recognized at the statement of financial position date is the present value of the defined benefit obligation. The defined benefit obligation is calculated annually by independent actuaries using the projected unit method. The present value of the defined benefit obligation is determined by discounting the estimated future cash outflows using an interest rate equal to the yield on high quality corporate bonds that are denominated in the currency in which the benefits will be paid, and that have a term to maturity approximating to the term of the related pension liability.

Actuarial gains and losses that arise are recognized in shareholders' equity and presented in the statement of other comprehensive income in the period they arise. Past service costs are recognized immediately to the extent that benefits are vested and are otherwise recognized over the average period until benefits are vested on a straight-line basis. Current service costs and any past service costs, together with the unwinding of the discount on plan liabilities, offset by the expected return on plan assets where applicable, are charged to operating expenses.

Source: Standard Chartered PLC annual report 2009 © Standard Chartered PLC

MULTIPLE-CHOICE QUESTIONS

1. An entity contributes to an industrial pension plan that provides a pension arrangement for its employees. A large number of other employers also contribute to the pension plan, and the entity makes contributions in respect of each employee. These contributions are kept separate from corporate assets and are used together with any investment income to purchase annuities for retired employees. The only obligation of the entity is to pay the annual contributions. This pension scheme is a

 (a) Multiemployer plan and a defined contribution scheme.
 (b) Multiemployer plan and a defined benefit scheme.
 (c) Defined contribution plan only.
 (d) Defined benefit plan only.

2. Which of these events will cause a change in a defined benefit obligation?

 (a) Changes in mortality rates or the proportion of employees taking early retirement.
 (b) Changes in the estimated salaries or benefits that will occur in the future.
 (c) Changes in the estimated employee turnover.
 (d) Changes in the discount rate used to calculate defined benefit liabilities and the value of assets.
 (e) All of the above.

3. An entity has decided to improve its defined benefit pension scheme. The benefit payable will be determined by reference to 60 years service rather than 80 years service. As a result, the defined benefit pension liability will increase by $10 million. The average remaining service lives of the employees is ten years. How should the increase in the pension liability by $10 million be treated in the financial statements?

 (a) The past service cost should be charged against retained profit.
 (b) The past service cost should be charged against profit or loss for the year.
 (c) The past service cost should be spread over the remaining working lives of the employees.
 (d) The past service cost should not be recognized.

4. Which of these elements are taken into account when determining the discount rate to be used?

 (a) Market yields at the statement of financial position date on high-quality corporate bonds.
 (b) Investment or actuarial risk.
 (c) Specific risk associated with the entity's business.
 (d) Risk that future experiences may differ from actuarial assumptions.

5. An entity operates a defined benefit plan that pays employees an annual benefit based on their number of years of service. The annual payment does allow the employer to vary the final benefit. Over the last five years the entity has used this flexibility to increase employees' pensions by the current growth in earnings per share. How will employees' benefit be calculated if they retire in the current period?

 (a) It will be based on the existing plan rules with no additional award.
 (b) It will be based on the existing plan rules plus the current rate of growth of earnings per share.
 (c) It will be based on the plan rules plus the current rate of inflation.
 (d) It will be based on the plan rules plus the increase in earnings per share anticipated over the remaining working lives of the employees.

6. Which of these assets should be included within the valuation of plan assets?

 (a) Unpaid contributions.
 (b) Unlisted corporate bonds that are redeemable but not transferable without the entity's permission.
 (c) A loan to the entity that cannot be assigned to a third party.
 (d) Investments in listed companies.

7. An entity has decided to protect its pension obligation with an insurance policy. The insurance policy permits the entity to cash in the insurance policy. Is this insurance policy a qualifying insurance policy that will be included in plan assets?

 (a) Yes.
 (b) No.

8. An entity uses International Financial Reporting Standards to prepare its financial statements, but the defined benefit obligation has been calculated using assumptions that are different from IFRS. The financial statements of the entity also do not take into account unrecognized past service costs. How should the entity measure its net pension liability?

 (a) The net present value of the defined benefit obligation less the fair value of the plan assets.
 (b) The net present value of the defined benefit obligation less the fair value of plan assets less the unrecognized past service costs.
 (c) The net present value of the defined benefit obligation less the fair value of the plan assets less the unrecognized past service costs. In addition, a review of the assumptions should be undertaken to remeasure the obligation.

(d) The value in the entity's statement of financial position will simply be used in the consolidated financial statements.

9. An entity operates a defined benefit pension plan and changes it on January 1, 20X4, to a defined contribution plan. The defined benefit pension plan still relates to past service but not to future service. The net pension liability after the plan amendment is $70 million, and the net pension liability before the amendment was $100 million. How should the entity account for this change?

(a) The entity recognizes a gain of $30 million.

(b) The entity does not recognize a gain.

(c) The entity recognizes a gain of $30 million over the remaining service lives of the employees.

(d) The entity recognizes the gain but applies the 10% corridor approach to it.

10. An entity on December 31, 20X5, changes its defined benefit pension plan to a defined contribution plan. The entity agrees with the employees to pay them $9 million in total on the introduction of a defined contribution plan. The employees forfeit any pension entitlement for the defined benefit plan. The pension liability recognized in the statement of financial position at December 31, 20X4, was $10 million. How should this curtailment be accounted for in the statement of financial position at December 31, 20X5?

(a) A settlement gain of $1 million should be shown.

(b) The pension liability should be credited to reserves and a cash payment of $9 million should be shown in expense in the statement of comprehensive income.

(c) The cash payment should go to reserves and the pension liability should be shown as a credit to the statement of comprehensive income.

(d) A credit to reserves should be made of $1 million.

11. The salaried employees are entitled to 30 days paid leave each year. The entitlement accrues evenly over the year and unused leave may be carried forward for one year. The holiday year is the same as the financial year. At September 30, 20X9, the entity has 100 salaried employees and the average unused holiday entitlement is two days per employee. 4% of employees leave without taking their entitlement and there is no cash payment when an employee leaves in respect of holiday entitlement. There are 240 working days in the year and the total annual salary cost is $2 million. What would be the accrual in the financial statements for holiday pay entitlement?

(a) $2 million

(b) $1.92

(c) $160,000

(d) $16,000

12. An entity has the following balances relating to its defined benefit plan:

- Present value of the obligation: $13 million
- Fair value of plan assets: $17 million
- Actuarial losses: $1.3 million unrecognized
- Past service cost: $1.2 million unrecognized
- Present value of available future refunds and reduction in future contributions: $0.1 million

Calculate the value that will be given to the net plan asset under IAS 19.

(a) $6.5 million

(b) $3.9 million

(c) $4 million

(d) $2.6 million

13. An entity has a defined benefit pension plan. As of January 1, 20X9, these values relate to the pension scheme:

- Fair value of plan assets: $2.5 million
- Present value of defined benefit obligation: $2 million
- Cumulative unrecognized actuarial gains: $1 million
- Average remaining working lives of employees: 20 years

At the end of the period at December 31, 20X9, the fair value of the plan assets has risen by $0.5 million. The present value of the defined benefit obligation has risen by $0.3 million. The actuarial gain is $1.2 million, and the average remaining working lives of the employees is 20 years. The entity wishes to use the full recognition approach for actuarial gains and losses. Show how the actuarial gain or loss for the period ending December 31, 20X9, could be recognized in the financial statements.

(a) $1.2 million

(b) $0.75 million

(c) $0.5 million

(d) $37,500

14. What would be the correct answer if the corridor approach was used?

(a) $1.2 million

(b) $0.75 million

(c) $0.5 million

(d) $37,500

Chapter 14

ACCOUNTING FOR GOVERNMENT GRANTS AND DISCLOSURE OF GOVERNMENT ASSISTANCE (IAS 20)

INTRODUCTION

Government grants or other types of government assistance are usually intended to encourage entities to embark on activities that they would not have otherwise undertaken. IAS 20 sets out the *accounting treatment and disclosure* of "government grants" and the *disclosure requirements* (only) of "government assistance."

Government assistance, according to the Standard, is action by the government aimed at providing economic benefits to some constituency by subsidizing entities that will provide them with jobs, services, or goods that might not otherwise be either available or available at a desired cost. Depending on the nature of the assistance given and the associated conditions, government assistance can be of many types, including grants, forgivable loans, and indirect or nonmonetary forms of assistance, such as technical advice.

A government grant is government assistance that entails the transfer of resources in return for compliance, either past or future, with certain conditions relating to the entity's operating activities, such as for remediating a polluted plant site.

SCOPE

IAS 20 deals with the accounting treatment and disclosure requirements of grants received by entities from government. It also mandates disclosure requirements of other forms of government assistance.

The Standard provides four exclusions:

1. Special problems arising in reflecting the effects of changing prices on financial statements or similar supplementary information
2. Government assistance provided in the form of tax benefits (including income tax holidays, investment tax credits, accelerated depreciation allowances, and concessions in tax rates)

3. Government participation in the ownership of the entity
4. Government grants covered by IAS 41

DEFINITIONS OF KEY TERMS
(in accordance with IAS 20)

Fair value. The amount for which an asset could be exchanged between a knowledgeable, willing buyer and a knowledgeable, willing seller in an arm's-length transaction.

Forgivable loans. Those loans that the lender undertakes to waive repayment of under certain prescribed conditions.

Government. For the purposes of IAS 20, refers not only to a government (of a country), as is generally understood, but also to government agencies and similar bodies, whether local, national, or international.

Government assistance. Action by a government aimed at providing an economic benefit to an entity or group of entities qualifying under certain criteria. It includes a government grant and other kinds of nonmonetary government assistance, such as providing, at no cost, legal advice to an entrepreneur for setting up a business in a free trade zone. It *excludes* benefits provided indirectly through action affecting trading conditions in general; for example, laying roads that connect the industrial area in which an entity operates to the nearest city or imposing trade constraints on foreign companies in order to protect domestic entrepreneurs in general.

Government grant. A form of government assistance that involves the transfer of resources to an entity in return for past or future compliance (by the entity) of certain conditions relating to its operating activities. It excludes

- Those forms of government assistance that cannot reasonably be valued
- Transactions with governments that cannot be distinguished from the normal trading transactions of the entity

Grants related to assets. Those government grants whose primary condition is that an entity qualifying for them should acquire (either purchase or construct) a long-term asset or assets. Subsidiary conditions may also be attached to such grants. Examples of subsidiary conditions include specifying the type of long-term assets, location of long-term assets, or periods during which the long-term assets are to be acquired or held.

Grants related to income. Government grants other than those related to assets.

GOVERNMENT GRANTS

Government grants are assistance provided by government by transfer of resources (either monetary or nonmonetary) to entities. In order to qualify as a government grant, the grant should be provided by the government, to an entity, in return for past or future compliance with conditions relating to the operating activities of the entity.

For quite some time, it has been unclear whether the provisions of IAS 20 would apply to government assistance aimed at encouraging or supporting business activities in certain regions or industry sectors, because related conditions may not specifically relate to the operating activities of the entity. Examples of such grants are government grants that involve transfer of resources to entities to operate in a particular area (i.e., an economically backward area) or a particular industry (i.e., an agriculture-based industry that, due to its low profitability, may not be a popular choice of entrepreneurs). The Standing Interpretations Committee's Interpretation, SIC 10, has clarified that "the general requirement to operate in certain regions or industry sectors in order to qualify for the government assistance constitutes such a condition in accordance with IAS 20." This Interpretation has set to rest the confusion as to whether such government assistance falls within the definition of government grants and thus whether the requirements of IAS 20 apply to such government assistance.

RECOGNITION OF GOVERNMENT GRANTS

Criteria for Recognition

Government grants are provided in return for past or future compliance with certain conditions. Thus grants should not be recognized until there is *reasonable assurance* that both:

- The entity will comply with the conditions attached to the grant.
- The grant(s) will be received.

Recognition Period

The Standard discusses two broad approaches with respect to the accounting treatment of government grants—the "capital approach" and the "income approach." It is fairly evident that IAS 20 is not in favor of the capital approach, which requires a government grant to be directly credited to the shareholders' equity. Supporting the income approach, the Standard sets out this rule for recognition of government grants: *"Government grants should be recognized as income, on a systematic and rational basis, over the periods necessary to match them with the related costs."* As a corollary, and by way of abundant precaution, the Standard reiterates that government grants should *not* be credited directly to shareholders' interests.

In setting out this rule, the Standard expands it further and lays down additional principles for recognition of grants under different conditions. These rules are explained in the case studies.

Principle 1: "Grants in recognition of specific costs are recognized as income over the same period as the relevant expense."

According to the Standard, grants in recognition of specific costs should be taken to income "over the period which matches the costs" using a "systematic and rational basis."

CASE STUDY 1

Facts

Brilliant Inc. received a grant of $60 million to compensate it for costs it incurred in planting trees over a period of five years. Brilliant Inc. will incur such costs in this manner:

Year	Costs
1	$ 2 million
2	$ 4 million
3	$ 6 million
4	$ 8 million
5	$10 million

Total costs thus incurred will aggregate to $30 million, whereas the grant received is $60 million.

Required

Based on the provisions of IAS 20, how would Brilliant Inc. treat the "grant" in its books?

Solution

Applying the principle outlined in the Standard for recognition of the grant, that is, recognizing the grant as income "over the period which matches the costs" using a "systematic and rational basis" (in this case, sum-of-the-years' digits amortization), the total grant would be recognized as

Year	Grant recognized
1	$ 60 × (2/30) = $ 4 million
2	$ 60 × (4/30) = $ 8 million
3	$ 60 × (6/30) = $12 million
4	$ 60 × (8/30) = $16 million
5	$ 60 × (10/30) = $20 million

Principle 2: "Grants related to depreciable assets are usually recognized as income over the periods and in the proportions in which depreciation on those assets is charged."

CASE STUDY 2

Facts

Intelligent Corp. received a grant of $150 million to install and run a windmill in an economically backward area. Intelligent Inc. has estimated that such a windmill would cost $250 million to construct. The secondary condition attached to the grant is that the entity should hire labor in the local market (i.e., from the economically backward area where the windmill is located) instead of employing workers from other parts of the country. It should maintain a ratio of 1:1 local workers to workers from outside in its labor force for the next five years. The windmill is to be depreciated using the straight-line method over a period of ten years.

Required

Advise Intelligent Corp. on the treatment of this grant in accordance with IAS 20.

Solution

The grant received by Intelligent Corp. will be recognized over a period of ten years. In each of the ten years, the grant will be recognized in proportion to the annual depreciation on the windmill. Thus $15 million will be recognized as income in each of the ten years. With regard to the secondary condition of maintenance of the ratio of 1:1 in the labor force, this contingency would need to be disclosed in the footnotes to the financial statements for the next five years (during which period the condition is in force), in accordance with disclosure requirements of IAS 37.

Principle 3: "Grants related to nondepreciable assets may also require the fulfillment of certain obligations and would then be recognized as income over periods which bear the cost of meeting the obligations."

CASE STUDY 3

Facts

Citimart Inc. was granted 5,000 acres of land in a village, located near the slums outside the city limits, by a local government authority. The condition attached to this grant was that Citimart Inc. should clean up this land and lay roads by employing laborers from the village in which the land is located. The government has fixed the minimum wage payable to the workers. The entire operation will take three years and is estimated to cost $100 million. This amount will be spent in this way: $20 million each in the first and second years and $60 million in the third year. The fair value of this land is currently $120 million.

Required

Based on the principles laid down for accounting and recognition of grants, how should this grant be treated in the books of Citimart Inc.?

Solution

Citimart Inc. would need to recognize the fair value of the grant over the period of three years in proportion to the cost of meeting the obligation. Thus, $120 million will be recognized as

Year	Grant recognized
1	$120 × (20/100) = $24 million
2	$120 × (20/100) = $24 million
3	$120 × (60/100) = $72 million

Principle 4: "Grants are sometimes received as part of a package of financial or fiscal aids to which a number of conditions are attached."

When different conditions are attached to different components of the grant, the terms of the grant would have to be evaluated in order to determine how the entity would earn the various elements of the grant. Based on that assessment, the total grant amount would then be apportioned.

CASE STUDY 4

Exuberant Inc. received a consolidated grant of $120 million. Three-fourths of the grant is to be utilized to purchase a college building for students from underdeveloped or developing countries. The balance of the grant is for subsidizing the tuition costs of those students for four years from the date of the grant.

The grant would first be apportioned as

| Grant related to assets (3/4) | = | $90 million |
| Grant related to income (1/4) | = | $30 million |

Required

Advise Exuberant Inc. on the treatment of the grant in accordance with IAS 20.

Solution

The grant related to assets would be recognized in income over the useful life of the college building, for example, ten years, using a systematic and rational basis. Assuming the college building is depreciated using the straight-line method, this portion of the grant (i.e., $90 million) would be recognized as income over a period of ten years at $9 million per year.

The grant related to income would be recognized over a period of four years. Assuming that the tuition subsidy will be offered evenly over the period of four years, this portion of the grant (i.e., $30 million) would be taken to income over a period of four years at $7.5 million per year.

Principle 5: "A government grant that becomes receivable as compensation for expenses or losses already incurred or for the purpose of giving immediate financial support to the entity with no future related costs should be recognized as income of the period in which it becomes receivable."

Sometimes grants are awarded for the purposes of giving immediate financial support to an entity, for example, to revive an insolvent commercial business (referred to as a sick unit in third-world countries). Such grants are not given as incentives to invest funds in specified areas or for a specified purpose from which the benefits will be derived over a period of time in the future. Instead such grants are awarded to compensate an entity for losses incurred in the past. Thus they should be recognized as income in the period in which the entity becomes eligible to receive such grants.

A grant may be awarded to an entity to compensate it for losses incurred in the past for operating out of an economically backward area that has been hit recently by an earthquake. During the period the entity operated in that area, the area experienced an earthquake, and thus the entity incurred massive losses. Such a grant received by the entity should be recognized as income in the year in which the grant becomes receivable.

NONMONETARY GRANTS

A government grant may not always be given in cash or cash equivalents. Sometimes a government grant may take the form of a transfer of a nonmonetary asset, such as a grant of a plot of land or a building in a remote backward area. In these circumstances, the Standard prescribes these optional accounting treatments:

- To account for both the grant and the asset at the fair value of the nonmonetary asset
- To record both the asset and the grant at a "nominal amount"

PRESENTATION OF GRANTS RELATED TO ASSETS

Presentation on the Balance Sheet

Government grants related to assets, including nonmonetary grants at fair value, should be presented in the balance sheet in either of two ways:

1. By setting up the grant as deferred income
2. By deducting the grant in arriving at the carrying amount of the asset

CASE STUDY 5

Facts

Taj Corp. received a grant related to a factory building that it bought in 2007. The total amount of the grant was $9 million. Taj Corp. acquired the building from an industrialist identified by the government. If Taj Corp. did not purchase the factory building, which was located in the slums of the city, it would have been repossessed by a government agency. Taj Corp. purchased the factory building for $27 million. The useful life of the building is not considered to be more than three years, mainly due to the fact that it was not properly maintained by the previous owner.

Solution

Under Option 1: Set up the grant as deferred income.

- The grant of $9 million would be set up initially as deferred income in 2007.
- At the end of 2007, $3 million would be recognized as income, and the balance of $6 million would be carried forward in the balance sheet.
- At the end of 2008, $3 million would be taken to income, and the balance of $3 million would be carried forward in the balance sheet.
- At the end of 2009, $3 million would be taken to income.

Under Option 2: The grant will be deducted from carrying value.

The grant of $9 million is deducted from the gross book value of the asset to arrive at the carrying value of $18 million. As the useful life is three years, annual depreciation of $6 million per year is recognized in comprehensive income for the years 2007, 2008, and 2009.

The effect on the operating results is the same whether the first option or the second option is chosen.

Under the second option, the grant is indirectly recognized in income through the reduced depreciation charge of $3 million per year. Under the first option, it is taken to income directly.

Presentation in the Statement of Cash Flows

When grants related to assets are received in cash, there is an inflow of cash to be shown under the investing activities section of the cash flow statement. Furthermore, there would also be an outflow resulting from the purchase of the asset. IAS 20 specifically requires that both these movements should be shown separately and not be netted. The Standard further clarifies that such movements should be shown separately regardless of whether or not the grant is deducted from the related asset for the purposes of the balance sheet presentation.

Presentation of Grants Related to Income

The Standard allows a free choice between two presentations.

Option 1: Grant presented as a credit in the statement of comprehensive income, either separately or under a general heading of other income

Option 2: Grant deducted in reporting the related expense

The Standard does not favor either option. It acknowledges the reasoning given in support of each approach by its supporters. The Standard considers both methods to be acceptable. However, it does recommend disclosure of the grant for a proper understanding of the financial statements. The Standard recognizes that the disclosure of the effect of the grants on any item of income or expense may be appropriate.

REPAYMENT OF GOVERNMENT GRANTS

When a government grant becomes repayable, for example, due to nonfulfillment of a condition attached to it, it should be treated as a change in estimate under IAS 8 and accounted for prospectively (as opposed to retrospectively).

Repayment of a grant related to income should

- First be applied against any unamortized deferred income (credit) set up in respect of the grant
- Be recognized immediately as an expense, to the extent that the repayment exceeds any such deferred income (credit), or in the case where no deferred credit exists

Repayment of a grant related to an asset:

- Should be recorded by increasing the carrying amount of the asset or reducing the deferred income balance by the amount repayable
- In the case where, the cumulative additional depreciation that would have been recognized to date as an expense in the absence of the grant should be recognized immediately as an expense

When a grant related to an asset becomes repayable, it would become incumbent upon the entity to assess whether any impairment in value of the asset (to which the repayable grant relates) has resulted. For example, a bridge is being constructed through funding from a government grant. During the construction period, because of nonfulfillment of the terms of the grant, the grant became repayable. Because the grant was provided to assist in the construction, it is possible that the entity may not be in a position to arrange funds to complete the project. In such a circumstance, the asset is impaired and may need to be written down to its recoverable value, in accordance with IAS 36.

GOVERNMENT ASSISTANCE

Government assistance includes government grants. IAS 20 deals with both accounting and disclosure of government grants but only with disclosure requirements of government assistance. Thus government assistance comprises government grants and other forms of government assistance (i.e., those not involving transfer of resources).

Excluded from the government assistance are certain forms of government benefits that cannot reasonably have a value placed on them, such as free technical or other professional advice. Also excluded from government assistance are government benefits that cannot be distinguished from the normal trading transactions of the entity. The reason for the second exclusion is obvious: Although the benefit cannot be disputed, any attempt to segregate it would necessarily be arbitrary.

DISCLOSURES

IAS 20 prescribes these three disclosures:

1. The accounting policy adopted for government grants, including the methods of presentation adopted in the financial statements
2. The nature and extent of government grants recognized in the financial statements and an indication of other forms of government assistance from which the entity has directly benefited
3. Unfulfilled conditions and other contingencies attached to government assistance that has been recognized

MULTIPLE-CHOICE QUESTIONS

1.   In the case of a nonmonetary grant, which of the following accounting treatments is prescribed by IAS 20?

    (a)   Record the asset at replacement cost and the grant at a nominal value.

    (b)   Record the grant at a value estimated by management.

    (c)   Record both the grant and the asset at fair value of the nonmonetary asset.

    (d)   Record only the asset at fair value; do not recognize the fair value of the grant.

2.   In the case of grants related to an asset, which of these accounting treatments (balance sheet presentation) is prescribed by IAS 20?

    (a)   Record the grant at a nominal value in the first year and write it off in the subsequent year.

    (b)   Either set up the grant as deferred income or deduct it in arriving at the carrying amount of the asset.

    (c)   Record the grant at fair value in the first year and take it to income in the subsequent year.

    (d)   Take it to the statement of comprehensive income and disclose it as an extraordinary gain.

3.   In the case of grants related to income, which of these accounting treatments is prescribed by IAS 20?

    (a)   Credit the grant to "general reserve" under shareholders' equity.

    (b)   Present the grant in the statement of comprehensive income as "other income"' or as a separate line item, or deduct it from the related expense.

    (c)   Credit the grant to "retained earnings" on the balance sheet.

    (d)   Credit the grant to sales or other revenue from operations in the statement of comprehensive income.

4.   Which of these disclosures is **not** required by IAS 20?

    (a)   The accounting policy adopted for government grants, including methods of presentation adopted in the financial statements.

    (b)   Unfulfilled conditions and other contingencies attached to government assistance.

    (c)   The names of the government agencies that gave the grants along with the dates of sanction of the grants by these government agencies and the dates when cash was received in the case of monetary grants.

    (d)   The nature and extent of government grants recognized in the financial statements and an indication of other forms of government assistance from which the entity has directly benefited.

5.   Which of the following is **not** specifically excluded from the purview of IAS 20?

    (a)   Government participation in ownership of the entity.

    (b)   Government grant covered by IAS 41.

    (c)   Government assistance provided in the form of tax benefits.

    (d)   Forgivable loan from the government.

Chapter 15

THE EFFECTS OF CHANGES IN FOREIGN EXCHANGE RATES (IAS 21)

OBJECTIVES

The purpose of IAS 21 is to set out how to account for transactions in foreign currencies and foreign operations. The Standard also shows how to translate financial statements into a presentation currency. The presentation currency is the currency in which the financial statements are presented. The Standard permits an entity to present its financial statements in any currency (or currencies). The key issues are the exchange rate(s) that should be used and where the effects of changes in exchange rates are reported in the financial statements.

> **DEFINITIONS OF KEY TERMS**
> **(in accordance with IAS 21)**
>
> **Exchange difference.** The difference resulting from translating a given number of units of one currency into another currency at different exchange rates.
>
> **Foreign operation.** A subsidiary, associate, joint venture, or branch whose activities are based or conducted in a country or currency other than those of the reporting entity.
>
> **Functional currency.** The currency of the primary economic environment in which the entity operates.
>
> **Closing rate.** The spot exchange rate at the end of the reporting period.
>
> **Spot rate.** The exchange rate for immediate delivery.
>
> **Presentation currency.** The currency that is used to present the financial statements.

FUNCTIONAL CURRENCY

The functional currency should be determined by looking at several factors. This currency should be the one in which the entity normally generates and spends cash and in which transactions are normally denominated. All transactions in currencies other than the functional currency are treated as transactions in foreign currencies. Five factors can be taken into account in making this decision.

The currency

1. That mainly influences the price at which goods and services are sold
2. Of the country whose competitive forces and regulations mainly influence the entity's pricing structure
3. That influences the costs of the entity
4. In which funds are generated
5. In which receipts from operating activities are retained

The first three items are generally considered to be the most influential in deciding the functional currency.

An entity will have to determine the functional currency of a foreign operation, such as a foreign subsidiary, and whether it is the same currency as that of the reporting entity. Such factors as whether the foreign entity is an extension of the reporting entity's business, what proportion of its transactions are with the reporting entity, and the nature of the cash flows will help determine the functional currency of the foreign operation.

The entity's functional currency reflects the transactions, events, and conditions under which the entity conducts its business. Once decided on, the functional currency does not change unless there is a change in the underlying nature of the transactions and relevant conditions and events.

If the functional currency is the currency of a hyperinflationary economy, the financial statements should be restated using IAS 29, *Financial Reporting in Hyperinflationary Economies*.

Where there is a change in the functional currency, it should be applied from the date of change. A change must be linked to a change in the nature of the underlying transactions. For example, a change in the major market may lead to a change in the currency that influences sales prices. The change is accounted for prospectively, not retrospectively.

RECORDING FOREIGN CURRENCY TRANSACTIONS USING THE FUNCTIONAL CURRENCY

Foreign currency transactions should be recorded initially at the spot rate of exchange at the date of the transaction. An approximate rate can be used. For example, in general, an average rate for a particular period can be used, but if exchange rates are fluctuating wildly, an average rate cannot be used.

Subsequently, at the end of each reporting period, foreign currency monetary amounts should be reported using the closing rate. Nonmonetary items measured at historical cost should be reported using the exchange rate at the date of the transaction. Nonmonetary items carried at fair value should be reported at the rate that existed when the fair values were determined.

It is possible that the carrying value for an item will have been determined by a comparison of two amounts that have been measured at different dates. For example, the cost of inventory can have been determined at one date and the net realizable value or recoverable amount at another date. The effect may be to change the amount of any impairment loss recognized in the functional currency.

PRACTICAL INSIGHT

FJA AG, a German company, discloses that the statements of comprehensive incomes of foreign operations are converted at annual average rates. This follows IAS 21, which allows a rate that approximates to actual exchange rates for the transaction, such as an average rate for the period, to be used to translate income and expense items of a foreign operation.

CASE STUDY 1

Facts

An entity buys inventory from a foreign supplier for €4 million. The functional currency of the entity is the dollar. The date of the order was March 31, 20X9, the date of shipping was April 7, 20X9, the date of the invoice was April 8, 20X9, the date the goods were received was April 15, 20X9, and the date the invoice was paid was May 31, 20X9.

Required

What is the date of the transaction for the purpose of recording the purchase of inventory?

Solution

Although IAS 2, *Inventories*, does not refer to the date of the initial recognition of inventory, IAS 39 says that a liability should be recognized when the entity becomes party to the contractual provisions of a contract. The date that the risks and rewards of ownership pass will essentially be the date of the transaction for these purposes.

It is unlikely that the ownership will pass on the date of the order, but it could pass on shipping, depending on the nature of the agreement. Similarly, it could pass on receipt of the goods, but it is unlikely to pass on receipt of the invoice or when payment is made.

Thus the date of the transaction in this case is likely to be the date of shipping or date of receipt, depending on when the risks and rewards of ownership pass and who would suffer loss if the inventory was damaged or lost in transit.

RECOGNITION OF EXCHANGE DIFFERENCES

Exchange differences arising on monetary items are normally reported in profit or loss in the period.

However, exchange differences arising on a monetary item that forms part of a reporting entity's net investment in a foreign operation shall be recognized in profit or loss in the separate financial statements of the reporting entity or the individual financial statements of the foreign operation, as appropriate. In the consolidated financial statements such exchange differences are recognized initially in other comprehensive income and reclassified from equity to profit or loss on disposal of the net investment.

Furthermore, when a gain or loss on a nonmonetary item is recognized in other comprehensive income, any exchange component of that gain or loss shall be recognized in other comprehensive income. In addition, when a gain or loss on a nonmonetary item is recognized in profit or loss, any exchange component of that gain or loss shall be recognized in profit or loss.

On the disposal of a foreign operation, the cumulative amount of the exchange differences relating to that foreign operation recognized in other comprehensive income and accumulated in the separate component of equity, shall be reclassified from equity to profit or loss (as a reclassification adjustment) when the gain or loss on disposal is recognized. Loss of control gives rise to recognition in profit or loss of the parent's share of deferred foreign exchange differences accumulated in the separate component of equity in accordance with IAS 21 for a net investment in a foreign subsidiary. The same principle applies when a parent loses control of a subsidiary that was classified as a foreign operation but retains an investment in that foreign operation. Thus, the entire cumulative gain or loss attributable to the parent is recognized in profit or loss on loss of control.

If there is a change in the parent's ownership interest in a subsidiary after control is obtained that does not result in a loss of control, deferred foreign exchange differences recognized directly in equity are reattributed between controlling and noncontrolling interest without recognizing a profit or loss. If the parent subsequently loses control of the subsidiary only the parent's share of deferred foreign exchange differences recognized previously in equity is recognized in profit or loss.

CASE STUDY 2

Facts

An entity purchases equipment from a foreign supplier for €6 million on March 31, 20X9, when the exchange rate was €2 = $1. The entity also sells goods to a foreign customer for €3.5 million on April 30, 20X9, when the exchange rate was €1.75 = $1. At the entity's year-end of May 31, 20X9, the amounts have not been paid. The closing exchange rate was €1.5 = $1. The entity's functional currency is the dollar.

Required

Calculate the exchange differences that would be recorded in profit or loss for the period ending May 31, 20X9.

Solution

The entity records the asset at a cost of $3 million at March 31, 20X9, and a liability of the same amount. At year-end, the amount has not been paid. Thus using the closing rate of exchange, the amount payable would be retranslated at $4 million, which would give an exchange loss of $1 million to be reported in profit or loss. The cost of the asset remains at $3 million before depreciation.

Similarly, the entity will record a sale of $2 million and an amount receivable of the same amount. At year-end, the receivable would be stated at $2.33 million, which would give an exchange gain of $0.33 million, which would be reported in profit or loss.

IAS 21 does not specify where exchange gains and losses should be shown in the statement of comprehensive income.

TRANSLATION TO THE PRESENTATION CURRENCY FROM THE FUNCTIONAL CURRENCY

An entity can present its financial statements in any currency. If the presentation currency differs from the functional currency, the financial statements are retranslated into the presentation currency.

If the financial statements of the entity are not in the functional currency of a hyperinflationary economy, then they are translated into the presentation currency in this way:

- Assets and liabilities (including any goodwill arising on the acquisition and any fair value adjustment) are translated at the closing rate at the date of that statement of financial position.
- The statement of comprehensive income is to be translated at the exchange rate at the date of the transactions. (Average rates are allowed if there is no great fluctuation in the exchange rates.)
- All exchange differences are recognized in other comprehensive income.

Any exchange difference that relates to the minority interest is recognized in the statement of financial position amount.

Special rules apply for translating into a different presentation currency, the results and financial position of an entity whose functional currency is the currency of a hyperinflationary economy. All amounts are translated at the closing spot rate. The one exception is that the comparative amounts will be shown as presented in the previous period.

When there is a change in an entity's functional currency, the entity shall apply the translation procedures applicable to the new functional currency prospectively from the date of the change.

CASE STUDY 3

Facts

An entity commenced business on January 1, 20X9, with an opening share capital of $2 million. The statement of comprehensive income and closing statement of financial position follow:

Statement of comprehensive income for the year ended December 31, 20X9

	$m
Revenue	32
Cost of sales	(10)
Gross profit	22
Distribution costs	(8)
Administrative expenses	(2)
Profit before tax	12
Tax expense	(4)
Profit for period	8

Statement of financial position at December 31, 20X9

	$m
Share capital	2
Retained earnings	8
	10
Trade payables	4
Total equity and liabilities	14
Land (nondepreciable) acquired December, 31 20X9	8
Inventories	4
Trade receivables	2
Total assets	14

The functional currency is the dollar, but the entity wishes to present its financial statements using the euro as its presentational currency. The entity translates the opening share capital at the closing rate. The exchange rates in the period were

	$1 =
January 1, 20X9	€1
December 31, 20X9	€2
Average rate	€1.5

Required

Translate the financial statements from the functional currency to the presentational currency.

Solution

Statement of comprehensive income for the year ended December 31, 20X9, at average rate

	(€1.5 = $1)
Revenue	48
Cost of sales	(15)
Gross profit	33
Distribution costs	(12)
Administrative expenses	(3)
Profit before tax	18
Tax expense	(6)
Profit for period	12

Statement of financial position at December 31, 20X9

	(€2 = $1)
Share capital (closing rate)	4
Retained earnings (average rate)	12
Exchange difference (see after table)	4
	20
Trade payables	8
Total equity and liabilities	28
Land (nondepreciable) acquired December 31, 20X9	16
Inventories	8
Trade receivables	4
Total assets	28

The exchange difference is calculated in this way:

The retained earnings if translated into euros would be €16 million. As the statement of comprehensive income has been translated using the average rate, the profit per that statement is €12 million, creating an exchange difference of €4 million.

The total exchange difference of €4 million, is shown as a component of equity.

TRANSLATION OF A FOREIGN OPERATION

When preparing group accounts, it is normal to deal with entities that utilize different currencies. The financial statements should be translated into the presentation currency.

Any goodwill and fair value adjustments are treated as assets and liabilities of the foreign entity and therefore are retranslated at each statement of financial position date at the closing spot rate.

Exchange differences on intragroup items are recognized in profit or loss unless the difference arises on the retranslation of an entity's net investment in a foreign operation when it is classified as equity.

Dividends paid in a foreign currency by a subsidiary to its parent company may lead to exchange differences in the parent's financial statements and will not be eliminated on consolidation but recognized in profit or loss.

PRACTICAL INSIGHT

Volkswagen discloses in its financial statements that it has adopted early revised IAS 21 regarding the requirement that goodwill in foreign operations should be translated at the closing rate. The company discloses that the cumulative effect of the change is a charge of €59 million to the translation reserve.

CASE STUDY 4

Facts

An entity has a foreign subsidiary whose functional currency is the euro. The functional currency of the entity is the dollar. On January 1, 20X9, when the exchange rate was $1= €1.5 the entity loans the subsidiary $3 million. At December 31, 20X9, the loan has not been repaid and is regarded as part of the net investment in the foreign subsidiary, as settlement of the loan is not planned or likely to occur in the foreseeable future. The exchange rate at December 31, 20X9, is $1 = €2, and the average rate for the year was $1 = €1.75.

Required

Explain how this loan would be treated in the entity's and group's financial statements.

Solution

There is no exchange difference in the entity's financial statements, as the loan has been made in dollars. In the foreign subsidiary's financial statements, the loan is translated into its own functional currency (euro) at the rate of $1= €1.5, or €4.5 million as of January 1, 20X8. At year-end, the closing rate will be used to translate this loan. This will result in the loan being restated at €6 million ($3 million × 2), giving an exchange loss of €1.5 million, which will be shown in the subsidiary's statement of comprehensive income.

In the group financial statements, this exchange loss will be translated at the average rate, as it is in the subsidiary's statement of comprehensive income, giving a loss of ($1.5/1.75 million), or $857,000. This will be recognized in equity.

There will be a further exchange difference (gain) arising between the amount included in the subsidiary's statement of comprehensive income at the average rate and at the closing rate: that is, $857,000 minus $750,000 (1.5 million euros/2), or $107,000.

Thus the overall exchange difference is $750,000. This will be recognized in other comprehensive income and accumulated in equity.

An alternative way of calculating this exchange loss follows. The loan at January 1, 20X9, is €4.5 million. On retranslation, this becomes $2.25 million at December 31, 20X9 (€4.5/2). The original loan was $3 million, so there is an exchange loss of ($3 − 2.25) million, or $0.75 million.

DISPOSAL OF A FOREIGN ENTITY

When a foreign operation is disposed of, the cumulative amount of the exchange differences recognized in other comprehensive income and accumulated in equity relating to that foreign operation shall be reclassified from equity to profit or loss when the gain or loss on disposal is recognized.

CASE STUDY 5

Facts

An entity has a 100% owned foreign subsidiary, which it carries at its original cost of $2 million. It sells the subsidiary on March 31, 20X9, for €5 million. As of March 31, 20X8, the balance on the exchange reserve was $300,000 credit. The functional currency of the entity is the dollar, and the exchange rate on March 31, 20X9, is $1 = €2. The net asset value of the subsidiary at the date of disposal was $2.4 million.

Required

Discuss the treatment of the disposal of the foreign subsidiary.

Solution

The subsidiary is sold for €5 million/2 or $2.5 million. In the parent entity's accounts, a gain of $0.5 million will be shown ($2.5 − $2 million).

In the group financial statements, the cumulative exchange gain will have to be shown in profit or loss together with the gain on disposal. The gain on disposal is $(2.5 − 2.4) million, or $100,000, which is the difference between the sale proceeds and the net asset value of the subsidiary. To this is added the cumulative exchange gain of $300,000 to give a total gain of $400,000, which will be included in the group statement of comprehensive income.

In 2008, amendments were made to IFRS 3, *Business Combinations,* and IAS 27, *Consolidated and Separate Financial Statements.* At the same time amendments were made to IAS 21, *The Effects of Changes in Foreign Exchange Rates.* The amendments specified that the loss of control of a subsidiary with a foreign operation should be treated as a disposal for the purposes of reclassifying the related accumulated exchange differences in equity to the profit or loss when the gain or loss on disposal was recognized. The same accounting treatment would be applied to the loss of joint control of a joint venture or the loss of significant influence over an associate. If an entity applies the IAS 27 amendments to an earlier period it should apply the amendments to IAS 21.

The amendments apply to annual periods beginning on or after July 1, 2009.

DISCLOSURE

An entity should disclose

- The amount of exchange differences recognized in profit or loss but not differences arising on financial instruments measured at fair value through profit or loss in accordance with IAS 39
- The net exchange differences classified in a separate component of equity and a reconciliation of the amount of such exchange differences at the beginning and end of the period

- When the presentation currency is different from the functional currency, disclosure of that fact together with the functional currency is required, as well as the reason for using a different presentation currency
- Any change in the functional currency of either the reporting entity or significant foreign operation and the reasons for the change

When an entity presents its financial statements in a currency that is different from its functional currency, it may describe those financial statements as complying with International Financial Reporting Standards (IFRS) only if they comply with all the requirements of each applicable Standard and Interpretation.

If an entity displays its financial statements or other financial information in a currency that is different from either its functional or presentation currency or if the requirements just listed are not met, then it should

- Clearly identify the information as supplementary information to distinguish it from the information that complies with IFRS.
- Disclose the currency in which the supplementary information is displayed.
- Disclose the entity's functional currency and the method of translation used to determine the supplementary information.

CASE STUDY 6

Jocatt Statement of Financial Position

December 31, 20X9

	€m
Assets:	
Noncurrent assets	
Property, plant, and equipment (PPE)	1,900
Financial assets	250
	2,150
Current assets	1,650
Total assets	3,800
Equity and liabilities:	
Share capital	1,000
Retained earnings	1,500
Total equity	2,500
Noncurrent liabilities	800
Current liabilities	500
Total liabilities	1,300
Total equity and liabilities	3,800

An entity acquired 60% of the share capital of Jocatt on January 1, 20X9 for €1,380 million when Jocatt's retained earnings were €1,100 million. The fair value of the identifiable net assets of Jocatt on January 1, 20X9, was €2,475 million and related to nondepreciable PPE. The fair value of the noncontrolling interest (NCI) in Jocatt at January 1, 20X9, was €1,250 million. The entity wishes to use the "full goodwill" method to prepare the group financial statements. Jocatt's profit for the year is €400 million.

The following exchange rates were in force:

	€ to $
January 1, 20X9	6
December 31, 20X9	5

The average rate for the year to December 31, 20X9, was €5.5 to $1.

Required

Calculate

1. Goodwill arising on the acquisition of Jocatt
2. Any exchange gain arising on goodwill at December 31, 20X9
3. Any exchange difference arising on the retranslation of Jocatt's net assets

Solution

a. Jocatt—translation and calculation of goodwill

	€ m	*€ m—fair value adj*	*Rate*	*$m*
Property, plant, and equipment	1,900	375	5	455
Financial assets	250		5	50
Current assets	1,650		5	330
				835

	€ m	*€ m—fair value adj*	*Rate*	*$m*
Share capital	1,000		6	167
Retained earnings—preacquisition	1,100		6	183
—postacquisition (balance)	400			162
Other equity		375	6	63
Noncurrent liabilities	800		5	160
Current liabilities	500		5	100
				835

The fair value adjustment at acquisition is 2,475 – (1,000 + 1,100) = €375 million.

Goodwill is measured using the full goodwill method.

	€ m	*Rate*	*$m*
Cost of acquisition	1,380	6	230
NCI	1,250	6	208
Less net assets acquired	(2,475)	6	413
Goodwill	155	6	26

b. Goodwill is treated as a foreign currency asset and is retranslated at the closing rate. Goodwill at December 31, 20X9, will be €155 million divided by 5, that is $31 million. Therefore an exchange gain of $5 million will be recorded in retained earnings ($3 million) and noncontrolling interest ($2 million).

c. Exchange difference on Jocatt's net assets

Arising on retranslation of opening net assets	*$m*
Opening rate €2,475m @ 6 = $412.5m	
Closing rate €2,475m @ 5 = $495m	
Difference	82.5
Arising on retranslation of profits for year	
€400m @5.5 = $73m	
€400m @ 5 = $80m	
Difference	7
Total	89.5 (say 90m)

The exchange difference is credited to exchange reserve ($54m) and NCI ($36m).

EXTRACTS FROM PUBLISHED FINANCIAL STATEMENTS

J. SAINSBURY PLC Financial Statements to March 21, 2009

Capital redemption and other reserves continued

Currency translation reserve represents the foreign exchange differences on the translation of the net assets of the Group's foreign operations from their functional currency to the presentation currency of the parent.

STANDARD CHARTERED PLC—Annual Report, 2009

Foreign currency translation

Both the parent company financial statements and the Group financial statements are presented in US dollars, which is the presentation currency of the Group and the functional and presentation currency of the Company.

Transactions and balances

Foreign currency transactions are translated into the functional currency using the exchange rates prevailing at the dates of the transactions. Foreign exchange gains and losses resulting from the settlement of such transactions, and from the translation at year-end exchange rates of monetary assets and liabilities denominated in foreign currencies, are recognized in the statement of comprehensive income. Nonmonetary assets and liabilities are translated at historical exchange rates if held at historical cost, or year-end exchange rates if held at fair value, and the resulting foreign exchange gains and losses are recognized in either the statement of comprehensive income or shareholders' equity depending on the treatment of the gain or loss on the asset or liability.

Group companies

The results and • nancial position of all the entities included in the Group financial statements that have a functional currency different from the Group's presentation currency are accounted for as follows:

- Assets and liabilities for each statement of financial position presented are translated at the closing rate at the statement of financial position date
- Income and expenses for each statement of comprehensive income are translated at average exchange rates or at the rates on the date of the transaction where exchange rates fluctuate significantly
- All resulting exchange differences arising since January 1, 2004 are recognized as a separate component of equity

On consolidation, exchange differences arising from the translation of the net investment in foreign entities, and of borrowings and other currency instruments designated as hedges of such investments, are taken to other comprehensive income. When a foreign operation is sold or capital repatriated they are recognized in the statement of comprehensive income as part of the gain or loss on disposal.

Goodwill and fair value adjustments arising on the acquisition of a foreign entity are treated as assets and liabilities of the foreign entity and translated at the closing rate.

Source: Standard Chartered PLC annual report 2009. © Standard Chartered PLC

MULTIPLE-CHOICE QUESTIONS

1. Which of these considerations would **not** be relevant in determining the entity's functional currency?
- (a) The currency that influences the costs of the entity.
- (b) The currency in which finance is generated.
- (c) The currency in which receipts from operating activities are retained.
- (d) The currency that is the most internationally acceptable for trading.

2. Foreign operations that are an integral part of the operations of the entity would have the same functional currency as the entity. Where a foreign operation functions independently from the parent, the functional currency will be
- (a) That of the parent.
- (b) Determined using the guidance for determining an entity's functional currency.
- (c) That of the country of incorporation.
- (d) The same as the presentation currency.

3. An entity started trading in country A, whose currency was the dollar. After several years the entity expanded and exported its product to country B, whose currency was the euro. The functional currency of the entity was deemed to be the dollar but by the end of 20X7, 80% of the business was conducted in country B using the euro. At the end of 20X6, 30% of the business was conducted in the euro. The functional currency should
- (a) Remain the dollar.
- (b) Change to the euro at the beginning of 20X7.
- (c) Change to the euro at the end of 20X7.
- (d) Change to the euro at the end of 20X7 if it is considered that the underlying transactions, events, and conditions of business have changed.

4. An entity started trading in country A, whose currency was the dollar. After several years the entity expanded and exported its product to country B, whose currency was the euro. The business was conducted through a subsidiary in country B. The subsidiary is essentially an extension of the entity's own business, and the directors of the two entities are common. The functional currency of the subsidiary is
- (a) The dollar.
- (b) The euro.
- (c) The dollar or the euro.
- (d) Difficult to determine.

5. An entity purchases plant from a foreign supplier for €3 million on January 31, 20X6, when the exchange rate was €2 = $1. At the entity's year-end of March 31, 20X6, the amount has not been paid. The closing exchange rate was €1.5 = $1. The entity's functional currency is the dollar. Which of the following statements is correct?
- (a) Cost of plant $2 million, exchange loss $0.5 million, trade payable $1.5 million.
- (b) Cost of plant $1.5 million, exchange loss $0.6 million, trade payable $2 million.
- (c) Cost of plant $1.5 million, exchange loss $0.5 million, trade payable $2 million.
- (d) Cost of plant $2 million, exchange loss $0.5 million, trade payable $2 million.

6. An entity acquired all the share capital of a foreign entity at a consideration of €9 million on June 30, 20X6. The fair value of the net assets of the foreign entity at that date was €6 million. The functional currency of the entity is the dollar. The financial year-end of the entity is December 31, 20X6. The exchange rates at June 30, 20X6, and December 31, 20X6, were €1.5 = $1 and €2 = $1 respectively. What figure for goodwill should be included in the financial statements for the year ended December 31, 20X6?
- (a) $2 million.
- (b) €3 million.
- (c) $1.5 million.
- (d) $3 million.

7. An entity has a subsidiary that operates in a country where the exchange rate fluctuates wildly and there are seasonal variations in the income and expenditure patterns. Which of the following rates of exchange would probably be used to translate the foreign subsidiary's statement of comprehensive income?
- (a) Year-end spot rate.
- (b) Average for the year.
- (c) Average of the quarter-end rates.
- (d) Average rates for each individual month of the year.

8. An entity has a subsidiary that operates in a foreign country. The subsidiary sold goods to the parent for €2.1 million. The functional currency of the entity is the dollar. The cost of the goods to the subsidiary was €1.2 million. The goods were recorded by the entity at $1.05 million (€2 = $1) and were all unsold at the year-end of December 31, 20X6. The exchange rate at that date was €1.5 = $1. What is the value of the intragroup profit that will be eliminated at December 31, 20X6?
- (a) $205,000
- (b) $600,000
- (c) $450,000
- (d) $350,000

9. An entity has a subsidiary that operates in a foreign country. The subsidiary issued a legal notice of a dividend to the parent of €2.4 million, and this was recorded in the parent entity's financial statements. The exchange rate at that date was €2 = $1. The functional currency of the entity is the dollar. At the date of receipt of the dividend, the exchange rate had moved to €3 = $1. The exchange difference arising on the dividend would be treated in which way in the financial statements?

(a) No exchange difference will arise, as it will be eliminated on consolidation.

(b) An exchange difference of $400,000 will be taken to equity.

(c) An exchange difference of $400,000 will be taken to the parent entity's statement of comprehensive income and the group statement of comprehensive income.

(d) An exchange difference of $400,000 will be taken to the parent entity's statement of comprehensive income only.

10. An entity acquired 60% of the share capital of a foreign entity on June 30, 20X6. The fair value of the net assets of the foreign entity at that date was €6 million. This value was €1.2 million higher than the carrying amount of the net assets of the foreign entity. The excess was due to the increase in value of nondepreciable land. The functional currency of the entity is the dollar. The financial year-end of the entity is December 31, 20X6. The exchange rates at June 30, 20X6, and December 31, 20X6, were €1.5 = $1 and €2 = $1 respectively. What figure for the fair value adjustment should be included in the group financial statements for the year ended December 31, 20X6?

(a) $600,000

(b) $800,000

(c) $2 million.

(d) $3 million.

11. An entity has a foreign subsidiary whose carrying value at cost is $35 million. It sells the subsidiary on December 31, 20X9 for €52 million. As at December 31, 20X9, the credit balance on the exchange reserve, which relates to this subsidiary was $8 million. The functional currency of the entity is the dollar and the exchange rate on December 31, 20X9 is $1 = €1.3. The net asset value of the subsidiary at the date of disposal was $34 million. What is the profit or loss on the sale of the subsidiary that will appear in the group statement of comprehensive income?

(a) $5 million

(b) $8 million

(c) $13 million

(d) $14 million

Chapter 16

BORROWING COSTS (IAS 23)

BACKGROUND

IAS 23, *Borrowing Costs,* prescribes the criteria for determining whether borrowing costs can be capitalized as part of the cost of acquiring, constructing, or producing a "qualifying asset." The Standard prescribes the capitalization of borrowing costs into the cost of a qualifying asset.

IAS 23 has been revised to eliminate the option available hitherto to recognize borrowing costs as an expense. This amendment to the standard was made as part of the efforts of the IASB and the US FASB towards convergence of their standards.

SCOPE

The Standard is to be applied in accounting for (i.e., recognizing) borrowing costs. Not all kinds of borrowing costs are to be capitalized. Borrowing costs that are *directly attributable* to the acquisition, construction, or production of a qualifying asset are to be capitalized as part of the cost of that asset.

The Standard applies only to borrowing costs relating to external borrowings and not to equity. Therefore, the Standard does not deal with the imputed or actual cost of equity, including preferred capital not classified as equity.

> **DEFINITIONS OF KEY TERMS**
> **(in accordance with IAS 23)**
>
> **Borrowing costs.** Include interest and other costs incurred by an entity in relation to borrowing of funds.
>
> **Qualifying asset.** An asset that necessarily takes a substantial period of time to get ready for its intended use or sale.

> ### PRACTICAL INSIGHT
>
> The concept of "qualifying asset" is difficult to understand and comprehend in the spirit of the Standard. Some entities inadvertently apply (or at least insist on applying) this Standard to borrowing costs relating to assets that are expensive to purchase. These entities get confused because to them the quantum of the borrowing costs relating to the cost of the asset probably justifies such accounting treatment. For instance, if an expensive machine is bought (as opposed to being built by the entity) and the cost of the machine is quite substantial, entities inadvertently apply the Standard and argue that it is appropriate to capitalize borrowing costs along with the cost of the plant. Their justification is that since the machine is very expensive, the borrowing costs relating to the purchase of the machine are also quite significant. Thus it would not be right on their part to expense these costs. These entities further argue that in expensing such borrowing costs, they are able to capture only part of the cost of the asset. The cost of financing is to be included in the cost of the purchase of the asset because without incurring that cost, the entity would not have been in a position to purchase such an expensive asset.
>
> In practice, auditors face such situations quite often, especially in developing countries, where the costs of borrowing are quite high compared to other economies.

BORROWING COSTS

Borrowing costs, as understood generally, refer to interest costs. However, borrowing costs as envisaged by the Standard are not just interest costs on short-term borrowings, such as bank overdrafts and notes payable, or long-term borrowings, such as term loans and real estate mortgages. Rather, borrowing costs also include other related costs, such as

- Amortization of discounts or premiums relating to borrowings
- Amortization of ancillary costs incurred in connection with the arrangement or borrowings
- Exchange differences arising from foreign currency borrowings to the extent that they are regarded as an adjustment to interest costs
- Finance charges in respect of finance leases recognized in accordance with IAS 17, *Leases*

CASE STUDY 1

Facts

On December 1, 2009, Compassionate Inc. began construction of homes for those families that were hit by the tsunami disaster and were homeless. The construction is expected to take 3.5 years. It is being financed by issuance of bonds for $7 million at 12% per annum. The bonds were issued at the beginning of the construction. The bonds carry a 1.5% issuance cost. The project is also financed by issuance of share capital with a 14% cost of capital. Compassionate Inc. is required under IAS 23 to capitalize borrowing costs.

Required

Compute the borrowing costs that need to be capitalized under IAS 23.

Solution

Since these homes are "qualifying assets," borrowing costs can be capitalized and are computed thus:

a.	Interest on $7 million bond	=	$7,000,000 ×12%	=	$840,000
b.	Amortization of issuance costs of the bond (using the straight-line method)	=	[(0.015 × $7,000,000)/3.5 years]	=	$30,000
	Total borrowing to be capitalized	=	$840,000 + $30,000	=	$870,000

QUALIFYING ASSETS

Assets that are ready for their intended use or sale when acquired are *not* qualifying assets as envisioned by this Standard. Qualifying assets, for the purposes of this Standard, *are assets that take a substantial period of time to get ready for their intended use*. Examples of qualifying assets include

- A toll bridge that takes a couple of years to construct before it is ready for use and is opened to the public
- A power plant that takes a substantial period of time to get ready for its intended use
- A hydroelectric dam that services the needs of a village and takes a considerable period of time to construct

Inventories that are routinely manufactured or are produced on a repetitive basis over a short period of time are obviously not qualifying assets. However, inventories that require a substantial period of time to bring to a saleable condition can be regarded as qualifying assets for the purposes of this Standard.

CASE STUDY 2

Facts

1. Magnificent Inc. engaged a consulting firm to advise it on many projects that it had been planning to undertake in order to diversify its operations and enhance its public image and ratings. With this mandate, the consulting firm set out to prepare a feasibility study for the construction of a shopping mall that would house anchor tenants such as world-class international designers and well-known global retail chains. The consulting firm advised Magnificent Inc. that this kind of a project would do wonders to its corporate image. This shopping mall had certain distinguishing features that were unique in many respects, and it could easily win the coveted title of the most popular commercial complex in the country. Based on this advice, Magnificent Inc. began construction of the shopping mall on a huge plot of land in the heart of the city. Substantial amounts were spent on its construction. Architects from around the globe competed for the project, and the construction was entrusted to the best construction firm in the country. The construction took over two years from the date the project was launched. The total cost of construction was financed by a term loan from an international bank.
2. The consulting firm also advised Magnificent Inc. to launch a car dealership that deals only in world-renowned, expensive brand names, such as Rolls-Royce and Alfa Romeo. According to the research study undertaken by the consulting firm, this would be yet another business to diversify and invest in, in order to enhance the corporate image of Magnificent Inc. with people who matter, as such an exclusive car dealership would cater only to the needs of the top management of multinational corporations (MNCs) operating in the country. Magnificent Inc. invested in this business by borrowing funds from major local banks. Besides the corporate guarantees Magnificent Inc. gave to the banks, they also insisted on depositing with the banks, title deeds of the cars as security for the loans until the entire loan amounts are paid.

Required

1. Would the shopping mall be considered a qualifying asset under the Standard? Would the interest expense on the term loan borrowed for the construction of the shopping mall qualify as eligible borrowing costs?
2. Would the expensive cars purchased by the car dealership be considered qualifying assets under the Standard, whereby Magnificent Inc. would be required to capitalize the borrowing costs, which are substantial compared to the costs of the cars? Would borrowing costs include the guarantee commission paid to banks for arranging corporate guarantees in addition to interest expense on bank loans?

Solution

1. Yes, the shopping mall would be considered a qualifying asset as envisaged by the Standard because construction took a substantial period of time. Furthermore, the interest expense on the funds borrowed for the construction of the shopping mall would qualify as eligible borrowing costs.

2. Although the cars purchased are expensive assets, because they are ready for use when purchased (and do not take a substantial period of time to get ready for their intended use), they are not qualifying assets. Neither the interest expense on bank borrowings nor the guarantee fees for corporate guarantees given to banks by Magnificent Inc. would be capitalized with the cost of cars and would be expensed in the year of acquisition of the cars.

RECOGNITION

Borrowing costs that are directly attributable to the acquisition, construction, or production of a qualifying asset shall be capitalized as part of the cost of that asset. Capitalization of borrowing costs that are directly attributable to the acquisition, construction, or production of a qualifying asset as part of the cost of the asset is possible only if both these conditions are met:

- It is probable that they will result in future economic benefits to the entity.
- The costs can be measured reliably.

(If borrowing costs do not meet these criteria, then they are expensed.)

Amendments to IAS 23 Effective January 1, 2009

During March 2007, the IASB issued amendments to IAS 23. These amendments eliminated the option available under the Standard to recognize borrowing costs as an expense. Under the revised Standard, to the extent that borrowing costs relate to the acquisition, construction, or production of a "qualifying asset," they should be capitalized as part of the cost of the asset. All other borrowing costs should be expensed as incurred.

The revised Standard is effective for annual periods beginning on or after January 1, 2009. Early application is permitted but retrospective application is not permitted.

These revisions to IAS 23 have been made as part of the IASB's efforts to converge with US GAAP. By amending IAS 23 and removing the option to expense borrowing costs relating to "qualifying assets," the principal difference between IAS 23 and SFAS 34 (US GAAP) has been eliminated.

BORROWINGS ELIGIBLE FOR CAPITALIZATION

When borrowings are taken specifically to acquire, construct, or produce an asset, the borrowing costs that relate to that particular qualifying asset are readily identifiable. In such circumstances, it is easy to quantify the borrowing costs that would need to be capitalized by using the process of elimination, that is, capitalizing the borrowing costs that would have been avoided had the expenditure on the qualifying asset not been made.

Difficulties arise, however, if borrowings and funding are organized centrally, say, within a group of companies. In such cases, a weighted-average capitalization rate may be applied to the expenditures on the qualifying asset.

When funds borrowed specifically to finance a qualifying asset are not utilized immediately, and instead the idle funds are invested temporarily until required, the borrowing costs that are capitalized should be reduced by any investment income resulting from the investment of idle funds.

Borrowing costs capitalized in a period cannot exceed the amount of borrowing costs incurred by the entity during that period.

CASE STUDY 3

Facts

A socially responsible multinational corporation (MNC) decided to construct a tunnel that will link two sides of the village that were separated by a natural disaster years ago. Realizing its role as a good corporate citizen, the MNC has been in this village for a couple of years exploring oil and gas in the nearby offshore area. The tunnel would take two years to build and the total capital outlay needed for the construction would be not less than $20 million. To allow itself a margin of safety, the MNC borrowed

$22 million from three sources and used the extra $2 million for its working capital purposes. Financing was arranged in this way:

- Bank term loans: $5 million at 7% per annum
- Institutional borrowings: $7 million at 8% per annum
- Corporate bonds: $10 million at 9% per annum

In the first phase of the construction of the tunnel, there were idle funds of $10 million, which the MNC invested for a period of six months. Income from this investment was $500,000.

Required

When MNC capitalizes borrowing costs under IAS 23, how would it treat the borrowing costs? How would it capitalize the borrowing costs, and what would it do with the investment income?

Solution

Under IAS 23, borrowing costs would be capitalized as part of the cost of the asset.

1. In order to capitalize the borrowing costs, a weighted-average cost of funds borrowed is computed:

    = ($5 million × 7%) + ($7 million × 8%) + ($10 million × 9%)/($5 million + $7 million + $10 million)
    = ($1.81 million/$22 million) × 100
    = 8.22 % per annum

2. Total borrowing cost = $20 million × 8.22 % per annum × 2 years

    = $1.644 million × 2 years
    = $3.288 million

3. Borrowing costs to be capitalized = Interest expense – Investment income (resulting from investment of idle funds)

    = $3,288,000 – $500,000
    = $2,788,000

EXCESS OF CARRYING AMOUNT OF THE QUALIFYING ASSET OVER THE RECOVERABLE AMOUNT

When the carrying amount or the expected ultimate cost of the qualifying asset exceeds its recoverable amount or net realizable value, the carrying amount is to be written down or written off in accordance with the requirements of other Standards, such as IAS 36, *Impairment of Assets*.

COMMENCEMENT OF CAPITALIZATION

Capitalization of borrowing costs shall commence when

- Expenditures for the asset are being incurred.
- Borrowing costs are being incurred.
- Activities necessary to prepare the asset for its intended use or sale are in progress.

SUSPENSION OF CAPITALIZATION

Capitalization shall be suspended during extended periods in which active development is interrupted unless that period is a necessary part of the process for the production of the asset. For example, capitalization would be suspended during an interruption to the construction of a bridge during very high water levels, which are common in the area where construction is taking place. However, capitalization of borrowing costs should *not* be suspended when there is only a temporary delay that is caused by certain expected and anticipated reasons, such as while an asset is getting ready for its intended use.

CESSATION OF CAPITALIZATION

Capitalization of borrowing costs shall cease when substantially all the activities necessary to prepare the asset for its intended use or sale are complete. If all that is left are minor modifications, such as decoration or routine administrative work, then the asset is considered to be substantially complete.

In some instances, such as a business park or extensive development, parts may become ready for use in stages. In such cases, capitalization ceases on those parts that are ready for use.

DISCLOSURE

An entity shall disclose the amount of borrowing costs capitalized during the period, and the capitalization rate used to determine the amount of borrowing costs eligible for capitalization.

EXTRACT FROM PUBLISHED FINANCIAL STATEMENTS

BARLOWORLD, Annual Report, 2009

Notes to Financial Statements

31. Borrowing costs

Borrowing costs (net of investment income earned on the temporary investment of specific borrowings pending their expenditure on qualifying assets) directly attributable to the acquisition, construction, or production of assets that necessarily take a substantial period of time to get ready for their intended use or sale, are added to the cost of those assets, until such time as the assets are substantially ready for their intended use or sale. All other borrowing costs are expensed in the period in which they are incurred.

MULTIPLE-CHOICE QUESTIONS

1. Borrowing costs shall be capitalized as part of the asset when
- (a) They relate to qualifying assets and the entity capitalizes them under IAS 23.
- (b) They relate to motor cars purchased for office use from a dealership in town.
- (c) They are not directly attributable to the acquisition of qualifying assets as defined under IAS 23.
- (d) They relate to the period after the qualifying assets are substantially ready for their intended use although some minor routine administrative work is still going on.

2. Which of the following may **not** be considered a "qualifying asset" under IAS 23?
- (a) A power generation plant that normally takes two years to construct.
- (b) An expensive private jet that can be purchased from a local vendor.
- (c) A toll bridge that usually takes more than a year to build.
- (d) A ship that normally takes one to two years to complete.

3. Which of the following costs may **not** be eligible for capitalization as borrowing costs under IAS 23?
- (a) Interest on bonds issued to finance the construction of a qualifying asset.
- (b) Amortization of discounts or premiums relating to borrowings that qualify for capitalization.
- (c) Imputed cost of equity.
- (d) Exchange differences arising from foreign currency borrowings to the extent that they are regarded as an adjustment to interest costs pertaining to a qualifying asset.

4. Capitalization of borrowing costs
- (a) Shall be suspended during temporary periods of delay.
- (b) May be suspended only during extended periods of delays in which active development is delayed.
- (c) Should never be suspended once capitalization commences.
- (d) Shall be suspended only during extended periods of delays in which active development is delayed.

5. Which of the following is **not** a disclosure requirement under IAS 23?
- (a) Accounting policy adopted for borrowing costs.
- (b) Amount of borrowing costs capitalized during the period.
- (c) Segregation of assets that are "qualifying assets" from other assets on the balance sheet or as a disclosure in the footnotes to the financial statements.
- (d) Capitalization rate used to determine the amount of borrowing costs eligible for capitalization.

Chapter 17

RELATED-PARTY DISCLOSURES
(IAS 24)

BACKGROUND AND INTRODUCTION

Related-party transactions are a normal and a common feature of business and commerce these days. However, in some cases, entities may enter into transactions with related parties at terms that unrelated parties might not enter into under normal circumstances. Thus the existence of a related-party relationship may have an effect on profit or loss and the financial position of an entity. In order to ensure "transparency" in financial reporting, most accounting standards around the world prescribe disclosures of transactions with related parties.

IAS 24, *Related-Party Disclosures*, is the Standard under the International Financial Reporting Standards (IFRS) that prescribes the requirements for the disclosure of related-party relationships in financial statements. The Standard was initially issued by the International Accounting Standards Committee (IASC), IASB's predecessor, in July 1984, and was reformatted by it in 1994. In 2003 the IASB issued a revised IAS 24 and the Standard was subsequently amended by amendments to IAS 19 and IAS 1. Recently, in November 2009, the IASB issued a revised IAS 24.

The purpose of the Standard is to make the reader of financial statements aware of the existence of related-party relationships and the extent to which an entity's financial position, profitability, or cash flows may have been affected by transactions with such parties. It should be noted that this is a *disclosure* Standard and *does not* deal with recognition or measurement issues, all of which are dealt with by other relevant Standards.

Related-party transactions generally are very sensitive subjects in most parts of the world. Often, and sometimes erroneously, it is believed that transactions with related parties are "not a good thing;" usually this is the case in unscrupulous corporate deals where transactions with related parties are used to manipulate the results of an operation or net assets for economic gain by a group of individuals in control of the entity. Although this may be true in some instances, especially in the recent highly publicized corporate scandals where the board of directors (i.e., "related parties") allegedly took the shareholders for a ride, in most cases there are valid economic and/or commercial reasons for dealing with related parties.

ILLUSTRATION

An example of related-party transactions is a group of companies (with a common parent) having diverse activities wherein entities within the group, in the normal course of business, enter into day-to-day transactions with other entities within the group. For instance, one entity within the group may supply goods or services to another but only after going through a tendering process in competition with third parties. In such a case, the transaction is transparent, as a bidding process was conducted and the price at which the transaction was entered into would in all likelihood have been at market, or arm's-length, pricing. This is what generally happens in the real world, and, in principle, there is nothing wrong with entering into such a transaction with entities within the group. The Standard merely requires entities that enter into such transactions with other related parties to so state in their financial statements.

It is important, however, that a reader of financial statements is made aware of all related-party relationships, transactions, and balances as such transactions may not always be at arm's length and may have occurred only, or indeed transactions may not have occurred, because of the position that a related party has—it can influence, or can be influenced by, that other party, which can impact the reported results, net assets, or cash flows.

SCOPE

The requirements of IAS 24 (revised 2009) are to be applied in

1. Identifying related-party relationships and transactions
2. Identifying outstanding balances, including commitments, between an entity and its related parties
3. Identifying the circumstances in which disclosure of items in 1 and 2 is required
4. Determining the disclosures that are to be made about those items

The Standard is very clear that its provisions apply to disclosure of related-party transactions and outstanding balances, including commitments, in the consolidated and *separate financial statements* of a parent company, venturer, or investor presented in accordance with IAS 27. Furthermore, transactions with other entities in a group are to be disclosed in an individual entity's financial statements, although such intragroup transactions are eliminated on consolidation in the financial statements of the group.

PRACTICAL INSIGHT

In separate financial statements of a parent company, presented on a "stand-alone" basis as permitted under IAS 27, transactions with its subsidiaries would be disclosed as related-party transactions. However, in "consolidated financial statements" of the parent company, there will be no related-party transactions or balances reported between members of the consolidated group, as all such items will have been eliminated upon consolidation by applying the procedures outlined in IAS 27, *Consolidated and Separate Financial Statements*.

DEFINITIONS OF KEY TERMS
(in accordance with IAS 24 [revised 2009], paragraph 9)

A **related-party** is a person or entity that is related to the entity that is preparing its financial statements ("reporting entity"). 1.   The following three points illustrate how a person or a close member of that person's family is related to a reporting entity if that person:

   a. Has control or joint control over the reporting entity.
   b. Has significant influence over the reporting entity.
   c. Is a member of the key management personnel of the reporting entity or the parent of the reporting entity.

2. An entity is related to a reporting entity if any of the seven following conditions applies:

   a. The entity and the reporting entity are members of the same group (which means that each parent, subsidiary, and fellow subsidiary is related to the others).

   b. One entity is an associate or joint venture of the other entity (or an associate or a joint venture of a member of a group of which the other entity is a member).

   c. Both entities are joint ventures of the same third party.

   d. One entity is a joint venture of a third party and the other entity is an associate of the third party.

   e. The entity is a postemployment benefit plan for the benefit of employees of either the reporting entity or an entity related to the reporting entity. If the reporting entity is itself such a plan, the sponsoring employers are also related to the reporting entity.

   f. The entity is controlled or jointly controlled by a person identified in 1.

   g. A person identified in 1 (a) has significant influence over the entity or is a member of the key management personnel of the entity (or of a parent of the entity).

Related-party transaction. A transfer of resources, services, or obligations between related parties, *regardless of whether a price is charged **or not.***

Close family members of a person. Those family members *who may be expected to influence, or be influenced by,* that person, in their dealings with the entity and include

1. The person's domestic partner and children
2. Children of the person's domestic partner
3. Dependents of the person or the person's domestic partner

Compensation. Includes all employee benefits (as described in IAS 19, *Employee Benefits,* and IFRS 2, *Share-Based Payments*). It also includes consideration paid on behalf of a parent of the entity in respect of the entity.

Control. The power to govern the financial and operating policies of an entity so as to obtain benefits from its activities.

Joint control. The contractually agreed sharing of control.

Significant influence. The power to participate in the financial and operating decisions of an entity, but not having control over those policies.

Key management personnel. Those persons having authority and responsibility for planning, directing, and controlling the activities of an entity, either directly or indirectly, and include directors (executive or otherwise) of that entity.

EXPLANATION AND FURTHER ELABORATION OF THE DEFINITIONS

Most of the definitions are a matter of common sense insofar as they specifically include parent companies (in relation to a subsidiary), subsidiaries (in relation to the parent), fellow subsidiaries, associates, joint ventures, and key management. However, a number of definitions require in-depth analysis to comprehend the real meaning behind the terminology used.

Interpretations and clarifications of the various aspects of the definitions follow to enable the Standard to be applied in its true spirit. In fact, this is a requirement of the Standard, as it categorically states that *"in considering each related-party relationship, attention is directed to the substance of the relationship and not merely the legal form"* (IAS 24 [revised 2009], paragraph 10).

The amendment to IAS 24 in November 2009 changed definitions including that of a "related party." Certain related-party relationships were affected by the changes in the definitions. To comprehend the significance of the changes let us examine the following case studies:

CASE STUDY 1

Facts

P Inc. (parent company) owns a subsidiary, S Corp.

Person C is the CEO, *"key management personnel,"* of S Corp.

Entity Z Ltd. is jointly controlled by Person C.

Required

Is S Corp. a related party of Z Ltd. for the purposes of the financial statements of Z Ltd.?

Solution

Yes, under IAS 24 (revised 2009), S Corp. is a related party of Z Ltd. for the purposes of the financial statements of Z Ltd.

CASE STUDY 2

Facts

John Smith (father) and John Doe (son) are related parties ("close members of the family") in accordance with IAS 24.

John Smith (father) is in "joint control" of Amazing Inc.

John Doe (son) has "joint control" over a joint venture, Good Ltd.

Required

Keeping in mind the latest amendments to IAS 24, for the purposes of the financial statements of Amazing Inc. and Good Ltd., are related-party disclosures required in terms of IAS 24 (revised 2009)?

Solution

1. For the purposes of the financial statements of Amazing Inc.: Good Ltd., the entity joint controlled by John Doe (son) is a related party and therefore related-party transactions between them would attract disclosure requirements of IAS 24.
2. For the purposes of the financial statements of Good Ltd.: Amazing Inc., the entity under "joint control" of John Smith (father), is a related party and therefore related-party transactions between them would attract disclosure requirements of IAS 24.

Key Management Personnel

Key management personnel include all those who have authority and responsibility for planning, directing, and controlling the activities of an entity. Therefore, these persons *need not necessarily be directors.* The definition does indeed include "directors, executive, or otherwise."

PRACTICAL INSIGHT

This broad definition will include nonexecutive directors (NEDs) and what in some jurisdictions are termed "shadow directors"—those persons in accordance with whose instructions the directors act, whether those persons are legally called directors or not. This definition also includes key management personnel of the entity's parent.

Thus in most cases it would be difficult to avoid the related-party label. However, the Standard does state that two entities are not related solely because they have a director or other key management personnel in common. This statement recognizes the increasing use by significant entities of nonexecutive directors in order to satisfy corporate governance issues and requirements. Doing this can quite easily result in entities having common directors, as often such persons are retired politicians, civil servants, or prominent corporate executives, any one of whom may sit on various boards in their "retirement."

However, it must be remembered that for management personnel to be "key," they must have authority and responsibility for planning, directing, and controlling the entity's activities. For many of these "professional" NEDs, this will not be the case.

Close Members of the Family of an Individual

The issue of "close members of the family of an individual" is a thorny one. International Accounting Standards have always been designed to cater to cross-border jurisdictions, but this issue has cross-cultural dimensions as well. Although the Standard provides a list of persons that "close members of the family of an individual" are purported to include, the wording of the definition makes it clear that the list is by no means exhaustive. This fact is obvious; the definition is an inclusive one that begins with the word "includes," thus announcing clearly that "related parties" not specifically mentioned in the definition are not necessarily excluded under this principle and should not automatically be ruled out. In other words, IAS 24 puts the onus on the person applying the Standard to apply the Standard correctly. The Standard says that "close members of the family of an individual" are those *who may be expected to influence, or be influenced by, that individual, in his dealings with the entity.* To put it differently, and to sum up, it appears that the *other* "related parties" not specifically mentioned in this part of the definition, but covered by inference (because the Standard says "includes"), are a matter of interpretation. The burden of applying (accurately) the principle enshrined in the Standard rests squarely on the entity applying the Standard. This task is an onerous one, as under IAS 1, a set of financial statements cannot be described as prepared in accordance with International Financial Reporting Standards (IFRS) unless the provisions of *each and every Standard are fully complied with.*

PRACTICAL INSIGHT

This principle allows *cross-cultural interpretation* of the expression "close member of the family of an individual." For example, regarding siblings: In some cultures, the younger sibling may always defer to the elder. In other cultures, this may not be the case. Furthermore, in some cultures, where the families are very closely knit, relatives other than sons or daughters could also be considered as "close members of the family" because they could very well influence the individual in his or her dealings with the entity. However, in other countries, where each individual independently makes business decisions, this may not be the case. According to one school of thought, this anomaly could, to some extent, be avoided if the Standard provided an exhaustive and prescribed list of "close members of the family of an individual" (as is the case in accounting standards of some countries).

PRACTICAL INSIGHT

Yet another "gray" area is that of "children" of an individual. The Standard states that children are related parties but does not clarify whether it is referring only to minors. If the definition is stretched to include even "adult children," it could give rise to disagreement based on the principle of substance over form. It may be possible to interpret this area in the light of one of the other elements of the definition of "close members of the family of the individual"—that of "dependents" of the individual. In some cases, parents may be dependent on a child for financial, emotional, or physical support; thus they are related parties. This interpretation could be extended to the definition of children also, so that if the children are not dependent, they are not necessarily related parties for the purposes of the Standard. This is, however, a very fine line to draw and possibly an aggressive interpretation.

PRACTICAL INSIGHT

According to one school of thought, by referring to "domestic partners" rather than "spouses," the Standard recognizes the trend in some cultures for persons to cohabit without marrying. For all intents and purposes, they are "spouses."

CASE STUDY 3

Facts

Interesting Inc. is a manufacturer of automobile spare parts. It transacts business through a business model that has worked for several years and has made the entity a successful enterprise that is rated in the top ten businesses in its field by a trade journal. Interesting Inc. believes in working with reliable and dependable vendors and also sells only to entities that it can either control or exercise significant influence over. The business model works in this way:

1. Interesting Inc. purchases everything it needs from Excellent Inc., a well-known supplier. Due to the high quality of the material that Excellent Inc. has provided over the last ten years, Interesting Inc. has never purchased from any other supplier. Thus it may be considered economically dependent on Excellent Inc.
2. Interesting Inc. sells 70% of its output to a company owned by a director and the balance to an entity that is its "associate" by virtue of Interesting Inc. owning 35% of the share capital of that company.
3. Interesting Inc. stores inventory in a warehouse that is leased from the wife of its director. The lease rentals are at arm's length.
4. Interesting Inc. has provided an interest-free loan to a company owned by the chief executive officer (CEO) of Interesting Inc. for the purposes of financing the purchase of delivery vans which the company owned by the CEO is using for transporting goods from the warehouse of the supplier to the warehouse used by Interesting Inc. for storing inventory.

Required

Based on the requirements of IAS 24, identify which transactions would need to be disclosed as related-party transactions under IAS 24.

Solution

Let us examine each of the transactions in order to determine whether they would warrant disclosure as a related-party transaction under IAS 24.

1. Notwithstanding the fact that Interesting Inc. purchases all its raw materials from Excellent Inc. and is economically dependent on it, Excellent Inc. does not automatically become a related party. Thus for the purpose of IAS 24, purchases made from Excellent Inc. are not considered related-party transactions.
2. 70% of the sales are to an entity owned by a "director" (i.e., an entity controlled by a key management person), and 30% of the sales are made to an entity that Interesting Inc. has "significant influence" over. Thus both sales are to related parties as defined in IAS 24 and would need to be disclosed as such.
3. The lease of the warehouse, although at arm's length, has been entered into with the wife (a "close member of the family") of a "director" (a key management person) and thus needs to be disclosed as a related-party transaction.
4. The interest-free loan to an entity owned by a director needs to be disclosed as a related-party transaction. The fact that it is interest-free may warrant disclosure because it may not be construed as an "arm's-length transaction" since Interesting Inc. would not normally provide unrelated parties with interest-free loans.

NOTE: IAS 24, paragraph 21, requires that "disclosures that related-party transactions were made on terms equivalent to those that prevail in arm's-length transactions are made only if such terms can be substantiated."

Furthermore, the rental expenses paid for hiring a delivery van belonging to an entity owned by a director also would need to be disclosed as a related-party transaction since these charges are paid to an entity "controlled" by a key management person.

Joint Ventures

The Standard clarifies that two parties to a joint venture are not related solely through their contractual relationship. The *joint venture* would be a related party of each venturer by definition, but, if the joint venture contract is the *only* relationship between the two venturers, this does not make them related.

Compensation to Key Management Personnel

In the past, it has always been arguable as to whether "directors' remuneration" was a related-party transaction. While in some jurisdictions law requires disclosure, it has been debated as to whether IAS 24 referred to such transactions. The Standard now makes very clear that such transactions are included, no matter how they are termed.

SCOPE EXCLUSIONS AND EXEMPTION

Exclusions

Although apparently some parties, by virtue of their relationship with the entity, may appear as related parties falling within the scope of IAS 24, the Standard clarifies that the following parties are not necessarily related parties as envisaged in the Standard:

- Providers of finance, trade unions, public utilities, and government departments and agencies (that do not control, jointly control, or significantly influence the reporting entity) are not necessarily related parties simply by virtue of their normal dealings with an entity, even if they participate in decision-making processes or affect freedom of action.
- Customers, suppliers, franchisors, distributors, or general agents with whom an entity transacts a significant volume of business are not related to an entity solely because the entity is economically dependent on them.
- Two entities are not related parties simply because they have common directors or other members of key management personnel in common.
- Two venturers are not related parties simply because they share joint control over a joint venture.

Partial Exemption for Government-Related Entities, Amendment to IAS 24 Effective for Periods Beginning on or after January 1, 2011 (with earlier application permitted)

The erstwhile provisions of IAS 24 (i.e., prior to the amendment made in November 2009) did not provide a specific exemption for disclosure of related-party transactions among government-related entities. In certain jurisdictions, particularly in China, a global economic player, this provided practical challenges in identifying and reporting related-party transactions. It was argued that in such jurisdictions the government does not exert influence (despite its ownership interests) to impact the economic outcomes of transactions between government-related entities as well as with the government itself and therefore this phenomenon required a specific clarification or an amendment to the Standard.

The IASB addressed these concerns by revising the Standard and providing a partial exemption for government-related entities from the general disclosure requirements of the Standard (explained later and outlined in paragraph 18 of IAS 24 [revised 2009]).

DISCLOSURES

In order to enable users of financial statements to better understand the financial position of an entity and to form a view about the effects of related-party transactions on an entity, IAS 24 has mandated extensive disclosure requirements with respect to related-party transactions.

IAS 24 (revised 2009), paragraph 21, provides examples of general disclosures of transactions with related parties:

- Purchases or sales of goods and sales of property or other assets
- Rendering or receiving of services
- Leases
- Transfers of research and developments, transfers under license agreements, and finance agreements
- Provision of guarantees or collateral
- Providing commitments to do something if a particular event occurs or does not occur
- Settlement of liabilities by a related party on behalf of the entity or by the entity on behalf of the related party

---

PRACTICAL INSIGHT

Participation by a parent or subsidiary in a defined benefit plan that shares risks between group entities is a related-parties transaction in accordance with a specific provision of paragraph 22 of IAS 24 (revised 2009).

According to IAS 24 (revised 2009), paragraph 13, an entity should disclose

- Relationships between parents and subsidiaries regardless of whether there have been any transactions between them.
- The name of the entity's parent and, if different, the ultimate controlling party. If neither the entity's parent nor the ultimate controlling party produces financial statements available for public use, the name of the "next most senior parent" that does so shall also be disclosed.

PRACTICAL INSIGHT

The Standard (IAS 24 [revised 2009], paragraph 16) clarifies the meaning of "next most senior parent"—it refers to the first parent in the group above the immediate parent that produces consolidated financial statements available for public use.

According to IAS 24 (revised 2009), paragraph 17, an entity should disclose "key management personnel" compensation in total and for each of these categories:

1. Short-term employee benefits
2. Postemployment benefits
3. Other long-term benefits
4. Termination benefits
5. Share-based payments

IAS 24 (revised 2009), paragraph 18, states that if there have been transactions between related parties, an entity should disclose the nature of the related-party relationship as well as information about the transactions and outstanding balances necessary for an understanding of the potential effect of the relationship on the financial statements. *At a minimum, disclosures shall include*

- The amount of the transactions
- The amount of outstanding balances:
  - Their terms and conditions
  - Whether they are secured or unsecured
  - The nature of the settlement consideration
  - Details of guarantees given or received
- Provisions for doubtful debts against balances outstanding
- Provisions for doubtful debts recognized as an expense

According to IAS 24 (revised 2009), paragraph 19, these disclosures are required to be *disclosed separately for each of these categories of related party:*

- Parent
- Entities with joint control or significant influence over the entity
- Subsidiaries
- Associates
- Joint ventures in which the entity is a venturer
- Key management personnel of the entity or its parent
- Other related parties

IAS 24 (revised 2009), paragraph 24, states that items of a *similar nature* may be *disclosed in aggregate* except when separate disclosure is necessary for an understanding of the effects of related-party transactions on the financial statements of the entity.

Government-Related Entities

In accordance with the latest revision to IAS 24, effective for periods beginning on or after January 1, 2011, a reporting entity is exempt from the disclosure requirements of paragraph 18 of IAS 24 (revised 2009) in terms of related-party transactions and outstanding balances, and commitments.

IAS 24 (revised 2009), paragraph 26, prescribes the following alternative disclosure requirements in case an exemption relating to government-related entities is applied by a reporting entity:

- The name of the government and the nature of its relationship with the reporting entity (i.e., control, joint control, or significant influence).
- The nature and amount of each individually significant transaction.
- For other transactions, that are collectively significant, a qualitative or quantitative indication of their extent.

According to IAS 24 (revised 2009), paragraph 27, in assessing the level of detail to be disclosed in accordance with the previously mentioned requirement of the Standard, the reporting entity should evaluate factors such as "closeness of the relationship" and "other factors" such as whether it is

- Significant in terms of size
- Carried out on nonmarket terms
- Outside normal day-to-day business operations, such as purchase and sale of businesses
- Disclosed to regulatory or supervisory authorities
- Reported to senior management
- Subject to shareholder approval

CASE STUDY 4

Facts

Zeeba Inc. is part of a major industrial group of companies and is known to accurately disclose related-party transactions in its financial statements prepared under IFRS. With the sweeping changes that were made to the various Standards under the International Accounting Standards Board's Improvements Project, the entity is seeking advice from IFRS specialists on whether the following transactions need to be reported under IAS 24 and, if so, to what extent, and how the related-party transactions footnote should be worded.

1. Remuneration and other payments made to the entity's chief executive officer (CEO) during the year 20XX were

   a. An annual salary of $2 million
   b. Share options and other share-based payments valued at $1 million
   c. Contributions to retirement benefit plan amounting to $1 million
   d. Reimbursement of his travel expenses for business trips totaling $1.2 million

2. Sales made during the year 20XX to

   a. Meifa, Inc., parent company: $35 million

   b. Deifa, Inc., associate: $25 million

3. Trade debtors at December 31, 20XX, include

   a. Due from Meifa, Inc.: Gross: $10 million, Net of provision: $7 million

   b. Due from Deifa, Inc.: $15 million (these receivables are fully backed by corporate guarantees from Deifa, Inc.)

Required

Please advise Zeeba, Inc. on related-party transactions that need to be disclosed and draft a sample related-party transactions footnote to guide the entity.

Solution

1. All the listed items are required to be disclosed in Zeeba, Inc.'s financial statements prepared under IFRS. The only *exception* is the *reimbursement of the travel expenses* of *the CEO amounting to $1.2 million*; as this sum is not "compensation," it is not required to be disclosed under IAS 24.

2. Footnote: Related-Party Transactions

   a. Zeeba, Inc. enters into related-party transactions in the normal course of business. During the year 20XX, these related-party transactions were entered into with related parties as defined under IAS 24. The transactions resulted in balances due from those two parties that, at December 31, 20XX, were

     (1) With the parent company (Meifa, Inc.)

Sales	$35 million
Included in trade debtors (due from parent company)	$10 million
Provision for doubtful debts	$ 3 million

     (2) With an "associate"

Sales	$25 million
Included in trade debtors (due from an associate)*	$15 million

         * *Amount due from an associate is secured by a corporate guarantee given by the associate.*

   b. For the year ended December 31, 20XX, Zeeba, Inc. made these payments to its CEO, part of the "key management personnel":

Short-term benefits (salary)	$2 million
Postemployment benefits (retirement benefit plan contribution)	$1 million
Share-based payments (stock options, etc.)	$1 million
Total	$4 million

EXTRACTS FROM PUBLISHED FINANCIAL STATEMENTS

BARLOWORLD, Annual Report, 2009

Related-Party Transactions

Various transactions are entered into by the company and its subsidiaries during the year with related parties. Unless specifically disclosed these transactions occurred under terms that are no less favorable than those entered into with third parties. Intragroup transactions are eliminated on consolidation.

The following is a summary of other transactions with related parties during the year and balances due at year-end:

R million	*Associates of the group*	*Joint ventures in which the group is a venture*
2009		
Goods and services sold to		
Bartrac Equipment		5
Barloworld Heftruck Verhuur B.V.		97
	--	**102**
Goods and services purchased from		
Barloworld Heftruck Verhuur B.V		11
	--	**11**

R million	Associates of the group	Joint ventures in which the group is a venture
Other transactions		
Management fees received from joint ventures		5
Other transactions	--	1
	--	**6**
Amount due (to)/from related parties as at end of year*		
Vostochnaya Technica Siberia loan		73
PhakisaWorld Fleet Solutions loan		2
Subaru Southern Africa (Pty) Limited		11
Barloworld Siyakhula (Pty) Limited	5	--
	5	**86**
2008		
Goods and services sold to		
Bartrac Equipment		87
The Used Equipment Co (Pty) Limited		9
Vostochnaya Technica UK		7
Energyst B.V.	3	--
Barloworld Heftruck Verhuur B.V		12
PhakisaWorld Fleet Solutions		101
	3	**216**
Goods and services purchased from		
The Used Equipment Co (Pty) Limited		94
Barloworld Heftruck Verhuur B.V		29
	--	**123**
Other Transactions		
Management fees received from joint ventures		11
	--	11
Amounts due (to)/from related parties as at end of year		
Vostochnaya Technica Siberia loan		275
PhakisaWorld Fleet Solutions loan		221
Other loans to joint venturers		10
		506
2007		
Goods and services sold to		
Barzem Enterprises (Pty) Limited	26	
Du Pont Barloworld (Pty) Limited (Herberts)	89	
International Paints (Pty) Limited	38	
NMI Durban South Motors (Pty) Limited		8
Sizwe Paints (Pty) Limited	20	
The Used Equipment Co (Pty) Limited		34
PhakisaWorld Fleet Solutions	39	
Other sales to related parties	6	--
	218	**42**
Goods and services purchased from		
NMI Durban South Motors (Pty) Limited		4
Du Pont Barloworld (Pty) Limited (Herberts)	4	
	4	**4**
Other transactions		
Management fees received from associates	4	--
	4	--
Amounts due (to)/from related parties as at end of year		
Barzem Enterprises (Pty) Limited	(15)	
Du Pont Barloworld (Pty) Limited (Herberts)	9	
International Paints (Pty) Limited	10	
NMI Durban South Motors (Pty) Limited		1
PhakisaWorld Fleet Solutions	22	
PhakisaWorld Fleet Solutions loan	184	
The Used Equipment Co (Pty) Limited		127
Vostochnaya Technica Siberia loan		100
Other loans to associates	19	
	229	**228**

Terms on other outstanding balances

Unless otherwise noted, all outstanding balances are payable within 30 days, unsecured, and not guaranteed.

Except for the impairment of the Finaltair loan, there are no doubtful debt provisions raised in respect of amounts due to/from related parties and no bad debts incurred during the year on these balances.

Associates and joint ventures

The loans to associates and joint ventures are repayable on demand and bear interest at market-related rates.

The loan to Finaltair was fully impaired during 2007 as per note 5.

Details of investments in associates and joint ventures are disclosed in notes 5, 39, and 40.

Subsidiaries

Details of investments in subsidiaries are disclosed in note 37.

Directors

Details regarding directors' remuneration and interests are disclosed in note 36, and share options are disclosed in note 34.

Transactions with key management and other related parties (excluding directors)

There were no material transactions with key management or close family members of related parties.

Shareholders

The principal shareholders of the company are disclosed on page 64.

Barloworld Medical Scheme

Contributions of R84 million were made to the Barloworld Medical Scheme on behalf of employees (2008: R73 million; 2007:R92 million.

HSBC HOLDING PLC, Annual Report, 2009

43. Related-Party Transactions

Related parties of the Group and HSBC Holdings include subsidiaries, associates, joint ventures, post-employment benefit plans for HSBC employees, key management personnel, close family members of key management personnel and entities which are controlled, jointly controlled or significantly influenced, or for which significant voting power is held, by key management personnel or their close family members.

Key management personnel are defined as those persons having authority and responsibility for planning, directing and controlling the activities of HSBC Holdings, being the Directors and Group Managing Directors of HSBC Holdings.

Compensation of Key Management Personnel

	HSBC		
	2009	*2008*	*2007*
	US$m	*US$m*	*US$m*
Short-term employee benefits	22	31	62
Postemployment benefits	3	5	4
Termination benefits	--	--	9
Share-based payments	27	16	40
	52	52	115

PRACTICAL INSIGHT

IAS 24 (revised 2009), paragraph 23, now clarifies that it is only permissible to make a disclosure that related-party transactions were made at an arm's length (i.e. on terms that are equivalent to those with "third parties") if such terms can be substantiated. In practice, it was noted that there was a tendency on the part of entities to make disclosures in their financial statements to the effect that "related party transactions are at arm's length" or were made on "normal terms." With such an explicit clarification within IAS 24 it is now incumbent upon the entity (and also auditors of the entity) to ensure that such disclosures would only be made if they can be substantiated.

Examples of how this requirement of the Standard could present challenges in practice are

1. Credit terms offered to related parties vis-á-vis third parties. If an entity offers 120 days' credit terms to sales made to a related party when it normally offers 60 days' credit terms to others it would be difficult for the entity to justify a disclosure to the effect in the financial statements of the entity that "related-party transactions are made at arm's length."

2. The pricing of related-party transactions is often a sensitive subject, particularly if pricing is not at arm's length. This area can be a difficult one that is open to judgment. For example, an entity may sell 60% of its production to a related party at unit prices substantially lower than what it charges other third parties for the balance 40% production. None of the third parties accounted for more than 5% of the sales. It may be very difficult to determine whether the volume discount was at a market rate. It can be even more difficult to determine arm's length if there are no sales to third parties. *In such cases, the Standard states that a transaction can be described as at arm's length only if it can be substantiated.* Thus it is the responsibility of the management to prove the market value of transactions if *it wishes to describe transactions as "at market value."*

MULTIPLE-CHOICE QUESTIONS

1. Which of the following is **not** a related party as envisaged by IAS 24?
    (a) A director of the entity.
    (b) The parent company of the entity.
    (c) A shareholder of the entity that holds 1% stake in the entity.
    (d) The son of the chief executive officer of the entity.

2. IAS 24 requires disclosure of compensation of key management personnel. Which of the following would **not** be considered "compensation" for this purpose?
    (a) Short-term benefits.
    (b) Share-based payments.
    (c) Termination benefits.
    (d) Reimbursement of out-of-pocket expenses.

3. To enable financial statement users to form a view about the effects of the related-party transactions, IAS 24 requires certain disclosures to be made. Which of the following disclosures is **not** a mandated disclosure under IAS 24?
    (a) Relationships between parents and subsidiaries irrespective of whether there have been transactions between those related parties.
    (b) Names of all the "associates" that an entity has dealt with during the year.
    (c) Name of the entity's parent and, if different, the ultimate controlling party.
    (d) If neither the entity's parent nor its ultimate controlling entity produces financial statements available for public use, then the name of the next most senior parent that does so.

4. If there have been related-party transactions during the year, an entity needs to make, at a minimum, certain disclosures. Which of the following is **not** a required minimum disclosure under IAS 24?
    (a) The amount of the related-party transactions.
    (b) The amount of the outstanding related-party balances and their terms and conditions along with details of guarantees given and received.
    (c) The amounts of similar transactions with unrelated (third) parties to establish that comparable related-party transactions have been entered at arm's length.
    (d) Provisions for doubtful debts related to the amount of outstanding related-party balances and expense recognized during the year in respect of bad or doubtful debts due from related parties.

5. The minimum disclosures prescribed under IAS 24 are to be made separately for certain categories of related parties. Which of the following is **not** among the list of categories specified under the Standard for the purposes of separate disclosure?
    (a) Entities with joint control or significant influence over the entity.
    (b) The parent company of the entity.
    (c) An entity that has a common director with the entity.
    (d) Joint ventures in which the entity is a venturer.

Chapter 18

ACCOUNTING AND REPORTING BY RETIREMENT BENEFIT PLANS (IAS 26)

INTRODUCTION

IAS 26 deals with accounting and reporting to all participants of a retirement benefit plan as a group, and not with reports that might be made to individuals about their particular retirement benefits. The Standard sets out the form and content of the general-purpose financial reports of retirement benefit plans. The Standard applies to

- **Defined contribution plans.** Where benefits are determined by contributions to the plan together with investment earnings thereon.
- **Defined benefit plans.** Where benefits are determined by a formula based on employees' earnings and/or years of service.

IAS 26 is sometimes confused with IAS 19, because both Standards address employee benefits. But there is a difference: While IAS 26 addresses the financial reporting considerations for the benefit plan itself, as the reporting entity, IAS 19 deals with employers' accounting for the cost of such benefits as they are earned by the employees. These Standards are thus somewhat related, but there will not be any direct interrelationship between amounts reported in benefit plan financial statements and amounts reported under IAS 19 by employers.

SCOPE

IAS 26 addresses the accounting and reporting by retirement benefit plans. It does not mandate the presentation of an annual report for the plan. However, the terms of a retirement plan may require that the plan present an annual report; in some jurisdictions this may be a statutory requirement. If such annual reports are prepared by a retirement plan, then the requirements of this Standard should be applied to them.

The retirement benefit plan is a separate entity, distinct from the employer of the plan's participants; the Standard treats it as such. The Standard also applies to retirement benefit plans that have sponsors other than the employer (e.g., trade associations or groups of employers). Furthermore, this Standard deals with accounting and reporting by retirement benefit plans to all participants as a group; it does not deal with reports to individual participants with respect to their retirement benefit entitlements.

Whether there are formal retirement benefit plans or informal retirement benefit arrangements, the Standard prescribes the same accounting for both. It is also worthy of mention that this Standard applies whether a separate fund is created or not and regardless of whether there are trustees. The requirements of this Standard also apply to retirement benefit plans with assets invested with an insurance company, unless the contract with the insurance company is in the name of a specified participant or a group of participants and the responsibility is solely of the insurance company.

DEFINITIONS OF KEY TERMS
(In accordance with IAS 26)

Actuarial present value of promised retirement benefits. The present value of the expected future payments by a retirement benefit plan to existing and past employees, attributable to the service already rendered.

Defined benefit plans. Retirement benefit plans whereby retirement benefits to be paid to plan participants are determined by reference to a formula usually based on employees' earnings and/or years of service.

Defined contribution plans. Retirement benefit plans whereby retirement benefits to be paid to plan participants are determined by contributions to a fund together with investment earnings thereon.

Funding. The transfer of assets to a separate entity (distinct from the employer's enterprise), the "fund," to meet future obligations for the payment of retirement benefits.

Net assets available for benefits. The assets of a retirement benefit plan less its liabilities other than the actuarial present value of promised retirement benefits.

Participants. The members of a retirement benefit plan and others who are entitled to benefits under the plan.

Retirement benefit plans. Formal or informal arrangements based on which an enterprise provides benefits for its employees on or after termination of service, which usually are referred to as termination benefits. These could take the form of annual pension payments or lump-sum payments. Such benefits, or the employer's contributions toward them, should however be determinable or possible of estimation in advance of retirement from the provisions of a document (i.e., based on a formal arrangement) or from the enterprise's practices (which is referred to as an informal arrangement).

Vested benefits. Entitlements, the rights to which, under the terms of a retirement benefit plan, are not conditional on continued employment.

DEFINED CONTRIBUTION PLANS

Retirement benefit plans can either be defined contribution plans or defined benefit plans. When the amount of the future benefits payable to the participants of the retirement benefit plan is determined by the contributions made by the participants' employer, the participants, or both, together with investment earnings thereon, such plans are defined contribution plans. Defined benefit plans guarantee certain defined benefits, often determined by a formula that takes into consideration factors such as number of years of service of employees and their salary level at the time of retirement, irrespective of whether the plan has sufficient assets; thus the ultimate responsibility for payment (which may be guaranteed by an insurance company, the government, or some other entity, depending on local law and custom) remains with the employer. In rare cases, a retirement benefit plan may contain characteristics of both defined contribution and defined benefit plans; for the purposes of this Standard, such a hybrid plan is deemed to be a defined benefit plan.

According to IAS 26, the report of a defined contribution plan should contain a "Statement of the Net Assets Available for Benefits" and a description of the funding policy. In preparing the statement of the net assets available for benefits, the plan investments should be carried at "fair value," which in the case of marketable securities would be their "market value." If an estimate of fair value is not possible, the entity must disclose why "fair value" has not been used.

PRACTICAL INSIGHT

In practice, in many cases, "plan assets" will have determinable market values, because in discharge of their fiduciary responsibilities, plan trustees generally will mandate that the retirement plans hold only marketable investments.

Example

An example of a statement of net assets available for plan benefits, for a defined contribution plan, is presented next.

Benevolent Corp. Defined Contribution Plan
STATEMENT OF NET ASSETS AVAILABLE FOR BENEFITS
December 31, 2009
(in thousands of US $)

Assets	
Investments at fair value:	
US government securities	$10,000
US municipal bonds	13,000
US equity securities	13,000
EU equity securities	13,000
US debt securities	12,000
EU corporate bonds	12,000
Others	11,000
Total investments	84,000
Receivables:	
Amounts due from stockbrokers on sale of securities	25,000
Accrued interest	15,000
Dividends receivable	12,000
Total receivables	52,000
Cash:	15,000
Total assets	151,000
Liabilities	
Accounts payable	
Amounts due to stockbrokers on purchase of securities	20,000
Benefits payable to participants—due and unpaid	21,000
Total accounts payable	41,000
Accrued expenses	21,000
Total liabilities	62,000
Net assets available for benefits	89,000

DEFINED BENEFIT PLANS

Defined benefit plans are those plans where the benefits are guaranteed amounts and amounts to be paid as retirement benefits are determined by reference to a formula, usually based on employees' earnings and/or number of years of service. The critical factors are thus the retirement benefits that are fixed or determinable, without regard to the adequacy of assets that may have been set aside for payment of the benefits. This clearly is different from the way defined contribution plans work; they provide the employees, upon retirement, amounts that have been set aside, plus or minus investment earnings or losses that have been accumulated thereon, however great or small that amount may be.

IAS 26 requires that the report of a defined benefit plan should contain one of the two following statements, *either*

1. A statement that shows

   a. The net assets available for benefits
   b. The actuarial present value of promised retirement benefits, distinguishing between vested and nonvested benefits
   c. The resulting excess or deficit

or

2. A statement of net assets available for benefits including *either*

   a. A note disclosing the actuarial present value of promised retirement benefits, distinguishing between vested and nonvested benefits, *or*
   b. A reference to this information in an accompanying actuarial report

IAS 26 recommends, but does not mandate, that in each of the three formats just described, a report of the trustees in the nature of a management or directors' report and an investment report may also accompany the statements.

The Standard does not make it incumbent upon the plan to use annual actuarial valuations. If an actuarial valuation has not been prepared on the date of the report, the most recent valuation should be used as the basis for preparing the financial statement. The Standard does, however, require that the date of the actuarial valuation used should be disclosed. Actuarial present values of promised benefits should be based either on current or projected salary levels; *whichever basis is used should also be disclosed.* Furthermore, the effect of any changes in actuarial assumptions that had a material impact on the actuarial present value of promised retirement benefits should also be disclosed. The report should explain the relationship between actuarial present values of promised benefits, the net assets available for benefits, and the policy for funding the promised benefits.

As in the case of defined contribution plans, investments of a defined benefit plan should be carried at fair value, which for marketable securities would be "market values."

Example

Examples of the alternative types of reports prescribed for a defined benefit plan follow.

Excellent Inc. Defined Benefit Plan
**STATEMENT OF NET ASSETS AVAILABLE FOR BENEFITS, ACTUARIAL
PRESENT VALUE OF ACCUMULATED RETIREMENT
BENEFITS AND PLAN EXCESS OR DEFICIT**
December 31, 2009
(in thousands of US $)

1. Statement of net assets available for benefits:

Assets	
Investments at fair value:	
US government securities	155,000
US municipal bonds	35,000
US equity securities	35,000
EU equity securities	35,000
US debt securities	25,000
EU corporate bonds	25,000
Others	15,000
Total investments	325,000
Receivables:	
Amounts due from stockbrokers on sale of securities	155,000
Accrued interest	55,000
Dividends receivable	25,000
Total receivables	235,000
Cash:	55,000
Total assets	615,000
Liabilities	
Accounts payable:	
Amounts due to stockbrokers on purchase of securities	150,000
Benefits payable to participants–due and unpaid	150,000
Total accounts payable	300,000
Accrued expenses:	120,000
Total liabilities	420,000
Net assets available for benefits	195,000

2. Actuarial present value of accumulated plan benefits:

Vested benefits	120,000
Nonvested benefits	30,000
Total	150,000

3. Excess of net assets available for benefits over actuarial present
   value of accumulated plan benefits   45,000

Excellent Inc. Defined Benefit Plan
STATEMENT OF CHANGES IN NET ASSETS AVAILABLE FOR BENEFITS
December 31, 2009
(in thousands of US $)

Investment income:	
Interest income	45,000
Dividend income	15,000
Net appreciation (unrealized gain) in fair value of investments	15,000
Total investment income	75,000
Plan contributions:	
Employer contributions	55,000
Employee contributions	50,000
Total plan contributions	105,000
Total additions to net asset value	180,000
Plan benefit payments:	
Pensions (annual)	25,000
Lump-sum payments on retirement	35,000
Severance pay	10,000
Commutation of superannuation benefits	15,000
Total plan benefit payments	85,000
Total deductions from net asset value	85,000
Net increase in asset value	95,000
Net assets available for benefits	
Beginning of year	100,000
End of year	195,000

ADDITIONAL DISCLOSURES REQUIRED BY THE STANDARD

In the case of both defined benefit plans and defined contribution plans, IAS 26 requires that the reports of a retirement benefit plan should also contain this information:

- A statement of changes in net assets available for benefits
- A summary of significant accounting policies
- A description of the plan and the effect of any changes in the plan during the period

Reports provided by retirement benefits plans may include any of the following five, if applicable:

1. A statement of net assets available for benefits disclosing

   a. Assets at the end of the period, suitably classified
   b. The basis of valuation of assets
   c. Details of any single investment exceeding either 5% of the net assets available for benefits or 5% of any class or type of security
   d. Details of any investment in the employer
   e. Liabilities other than the actuarial present value of promised retirement benefits

2. A statement of changes in net assets available for benefits showing

   a. Employer contributions
   b. Employee contributions
   c. Investment income such as interest and dividends
   d. Other income

    e. Benefits paid or payable (analyzed, e.g., as retirement, death, and disability benefits, and lump-sum payments)

    f. Administrative expenses

    g. Other expenses

    h. Taxes on income

    i. Profits and losses on disposal of investments and changes in value of investments

    j. Transfers from and to other plans

3. A description of the funding policy.
4. For defined benefit plans, the actuarial present value of promised retirement benefits (which may distinguish between vested benefits and nonvested benefits) based on the benefits promised under the terms of the plan, on service rendered to date and using either current salary levels or projected salary levels. This information may be included in an accompanying actuarial report to be read in conjunction with the related information.
5. For defined benefit plans, a description of the significant actuarial assumptions made and the method used to calculate the actuarial present value of promised retirement benefits.

According to the Standard, since the report of a retirement benefit plan contains a description of the plan, either as part of the financial information or in a separate report, it may contain any of the following seven:

1. The names of the employers and the employee groups covered
2. The number of participants receiving benefits and the number of other participants, classified as appropriate
3. The type of plan—defined contribution or defined benefit
4. A note as to whether participants contribute to the plan
5. A description of the retirement benefits promised to participants
6. A description of any plan termination terms
7. Changes in items 1. through 6. during the period covered by the report

Furthermore, it is not uncommon to refer to other documents that are readily available to users in which the plan is described, and to include in the report only information on subsequent changes.

MULTIPLE-CHOICE QUESTIONS

1. IAS 26 deals with
   (a) Employers' accounting for the cost of retirement benefits.
   (b) General-purpose financial statements of financial reports of retirement benefit plans.
   (c) Only defined contribution plans and not defined benefit plans.
   (d) Only defined benefit plans and not defined contribution plans.

2. In rare circumstances, when a retirement benefit plan has attributes of both defined contribution and defined benefit plans, according to IAS 26 it is deemed
   (a) Defined benefit plan.
   (b) Defined contribution plan.
   (c) Neither a defined benefit nor a defined contribution plan.
   (d) For aspects of the hybrid plan that are similar to a defined benefit plan: provisions of IAS 26 applicable to such plans are to be applied; for aspects of the hybrid plan that are similar to a defined contribution plan, provisions of IAS 26 that apply to such plans are to be applied.

3. In the case of a defined benefit plan, IAS 26
   (a) Makes it incumbent upon the plan to obtain an actuarial valuation.
   (b) Does not make it incumbent upon the plan to obtain an actuarial valuation.
   (c) Allows the plan to estimate the present value of future benefits based on valuations done by other similar plans.
   (d) Allows the plan to add a percentage based on consumer price index to the previous year's valuation of actuarial valuation.

Chapter 19

CONSOLIDATED AND SEPARATE
FINANCIAL STATEMENTS (IAS 27)

SCOPE

The Standard is to be applied in preparing the consolidated financial statements of groups of companies controlled by a parent entity. The objective of IAS 27 is to enhance the relevance, reliability, and comparability of the information that a parent entity provides in its separate financial statements and in its consolidated financial statements for a group of entities under its control. The Standard specifies

1. The circumstances in which an entity must consolidate the financial statements of another entity (being a subsidiary).
2. The accounting for changes in the level of ownership interest in a subsidiary.
3. The accounting for the loss of control of a subsidiary.
4. The information that an entity must disclose to enable users of the financial statements to evaluate the nature of the relationship between the entity and its subsidiaries.

DEFINITIONS OF KEY TERMS
(in accordance with IAS 27)

Consolidated financial statements. The financial statements of a group shown as those of a single economic entity.

Subsidiary. An entity controlled by another entity.

Parent. An entity that has one or more subsidiaries.

Control. The power to govern the financial and operating policies of an entity.

Noncontrolling interest. The portion of the equity interest not owned by the parent.

PRESENTATION OF FINANCIAL STATEMENTS

Financial statements should be presented by the parent entity unless these four conditions are met:

1. A parent is the wholly owned subsidiary or is a partially owned subsidiary of another entity and its other owners do not object to the parent not preparing consolidated financial statements.
2. The parent's equity or debt capital is not traded on a public market.
3. The parent did not file nor is it filing its financial statements with a securities commission or other regulator for the purpose of issuing shares.
4. The ultimate or intermediate parent of the parent produces consolidated financial statements that comply with International Financial Reporting Standards (IFRS) and that are for public use.

There is a limited exception available to some nonpublic entities. However, that exception does not relieve venture capital organizations, mutual funds, unit trusts, and similar entities from consolidating their subsidiaries.

CONSOLIDATED FINANCIAL STATEMENTS

All subsidiaries of the parent should be consolidated. Control is presumed to exist when the parent owns either directly or indirectly more than half of the voting rights of the entity.

In exceptional circumstances, if it can be demonstrated that such ownership does not constitute control, then the parent/subsidiary relationship does not exist. Even if less than half or even half of the voting rights is acquired, it is still possible for control to exist where there is power:

- Over more than half of the voting rights because of an agreement with other investors
- To govern the financial and operating policies of the entity by law or by agreement
- To appoint or remove the majority of the members of the board of directors and control of the entity is by that board
- To cast the majority of votes at a meeting of the board of directors and control is exercised by that board

---

PRACTICAL INSIGHT

TPSA, a Polish entity, discloses in its financial statements that it has a 66% subsidiary; the remaining 34% is held by another party. TPSA had the right to nominate four out of six members of the subsidiary's management board, although the minority shareholder had a blocking right in various circumstances. The articles were changed so that members of the board were nominated equally by TPSA and the minority shareholder. The view taken by TPSA was that the blocking rights were not intended to deprive it of its ability to control the subsidiary and have never been used as such. TPSA considers that it continues to exercise control under IAS 27 and continues to consolidate the subsidiary.

A subsidiary cannot be excluded from consolidation because its business is dissimilar from that of the other entities within the group.

An entity loses control when it loses the power to govern its financial and operating policies. This could occur, for example, where a subsidiary becomes subject to the control of the government, a regulator, a court of law, or as a result of a contractual agreement.

The Standard does not require the consolidation of a subsidiary where the control is intended to be temporary. There should be evidence that the subsidiary has been acquired with the intention to dispose of it within 12 months and that management is actively seeking a buyer.

A subsidiary that has previously been excluded from consolidation and is not disposed of within the 12-month period must be consolidated from the date of acquisition.

A subsidiary that is operating under severe long-term restrictions that impair its ability to transfer funds to the parent should not be excluded from consolidation. Control must be lost for the exclusion to happen.

CASE STUDY 1

Facts

There are currently severe restrictions on the repatriation of dividends from a subsidiary located in Country A. As a result, the directors of the parent entity wish to deconsolidate the subsidiary as they feel that this restriction may be in place for several years. Two subsidiaries located in the country are individually immaterial but collectively material. The directors also wish to deconsolidate these entities.

Required

Can the results of these subsidiaries be deconsolidated?

Solution

Control must be lost for deconsolidation to occur, and the impairment of the ability to transfer funds is not sufficient reason. Therefore, the subsidiary should be consolidated. Also, IFRS do not apply to immaterial items, but the two subsidiaries should be taken together and in this instance are material. Hence this is also not a reason for deconsolidation.

ACCOUNTING PROCEDURES

The group must use uniform accounting policies for reporting transactions, without exception.

CASE STUDY 2

Facts

A French parent entity uses a revaluation method to value its property, but an American subsidiary uses the cost basis for valuation. The directors feel that it is not practical to keep revaluing the property of the American subsidiary and wish to discontinue revaluing the property on consolidation.

Required

Must uniform accounting policies be used under IAS 27?

Solution

Uniform accounting policies must be used by the group. There are no exceptions under IAS 27, even if it is not practical to use uniform policies.

In preparing consolidated financial statements, an entity combines the financial statements of the parent and its subsidiaries line by line by adding together like items of assets, liabilities, equity, income, and expenses. In order that the consolidated financial statements present financial information about the group as that of a single economic entity, the following steps are then taken:

1. The carrying amount of the parent's investment in each subsidiary and the parent's portion of equity of each subsidiary are eliminated
2. Noncontrolling interests in the profit or loss of consolidated subsidiaries for the reporting period are identified
3. Noncontrolling interests in the net assets of consolidated subsidiaries are identified separately from the parent's ownership interests in them. Noncontrolling interests in the net assets consist of the following two items:

   a. The amount of those noncontrolling interests at the date of the original combination calculated in accordance with IFRS 3.
   b. The noncontrolling interests' share of changes in equity since the date of the combination.

Noncontrolling interests must be presented in the consolidated statement of financial position within equity separately from the equity of the owners of the parent. Total comprehensive income must be attributed to the owners of the parent and to the noncontrolling interests even if this results in the noncontrolling interests having a deficit balance.

All intergroup transactions, balances, income, and expenditures should be eliminated in full. Any intergroup losses on items may be indicative of an impairment loss and may require recognition in the consolidated financial statements.

The financial statements of the parent and its subsidiaries should be prepared using the same reporting date. If the reporting dates are different, the subsidiary should prepare additional financial statements for consolidation purposes as of the same date of the parent entity, unless it is impracticable to do so. In this case, adjustments must be made for the effects of significant transactions that have occurred between the date of the subsidiary's and the date of the parent entity's financial statements. The difference between these dates should never be more than three months.

PRACTICAL INSIGHT

Agrana Beteiligung AG, an Austrian entity, states that those subsidiaries' financial statements with different year-ends all fell within the three-month window. The ends of the reporting periods of all subsidiaries have been harmonized to the end of February. A note in the financial statements cautions that this should be taken into account for comparability purposes and discloses an increase in revenue of €40 million and an increase in profit after tax of €2 million.

If the loss that is applicable to the minority exceeds the noncontrolling interest in the equity of the subsidiary, then the excess and any further losses attributable to the minority are charged to the group, unless the minority has a binding obligation to make good the losses.

When such a subsidiary subsequently reports profits, all such profits will be attributable to the group until the minority's share of losses, which have been absorbed by the group, have been recovered.

In the separate financial statements of the parent entity, investments in subsidiaries, associates, and jointly controlled entities should be accounted for by either measuring the investments at cost or in accordance with IAS 39. Any such items that are classified as held for sale should be accounted for in accordance with IFRS 5.

Investments in jointly controlled entities and associates that are accounted for in accordance with IAS 39 in the consolidated financial statements (i.e., when a subsidiary ceases to be a subsidiary, associate, or joint venture) must be accounted for in the same way in the investor's separate financial statements.

CHANGES IN THE OWNERSHIP INTERESTS

The revised Standard moves IFRS to the use of the economic entity model. Current practice is the parent company approach. The economic entity approach treats all providers of equity capital as shareholders of the entity, even when they are not shareholders in the parent company. The parent company approach sees the financial statements from the perspective of the parent company shareholders.

For example, disposal of a partial interest in a subsidiary in which the parent company retains control does not result in a gain or loss but in an increase or decrease in equity under the economic entity approach. Purchase of some or all of the noncontrolling interest is treated as a treasury transaction and accounted for in equity. A partial disposal of an interest in a subsidiary in which the parent company loses control but retains an interest as an associate creates the recognition of gain or loss on the entire interest. A gain or loss is recognized on the part that has been disposed of and a further holding gain is recognized on the interest retained, being the difference between the fair value of the interest and the book value of the interest. The gains are recognized in the statement of comprehensive income. Amendments to IAS 28, *Investments in Associates,* and IAS 31, *Interests in Joint Ventures,* extend this treatment to associates and joint ventures.

CASE STUDY 3

On January 1, 20X9, Race acquired 70% of the equity interests of Pine, a public limited company. The purchase consideration comprised cash of $360 million. The fair value of the identifiable net assets was $480 million. The fair value of the noncontrolling interest in Pine was $210 million on January 1, 20X9. Race wishes to use the "full goodwill" method for all acquisitions. Race acquired a further 10% interest from the noncontrolling interests (NCI) in Pine on December 31, 20X9, for a cash consideration of $85 million. The carrying value of the net assets of Pine was $535 million at December 31, 20X9.

Required

How should the further interest be accounted for?

Solution

The net assets of Pine have increased by $(535 – 480) million, that is, $55 million and therefore the NCI has increased by 30% of $55 million, that is, $16.5 million. However Race has purchased an additional 10% of the shares and this is treated as a treasury transaction. There is no adjustment to goodwill on the further acquisition.

	$m	$m
Fair value of consideration for 70% interest	360	
Fair value of noncontrolling interest	210	570
Fair value of identifiable net assets		(480)
Goodwill		90

	$m
Pine January 1, 20X9 NCI	210
Share of increase in net assets in postacquisition period	16.5
Net assets December 31, 20X9	226.5
Transfer to equity of Race (10/30 × 226.5)	(75.5)
Balance at December 31, 20X9–NCI	151
Fair value of consideration	85
Charge to NCI	(75.5)
Negative movement in equity	9.5

Race has effectively purchased a further share of the NCI with the premium paid for that share naturally being charged to equity. The situation is comparable to when a parent company sells part of its holding but retains control.

CASE STUDY 4

Facts as in Case Study 3 but instead of acquiring a further 10%, Race had disposed of a 10% interest of the noncontrolling interests in Pine on December 31, 20X9, for a cash consideration of $65 million. The carrying value of the net assets of Pine was $535 million at December 31, 20X8.

Required

Account for the disposal of the interest in Pine.

Solution

	$m
Pine net assets at January 1, 20X9	480
Increase in net assets	55
Net assets at December 31, 20X9	535
Fair value of consideration	65
Transfer to NCI [10% × (535 net assets + 90 goodwill)]	(62.5)
Positive movement in equity	2.5

The parent has effectively sold 10% of the carrying value of the net assets (including goodwill) of the subsidiary ($62.5m) at December 31, 20X9, for a consideration of $65 million, giving a profit of $2.5 million, which is taken to equity.

When an entity loses control of a subsidiary it derecognizes the assets and liabilities and related equity components of the former subsidiary. Any gain or loss is recognized in profit or loss. Any investment retained in the former subsidiary is measured at its fair value at the date when control is lost. IAS 27 sets out the six adjustments to be made when a parent loses control of a subsidiary.

1. Derecognize the carrying amount of assets (including goodwill), liabilities, and non-controlling interests.
2. Recognize the fair value of consideration received.
3. Recognize any distribution of shares to owners.
4. Reclassify to profit or loss any amounts (i.e., the entire amount, not a proportion) relating to the subsidiary's assets and liabilities previously recognized in other comprehensive income as if the assets and liabilities had been disposed of directly.
5. Recognize any resulting difference as a gain or loss in profit or loss attributable to the parent.
6. Recognize the fair value of any residual interest.

CASE STUDY 5

On January 1, 20X9, Race had acquired a 90% interest in Mine, a public limited company for a cash consideration of $80 million. Mine's identifiable net assets had a fair value of $74 million and the NCI had a fair value of $6 million. Race uses the full goodwill method. On December 31, 20X9, Race disposed of 65% of the equity of Mine (no other investor obtained control as a result of the disposal) when its identifiable net assets were $83 million. Of the increase in net assets $6 million had been reported in profit or loss and $3 million had been reported in comprehensive income. The sale proceeds were $65 million and the remaining equity interest was fair valued at $25 million. After the disposal, Mine is classified as an associate under IAS 28, *Investments in Associates*.

Required

Show the gain or loss on disposal of Mine.

Solution

The gain recognized in profit or loss would be as follows:

	$m
Fair value of consideration	65
Fair value of residual interest to be recognized as an associate	25
Gain reported in comprehensive income	3
Value of NCI (10% of 83)	8.3
	101.3
Less: Net assets and goodwill derecognized	
Net assets	(83)
Goodwill (80 + 6 – 74)	(12)
Gain on disposal to profit or loss	6.3

After the sale of the interest, the holding in the associate will be fair valued at $25 million.

Separate Financial Statements

When an entity elects, or is required by local regulations, to present separate financial statements, investments in subsidiaries, jointly controlled entities, and associates, must be accounted for at cost or in accordance with IAS 39, *Financial Instruments: Recognition and Measurement*. The parent/investor shall apply the same accounting for each category of investments. Investments that are classified as held for sale in accordance with IFRS 5 shall be accounted for in accordance with that IFRS (IAS 27.37). Investments carried at cost should be measured at the lower of their carrying amount and fair value less costs to sell. The measurement of investments accounted for in accordance with IAS 39 is not changed in such circumstances (IAS 27.38). An entity shall recognize a dividend from a subsidiary, jointly controlled entity, or associate in profit or loss in its separate financial statements when its right to receive the dividend in established (IAS 27.38A).

DISCLOSURES

Disclosure requirements under this Standard are quite extensive. These disclosures must be made in consolidated financial statements:

1. The nature of the relationship between the parent and a subsidiary when the parent does not own, directly or indirectly through subsidiaries, more than half of the voting power
2. The reasons why the ownership, directly or indirectly through subsidiaries, of more than half of the voting or potential voting power of an investee does not constitute control
3. The reporting date of the financial statements of a subsidiary when such financial statements are used to prepare consolidated financial statements and are of a reporting date or for a period that is different from that of the parent, and the reason for using a different reporting date or period
4. The nature and extent of any significant restrictions on the ability of subsidiaries to transfer funds to the parent in the form of cash dividends or to repay loans or advances

These disclosures are required where separate financial statements are prepared for a parent that elects not to prepare consolidated financial statements:

1. The fact that the financial statements are separate financial statements and that the exemption from consolidation has been used; the name and country of incorporation or residence of the entity whose consolidated financial statements that comply with IFRS have been produced for public use; and the address where those consolidated financial statements are obtainable
2. A list of significant investments in subsidiaries, jointly controlled entities, and associates, including the name, country of incorporation or residence, proportion of ownership interest, and, if different, proportion of voting power held
3. A description of the method used to account for the investments in 2

These disclosures are required where a parent, investor in a jointly controlled entity, or investor in an associate prepared separate financial statements:

1. The fact that the statements are separate financial statements and the reasons why those statements are prepared if not required by law
2. A list of significant investments in subsidiaries, jointly controlled entities, and associates, including the name, country of incorporation or residence, proportion of ownership interest and, if different, proportion of voting power held
3. A description of the method used to account for the investments under 2

CASE STUDY 6

Facts

Entity X is preparing its group accounts for the year ended December 31, 20X9, and has acquired investments in three companies. The details are set out next.

1. Entity Y

The whole of the share capital of Y was acquired on July 1, 20X9, with a view to selling the subsidiary within a year. At the date of acquisition, the estimated fair value less cost to sell of Y is $27 million. (The fair value of the liabilities is $8 million.) At year-end, (December 31, 20X9), the estimated fair value less costs to sell is $26 million. (The fair value of the liabilities is $7 million.)

2. Entity Z

X has acquired, on August 1, 20X9, 48% of Z, which is a major supplier of X. X has a written agreement with another major shareholder, which owns 30% of the share capital of Z, whereby X can receive as much of Z's production as it wishes. X has also made a substantial loan to Z, which is repayable on demand. If repaid currently, Z would be insolvent.

3. Entity W

X has acquired 45% of the voting shares of W on September 1, 20X9. The other shares are owned by V (25%) and T (30%). V and T are both institutional investors and have representation on the board of directors. X can appoint four members of the board; V and T appoint three each. The effective power to set W's operating policies lies with the four directors appointed by X. However, if there is to be any change in the capital structure of the company, then the full board (ten directors) must vote in favor of the proposal.

Required

Discuss how these three investments should be treated in the consolidated financial statements of X group for year ended December 31, 20X9.

Solution

Entity Y, which was acquired on July 1, 20X9, will have to be accounted for under IFRS 5. It will meet the criteria as being held for sale and, therefore, must be accounted for in this way.

Initially, the fair value of the assets would be recorded at $27 million plus $8 million, which is $35 million. The fair value of the liabilities would be recorded at $8 million. At the end of the reporting period X will have to remeasure the investment in entity Y at the lower of its cost and fair value less cost to sell, which will be $26 million. The assets and liabilities will have to be presented separately in the consolidated financial statements from any other assets and liabilities. The total assets at year-end December 31 will be shown separately as $33 million and the total liabilities will be shown separately as $7 million. Obviously the subsidiary is not consolidated as such.

X owns 48% of the voting shares and has the power to control who has access to the operating capacity of Z by virtue of a written agreement with another shareholder that owns 30% of the share capital. There will be a presumption that X will have significant influence over Z through its ability to demand repayment of a substantial loan. Therefore, X should consolidate Z. X has the power to govern the financial and operating policies of the entity through agreement and through its relationship with Z.

Regarding entity W, X has 45% of the voting power, V has 25%, and T has 30%, but V and T are institutional investors, and the directors who represent these investors have no effective power. Substantial power lies with the four directors of W. Although the full board retains some powers, these powers are limited. The four directors representing W have effective control over most of the financing and operating policies, which would represent a significant part of the decision making. X has effective control over V through its control over the board of directors and decision making. Therefore, W should be consolidated.

SIC 12, *Consolidation—Special-Purpose Entities,* addresses the situation where a special-purpose entity should be consolidated by a reporting entity under the consolidation principles in IAS 27. Under SIC 12, an entity must consolidate a special-purpose entity (SPE) when, in substance, the entity controls the SPE.

IFRIC 5, *Rights to Interests Arising from Decommissioning Activities, Restoration and Environmental Funds,* states that where an entity recognizes a decommissioning obligation under IFRS and contributes to a fund to segregate assets to pay for the obligation, it should apply IAS 27, SIC 12, IAS 28, and IAS 31 to determine whether the funds should be consolidated, proportionately consolidated, or accounted for under the equity method.

IFRIC 17, *Distributions of Noncash Assets to Owners,* applies to the entity making the distribution, not to the recipient. It applies when noncash assets are distributed to owners or when the owner is given a choice of taking cash in lieu of the noncash assets.

IFRIC 17 clarifies in the following five items that

1. A dividend payable should be recognized when the dividend is appropriately authorized and is no longer at the discretion of the entity
2. An entity should measure the dividend payable at the fair value of the net assets to be distributed
3. An entity should remeasure the liability at each reporting date and at settlement, with changes recognized directly in equity
4. An entity should recognize the difference between the dividend paid and the carrying amount of the net assets distributed in profit or loss, and should disclose it separately
5. An entity should provide additional disclosures if the net assets being held for distribution to owners meet the definition of a discontinued operation

IFRIC 17 applies to pro rata distributions of noncash assets (all owners are treated equally) but does not apply to common control transactions.

In September 2010, the IASB published a staff draft of a forthcoming consolidation standard. Control would be defined as power to direct the activities of another entity to generate returns for the reporting entity. Power would be the current ability to direct the activities of an entity that significantly affect the returns. Power need not be absolute, need not have been exercised, and would be assessed on the basis of current facts and circumstances. The activities in the control definition are those activities of an entity that significantly affect the returns.

The reporting entity can have the current ability to direct the activities by having

- More than half of the voting rights in an entity controlled by voting rights
- Contractual rights within other contractual arrangements that related to the substantive activities of the entity
- A combination of contractual rights within other contractual arrangements and holding voting rights in the entity.
- By holding less than half of the voting rights in an entity considering relevant facts and circumstances.

A reporting entity that holds less than half of the voting right in an entity may need to rely on other indicators of power to provide evidence of having the ability to direct, such as whether it can obtain additional voting rights.

EXTRACTS FROM PUBLISHED FINANCIAL STATEMENTS

BARLOWORLD Annual Report, 2009

Consolidated financial statements

Interests in subsidiaries

The consolidated financial statements incorporate the assets, liabilities, income, expenses, and cash flows of the Company and all entities controlled by the Company as if they are a single economic entity. Control is achieved where the Company has the power to govern the financial and operating policies of an entity so as to obtain benefits from its activities.

The results of subsidiaries acquired or disposed of during the period are included in the consolidated statement of comprehensive income from the date of acquisition or up to the date of disposal.

Intercompany transactions and the resulting unrealized profits and balances between group entities are eliminated on consolidation.

Minority interests in the net assets of consolidated subsidiaries are shown separately from the group equity therein. It consists of the amount of those interests at acquisition plus the minorities' subsequent share of changes in equity of the subsidiary. On acquisition date, the minorities' interest is measured at the proportion of the fair values of the identifiable assets and liabilities acquired. Losses applicable to minorities in excess of its interest in the subsidiaries' equity are allocated against the group's interest except to the extent that the minorities have a binding obligation and the financial ability to cover losses. Minorities are considered to be equity participants and all transactions with minorities are recorded directly within equity.

UNILEVER Annual Report, 2009

Basis of consolidation

Due to the operational and contractual arrangements referred to previously in these statements, NV and PLC form a single reporting entity for the purposes of presenting consolidated accounts. Accordingly, the accounts of Unilever are presented by both NV and PLC as their respective consolidated accounts. Group companies included in the consolidation are those companies controlled by NV or PLC. Control exists when the Group has the power to govern the financial and operating policies of an entity so as to obtain benefits from its activities. The net assets and results of acquired businesses are included in the consolidated accounts from their respective dates of acquisition, being the date on which the Group obtains control. The results of disposed businesses are included in the consolidated accounts up to their date of disposal, being the date control ceases. Intercompany transactions and balances are eliminated.

MULTIPLE-CHOICE QUESTIONS

1. X has control over the composition of Y's board of directors. X owns 49% of Y and is the largest shareholder. X has an agreement with Z, which owns 10% of Y, whereby Z will always vote in the same way as X. Can X exercise control over Y?

    (a) X cannot exercise control because it owns only 49% of the voting rights.

    (b) X cannot exercise control because it can control only the makeup of the board and not necessarily the way the directors vote.

    (c) X can exercise control solely because it has an agreement with Z for the voting rights to be used in whatever manner X wishes.

    (d) X can exercise control because it controls more than 50% of the voting power, and it can govern the financial and operating policies of Y through its control of the board of directors.

2. X owns 50% of Y's voting shares. The board of directors consists of six members; X appoints three of them and Y appoints the other three. The casting vote at meetings always lies with the directors appointed by X. Does X have control over Y?

    (a) No, control is equally split between X and Z.

    (b) Yes, X holds 50% of the voting power and has the casting vote at board meetings in the event that there is not a majority decision.

    (c) No, X owns only 50% of the entity's shares and therefore does not have control.

    (d) No, control can be exercised only through voting power, not through a casting vote.

3. Z has sold all of its shares to the public. The company was formerly a state-owned entity. The national regulator has retained the power to appoint the board of directors. An overseas entity acquires 55% of the voting shares, but the regulator still retains its power to appoint the board of directors. Who has control of the entity?

    (a) The national regulator.

    (b) The overseas entity.

    (c) Neither the national regulator nor the overseas entity.

    (d) The board of directors.

4. A has acquired an investment in a subsidiary, B, with the view to dispose of this investment within six months. The investment in the subsidiary has been classified as held-for-sale and is to be accounted for in accordance with IFRS 5. The subsidiary has never been consolidated. How should the investment in the subsidiary be treated in the financial statements?

    (a) Purchase accounting should be used.

    (b) Equity accounting should be used.

    (c) The subsidiary should not be consolidated but IFRS 5 should be used.

    (d) The subsidiary should remain off the statement of financial position.

5. A manufacturing group has just acquired a controlling interest in a football club that is listed on a stock exchange. The management of the manufacturing group wishes to exclude the football club from the consolidated financial statements on the grounds that its activities are dissimilar. How should the football club be accounted for?

    (a) The entity should be consolidated as there is no exemption from consolidation on the grounds of dissimilar activities.

    (b) The entity should not be consolidated using the purchase method but should be consolidated using equity accounting.

    (c) The entity should not be consolidated and should appear as an investment in the group accounts.

    (d) The entity should not be consolidated; details should be disclosed in the financial statements.

6. In the separate financial statements of a parent entity, investments in subsidiaries that are not classified as held-for-sale should be accounted for

    (a) At cost.

    (b) In accordance with IAS 39.

    (c) At cost or in accordance with IAS 39.

    (d) Using the equity method.

7. Which of the following is **not** a valid condition that will exempt an entity from preparing consolidated financial statements?

    (a) The parent entity is a wholly owned subsidiary of another entity.

    (b) The parent entity's debt or equity capital is not traded on the stock exchange.

    (c) The ultimate parent entity produces consolidated financial statements available for public use that comply with IFRS.

    (d) The parent entity is in the process of filing its financial statements with a securities commission.

8. Entity X controls an overseas entity Y. Because of exchange controls, it is difficult to transfer funds out of the country to the parent entity. X owns 100% of the voting power of Y. How should Y be accounted for?

    (a) It should be excluded from consolidation and the equity method should be used.

    (b) It should be excluded from consolidation and stated at cost.

    (c) It should be excluded from consolidation and accounted for in accordance with IAS 39.

(d) It is not permitted to be excluded from consolidation because control is not lost.

9. Partial sale of an investment in a subsidiary, which does not result in a change of control, is treated as follows

(a) It is recorded directly in income.

(b) It is recorded directly in equity.

(c) It results in the adjustment of the goodwill.

(d) It results in the revaluation of the whole of the equity interest.

10. Partial sale of a subsidiary, which results in the retention of significant influence so that the remaining investment constitutes an associate, is dealt with as follows:

(a) It is recorded directly in income.

(b) It is recorded directly in equity.

(c) It results in the retained interest being measured at fair value and a gain or loss calculated on the disposal of the subsidiary.

(d) It results in the revaluation of the whole of the equity interest.

11. A company has finalized the deferred tax calculation on 01/10/X9 in relation to its acquisition of a subsidiary on 01/01/X9. The adjustment required will

(a) Be adjusted through income.

(b) Be ignored as it is too long since the acquisition.

(c) Be adjusted through equity.

(d) Affect the calculation of goodwill.

12. On January 1, 20X9, A acquired a 60% interest in B for $80 million. A already held a 10% interest which had been acquired for $12 million but which was fair valued at $15 million at January 1, 20X9. The fair value of the noncontrolling interest at January 1, 20X9, was $47 million and the fair value of the identifiable net assets of B was $130 million. The goodwill would be as follows using the full goodwill method:

(a) $1 million.

(b) $12 million.

(c) $35 million.

(d) $38 million.

13. On January 1, 20X9, A acquired a 60% interest in B for $80 million. A already held a 10% interest which had been acquired for $12 million but which was fair valued at $15 million at January 1, 20X9. The fair value of the noncontrolling interest at January 1, 20X9, was $47 million and the fair value of the identifiable net assets of B was $130 million. A gain relating to the revaluation of the original equity interest would be recorded as follows:

(a) $3 million.

(b) $12 million.

(c) $35 million.

(d) $38 million.

14. Where should noncontrolling interests be presented in the consolidated statement of financial position?

(a) Within long-term liabilities.

(b) In between long-term liabilities and current liabilities.

(c) Within the parent shareholders' equity.

(d) Within equity but separate from the parent shareholders' equity.

Chapter 20

INVESTMENTS IN ASSOCIATES
(IAS 28)

BACKGROUND AND INTRODUCTION

This Standard is to be applied to all accounting for investments in associates but does not apply to investments in associates held by a venture capital organization, a mutual fund, a unit trust, and a similar entity, including investment-linked insurance funds, where these investments upon initial recognition are designated at fair value through profit or loss or classified as held for trading and accounted for in accordance with IAS 39.

> ## DEFINITIONS OF KEY TERMS
> ### (in accordance with IAS 28)
>
> **Associate.** An entity in which an investor has significant influence but which is neither a subsidiary nor an interest in a joint venture.
>
> **Significant influence.** The power to participate in the financial and operating policy decisions of the investee but not to control them; that control includes joint control over those policies.
>
> **Equity method.** A method of accounting by which an investment is initially recognized at cost and adjusted thereafter to reflect the post acquisition change in the investor's share of the net assets of the investee. The profit or loss attributable to the investment in the associate is included in the investor's statement of comprehensive income.

SIGNIFICANT INFLUENCE

It is presumed that the investor has significant influence if it holds directly or indirectly 20% or more of the voting power of the associate unless it can be clearly shown that significant influence does not exist. If the holding is less than 20%, the investor will be presumed not to have significant influence unless such influence can be shown. If a substantial or even a majority ownership is held by another investor, this does not necessarily mean that significant influence cannot arise through a holding of 20% or more.

Significant influence is normally created in one of these ways:

- Representation on the board of directors
- Participation in the policy-making process
- Material transactions occurring between the two entities
- The changing over of management
- The provision of essential technical information

The existence of potential voting rights, for example, through the ownership of share-warrants, share-call options, and the like, must be considered when assessing whether an entity has significant influence. Where these potential voting rights are not currently exercisable, they will not be taken into account.

Significant influence is lost when the investor loses the power to participate in the financial and operating policy decisions of the investee. This can occur without the loss of voting power or without a change in the ownership levels. It could occur, for example, where the associate is subject to government control or regulation as the result of a contractual agreement.

CASE STUDY 1

Facts

X owns 60% of the voting rights of Y, Z owns 19% of the voting rights of Y, and the remainder are dispersed among the public. Z also is the sole supplier of raw materials to Y and has a contract to supply certain expertise regarding the maintenance of Y's equipment.

Required

What is the relationship between Z and Y?

Solution

Z may be able to exercise significant influence over Y, and therefore it may have to be treated as an associate. Although Z owns only 19% of the voting rights, it is the sole supplier of raw materials to Y and provides expertise in the form of maintenance of Y's equipment.

EQUITY METHOD

Under the equity method, the investment in the associate is recognized initially at cost, and then the carrying amount is adjusted to recognize the investor's share of profit or loss of the investee after that date. The investor's share of the profit or loss of the associate is recognized in the statement of comprehensive income. Adjustments to the carrying amount may be necessary for distributions received or through changes in the investor's interest in the investee or changes arising from the revaluation of property, plant, and equipment, for example.

CASE STUDY 2

Facts

A acquires 25% of the voting shares of B on January 1, 20X9. The purchase consideration was $10 million, and A has significant influence over B. The retained earnings of B were $15 million at the date of acquisition, and the A group has several other subsidiaries. The retained earnings of B at December 31, 20X9, were $21 million.

Required

Calculate the carrying value of the investment in B in the group financial statements at December 31, 20X9.

Solution

	$m
Cost of investment	10.0
Share of post acquisition reserves 25% of ($21 – $15)m	1.5
	11.5

The share of the postacquisition reserves will be credited to the retained earnings of the group. Goodwill in an associate is not separately recognized. The entire carrying amount is tested for impairment.

In the consolidated statement of comprehensive income, income from associates for the year is reported after profit from operations, just before profit before tax.

CASE STUDY 3

Facts

Company A sells inventory to its 30%-owned associate, B. The inventory had cost A $200,000 and was sold for $300,000. B also has sold inventory to A. The cost of this inventory to B was $100,000, and it was sold for $120,000.

Required

How would the intercompany profit on these transactions be dealt with in the financial statements if none of the inventory had been sold at year-end?

Solution

Company A to Company B

	$000
The intergroup profit is $(300 – 200)	100
Profit reported would be 100 × 70/100 =	70

The remaining profit would be deferred until the sale of the inventory.

Company B to Company A

The profit made by B would be $(120 – 100) = 20

An amount of 20 × 30/100 would be eliminated from the carrying value of the investment, that is, $6,000.

The alternative is to eliminate the whole of the profit from B's profit for the period and then calculate the profit attributable to the associate.

EXCEPTIONS TO THE EQUITY METHOD

An investment in an associate should be accounted for using the equity method except in these three exceptional circumstances:

1. Where the investment is classified as held-for-sale in accordance with IFRS 5
2. Where a parent does not have to present consolidated financial statements because of the exemption in IAS 27
3. The investor need not use the equity method if *all* of these criteria apply:

    a. The investor is a wholly owned subsidiary or is a partially owned subsidiary of another entity and its owners have been informed about and do not object to the investor not applying the equity method. The owners in this case are all of those entitled to vote.
    b. The investor's debt or equity instruments are not traded in a public market.
    c. The investor did not file, nor is it in the process of filing, its financial statements with a securities commission or other regulatory body for the purpose of issuing any class of financial instrument in a public market.
    d. The ultimate or any intermediate parent of the investor produces consolidated financial statements that are available for public use and that comply with IFRS.

INVESTOR CEASES TO HAVE SIGNIFICANT INFLUENCE

If the investor ceases to have significant influence over an associate, then the equity method should not be used and the investment should be accounted for using IAS 39, provided that the associate does not become a subsidiary or a joint venture.

On the loss of significant influence, the investor measures at fair value any investment the investor retains in the former associate. The investor recognizes in profit or loss any difference between the following two:

1. The fair value of any retained investment and any proceeds from the disposing of the part interest in the associate.
2. The carrying amount of the investment at the date when significant influence is lost.

When an investment ceases to be an associate and is accounted for in accordance with IAS 39, the fair value of the investment at the date when it ceases to be an associate is regarded as its fair value on initial recognition as a financial asset in accordance with IAS 39.

If an investor loses significant influence over an associate, the investor accounts for all amounts recognized in other comprehensive income in relation to that entity on the same basis as if the associate had directly disposed of the related assets or liabilities. Hence, if a gain or loss previously recognized in other comprehensive income would be reclassified to profit or loss on the disposal of the related assets or liabilities, the investor reclassifies the gain or loss from equity to profit or loss (as a reclassification adjustment). If an investor's ownership interest in an associate is reduced, but the investment continues to be an associate, the investor reclassifies to profit or loss only a proportionate amount of the gain or loss previously recognized in other comprehensive income.

CASE STUDY 4

Facts

Company X owns 22% of Company Y and is entitled to appoint two directors to the board, which consists of eight members. The remaining 78% of the voting rights are held by two other companies, each of which is entitled to appoint three directors. The board makes decisions on the basis of a simple majority. Because board meetings are often held at very short notice, Company X does not always have representation on the board. Often the suggestions of the representative of Company X are ignored, and the decisions of the board seem to take little notice of any representations made by the directors from Company X.

Required

What is the relationship between Company X and Company Y?

Solution

Company X is unable to exercise significant influence, as its directors seem to be ignored at board meetings. Therefore, the equity method should not be used.

CASE STUDY 5

Facts

Angel has a 36% holding in Dust. It sells 75% of its holding for $15 million. The carrying value of the associate including goodwill at the date of the sale is $18 million and Dust has available for sale reserve of $1 million. The fair value of the remaining holding in Dust is $5 million.

Required

Account for the disposal of Dust in the financial statements of Angel.

Solution

On disposal Angel will recognize the remaining financial asset in Dust at a value of $5 million. It will record the consideration received of $15 million, derecognize the associate's value of $18 million and reclassify the available for sale reserves to profit or loss as part of the gain or loss on disposal.

As a result, the gain on disposal is ($15 + $5 – $18 + $1), that is, $3 million.

CASE STUDY 6

Facts

Angel has another associate, Buttle, and owns 30% of the share capital. The fair value of Buttle's net assets at acquisition was $46 million and the initial carrying amount including goodwill in Angel's books was $12 million. The carrying amount of the investment at December 31, 20X9, is $27 million and Buttle's net assets are fair valued at $60 million. Buttle issues new shares so that Angel's holding is reduced to 20%, as Angel did not subscribe for the new shares which raised $60 million.

Required

Discuss the accounting for Buttle on the issue of the new shares.

Solution

The dilution in ownership means effectively that Angel has disposed of one third of its interest in Buttle. A gain or loss is calculated by comparing the carrying value of the disposed interest (1/3 of $27m) that is, $9 million with Angel's share of the proceeds of issue of the shares (20% of $60m) that is, $12 million. The gain on dilution is $3 million.

A portion of the carrying value of the associate is derecognized (1/3 of $27m), that is, $9 million including goodwill of $4 million (1/3 of $12m). The share of the proceeds ($12m) is added to the carrying value of the investment in the associate because of the increase in the net assets of Buttle. The net effect is that the carrying value of the associate increases by $3 million which is the gain on dilution.

ACQUISITION OF AN ASSOCIATE AND ACCOUNTING TREATMENT

When an investment in an associate is acquired, any difference between the cost of the investment and the investor's share of the net fair value of the associate's net assets and contingent liabilities is accounted for in accordance with IFRS 3. Thus, any goodwill relating to the associate will be included in the carrying value of the investment.

IFRS 3 and, therefore, IAS 28 do not allow amortization of that goodwill. Negative goodwill is excluded from the carrying amount of the investment. This amount should be included as income in determining the investor's share of the associate's profit or loss for the period in which the investment was acquired.

After acquisition, adjustments will be made to the investor's share of the associates' profits or losses for such events as impairment losses incurred by the associate.

In determining the investor's share of profits or losses, the most recently available financial statements of the associate are used. If the reporting dates of the investor and the associate are different, both should prepare financial statements as of the date as those of the investor unless it is impracticable to do so.

If financial statements are prepared to a different reporting date, then adjustments should be made for any significant transactions or events that occurred between the date of the associate's financial statements and the date of the investor's financial statements. The difference between the reporting dates should not be more than three months.

If the associate uses accounting policies that are different from those of the investor, the associate's financial statements should be adjusted and the investor's accounting policies should be used.

If the investor's share of losses of an associate equals or exceeds its interest in the associate, then the investor should not recognize its share of any further losses.

The interest in the associate is essentially the carrying amount of the investment using the equity method together with any other long-term interests that are essentially part of the investor's net investment in the associate. An example is a long-term loan from the investor to the associate. Long-term interests in this context do not include trade receivables or payables or any secured long-term receivables. Losses recognized in excess of the investor's investment in ordinary shares should be applied to the other elements of the investor's interest in the associate in the order of their priority in liquidation.

When the investor's interest is reduced to zero, any additional losses are provided for and liabilities recognized only to the extent that the investor has a legal or constructive obligation or has made payments on behalf of the associate. When the associate reports profits, the investor can recognize its share of those profits only after its share of the profits equals the share of the losses not yet recognized.

PRACTICAL INSIGHT
November AG Gesellschaft fur Molekulare Medizin, a German company, accounted for an associate under the equity method. As a result of the associate's uncertain financing, the investment was written down to €1. The write-down was classified as depreciation but should have been treated as an impairment loss in the statement of comprehensive income.

IMPAIRMENT LOSSES

Impairment indicators in IAS 39 apply to investments in associates. Because the goodwill is included in the carrying amount of the investment in an associate and is not separately recognized, it cannot be tested for impairment separately by applying IAS 36. Instead the entire carrying amount of the investment is tested for impairment under IAS 36 by comparing the recoverable amount with the carrying amount.

Each associate must be assessed individually regarding the recoverable amount of that investment unless the associate does not generate independent cash flows.

An investment in an associate is accounted for in the investor's separate financial statements in accordance with IAS 27.

CASE STUDY 7

Facts

A acquired 30% of the issued capital of B for $1 million on December 31, 20X7. The accumulated profits at that date were $2 million. A appointed three directors to the board of B, and A intends to hold the investment for a significant period of time. The companies prepare their financial statements to December 31 each year. The abbreviated statement of financial position of B on December 31, 20X9, is

Sundry net assets	$6 million
Issued share capital of $1	$1 million
Share premium	$2 million
Retained earnings	$3 million

B had made no new issues of shares since the acquisition of the investment by A. The recoverable amount of net assets of B is deemed to be $7 million. The fair value of the net assets at the date of acquisition was $5 million.

Required

What amount should be shown in A's consolidated statement of financial position at December 31, 20X9, for the investment in B?

Solution

	$m
Investment in associate (30% × $6 million)	1.8
Alternative calculation	
Cost	1.0
Postacquisition profits 30% (3 – 2)	0.3
Negative goodwill (30% of $5 million) – $1 million	<u>0.5</u>
	<u>1.8</u>

The negative goodwill will be credited to income.

An impairment test would prove that the carrying amount of the investment is not impaired.

	$m
Recoverable amount $7 million × 30%	2.1
Carrying value of investment	1.8

(Goodwill should not be impairment tested separately but included in the carrying value of the investment.)

SEPARATE FINANCIAL STATEMENTS

IAS 28 cross-refers to IAS 27, as that Standard specifies the accounting and disclosures required for investments in associates in an investor's separate financial statements. IAS 27 requires that such investments should be accounted for either at cost or in accordance with IAS 39.

Separate financial statements are defined in IAS 28 as the investor's own financial statements in which investments are accounted at cost or in accordance with IAS 39. Associates are not equity accounted in separate statements. Separate financial statements are presented in addition to consolidated financial statements.

IAS 27 and IAS 28 do not mandate which entities produce separate financial statements. An entity may voluntarily elect, or be required by local regulations, to present separate financial statements.

Investors that are exempt from the requirement to consolidate or equity account their investments may present separate financial statements as their only financial statements.

DISCLOSURES

Under IAS 28, these disclosures are mandated:

- Fair value of investment in associates for which there are published price quotations.
- Summarized financial information of associates, including the aggregated amounts of assets, liabilities, revenues, and profit or loss.
- Reasons why investments of less than 20% are accounted for by the equity method or when investments of more than 20% are not accounted for by the equity method.
- The reporting date of the financial statements of an associate that is different from that of the investor and the reasons why.
- Nature and extent of any significant restrictions on the ability of associates to transfer funds to the investor in the form of cash dividends, or repayment of loans or advances.
- Unrecognized share of losses of an associate, both for the period and cumulatively, if an investor has discontinued recognition of its share of losses of an associate.
- Reasons why an associate is not accounted for using the equity method.
- Summarized financial information of associates, either individually or in groups that are not accounted for using the equity method, including the amounts of total assets, total liabilities, revenues, and profit or loss.
- Equity method investment should be classified as noncurrent assets.
- The investor's share of the profit or loss of equity method investments, and the carrying amount of those investments, must be separately disclosed.

- The investor's share of any discontinued operations of such associates should be separately disclosed.
- The investor's share of changes recognized directly in the associate's equity are also recognized directly in equity by the investor, and disclosed in the statement of changes in equity as required by IAS 1, *Presentation of Financial Statements.*

In addition, in accordance with IAS 37, these points should also be disclosed

- Investor's share of the contingent liabilities of an associate incurred jointly with other investors.
- Any contingent liabilities that may arise because the investor is severally liable for all or part of the liabilities of the associate.

EXTRACTS FROM PUBLISHED FINANCIAL STATEMENTS

UNILEVER Annual Report, 2009

Other noncurrent assets	€ million 2009	€ million 2008
Interest in net assets of joint ventures	60	73
Interest in net assets of associates	42	67
Other noncurrent financial assets[a]:	485	904
Held-to-maturity investments[b]	--	472
Loans and receivables	2	9
Available-for-sale financial assets[c][d]	436	370
Financial assets at fair value through profit or loss[d]	47	53
Long-term trade and other receivables[e]	212	171
Fair value of biological assets	32	31
Other nonfinancial assets	186	180
	1,017	1,426

[a] Predominantly consist of investments in a number of companies and financial institutions in India, Europe, and the United States, including €129 million (2008: €146 million) of assets in a trust to fund benefit obligations in the United States.

[b] During 2009 €436 million of held-to-maturity investments were reclassified as available for sale in relation to the closure of an employee savings program.

[c] Includes unlisted preferred shares arising in connection with US laundry disposal.

[d] Methods of valuation techniques used to determine fair values are given in note 15 on page 108.

[e] Classified as loans and receivables.

Movements during 2009 and 2008	€ million 2009	€ million 2008
Joint ventures[f]		
January 1	73	150
Additions	--	--
Dividends received/reductions[g]	(145)	(202)
Share in net profit	111	125
Currency retranslation	21	--
December 31	60	73
Associates[h]		
January 1	67	44
Acquisitions/(disposals)	--	22
Dividends received/reductions	(32)	(22)
Share in net profit	4	6
Currency retranslation	3	(14)
	42	36
Of which: Net liabilities of JohnsonDiversey reclassified to provisions	--	31
December 31	42	67

[f] Our principal joint ventures are Unilever Jerónimo Martins in Portugal, Pepsi/Lipton International and the Pepsi/Lipton Partnership in the United States.

[g] A reduction of €110 million in carrying value of Pepsi/Lipton International was recorded in relation to the extension of the Pepsi/Lipton joint venture for ready-to-drink tea in January 2008.

[h] Associates as at December 31, 2009, primarily comprise our investment in Langholm Capital Partners. Other Unilever Ventures assets (excluding Langholm) are included under Other noncurrent financial assets above.

BARLOWORLD Annual Report, 2009

Interests in associates and joint ventures

The consolidated financial statements incorporate the assets, liabilities, income, and expenses of associates and joint ventures using the equity method of accounting, applying the group's accounting policies, from the acquisition date to the disposal date (except when the investment is classified as held-for-sale, in which case it is accounted for as a Noncurrent Asset Held For Sale). The most recent audited annual financial statements of associates and joint ventures are used, which are all within three months of the year-end of the group. Adjustments are made to the associate's or joint venture's financial results for material transactions and events in the intervening period. Losses of associates and joint ventures in excess of the group's interest are not recognized unless there is a binding obligation to contribute to the losses.

Goodwill arising on the acquisition of associates and joint ventures is included in the carrying amount of the associate and accounted for in accordance with the accounting policy for goodwill as set out in note 17 below with the exception of impairment testing which is done in accordance with note 35 below and not done separately from the investment.

Where a group entity transacts with an associate or a jointly controlled entity of the group, unrealized profits and losses are eliminated to the extent of the group's interest in the relevant associate or jointly controlled entity.

MULTIPLE-CHOICE QUESTIONS

1. An entity has bought a 25% share in another entity with a view to selling that investment within six months. The investment has been classified as held-for-sale in accordance with IFRS 5. How should the investment be treated in the final year accounts?

    (a) It should be equity accounted.

    (b) The assets and liabilities should be presented separately from other assets in the statement of financial position under IFRS 5.

    (c) The investment should be dealt with under IAS 29.

    (d) Purchase accounting should be used for this investment.

2. The Standard does not require the equity method to be applied when the associate has been acquired and held with a view to its disposal within a certain time period. What is the period within which the associate must be disposed of?

    (a) Six months.

    (b) Twelve months.

    (c) Two years.

    (d) In the near future.

3. How is goodwill arising on the acquisition of an associate dealt with in the financial statements?

    (a) It is amortized.

    (b) It is impairment tested individually.

    (c) It is written off against profit or loss.

    (d) Goodwill is not recognized separately within the carrying amount of the investment.

4. An investor must apply the requirements of IAS 39 in determining whether it is necessary to recognize any impairment loss in the investment in an associate. How is the impairment test carried out?

    (a) The goodwill is separated from the rest of the investment and is impairment tested individually.

    (b) The entire carrying amount of the investment is tested for impairment under IAS 36 by comparing its recoverable amount with its carrying amount.

    (c) The carrying value of the investment should be compared with its market value.

    (d) The recoverable amounts of all investments in associates should be assessed together to determine whether there has been an impairment on all investments.

5. What should happen when the financial statements of an associate are not prepared to the same date as the investor's accounts?

    (a) The associate should prepare financial statements for the use of the investor at the same date as those of the investor.

    (b) The financial statements of the associate prepared up to a different accounting date will be used as normal.

    (c) Any major transactions between the date of the financial statements of the investor and that of the associate should be accounted for.

    (d) As long as the gap is not greater than three months, there is no problem.

6. If the investor ceases to have significant influence over an associate, how should the investment be treated?

    (a) It should still be treated using equity accounting.

    (b) It should be treated in accordance with IAS 39.

    (c) The investment should be frozen at the date at which the investor ceases to have significant influence.

    (d) The investment should be treated at cost.

7. If there is any excess of the investor's share of the net fair value of the associate's identifiable assets and contingent liabilities over the cost of the investment, that is, negative goodwill, how should that excess be treated?

    (a) It should be included in the carrying amount of the investment.

    (b) It should be written off against retained earnings.

    (c) It should be included as income in the determination of the investor's share of the associate's profit or loss for the period.

    (d) It should be disclosed separately as part of the investor's equity.

8. What accounting method should be used for an investment in an associate where it is operating under severe long-term restrictions—for example where the government of a company has temporary control over the associate?

    (a) IAS 39 should be applied.

    (b) The equity method should be applied if significant influence can be exerted.

    (c) The associate should be shown at cost.

    (d) Proportionate consolidation should be used.

9. An investor sells inventory for cash to a 25% associate. The inventory cost the investor $6 million and is sold to the associate for $10 million. None of the inventory has been sold at year-end. How much of the profit on the transaction would be reported in the group accounts?

    (a) $4 million.

    (b) $1 million.

(c) $3 million.

(d) Zero.

10. On the loss of significant influence, the investor measures at fair value any investment the investor retains in the former associate. The investor recognizes in profit or loss any difference between

(a) The initial carrying value of any retained investment, any proceeds from disposing of the part interest in the associate and the carrying amount of the investment at the date when significant influence is lost.

(b) The fair value of any retained investment and the carrying amount of the investment at the date when significant influence is lost.

(c) Any proceeds from the disposing of the part interest in the associate and the carrying amount of the investment at the date when significant influence is lost.

(d) The fair value of any retained investment, any proceeds from the disposing of the part interest in the associate and the carrying amount of the investment at the date when significant influence is lost.

11. When an investment ceases to be an associate and is accounted for in accordance with IAS 39, the fair value of the investment at the date when it ceases to be an associate

(a) Is regarded as its cost on initial recognition as a financial asset in accordance with IAS 39.

(b) Is regarded as its fair value on initial recognition as a financial asset in accordance with IAS 39.

(c) Is regarded as its fair value on initial recognition as a financial liability in accordance with IAS 39.

(d) Is regarded as its amortized cost on initial recognition as an available for sale investment in accordance with IAS 39.

12. A has a 24% holding in B. It sells 50% of its holding for $5 million. The carrying value of the associate including goodwill at the date of the sale is $8 million and B has an available for sale reserve of $1 million. The fair value of the remaining holding in B is $2 million. On the disposal A will recognize

(a) The remaining financial asset in B at a value of $5 million and a loss on disposal of $2 million.

(b) The remaining financial asset in B at a value of $2 million and a loss on disposal of $2 million.

(c) The remaining financial asset in B at a value of $2 million and a gain on disposal of $2 million.

(d) The remaining financial asset in B at a value of $2 million and a loss on disposal of $1 million.

13. Angel has an associate Buttle and owns 40% of the share capital. The fair value of Buttle's net assets at acquisition was $6 million and the initial carrying amount including goodwill in Angel's books was $2.2 million. The carrying amount of the investment at December 31, 20X9 is $2.8 million and Buttle's net assets are fair valued at $9 million. Buttle issues new shares so that Angel's holding is reduced to 20% as Angel did not subscribe for the new shares which raised $8 million. The accounting for Buttle on the issue of the new shares will be

(a) The carrying value of the associate decreases by $0.2 million and the loss on dilution is $0.2 million.

(b) The carrying value of the associate increases by $2.2 million and the gain on dilution is $2.2 million.

(c) The carrying value of the associate increases by $0.2 million and the gain on dilution is $0.2 million.

(d) The carrying value of the associate decreases by $2.2 million and the gain on dilution is $2.2 million.

Chapter 21

FINANCIAL REPORTING IN HYPERINFLATIONARY ECONOMIES (IAS 29)

SCOPE

This Standard deals with the measurement problems of entities that are reporting in the currency of a hyperinflationary economy. In this situation, financial information reported in historical terms would present a distorted picture of the entity's performance and financial position. This Standard sets out procedures for adjusting the financial information for the effects of hyperinflation.

DEFINITION OF HYPERINFLATION

The Standard does not define hyperinflation but sets out the general characteristics of a hyperinflationary economy.

These characteristics would include the following five:

1. Where the preference is to keep wealth in nonmonetary assets or in a stable foreign currency. Any local currency would be immediately invested in order to attempt to maintain its purchasing power.
2. Where prices are quoted in a stable foreign currency and the population regards monetary amounts in that currency, as effectively a local currency.
3. Where transactions are priced at an amount that includes compensation for the future expected loss of the purchasing power of the local currency. This characteristic would be taken into account even if the credit period is quite short.
4. Where prices, wages, and interest rates are closely linked to a price index.
5. Where cumulative inflation rates over a period of three years approach or exceed 100%.

Although IAS 29 sets out the characteristics that may indicate a hyperinflationary economy, it also states that judgment will have to be used in determining whether restatement of the financial statements of the entity is required.

CEASING TO BE HYPERINFLATIONARY

Likewise, judgment will be required in determining whether an economy is no longer hyperinflationary. The criteria used for this is whether the cumulative inflation rate drops below 100% in a three-year period.

When the economy ceases to have hyperinflation, then the entity should discontinue preparing financial statements in accordance with IAS 29. If possible, all entities in that environment should cease to apply the Standard from the same date.

The carrying amounts in subsequent financial statements will be taken as the amounts expressed in the measuring unit current at the end of the previous year.

FUNCTIONAL CURRENCY AND HYPERINFLATION

The functional currency should be based on the economic circumstances relevant to the entity and not based on choice. If the functional currency is one of a hyperinflationary economy, the financial statements should be stated in terms of the measurement unit current at the end of the reporting period.

PRACTICAL INSIGHT

Wella AG discloses in its 2002 accounts that the functional currency of foreign subsidiaries is normally the national currency, as the subsidiaries operate independently. The entity also states that the financial statements of subsidiaries operating in Turkey have been restated to reflect the purchasing power at the end of the reporting period.

If a parent entity operates in a hyperinflationary economy but a subsidiary does not, then the parent's results should be restated for hyperinflation but the subsidiary's results need not be restated but should comply with IAS 21.

If a subsidiary is operating in a hyperinflationary economy and the parent entity is not, then the parent entity would prepare financial statements using IFRS and the subsidiary would use IAS 29.

RESTATEMENT OF FINANCIAL STATEMENTS: STATEMENT OF FINANCIAL POSITION

IAS 29 requires the restatement of financial statements including the cash flow statements and requires the use of a general price index.

PRACTICAL INSIGHT

Turkiye Petrol Rafanerileri published in its accounts that cumulative inflation in Turkey was 227% for the three years to December 2002. The entity restates comparatives and discloses that it uses the Turkish countryside wholesale prices index.

It is preferable that all entities in the same country use the same index.

Monetary items are already stated in the measuring unit at the end of the reporting periods and are therefore not restated.

All nonmonetary items are restated using the change in the general price index between the date that those items were acquired and the current reporting date, unless they are carried at current values (e.g., net realizable value and market value) at the reporting date, in which case they are not restated.

Any gain or loss on the restatement of nonmonetary items is included in the statement of comprehensive income. It is a requirement to disclose this net gain or loss separately.

The index is applied from the dates on which accounting for hyperinflation was first applicable to these items.

Some nonmonetary assets are carried at values determined at an earlier date than that of the financial statements. Examples are the revaluation of property or equipment. In this case, the carrying amounts are restated from the date the assets were revalued.

The restated amounts are compared to (1) recoverable amounts in the case of noncurrent assets, (2) net realizable value in the case of inventory, (3) market value in the case of current investments, and reduced if they exceed the aforementioned values.

An associate operating in the hyperinflationary economy should have its financial statements restated in accordance with IAS 29.

Opening owners' equity should be restated using the Standard, but retained earnings and revaluation surplus should not be restated. Any revaluation surplus arising prior to the application of the Standard is eliminated. Restated retained earnings are the balancing figure in the restated statement of financial position.

STATEMENT OF COMPREHENSIVE INCOME

The statement of comprehensive income is expressed in terms of the measuring unit at the reporting date. Therefore, amounts need to be restated from the dates they were initially recorded.

PRACTICAL INSIGHT

Norilsk Nicket, a Russian entity, disclosed that the economy of the Russian Federation was considered to be hyperinflationary even though a rate of inflation was not published. Norilsk Nicket showed a table of conversion factors taken from the consumer price index. It also disclosed that the economy has ceased to be hyperinflationary and that it will now measure its noncurrent assets and liabilities at cost.

CASE STUDY 1

Facts

An entity keeps three weeks' inventory of raw materials on hand and has a substantial amount of finished goods inventory. The entity operates in a hyperinflationary environment.

Required

Advise the entity as to how to restate its inventory.

Solution

A general price index should be used, but the problem will be maintaining records of the acquisition dates of the raw materials and the nature and timing of the conversion cost to finished inventory. Systems need to be developed to accumulate this information in order to use general price indices. If there are low inventory levels, the problem is minimized. In this case, the general price indices for the most recent month will be used together with the aged inventory lists to restate inventory.

The gain or loss on the net monetary position is included in net income.

SUNDRY POINTS

Current cost financial statements. The statement of financial position is not restated, but the statement of comprehensive income needs restating into the measuring unit at the reporting date using a general price index.

Taxation. There may be deferred tax consequences of the restatement of the carrying values of assets and liabilities.

CASE STUDY 2

Facts

Z operates in a hyperinflationary economy. Its statement of financial position at December 31, 20X9, follows:

	m zlotys
Property, plant, and equipment	900
Inventory	2,700
Cash	350
Share capital (issued 20X1)	400
Retained earnings	2,350
Noncurrent liabilities	500
Current liabilities	700

The general price index had moved in this way:

	December 31
20X1	100
20X2	130
20X3	150
20X4	240
20X5	300

The property, plant, and equipment was purchased on December 31, 20X7, and there is six months' inventory held. The noncurrent liabilities were a loan raised on March 31, 20X9.

Required

Show the statement of financial position of Z after adjusting for hyperinflation.

Solution

	m zlotys
Property, plant, and equipment (900 × 300/150)	1,800
Inventory (300/270) × 2,700	3,000
Cash	350
	5,150
Share capital (300/100 × 400)	1,200
Retained earnings (balance)	2,750
Noncurrent liabilities	500
Current liabilities	700
	5,150

The inventory had been restated assuming that the index has increased proportionately over time. The loan is a monetary item and therefore is not restated. If the loan had been index linked, then it would have been restated in accordance with the loan agreement.

Consistency of Terminology with Other IFRS

The IASB has identified that paragraph 6 of IAS 29, *Financial Reporting in Hyperinflationary Economies,* contained an out-of-date description of the measurement basis used in financial statements. For example, it says assets and liabilities are at cost except "to the extent that property, plant, and equipment and investments may be revalued." In other words, it does not reflect that there are now several other statement of financial position categories that may or must be measured on the basis of a current value (such as fair value) rather than a historical value. The IASB also believes the Standard uses some out-of-date or inconsistent terminology. In particular, it

1. Uses the term "market value" in IAS 29 to describe existing measurement practice instead of the defined term "fair value."
2. Uses the terms "results of operations" and "net income" when other standards use the term "profit or loss."
3. Refers to "investments" as nonmonetary assets carried at cost. Most investments are now measured at fair value in accordance with IAS 39.

The IASB has therefore updated IAS 29's descriptions of current practice. IAS 29 is amended to clarify that a number of assets and liabilities may or must be measured on the basis of a current value rather than a historical value.

Entities that prepare financial statements on the historical cost basis of accounting *do so* without regard either to changes in the general level of prices or to increases in specific prices of assets held. *The exceptions to this are those assets that the entity is required to or chooses to measure on a fair value or revaluation basis; for example,* property, plant, and equipment may be revalued *and biological assets must be measured at fair value.* Some entities, however, present financial statements that are based on a current cost approach that reflects the effects of changes in the specific prices of assets held.

The previously mentioned amended guidance reflects the fact that a number of assets and liabilities are measured at fair value rather than historical cost.

The following countries should continue to be considered highly inflationary as of September 30, 2009:

Myanmar
Zimbabwe

The following country should be considered highly inflationary for periods beginning on or after December 1, 2009:

Venezuela

The following countries are on the Task Force's inflation "watch list":

Democratic Republic of Congo
Ethiopia
Guinea
Iran
Iraq
Sao Tome and Principe
Seychelles

The IASB proposed (September 2010) adding an exemption to IFRS 1 that an entity can apply at the date of transition to IFRS after being subject to severe hyperinflation. This exemption would allow an entity to measure assets and liabilities at fair value and use that fair value as the deemed cost of those assets and liabilities in the opening IFRS statement of financial position.

DISCLOSURE

This information has to be disclosed under IAS 29:

1. That the financial statements and other corresponding period data have been restated for changes in the general purchasing power of the reporting currency
2. The basis on which the financial statements are prepared, that is, based on historical cost or current cost approach
3. The nature and level of the price index at the end of the reporting period and any movements on this index in the current and previous reporting period

IFRIC 7, *Applying the Restatement Approach under IAS 29, "Financial Reporting in Hyperinflationary Economies,"* states that in the period in which the economy of an entity's functional currency becomes hyperinflationary, the entity shall apply the requirements of IAS 29 as if the economy had always been hyperinflationary. The effect is that restatements of nonmonetary items carried at historical cost are made from the dates they were first recognized; for other nonmonetary items the restatements are made from the dates of the revised current values. Deferred tax items are remeasured in accordance with IAS 12 after restating the nominal carrying amounts of the nonmonetary items in the opening statement of financial position by applying the measuring unit at that date. These items are restated for the change in the measuring unit from the date of the opening statement of financial position to the date of the closing statement of financial position.

MULTIPLE-CHOICE QUESTIONS

1. An entity has several subsidiaries that operate in a hyperinflationary economy, which uses the zloty as its local currency. Management wishes to show the financial statements in US dollars. Many of the operations of the entity are within countries that are not hyperinflationary, and these subsidiaries use the euro as their functional currency. What currency should the entity use to present its consolidated financial statements?

   (a) US dollars.
   (b) The zloty.
   (c) The euro.
   (d) The entity may use any currency.

2. An entity has a subsidiary that operates in a hyperinflationary economy. The subsidiary's financial statements are measured in terms of the local currency, which is the zloty. The subsidiary's financial statements have been restated in accordance with IAS 29. The parent is located in the United States and prepares the consolidated financial statements in US dollars. Which of the following accounting procedures is correct in terms of the consolidation of the subsidiary's financial statements?

   (a) The subsidiary's financial statements should be prepared using the zloty and then retranslated into US dollars.
   (b) The subsidiary's financial statements should be prepared using the zloty, then restated according to IAS 29, and then retranslated into US dollars at closing rates.
   (c) The subsidiary's financial statements should be remeasured in US dollars, then restated according to IAS 29 and consolidated.
   (d) The subsidiary's financial statements should be deconsolidated and not included in the consolidated financial statements.

3. An entity is trying to determine which assets and which liabilities are monetary and nonmonetary. Which of the following assets or liabilities are nonmonetary?

   (a) Trade receivables.
   (b) Deferred tax liabilities.
   (c) Accrued expenses and other payables.
   (d) Taxes payable.

4. Property was purchased on December 31, 20X5, for 20 million zlotys. The general price index in the country was 60.1 on that date. On December 31, 20X7, the general price index had risen to 240.4. If the entity operates in a hyperinflationary economy, what would be the carrying amount in the financial statements of the property after restatement?

   (a) 20 million zlotys.
   (b) 1,200.2 million zlotys.

   (c) 80 million zlotys.
   (d) 4,808 million zlotys.

5. The following "equity" relates to an entity operating in a hyperinflationary economy:

	Before IAS 29	*After restatement*
Share capital	100	170
Revaluation reserve	20	--
Retained earnings	30	--
	150	270

What would be the balances on the revaluation reserve and retained earnings after the restatement for IAS 29?

   (a) Revaluation reserve 0, retained earnings 100.
   (b) Revaluation reserve 100, retained earnings 0.
   (c) Revaluation reserve 20, retained earnings 80.
   (d) Revaluation reserve 70, retained earnings 30.

6. The IASB has updated IAS 29's descriptions of current practice. IAS 29 is amended to clarify that a number of assets and liabilities may or must be measured on the basis of

   (a) Historical cost rather than current value.
   (b) Current value rather than a historical value.
   (c) Net realizable value.
   (d) Amortized cost.

Chapter 22

INTERESTS IN JOINT VENTURES
(IAS 31)

SCOPE

The Standard applies to accounting for interests in joint ventures and the financial reporting of assets, liabilities, income, and expenses of the joint ventures in the accounts of the venturers.

It does not apply to investments in jointly controlled entities held by venture capital organizations, mutual funds, unit trusts, and other similar entities or items that are accounted for at fair value through profit and loss or classified as held-for-trading under IFRS 9 and IAS 39.

A venturer does not have to apply proportionate consolidation or the equity method in these circumstances:

1. Where the interest is classified as held for sale under IFRS 5.
2. Where a parent is exempt from preparing consolidated financial statements by IAS 27. In the separate financial statements prepared by the parent, the investment in the jointly controlled entity may be accounted for by the cost method or under IFRS 9 and IAS 39.
3. If *all* four of the following apply:

   a. The venturer is a wholly owned subsidiary or a partially owned subsidiary by another entity and its owners have been informed and do not object to the venturer not applying proportionate consolidation or the equity method.
   b. The venturer's debt or equity capital is not traded on a public market.
   c. The venturer has not filed nor is filing its financial statements with a security commission for the purpose of issuing any class of financial instrument.
   d. The ultimate or intermediate parent produces consolidated financial statements in accordance with International Financial Reporting Standards (IFRS).

DEFINITIONS OF KEY TERMS
(in accordance with IAS 31)

   Joint venture. A contractual agreement between two or more parties that undertake an economic activity that is subject to joint control.
   Joint control. The contractually agreed sharing of control over economic activity that exists when the strategic decisions relating to the activity require unanimous consent of the parties involved.
   Control. The power to govern the financial and operating policies so as to obtain benefits.
   Venturer. A party to a joint venture who has joint control over that joint venture.
   Investor in a joint venture. A party to a joint venture who does not have joint control over that venture.

DIFFERENT FORMS OF JOINT VENTURE

There are three different forms of joint venture set out in the IAS.

1. Jointly controlled operations
2. Jointly controlled assets
3. Jointly controlled entities

In all of these cases, there must be a contractual arrangement that establishes joint control.

The contractual arrangement is important; if there is no contractual arrangement to establish the joint control, the investments are not deemed to be joint ventures under IAS 31.

Contractual arrangements can be created in different ways. They can be by contract or via discussions (minuted) among the venturers, or they may be set out in the articles of the entity.

The contractual arrangement usually should be in writing and deal with the nature of the activities, the appointment of the board of directors, the capital contributions by the venturers, and the sharing of profits and losses of the joint ventures. The key thing is that no single venturer should be in a position to control the activities.

JOINTLY CONTROLLED OPERATIONS

In jointly controlled operations, a separate entity is not established. Each venturer uses its own assets, incurs its own expenses and liabilities, and raises its own financing. The agreement between the venturers normally would set out the details of how the revenue and expenses were going to be shared.

An example of this type of agreement may be where two entities agree to develop and manufacture a high-speed train where, for example, the engine may be developed by one venturer and the carriages by another. Each venturer would pay the costs and take a share of the revenue from the sale of the trains according to the agreement. Here each venturer will show in its financial statements the assets that it controls, the liabilities that it incurs, together with the expenses that it incurs and its share of the income from the sale of goods or services.

Because each joint venturer is simply recording its own assets and liabilities and expenses that have been incurred and its share of the joint venture income, there are no adjustments or other consolidation procedures used in respect of these items.

JOINTLY CONTROLLED ASSETS

With jointly controlled assets, the venturers jointly control and often jointly own assets that are given to the joint venture. Each venturer may take a share of the assets' output, and each venturer will bear a share of the expenses that are incurred.

Normally this will not involve the establishment of a company or partnership or any other business entity. Each venturer controls its economic benefits through its share of the asset.

An example of this type of venture is in the oil industry, where a number of oil companies jointly own a pipeline. The pipeline will be used to transport the oil, and each venturer agrees to bear part of the expenses of operating the pipeline. The financial statements of each venturer will show its share of the joint assets, any liabilities it has incurred directly, and its share of any joint liabilities together with any income from the sale or usage of its share of the output of the joint venture. Additionally any share of the expenses incurred by the joint venturer or expenses incurred directly will be shown in the financial statements.

The accounting treatment of jointly controlled assets is based on the substance of the transaction and its economic reality and quite often the legal form of the joint venture. It is unlikely that separate financial statements will be prepared for the joint venture, although a record may be kept of any expenses incurred.

JOINTLY CONTROLLED ENTITIES

A jointly controlled entity normally involves the setting up of a company or partnership or other entity in which each of the joint venturers has an interest. The key thing about this type of entity is that there is a contractual arrangement that establishes the joint control over it.

Each venturer normally would contribute assets and other resources to the jointly controlled entity. These assets and resources would be included in the accounting records of the venturer and recognized as an investment in the jointly controlled entity. An example is where an entity enters into an agreement with a foreign government to set up a manufacturing business. The separate entity will be jointly controlled by the joint venturer and the government of the foreign country.

A jointly controlled entity will maintain its own accounting records and will prepare its own financial statements.

IAS 31 allows two accounting treatments for an investment in the jointly controlled entity.

1. Proportionate consolidation
2. The equity method of accounting

On the loss of joint control, the investor must measure at fair value any investment retained in the former jointly controlled entity. The investor must recognize in profit or loss any difference between

1. The fair value of any retained investment and any proceeds from the disposing of the part interest in the jointly controlled entity
2. The carrying amount of the investment at the date when joint control is lost

When an investment ceases to be a jointly controlled entity and is accounted for under IFRS 9 and IAS 39, the fair value of the investment when it ceases to be a jointly controlled entity is regarded as its fair value on initial recognition as a financial asset.

If an investor loses joint control of an entity, the investor must account for all amounts recognized in other comprehensive income in relation to that entity on the same basis required as if the jointly controlled entity had directly disposed of the related assets or liabilities. Thus, if a gain or loss previously recognized in other comprehensive income would be reclassified to profit or loss on the disposal of the related assets or liabilities, the investor reclassifies the gain or loss from equity to profit or loss (as a reclassification adjustment) when the investor loses joint control of the entity.

PROPORTIONATE CONSOLIDATION

Under the proportionate consolidation method of accounting, the statement of financial position of the venturer includes its share of the net assets of the joint venture and the statement of comprehensive income includes its share of the income and expenses of the joint venture.

Different reporting formats may be used to present proportionate consolidation of financial statements.

- The venturer may combine each of its share of the assets and liabilities, income, and expenses of the jointly controlled entity with similar items in its financial statements.
- The venturer may include separate line items for the same items.

EQUITY METHOD

The equity method is described in Chapter 20 dealing with IAS 28, *Investments in Associates*. If the venturer ceases to have control at any time or ceases to have significant influence in a jointly controlled entity, then the equity method should be discontinued.

CASE STUDY 1

Facts

Three entities decide to form a joint venture. The entities have these holdings in the joint venture: Aztec holds 25% of the equity shares, Matex owns 35% of the equity shares, and Azure owns 40% of the equity shares. The agreement among the companies is such that decisions can be made only with a 60% majority. Each company has equal representation on the management board.

Required

Discuss the way in which the entities' holdings in the joint venture should be accounted for.

Solution

The structure of the joint venture means that each venturer has the opportunity to control the joint venture and, therefore, exercise control. Only two of the joint venturers must be in agreement to achieve a 60% majority. They should use either equity accounting or proportionate consolidation. Additionally each entity has equal representation on the management board.

EXCEPTION TO THE USE OF THE EQUITY METHOD AND PROPORTIONATE CONSOLIDATION

If the jointly controlled entity becomes classified as held for sale under IFRS 5, it has to be accounted for using that Standard. Similarly if the jointly controlled entity becomes a subsidiary or an associate, then the respective standards should be used.

In the separate financial statements of the venturer, any interest in a jointly controlled entity should be accounted for either at cost or under IAS 39.

If an asset is contributed or sold to the jointly controlled entity and the asset is still retained by the joint venture, then the venturer should recognize only that portion of the gain that is attributable to the other venturers (assuming that the risks and rewards of ownership have passed).

However, the venturer should recognize the full amount of any loss incurred when this sale provides evidence of a reduction in the net realizable value of current assets or an impairment loss.

When the venturer purchases assets from a jointly controlled entity, it should not recognize its share of the gain until it resells the asset to a third party.

FINANCIAL STATEMENTS OF AN INVESTOR

Where the interest in the joint venture is classified as that of an investor in a joint venture (i.e., the investor does not have joint control), then it should be reported as interest in the joint venture in accordance with either IAS 28, or IAS 39.

SEPARATE FINANCIAL STATEMENTS

Separate financial statements are the investor's own financial statements in which investments are accounted for on the basis of the direct equity interest. The term direct equity interest means at cost or in accordance with IFRS 9 and IAS 39. Jointly controlled entities are not proportionately consolidated or equity accounted in separate financial statements.

IAS 27 and IAS 31 do not mandate which entities produce separate financial statements, but specify the accounting and disclosures required when an entity elects, or is required, by local regulations, to present separate financial statements. Where separate financial statements are produced, they are presented in addition to consolidated financial statements or "economic interest" financial statements. Investors that are exempt from the requirement to consolidate, proportionately consolidate, or equity account their investments may present separate financial statements as their only financial statements.

CASE STUDY 2

Facts

Albion and Board decide to form a joint venture but do not sign a written agreement regarding the control of the joint venture. However, minutes of the meeting where the relationship was discussed have been signed by the parties. Each company owns 50% of the equity shares and provides equal numbers of directors to the management board. There is an understanding that the shares in the joint venture cannot be sold unless first offered to the other shareholder.

Required

Discuss whether it is possible for joint control to exist if there is no written contract.

Solution

Joint control will exist in this case because the substance of the arrangement is that of joint control, and the Standard says that the existence of a contractual arrangement can be shown in a number of ways, one of which is minutes of discussions between the venturers. The existence of a contractual obligation establishes joint control over the venture so that no single venturer can be in a position to control the venture. Each company owns 50% of the equity and provides equal numbers to the board. Also, the shares should be offered to the other shareholder first before selling.

TRANSACTIONS BETWEEN A VENTURER AND A JOINT VENTURE

When a venturer contributes or sells assets to a joint venture and where the assets are retained by the joint venture, the venturer should recognize only the proportion of the gain or loss that is attributable to the interests of the other venturers.

When a venturer purchases assets from a joint venture, the venturer should not recognize its share of the profit or loss of the joint venture from the transaction, until it resells the assets to an independent third party.

The full amount of any loss is recognized if the transaction provides evidence of a reduction in the net realizable value of current assets or an impairment loss.

CASE STUDY 3

B has entered into an agreement with J, and H, both public limited companies on December 1, 20X8. Each of the companies holds one third of the equity in an entity, W, a public limited company, which operates offshore oil rigs. Any decisions regarding the operating and financial policies relating to W have to be approved by two thirds of the venturers. B wants to account for the interest in the entity by using proportionate consolidation, and wishes advice on the matter.

The oil rigs of W started operating on December 1, 19X8 and are measured under the cost model. The useful life of the rigs is 40 years. The initial cost of the rigs was $240 million, which included decommissioning costs (discounted) of $20 million. At December 1, 20X8, the carrying amount of the decommissioning liability has grown to $32.6 million, but the net present value of the decommissioning liability has decreased to $18.5 million as a result of the increase in the risk-adjusted discount rate from 5% to 7%. B is unsure how to account for the oil rigs in the financial statements of W for the year ended November 30, 20X9. B owns a 10% interest in a pipeline, which is used to transport the oil from the offshore oil rig to a refinery on the land. B has joint control over the pipeline and has to pay its share of the maintenance costs. B has the right to use 10% of the capacity of the pipeline. B wishes to show the pipeline as an investment in its financial statements

Required

Discuss the accounting treatment of the above items.

Solution

A jointly controlled entity is a corporation, partnership, or other entity in which two or more venturers have an interest, under a contractual arrangement that establishes joint control over the entity (IAS 31.24).

IAS 31 allows two treatments of accounting for an investment in jointly controlled entities:

1. Proportionate consolidation.
2. Equity method of accounting.

Joint control is the contractually agreed sharing of control over an economic activity and only exists when strategic, financial, and operating decisions relating to the activity require the unanimous consent of the parties sharing control, that is, the venturers (IAS 31 Para 3). Thus B cannot use proportionate consolidation, as W is not jointly controlled. A decision can be made by gaining the approval of two thirds of the venturers and not by unanimous agreement. Two out of the three venturers can make the decision. Thus each investor must account for their interest in the entity as an associate since they have significant influence but not control. Equity accounting will be used.

One of the key differences between decommissioning costs and other costs of acquisition is the timing of costs. Decommissioning costs will not become payable until some future date. Consequently, there is likely to be uncertainty over the amount of costs that will be incurred. Management should record its best estimate of the entity's obligations (IAS 16.16). Discounting is used to address the impact of the delayed cash flows. The amount capitalized, as part of the assets will be the amount estimated to be paid, discounted to the date of initial recognition. The related credit is recognized in provisions. An entity that uses the cost model records changes in the existing liability and changes in discount rate are added to, or deducted from, the cost of the related asset in the current period (IFRIC 1.5). Thus in the case of W, the accounting for the decommissioning is as follows.

The carrying amount of the asset will be

	$m
Carrying amount at December 1, 20X8	
(240 – depreciation 60 – 14.1 decrease in decommissioning costs)	165.9
Less depreciation 165.9 ÷ 30 years	(5.5)
Carrying amount at November 30, 20X9	160.4
Finance cost ($32.6 million – $14.1 million) at 7%	1.3
Decommissioning liability will be ($32.6m – $14.1m)	18.5
Decommissioning liability at November 30, 20X9	19.8

Jointly controlled assets involve the joint control, and often the joint ownership, of assets dedicated to the joint venture. Each venturer may take a share of the output from the assets and each bears a share of the expenses incurred (IAS 31 Para 18). IAS 31 requires that the venturer should recognize in its financial statements its share of the joint assets, any liabilities that it has incurred directly, and its share of any liabilities incurred jointly with other venturers, income from the sale or use of its share of the output of the joint venture, its share of expenses incurred by the joint venture, and expenses incurred directly in the respect of its interest in the joint venture (IAS 31 Para 21). The pipeline is a jointly controlled asset. Therefore, B should not show the asset as an investment but as property, plant, and equipment. Any liabilities or expenses incurred should be shown also.

CASE STUDY 4

Entity A holds a 40% interest in entity B and exercises joint control over B. A uses proportionate consolidation to account for its interest in B. A has loaned B $10 million and both entities recognize the loan at its amortized cost of $9 million.

Required

How should A account for the loan to B?

Solution

The loan to B should be eliminated from A's accounts to the extent of A's interest. This represents the intercompany element, which should be eliminated. The amount shown in A's accounts would be 60% of $9 million, which would be $54 million.

CASE STUDY 5

A is an entity jointly controlled by B and C. B owns 60% and C owns 40% of A. Both entities use proportionate consolidation. On December 31, 20X9, B sells PPE for $2 million to A. The PPE has a carrying value of $1.2 million in B's books.

Required

What are the accounting entries for this transaction?

Solution

B would recognize a gain equal to the amount of profit attributable to the other venturer. That is $(2 − 1.2) million × 40% which is $0.32 million. Only 40% of the gain is reported in B's financial statements. The unrealized proportion of the gain is eliminated against B's share of the asset now carried in the statement of financial position of A. B's share of the asset will be 60% × $2 million, that is, $1.2 million less the unrealized gain of $0.48 million. That is $0.72 million. This actually represents B's original share of the asset had the gain not been recorded. When the PPE is sold by A, the profit eliminated can be recognized ($0.48 million).

DISCLOSURE

A venturer has to disclose specific information about contingent liabilities relating to its interest in the joint venture and also this information:

- Capital commitments and contingent liabilities relating to its interests in joint ventures.
- A list and descriptions of interests in significant joint ventures and the proportion of the ownership interest that is held in jointly controlled entities. If the line-by-line format is used for proportionate consolidation or if the equity method is used, then the venturer should disclose the aggregate amount of current assets, long-term assets, current liabilities, and income and expenses relating to its interests in joint ventures.
- The method that is used to recognize the interests in jointly controlled entities.

PRACTICAL INSIGHT

Holcim S.A., a Swiss entity, uses proportionate consolidation to account for an investment in a joint venture. The entity chooses to consolidate its share of the assets, liabilities, income, and expenses on a line-by-line basis rather than showing them as separate line items. This seems to be the practice of many companies using IFRS.

SIC 13, *Jointly Controlled Entities—Nonmonetary Contributions by Venturers,* clarifies the circumstances in which the appropriate portion of gains or losses resulting from a contribution of a nonmonetary asset to a jointly controlled entity (JCE) in exchange for an equity interest in the JCE should be recognized by the venturer in the statement of comprehensive income.

EXTRACTS FROM PUBLISHED FINANCIAL STATEMENTS

UNILEVER PLC Annual Report, 2009

Other noncurrent assets	€ million 2009	€ million 2008
Interest in net assets of joint ventures	**60**	73
Interest in net assets of associates	**42**	67
Other noncurrent financial assets[a]	**485**	904
Held-to-maturity investments[b]	**--**	472
Loans and receivables	**2**	9
Available-for-sale financial assets[c][d]	**436**	370
Financial assets at fair value through profit or loss[d]	**47**	53
Long-term trade and other receivables[e]	**212**	171
Fair value of biological assets	**32**	31
Other nonfinancial assets	**186**	180
	1,017	1,426

[a] *Predominantly consist of investments in a number of companies and financial institutions in India, Europe, and the United States, including €129 million (2008: €146 million) of assets in a trust to fund benefit obligations in the United States.*

[b] *During 2009 €436 million of held-to-maturity investments were reclassified as available for sale in relation to the closure of an employee savings program.*

[c] *Includes unlisted preferred shares arising in connection with US laundry disposal.*

[d] *Methods of valuation techniques used to determine fair values are given in note 15 on page 108.*

[e] *Classified as loans and receivables.*

Movements during 2009 and 2008	€ million 2009	€ million 2008
Joint ventures[f]		
January 1	**73**	150
Additions	**--**	--
Dividends received/reductions[g]	**(145)**	(202)
Share in net profit	**111**	125
Currency retranslation	**21**	--
December 31	**60**	73
Associates[h]		
January 1	**67**	44
Acquisitions/(disposals)	**--**	22
Dividends received/reductions	**(32)**	(22)
Share in net profit	**4**	6
Currency retranslation	**3**	(14)
	42	36
Of which: Net liabilities of JohnsonDiversey reclassified to provisions	**--**	31
December 31	**42**	67

[f] *Our principal joint ventures are Unilever Jerónimo Martins in Portugal, Pepsi/Lipton International and the Pepsi/Lipton Partnership in the United States.*

[g] *A reduction of €110 million in carrying value of Pepsi/Lipton International was recorded in relation to the extension of the Pepsi/Lipton joint venture for ready-to-drink tea in January 2008.*

[h] *Associates as at December 31, 2009, primarily comprise our investment in Langholm Capital Partners. Other Unilever Ventures assets (excluding Langholm) are included under "Other noncurrent financial assets" above.*

Analysis of listed and unlisted investments	€ million 2009	€ million 2008
Investments listed on a recognized stock exchange	60	344
Unlisted investments	425	560
	485	904

Other income from noncurrent investments	€ million 2009	€ million 2008	€ million 2007
Income from other noncurrent investments	**47**	19	19
Profit/(loss) on disposal[i]	**327**	69	20
	374	88	39

[i] *For 2008 includes disposal of Palmci plantations.*

For 2009 includes €327 million profit from the disposal of the majority of our equity interest in JohnsonDiversey.

The joint ventures and associates have no significant contingent liabilities to which the Group is exposed, and the Group has no significant contingent liabilities in relation to its interest in the joint ventures and associates.

The Group has no outstanding capital commitments to joint ventures.

J. SAINSBURY Annual Report, 2009

Investment in joint ventures continued

The Group's principal joint ventures were

	Year-end	Share of ordinary allotted capital	Country of registration or incorporation
BL Sainsbury Superstores Limited (property investment — UK)	March 31	50%	England
The Harvest Limited Partnership (property investment — UK)	March 31	50%	England
Sainsbury's Bank plc (financial services — UK)	December 31	50%	England

Where relevant, management accounts for the joint ventures have been used to include the results up to March 21, 2009.

The Group's share of the assets, liabilities, income, and expenses of its joint ventures are detailed below:

	2009 £m	2008 £m
Noncurrent assets	**1,398**	1,069
Current assets	**1,494**	2,405
Current liabilities	**(1,800)**	(2,896)
Noncurrent liabilities	**(809)**	(430)
Net assets	**283**	148
Income	**239**	237
Expenses	**(350)**	(239)
Loss after tax	**(111)**	(2)

Investments in joint ventures at March 21, 2009, include £5 million of goodwill (2008: £nil).

BP PLC Annual Report, 2009

Interests in joint ventures

A joint venture is a contractual arrangement whereby two or more parties (venturers) undertake an economic activity that is subject to joint control. Joint control exists only when the strategic financial and operating decisions relating to the activity require the unanimous consent of the venturers. A jointly controlled entity is a joint venture that involves the establishment of a company, partnership, or other entity to engage in economic activity that the group jointly controls with its fellow venturers. The results, assets and liabilities of a jointly controlled entity are incorporated in these financial statements using the equity method of accounting. Under the equity method, the investment in a jointly controlled entity is carried in the balance sheet at cost, plus postacquisition changes in the group's share of net assets of the jointly controlled entity, less distributions received, and less any impairment in value of the investment. Loans advanced to jointly controlled entities are also included in the investment on the group balance sheet. The group income statement reflects the group's share of the results after tax of the jointly controlled entity. Financial statements of jointly controlled entities are prepared for the same reporting year as the group. Where necessary, adjustments are made to those financial statements to bring the accounting policies used into line with those of the group. Unrealized gains on transactions between the group and its jointly controlled entities are eliminated to the extent of the group's interest in the jointly controlled entities. Unrealized losses are also eliminated unless the transaction provides evidence of an impairment of the asset transferred. The group assesses investments in jointly controlled entities for impairment whenever events or changes in circumstances indicate that the carrying value may not be recoverable. If any such indication of impairment exists, the carrying amount of the investment is compared with its recoverable amount, being the higher of its fair value less costs to sell and value in use. Where the carrying amount exceeds the recoverable amount, the investment is written down to its recoverable amount. The group ceases to use the equity method of accounting on the date from which it no longer has joint control or significant influence over the joint venture, or when the interest becomes held for sale. Certain of the group's activities, particularly in the Exploration and Production segment, are conducted through joint ventures where the venturers have a direct ownership interest in, and jointly control, the assets of the venture. BP recognizes, on a line-by-line basis in the consolidated financial statements, its share of the assets, liabilities, and expenses of these jointly controlled assets, along with the group's income from the sale of its share of the output and any liabilities and expenses incurred in relation to the venture.

MULTIPLE-CHOICE QUESTIONS

1. A joint venture is exempt from using the equity method or proportionate consolidation in certain circumstances. Which of the following circumstances is **not** a legitimate reason for not using the equity method or proportionate consolidation?

(a) Where the interest is held for sale under IFRS 5.

(b) Where the exception in IAS 27 applies regarding an entity not being required to present consolidated financial statements.

(c) Where the venturer is wholly owned, is not a publicly traded entity and does not intend to be, the ultimate parent produces consolidated accounts, and the owners do not object to the nonusage of the accounting methods.

(d) Where the joint venture's activities are dissimilar from those of the parent.

2. In the case of a jointly controlled operation, a venturer should account for its interest by

(a) Using the equity method or proportionate consolidation.

(b) Recognizing the assets and liabilities, expenses and income that relate to its interest in the joint venture.

(c) Showing its share of the assets that it jointly controls, any liabilities incurred jointly or severally, and any income or expense relating to its interest in the joint venture.

(d) Using the purchase method of accounting.

3. In the case of jointly controlled assets, a venturer should account for its interest by

(a) Using the equity method or proportionate consolidation.

(b) Recognizing the assets and liabilities, expenses and income that relate to its interest in the joint venture.

(c) Showing its share of the assets that it jointly controls, any liabilities incurred jointly or severally, and any income or expense relating to its interest in the joint venture.

(d) Using the purchase method of accounting.

4. In the case of jointly controlled entities, a venturer should account for its interest by

(a) Using the equity method or proportionate consolidation.

(b) Recognizing the assets and liabilities, expenses and income that relate to its interest in the joint venture.

(c) Showing its share of the assets that it jointly controls, any liabilities incurred jointly or severally, and any income or expense relating to its interest in the joint venture.

(d) Using the purchase method of accounting.

5. The exemption from applying the equity method or proportionate consolidation is available in the following circumstances

(a) Where severe long-term restrictions impair the ability to transfer funds to the investor.

(b) Where the interest is acquired with a view to resale within 12 months.

(c) Where the activities of the venturer and joint venture are dissimilar.

(d) Where the venturer does not exert significant influence.

6. Under proportionate consolidation, the noncontrolling interest in the venture is

(a) Shown as a deduction from the net assets.

(b) Shown in the equity of the venturer.

(c) Shown as part of long-term liabilities of the venturer.

(d) Not included in the financial statements of the venturer.

7. A company has a 40% share in a joint venture and loans the venture $2 million. What figure will be shown for the loan in the statement of financial position of the venturer?

(a) $2 million.

(b) $800,000

(c) $1.2 million.

(d) Zero.

8. A is an entity jointly controlled by B and C. B owns 52% and C owns 48% of A. Both entities use proportionate consolidation. On December 31, 20X9, B sells PPE for $12 million to A. The PPE has a carrying value of $8 million in B's books. What gain would be shown in the financial records of B?

(a) $1.92 million.

(b) $2.08 million.

(c) $3.84 million.

(d) $4 million.

9. Entity A holds a 60% interest in entity B and exercises joint control over B. A uses proportionate consolidation to account for its interest in B. A has loaned B $15 million and both entities recognize the loan at its amortized cost of $12 million. How should A recognize the loan to B in its financial statements?

(a) The loan to B should be eliminated from A's accounts to the extent of $9 million.

(b) The loan to B should be eliminated from A's accounts to the extent of $7.2 million.

(c) The loan to B should be eliminated from A's accounts to the extent of $6 million.

(d) The loan to B should be eliminated from A's accounts to the extent of $4.8 million.

10. On the loss of joint control, the investor must measure at fair value any investment retained in the former jointly controlled entity. The investor must recognize in profit or loss any difference between

(a) The net realizable value of any retained investment plus any proceeds from disposing of the part interest in the jointly controlled entity and the carrying amount of the investment at the date when joint control is lost.

(b) The fair value of any retained investment plus any proceeds from disposing of the part interest in the jointly controlled entity and the carrying amount of the investment at the date when joint control is lost.

(c) The original cost of any retained investment plus any proceeds from disposing of the part interest in the jointly controlled entity and the carrying amount of the investment at the date when joint control is lost.

(d) The fair value of any retained investment plus any proceeds from disposing of the part interest in the jointly controlled entity and the fair value of the investment at the date when joint control is lost.

Chapter 23

FINANCIAL INSTRUMENTS: PRESENTATION (IAS 32)

INTRODUCTION

IAS 32, *Financial Instruments: Presentation,* addresses the presentation of financial instruments as financial liabilities or equity. IAS 32 includes requirements for

- The presentation of financial instruments as either financial liabilities or equity, including:

  - When a financial instrument should be presented as a financial liability or equity instrument by the issuing entity
  - How to separate and present the components of a compound financial instrument that contains both liability and equity elements
  - The accounting treatment of reacquired equity instruments of the entity ("treasury shares")

- The presentation of interest, dividends, losses, and gains related to financial instruments
- The circumstances in which financial assets and financial liabilities should be offset

IAS 32 complements the requirements for recognizing and measuring financial assets and financial liabilities in IFRS 9, *Financial Instruments,* and IAS 39, *Financial Instruments: Recognition and Measurement,* and the disclosure requirements for financial instruments in IFRS 7, *Financial Instruments: Disclosures.*

Prior to the issuance of IFRS 7, IAS 32 contained both presentation and disclosure requirements and was entitled *Financial Instruments: Disclosure and Presentation.* IFRS 7, which became effective for annual periods beginning on or after January 1, 2007, relocates the disclosure requirements in IAS 30 and IAS 32 to IFRS 7. Therefore, IASB shortened the title of IAS 32 to *Financial Instruments: Presentation.*

SCOPE

IAS 32 applies to all entities in the presentation of both

- Financial instruments
- Certain net settled contracts to purchase or sell nonfinancial items

DEFINITIONS OF KEY TERMS
(in accordance with IAS 32)

Financial instrument. Any contract that gives rise to a financial asset of one entity and a financial liability or equity instrument of another entity.

Puttable financial instruments. A puttable financial instrument includes an instrument where the issuer of the instrument has the obligation to buy-back the instrument on exercise of the put option by the holder of the instrument.

In this definition, "contract" refers to an agreement between two parties that the parties have little, if any, discretion to avoid, usually because the agreement is enforceable by law. An asset or liability that is not contractual (e.g., an obligation to pay income taxes) is not a financial instrument even though it may result in the receipt or delivery of cash.

The term "financial instrument" encompasses equity instruments, financial assets, and financial liabilities. These three terms all have specific definitions that help entities determine which items should be accounted for as financial instruments.

Equity instrument. Any contract that evidences a residual interest in the assets of an entity after deducting all of its liabilities.

This definition reflects the basic accounting equation that states that equity equals assets less liabilities.

Example

Examples of equity instruments include

- Ordinary shares (that cannot be put back to the issuer by the holder)
- Preference shares (that cannot be redeemed by the holder or provide for nondiscretionary dividends)
- Warrants or written call options (that allow the holder to subscribe for—or purchase—a fixed number of nonputtable ordinary shares in exchange for a fixed amount of cash or another financial asset)

The definition of an equity instrument is brief and succinct, but the definitions of "financial asset" and "financial liability" are more complex. Summaries of the IAS 32 definitions for those terms follow.

Financial asset. Any asset that is

1. Cash
2. An equity instrument of another entity
3. A contractual right to receive cash or another financial asset from another entity, or to exchange financial assets or financial liabilities with another entity under conditions that are potentially favorable to the entity
4. A contract that may or will be settled in the entity's own equity instrument and is not classified as an equity instrument of the entity (discussed ahead)

Example

Examples of assets that meet the definition of a financial asset are

- Cash (see 1. in the preceding list)
- Investment in shares or other equity instrument issued by other entities, (see 2. in the preceding list)
- Receivables (see 3. in the preceding list)
- Loans to other entities (see 3. in the preceding list)
- Investments in bonds and other debt instruments issued by other entities (see 3. in the preceding list)
- Derivative financial assets (see 3. in the preceding list)
- Some derivatives on own equity (see 4. in the preceding list)

Financial liability. Any liability that is

1. A contractual obligation to deliver cash or another financial asset to another entity; or to

exchange financial assets or financial liabilities with another entity under conditions that are potentially unfavorable to the entity

2. A contract that will or may be settled in the entity's own equity instruments and is not classified as an equity instrument of the entity (discussed ahead)

Example

Examples of liabilities that meet the definition of financial liabilities are

- Payables (e.g., trade payables) (see 1. previous paragraph)
- Loans from other entities (see 1. previous paragraph)
- Issued bonds and other debt instruments issued by the entity (see 1. previous paragraph)
- Derivative financial liabilities (see 1. previous paragraph)
- Obligations to deliver own shares worth a fixed amount of cash (see 2. previous paragraph)
- Some derivatives on own equity (see 2. previous paragraph)

It follows from the definitions that these assets and liabilities are not financial instruments:

- *Physical assets* (e.g., inventories, property, plant, and equipment). Control of physical assets creates an opportunity to generate a cash inflow but does not give rise to a present right to receive cash or another financial asset.
- *Leased assets.* Control of leased assets creates an opportunity to generate a cash inflow but does not give rise to a present right to receive cash or another financial asset.
- *Intangible assets* (e.g., patents and trademarks). Control of intangible assets creates an opportunity to generate a cash inflow but does not give rise to a present right to receive cash or another financial asset.
- *Prepaid expenses.* Such assets are associated with the receipt of goods or services. They do not give rise to a present right to receive cash or another financial asset.
- *Deferred revenue.* Such liabilities are associated with the future delivery of goods or services. They do not give rise to a contractual obligation to pay cash or another financial asset.
- *Warranty obligations.* Such liabilities are associated with the future delivery of goods or services. They do not give rise to a contractual obligation to pay cash or another financial asset.
- *Income tax liabilities (or assets).* Such liabilities (or assets) are not contractual but are imposed by statutory requirements.
- *Constructive obligations.* Such obligations do not arise from contracts. (A constructive obligation is defined by IAS 37 as an obligation that derives from an entity's actions where: (1) by an established pattern of past practice, published policies, or a sufficiently specific current statement, the entity has indicated to other parties that it will accept certain responsibilities; and (2) as a result, the entity has created a valid expectation on the part of those other parties that it will discharge those responsibilities.)

Apart from items that meet the definition of financial instruments, IAS 32, IFRS 9, IAS 39, and IFRS 7 also apply to some contracts that do not meet the definition of a financial instrument but have characteristics similar to derivative financial instruments. This *expands* the scope of IAS 32, IFRS 9, IAS 39, and IFRS 7 to contracts to purchase or sell nonfinancial items (e.g., gold, electricity, or gas) at a future date when, and only when, a contract has both of these two characteristics: (1) it can be settled net in cash or some other financial instrument, and (2) it is not for receipt or delivery of the nonfinancial item in accordance with the entity's expected purchase, sale, or usage requirements. The chapter on IAS 39 provides a more detailed discussion.

IAS 32 has scope exceptions for some items that meet the definition of a financial instrument, because they are accounted for under other IFRS. Such scope exceptions are listed in the table.

Scope Exception	*Applicable Standard*
Interests in subsidiaries	IAS 27, *Consolidated and Separate Financial Statements*
Interests in associates	IAS 28, *Investments in Associates*
Interests in joint ventures	IAS 31, *Interests in Joint Ventures*

Scope Exception	*Applicable Standard*
Employee benefit plans	IAS 19, *Employee Benefits*
Share-based payment transactions	IFRS 2, *Share-Based Payment*
Contracts for contingent consideration in	
business combinations	IFRS 3, *Business Combinations*
Insurance contracts	IFRS 4, *Insurance Contracts*

Unlike IAS 39, IAS 32 has no scope exception for an entity's issued equity instruments that are classified in the equity section of the balance sheet (e.g., an entity's share capital).

CASE STUDY 1

This case illustrates how to apply the definition of a financial instrument and the scope of IAS 32.

Facts

Company A is evaluating whether each of these items is a financial instrument and whether it should be accounted for under IAS 32:

1. Cash deposited in banks
2. Gold bullion deposited in banks
3. Trade accounts receivable
4. Investments in debt instruments
5. Investments in equity instruments, where Company A does not have significant influence over the investee
6. Investments in equity instruments, where Company A has significant influence over the investee
7. Prepaid expenses
8. Finance lease receivables or payables
9. Deferred revenue
10. Statutory tax liabilities
11. Provision for estimated litigation losses
12. An electricity purchase contract that can be net settled in cash
13. Issued debt instruments
14. Issued equity instruments

Required

Help Company A to determine (1) which of the previous items meets the definition of a financial instrument and (2) which of the previous items falls within the scope of IAS 32.

Solution

1. Yes, cash deposited in a bank is a financial instrument. If an entity deposits cash in a bank, it is a financial asset of the entity and a financial liability of the bank, because the bank has a contractual obligation to repay the cash to the entity. It falls within the scope of IAS 32.
2. No, gold is not a financial instrument. It is a commodity. It is outside the scope of IAS 32.
3. Yes, a trade accounts receivable is a financial instrument. Trade accounts receivable is a financial asset because the holder has a contractual right to receive cash. It falls within the scope of IAS 32.
4. Yes, an investment in a debt instrument is a financial instrument. Investments in debt instruments are financial assets because the investor has a contractual right to receive cash. It falls within the scope of IAS 32.
5. Yes, an investment in an equity instrument is a financial instrument. Investments in equity instruments are financial assets because the investor holds an equity instrument issued by another entity. It falls within the scope of IAS 32.
6. While an investment in an equity instrument is a financial instrument (a financial asset), if the investor has significant influence, joint control, or control over the investee, the investment generally is scoped out of IAS 32 and instead accounted for as an investment in an associate, joint venture, or subsidiary.
7. No, prepaid expenses are not financial instruments because they will not result in the delivery or exchange of cash or other financial instruments. They are outside the scope of IAS 32.
8. Yes, finance lease receivables or payables are financial instruments. They are within the scope of IAS 32. (However, they are scoped out of IAS 39 except for recognition and measurement of impairment of finance lease receivables.)

9. No, deferred revenue does not meet the definition of a financial instrument. Deferred revenue is outside the scope of IAS 32.

10. No, deferred taxes do not meet the definition of a financial instrument, because they do not arise from contractual rights or obligations, but from statutory requirements. They are outside the scope of IAS 32.

11. No, provisions do not meet the definition of a financial instrument, because they do not arise as a result of contractual rights or obligations. They are outside the scope of IAS 32.

12. Even though an electricity purchase contract does not meet the definition of a financial instrument, it is included in the scope of IAS 32 (and IFRS 9 and IAS 39) if it can be settled net in cash unless it will be settled by delivery to meet the entity's normal purchase, sale, or usage requirements.

13. Yes, an issued debt instrument meets the definition of a financial liability. It is within the scope of IAS 32.

14. Yes, an issued equity instrument is a financial instrument that falls within the scope of IAS 32. However, although an issued equity instrument meets the definition of a financial instrument, there is a specific scope exception for issued equity instruments in IAS 39 (and IFRS 9).

PRESENTATION OF LIABILITIES AND EQUITY

Classification as Liabilities or Equity

A key issue addressed by IAS 32 is how an issuer of a financial instrument determines whether the instrument should be classified as an equity instrument or a financial liability (or, in a few cases, a financial asset). IAS 32 provides this principle:

- The issuer of a financial instrument shall classify the instrument, or its component parts, on initial recognition as a financial liability, a financial asset, or an equity instrument in accordance with the substance of the contractual arrangement and the definitions of a financial liability, a financial asset, and an equity instrument.

This principle highlights the need to consider not only the legal form of an instrument but also the substance of the contractual arrangement associated with the instrument when determining whether an instrument should be classified and presented as liabilities or equity. When substance and legal form of an instrument are different, substance governs the classification and presentation.

A critical feature in differentiating a financial liability from an equity instrument is the existence of a contractual obligation that meets the definition of a financial liability. If there is an obligation to deliver cash or another financial asset, the instrument usually meets the definition of a financial liability, even though its form may be that of an equity instrument. It does not matter whether the obligation is conditional on the counterparty exercising a right to require payment. An obligation to deliver cash or another financial asset usually is a financial liability even though the obligation may be contingent upon the holder exercising a right to require the delivery of cash or another financial asset.

Example

Examples of financial instruments that have the form of equity instruments, but in substance meet the definition of a financial liability and therefore should be accounted for as financial liabilities, are

- A preference share that provides for mandatory redemption by the issuer for a fixed amount at a fixed or determinable future date. This is a financial liability of the issuer because the issuer has an obligation to pay cash or another financial asset.
- A preference share that gives the holder the right to require the issuer to redeem the instrument at or after a particular date for a fixed amount. This is a financial liability of the issuer because the issuer has an obligation to pay cash or another financial asset.
- A financial instrument that gives the holder the right to put the instrument back to the issuer for a fixed amount of cash or another financial asset. This is a financial liability of the issuer because the issuer has an obligation to pay cash or another financial asset.

CASE STUDY 2

This case illustrates the application of the principle for how to distinguish between liabilities and equity.

Facts

During 2004, Entity A has issued a number of financial instruments. It is evaluating how each of these instruments should be presented under IAS 32:

1. A perpetual bond (i.e., a bond that does not have a maturity date) that pays 5% interest each year
2. A mandatorily redeemable share with a fixed redemption amount (i.e., a share that will be redeemed by the entity at a future date)
3. A share that is redeemable at the option of the holder for a fixed amount of cash
4. A sold (written) call option that allows the holder to purchase a fixed number of ordinary shares from Entity A for a fixed amount of cash

Required

For each of the above instruments, discuss whether it should be classified as a financial liability and, if so, why.

Solution

1. An issued perpetual bond (i.e., a bond that does not have a maturity date) that pays 5% interest each year should be classified as a financial liability. Because the instrument contains an obligation to pay interest, it meets the definition of a financial liability.
2. An issued mandatorily redeemable share (i.e., a share that will be redeemed by the entity at a future date) with a fixed redemption amount should be classified as a financial liability. Because the instrument contains an obligation to pay a fixed amount of cash or other financial assets on redemption of the share, it meets the definition of a financial liability.
3. An issued share that is redeemable for a fixed amount of cash at the option of the holder should be classified as a financial liability. Because the entity cannot avoid settlement through delivery of cash should the holder demand redemption, the share meets the definition of a financial liability.
4. A sold (written) call option that allows the holder to purchase a fixed number of ordinary shares from Entity A for a fixed amount of cash should be classified as equity. As discussed later in this chapter, a contract that will or may be settled in own equity is classified as equity if it provides for the exchange of a fixed number of own equity instruments for a fixed amount of cash.

Interpretation 2, *Members' Shares in Cooperative Entities and Similar Instruments*, of the International Financial Reporting Interpretations Committee (IFRIC) addresses the application of IAS 32's classification requirements to financial instruments issued to members of cooperative entities that evidence the members' ownership interests in the entity ("members' shares"). In some cases, such shares give the member the right to request redemption for cash or another financial asset. In such cases, IFRIC Interpretation 2 clarifies that members' shares are equity if

1. The entity has an unconditional right to refuse redemption of the members' shares.
2. Redemption is unconditionally prohibited by local law, regulation, or the entity's governing charter.

If an unconditional prohibition is partial (e.g., redemption of members' shares is prohibited if redemption would cause the number of members' shares or amount of paid-in capital from members' shares to fall below a specified level), members' shares in excess of the prohibition against redemption are liabilities, unless the entity has the unconditional right to refuse redemption.

Example

A cooperative bank has issued members' shares that give members the right to vote and participate in dividend distributions. Members also have the right to request redemption of the shares for cash. The charter of the cooperative bank states that the entity has the right to refuse redemption at its sole discretion, but the entity has never refused to redeem members' shares in the past. Nevertheless, the members' shares are equity because the entity has the unconditional right to refuse redemption.

In February 2008, IASB published an amendment to IAS 32 to make a limited exception to the principle that instruments that contain an obligation to deliver cash or other financial assets always should be classified as financial liabilities. This exception applies to instruments that represent the residual interest in the net assets of the entity and that meet certain specified conditions. Under this exception, some puttable financial instruments and some financial instruments that impose on the entity an obligation to deliver to another party a pro rata share of the net assets of the entity only on liquidation are classified as equity.

Puttable Financial Instruments and Obligations Arising on Liquidation—Amendments Effective 2009

Effective January 1, 2009, IAS 32 *Financial Instruments: Presentation,* has been amended to address the classification of (1) puttable financial instruments and (2) obligations arising only on liquidation, with the objective of providing a "short-term, limited scope amendment" designed to avoid outcomes arising under the general principles of IAS 32 that were counterintuitive.

Puttable financial instruments. A puttable financial instrument includes an instrument where the issuer of the instrument has the obligation to buy back the instrument on exercise of the put option by the holder of the instrument.

Example

A Cooperative Society of farmers issued a financial instrument to the constituent farmers. The financial instrument provides to the farmer, in proportion to the holding, a right in the residual interest of the Society. Also, according to the terms of the instrument, a farmer who held the instrument had the option to "put" or "sell back" the instrument to the Society for cash. Such an instrument would qualify as a puttable instrument.

Generally, any instrument that results in a contractual obligation to deliver cash or another financial asset would qualify as a financial liability. In the previous example, by this general definition, the puttable instrument would then qualify as a financial liability since there is an obligation to buy back the instrument for cash upon exercise of the put option by the holder. However, in this case, the entire equity of the entity (the Cooperative Society in the previous example) would then have to be reclassified as a liability. This would result in the entity having no equity at all, which the Board concluded was counterintuitive.

To avoid such outcomes, the Board provided a limited-scope amendment allowing such instruments to be classified as equity provided the instruments meet certain stringent conditions.

Thus, puttable financial instruments are presented as equity only if all four of the following criteria are met:

1. The holder is entitled to a pro rata share of the entity's net assets on liquidation.
2. The instrument is in the class of instruments that is the most subordinate and all instruments in that class have identical features.
3. The instrument has no other characteristics that would have met the definition of a financial liability.
4. The total expected cash flows attributable to the instrument over its life are based substantially on the profit or loss, the change in the recognized net assets or the change in the fair value of the recognized and unrecognized net assets of the entity (excluding any effects of the instrument itself).

In addition to the criteria set out in the previous paragraph, the entity must have no other instrument that has terms equivalent to criterion 4 aforementioned, and that has the effect of substantially restricting or fixing the residual return to the holders of the puttable financial instruments.

Obligations only arising on liquidation. Some financial instruments include a contractual obligation for the issuing entity to delivery to another entity a pro rata share of its net assets only on liquidation. The obligation arises because liquidation either is certain to occur and outside the control of the entity or is uncertain to occur but is at the option of the instrument holder.

Example

A Cooperative Society of farmers issued a financial instrument to the constituent farmers. The financial instrument provides to the farmer, a right to receive pro rata share of net assets in cash in the event of liquidation. The Cooperative Society has been incurring losses in the past and management has taken necessary steps to liquidate the entity. Since liquidation is now certain to occur, there is an obligation to deliver to another entity a pro rata share of net assets. Such an obligation would qualify as an obligation only arising on liquidation.

The criteria for equity classification for instruments that impose on the entity an obligation to deliver to another party a pro rata share of the net assets of the entity only on liquidation are the same as those relating to puttable instruments except criteria 3 and 4 (previously mentioned) do not apply. Criterion 3 does not apply because, if there is a component of the instrument that meets the definition of a liability (other than the right at liquidation itself), this will be recognized separately as a financial liability and the instrument will be presented as a compound instrument, that is, with both liability and equity components. Criterion 4 does not apply because should any cash flows be paid to the holder of the instrument during the instrument's life, this will reduce the amount ultimately payable at liquidation.

Split Accounting for Compound Instruments

Sometimes issued nonderivative financial instruments contain both liability and equity elements. In other words, one component of the instrument meets the definition of a financial liability and another component of the instrument meets the definition of an equity instrument. Such instruments are referred to as compound instruments. The approach to accounting for compound instruments is to apply split accounting, that is, to present the liability and equity elements separately. IAS 32 provides this principle: The issuer of a nonderivative financial instrument shall evaluate the terms of the financial instrument to determine whether it contains both a liability and an equity component. Such components shall be classified separately as financial liabilities, financial assets, or equity instruments.

Example

To illustrate, a bond that is convertible into a fixed number of ordinary shares of the issuer is a compound instrument. From the perspective of the issuer, a convertible bond has two components:

1. An obligation to pay interest and principal payments on the bond as long as it is not converted. This component meets the definition of a financial liability, because the issuer has an obligation to pay cash.
2. A sold (written) call option that grants the holder the right to convert the bond into a fixed number of ordinary shares of the entity. This component meets the definition of an equity instrument.

PRACTICAL INSIGHT

Instruments that from the issuer's perspective have both liability and equity elements are from the holder's perspective often financial assets that contain embedded derivatives under IAS 39. However, split accounting under IAS 32 is different from embedded derivatives accounting under IAS 39 because, under IAS 39, an embedded derivative is separated and accounted for as a financial asset or financial liability at fair value, while under IAS 32, an embedded derivative that meets the definition of an equity instrument is classified and presented as own equity.

By requiring split accounting for the components of compound instruments, IAS 32 ensures that financial liabilities and equity instruments are accounted for in a consistent manner irrespective of whether they are transacted together in a single, compound instrument (e.g., a convertible bond) or transacted separately as two freestanding contracts (i.e., a bond and an issued share warrant).

To determine the initial carrying amounts of the liability and equity components, entities apply the so-called with-and-without method. The fair value of the instrument is determined first including the equity component. The fair value of the instrument as a whole generally equals the proceeds (consideration) received in issuing the instrument. The liability component is then measured separately without the equity component. The equity component is assigned the residual amount after deducting from the fair value of the compound instrument as a whole the amount separately determined for the liability component. That is

> Fair value of compound instrument
> – Fair value of liability component (= its initial carrying amount)
> = Initial carrying amount of equity component

The opposite is not permitted; that is, it is not appropriate to determine the fair value of the equity component first and then allocate the residual to the liability component.

The sum of the initially recognized carrying amounts of the liability and equity components always equals the amount that would have been assigned to the instrument as a whole.

Example

Entity A issues a bond with a principal amount of $100,000. The holder of the bond has the right to convert the bond into ordinary shares of Entity A. On issuance, Entity A receives proceeds of $100,000. By discounting the principal and interest cash flows of the bond using interest rates for similar bonds without an equity component, Entity A determines that the fair value of a similar bond without any equity component would have been $91,000. Therefore, the initial carrying amount of the liability component is $91,000. The initial carrying amount of the equity component is computed as the difference between the total proceeds (fair value) of $100,000 and the initial carrying amount of the liability component of $91,000. Thus, the initial carrying amount of the equity component is $9,000. Entity A makes this journal entry:

Cash	100,000	
Financial liability		91,000
Equity		9,000

The subsequent accounting for the liability component is governed by IAS 39. For instance, if the liability component is measured at amortized cost, the difference between the initial carrying amount of the liability component ($91,000 in the example) and the principal amount at maturity ($100,000 in the example) is amortized to profit or loss as an adjustment of interest expense in accordance with the effective interest method. This has the effect of increasing interest expense as compared with the stated interest rate on the bond.

The accounting for the equity component is outside the scope of IAS 39. Equity is not remeasured subsequent to initial recognition.

Classification of the liability and equity components of a convertible debt instrument is not revised as a result of a change in the likelihood that the equity conversion option will be exercised.

CASE STUDY 3

This case illustrates the accounting for issued convertible debt instruments.

Facts

On October 31, 20X5, Entity A issues convertible bonds with a maturity of five years. The issue is for a total of 1,000 convertible bonds. Each bond has a par value of $100,000, a stated interest rate is 5% per year, and is convertible into 5,000 ordinary shares of Entity A. The convertible bonds are issued at par. The per-share price for an Entity A share is $15. Quotes for similar bonds issued by Entity A without a conversion option (i.e., bonds with similar principal and interest cash flows) suggest that they can be sold for $90,000.

Required

1. Indicate how Entity A should account for the compound instrument on initial recognition.
2. Determine whether the effective interest rate will be higher, lower, or equal to 5%.

Solution

Entity A should separate the liability and equity components of the convertible bonds using the with-and-without method. First, it should determine the fair value of the liability element. This is equal to $90,000 because similar bonds without an equity component sell for $90,000. Accordingly, the initial carrying amount of the liability component is $90,000. Second, it should determine the initial carrying amount of the equity component. This is equal to the difference between the total proceeds received from the bond of $100,000 and the initially allocated amount to the liability component of $90,000. Therefore, the carrying amount of the equity component is $10,000. The journal entry is

Cash	100,000	
Financial liability		90,000
Equity		10,000

The effective interest rate is higher than 5% because it includes amortization of the difference between the initial carrying amount of the liability component of $90,000 and the principal amount of the liability of $100,000. (The effective interest rate is 7.47%.)

Instruments That Will or May Be Settled in Own Equity

Sometimes entities enter into contracts that will or may be settled in equity instruments issued by the entity ("own equity").

Example

A contract may specify that the entity is required to deliver as many of the entity's own equity instruments as are equal in value to $100,000 on a future date. In that case, the number of shares that will be delivered will vary based on changes in the share price. If the share price increases, fewer shares will be delivered. If the share price decreases, more shares will be delivered.

Alternatively, a contract may specify that the entity is required to deliver as many of the entity's own equity instruments as are equal in value to the value of 100 ounces of gold on a future date. In that case, the number of shares that will be delivered will vary based on changes in both the share price and the gold price. If the share price increases, fewer shares will be delivered. If the share price decreases, more shares will be delivered. If the gold price increases, more shares will be delivered. If the gold price decreases, fewer shares will be delivered.

Contracts that will or may be settled in the entity's own equity instruments are classified as equity instruments of the entity if they

- Are nonderivative contracts and will be settled by issuance of a fixed number of the entity's own equity instruments
- Are derivative contracts and will be settled by the exchange of a fixed number of the entity's own equity instruments and a fixed amount of cash

Because such instruments are classified as own equity, any consideration received for such an instrument is added directly to equity and any consideration paid is deducted directly from equity. Changes in fair value of such instruments are not recognized.

Example

Examples of instruments that will or may be settled in own equity and are classified as equity instruments of the entity are

- An issued (written) call option or warrant that gives the holder the right to purchase a fixed number of equity instruments of the entity (e.g., 1,000 shares) for a fixed price (e.g., $100). If the proceeds from issuing the call option is $9,000, the entity makes this journal entry:

Cash	9,000	
Equity		9,000

- A purchased call option that gives the entity the right to repurchase a fixed number of its own issued equity instruments (e.g., 1,000 shares) for a fixed price (e.g., $100). If the price for purchasing the call option is $9,000, the entity makes this journal entry:

Equity	9,000	
Cash		9,000

- A forward contract to sell a fixed number of equity instruments (e.g., 1,000 shares) of the entity to another entity for a fixed exercise price at a future date (e.g., $100). If the forward is entered into at a zero fair value, no journal entry is required until settlement of the transaction.

If, however, there is any variability in the amount of cash or own equity instruments that will be received or delivered under such a contract (e.g., based on the share price, the price of gold, or some other variable), the contract is a financial asset or financial liability, as applicable.

Example

Examples of instruments that are classified as financial liabilities are

- A contract that requires the entity to deliver as many of the entity's own equity instruments as are equal in value to $100,000 on a future date
- A contract that requires the entity to deliver as many of the entity's own equity instruments as are equal in value to the value of 100 ounces of gold on a future date
- A contract that requires the entity to deliver a fixed number of the entity's own equity instruments in return for an amount of cash calculated to equal the value of 100 ounces of gold on a future date

If a financial instrument requires the issuer to repurchase its own issued equity instruments for cash or other financial assets, there is a financial liability for the present value of the repurchase price (redemption amount). The liability is recognized by reclassifying the amount of the liability from equity. Subsequently, the liability is accounted for under IAS 39. If it is classified as a financial liability measured at amortized cost, the difference between the repurchase price and the present value of the repurchase price is amortized to profit or loss as an adjustment to interest expense using the effective interest rate method.

Example

On January 1, 20X7, Entity A enters into a forward contract that requires the entity to repurchase 1,000 shares for $60,000 on December 31, 20X7. No consideration is paid or received at inception of the contract. The market interest rate is 10%, such that the present value of the payment is $54,545 [= 60,000/(1 + 10%)]. Therefore, the entity makes this journal entry on initial recognition to recognize its liability for the repurchase price:

Equity	54,545	
Liability		54,545

On December 31, 20X7, Entity A makes this entry to recognize the amortization in accordance with the effective interest method:

Interest expense	6,565	
Liability		6,565

Finally, on December 31, 20X7, Entity A settles the forward contract and makes this journal entry:

Liability	60,000	
Cash		60,000

If a derivative financial instrument gives one party a choice over how it is settled, it is a financial asset or financial liability unless all of the settlement alternatives would result in it being an equity instrument.

Example

One example of a contract that would be classified as a financial liability because it provides for a choice of settlement is a written call option on own equity that the entity can decide to settle by either of the following:

1. By issuing a fixed number of own equity instruments in return for a fixed amount of cash.
2. Net in cash, in an amount equal to the difference between (a) the value of a fixed number of own equity instruments and (b) a fixed amount.

Such a financial liability would be accounted for as a derivative at fair value.

If the contract had not included a net settlement alternative (2 in the preceding list), it would have been classified as an equity instrument because it would not have contained any variability in the amount of cash or the number of equity instruments that would have been exchanged.

Treasury Shares

Treasury shares are shares that are not currently outstanding. When an entity reacquires an outstanding share or other equity instrument, the consideration paid is deducted from equity. No gain or loss is recognized in profit or loss even if the reacquisition price differs from the amount at which the equity instrument was originally issued. Similarly, if the entity subsequently resells the treasury share, no gain or loss is recognized in profit or loss even if the proceeds at reissuance differ from the consideration paid when the treasury shares were reacquired previously. The amount of treasury shares is disclosed separately either in the notes or on the face of the balance sheet.

Example

On January 15, 20X5, Entity A issues 100 shares at a price of $50 per share, resulting in total proceeds of $5,000. It makes this journal entry:

Cash	$5,000	
Equity		$5,000

On August 15, 20X5, Entity A reacquires 20 of the shares at a price of $100 per share, resulting in a total price paid of $2,000. It makes this journal entry:

Equity	$2,000	
Cash		$2,000

On December 15, 20X5, Entity A reissues 15 of the 20 shares it reacquired on August 15, 20X5, at a price of $200 per share, resulting in total proceeds of $3,000. It makes this journal entry:

Cash	$3,000	
Equity		$3,000

CASE STUDY 4

This case illustrates the effect on equity of treasury share transactions.

Facts

- At the beginning of 20X4, the amount of equity is $534,000.
- These transactions occur during 20X4:

  - February 15: Dividends of $10,000 are paid.
  - March 14: 10,000 shares are sold for $14 per share.
  - June 6: 2,000 shares are repurchased for $16 per share.
  - October 8: 2,000 shares previously repurchased are resold for $18 per share.

- Profit or loss for the year 20X4 is $103,000.
- No other transactions affect the amount of equity during the year.

Required

Indicate the effect of these transactions on the amount of equity and determine the amount of equity outstanding at the end of the year.

Solution

Date		*Equity*
January 1, 20X4	Equity: opening balance	$534,000
February 15, 20X4	Dividend paid	– 10,000
March 14, 20X4	Issuance of equity	+140,000
June 6, 20X4	Repurchase of equity	– 32,000
October 8, 20X4	Issuance of equity	+ 36,000
December 31, 20X4	Profit or loss	+103,000
December 31, 20X4	Equity: closing balance	$771,000

PRESENTATION OF INTEREST, DIVIDENDS, LOSSES, AND GAINS

The classification of an issued financial instrument as either a financial liability or an equity instrument determines whether interest, dividends, gains, and losses relating to that instrument are recognized in profit or loss or directly in equity.

- Dividends to holders of outstanding shares that are classified as equity are debited by the entity directly to equity.
- Dividends to holders of outstanding shares that are classified as financial liabilities are recognized in the same way as interest expense on a bond.
- Gains and losses associated with redemptions of financial liabilities are recognized in profit or loss.
- Redemptions and refinancings of equity instruments of the entity are recognized as changes in equity.
- Changes in the fair value of equity instruments of the entity are not recognized in the financial statements.
- Generally, costs incurred in issuing or acquiring own equity instruments are not expensed but accounted for as a deduction from equity. Such costs include regulatory fees, legal fees, advisory fees, and other transaction costs that are directly attributable to the equity transaction and that otherwise would have been avoided.

Offsetting of a Financial Asset and a Financial Liability

Generally, it is inappropriate to net financial assets and financial liabilities and present only the net amount in the balance sheet.

Example

Entity A has $120,000 of financial assets that are held for trading and $30,000 of financial liabilities that are held for trading. It would be inappropriate for Entity A to present only the net amount of $90,000 as a financial asset. Instead it should present a financial asset of $120,000 and a financial liability of $30,000.

IAS 32 requires a financial asset and a financial liability to be offset with the net amount presented as an asset or liability in the balance sheet when, and only when, these *two* conditions are met:

1. *A right of set-off.* The entity currently has a legally enforceable right to set off the recognized amounts. This means that the entity has an unconditional legal right, supported by contract or otherwise, to settle or otherwise eliminate all or a portion of an amount due to another party by applying an amount due from that other party.
2. *Intention to settle net or simultaneously.* The entity intends either to settle on a net basis or to realize the asset and settle the liability simultaneously.

These two conditions reflect the view that when an entity has the right to receive or pay a single amount and intends to do so, it has, in effect, only a single financial asset or financial liability. When both conditions are met, net presentation reflects more appropriately the entity's expected future cash flows from settling the asset and the liability. When either or both of the two conditions are not met, financial assets and financial liabilities are presented separately. In those cases, separate presentation better reflects the entity's expected future cash flows and associated risks.

CASE STUDY 5

This case illustrates the application of the conditions for offsetting of financial assets and financial liabilities.

Facts

Entity A has a legal right to set off cash flows due to Entity B (i.e., payables of Entity A) against amounts due from Entity B (i.e., receivables of Entity A). Entity A has these payables to Entity B: $1,000,000 on March 31, $3,000,000 on June 30, and $2,500,000 on October 31. Entity A has these receivables from Entity B: $500,000 on January 15, $4,000,000 on June 30, and $1,000,000 on December 15.

Required

Indicate the extent to which Entity A can set off the aforementioned receivables and payables in its statement of financial position, assuming it has an intention to settle offsetting amounts net or simultaneously on each settlement date.

Solution

Entity A can offset the $3,000,000 to be received and paid on June 30 because it has a legal right and intention to settle that amount net or simultaneously. It cannot offset the payments on January 15, March 31, October 31, and December 15 or the remaining payment of $1,000,000 on June 30. Accordingly, ignoring the time value of money, Entity A should present assets of $2,500,000 and liabilities of $3,500,000.

AMENDMENTS TO IAS 32—CLASSIFICATION OF "RIGHTS ISSUES"—EFFECTIVE 2010

Effective February 1, 2010, IAS 32 has been amended to allow classification of rights, options, and warrants denominated in a foreign currency as equity instruments.

A financial instrument otherwise meeting the definition of equity instruments, issued to acquire a fixed number of an entity's own nonderivative equity instruments for a fixed amount in any currency are classified as equity instruments, provided the offer is made pro rata to all existing owners of the same class of the entity's own nonderivative equity instruments.

Example

An entity whose functional currency is the euro issued share warrants whereby the holder of each warrant is entitled to acquire one equity share of the entity for a price of US$15 per share. The offer is made by the entity to all existing owners of the equity shares.

Generally, a derivative instrument relating to issue of an entity's own instruments is classified as equity only if it results in the exchange of a fixed number of equity instruments for a fixed amount of cash or other financial asset. In this example, it could have been argued that since the cash would be received in US dollars, the amount of cash received in the functional currency, euro, was variable. Hence it could have been argued that the instrument should be classified as liability and not equity.

The Board considered the argument and held that such transactions represent transactions with equity owners in their capacity as owners. Hence the Board concluded that such instruments, if issued pro rata to all existing owners, would quality as equity.

EXTRACTS FROM FINANCIAL STATEMENTS

BP PLC, Annual Report, 2009

Notes on Financial Statements

24. Financial instruments and financial risk factors

The accounting classification of each category of financial instruments, and their carrying amounts, are set out below.

At December 31	Note	Loans and receivables	Available-for-sale financial assets	At fair value through profit and loss	Derivative hedging instruments	Financial liabilities measured at amortized cost	*$ million* *2009* Total carrying amount
Financial assets							
Other investments	25	--	1,567	--	--	--	1,567
Loans		1,288	--		--	--	1,288
Trade and other receivables	27	31,016	--	--	--	--	31,016

	Note	Loans and receivables	Available-for-sale financial assets	At fair value through profit and loss	Derivative hedging instruments	Financial liabilities measured at amortized cost	$ million Total carrying amount
Derivative financial instruments	31	--	--	--	972	--	8,932
Cash and cash equivalents	28	6,570	1,769	7,960	--	--	8,339
				--			
Financial liabilities							
Trade and other payables	30	--	--	--	--	(34,325)	(34,325)
Derivative financial instruments	31	--	--	(7,389)	(766)	--	(8,155)
Accruals		--	--	--	--	(6,905)	(6,905)
Finance debt	32	--	--	--	--	(34,627)	(34,627)
		38,874	3,336	571	206	(75,857)	(32,870)

At December 31	Note	Loans and receivables	Available-for-sale financial assets	At fair value through profit and loss	Derivative hedging instruments	Financial liabilities measured at amortized cost	$ million 2008 Total carrying amount
Financial assets							
Other investments	25	--	855	--	--	--	855
Loans		1,163	--	--	--	--	1,163
Trade and other receivables	27	29,489	--	--	--	--	29,489
Derivative financial instruments	31	--	--	12,501	1,063	--	13,564
Cash and cash equivalents	28	5,609	2,588	--	--	--	8,197
Financial liabilities							
Trade and other payables	30	--	--	--	--	(33,140)	(33,140)
Derivative financial instruments	31	--	--	(13,173)	(2,075)	--	(15,248)
Accruals		--	--	--	--	(7,527)	(7,527)
Finance debt	32	--	--	--	--	(33,204)	(33,204)
		36,261	3,443	(672)	(1,012)	(73,871)	(35,851)

The fair value of finance debt is shown in Note 32. For all other financial instruments, the carrying amount is either the fair value, or approximates the fair value.

Financial risk factors

The group is exposed to a number of different financial risks arising from natural business exposures as well as its use of financial instruments including: market risks relating to commodity prices, foreign currency exchange rates, interest rates and equity prices; credit risk; and liquidity risk.

The group financial risk committee (GFRC) advises the group chief financial officer (CFO) who oversees the management of these risks. The GFRC is chaired by the CFO and consists of a group of senior managers including the group treasurer and the heads of the finance, tax and the integrated supply and trading functions. The purpose of the committee is to advise on financial risks and the appropriate financial risk governance framework for the group. The committee provides assurance to the CFO and the group chief executive (GCE), and via the GCE to the board, that the group's financial risk-taking activity is governed by appropriate policies and procedures and that financial risks are identified, measured and managed in accordance with group policies and group risk appetite.

The group's trading activities in the oil, natural gas and power markets are managed within the integrated supply and trading function, while activities in the financial markets are managed by the treasury function. All derivative activity is carried out by specialist teams that have the appropriate skills, experience and supervision. These teams are subject to close financial and management control.

The integrated supply and trading function maintains formal governance processes that provide oversight of market risk associated with trading activity. These processes meet generally accepted industry practice and reflect the principles of the Group of Thirty Global Derivatives Study recommendations. A policy and risk committee monitors and validates limits and risk exposures, reviews incidents and validates risk-related policies, methodologies and procedures. A commitments committee approves value-at-risk delegations, the trading of new products, instruments and strategies and material commitments.

In addition, the integrated supply and trading function undertakes derivative activity for risk management purposes under a separate control framework as described more fully below.

(a) Market risk

Market risk is the risk or uncertainty arising from possible market price movements and their impact on the future performance of a business. The market price movements that the group is exposed to include oil, natural gas and power prices (commodity price risk), foreign currency exchange rates, interest rates, equity prices, and other indices that could adversely affect the value of the group's financial assets, liabilities or expected future cash flows. The group enters into derivatives in a well established entrepreneurial trading operation. In addition, the group has developed a control framework aimed at managing the volatility inherent in certain of its natural business exposures. In accordance with this control framework the group enters into various transactions using derivatives for risk management purposes.

The group measures market risk exposure arising from its trading positions using value-at-risk techniques. These techniques are based on a variance/covariance model or a Monte Carlo simulation and make a statistical assessment of the market risk arising from possible future changes in market prices over a 24-hour period. The calculation of the range of potential changes in fair value takes into account a snapshot of the end-of-day exposures and the history of one-day price movements, together with the correlation of these price movements. The value-at-risk measure is supplemented by stress testing and tail risk analysis.

The trading value-at-risk model is used for derivative financial instrument types such as: interest rate forward and futures contracts, swap agreements, options and swaptions; foreign exchange forward and futures contracts, swap agreements and options; and oil, natural gas and power price forwards, futures, swap agreements and options. Additionally, where physical commodities or nonderivative forward contracts are held as part of a trading position, they are also reflected in the value-at-risk model. For options, a linear approximation is included in the value-at-risk models when full revaluation is not possible.

The value-at-risk table does not incorporate any of the group's natural business exposures or any derivatives entered into to risk manage those exposures. Market risk exposure in respect of embedded derivatives is also not included in the value-at-risk table. Instead separate sensitivity analyses are disclosed below.

Value-at-risk limits are in place for each trading activity and for the group's trading activity in total. The board has delegated an overall limit of $100 million value at risk in support of this trading activity. The high and low values at risk indicated in the table below for each type of activity are independent of each other through the portfolio effect the high value at risk for the group as a whole is lower than the sum of the highs for the constituent parts. The potential movement in fair values is expressed to a 95% confidence interval. This means that, in statistical terms, one would expect to see a decrease in fair values greater than the trading value at risk on one occasion per month if the portfolio were left unchanged.

$ million

Value at risk for 1 day at 95% confidence interval	2009				2008			
	High	*Low*	*Average*	*Year-end*	*High*	*Low*	*Average*	*Year-end*
Group trading	**79**	**24**	**45**	**30**	76	20	37	69
Oil price trading	**75**	**9**	**29**	**12**	69	12	25	63
Natural gas price trading	**70**	**15**	**33**	**31**	50	12	24	23
Power price trading	**14**	**3**	**5**	**5**	14	3	7	4
Currency trading	**4**	**--**	**2**	**2**	4	--	2	--
Interest rate trading	**7**	**--**	**3**	**3**	7	--	2	1
Other trading	**4**	**1**	**2**	**3**	5	1	2	2

The major components of market risk are commodity price risk, foreign currency exchange risk, interest rate risk and equity price risk, each of which is discussed below.

(i) Commodity price risk

The group's integrated supply and trading function uses conventional financial and commodity instruments and physical cargoes available in the related commodity markets. Oil and natural gas swaps, options and futures are used to mitigate price risk. Power trading is undertaken using a combination of over-the-counter forward contracts and other derivative contracts, including options and futures. This activity is on both a stand-alone basis and in conjunction with gas derivatives in relation to gas generated power margin. In addition, NGLs are traded around certain US inventory locations using over-the-counter forward contracts in conjunction with over-the-counter swaps, options and physical inventories. Trading value-at-risk information in relation to these activities is shown in the table above.

As described above, the group also carries out risk management of certain natural business exposures using over-the-counter swaps and exchange futures contracts. Together with certain physical supply contracts that are classified as derivatives, these contracts fall outside of the value-at-risk framework. For these derivative contracts the sensitivity of the net fair value to an immediate 10% increase or decrease in all reference prices would have been $73 million at December 31, 2009 (2008 $90 million). This figure does not include any corresponding economic benefit or disbenefit that would arise from the natural business exposure which would be expected to offset the gain or loss on the over-the-counter swaps and exchange futures contracts mentioned above.

In addition, the group has embedded derivatives relating to certain natural gas contracts. The net fair value of these contracts was a liability of $1,331 million at December 31, 2009 (2008 liability of $1,867 million). Key information on the natural gas contracts is given below.

At December 31	2009	2008
Remaining contract terms	9 months to 8 years 9 months	1 year 9 months to 9 years 9 months
Contractual/notional amount	2,460 million therms	3,585 million therms
Discount rate–nominal risk free	4.0%	2.5%

For these embedded derivatives the sensitivity of the net fair value to an immediate 10% favorable or adverse change in the key assumptions is as follows.

| | | 2009 | | | | | 2008 $ million | |
At December 31	Gas price	Oil price	Power price	Discount rate	Gas price	Oil price	Power price	Discount rate
Favorable 10% change	175	26	23	20	291	81	27	16
Unfavorable 10% change	(215)	(43)	(19)	(20)	(289)	(81)	(27)	(16)

The sensitivities for risk management activity and embedded derivatives are hypothetical and should not be considered to be predictive of future performance. In addition, for purposes of this analysis, in the above table, the effect of a variation in a particular assumption on the fair value of the embedded derivatives is calculated independently of any change in another assumption. In reality, changes in one factor may contribute to changes in another, which may magnify or counteract the sensitivities. Furthermore, the estimated fair values as disclosed should not be considered indicative of future earnings on these contracts.

(ii) Foreign currency exchange risk

Where the group enters into foreign currency exchange contracts for entrepreneurial trading purposes the activity is controlled using trading value-at-risk techniques as explained above. This activity is described as currency trading in the value-at-risk table above.

Since BP has global operations, fluctuations in foreign currency exchange rates can have significant effects on the group's reported results. The effects of most exchange rate fluctuations are absorbed in business operating results through changing cost competitiveness, lags in market adjustment to movements in rates and conversion differences accounted for on specific transactions. For this reason, the total effect of exchange rate fluctuations is not identifiable separately in the group's reported results. The main underlying economic currency of the group's cash flows is the US dollar. This is because BP's major product, oil, is priced internationally in US dollars. BP's foreign currency exchange management policy is to minimize economic and material transactional exposures arising from currency movements against the US dollar. The group coordinates the handling of foreign currency exchange risks centrally, by netting off naturally occurring opposite exposures wherever possible, and then dealing with any material residual foreign currency exchange risks.

The group manages these exposures by constantly reviewing the foreign currency economic value at risk and managing such risk to keep the 12-month foreign currency value at risk below $200 million. At December 31, 2009, the foreign currency value at risk was $140 million (2008: $70 million). At no point over the past three years did the value at risk exceed the maximum risk limit. The most significant exposures relate to capital expenditure commitments and other UK and European operational requirements, for which a hedging program is in place and hedge accounting is claimed as outlined in Note 31.

For highly probably forecast capital expenditures the group locks in the US dollar cost of non-US dollar supplies by using currency forwards and futures. The main exposures are sterling, Canadian dollar, euro, Norwegian krone, Australian dollar, Korean won, and at December 31, 2009, open contracts were in place for $800 million sterling, $491 million Canadian dollar, $299 million euro, $240 million Norwegian krone, $215 million Australian dollar, $51 million Korean won, and $41 million Singapore dollar capital expenditures maturing within six years, with over 65% of the deals maturing within two years (2008: $949 million sterling, $712 million Canadian dollar, $553 million euro, $392 million Norwegian krone, $303 million Australian dollar, and $187 million Korean won capital expenditures maturing within seven years with over 65% of the deals maturing within two years).

For other UK, European, Canadian and Australian operational requirements the group uses cylinders and currency forwards to hedge the estimated exposures on a 12-month rolling basis. At December 31, 2009, the open positions relating to cylinders consisted of receive sterling, pay US dollar, purchased call and sold put options (cylinders) for $1,887 million (2008: $1,660 million); receive euro, pay US dollar cylinders for $1,716 million (2008: $1,612 million); receive Canadian dollar, pay US dollar cylinders for $300 million (2008: $250 million); and receive Australian dollar, pay US dollar cylinders for $297 million (2008: $455 million). At December 31, 2009, there were no open positions relating to currency forwards (2008: buy sterling, sell US dollar currency forwards for $816 million; buy euro, sell US dollar currency forwards for $141 million; buy Canadian dollar, sell US dollar, currency forwards for $50 million; and buy Australian dollar, sell US dollar currency forwards for $90 million).

In addition, most of the group's borrowings are in US dollars or are hedged with respect to the US dollar. At December 31, 2009, the total foreign currency net borrowings not swapped into US dollars amounted to $465 million (2008: $1,037 million). Of this total, $113 million was denominated in currencies other than the functional currency of the individual operating unit being entirely Canadian dollars (2008: $92 million, being entirely Canadian dollars). It is estimated that a 10% change in the corresponding exchange rates would result in an exchange gain or loss in the income statement of $11 million (2008: $9 million).

(iii) Interest rate risk

Where the group enters into money market contracts for entrepreneurial trading purposes the activity is controlled using value-at-risk techniques as described above. This activity is described as interest rate trading in the value-at-risk table above.

BP is also exposed to interest rate risk from the possibility that changes in interest rates will affect future cash flows or the fair values of its financial instruments, principally finance debt.

While the group issues debt in a variety of currencies based on market opportunities, it uses derivatives to swap the debt to a US dollar floating rate exposure but in certain defined circumstances maintains a fixed rate exposure for a proportion of debt. The proportion of floating rate debt net of interest rate swaps at December 31, 2009, was 63% of total finance debt outstanding (2008: 72%). The weighted-average interest rate on finance debt at December 31, 2009, is 2% (2008: 3%) and the weighted-average maturity of fixed rate debt is four years (2008: three years).

The group's earnings are sensitive to changes in interest rates on the floating rate element of the group's finance debt. If the interest rates applicable to floating rate instruments were to have increased by 1% on January 1, 2010, it is estimated that the group's profit before taxation for 2010 would decrease by approximately $219 million (2008: $239 million decrease in 2009). This assumes that the amount and mix of fixed and floating rate debt, including finance leases, remains unchanged from that in place at December 2009 and that the change in interest rates is effective from beginning of the year. Where the interest rate applicable to an instrument is reset during a quarter it is assumed that this occurs at the beginning of the quarter and remains unchanged for the rest of the year. In reality, the fixed/floating rate mix will fluctuate over the year and interest rates will change continually. Furthermore, the effect on earnings shown by this analysis does not consider the effect of any other changes in general economic activity that may accompany such an increase in interest rates.

(iv) Equity price risk

The group holds equity investments, typically made for strategic purposes, that are classified as noncurrent available-for-sale financial assets and are measured initially at fair value with changes in fair value recognized in other comprehensive income. Accumulated fair value changes are recycled to the income statement on disposal, or when the investment is impaired. No impairment losses have been recognized in 2009 (2008: $546 million and 2007: nil) relating to listed noncurrent available-for-sale investments. For further information see Note 25.

At December 31, 2009, it is estimated that an increase of 10% in quoted equity prices would result in an immediate credit to other comprehensive income of $130 million (2008: $59 million credit to other comprehensive income), whilst a decrease of 10% in quoted equity prices would result in an immediate charge to other comprehensive income of $130 million (2008: $48 million charge to profit or loss and $11 million charge to other comprehensive income).

At December 31, 2009, 73% (2008: 56%) of the carrying amount of noncurrent available-for-sale financial assets represented the group's stake in Rosneft, thus the group's exposure is concentrated on changes in the share price of this equity in particular.

(b) Credit risk

Credit risk is the risk that a customer or counterparty to a financial instrument will fail to perform or fail to pay amounts due causing financial loss to the group and arises from cash and cash equivalents, derivative financial instruments and deposits with financial institutions and principally from credit exposures to customers relating to outstanding receivables.

The group has a credit policy, approved by the CFO, that is designed to ensure that consistent processes are in place throughout the group to measure and control credit risk. Credit risk is considered as part of the risk-reward balance of doing business. On entering into any business contract the extent to which the arrangement exposes the group to credit risk is considered. Key requirements of the policy are formal delegated authorities to the sales and marketing teams to incur credit risk and to a specialized credit function to set counterparty limits; the establishment of credit systems and processes to ensure that counterparties are rated and limits set, and systems to monitor exposure against limits and report regularly on those exposures, and immediately on any excesses, and to track and report credit losses. The treasury function provides a similar credit risk management activity with respect to group-wide exposures to banks and other financial institutions.

In the current economic environment the group has placed increased emphasis on the management of credit risk. Policies and procedures were reviewed in 2008 and credit exposures arising from physical commodity and derivative transactions with banks and other counterparties have been reduced in 2008 and 2009, mainly through netting and collateral arrangements.

Before trading with a new counterparty can start, its creditworthiness is assessed and a credit rating is allocated that indicates the probability of default, along with a credit exposure limit. The assessment process takes into account all available qualitative and quantitative information about the counterparty and the group, if any, to which the counterparty belongs. The counterparty's business activities, financial resources and business risk management processes are taken into account in the assessment, to the extent that this information is publicly available or otherwise disclosed to BP by counterparty, together with external credit ratings, if any, including ratings prepared by Moody's Investor Service and Standard & Poor's. Creditworthiness continues to be evaluated after transactions have been initiated and a watchlist of higher-risk counterparties is maintained.

The group does not aim to remove credit risk but expects to experience a certain level of credit losses. The group attempts to mitigate credit risk by entering into contracts that permit netting and allow for termination of the contract on the occurrence of certain events of default. Depending on the creditworthiness of the counterparty, the group may require collateral or other credit enhancements such as cash deposits or letters of credit and parent company guarantees. Trade receivables and payables, and derivative assets and liabilities are presented on a net basis where unconditional netting arrangements are in place with counterparties and where there is an intent to settle amounts due on a net basis. The maximum credit exposure associated with financial assets is equal to the carrying amount. At December 31, 2009, the maximum credit exposure was $49,575 million (2008: $52,413 million). Collateral received and recognized in the balance sheet at the year-end was $4,549 million (2008: $1,121 million) and collateral held off-balance-sheet was $48 million (2008: $203 million). Credit exposure exists in relation to guarantees issued by group companies under which amounts outstanding at December 31, 2009, were $319 million (2008: $223 million) in respect of liabilities of jointly controlled entities and associates and $667 million (2008: $613 million) in respect of liabilities of other third parties.

Notwithstanding the processes described above, significant unexpected credit losses can occasionally occur. Exposure to unexpected losses increases with concentrations of credit risk that exist when a number of counterparties are involved in similar activities or operate in the same industry sector or geographical area, which may result in their ability to meet contractual obligations being impacted by changes in economic, political or other conditions. The group's principal customers, suppliers and financial institutions with which it conducts business are located throughout the world. In addition, these risks are managed by maintaining a group watchlist and aggregating multisegment exposures to ensure that a material credit risk is not missed.

Reports are regularly prepared and presented to the GFRC that covers the group's overall credit exposure and expected loss trends, exposure by segment, and overall quality of the portfolio. The reports also include details of the largest counterparties by exposure level and expected loss, and details of counterparties on the group watchlist.

Some mitigation of credit exposure is achieved by: netting arrangements; credit support agreements which require the counterparty to provide collateral or other credit risk mitigation; and credit insurance and other risk transfer instruments.

For the contracts comprising derivative financial instruments in an asset position at December 31, 2009, it is estimated that over 80% (2008: over 80%) of the unmitigated credit exposure is to counterparties of investment grade credit quality.

Trade and other receivables of the group are analyzed in the table below. By comparing the BP credit ratings to the equivalent external credit ratings, it is estimated that approximately 55-60% (2008: approximately 60-65%) of the unmitigated trade receivables portfolio exposure is of investment grade credit quality. With respect to the trade and other receivables that are neither impaired nor past due, there are no indications as of the reporting date that the debtors will not meet their payment obligations.

The group does not typically renegotiate the terms of trade receivables; however, if a renegotiation does take place, the outstanding balance is included in the analysis based on the original payments terms. There were no significant renegotiated balances outstanding at December 31, 2009, or December 31, 2008.

		$ million
Trade and other receivables at December 31	*2009*	*2008*
Neither impaired nor past due	29,426	25,838
Impaired (net of valuation allowance)	91	73
Not impaired and past due in the following periods		
Within 30 days	808	1,323
31 to 60 days	151	489
61 to 90 days	76	596
Over 90 days	464	1,170
	31,016	29,489

The movement in the valuation allowance for trade receivables is set out below.

		$ million
Trade and other receivables at December 31	*2009*	*2008*
At January 1	391	406
Exchange adjustments	12	(32)
Charge for the year	157	191
Utilization	(130)	(174)
At December 31	430	391

(c) Liquidity risk

Liquidity risk is the risk that suitable sources of funding for the group's business activities may not be available. The group's liquidity is managed centrally with operating units forecasting their cash and currency requirements to the central treasury function. Unless restricted by local regulations, subsidiaries pool their cash surpluses to treasury, which will then arrange to fund other subsidiaries' requirements, or invest any net surplus in the market or arrange for necessary external borrowings, while managing the group's overall net currency positions.

In managing its liquidity risk, the group has access to a wide range of funding at competitive rates through capital markets and banks. The group's treasury function centrally coordinates relationships with banks, borrowing requirements, foreign exchange requirements and cash management. The group believes it has access to sufficient funding through the commercial paper markets and by using undrawn committed borrowing facilities to meet foreseeable borrowing requirements. At December 31, 2009, the group had substantial amounts of undrawn borrowing facilities available, including committed facilities of $4,950 million, of which $4,550 million are in place through to the fourth quarter of 2011, unchanged from the position as at December 31, 2008. These facilities are with a number of international banks and borrowings under them would be at preagreed rates.

The group has in place a European Debt Issuance Program (DIP) under which the group may raise $20 billion of debt for maturities of one month or longer. At December 31, 2009, the amount drawn down against the DIP was $11,403 million (2008: $10,334 million). In addition, the group has in place an unlimited US Shelf Registration under which it may raise debt with maturities of one month or longer.

The group has long-term debt ratings of Aa1 (stable outlook) and AA (stable outlook), assigned respectively by Moody's and Standard and Poor's, unchanged from 2008.

Despite recent increased uncertainty in the financial markets, including a lack of liquidity for some borrowers, we have been able to issue $11 billion of long-term debt during 2009 and issue short-term commercial paper at competitive rates, as and when required. As an additional precautionary measure, we have increased and maintained the cash and cash equivalents held by the group to $8.3 billion at the end of 2009 and $8.2 billion at the end of 2008, compared with $3.6 billion at the end of 2007.

The amounts shown for finance debt in the table below include expected interest payments on borrowings and future minimum lease payments with respect to finance leases.

MULTIPLE-CHOICE QUESTIONS

1. Are there any circumstances when a contract that is not a financial instrument would be accounted for as a financial instrument under IAS 32, IFRS 9, and IAS 39?

(a) No. Only financial instruments are accounted for as financial instruments.

(b) Yes. Gold, silver, and other precious metals that are readily convertible to cash are accounted for as financial instruments.

(c) Yes. A contract for the future purchase or delivery of a commodity or other nonfinancial item (e.g., gold, electricity, or gas) generally is accounted for as a financial instrument if the contract can be settled net.

(d) Yes. An entity may designate any nonfinancial asset that can be readily convertible to cash as a financial instrument.

2. Which of the following assets is **not** a financial asset?

(a) Cash.

(b) An equity instrument of another entity.

(c) A contract that may or will be settled in the entity's own equity instrument and is not classified as an equity instrument of the entity.

(d) Prepaid expenses.

3. Which of the following liabilities is a financial liability?

(a) Deferred revenue.

(b) A warranty obligation.

(c) A constructive obligation.

(d) An obligation to deliver own shares worth a fixed amount of cash.

4. Which of the following statements best describes the principle for classifying an issued financial instrument as either a financial liability or equity?

(a) Issued instruments are classified as liabilities or equity in accordance with the substance of the contractual arrangement and the definitions of a financial liability, financial asset, and an equity instrument.

(b) Issued instruments are classified as liabilities or equity in accordance with the legal form of the contractual arrangement and the definitions of a financial liability and an equity instrument.

(c) Issued instruments are classified as liabilities or equity in accordance with management's designation of the contractual arrangement.

(d) Issued instruments are classified as liabilities or equity in accordance with the risk and rewards of the contractual arrangement.

5. Which of the following instruments would **not** be classified as a financial liability?

(a) A preference share that will be redeemed by the issuer for a fixed amount of cash on a future date (i.e., the entity has an outstanding share that it will repurchase at a future date).

(b) A contract for the delivery of as many of the entity's ordinary shares as are equal in value to $100,000 on a future date (i.e., the entity will issue a variable number of own shares in return for cash at a future date).

(c) A written call option that gives the holder the right to purchase a fixed number of the entity's ordinary shares in return for a fixed price (i.e., the entity would issue a fixed number of own shares in return for cash, if the option is exercised by the holder, at a future date).

(d) An issued perpetual debt instrument (i.e., a debt instrument for which interest will be paid for all eternity, but the principal will not be repaid).

6. What is the principle of accounting for a compound instrument (e.g., an issued convertible debt instrument)?

(a) The issuer shall classify a compound instrument as either a liability or equity based on an evaluation of the predominant characteristics of the contractual arrangement.

(b) The issuer shall classify the liability and equity components of a compound instrument separately as financial liabilities, financial assets, or equity instruments.

(c) The issuer shall classify a compound instrument as a liability in its entirety, until converted into equity, unless the equity component is detachable and separately transferable, in which case the liability and equity components shall be presented separately.

(d) The issuer shall classify a compound instrument as a liability in its entirety, until converted into equity.

7. How are the proceeds from issuing a compound instrument allocated between the liability and equity components?

(a) First, the liability component is measured at fair value, and then the remainder of the proceeds is allocated to the equity component (with-and-without method).

   (b) First, the equity component is measured at fair value, and then the remainder of the proceeds is allocated to the liability component (with-and-without method).

   (c) First, the fair values of both the equity component and the liability component are estimated. Then the proceeds are allocated to the liability and equity components based on the relation between the estimated fair values (relative fair value method).

   (d) The equity component is measured at its intrinsic value. The liability component is measured at the par amount less the intrinsic value of the equity component.

8. What is the accounting for treasury share transactions?

   (a) On repurchase of treasury shares, a gain or loss is recognized equal to the difference between the amount at which the shares were issued and the repurchase price for the shares.

   (b) On reissuance of treasury shares, a gain or loss is recognized equal to the difference between the previous repurchase price and the reissuance price.

   (c) On repurchase or reissuance of previously repurchased own shares, no gain or loss is recognized.

   (d) Treasury shares are accounted for as financial assets in accordance with IAS 39.

9. What are the conditions for offsetting (net presentation) of financial assets and financial liabilities?

   (a) A legal right of set-off.

   (b) A legal right of set-off and an intention to settle net or simultaneously.

   (c) The existence of a clearing mechanism or other market mechanism for net settlement and an expectation of net settlement.

   (d) A netting agreement and an expectation of net settlement.

Chapter 24

FINANCIAL INSTRUMENTS: RECOGNITION AND MEASUREMENT (IAS 39)

INTRODUCTION

IAS 39, *Financial Instruments: Recognition and Measurement*, addresses the accounting for financial assets and financial liabilities. More specifically, IAS 39 contains requirements for

- When a financial asset or financial liability should first be recognized in the statement of financial position
- When a financial asset or a financial liability should be derecognized (i.e., removed from the statement of financial position)
- How a financial asset or financial liability should be classified into one of the categories of financial assets or financial liabilities
- How a financial asset or financial liability should be measured, including

  - When a financial asset or financial liability should be measured at cost, amortized cost, or fair value in the statement of financial position
  - When to recognize and how to measure impairment of a financial asset or group of financial assets
  - Special accounting rules for hedging relationships involving a financial asset or financial liability

- How a gain or loss on a financial asset or financial liability should be recognized either in profit or loss or in other comprehensive income

IAS 39 does not deal with presentation of issued financial instruments as liabilities or equity, nor does it deal with disclosures that entities should provide about financial instruments. Presentation issues are addressed in IAS 32, *Financial Instruments: Presentation*; disclosure issues are addressed in IFRS 7, *Financial Instruments: Disclosures*.

Many view IAS 39 as one of the most complex Standards, if not the most complex one, to apply in practice. More complex areas include the application of the derecognition requirements for financial assets, fair value measurement, and the designation and measurement of hedging relationships.

SCOPE

In general, IAS 39 applies to all entities in the accounting for both

- Financial instruments
- Other contracts, which are specifically included in the scope

Financial Instruments

IAS 39 applies in the accounting for all financial instruments except for those financial instruments specifically exempted. As discussed in the chapter on IAS 32, a *financial instrument* is defined as any contract that gives rise to a financial asset of one entity and a financial liability or equity instrument of another entity. Thus, financial instruments include financial assets, financial liabilities, and equity instruments.

Example

Financial assets within the scope of IAS 39 include

- Cash
- Deposits in other entities
- Receivables (e.g., trade receivables)
- Loans to other entities
- Investments in bonds and other debt instruments issued by other entities
- Investments in shares and other equity instruments issued by other entities

Financial liabilities within the scope of IAS 39 include

- Deposit liabilities
- Payables (e.g., trade payables)
- Loans from other entities
- Bonds and other debt instruments issued by the entity

Apart from the preceding traditional types of financial instruments, IAS 39 also applies to more complex, derivative financial instruments (e.g., call options, put options, forwards, futures, and swaps). Derivatives are contracts that allow entities to speculate on—or hedge against—future changes in market factors at a relatively low or no initial cost.

Example

Derivative financial instruments within the scope of IAS 39 include

- A purchased call option to purchase (call) a financial asset at a fixed price at a future date. The call option gives the entity the right, but not the obligation, to purchase the asset.
- A purchased put option to sell (put) a financial asset at a fixed price at a future date. The put option gives the entity the right, but not the obligation, to sell the asset.
- A forward contract for the purchase (or sale) of a financial asset at a fixed price at a future date.
- An interest rate swap under which the entity pays a floating interest rate and receives a fixed interest rate on a specified notional amount.

Other Contracts within the Scope of IAS 39

Apart from items that meet the definition of financial instruments, IAS 39 also applies to some contracts that do not meet the definition of a financial instrument but have characteristics similar to derivative financial instruments. This *expands* the scope of IAS 39 to contracts to purchase or sell nonfinancial items (e.g., gold, electricity, or gas) at a future date when, and only when, they have *both* of these two characteristics:

1. The contract is subject to potential *net settlement*. Specifically, when the entity can settle the contract net in cash, or by some other financial instrument, or by exchanging financial instruments rather than by delivering or receiving the underlying nonfinancial item, the contract is subject to potential net settlement.

2. The contract is not part of the entity's expected purchase, sale, or usage requirements (i.e., the contract is not a "normal" purchase or sale). Specifically, when the contract is entered into and held for the purpose of making or taking delivery of the nonfinancial item (e.g., gold, electricity, or gas) in accordance with the entity's expected purchase, sale, or usage requirements, it is not within the scope of IAS 39.

By including contracts that meet the preceding two characteristics in the scope of IAS 39, derivatives are accounted for under IAS 39 whether they meet the definition of financial instrument or not.

Example

If an entity today (e.g., 1/1/X6) enters into a contract to purchase gold at a fixed price (e.g., €100) at a certain date in the future (e.g., 1/1/X7), the contract would be within the scope of IAS 39 if the entity could settle the contract net in cash and the entity does not expect to use the gold in its business activities. In that case, the contract is sufficiently similar to a derivative financial instrument that it is appropriate to recognize and measure in accordance with IAS 39. Recognition and measurement requirements are discussed later in this chapter.

If, however, the entity enters into a contract to purchase electricity and the purpose is to take delivery of the electricity in accordance with the entity's expected usage requirements, that contract would be outside the scope of IAS 39. Such a contract would instead be accounted for as an executory contract and usually not recognized until one of the parties has performed under the contract.

CASE STUDY 1

This case illustrates the application of IAS 39 to items other than financial instruments.

Entity A enters into a contract to purchase 5 million pounds of copper for a fixed price at a future date. Copper is actively traded on the metals exchange and is readily convertible to cash.

Required

Discuss whether this contract falls within the scope of IAS 39.

Solution

This contract potentially is within the scope of IAS 39 because it is a contract to buy or sell a nonfinancial item (copper) and the contract is subject to potential net settlement. Under IAS 39, a contract is considered to be subject to potential net settlement if the nonfinancial item that will be delivered is readily convertible to cash. This condition is met in this case because the nonfinancial item is traded on an active market.

Therefore, the contract is within the scope of IAS 39 unless it is a "normal purchase or sale." There is not sufficient information in the question to determine whether it is a "normal purchase or sale." The contract would be considered to be a normal purchase or sale if the entity intends to settle the contract by taking delivery of the nonfinancial item and has no history of

- Settling net
- Entering into offsetting contracts
- Selling shortly after delivery in order to generate a profit from short-term fluctuations in price or dealer's margin

Scope Exceptions

IAS 39 does not apply to an entity's own issued equity instruments that are classified in the equity section of the entity's statement of financial position (e.g., ordinary shares, preference shares, warrants, and share options classified in equity). Investments in equity instruments issued by other entities, however, are financial assets and within the scope of IAS 39 unless some other scope exception applies.

IAS 39 also provides scope exceptions for some other items that meet the definition of a financial instrument, because they are accounted for under other International Accounting Standards

(IAS) or International Financial Reporting Standards (IFRS). Such scope exceptions are listed in the following table.

Scope exception	*Applicable standard*
Lease receivables and lease payables	IAS 17, *Leases*
Employee benefit plans	IAS 19, *Employee Benefits*
Interests in subsidiaries	IAS 27, *Consolidated and Separate Financial Statements*
Interests in associates	IAS 28, *Investments in Associates*
Interests in joint ventures	IAS 31, *Interests in Joint Ventures*
Share-based payment transactions	IFRS 2, *Share-Based Payment*
Contingent consideration in business combinations	IFRS 3, *Business Combinations*
Insurance contracts	IFRS 4, *Insurance Contracts*

CLASSIFICATION OF FINANCIAL ASSETS AND FINANCIAL LIABILITIES INTO CATEGORIES

In order to determine the appropriate accounting for a financial asset or financial liability, the asset or liability must first be classified into one of the categories specified by IAS 39. There are four categories of financial assets and two categories of financial liabilities. The classification of a financial asset or financial liability determines

- Whether the asset or liability should be measured at cost, amortized cost, or fair value in the statement of financial position
- Whether a gain or loss should be recognized immediately in profit or loss or in other comprehensive income (with recognition in profit or loss at a later point in time)

Financial Assets

An entity is required to classify its *financial assets* into one of these four categories:

1. Financial assets at fair value through profit or loss (FVTPL)
2. Held-to-maturity investments (HTM)
3. Loans and receivables (L&R)
4. Available-for-sale financial assets (AFS)

The first category—*financial assets at fair value through profit or loss*—includes financial assets that the entity either (1) holds for trading purposes or (2) otherwise has elected to classify into this category.

Financial assets that are held for trading are always classified as financial assets at fair value through profit or loss. A financial asset is considered to be held for trading if the entity acquired or incurred it principally for the purpose of selling or repurchasing it in the near term or it is part of a portfolio of financial assets subject to trading. Trading generally reflects active and frequent buying and selling with an objective to profit from short-term movements in price or dealer's margin. In addition, derivative assets are always treated as held for trading unless they are designated and effective hedging instruments. The designation of hedging instruments is discussed later in this chapter.

Financial assets other than those held for trading may also be classified selectively on initial recognition as financial assets at fair value through profit or loss. This ability to selectively classify financial instruments as items measured at fair value with changes in fair value recognized in profit or loss is referred to as the fair value option. This fair value option may be applied only at initial recognition and only if specified conditions are met:

- Where such designation eliminates or significantly reduces a measurement or recognition inconsistency (sometimes referred to as an accounting mismatch) that would otherwise arise from measuring assets or liabilities or recognizing the gains and losses on them on different bases.

- For a group of financial assets, financial liabilities, or both that are managed and evaluated on a fair value basis in accordance with a documented risk management or investment strategy, and information is provided internally on that basis.
- For an instrument that contains an embedded derivative (unless that embedded derivative does not significantly modify the instrument's cash flows under the contract or it is clear with little or no analysis that separation of the embedded derivative is prohibited).

The second category—*held-to-maturity investments*—includes financial assets with fixed or determinable payments and fixed maturity that the entity has the positive intention and ability to hold to maturity. This category is intended for investments in bonds and other debt instruments that the entity will not sell before their maturity date irrespective of changes in market prices or the entity's financial position or performance. For instance, a financial asset cannot be classified as held to maturity if the entity stands ready to sell the financial asset in response to changes in market interest rates or risks or liquidity needs. Since investments in shares and other equity instruments generally do not have a maturity date, such instruments cannot be classified as held-to-maturity investments.

If an entity sells or reclassifies more than an insignificant amount of held-to-maturity investments (i.e., a very small amount in proportion to the total amount of held-to-maturity investments) prior to maturity, such sales or reclassifications normally will disqualify the entity from using the held-to-maturity classification for any financial assets during the following two-year period. This is because sales of held-to-maturity investments call into question (or "taint") the entity's intentions with respect to holding such investments.

There are a few exceptions, where sales do not disqualify use of the held-to-maturity classification, including

- Sales that are so close to maturity that changes in the market rate of interest would not have a significant effect on the financial asset's fair value
- Sales that occur after the entity has collected substantially all of the financial asset's original principal through scheduled payments or prepayments
- Sales that are attributable to an isolated event that is beyond the entity's control, is non-recurring, and could not have been reasonably anticipated by the entity (e.g., a significant deterioration in the issuer's creditworthiness)

In order to be classified as held to maturity, a financial asset must also be quoted in an active market. This condition distinguishes held-to-maturity investments from loans and receivables. Loans and receivables and financial assets that are held for trading, including derivatives, cannot be classified as held-to-maturity investments.

The third category—*loans and receivables*—includes financial assets with fixed or determinable payments that do not have a quoted price in an active market. For example, an entity may classify items such as account receivables, note receivables, and loans to customers in this category. Financial assets with a quoted price in an active market and financial assets that are held for trading, including derivatives, cannot be classified as loans and receivables. In addition, financial assets for which the holder may not recover substantially all of its investment (other than because of credit deterioration) cannot be classified as loans and receivables. In addition to not being quoted in an active market, loans and receivables differ from held-to-maturity investments in that there is no requirement that the entity demonstrates a positive intention and ability to hold loans and receivables to maturity.

The fourth category—*available-for-sale financial assets*—includes financial assets that do not fall into any of the other categories of financial assets or that the entity otherwise has elected to classify into this category. For example, an entity could classify some of its investments in debt and equity instruments as available-for-sale financial assets. Financial assets that are held for trading, including derivatives, cannot be classified as available-for-sale financial assets.

CASE STUDY 2

This case illustrates how to classify a financial asset or financial liability into one of the categories of financial assets or financial liabilities.

Facts

Entity A is considering how to classify these financial assets and financial liabilities:

1. An accounts receivable that is not held for trading.
2. An investment in an equity instrument quoted in an active market that is not held for trading.
3. An investment in an equity instrument that is not held for trading and does not have a quoted price, and whose fair value cannot be reliably measured.
4. A purchased debt security that is not quoted in an active market and that is not held for trading.
5. A purchased debt instrument quoted in an active market that Entity A plans to hold to maturity. If market interest rates fall sufficiently, Entity A will consider selling the debt instrument to realize the associated gain.
6. A "strategic" investment in an equity instrument that is not quoted in an active market. Entity A has no intention to sell the investment.
7. An investment in a financial asset that is held for trading.

Required

Indicate into which category or categories each item can be classified. Please note that some of the items can be classified into more than one category.

Solution

1. An accounts receivable that is not held for trading should be classified into the category of loans and receivables, unless the entity elects to designate it as either at fair value through profit or loss or available for sale.
2. An investment in an equity instrument that has a quoted price and that is not held for trading should be classified as an available-for-sale financial asset, unless the entity elects to designate it as at fair value through profit or loss.
3. An investment in an equity instrument that is not held for trading and does not have a quoted price, and whose fair value cannot be reliably measured, should be classified as an available-for-sale financial asset.
4. A purchased debt security that is not quoted in an active market and that is not held for trading should be classified into the category, loans and receivables unless the entity designates it as either at fair value through profit or loss or available for sale.
5. This purchased debt instrument should be classified as available for sale unless the entity elects to designate it as at fair value through profit or loss. Even though the debt instrument is quoted in an active market and Entity A plans to hold it to maturity, Entity A cannot classify it as held to maturity because Entity A will consider selling the debt instrument if market interest rates fall sufficiently.
6. A "strategic" investment in an equity instrument that is not quoted in an active market and for which there is no intention to sell should be classified as available for sale unless Entity A designates it as at fair value through profit or loss.
7. An investment in a financial asset that is held for trading should be classified into the category of financial asset at fair value through profit or loss.

Financial Liabilities

There are two principal categories of financial liabilities:

1. Financial liabilities at fair value through profit or loss (FVTPL)
2. Financial liabilities measured at amortized cost

Additionally, IAS 39 provides accounting requirements for issued financial guarantee contracts and commitments to provide a loan at a below-market interest rate.

Financial liabilities at fair value through profit or loss include financial liabilities that the entity either has incurred for trading purposes or otherwise has elected to classify into this category.

Derivative liabilities are always treated as held for trading unless they are designated and effective hedging instruments. The designation of hedging instruments is discussed later in this chapter.

An example of a liability held for trading is an issued debt instrument that the entity intends to repurchase in the near term to make a gain from short-term movements in interest rates. Another example of a liability held for trading is the obligation that arises when an entity sells a security that it has borrowed and does not own (a so-called short sale).

As with financial assets, the ability to selectively classify financial instruments as items measured at fair value with changes in fair value recognized in profit or loss is referred to as the fair value option. This fair value option may be applied only at initial recognition and only if any of these conditions are met:

- Such designation eliminates or significantly reduces a measurement or recognition inconsistency (sometimes referred to as an accounting mismatch) that would otherwise arise from measuring assets or liabilities or recognizing the gains and losses on them on different bases.
- A group of financial assets, financial liabilities, or both are managed and evaluated on a fair value basis in accordance with a documented risk management or investment strategy, and information is provided internally on that basis.
- An instrument contains an embedded derivative (unless that embedded derivative does not significantly modify the instrument's cash flows under the contract or it is clear with little or no analysis that separation of the embedded derivative is prohibited).

The second category of financial liabilities is *financial liabilities measured at amortized cost.* It is the default category for financial liabilities that do not meet the definition of financial liabilities at fair value through profit or loss. For most entities, most financial liabilities will fall into this category. Examples of financial liabilities that generally would be classified in this category are account payables, note payables, issued debt instruments, and deposits from customers.

In addition to the two categories of financial liabilities just listed, IAS 39 also addresses the measurement of certain issued financial guarantee contracts and loan commitments. A *financial guarantee contract* is a contract that requires the issuer to make specified payments to reimburse the holder for a loss it incurs because a specified debtor fails to make payment when due in accordance with the original or modified terms of a debt instrument. After initial recognition, IAS 39 requires issued financial guarantee contracts to be measured at the higher of (a) the amount determined in accordance with IAS 37, *Provisions, Contingent Liabilities and Contingent Assets*, and (b) the amount initially recognized less, when appropriate, cumulative amortization. A similar requirement applies to issued commitments to provide a loan at a below-market interest rate.

Reclassifications

IAS 39 severely restricts the ability to reclassify financial assets and financial liabilities from one category to another. Reclassifications into or out of the FVTPL category are not permitted. Reclassifications between the AFS and HTM categories are possible, although reclassifications of more than an insignificant amount of HTM investments normally would necessitate reclassification of all remaining HTM investments to AFS. An entity also cannot reclassify from L&R to AFS.

Without these restrictions on reclassifications, there is a concern that entities would be able to manage earnings (i.e., adjust the figures reported in profit or loss at will) by selectively reclassifying financial instruments. For instance, if the entity desired to increase profit or loss in a period, it would reclassify assets on which it could recognize a gain following reclassification (e.g., if an asset measured at amortized cost has a higher fair value).

Summary

The next table summarizes IAS 39's classification requirements and provides examples of financial assets and financial liabilities in the different categories.

Category	*Classification requirements*	*Examples*
Financial assets at fair value through profit or loss	Financial assets that are either (1) held for trading or (2) electively designated into the category	Derivative assets and investments in debt and equity securities that are held in a trading portfolio
Available-for-sale financial assets	Financial assets that are either (1) electively designated into the category or (2) do not fall into any other category	Investments in debt and equity securities that do not fall into any other category
Held-to-maturity investments	Quoted financial assets with fixed or determinable payments for which the entity has an intent and ability to hold to maturity	Investments in quoted debt securities for which the entity has an intent and ability to hold to maturity
Loans and receivables	Unquoted financial assets with fixed or determinable payments	Accounts receivable, notes receivable, loan assets, and investments in unquoted debt securities
Financial liabilities at fair value through profit or loss	Financial liabilities that are either (1) held for trading or (2) electively designated into the category	Derivative liabilities and other trading liabilities
Financial liabilities at amortized cost	All financial liabilities other than those at fair value through profit or loss	Accounts payable, notes payable, and issued debt securities

RECOGNITION

The term "recognition" refers to when an entity should record an asset or liability initially on its statement of financial position.

The principle for recognition under IAS 39 is that an entity should recognize a financial asset or financial liability on its statement of financial position when, and only when, the entity becomes a party to the contractual provisions of the instrument. This means that an entity recognizes *all* of its contractual rights and obligations that give rise to financial assets or financial liabilities on its statement of financial position.

A consequence of IAS 39's recognition requirement is that a contract to purchase or sell a financial instrument at a future date is itself a financial asset or financial liability that is recognized in the statement of financial position today. The contractual rights and obligations are recognized when the entity becomes a party to the contract *rather* than when the transaction is settled. Accordingly, derivatives are recognized in the financial statements even though the entity may have paid or received nothing on entering into the derivative.

Planned future transactions and other expected transactions, no matter how likely, are not recognized as financial assets or financial liabilities because the entity has not yet become a party to a contract. Thus, a forecast transaction is not recognized in the financial statements even though it may be highly probable. In the absence of any right or obligation, there is no financial asset or financial liability to recognize.

CASE STUDY 3

This case illustrates the application of the principle for recognition of a financial asset or financial liability.

Facts

Entity A is evaluating whether each of the next items should be recognized as a financial asset or financial liability under IAS 39:

1. An unconditional receivable.
2. A forward contract to purchase a specified bond at a specified price at a specified date in the future.
3. A planned purchase of a specified bond at a specified date in the future.

4. A firm commitment to purchase a specified quantity of gold at a specified price at a specified date in the future. The contract cannot be net settled.
5. A firm commitment to purchase a machine that is designated as a hedged item in a fair value hedge of the associated foreign currency risk.

Required

Help Entity A by indicating whether each of the aforementioned items should be recognized as an asset or liability under IAS 39.

Solution

1. Entity A should recognize the unconditional receivable as a financial asset.
2. In principle, Entity A should recognize the forward contract to purchase a specified bond at a specified price at a specified date in the future as a financial asset or financial liability. However, the initial carrying amount may be zero because forward contracts usually are agreed on terms that give them a zero fair value at inception.
3. Entity A should not recognize an asset or liability for a planned purchase of a specified bond at a specified date in the future, because it does not have any present contractual right or obligation.
4. Entity A should not recognize an asset or liability for a firm commitment to purchase a specified quantity of gold at a specified price at a specified date in the future. The contract is not a financial instrument but is instead an executory contract. Executory contacts are generally not recognized before they are settled under existing standards. (Firm commitments that are financial instruments or that are subject to net settlement, however, are recognized on the commitment date under IAS 39.)
5. Normally, a firm commitment to purchase a machine would not be recognized as an asset or liability because it is an executory contract. Under the hedge accounting provisions of IAS 39, however, Entity A would recognize an asset or liability for a firm commitment that is designated as a hedged item in a fair value hedge to the extent there have been changes in the fair value of the firm commitment attributable to the hedged risk (i.e., in this case, foreign currency risk).

DERECOGNITION

The term "derecognition" refers to when an entity should remove an asset or liability from its statement of financial position. The derecognition requirements in IAS 39 set out the conditions that must be met in order to derecognize a financial asset or financial liability and the computation of any gain or loss on derecognition. There are separate derecognition requirements for financial assets and financial liabilities.

Derecognition of Financial Assets

Under IAS 39, derecognition of a financial asset is appropriate if either one of these two criteria is met:

1. The contractual rights to the cash flows of the financial asset have expired.
2. The financial asset has been transferred (e.g., sold) and the transfer qualifies for derecognition based on an evaluation of the extent of transfer of the risks and rewards of ownership of the financial asset.

The first criterion for derecognition of a financial asset is usually easy to apply. The contractual rights to cash flows may expire, for instance, because a customer has paid off an obligation to the entity or an option held by the entity has expired worthless. In these cases, derecognition is appropriate because the rights associated with the financial asset no longer exist.

The application of the second criterion for derecognition of financial assets is often more complex. It relies on an assessment of the extent to which the entity has transferred the risks and rewards of ownership of the asset and, if that assessment is not conclusive, an assessment of whether the entity has retained control of the transferred financial asset.

More specifically, when an entity sells or otherwise transfers a financial asset to another party, the entity (transferor) must evaluate the extent to which it has transferred the *risks and rewards of ownership* of the transferred financial asset to the other party (transferee). This evaluation is based on a comparison of the exposure to the variability in the amounts and timing of the net cash flows of the asset before and after the transfer of the asset.

IAS 39 distinguishes among three types of transfers:

1. The entity has *retained* substantially all risks and rewards of ownership of the transferred asset.
2. The entity has *transferred* substantially all risks and rewards of ownership of the transferred asset.
3. The entity has neither retained nor transferred substantially all risks and rewards of ownership of the transferred asset (i.e., cases that fall between situations 1. and 2. above).

If an entity transfers substantially all risks and rewards of ownership of a transferred financial asset—situation 2. above—the entity derecognizes the financial asset in its entirety.

Example

Examples of transactions where an entity has transferred substantially all risks and rewards of ownership—situation 2. above—include

- A sale of a financial asset where the seller (transferor) does not retain any rights or obligations (e.g., an option or guarantee) associated with the asset sold
- A sale of a financial asset where the transferor retains a right to repurchase the financial asset, but the repurchase price is set as the current fair value of the asset on the repurchase date
- A sale of a financial asset where the transferor retains a call option to repurchase the transferred asset, at the transferor's option, but that option is deep-out-of-the-money (i.e., it is not probable that the option will be exercised)
- A sale of a financial asset where the transferor writes a put option that obligates it to repurchase the transferred asset, at the transferee's option, but that option is deep-out-of-the-money

On derecognition, if there is a difference between the consideration received and the carrying amount of the financial asset, the entity recognizes a gain or loss in profit or loss on the sale. For a derecognized financial asset classified as available for sale, the gain or loss is adjusted for any unrealized holding gains or losses that previously have been recognized in other comprehensive income for that financial asset.

Example

If the carrying amount of a financial asset is $26,300 and the entity sells it for cash of $26,500 in a transfer that qualifies for derecognition, an entity makes these entries:

Cash	26,500	
Asset		26,300
Gain on sale		200

If the asset sold was an AFS financial asset, the entries would look differently. Changes in fair value of available-for-sale (AFS) financial assets are not recognized in profit or loss, but in other comprehensive income until realized. If changes in fair value of $2,400 had previously been recognized in other comprehensive income, the entity would make these entries on derecognition, assuming the carrying amount was $26,300 and the sale price was $26,500:

Cash	26,500	
Available-for-sale gains recognized in other		
comprehensive income	2,400	
Asset		26,300
Gain on sale		2,600

If an entity transfers a financial asset but retains substantially all risks and rewards of ownership of the financial asset—situation 1. above—IAS 39 requires the entity to continue to recognize the financial asset in its entirety. No gain or loss is recognized as a result of the transfer. This situation is sometimes referred to as a failed sale.

Example

Examples of transactions where an entity retains substantially all risks and rewards of ownership—situation 1.—include

- A sale of a financial asset where the asset will be returned to the transferor for a fixed price at a future date (e.g., a sale and repurchase [repo] transaction)
- A securities lending transaction
- A sale of a group of short-term accounts receivables where the transferor issues a guarantee to compensate the buyer for any credit losses incurred in the group and there are no other substantive risks transferred
- A sale of a financial asset where the transferor retains a call option to repurchase the transferred asset, at the transferor's option, where the option is deep-in-the-money (i.e., it is highly probable that the option will be exercised)
- A sale of a financial asset where the transferor issues (writes) a put option that obligates it to repurchase the transferred asset, at the transferee's option, where the option is deep-in-the money
- A sale of a financial asset where the transferor enters into a total return swap with the transferee that returns all increases in fair value of the transferred asset to the transferor and provides the transferee with compensation for all decreases in fair value

Example

An entity sells an asset for a fixed price but simultaneously enters into a forward contract to repurchase the transferred financial asset in one year at the same price plus interest. In this case, even though the entity has transferred the financial asset, there has been no significant change in the entity's exposure to risk and rewards of the asset. Due to the agreement to repurchase the asset for a fixed price on a future date, irrespective of what the market price of the asset may be on that date, the entity continues to be exposed to any increases or decreases in the value of the asset in the period between the sale and the repurchase. In substance, therefore, a repurchase transaction is similar to a borrowing of an amount equal to the fixed price plus interest with the transferred asset serving as collateral to the transferee.

For example, if an entity sells a financial asset for $14,300 in cash and at the same time enters into an agreement with the buyer to repurchase the asset in three months for $14,500, the sale would not qualify for derecognition. The asset would continue to be recognized, and the seller would instead recognize a borrowing from the buyer, as follows:

Cash	14,300	
Borrowing		14,300

In the period between the sale and repurchase of the financial asset, the entity would accrue interest expense on the borrowing for the difference between the sale price ($14,300) and repurchase price ($14,500):

Interest expense	200	
Borrowing		200

On the date of the repurchase, the entity would record the repurchase as follows:

Borrowing	14,500	
Cash		14,500

The evaluation of the extent to which derecognition of a financial asset is appropriate becomes more complex when the entity has retained some risks and rewards of ownership of a financial asset and transferred others. To do this evaluation, it may be necessary to perform a quantitative comparison of the entity's exposure before and after the transfer to the risks and rewards of the transferred asset. If the evaluation results in the conclusion that the entity has neither retained nor transferred substantially all risks and rewards of ownership—situation 3. above—derecognition depends on whether the entity has retained *control* of the transferred financial asset. An entity has lost control if the other party (the transferee) has the practical ability to sell the asset in its entirety to a third party without attaching any restrictions to the transfer.

If the transferor has *lost control* of the transferred asset, the financial asset is derecognized in its entirety. If there is a difference between the asset's carrying amount (adjusted for any deferred unrealized holding gains and losses in equity) and the payment received, a gain or loss is recognized in the same way as in situation 1.

If the transferor has *retained control* over the transferred asset, the entity continues to recognize the asset to the extent of its *continuing involvement*. The continuing involvement is determined based on the extent to which the entity continues to be exposed to changes in amounts and timing of the net cash flows of the transferred asset (i.e., based on its nominal or maximum exposure to changes in net cash flows of the transferred asset).

Example

An example of a transaction where an entity neither retains nor transfers substantially all of the risks and rewards of ownership—situation 3.—is

- A sale of a group of accounts receivables where the transferor issues a guarantee to compensate the buyer for any credit losses incurred in the group up to a maximum amount that is less than the expected credit losses in the group

For instance, if an entity sells a loan portfolio that has a carrying amount of $100,000 for $99,000 and provides the buyer with a guarantee to compensate the buyer for any impairment losses up to $1,000 when expected losses based on historical experience is $3,000, the entity may determine that it has neither retained nor transferred substantially all risks and rewards of ownership. Therefore, it must evaluate whether it has retained control of the transferred asset. If the entity has retained control, the seller would continue to recognize $1,000 as an asset and a corresponding liability to reflect its continuing involvement in the asset (i.e., the maximum amount it may pay under the guarantee) and derecognize the remainder of the carrying amount of the loan portfolio of $99,000.

The following table summarizes the accounting treatments for the three types of transfers just described.

Situation		Accounting treatment
The transferor has retained substantially all risks and rewards—situation 1. above.		Continued recognition of the transferred asset. Any consideration received is recognized as a borrowing.
The transferor has neither retained nor transferred substantially all risks and rewards—situation 3. above.	The transferor has retained control.	Continued recognition of the transferred asset to the extent of the transferor's continuing involvement in the asset. The transferor recognizes a gain or loss for any part that qualifies for derecognition.
	The transferor has lost control.	Derecognition. The transferor recognizes any resulting gain or loss.
The transferor has transferred substantially all risks and rewards—situation 2. above.		Derecognition. The transferor recognizes any resulting gain or loss.

Pass-Through Arrangements

It is not always necessary for an entity actually to transfer its rights to receive cash flows from a financial asset in order for the asset to qualify for derecognition under IAS 39. Under certain conditions, contractual arrangements where an entity continues to collect cash flows from a financial asset it holds, but immediately passes on those cash flows to other parties, may qualify for derecognition if the entity is acting more like an agent (or "postbox") than a principal in the arrangement. Under such circumstances, the entity's receipts and payments of cash flows may not meet the definitions of assets and liabilities.

Thus, IAS 39 specifies that when an entity retains the contractual rights to receive the cash flows of a financial asset (the "original asset"), but assumes a contractual obligation to pay those cash flows to one or more entities (the "eventual recipients"), the entity treats the transaction as a transfer of a financial asset if, and only if, *all* of these three conditions are met:

1. The entity has no obligation to pay amounts to the eventual recipients unless it collects equivalent amounts from the original asset. Short-term advances by the entity with the right of full recovery of the amount lent plus accrued interest at market rates do not violate this condition.
2. The entity is prohibited by the terms of the transfer contract from selling or pledging the original asset other than as security to the eventual recipients for the obligation to pay them cash flows.
3. The entity has an obligation to remit any cash flows it collects on behalf of the eventual recipients without material delay. In addition, the entity is not entitled to reinvest such cash

flows, except for investments in cash or cash equivalents during the short settlement period from the collection date to the date of required remittance to the eventual recipients, and interest earned on such investments is passed to the eventual recipients.

For arrangements that meet these conditions, the requirements regarding evaluating transfer of risks and rewards just described are applied to the assets subject to that arrangement to determine the extent to which derecognition is appropriate. If the three conditions are not met, the asset continues to be recognized.

Consolidation

In consolidated financial statements, the derecognition requirements are applied from the perspective of the consolidated group. Before applying the derecognition principles in IAS 39, therefore, an entity applies IAS 27 and SIC 12, *Consolidation—Special-Purpose Entities,* to determine which entities should be consolidated. Special-purpose entities (SPEs) are entities that are created to accomplish a narrow and well-defined objective and often have legal arrangements that impose strict and sometimes permanent limits on the decision-making powers of the governing board, trustee, or management of the SPEs. For instance, SPEs often are created by transferors of financial assets to effect a securitization of those financial assets. Under SIC 12, the evaluation of whether an SPE should be consolidated is based on an evaluation of whether the substance of the relationship indicates that the SPE is controlled. Four indicators are: (1) the activities are conducted according to specific business needs, so that the entity obtains benefits; (2) decision-making powers including by autopilot to obtain the majority of the benefits; (3) the rights to obtain the majority of the benefits; and (4) the majority of the residual or ownership risks. Where an SPE is required to be consolidated, a transfer of a financial asset to that SPE from the parent or another entity within the group does not qualify for derecognition in the consolidated financial statements. The assets are derecognized only to the extent the SPE in turn sells the transferred assets to a third party or enters into a pass-through arrangement and that sale or arrangement meets the condition for derecognition.

Summary

The eight steps that are involved in the evaluation of whether to derecognize a financial asset under IAS 39 are

1. Consolidate all subsidiaries (including any SPE).
2. Determine whether the derecognition principles are applied to a part or all of an asset (or group of similar assets).
3. Have the rights to the cash flows from the asset expired? If yes, derecognize the asset. If no, go to step 4.
4. Has the entity transferred its rights to receive the cash flows from the asset? If yes, go to 6. If no, go to step 5.
5. *Has the entity assumed an obligation to pay the cash flows from the asset that meets the three conditions?* As discussed in the previous section, the three conditions are that (a) the transferor has no obligation to pay cash flows unless it collects equivalent amounts from the original asset, (b) the transferor is prohibited from selling or pledging the original asset, and (c) the transferor has an obligation to remit the cash flows without material delay. If yes, go to step 6. If no, continue to recognize the asset.
6. Has the entity transferred substantially all risks and rewards? If yes, derecognize the asset. If no, go to step 7.
7. *Has the entity retained substantially all risks and rewards?* If yes, continue to recognize the asset. If no, go to step 8.
8. *Has the entity retained control of the asset?* If yes, continue to recognize the asset to the extent of the entity's continuing involvement. If no, derecognize the asset.

The flowchart illustrates these steps.

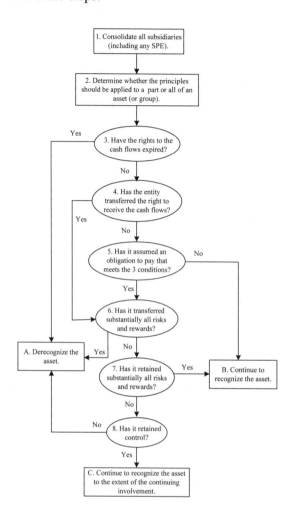

CASE STUDY 4

This case illustrates the application of the principle for derecognition of financial assets

Facts

During the reporting period, Entity A has sold various financial assets:

1. Entity A sells a financial asset for $10,000. There are no strings attached to the sale, and no other rights or obligations are retained by Entity A.
2. Entity A sells an investment in shares for $10,000 but retains a call option to repurchase the shares at any time at a price equal to their current fair value on the repurchase date.
3. Entity A sells a portfolio of short-term account receivables for $100,000 and promises to pay up to $3,000 to compensate the buyer if and when any defaults occur. Expected credit losses are significantly less than $3,000, and there are no other significant risks.
4. Entity A sells a portfolio of receivables for $10,000 but retains the right to service the receivables for a fixed fee (i.e., to collect payments on the receivables and pass them on to the buyer of the receivables). The servicing arrangement meets the pass-through conditions.
5. Entity A sells an investment in shares for $10,000 and simultaneously enters into a total return swap with the buyer under which the buyer will return any increases in value to Entity A and Entity A will pay the buyer interest plus compensation for any decreases in the value of the investment.
6. Entity A sells a portfolio of receivables for $100,000 and promises to pay up to $3,000 to compensate the buyer if and when any defaults occur. Expected credit losses significantly exceed $3,000.

Required

Help Entity A by evaluating the extent to which derecognition is appropriate in each of the aforementioned cases.

Solution

1. Entity A should derecognize the transferred financial asset, because it has transferred all risks and rewards of ownership.
2. Entity A should derecognize the transferred financial asset, because it has transferred substantially all risks and rewards of ownership. While Entity A has retained a call option (i.e., a right that often precludes derecognition), the exercise price of this call option is the current fair value of the asset on the repurchase date. Therefore, the value of the call option should be close to zero. Accordingly, Entity A has not retained any significant risks and rewards of ownership.
3. Entity A should continue to recognize the transferred receivables because it has retained substantially all risks and rewards of the receivables. It has kept all expected credit risk, and there are no other substantive risks.
4. Entity A should derecognize the receivables because it has transferred substantially all risks and rewards. Depending on whether Entity A will obtain adequate compensation for the servicing right, Entity A may have to recognize a servicing asset or servicing liability for the servicing right.
5. Entity A should continue to recognize the sold investment because it has retained substantially all the risks and rewards of ownership. The total return swap results in Entity A still being exposed to all increases and decreases in the value of the investment.
6. Entity A has neither retained nor transferred substantially all risks and rewards of the transferred assets. Therefore, Entity A needs to evaluate whether it has retained or transferred control. Assuming the receivables are not readily available in the market, Entity A would be considered to have retained control over the receivables. Therefore, it should continue to recognize the continuing involvement it has in the receivables, that is, the lower of (1) the amount of the asset ($100,000) and (2) the maximum amount of the consideration received it could be required to repay ($3,000).

Derecognition of Financial Liabilities

The derecognition requirements for financial liabilities are different from those for financial assets. There is no requirement to assess the extent to which the entity has retained risks and rewards in order to derecognize a financial liability. Instead, the derecognition requirements for financial liabilities focus on whether the financial liability has been extinguished. This means that derecognition of a financial liability is appropriate when the obligation specified in the contract is discharged or is cancelled or expires. Absent legal release from an obligation, derecognition is not appropriate even if the entity were to set aside funds in a trust to repay the liability (so-called in-substance defeasance).

If a financial liability is repurchased (e.g., when an entity repurchases in the market a bond that it has issued previously), derecognition is appropriate even if the entity plans to reissue the bond in the future. If a financial liability is repurchased or redeemed at an amount different from its carrying amount, any resulting extinguishment gain or loss is recognized in profit or loss.

An extinguishment gain or loss is also recognized if an entity exchanges the original financial liability for a new financial liability with substantially different terms or substantially modifies the terms of an existing financial liability. In those cases, the extinguishment gain or loss equals the difference between the carrying amount of the old financial liability and the initial fair value (plus transaction costs) of the new financial liability. An exchange or modification is considered to have substantially different terms if the difference in present value of the cash flows under the old and new terms is at least ten percent, discounted using the original effective interest rate of the original debt instrument.

CASE STUDY 5

This case illustrates the application of the principle for derecognition of financial liabilities.

Facts

1. A put option written by Entity A expires.
2. Entity A owes Entity B $50,000 and has set aside that amount in a special trust that it will not use for any purpose other than to pay Entity B.
3. Entity A pays Entity B $50,000 to discharge an obligation to pay $50,000 to Entity B.

Required

Evaluate the extent to which derecognition is appropriate in each of the previous cases.

Solution

1. Derecognition is appropriate because the option liability has expired. Therefore, the entity no longer has an obligation and the liability has been extinguished.
2. Derecognition is not appropriate because Entity A still owes Entity B $50,000. It has not obtained legal release from paying this amount.
3. Derecognition is appropriate because Entity A has discharged its obligation to pay $50,000.

MEASUREMENT

The term "measurement" refers to the determination of the carrying amount of an asset or liability in the statement of financial position. The measurement requirements in IAS 39 also address whether gains and losses on financial assets and financial liabilities should be included in profit or loss or recognized in other comprehensive income.

The following sections discuss these aspects of measurement of financial assets and financial liabilities:

- Initial measurement (measurement when a financial asset or financial liability is first recognized).
- Subsequent measurement (measurement subsequent to initial recognition). This subsection also discusses how to determine cost, amortized cost, and fair value.
- Impairment (adjustments to the measurement due to incurred losses).

The measurement of an asset or liability may also be adjusted because of a designated hedging relationship. Hedge accounting is discussed later in this chapter.

Initial Measurement

When a financial asset or financial liability is recognized initially in the statement of financial position, the asset or liability is measured at fair value (plus transaction costs in some cases). *Fair value* is the amount for which an asset could be exchanged, or a liability settled, between knowledgeable, willing parties in an arm's-length transaction. In other words, fair value is an actual or estimated transaction price on the reporting date for a transaction taking place between unrelated parties that have adequate information about the asset or liability being measured.

Since fair value is a market transaction price, on initial recognition fair value generally is assumed to equal the amount of consideration paid or received for the financial asset or financial liability. Accordingly, IAS 39 specifies that the best evidence of the fair value of a financial instrument at initial recognition generally is the transaction price. An entity may be able to overcome that presumption based on observable market data. In other words, if there is a difference between the transaction price and fair value as evidenced by comparison with other observable current market transactions in the same instrument or based on a valuation technique incorporating only observable market data, an immediate gain or loss on initial recognition results.

Developments—Fair Value. In response to the recommendations of the Financial Stability Forum in their report "Enhancing Market and Institutional Resilience," the IASB formed an expert advisory panel. The IASB's Expert Advisory Panel (EAP) has since issued guidance on fair value measurements. The report of the EAP is meant as educational guidance for measuring and disclosing fair values but does not establish new requirements. Further guidance from the IASB on fair values is awaited.

Transaction costs may arise in the acquisition, issuance, or disposal of a financial instrument. Transaction costs are incremental costs, such as fees and commissions paid to agents, advisers, brokers and dealers; levies by regulatory agencies and securities exchanges; and transfer taxes and duties. Except for those financial assets and financial liabilities measured at fair value through profit or loss, transaction costs that are directly attributable to the acquisition or issue of a financial asset or financial liability are capitalized (i.e., they are added to fair value and included in the initial measurement of the financial asset or financial liability and expensed over the life of the item, when impairment occurs, or on derecognition, as appropriate). Transaction costs are expensed immediately for financial assets or financial liabilities measured at fair value, because the payment of transaction costs does not result in any increase in future economic benefits to the entity (i.e., you cannot sell a financial asset at a higher price because you have paid transaction costs).

Example

Entity A purchases 100 shares of Entity B with a quoted price of $124 for a total consideration of $12,400. In addition, Entity A incurs transaction costs in the form of broker fees of $100 to acquire the shares. Entity A classifies the shares as at fair value through profit or loss. In this case, Entity A would make these journal entries on initial recognition:

Financial assets at fair value through profit or loss	12,400	
Fee expense	100	
Cash		12,500

(To recognize acquisition of 100 shares at fair value of $12,400)

If Entity A had classified the shares of Entity B as available for sale (i.e., a category for which changes in fair value are not recognized in profit or loss), the transaction costs would have been included in the initial measurement of the financial asset:

Available-for-sale financial asset	12,500	
Cash		12,500

(To recognize acquisition of 100 shares at fair value plus transaction costs of $12,500)

The same requirements apply to financial liabilities. For instance, if Entity A issues bonds for total proceeds of $17,100 and incurs transaction costs of $300 in issuing the bonds, it would make these journal entries, assuming the bonds are not measured at fair value through profit or loss:

Bonds	16,800	
Cash		16,800

(To recognize issuance of bonds for net proceeds of $16,800)

There may be a difference between the fair value and the consideration received or paid for related-party transactions or transactions where the entity expects to obtain some other benefits. If there is a difference between the consideration paid or received and the initial amount recognized for the financial asset or financial liability, that difference is recognized in profit or loss (unless it qualifies as some other type of asset or liability).

PRACTICAL INSIGHT

When goods or services are sold, the seller often gives the buyer some specified time to pay the invoice amount, such as 60 days, with no stated interest. This means that the seller obtains a short-term receivable and that the buyer obtains a short-term payable that meet the definition of financial instruments and are accounted for under IAS 39. Conceptually, such a receivable or payable should be measured at its present value (i.e., the present value of the invoice amount discounted using applicable current market interest rates). In that case, interest would be accrued over the term of the receivable for the difference between the initial present value and the invoice amount. As a practical accommodation, however, IAS 39 permits measuring short-term receivables and short-term payables with no stated interest at the original invoice amount if the effect of discounting is immaterial. For longer-term receivables or payables that do not pay interest or pay a below-market interest, IAS 39 does require measurement initially at the present value of the cash flows to be received or paid.

CASE STUDY 6

This case illustrates how to measure a financial asset or financial liability on initial recognition.

Facts

During 20X5, Entity A acquires and incurs these financial assets and financial liabilities:

1. A debt security that is held for trading is purchased for $50,000. Transaction costs of $200 are incurred.
2. Equity securities classified as at fair value through profit or loss are purchased for $20,000. The dealer fee paid is $375.
3. A bond classified as available for sale is purchased at a premium to par. The par value is $100,000 and the premium is $1,000 (such that the total amount paid is $101,000). In addition, transaction costs of $1,500 are incurred.
4. A bond measured at amortized cost is issued for $30,000. Issuance costs are $600.

Required

Determine the initial carrying amount of each of these financial instruments.

Solution

1. The initial carrying amount is $50,000. The transaction costs of $200 are expensed. This treatment applies because the debt security is classified as held for trading and, therefore, measured at fair value with changes in fair value recognized in profit or loss.
2. The initial carrying amount is $20,000. The dealer fee of $375 is expensed as a transaction cost. This treatment applies because the equity securities are classified as at fair value with changes in fair value recognized in profit or loss.
3. The initial carrying amount is $102,500 (i.e., the sum of the amount paid for the securities and the transaction costs). This treatment applies because the bond is not measured at fair value with changes in fair value recognized in profit or loss.
4. The initial carrying amount is $29,400 (i.e., the amount received from issuing the bond less the transaction costs paid). For liabilities, transaction costs are deducted, not added, from the initial carrying amount. This treatment applies because the bond is not measured at fair value with changes in fair value recognized in profit or loss.

Subsequent Measurement

Subsequent to initial recognition, financial assets and financial liabilities are measured using one of these three measurement attributes:

1. Cost
2. Amortized cost
3. Fair value

Whether a financial asset or financial liability is measured at cost, amortized cost, or fair value depends on its classification into one of the four categories of financial assets or two categories of financial liabilities defined by IAS 39 and whether its fair value can be reliably determined.

Because different categories are measured in different ways under IAS 39, the measurement requirements of IAS 39 are often characterized as a mixed measurement approach. Conceptually, an alternative approach would be to measure all financial assets and financial liabilities in the same way (e.g., at fair value). A benefit of such an approach is that some of the complexity of IAS 39 could be eliminated, because the need for classification and hedge accounting guidance would decrease. There is little consensus currently, however, for moving to an alternative approach in the near future. For instance, some believe that fair values are not sufficiently reliable in all cases to include them in the primary financial statements.

Cost

Cost is the amount for which an asset was acquired or a liability incurred, including transaction costs (i.e., fees or commissions paid).

Example

If an entity purchases a financial asset for a price of $230 and, in addition, incurs $20 of costs that are directly attributable to the acquisition, the cost for that asset equals $250.

Subsequent to initial recognition, only one type of financial instrument is measured at cost under IAS 39: investments in unquoted equity instruments that cannot be reliably measured at fair value, including derivatives that are linked to and must be settled by such unquoted equity instruments. For instance, an entity may conclude that fair value is not reliably measurable for an investment in a nonpublic entity ("private equity" investment). In that case, the entity is required to measure the investment at cost.

Example

Entity A purchases a 10% holding of the ordinary shares in a nonpublic, start-up entity for a total cost of $250 paid in cash.

Thus, on initial recognition, it debits financial assets $250 and credits cash $250.

Financial asset	250	
Cash		250

There is no active market for the shares, and Entity A determines that it is not possible to reliably estimate the fair value of the shares using valuation techniques. In that case, Entity A should continue to measure the investment at its cost of $250 at each subsequent reporting date for as long as the asset is held, assuming that the asset does not become impaired.

While an investment measured at cost is held, unrealized holding gains or losses are normally not recognized in profit or loss. However, any cash dividends received are reported as dividend income.

Example

If Entity A receives a cash dividend of $10, it makes this journal entry:

Cash	10	
Dividend income		10

When an investment held at cost is sold or otherwise derecognized, any difference between its carrying amount and the consideration received is recognized in profit or loss.

Example

If Entity A sells an investment that is held at cost and that is carried in the statement of financial position at $120, for cash of $170, it would recognize a realization gain of $50:

Cash	170	
Financial asset		120
Gain on sale		50

CASE STUDY 7

This case illustrates when an investment would be measured at cost.

Facts

During 20X6, Entity A acquired these financial instruments:

1. A share quoted on a stock exchange
2. A bond quoted in an active bond market

3. A bond that is not quoted in an active market
4. A share that is not quoted in an active market but whose fair value can be estimated using valuation techniques
5. A share that is not quoted in an active market and whose fair value cannot be measured reliably
6. A derivative that is linked to and must be settled by an unquoted equity instrument whose fair value cannot be measured reliably

Required

Indicate which of the previous items would be measured at cost.

Solution

Only 5. and 6. would be measured at cost.

1. A share quoted on a stock exchange would always be measured at fair value, assuming the market is active.
2. A bond quoted in an active bond market would be measured at fair value or amortized cost, depending on its classification.
3. A bond that is not quoted in an active market would be measured at fair value or amortized cost, depending on its classification.
4. A share that is not quoted in an active market, but whose fair value can be estimated using valuation techniques, would always be measured at fair value.
5. A share that is not quoted in an active market and whose fair value cannot be measured reliably would be measured at cost.
6. A derivative that is linked to and must be settled by an unquoted equity instrument whose fair value cannot be measured reliably would be measured at cost.

Amortized Cost

Amortized cost is the cost of an asset or liability as adjusted, as necessary, to achieve a constant effective interest rate over the life of the asset or liability (i.e., constant interest income or constant interest expense as a percentage of the carrying amount of the financial asset or financial liability).

Example

If the amortized cost of an investment in a debt instrument for which no interest or principal payments are made during the year at the beginning of 20X4 is $100,000 and the effective interest rate is 12%, the amortized cost at the end of 20X4 is $112,000 [100,000 + (12% × 100,000)].

Subsequent to initial measurement, these categories of financial assets and financial liabilities are measured at amortized cost in the statement of financial position:

• Held-to-maturity investments
• Loans and receivables
• Financial liabilities not measured at fair value through profit or loss

It is not possible to compute amortized cost for instruments that do not have fixed or determinable payments, such as for equity instruments. Therefore, such instruments cannot be classified into these categories.

For held-to-maturity investments and loans and receivables, income and expense items include interest income and impairment losses. In addition, if a held-to-maturity investment or loan or receivable is sold, the realized gain or loss is recognized in profit or loss. Note, however, that, as discussed, sales of held-to-maturity investments normally will disqualify the entity from using that classification for any other assets that would otherwise have been classified as held to maturity.

Financial liabilities measured at amortized cost are all financial liabilities other than those measured at fair value. For financial liabilities measured at amortized cost, the most significant item of expense is interest expense. In addition, if financial liabilities are repaid or repurchased before their maturity, extinguishment gains or losses will result if the repurchase price is different from the carrying amount.

In order to determine the amortized cost of an asset or liability, an entity applies the *effective interest rate method*. The effective interest rate method also determines how much interest income or interest expense should be reported in each period for a financial asset or financial liability.

The effective interest rate method allocates the contractual (or, when an asset or liability is prepayable, the estimated) future cash payments or receipts through the expected life of the financial instrument or, when appropriate, a shorter period, in order to achieve a *constant* effective interest rate (yield) in each period over the life of the financial instrument.

The *effective interest rate* is the internal rate of return of the cash flows of the asset or liability, including the initial amount paid or received, interest payments, and principal repayments.

PRACTICAL INSIGHT

The effective interest rate can be computed using a calculator or spreadsheet program. In mathematical terms, the effective interest is found by setting up this equation and solving for the interest rate (*y*) that equates (1) the initial carrying amount of the asset or liability (*PV*) with (2) the present value of the estimated future interest and principal cash flows (*CF*) in each period (i).

$$PV = \sum_{i=1}^{N} \frac{CF_i}{(1+y)^i}$$

In some cases, the effective interest rate will equal the stated interest rate of the asset or liability. This is often the case for loans and long-term note receivables or payables where the initial proceeds equals the principal and the entity was party to the contractual terms at its inception. For such assets, amortized cost equals cost and will be the same in each period. In other cases, the effective interest rate differs from the stated interest rate. This is the case when a debt security is purchased or issued at a premium (higher price) or discount (lower price) to the stated principal (par) amount. In those cases, it is usually necessary to compute the effective interest rate and prepare an amortization schedule in order to determine amortized cost in each period.

Example

This amortization schedule example illustrates how the effective interest method allocates the estimated future cash payments or receipts in order to achieve a constant effective interest rate (yield) in each period over the life of a financial instrument.

Assume that a debt security has a stated principal amount of $100,000, which will be repaid by the issuer at maturity in five years, and a stated coupon interest rate of 6% per year payable annually at the end of each year until maturity (i.e., $6,000 per year). Entity A purchases the debt security in the market on January 1, 20X1, for $93,400 (including transaction costs of $100), that is, at a discount of $6,600 to its principal (par) amount of $100,000. Entity A classifies the debt security as held to maturity and makes this journal entry:

Held-to-maturity investments	93,400	
Cash		93,400

Based on the cash flows of the debt security (i.e., an initial outflow of $93,400, five annual interest cash inflows of $6,000, and one principal cash inflow at maturity of $100,000), it can be shown that the effective interest rate (internal rate of return) of the investment in the debt security is approximately 7.64%. This is the only discount rate that will give a present value of the future cash flows that equals the purchase price.

Based on the effective interest rate of 7.64%, the amortized cost and reported interest income in each year over the life of the financial asset can be computed as indicated in this amortization schedule:

Year	(A) Beginning-of-period amortized cost	(B) Interest cash inflows (at 6%) and principal cash inflow	(C) Reported interest income [=(A) × 7.64%]	(D) Amortization of debt discount [=(C) – (B)]	(E) End-of-period amortized cost [=(A)+(D)]
20X1	93,400	6,000	7,133	1,133	94,533
20X2	94,533	6,000	7,220	1,220	95,753
20X3	95,753	6,000	7,313	1,313	97,066

Year	(A) Beginning-of-period amortized cost	(B) Interest cash inflows (at 6%) and principal cash inflow	(C) Reported interest income [=(A) × 7.64%]	(D) Amortization of debt discount [=(C) – (B)]	(E) End-of-period amortized cost [=(A)+(D)]
20X4	97,066	6,000	7,413	1,413	98,479
20X5	98,479	106,000	7,521	1,521	0.00

At the end of 20X1, Entity A makes this journal entry:

Cash	6,000	
Held-to-maturity investment	1,133	
Interest income		7,133

At the end of 20X2, Entity A makes this journal entry:

Cash	6,000	
Held-to-maturity investment	1,220	
Interest income		7,220

At the end of 20X3, Entity A makes this journal entry:

Cash	6,000	
Held-to-maturity investment	1,313	
Interest income		7,313

At the end of 20X4, Entity A makes this journal entry:

Cash	6,000	
Held-to-maturity investment	1,413	
Interest income		7,413

At the end of 20X5, Entity A makes this journal entry:

Cash	106,000	
Held-to-maturity investment	98,479	
Interest income		7,521

If the reporting period does not coincide with the interest payment dates (e.g., if interest is paid twice annually, on May 30 and November 30, while the reporting period ends on December 31), the amortization schedule is prepared using interest periods rather than reporting periods. The amounts computed as interest income in each interest period are then allocated to reporting periods.

Example

If interest income computed using the effective interest method for the interest period between November 30, 20X5, and May 30, 20X6, is $240,000, then one-sixth of that would be allocated to the 20X5 reporting period (i.e., $40,000) and five-sixths would be allocated to the 20X6 reporting period (i.e., $200,000).

On December 31, 20X5, this journal entry would be made:

Interest receivable	40,000	
Interest income		40,000

When interest is received on May 30, 20X6, this journal entry would be made:

Cash	240,000	
Interest income		200,000
Interest receivable		40,000

CASE STUDY 8

This case illustrates how to determine the amortized cost of a financial instrument, including the preparation of an amortization schedule.

Facts

On January 1, 20X5, Entity A purchases a bond in the market for $53,993. The bond has a principal amount of $50,000 that will be repaid on December 31, 20X9. The bond has a stated rate of 10% payable annually, and the quoted market interest rate for the bond is 8%.

Required

Indicate whether the bond was acquired at a premium or a discount. Prepare an amortization schedule that shows the amortized cost of the bond at the end of each year between 20X5 and 20X9 and reported interest income in each period.

Solution

The bond was acquired at a premium to par because the purchase price is higher than the par amount. An amortization schedule that shows the amortized cost of the bond at the end of each year between 20X5 and 20X9 and reported interest income in each period follows.

Year	(A) Beginning-of-period amortized cost	(B) Interest cash inflows (at 10%) and principal cash inflow	(C) Reported interest income [= (A) × 8%]	(D) Amortization of debt premium [= (C) − (B)]	(E) End-of-period amortized cost [= (A) − (D)]
20X5	53,993	5,000	4,319	681	53,312
20X6	53,312	5,000	4,265	735	52,577
20X7	52,577	5,000	4,206	794	51,784
20X8	51,784	5,000	4,143	857	50,926
20X9	50,926	55,000	4,074	926	0

Fair Value

As already indicated, *fair value* is defined as the amount for which an asset could be exchanged, or a liability settled, between knowledgeable, willing parties in an arm's-length transaction.

Three categories of financial assets and financial liabilities normally are measured at fair value in the statement of financial position:

1. Financial assets at fair value through profit or loss
2. Available-for-sale financial assets
3. Financial liabilities at fair value through profit or loss

Financial assets and financial liabilities in these categories include investments in debt instruments, investments in equity instruments, and issued debt instruments that are classified or designated into a category measured at fair value. However, there is one exception to fair value measurement in these categories. This exception applies to investments in equity instruments that are not quoted in an active market and cannot be reliably measured at fair value (or are derivatives that are linked to—and must be settled in—such an instrument). Such instruments are measured at cost instead of fair value.

The recognition of income and expense items in profit or loss differs among the categories measured at fair value.

- For financial assets at fair value through profit or loss and financial liabilities at fair value through profit or loss, all changes in fair value are recognized in profit or loss when they occur. This includes unrealized holding gains and losses.
- For available-for-sale financial assets, unrealized holding gains and losses are recognized in other comprehensive income until they are realized or impairment occurs. Only interest income and dividend income, impairment losses, and certain foreign currency gains and losses are recognized in profit or loss while available-for-sale financial assets are held. When gains or losses are realized (e.g., through a sale), the associated unrealized holding gains and losses that were previously recognized in other comprehensive income are reclassified to profit or loss.

IAS 39 establishes this hierarchy for determining fair value:

1. The existence of a *published price quotation* in an active market is the best evidence of fair value, and when such quotations exist, they are used to determine fair value. A financial instrument is regarded as quoted in an active market if quoted prices are readily and regularly available from an exchange, dealer, broker, industry group, pricing service, or regulatory

agency, and those prices represent actual and regularly occurring market transactions on an arm's-length basis.

Except for offsetting positions, assets are measured at the currently quoted bid price and liabilities are measured at the currently quoted asking price. When an entity has assets and liabilities with offsetting market risks, it may use midmarket prices for the offsetting positions. When current bid and asking prices are unavailable, the price of the most recent transaction provides evidence of fair value as long as there has not been a significant change in economic conditions since the time of the transaction. If circumstances have changed (e.g., a significant change in the risk-free interest rate) or the entity can demonstrate the last transaction does not reflect fair value (e.g., because it was not on arm's-length terms but a distress sale), the last transaction price is adjusted, as appropriate.

The fair value of a portfolio of financial instruments is the product of the number of units of the instrument and its quoted market price. Therefore, portfolio factors are not considered in determining fair value. For instance, a control premium associated with holding a controlling interest or a liquidity discount associated with holding a large block of instruments that cannot be rapidly sold in the market would not be considered in determining fair value. Although such factors may affect the price that is paid for a group of instruments in an actual transaction, the effect of such factors is in practice difficult to quantify.

2. For assets or liabilities that are not quoted in active markets, fair value is determined using *valuation techniques*, such as discounted cash flow models or option pricing models. Such valuation techniques estimate the price that would have been paid in an arm's-length transaction motivated by normal business considerations at the reporting date. If an entity uses a valuation technique to determine fair value, that technique should incorporate all factors that market participants would consider in setting a price, be consistent with accepted economic methodologies for pricing financial instruments, and maximize the use of market inputs.

The fair value of financial liabilities incorporates the effect of the entity's own credit risk; that is, the higher the credit risk, the lower the fair value of the liability. However, the fair value of a financial liability that has a demand feature (e.g., a demand deposit liability) is not lower than the amount repayable on demand, discounted from the first date the amount could be required to be repaid.

PRACTICAL INSIGHT

Often the fair value of a debt instrument that does not have a quoted rate or price can be determined by scheduling the cash flows and discounting them using the applicable current market interest rate for debt instruments that have substantially the same terms and characteristics (similar remaining maturity, cash flow pattern, credit quality, currency risk, collateral, and interest basis) for which quoted rates in active markets exist. These and other techniques for determining fair value are discussed in finance and valuation textbooks.

Examples

Financial Assets at Fair Value through Profit or Loss

Assume Entity A on December 15, 2006, acquires 1,000 shares in Entity B at a per share price of $55 for a total of $55,000 and classifies them as at fair value through profit or loss. On December 31, 2006, the quoted price of Entity B increases to $62, such that the fair value of all shares held in Entity B now equals $62,000. On January 1, 2007, Entity A sells the shares for a total of $62,000. In this case, the journal entries would be

December 15, 2006		
Financial assets at fair value through profit or loss	55,000	
Cash		55,000
December 31, 2006		
Financial assets at fair value through profit or loss	7,000	
Profit or loss		7,000

<u>January 1, 2007</u>

Cash	62,000	
Financial assets at fair value through profit or loss		62,000

Available-for-Sale Financial Assets

If Entity A instead had classified the shares as available for sale, the journal entries would be

<u>December 15, 2006</u>

Available-for-sale financial assets	55,000	
Cash		55,000

<u>December 31, 2006</u>

Available-for-sale financial assets	7,000	
Other comprehensive income		7,000

<u>January 1, 2007</u>

Cash	62,000	
Other comprehensive income	7,000	
Available-for-sale financial assets		62,000
Gain on sale (available-for-sale financial asset)		7,000

CASE STUDY 9

This case illustrates how to determine the fair value of a financial instrument.

Facts

Entity A is considering how to determine the fair value of the following financial instruments:

1. A share that is actively traded on a stock exchange
2. A share for which no active market exists but for which quoted prices are available
3. A loan asset originated by the entity
4. A bond that is not actively traded but whose fair value can be determined by reference to quoted interest rates for government bonds
5. A complex derivative that is tailor-made for the entity

Required

In each of these cases, discuss whether fair value would be determined using a quoted market price or a valuation technique under IAS 39.

Solution

1. The fair value of a share that is actively traded on a stock exchange equals the quoted market price.
2. The fair value of a share for which no active market exists, but for which quoted prices are available, would be determined using a valuation technique.
3. The fair value of a loan asset originated by the entity would be determined using a valuation technique.
4. The fair value of a bond that is not actively traded, but whose fair value can be determined by reference to quoted interest rates for government bonds, would be determined using a valuation technique.
5. The fair value of a complex derivative that is tailor-made to the entity would be determined using a valuation technique.

CASE STUDY 10

This case illustrates how to account for available-for-sale financial assets.

Facts

On August 1, 2006, Entity A purchased a two-year bond, which it classified as available for sale. The bond had a stated principal amount of $100,000, which Entity A will receive on August 1, 2008. The stated coupon interest rate was 10% per year, which is paid semiannually on December 31 and July 31. The bond was purchased at a quoted annual yield of 8% on a bond-equivalent yield basis.

Required

1. What price did Entity A pay for the bond? (Hint: Compute the present value using a semiannual yield and semiannual periods.)
2. Did Entity A purchase the bond at par, at a discount, or at a premium?
3. Prepare the journal entry at the date Entity A purchased the bond. (Entity A paid cash to acquire the bond. Assume that no transaction costs were paid.)
4. Prepare a bond amortization schedule for years 2006 to 2008. For each period, show cash interest receivable, recognized interest revenue, amortization of any bond discount or premium, and the carrying amount of the bond at the end of the period.
5. Prepare the journal entries to record cash interest receivable and interest revenue on July 31, 2007.
6. If the quoted market yield for the bond changes from 8% to 9% on December 31, 2007, should Entity A recognize an increase, a decrease, or no change in the carrying amount of the bond on that date? If you conclude that the carrying amount should change, compute the change and prepare the corresponding journal entries.

Solution

1. Entity A paid a price of $103,629.90 for the bond. This price is determined by discounting the interest and principal cash flows using the yield at which the bond was purchased (i.e., 8%). More specifically, you can compute the price by the following three steps:

   a. Computing the interest and principal cash flows and preparing a schedule showing the amounts and timing of the cash flows (column 1 ahead)
   b. Determining the discount factors to use for a discount rate of 8% per year (column 2 ahead)
   c. Multiplying each cash flow with its corresponding discount factor (column 3 ahead)

   Since the stated coupon rate is 10% per year on a stated principal amount of $100,000, the total annual interest payment is $10,000 and the semiannual interest payment is half of that (i.e., $10,000/2 = $5,000).

   On a bond-equivalent yield basis, the semiannual effective yield is simply half of the annual effective yield (i.e., 8%/2 = 4%). In other words, the semiannual effective yield is not compounded, but doubled, to arrive at the quoted annual yield. This convention is commonly used in the marketplace.

Date	(1) Cash flow	(2) Discount factor	(3) Present value
12/31/2006	$5,000	$1/(1 + 0.04) = 0.9615$	$4,807.69
7/31/2007	$5,000	$1/(1 + 0.04)^2 = 0.9246$	$4,622.78
12/31/2007	$5,000	$1/(1 + 0.04)^3 = 0.8890$	$4,444.98
7/31/2008	($100,000 + $5,000)	$1/(1 + 0.04)^4 = 0.8548$	$89,754.44
Total			$103,629.90

   Alternatively, you can use a discount factor for the principal payment and an annuity factor for the interest cash flows to compute the present value of the cash flows.

2. Entity A purchased the bond at a premium. The amount of the premium is $3,629.90. When a bond is purchased at a price that is higher than its stated principal amount, it is said to be purchased at a premium. This occurs when the yield at which the bond is purchased is lower than the stated coupon yield, for instance, because market interest rates have declined since the bond was originally issued.

3. *January 1, 2005*

Available-for-sale financial asset	103,629.90	
Cash		103,629.90

   (To record purchase of bond that is classified as available for sale)

   This amount is computed in question 1.

4.

	(1) Cash interest receipts	(2) Interest revenue	(3) Amortization of premium	(4) Carrying amount
1/8/2006	--	--	--	103,629.90
12/31/2006	5,000.00	4,145.20	854.80	102,775.09
7/31/2007	5,000.00	4,111.00	889.00	101,886.09
12/31/2007	5,000.00	4,075.44	924.56	100,961.54
7/31/2008	5,000.00	4,038.46	961.54	100,000.00

Cash interest received (column 1) is computed as the stated nominal amount multiplied by the stated coupon interest rate for half a year (i.e., $100,000 \times 10\% \times \frac{1}{2}$). Interest revenue reported in the income statement (column 2) is computed as the carrying amount in the previous period (column 4) times the effective interest rate (yield) at inception for half a year (i.e., previous carrying amount $\times 10\% \times \frac{1}{2}$). The amortization of the premium (column 3) is the difference between cash interest (column 1) and interest revenue (column 2). The carrying amount (column 4) equals the previous carrying amount (column 4) less the amortization of the premium during the period (column 3).

5.   *July 31, 2007*

Interest receivable	5,000.00	
Available-for-sale financial asset		889.00
Interest revenue		4,111.00

(To record interest revenue for the first half of 2007)

6. An increase in the current market yield of a bond results in a decrease in its fair value (an unrealized holding loss). Since the bond is classified as available for sale, Entity A should recognize this change in fair value in other comprehensive income, but not in profit or loss.

The new fair value is computed as the present value of the remaining cash flows discounted using the new quoted annual yield divided by half to obtain the semiannual yield (i.e., $9\%/2 = 4.5\%$):

$$(\$100,000 + \$5,000)/1.045 = \$100,478.47$$

Since the carrying amount absent the change in interest rates would have been $100,961.54, an unrealized holding loss of $483.07 has occurred. The journal entries are

December 31, 2007

Other comprehensive income	483.07	
Available-for-sale financial asset		483.07

(To record the unrealized holding loss)

Summary

Category	Measurement in the balance sheet	Income and expense items recognized in profit or loss
Financial assets at fair value through profit or loss	Fair value	• All changes in fair value • Interest income • Dividend income
Available-for-sale financial assets	Fair value	• Realized gains and losses • Impairment losses • Foreign currency gains and losses (for monetary items) • Interest income • Dividend income
Investments in unquoted equity instruments that cannot be reliably measured	Cost	• Realized gains and losses • Impairment losses • Dividend income
Held-to-maturity investments	Amortized cost	• Realized gains and losses • Impairment losses • Foreign currency gains and losses • Interest income

Category	Measurement in the balance sheet	Income and expense items recognized in profit or loss
Loans and receivables	Amortized cost	• Realized gains and losses • Impairment losses • Foreign currency gains and losses • Interest income
Financial liabilities at fair value through profit or loss	Fair value	• All changes in fair value • Interest expense
Financial liabilities at amortized cost	Amortized cost	• Realized gains and losses • Foreign currency gains and losses • Interest expense

Impairment

IAS 39 requires an entity to assess at each reporting date whether there is any *objective evidence* that a financial asset or group of financial assets is impaired. Objective evidence that a financial asset or group of financial assets is impaired includes observable data about these loss events:

1. Significant financial difficulty of the issuer or obligor.
2. A breach of contract, such as a default or delinquency in interest or principal payments.
3. A troubled debt restructuring.
4. It becomes probable that the borrower will enter bankruptcy or other financial reorganization.
5. The disappearance of an active market for that financial asset because of financial difficulties.
6. Observable data indicating that there is a measurable decrease in the estimated future cash flows from a group of financial assets since the initial recognition of those assets, although the decrease cannot yet be identified with the individual financial assets in the group (i.e., a loss that is incurred but not yet reported). Such data may include changes in unemployment rates or property prices that affect borrowers in a group.

For investments in equity instruments that are classified as available for sale, a significant or prolonged decline in the fair value below its cost is also objective evidence of impairment.

PRACTICAL INSIGHT

IAS 39 does not provide any bright line or rule of thumb to determine what constitutes a "significant or prolonged decline" in the fair value below its cost. This is a matter of judgment. With the promulgation of IFRS 9 this issue is expected to be resolved.

If any objective evidence of impairment exists, the entity recognizes any associated impairment loss in profit or loss. Only losses that have been *incurred* can be reported as impairment losses. This means that losses expected from future events, no matter how likely, are not recognized. A loss is incurred only if both of these two conditions are met:

1. There is objective evidence of impairment as a result of one or more events that occurred after the initial recognition of the asset (a "loss event").
2. The loss event has an impact on the estimated future cash flows of the financial asset or group of financial assets that can be reliably estimated.

The impairment requirements apply to these types of financial assets:

- Loans and receivables
- Held-to-maturity investments
- Available-for-sale financial assets
- Investments in unquoted equity instruments whose fair value cannot be reliably measured

The only category of financial assets that is not subject to testing for impairment is financial assets at fair value through profit or loss, because any declines in value for such assets are recognized immediately in profit or loss irrespective of whether there is any objective evidence of impairment. Financial liabilities are not subject to testing for impairment.

For loans and receivables and held-to-maturity investments, impaired assets are measured at the present value of the estimated future cash flows discounted using the original effective interest rate of the financial assets (i.e., the effective interest rate that is used to determine amortized cost). Any difference between the previous carrying amount and the new measurement of the impaired asset is recognized as an impairment loss in profit or loss. This would be the case if the estimated future cash flows have decreased.

Example

Assume Entity A at the beginning of 2006 originates a five-year loan for $10,000 that has a stated interest rate of 7% to be received at the end of each year and a principal amount of $10,000 to be received at maturity. The original effective interest rate is also 7%. At the beginning of 2010, Entity A determines that there is objective evidence of impairment due to significant financial difficulties of the borrower and estimates that remaining estimated future cash flows are $5,000 instead of $10,700 (i.e., interest for 2010 of $700 and principal of $10,000). In this case, Entity A measures the impaired asset at the beginning of 2010 at the present value of the estimated future cash flows discounted using the original effective interest rate. Inserting the actual amounts gives $5,000 discounted for one year at 7%, or 5,000/1.07, which results in a present value of $4,673. Accordingly, the impairment loss to be recognized at the beginning of 2010 equals $5,327 (= 10,000 − 4,673). If Entity A reduces the asset directly rather than through an allowance account, it would make this journal entry:

Impairment loss	5,327	
Loans and receivables		5,327

After this, the statement of financial position will show an asset for the loan of $4,673.

IAS 39 requires accrual of interest on impaired loans and receivables at the original effective interest rate. In this case, therefore, Entity A would accrue interest at 7% on the beginning carrying amount of $4,673 (i.e., $327 during 2010). Assuming the expectations at the beginning of the year turn out to be accurate, Entity A would make these entries at the end of year 2010:

Cash	5,000	
Interest income		327
Loans and receivables		4,673

For individually significant loans and receivables and held-to-maturity investments, an entity first assesses whether any objective evidence of impairment exists at the individual asset level. If no objective evidence of impairment exists for an individual asset, the entity groups the assessed asset together with other assets that have similar credit-risk characteristics. It then assesses whether any objective evidence of impairment exists at the group level. This two-step approach of first assessing at an individual level and then at a group level applies because impairment that does not yet meet the threshold for recognition when an individual asset is assessed may be evident when that asset is grouped with other similar financial assets (i.e., losses have been incurred but not yet been reported at the individual asset level).

For loans and receivables and held-to-maturity investments that are not individually significant, an entity has a choice whether to do an individual evaluation of specific financial assets or a collective evaluation of groups with similar credit-risk characteristics. Irrespective of whether it makes an individual evaluation, an entity is required to do an assessment at the group level for assets that have not been individually identified as impaired.

Example

An entity may observe that there is an increased number of late payments in a group of mortgage loans that have not been individually identified as impaired. Based on this data, the entity may determine that it has objective evidence of impairment because its past experience indicates that an increase in the number of late payments results in a measurable decrease in the estimated future cash flows in the group. In this case, the entity should measure any resulting impairment loss based on historical loss experience for assets with similar credit-risk characteristics adjusted, if necessary, for changes in conditions that affect losses.

For available-for-sale financial assets, impaired assets continue to be measured at fair value. Any unrealized holding losses that had previously been recognized in other comprehensive income are reclassified as an impairment loss to profit or loss.

Example

Assume Entity A has an investment in a debt security that it has classified as available for sale and that it had initially acquired for $100,000. Due to a decrease in fair value, the current carrying amount of the investment is $80,100 and Entity A has an unrealized holding loss of $19,900 recognized in other comprehensive income. (An unrealized holding loss on an available-for-sale financial asset would be accumulated in other comprehensive income.) Due to significant financial difficulties of Entity A, the debt security has been downgraded by the rating agencies, and it appears likely that the issuer of the debt security will not be able to repay all principal and interest on the bond. Therefore, Entity A determines that there is objective evidence of impairment equal to the unrealized holding loss previously recognized in other comprehensive income. In this case, Entity A would make these entries:

Impairment loss	19,900	
Other comprehensive income		19,900

After this, the statement of financial position will still show an asset of $80,100, but the amount of the unrealized holding loss that had previously been deferred in other comprehensive income would now have been recognized as an impairment loss in profit or loss.

For investments in unquoted equity instruments that cannot be reliably measured at fair value, impaired assets are measured at the present value of the estimated future cash flows discounted using the current market rate of return for a similar financial asset. Any difference between the previous carrying amount and the new measurement of the impaired asset is recognized as an impairment loss in profit or loss.

Reversals of Impairment Losses

Impairment losses for loans and receivables, held-to-maturity investments, and investments in debt instruments classified as available for sale are reversed through profit or loss if the impairment losses decrease and the decrease can be objectively related to an event occurring after the impairment was recognized (e.g., an improvement in an external credit rating). In other words, a gain would be recognized in profit or loss to reverse some or all of the previously recognized impairment loss in these circumstances. Such reversals are limited to what the asset's amortized cost would have been had the impairment not been recognized at the date the impairment loss is reversed.

Impairment losses for investments in equity instruments are never reversed in profit or loss until the investments are sold. A reason for the difference in treatment of reversals between investments in equity and debt instruments is that it is more difficult to objectively distinguish reversals of impairment losses from other increases in fair value for investments in equity instruments.

In 2006, the International Financial Reporting Interpretations Committee (IFRIC) issued IFRIC 10, *Interim Financial Reporting and Impairment.* This Interpretation clarifies that an entity shall not reverse an impairment loss recognized in a previous interim period in respect of an investment in either an equity instrument or a financial asset carried at cost. This applies even if a loss would not have been recognized, or a smaller loss would have been recognized, had an impairment assessment been made only at a subsequent reporting date.

Recognition of Interest Income on Impaired Financial Assets

Interest income on financial assets that have been identified as impaired are recognized using the discount rate the entity used to measure the impairment loss, that is, the original effective interest rate for financial assets measured at amortized cost. This means that the reporting of interest income is not suspended when an impairment occurs. Instead the original effective interest rate is applied against the written-down amount to determine the amount of interest income that should be reported in the subsequent period.

Summary

Categories of financial assets	At what amount are impaired assets measured in the balance sheet?	What is the amount of the impairment loss recognized in profit or loss?	Would impairment losses ever be reversed through profit or loss while the impaired asset is still held?
Loans and receivables	Present value of estimated future cash flows discounted using the *original* effective interest rate	The difference between the previous carrying amount and the new carrying amount	Yes, if the amount of the impairment loss decreases and the decrease can be objectively related to an event occurring after impairment was recognized
Held-to-maturity investments	Present value of estimated future cash flows discounted using the *original* effective interest rate	The difference between the previous carrying amount and the new carrying amount	Yes, if the amount of the impairment loss decreases and the decrease can be objectively related to an event occurring after impairment was recognized
Available-for-sale financial assets: investments in debt instruments	Fair value	The amount of unrealized holding losses previously recognized in other comprehensive income	Yes, if the amount of the impairment loss decreases and the decrease can be objectively related to an event occurring after impairment was recognized
Available-for-sale financial assets: investments in equity instruments	Fair value	The amount of unrealized holding losses previously recognized in other comprehensive income	No
Investments in unquoted equity instruments that cannot be reliably measured at fair value	Present value of estimated future cash flows discounted using the *current* market rate of return for a similar financial asset	The difference between the previous carrying amount and the new carrying amount	No

CASE STUDY 11

This case illustrates how to account for impairment of loans and receivables.

Facts

Entity A has a loan asset whose initial carrying amount is $100,000 and whose effective interest rate is 8%. On January 1, 20X5, Entity A determines that the borrower will probably enter into bankruptcy, and expects to collect only $20,000 of remaining principal and interest cash flows. Entity A expects to recover this amount at the end of 20X5.

Required

Determine the amount that Entity A should record as an impairment loss during 20X5 and the amount of interest income that would be reported during 20X5, if any.

Solution

On January 1, 20X5, Entity A should recognize an impairment loss of $81,481. The present value of the estimated future cash flows is $18,519 (= $20,000/1.08). The difference between the previous carrying amount of the asset ($100,000) and the present value of the estimated future cash flows ($18,519) is $81,481. The journal entry is

Impairment loss	81,481	
Loans and receivables		81,481

During 20X5, Entity A should recognize interest income of $1,481. This is computed by multiplying the original effective interest rate with the carrying amount (= 8% × 18,519). The journal entry is

Loans and receivables	$1,481	
Interest income		$1,481

DERIVATIVES

Derivatives are contracts such as options, forwards, futures, and swaps. Because they are often entered into at no cost, many times derivatives were not recognized in financial statements prior to IAS 39. The potential gains and losses that may arise on settlement of derivatives, however, bear little relation to their initial cost and can be significant. To provide more useful information about derivatives, therefore, IAS 39 requires derivatives to be measured at fair value in the statement of financial position (unless, as already discussed, they are linked to and must be settled by an investment in an unquoted equity instrument that cannot be reliably measured at fair value).

Determining whether changes in fair value of a derivative should be recognized either in profit or loss or in other comprehensive income in part depends on whether the entity uses the derivative to speculate or offset risk. As a general rule, changes in fair value of a derivative are recognized in profit or loss. However, when the derivative is used to offset risk and special hedge accounting conditions are met, some or all changes in fair value are recognized in other comprehensive income.

To enable entities to properly identify derivatives, IAS 39 provides this definition:

Derivative. A financial instrument or other contract with all three of the following characteristics:

1. Its value changes in response to the change in a specified interest rate, financial instrument price, commodity price, foreign exchange rate, index of prices or rates, credit rating, credit index, or other variable (sometimes called the *"underlying"*).

   For instance, a call option that gives the holder a right to purchase a share for a fixed price increases in value when the price of that share increases. In that case, the share price is an underlying that affects the value of the option.

2. It requires no *initial net investment* or an initial net investment that is smaller than would be required for other types of contracts that would be expected to have a similar response to changes in market factors.

   For instance, a call option on a share can usually be purchased for an amount much smaller than what would be required to purchase the share itself.

3. It is *settled* at a future date.

   For instance, a call option on a share is settled on the future date on which the holder may exercise the call option to purchase the share for a fixed price. Under IAS 39, the expiration of an option is also considered to be a form of settlement.

Example

Assume Entity A enters into a call option contract on December 15, 20X5, that gives it a right, but not an obligation, to purchase 1,000 shares issued by Entity B on April 15, 20X6, at an exercise price (i.e., strike price) of $100 per share. The cost Entity A pays for each option is $3. Therefore, Entity A makes this journal entry on December 15, 20X5:

Derivative asset	3,000	
Cash		3,000
(To record the purchase of 1,000 call options for $3.00 per option)		

Market data suggests that Entity A could sell each option for $4. Therefore, on December 31, 20X5, Entity A makes these journal entries to recognize the increase in fair value:

Derivative asset	1,000	
Derivative gain		1,000
(To record the increase in fair value of $1.00 per option)		

On April 15, 20X6, the fair value of each option is $10. The share price on this date is $110. Since the share price is higher than the exercise price, Entity A decides to exercise the option by buying 1,000 shares for $100 per share. Under IAS 39, financial assets are initially recognized at fair value, so the shares are recognized at their fair value of $110 per share rather than the option exercise price of $100 per share. In addition, the option asset is derecognized. Entity A makes these journal entries:

Derivative asset	6,000	
Derivative gain		6,000

(To record the increase in fair value of $6.00 per option)

Investment in shares of Entity B	110,000	
Cash		100,000
Derivative asset		$10,000

(To record exercise and derecognition of call options and receipt of shares)

As discussed previously, there is an exception to the requirement to measure derivatives at fair value for derivatives that are linked to and must be settled by an investment in an unquoted equity instrument that cannot be reliably measured at fair value. For instance, an option to buy shares in a start-up entity that is not publicly traded may qualify for this exception. If the fair value cannot be reliably measured, such a derivative would be measured at cost instead of fair value (i.e., close to zero in many cases).

CASE STUDY 12

This case illustrates how to account for derivatives.

Facts

On January 1, 20X6, Entity A enters into a forward contract to purchase on January 1, 20X8, a specified number of barrels of oil at a fixed price. Entity A is speculating that the price of oil will increase and plans to net settle the contract if the price increases. Entity A does not pay anything to enter into the forward contract on January 1, 20X6. Entity A does not designate the forward contract as a hedging instrument. At the end of 20X6, the fair value of the forward contract has increased to $400,000. At the end of 20X7, the fair value of the forward contract has declined to $350,000.

Required

Prepare the appropriate journal entries on January 1, 20X6, December 31, 20X6, and December 31, 20X7.

Solution

The journal entries are

January 1, 20X6
No entry is required.

December 31, 20X6

Derivative asset	400,000	
Gain		400,000

December 31, 20X7

Loss	50,000	
Derivative asset		50,000

Embedded Derivatives

Sometimes derivatives are embedded in other types of contracts. For instance, one or more derivative features may be embedded in a loan, bond, share, lease, insurance contract, or purchase, or sale contract. When a derivative feature is embedded in a nonderivative contract, the derivative is referred to as an *embedded derivative* and the contract in which it is embedded is referred to as a *host contract.*

Example

An entity may issue a bond with interest or principal payments that are indexed to the price of gold (e.g., the interest payments increase and decrease with the price of gold). Such a bond is a contract that combines a host debt instrument and an embedded derivative on the price of gold.

To achieve consistency in the accounting for derivatives (whether embedded or not) and to prevent entities from circumventing the recognition and measurement requirements for derivatives merely by embedding them in other types of contracts, entities are required to identify any embedded derivatives and account for them separately from their hosts' contracts if these three conditions are met:

1. On a stand-alone basis, the embedded feature meets the definition of a derivative.
2. The combined (hybrid) contract is not measured at fair value with changes in fair value recognized in profit or loss (i.e., if the combined contract is already accounted for similar to a derivative, there is no need to separate the embedded feature).
3. The economic characteristics and risks of the embedded feature are *not* closely related to the economic characteristics and risks of the host contract.

When any of these three conditions is not met, the embedded derivative is not separated (i.e., only if all conditions are met is an embedded derivative separated). When all of these conditions are met, the embedded derivative is separated (i.e., bifurcated) from the host contract and accounted for like any other derivative. The host instrument is accounted for under the accounting requirements that apply to the host instrument as if it had no embedded derivative.

The flowchart illustrates these three conditions.

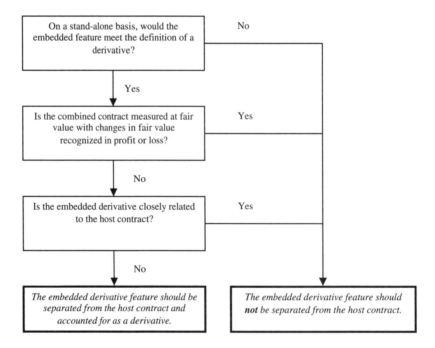

Example

A convertible bond is an instrument that combines both a host debt instrument and an equity conversion option (i.e., an option that enables the holder [investor] to convert the bond into a predetermined number of shares on specified conditions). In this case, the investor usually would be required to separate the equity conversion option from the investment in the host debt instrument and account for the equity conversion option separately as a derivative.

To help in the evaluation of whether an embedded feature is closely related—condition 3. above—IAS 39 provides examples of when the economic characteristics and risks would be considered to be closely related or not. Generally, for an embedded feature in a host debt contract to be considered closely related, the embedded feature must have primarily debt characteristics.

Example

Features that would be considered not closely related to the host contract are

- An equity conversion option embedded in a convertible bond instrument that allows the holder to convert the instrument into shares of the issuer
- A call option embedded in an investment in an equity instrument that allows the issuer to repurchase the instrument
- A bond that has a principal amount or interest payments that varies based on a commodity or equity price index
- A credit derivative embedded in a debt instrument that reduces the principal amount of the bond if a third party defaults
- Sales or purchase contracts that require payments in a foreign currency other than (a) the functional currency of any substantial party to the contract, (b) the currency in which the related good or service is routinely denominated (i.e., US dollars for crude oil), or (c) a currency that is commonly used in transactions in the local economic environment in which the transaction takes place

Features that would be considered closely related to a host contract are

- A call, put, or prepayment option embedded in a host debt contract (i.e., a loan) provided the exercise price is approximately equal to the contract's amortized cost
- An inflation index embedded in a host lease contract
- An embedded cap or floor on the level of interest paid or received on a variable debt instrument (provided the cap is equal to or above the initial market interest rate or the floor is equal to or below the initial market interest rate)

Example

Entity A invests $100,000 in a convertible debt instrument issued by Entity B that pays fixed interest of 7% and that can be converted into 1,000 shares in Entity B in five years at Entity A's option. Otherwise, the bond will pay $100,000 at maturity. Entity A classifies the investment as available for sale. In this case, Entity A would be required to separate the equity conversion option (the embedded derivative) from the host debt instrument because (1) the instrument contains an embedded derivative, (2) the instrument is not measured at fair value with changes in fair value recognized in profit or loss, and (3) equity and debt characteristics are not closely related. If the estimated fair value of the equity conversion option at initial recognition is $13,000, the journal entry on initial recognition is

Available-for-sale investment	87,000	
Derivative asset	13,000	
Cash		100,000

(To record the investment in the convertible debt instrument)

Subsequently, the equity conversion option is accounted for as a derivative at fair value with changes in fair value recognized in profit or loss, while the host debt instrument is accounted for as an available-for-sale financial asset at fair value with changes in fair value recognized in other comprehensive income. Moreover, the difference between the initial carrying amount and the principal amount of the available-for-sale financial asset (i.e., $13,000) is amortized to profit or loss using the effective interest rate method.

If an entity is required to separate an embedded derivative but is unable to reliably measure the embedded derivative, it is required to treat the entire hybrid instrument as a financial asset or financial liability that is held for trading (i.e., generally to measure it at fair value with changes in fair value recognized in profit or loss).

CASE STUDY 13

This case illustrates when to separate embedded derivatives.

Facts

Entity A is seeking to identify embedded derivatives that are required to be separated under IAS 39. It is considering whether these contracts contain embedded derivatives:

1. An investment in a bond whose interest payments are linked to the price of gold. The bond is classified as at fair value through profit or loss.
2. An investment in a bond whose interest payments are linked to the price of silver. The bond is classified as available for sale.
3. An investment in a convertible debt instrument that is classified as available for sale.
4. A lease contract that has a rent adjustment clause based on inflation.
5. An issued convertible debt instrument.

Required

Identify any embedded derivatives in these cases and, in each case, determine whether any identified embedded derivative requires separate accounting.

Solution

1. An investment in a bond whose interest payments are linked to the price of gold contains an embedded derivative on gold. However, because the bond is classified as at fair value through profit or loss, the embedded derivative should not be separated.
2. An investment in a bond whose interest payments are linked to the price of silver contains an embedded derivative on silver. Because the bond is not measured at fair value with changes in fair value recognized in profit or loss and a commodity derivative is not closely related to a host debt contract, the embedded derivative is separated and accounted for as a derivative.
3. An investment in a convertible debt instrument that is classified as available for sale contains an embedded equity conversion option. Because the bond is not measured at fair value with changes in fair value recognized in profit or loss and an equity conversion option is not closely related to a host debt contract, the embedded derivative is separated and accounted for as a derivative.
4. A lease contract that has a rent adjustment clause based on inflation contains an embedded derivative on inflation. However, the embedded derivative is not separated from the lease contract because a rent adjustment clause based on inflation is considered to be closely related to the host lease contract.
5. An issued convertible debt instrument contains an embedded equity conversion option. However, the equity conversion option generally is not accounted for as a derivative but is separated as an equity component in accordance with IAS 32 and accounted for as own equity.

Interpretation 9, *Reassessment of Embedded Derivatives,* of the International Financial Reporting Interpretations Committee clarifies that an entity is required to assess whether an embedded derivative is required to be separated and accounted for as a derivative when the entity first becomes a party to the contract that contains the potential embedded derivative. The entity is precluded from subsequently reassessing whether the contract contains an embedded derivative unless there is a change in the terms of the contract that significantly modifies the cash flows that otherwise would be required under the contract.

HEDGE ACCOUNTING

Hedging is a risk management technique that involves using one or more derivatives or other hedging instruments to offset changes in fair value or cash flows of one or more assets, liabilities, or future transactions. IAS 39 contains special accounting principles for hedging activities. When certain conditions are met, entities are permitted to depart from some of the ordinary accounting requirements and instead apply *hedge accounting* to assets and liabilities that form part of hedging relationships. These requirements are optional (i.e., entities are not required to apply hedge accounting unless they decide to do so). The effect of hedge accounting is that gains and losses on the hedging instrument and the hedged item are recognized in the same periods (i.e., gains and losses are matched).

Hedging Relationships

A *hedging relationship* has two components:

1. A *hedging instrument.* A hedging instrument is a derivative or, for a hedge of the risk of changes in foreign currency exchange rates, a nonderivative financial asset or nonderivative financial liability. To be designated as a hedging instrument, the fair value or cash flows of

the hedging instrument should be expected to offset changes in the fair value or cash flows of the hedged item. In addition, the hedging instrument must be with an external party (i.e., an internal derivative with another division does not qualify as a hedging instrument) and not be a written option (or net written option).

2. A *hedged item*. A hedged item is an asset, liability, firm commitment, highly probable forecast transaction, or net investment in a foreign operation. To be designated as a hedged item, the designated hedged item should expose the entity to risk of changes in fair value or future cash flows.

IAS 39 identifies three types of hedging relationships:

1. Fair value hedges
2. Cash flow hedges
3. Hedges of a net investment in a foreign operation

Accounting Treatment

Hedge accounting links the accounting for (1) the hedging instrument and (2) the hedged item to allow offsetting changes in fair value or cash flows to be recognized in the financial statements in the same time periods. Generally, hedge accounting involves either one of these two accounting treatments:

1. Changes in fair value of the *hedged item* are recognized in the current period to offset the recognition of changes in the fair value of the hedging instrument. This is the accounting treatment for fair value hedges.
2. Changes in fair value of the hedging instrument are recognized in other comprehensive income to the extent that the hedge is effective and released to profit or loss in the time periods in which the hedged item impacts profit or loss. This is the accounting treatment for cash flow hedges and hedges of net investments in foreign operations.

PRACTICAL INSIGHT

Hedge accounting is not always necessary to reflect the effect of hedging activities in the financial statements. When consistent accounting principles apply to offsetting positions (e.g., when both the hedging instrument and the hedged item are accounted for at fair value or at amortized cost), there is no need for an entity to apply hedge accounting to achieve consistent accounting for the offsetting positions.

Hedge Accounting Conditions

As discussed, hedge accounting is optional and allows entities to defer or accelerate the recognition of gains and losses under otherwise applicable accounting requirements. To prevent abuse, therefore, IAS 39 limits the use of hedge accounting to situations where special hedge accounting conditions are met. To qualify for hedge accounting, the hedging relationship should meet three conditions related to the designation, documentation, measurement, and effectiveness of the hedging relationships. These three conditions are

1. There is formal designation and documentation of the hedging relationship and the entity's risk management objective and strategy for undertaking the hedge. Hedge accounting is permitted only from the date such designation and documentation is in place.
2. The hedging relationship is effective, which means
   a. The hedge is expected to be highly effective in achieving offsetting changes in fair value or cash flows attributable to the hedged risk ("prospective" effectiveness).
   b. The effectiveness of the hedge can be measured reliably.
   c. The hedge is assessed on an ongoing basis and determined actually to have been highly effective throughout the financial reporting periods for which the hedge was designated ("retrospective" effectiveness).

3. For cash flow hedges of forecast transactions, the hedged forecast transaction must be highly probable and must present an exposure to variations in cash flows that could ultimately affect profit or loss.

Example

The designation and documentation of a hedging relationship should include identification of

- The hedging instrument(s)
- The hedged item(s) or transaction(s)
- The nature of the risk(s) being hedged
- How the entity will assess the hedging instrument's effectiveness in offsetting the exposure to changes in the hedged item's fair value or the hedged transaction's cash flows attributable to the hedged risk

CASE STUDY 14

This case considers the reasons and conditions for hedge accounting.

Required

1. Describe the three types of hedging relationships specified by IAS 39.
2. Discuss in what circumstances entities may want to apply hedge accounting.
3. Discuss the conditions for hedge accounting.

Solution

1. IAS 39 identifies three types of hedging relationships:

   a. *Fair value hedges* are hedges of the exposure to changes in fair value of a recognized asset or liability or an unrecognized firm commitment that is attributable to a particular risk and that could affect profit or loss. Under fair value hedge accounting, if the hedged item is otherwise measured at cost or amortized cost, the measurement of the hedged item is adjusted for changes in its fair value attributable to the hedged risk. These changes are recognized in profit or loss. If the hedged item is an available-for-sale financial asset, changes in fair value that would otherwise have been included in other comprehensive income are recognized in profit or loss.

   b. *Cash flow hedges* are hedges of the exposure to variability in cash flows that is attributable to a particular risk associated with a recognized asset or liability or a highly probable forecast transaction and could affect profit or loss. Under cash flow hedge accounting, changes in the fair value of the hedging instrument attributable to the hedged risk are recognized in other comprehensive income to the extent the hedge is effective (rather than being recognized immediately in profit or loss).

   c. Hedges of net investments in foreign operations are accounted for like cash flow hedges.

2. Entities may want to use hedge accounting to avoid mismatches in the recognition of gains and losses on related transactions. When an entity uses a derivative (or other instrument measured at fair value) to hedge the value of an asset or liability measured at cost or amortized cost or not recognized at all, accounting that is not reflective of the entity's financial position and financial performance may result because of the different measurement bases used for the hedging instrument and the hedged item. The normally applicable accounting requirements would include the changes in fair value of a derivative in profit or loss but not the changes in fair value of the hedged item in profit or loss. In addition, when an entity uses a derivative (or other instrument measured at fair value) to hedge a future expected transaction, the entity would like to defer the recognition of the change in fair value of the derivative until the future transaction affects profit or loss. Otherwise, the changes in fair value of a derivative hedging instrument would be recognized in profit or loss without a corresponding offset associated with the hedged item.

3. The hedge accounting conditions are

   a. There is formal designation and documentation of the hedging relationship and the entity's risk management objective and strategy for undertaking the hedge. Hedge accounting is permitted only from the date such designation and documentation is in place.

   b. The hedge is expected to be highly effective in achieving offsetting changes in fair value or cash flows attributable to the hedged risk.

c. The effectiveness of the hedge can be measured reliably.

d. The hedge is assessed on an ongoing basis and determined actually to have been highly effective throughout the financial reporting periods for which the hedge was designated.

e. For cash flow hedges, a hedged forecast transaction must be highly probable and must present an exposure to variations in cash flows that could ultimately affect profit or loss.

Fair Value Hedge

A *fair value hedge* is a hedge of the exposure to changes in fair value of a recognized asset or liability or an unrecognized firm commitment that is attributable to a particular risk and that could affect profit or loss. (A firm commitment is a binding agreement for the exchange of a specified quantity of resources at a specified price on a specified future date or dates.)

Fair value hedge accounting involves this accounting:

- The hedging instrument is measured at fair value with changes in fair value recognized in profit or loss.
- If the hedged item is otherwise measured at cost or amortized cost (e.g., because it is classified as a loan or receivable), the measurement of the hedged item is adjusted for changes in its fair value attributable to the hedged risk. These changes are recognized in profit or loss.
- If the hedged item is an available-for-sale financial asset, changes in fair value that would otherwise have been recognized in other comprehensive income are recognized in profit or loss.

Under fair value hedge accounting, changes in the fair value of the hedging instrument and of the hedged item are recognized in profit or loss at the same time. The result is that there will be no (net) impact on profit or loss of the hedging instrument and the hedged item if the hedge is fully effective, because changes in fair value will offset each other. If the hedge is not 100% effective (i.e., the changes in fair value do not fully offset), such ineffectiveness is automatically reflected in profit or loss.

Example

Fair value hedges include

- A hedge of the exposure to changes in the fair value of a fixed interest rate loan due to changes in market interest rates. Such a hedge could be entered into by either the borrower or the lender.
- A hedge of the exposure to changes in the fair value of an available-for-sale investment.
- A hedge of the exposure to changes in the fair value of a nonfinancial asset (e.g., inventory).
- A hedge of the exposure to changes in the fair value of a firm commitment to purchase or sell a nonfinancial item (e.g., a contract to purchase or sell gold for a fixed price on a future date).

Example

On January 1, 20X5, Entity A purchases a five-year bond that has a principal amount of $100,000 and pays annually a fixed interest rate of 5% per year (i.e., $5,000 per year). Entity A classifies the bond as an available-for-sale financial asset. Current market interest rates for similar five-year bonds are also 5% such that the fair value of the bond and the carrying amount of the bond on the acquisition date is equal to its principal amount of $100,000.

Because the interest rate is fixed, Entity A is exposed to the risk of declines in fair value of the bond. If market interest rates increase above 5%, for example, the fair value of the bond will decrease below $100,000. This is because the bond would pay a lower fixed interest rate than equivalent alternative investments available in the market (i.e., the present value of the principal and interest cash flows discounted using market interest rates would be less than the principal amount of the bond).

To eliminate the risk of declines in fair value due to increases in market interest rates, Entity A enters into a derivative to hedge (offset) this risk. More specifically, on January 1, 20X5, Entity A enters into an interest rate swap to exchange the fixed interest rate payments it receives on the bond for floating interest rate payments. If the derivative hedging instrument is effective, any declines in the fair value of the bond should be offset by opposite increases in the fair value of the derivative instrument. Entity A designates and documents the swap as a hedging instrument of the bond.

On entering into the swap on January 1, 20X5, the swap has a net fair value of zero. (In practice, swaps usually are entered into at a zero fair value. This is achieved by setting the interest payments that will be paid and received such that the present value of the expected floating interest payments Entity A will receive exactly equals the present value of the fixed interest payments Entity A will pay because of the swap agreement.) Therefore, no journal entry is required on this date.

At the end of 20X5, the bond has accrued interest of $5,000. Entity A makes this journal entry:

Interest receivable	5,000	
Interest income		5,000

In addition, market interest rates have increased to 6%, such that the fair value of the bond has decreased to $96,535. Because the bond is classified as available for sale, the decrease in fair value would normally have been recognized in other comprehensive income rather than in profit or loss. However, since the bond is classified as a hedged item in a fair value hedge of the exposure to interest rate risk, this change in fair value of the bond is instead recognized in profit or loss:

Hedging loss (hedged item)	3,465	
Available-for-sale financial asset		3,465

At the same time, Entity A determines that the fair value of the swap has increased by $3,465 to $3,465. Since the swap is a derivative, it is measured at fair value with changes in fair value recognized in profit or loss. Therefore, Entity A makes this journal entry:

Swap asset	3,465	
Hedging gain (hedging instrument)		3,465

Since the changes in fair value of the hedged item and the hedging instrument exactly offset, the hedge is 100% effective, and the net effect on profit or loss is zero.

CASE STUDY 15

This case illustrates the accounting for a fair value hedge.

Facts

Entity A has originated a 5% fixed rate loan asset that is measured at amortized cost ($100,000). Because Entity A is considering whether to securitize the loan asset (i.e., to sell it in a securitization transaction), it wants to eliminate the risk of changes in the fair value of the loan asset. Thus, on January 1, 20X6, Entity A enters into a pay-fixed, receive-floating interest rate swap to convert the fixed interest receipts into floating interest receipts and thereby offset the exposure to changes in fair value. Entity A designates the swap as a hedging instrument in a fair value hedge of the loan asset.

Market interest rates increase. At the end of the year, Entity A receives $5,000 in interest income on the loan and $200 in net interest payments on the swap. The change in the fair value of the interest rate swap is an increase of $1,300. At the same time, the fair value of the loan asset decreases by $1,300.

Required

Prepare the appropriate journal entries at the end of the year. Assume that all conditions for hedge accounting are met.

Solution

Cash	5,000	
Interest income		5,000
(To record interest income on the loan)		

Cash	200	
Interest income		200
(To record the net interest settlement of the swap)		

Derivative	1,300	
Hedging gain		1,300
(To record the increase in the fair value of the swap)		

Hedging loss	1,300	
Loan asset		1,300

(To record the decrease in the fair value of the loan asset attributable to the hedged risk)

Cash Flow Hedge

A *cash flow hedge* is a hedge of the exposure to variability in cash flows that

- Is attributable to a particular risk associated with a recognized asset or liability or a highly probable forecast transaction (A forecast transaction is an uncommitted but anticipated future transaction).
- Could affect profit or loss.

Cash flow hedge accounting involves this accounting:

- Changes in the fair value of the hedging instrument attributable to the hedged risk are recognized in other comprehensive income to the extent that the hedge is effective (rather than being recognized immediately in profit or loss).
- The accounting for the hedged item is not adjusted.
- If a hedge of a forecast transaction subsequently results in the recognition of a nonfinancial asset or nonfinancial liability (or becomes a firm commitment for which fair value hedge accounting is applied), the entity has an accounting policy choice of whether to reclassify the associated gains and losses that were recognized in other comprehensive income to profit or loss as a reclassification adjustment in the same period or periods during which the asset acquired or the liability assumed affects profit or loss or to remove the associated gains and losses that were recognized in other comprehensive income and include them in the initial cost or other carrying amount of the asset or liability (a so-called basis adjustment).
- If a hedge of a forecast transaction subsequently results in the recognition of a financial asset or financial liability, the gains and losses recognized in other comprehensive income remain there.
- When the hedged item affects profit or loss (e.g., through depreciation or amortization), any corresponding amount previously recognized in other comprehensive income is reclassified to profit or loss ("recycled").

To the extent the cash flow hedge is not fully effective, the ineffective portion of the change in fair value of the derivative is recognized immediately in profit or loss.

Example

Cash flow hedges include

- A hedge of the exposure to variable interest cash flows on a bond that pays floating interest payments
- A hedge of the cash flows from a forecast sale of an asset
- A hedge of the foreign currency exposure associated with a firm commitment to purchase or sell a nonfinancial item

Example

Entity A has the euro as its functional currency. It expects to purchase a machine for $10,000 on October 31, 20X6. Accordingly, it is exposed to the risk of increases in the dollar rate. If the dollar rate increases before the purchase takes place, the entity will have to pay more euros to obtain the $10,000 that it will have to pay for the machine. To offset the risk of increases in the dollar rate, the entity enters into a forward contract on April 30, 20X6, to purchase $10,000 in six months for a fixed amount (€8,000). Entity A designates the forward contract as a hedging instrument in a cash flow hedge of its exposure to increases in the dollar rate. At inception, the forward contract has a fair value of zero, so no journal entry is required.

On July 31 the dollar has appreciated, such that $10,000 for delivery on October 31, 20X6, costs €9,000 on the market. Therefore, the forward contract has increased in fair value to €1,000 (i.e., the difference between the committed price of €8,000 and the current price of €9,000 (ignoring, for simplicity, the effect of differences in interest rates between the two currencies). Entity A still expects to purchase the machine for $10,000, so it concludes that the hedge is 100% effective. Because the hedge is fully effective, the entire change in the fair value of the hedging instrument is recognized in other comprehensive income. Entity A makes this entry:

Forward asset	1,000	
Other comprehensive income		1,000

On October 31, 20X6, the dollar rate has further increased, such that $10,000 cost €9,500 in the spot market. Therefore, the fair value of the forward contract has increased to €1,500 (i.e., the difference between the committed price of €8,000 and the spot price of €9,500). It still expects to purchase the machine for $10,000 and makes this journal entry:

Forward asset	500	
Other comprehensive income		500

The forward contract is settled and Entity A makes this entry:

Cash	1,500	
Forward asset		1,500

Entity A purchases the machine for $10,000 (€9,500) and makes this journal entry:

Machine	9,500	
Accounts Payable		9,500

Depending on Entity A's accounting policy, the deferred gain or loss recognized in other comprehensive income of €1,500 should either (1) remain there and be released as the machine is depreciated or otherwise affects profit or loss or (2) be deducted from the initial carrying amount of the machine. Assuming the latter treatment, Entity A would make this journal entry:

Other comprehensive income	1,500	
Machine		1,500

The net effect of the cash flow hedge is to lock in a price of €8,000 for the machine.

Example

At the beginning of 20X0, Entity B issues a 10-year liability with a principal amount of $100,000 for $100,000 (i.e., at par). The bond pays floating interest that resets each year as market interest rates change. Entity B measures the liability at amortized cost ($100,000). Because the interest rate regularly resets to market interest rates, the fair value of the liability remains approximately constant irrespective of how market interest rates change. However, Entity B wishes to convert the floating rate payments to fixed rate payments in order to hedge its exposure to changes in cash flows due to changes in market interest rates over the life of the liability.

To hedge the exposure, Entity B enters into a five-year interest rate swap under which the entity pays fixed rate payments (5%) and in return receives floating rate payments that exactly offset the floating rate payments it makes on the liability. Entity B designates and documents the swap as a cash flow hedge of its exposure to variable interest payments on the bond. On entering into the interest rate swap, it has a fair value of zero. The effect of that interest rate swap is to offset the exposure to changes in interest cash flows to be paid on the liability. In effect, the interest rate swap converts the liability's floating rate payments into fixed rate payments, thereby eliminating the entity's exposure to changes in cash flows attributable to changes in interest rates resulting from the liability.

At the end of 20X5, the bond has accrued interest of $6,000. Entity B makes this journal entry:

Interest expense	6,000	
Bond interest payable		6,000

At the same time, a net interest payment of $1,000 has accrued under the swap for the year. Therefore, Entity A makes this journal entry:

Swap interest receivable	1,000	
Interest expense		1,000

The net effect on profit or loss is fixed net interest expense of $5,000 (= 6,000 − 1,000).

Because the swap is a derivative, it is measured at fair value. Entity B determines that the fair value of the swap (excluding accrued interest) has increased by $5,200. As the swap is designated as a hedging instrument in a cash flow hedge, the change in fair value is not recognized in profit or loss but in other comprehensive income to the extent that the swap is effective. In this case, Entity B determines that the swap is 100% effective. Therefore, Entity B makes this journal entry:

Swap asset	5,200	
Equity (hedging reserve)		5,200

Because the fair value of the swap will converge to zero by its maturity, the hedging reserve for the swap will also converge to zero by its maturity to the extent the hedge remains in place and is effective.

CASE STUDY 16

This case illustrates the accounting for a cash flow hedge.

Facts

Entity A is a producer of widgets. To hedge the risk of declines in the price of 100 widgets that it expects to sell on December 31, 20X8, Entity A on January 1, 20X7, enters into a net-settled forward contract on 100 widgets for delivery on December 31, 20X8. During 20X7, the change in the fair value of the forward contract is a decrease of $8,000. During 20X8, the change in the fair value of the forward contract is an increase of $2,000. On December 31, 20X8, Entity A settles the forward contract by paying $6,000. At the same time, it sells 100 widgets to customers for $93,000.

Required

Prepare the appropriate journal entries on January 1, 20X7, December 31, 20X7, and December 31, 20X8. Assume that all conditions for hedge accounting are met and that the hedging relationship is fully effective (100%).

Solution

January 1, 20X7
No entry required.

December 31, 20X7

Other comprehensive income	8,000	
Derivative liability		8,000

(To record the decrease in fair value of the hedging instrument)

December 31, 20X8

Derivative liability	2,000	
Other comprehensive income		2,000

(To record the increase in fair value of the hedging instrument)

Derivative liability	6,000	
Cash		6,000

(To record the settlement of the hedging instrument)

Cash	93,000	
Other comprehensive income		6,000
Sales revenue		87,000

(To record the sale and the associated amount recognized in other comprehensive income related to the hedge of the sale)

Hedge of a Net Investment in a Foreign Operation

IAS 21 defines a foreign operation as an entity that is a subsidiary, associate, joint venture, or branch of a reporting entity, the activities of which are based or conducted in a country or currency other than those of the reporting entity. A net investment in a foreign operation is the amount of the reporting entity's interest in the net assets of that operation. A hedge of a net investment in a foreign operation is accounted for like a cash flow hedge. In a hedge of a net investment, therefore, changes in fair value of the hedging instrument are recognized in other comprehensive income to the extent that the hedge is effective (rather than being recognized immediately in profit or loss) and recognized in profit or loss on the disposal of the net investment.

Example

To hedge its net investment in a foreign operation that has the Japanese yen as its functional currency, Entity A borrows ¥100,000,000. Assuming all hedge accounting conditions are met, Entity A may designate its borrowing as a hedging instrument in a hedge of the net investment. As a result, foreign currency gains and losses on the borrowing that would otherwise have been included in profit or loss under IAS 21 would instead be recognized in other comprehensive income to the extent that the hedge is effective until the disposal of the net investment.

Hedge Effectiveness Assessment and Measurement

As mentioned, two of the conditions for hedge accounting are that the hedge is

- Expected to be highly effective in achieving offsetting changes in fair value or cash flows during the period for which the hedge is designated (*prospective effectiveness*)
- Determined actually to have been highly effective throughout the reporting period for which the hedge was designated (*retrospective effectiveness*)

Generally, a hedge is viewed as being highly effective if actual results are within a range of 80% and 125%.

Example

If actual results are such that the gain on the hedging instrument is $90 and the loss on the hedged item is $100, the degree of offset is 90% (= 90/100), or 111% (= 100/90). The hedge would be considered to be highly effective because the degree of offset is between 80% and 125%.

Hedge effectiveness is important not only as a condition for hedge accounting, but also because the measurement of hedge effectiveness determines how much ineffectiveness will be reflected in profit or loss. To the extent that the changes do not fully offset, such differences reflect ineffectiveness that generally should be included in profit or loss. Such ineffectiveness may exist even though a hedge is determined to be highly effective based on the prospective or retrospective hedge effectiveness assessment for purposes of continued qualification for hedge accounting.

Example

If, for a fair value hedge, the gain on the hedging instrument is $90 and the loss on the hedged item is $100, a net loss of $10 would be included in profit or loss.

For a qualifying cash flow hedge, ineffectiveness is included in profit or loss only to the extent that the cumulative gain or loss on the hedging instrument exceeds the cumulative gain or loss on the hedged item since the inception of the hedging relationship (overhedging). If the cumulative gain or loss on the hedged item exceeds the cumulative gain or loss on the hedging instrument (underhedging), no ineffectiveness is reported. This is because—for a cash flow hedge—the hedged item is a future transaction that does not qualify for accounting recognition.

Example

If, for a cash flow hedge, the gain on the hedging instrument in the first period after designation is $490 and the loss on the hedged item is $100, no ineffectiveness is included in profit or loss, because the cumulative gain or loss on the hedged item exceeds the cumulative gain or loss on the hedging instrument ("underhedging").

If instead the loss on the hedging instrument in the first period after designation is $100 and the gain on the hedged item is $90, a loss of $10 is included in profit or loss due to ineffectiveness, because the cumulative gain or loss on the hedging instrument exceeds the cumulative gain or loss on the hedged item ("overhedging").

Discontinuation of Hedge Accounting

In any of these circumstances, an entity should discontinue hedge accounting prospectively:

- The hedging instrument expires or is sold, terminated, or exercised.
- The hedge no longer meets the hedge accounting conditions.
- The entity revokes the hedge designation.
- A hedged forecasted transaction is no longer expected to occur.

For discontinued fair value hedges, any previous hedge accounting adjustment to the carrying amount of hedged interest-bearing assets or liabilities, are amortized over the remaining maturity of those assets and liabilities. Other hedge accounting adjustments to the carrying amount of hedged items remain in the carrying amount.

For discontinued cash flow hedges, hedging gains and losses that have been recognized in other comprehensive income remain in equity until the hedged item affects profit or loss unless

- A forecast transaction is no longer expected to occur, in which case the deferred gain or loss is recognized immediately in profit or loss.
- A forecast transaction results in the recognition of a nonfinancial asset or nonfinancial liability and the entity has made an accounting policy choice to include those deferred gains and losses in the initial carrying amount of the nonfinancial asset or nonfinancial liability.

Macrohedging

One issue that has been the subject of considerable debate is the hedge accounting treatment of derivatives that are used to manage interest rate risk on a net, portfolio basis ("macrohedging"). For instance, banks, as part of their asset-liability management activities, for risk management purposes may wish to offset risk exposures on a net basis. However, IAS 39 does not permit an entity to designate a net position (i.e., a net amount of assets less liabilities or a net amount of cash inflows less cash outflows) as a hedged item because of difficulties associated with assigning hedge accounting adjustments to individual hedged assets or liabilities and measuring effectiveness.

PRACTICAL INSIGHT

It is often possible to qualify for cash flow hedge accounting for hedges of a net exposure by designating as the hedged item the exposure to changes in cash flows associated with a forecast bottom level portion of cash inflows or cash outflows in a particular future time period. For instance, if the entity forecasts cash inflows of $100 and cash outflows of $120 on a macro basis, it may designate a cash flow hedge for the interest rate risk associated with the refinancing or reinvestment of the first $20 of cash outflows in a particular period. In that case, as long as the entity has at least $20 of cash outflows in that period, the hedge may be considered effective.

In 2004, the IASB issued amendments to IAS 39 to relax the hedge accounting requirements associated with portfolio hedges of interest rate risk on a fair value hedge accounting basis. Those amendments provide a methodology for how to achieve fair value hedge accounting for portfolio hedges of interest rate risk.

RECENT AMENDMENTS TO IAS 39

Reclassification of Financial Assets

The amendment on reclassification of financial assets is a response to calls from the investor community to create a "level playing field" with US GAAP regarding the ability of an entity to reclassify financial assets. The changes to IAS 39 permit an entity to reclassify nonderivative financial assets out of the "fair value through profit or loss" (FVTPL) and "available-for-sale" (AFS) categories in limited circumstances.

Financial liabilities, derivatives, and financial assets that are designated as at FVTPL on initial recognition under the "fair value option" cannot be reclassified.

The amendments therefore only permit reclassification of debt and equity financial assets subject to meeting specified criteria.

The amendments do not permit reclassification into FVTPL after initial recognition.

Reclassification out of FVTPL and AFS. A financial asset within the scope of these amendments can only be reclassified out of FVTPL or AFS if specified criteria are met.

A debt instrument classified as AFS that would have met the definition of L&R (if it had not been designated as AFS) may be reclassified to the L&R category if the entity has the intention and ability to hold the financial asset for the foreseeable future or until maturity.

Any other debt instrument, or any equity instrument, may be reclassified from FVTPL to AFS, or from FVTPL to HTM (in the case of debt instruments only), if the financial asset is no longer held for the purpose of selling in the near term—but only in "rare" circumstances. In its press release the IASB mentioned that market conditions in the third quarter of 2008 would qualify as a "rare" circumstance.

It should be noted that the amendments do not refer to the reclassification of AFS debt instruments to HTM because IAS 39 already permitted such reclassifications.

Measurement at the reclassification date. All reclassifications must be made at the fair value of the financial asset at the date of reclassification. Any previously recognized gains or losses cannot be reversed. The fair value at the date of reclassification becomes the new cost or amortized cost of the financial asset, as applicable.

Effective date. These amendments are effective from July 1, 2008 as follows:

- For reclassifications made before November 1, 2008, an entity can reclassify a financial asset with effect from July 1, 2008, or any date thereafter until October 31, 2008.
- Reclassifications made on or after November 1, 2008, will take effect only from the date when the reclassification is made.

Amendment to IAS 39 and IFRIC 9: Clarification Regarding Reassessment of Embedded Derivatives

Following the amendments to IAS 39 in October 2008 relating to reclassifications out of the FVTPL category for certain held-for-trading financial assets in limited circumstances, IFRIC 9, *Reassessment of Embedded Derivatives,* and IAS 39 were amended whereby an entity is required to assess whether an embedded derivative is closely related to the host contract at the date of reclassification. The amendment is effective for periods commencing on or after June 30, 2009.

Under the revised IFRIC 9, reassessment of embedded derivatives is required in the following two circumstances:

1. When there is a change in the terms of the contract that significantly modifies the cash flows that otherwise would be required under the contract.
2. When there is a reclassification of a financial asset out of the FVTPL category.

Amendments to IAS 39—Eligible Hedged Items

The amendments to IAS 39 provide clarification on two issues in relation to hedge accounting. The amendments are effective for periods on or after July 1, 2009.

Identifying inflation as a hedged risk. Inflation may only be hedged in instances where changes in inflation are a contractually specified component of cash flows of a recognized financial instrument and such component is separately identifiable and reliably measurable.

Example

A company issues an inflation-linked debt. In this case, since inflation is a separately identifiable and reliably measurable component of cash flows, such cash flow exposure to changes in future inflation may be cash flow hedged.

A company issues a fixed-rate debt. In this case, the company cannot designate an inflation component in a fair value hedge since inflation in this case is not a separately identifiable and reliably measurable component of cash flows of the instrument. In this case however, the risk-free or benchmark interest rate portion of the fair value of the instrument will normally be separately identifiable and reliably measurable and hence may be hedged.

Hedging with options. IAS 39 permits an entity to designate purchased options as a hedging instrument. The amendments clarify that the intrinsic value, not the time value, of an option reflects a one-sided risk and therefore if an option is designated as a hedge in its entirety, the time value component would lead to hedge ineffectiveness. An entity may choose to exclude time value at the time of hedge designation in order to improve hedge effectiveness. In such circumstances, changes in the time value of the option will be recognized immediately in profit or loss.

EXTRACTS FROM PUBLISHED FINANCIAL STATEMENTS

UNILEVER GROUP, Year Ended December 31, 2009

Notes to the Financial Statements

Financial assets

The classification of financial assets is determined at initial recognition depending on the purpose for which they were acquired. Any impairment is recognized in the income statement as it arises.

Held-to-maturity investments

Held-to-maturity investments are assets with set cash flows and fixed maturities which Unilever intends to hold to maturity. They are held at cost plus interest using the effective interest method, less any impairments.

Loans and receivables

Loans and receivables have set payments and are not quoted in an active market. They arise when the Group provides money, goods or services. Loans and receivables are included in the balance sheet at amortized cost.

Short-term loans and receivables are initially measured at original invoice amount less any impairments.

Financial asset at fair value through profit or loss

A financial asset is in this category if it is intended to be sold in the short term. They are current assets if they are expected to be realized within 12 months. Transaction costs related to the purchase of the assets are expensed as incurred. Derivatives are classified here unless they are designated as hedges. Gains and losses arising from changes in value are included in the income statement.

Available-for-sale financial assets

Available-for-sale financial assets are assets that are designated in this category or not classified in any of the other categories. They are noncurrent assets unless the Group intends to dispose of them within 12 months. Changes in value are recognized in equity until the investment is sold or impaired, when they are included in the income statement.

Interest on available-for-sale securities is calculated using the effective interest rate method and recognized within other income. Dividends on equity investments are also recognized within other income.

Financial liabilities

Financial liabilities are recognized initially at fair value, net of transaction costs. They are subsequently held at amortized cost unless they are part of a fair value hedge. Any difference between the amount on initial recognition and the redemption value is recognized in the income statement using the effective interest method.

Short-term financial liabilities are measured at original invoice amount.

Derivatives

Derivatives are measured on the balance sheet at fair value and are used primarily to manage the risks of changes in exchange and interest rates. The Group uses foreign exchange forward contracts, interest rate swap contracts and forward rate agreements to hedge these exposures. The Group also uses commodity contracts to hedge some raw materials. Contracts that can be settled in cash are treated as financial instruments. The Group does not use derivative financial instruments for speculative purposes.

Changes in the fair value of derivatives that do not qualify for hedge accounting are recognized in the income statement as they arise.

Cash flow hedges

Changes in the value of derivatives used as hedges of future cash flows are recognized in equity with any ineffective portion recognized in the income statement. If the cash flow hedge results in the recognition of a nonfinancial asset or a liability, the gain or loss on the derivative is included in the initial measurement of that asset or liability. For other cash flow hedges, amounts deferred in equity are taken to the income statement when the hedged item affects profit or loss.

When a hedging instrument no longer qualifies for hedge accounting, any cumulative gain or loss is retained in equity until the forecasted transaction occurs. If a hedged transaction is no longer expected to occur, the cumulative gain or loss is transferred to the income statement.

Fair value hedges

In an effective fair value hedge, the hedged item is adjusted for changes in fair value, with the corresponding entry in the income statement. Gains and losses on the hedging instrument are recognized in the income statement. In a fully effective hedge the adjustments to the income statement are of equal and opposite value. For nonderivatives only the foreign currency element can be a hedging instrument.

Net investment hedges

Net investment hedges are hedges of exchange risks from investments in foreign subsidiaries. Gains and losses are recognized in equity. The accumulated gains and losses are taken to the income statement when the foreign operation is sold or partially disposed.

Valuation principles

The fair values of quoted investments are based on current bid prices. For listed securities where the market is not liquid, and for unlisted securities, the Group uses valuation techniques. These include the use of recent arm's length transactions, reference to other instruments that are substantially the same and discounted cash flow calculations.

Impairment of financial instruments

At each balance sheet date the Group assesses whether there is evidence that financial assets are impaired. A significant or prolonged fall in value below cost is considered in determining whether an asset is impaired. For available-for-sale financial assets, the cumulative loss is removed from equity and recognized in the income statement. Any subsequent reversals of impairment losses on available-for-sale equity instruments are not recognized in the income statement.

MULTIPLE-CHOICE QUESTIONS

1. The scope of IAS 39 includes all of the following items except
  (a) Financial instruments that meet the definition of a financial asset.
  (b) Financial instruments that meet the definition of a financial liability.
  (c) Financial instruments issued by the entity that meet the definition of an equity instrument.
  (d) Contracts to buy or sell nonfinancial items that can be settled net.

2. Which of the following is **not** a category of financial assets defined in IAS 39?
  (a) Financial assets at fair value through profit or loss.
  (b) Available-for-sale financial assets.
  (c) Held-for-sale investments.
  (d) Loans and receivables.

3. All of the following are characteristics of financial assets classified as held-to-maturity investments except
  (a) They have fixed or determinable payments and a fixed maturity.
  (b) The holder can recover substantially all of its investment (unless there has been credit deterioration).
  (c) They are quoted in an active market.
  (d) The holder has a demonstrated positive intention and ability to hold them to maturity.

4. Which of the following items is **not** precluded from classification as a held-to-maturity investment?
  (a) An investment in an unquoted debt instrument.
  (b) An investment in a quoted equity instrument.
  (c) A quoted derivative financial asset.
  (d) An investment in a quoted debt instrument.

5. All of the following are characteristics of financial assets classified as loan and receivables except
  (a) They have fixed or determinable payments.
  (b) The holder can recover substantially all of its investment (unless there has been credit deterioration).
  (c) They are not quoted in an active market.
  (d) The holder has a demonstrated positive intention and ability to hold them to maturity.

6. What is the principle for recognition of a financial asset or a financial liability in IAS 39?

  (a) A financial asset is recognized when, and only when, it is probable that future economic benefits will flow to the entity and the cost or value of the instrument can be measured reliably.
  (b) A financial asset is recognized when, and only when, the entity obtains control of the instrument and has the ability to dispose of the financial asset independent of the actions of others.
  (c) A financial asset is recognized when, and only when, the entity obtains the risks and rewards of ownership of the financial asset and has the ability to dispose of the financial asset.
  (d) A financial asset is recognized when, and only when, the entity becomes a party to the contractual provisions of the instrument.

7. In which of the following circumstances is derecognition of a financial asset **not** appropriate?
  (a) The contractual rights to the cash flows of the financial assets have expired.
  (b) The financial asset has been transferred and substantially all the risks and rewards of ownership of the transferred asset have also been transferred.
  (c) The financial asset has been transferred and the entity has retained substantially all the risks and rewards of ownership of the transferred asset.
  (d) The financial asset has been transferred and the entity has neither retained nor transferred substantially all the risks and rewards of ownership of the transferred asset. In addition, the entity has lost control of the transferred asset.

8. Which of the following transfers of financial assets qualify for derecognition?
  (a) A sale of a financial asset where the entity retains an option to buy the asset back at its current fair value on the repurchase date.
  (b) A sale of a financial asset where the entity agrees to repurchase the asset in one year for a fixed price plus interest.
  (c) A sale of a portfolio of short-term accounts receivables where the entity guarantees to compensate the buyer for any losses in the portfolio.
  (d) A loan of a security to another entity (i.e., a securities lending transaction).

9. Which of the following is **not** a relevant consideration when evaluating whether to derecognize a financial liability?
  (a) Whether the obligation has been discharged.
  (b) Whether the obligation has been canceled.

   (c) Whether the obligation has expired.

   (d) Whether substantially all the risks and rewards of the obligation have been transferred.

10. At what amount is a financial asset or financial liability measured on initial recognition?

   (a) The consideration paid or received for the financial asset or financial liability.

   (b) Acquisition cost. Acquisition cost is the consideration paid or received plus any directly attributable transaction costs to the acquisition or issuance of the financial asset or financial liability.

   (c) Fair value. For items that are not measured at fair value through profit or loss, transaction costs are also included in the initial measurement.

   (d) Zero.

11. In addition to financial assets at fair value through profit or loss, which of the following categories of financial assets is measured at fair value in the statement of financial position?

   (a) Available-for-sale financial assets.

   (b) Held-to-maturity investments.

   (c) Loans and receivables.

   (d) Investments in unquoted equity instruments.

12. What is the best evidence of the fair value of a financial instrument?

   (a) Its cost, including transaction costs directly attributable to the purchase, origination, or issuance of the financial instrument.

   (b) Its estimated value determined using discounted cash flow techniques, option pricing models, or other valuation techniques.

   (c) Its quoted price, if an active market exists for the financial instrument.

   (d) The present value of the contractual cash flows less impairment.

13. Is there any exception to the requirement to measure at fair value, financial assets classified as at fair value through profit or loss or available for sale?

   (a) No. Such assets are always measured at fair value.

   (b) Yes. If the fair value of such assets increases above cost, the resulting unrealized holding gains are not recognized but deferred until realized.

   (c) Yes. If the entity has the positive intention and ability to hold assets classified in those categories to maturity, they are measured at amortized cost.

   (d) Yes. Investments in unquoted equity instruments that cannot be reliably measured at fair value (or derivatives that are

linked to and must be settled in such unquoted equity instruments) are measured at cost.

14. What is the effective interest rate of a bond or other debt instrument measured at amortized cost?

   (a) The stated coupon rate of the debt instrument.

   (b) The interest rate currently charged by the entity or by others for similar debt instruments (i.e., similar remaining maturity, cash flow pattern, currency, credit risk, collateral, and interest basis).

   (c) The interest rate that exactly discounts estimated future cash payments or receipts through the expected life of the debt instrument or, when appropriate, a shorter period to the net carrying amount of the instrument.

   (d) The basic, risk-free interest rate that is derived from observable government bond prices.

15. Which of the following is not objective evidence of impairment of a financial asset?

   (a) Significant financial difficulty of the issuer or obligor.

   (b) A decline in the fair value of the asset below its previous carrying amount.

   (c) A breach of contract, such as a default or delinquency in interest or principal payments.

   (d) Observable data indicating that there is a measurable decrease in the estimated future cash flows from a group of financial assets although the decrease cannot yet be associated with any individual financial asset.

16. Under IAS 39, all of the following are characteristics of a derivative except

   (a) It is acquired or incurred by the entity for the purpose of generating a profit from short-term fluctuations in market factors.

   (b) Its value changes in response to the change in a specified underlying (e.g., interest rate, financial instrument price, commodity price, foreign exchange rate, etc.).

   (c) It requires no initial investment or an initial net investment that is smaller than would be required for other types of contracts that would be expected to have a similar response to changes in market factors.

   (d) It is settled at a future date.

17. Under IAS 39, is a derivative (e.g., an equity conversion option) that is embedded in another contract (e.g., a convertible bond) accounted for separately from that other contract?

(a) Yes. IAS 39 requires all derivatives (both freestanding and embedded) to be accounted for as derivatives.

(b) No. IAS 39 precludes entities from splitting financial instruments and accounting for the components separately.

(c) It depends. IAS 39 requires embedded derivatives to be accounted for separately as derivatives if, and only if, the entity has embedded the derivative in order to avoid derivatives accounting and has no substantive business purpose for embedding the derivative.

(d) It depends. IAS 39 requires embedded derivatives to be accounted for separately if, and only if, the economic characteristics and risks of the embedded derivative and the host contract are not closely related and the combined contract is not measured at fair value with changes in fair value recognized in profit or loss.

18. Which of the following is **not** a condition for hedge accounting?

(a) Formal designation and documentation of the hedging relationship and the entity's risk management objective and strategy for undertaking the hedge at inception of the hedging relationship.

(b) The hedge is expected to be highly effective in achieving offsetting changes in fair value or cash flows attributable to the hedged risk, the effectiveness of the hedge can be reliably measured, and the hedge is assessed on an ongoing basis and determined actually to have been effective.

(c) For cash flow hedges, a forecast transaction must be highly probable and must present an exposure to variations in cash flows that could ultimately affect profit or loss.

(d) The hedge is expected to reduce the entity's net exposure to the hedged risk, and the hedge is determined actually to have reduced the net entity-wide exposure to the hedged risk.

19. What is the accounting treatment of the hedging instrument and the hedged item under fair value hedge accounting?

(a) The hedging instrument is measured at fair value, and the hedged item is measured at fair value with respect to the hedged risk. Changes in fair value are recognized in profit or loss.

(b) The hedging instrument is measured at fair value, and the hedged item is measured at fair value with respect to the hedged risk. Changes in fair value are recognized in other comprehensive income to the extent that the hedge is effective.

(c) The hedging instrument is measured at fair value with changes in fair value recognized in other comprehensive income to the extent that the hedge is effective. The accounting for the hedged item is not adjusted.

(d) The hedging instrument is accounted for in accordance with the accounting requirements for the hedged item (i.e., at fair value, cost or amortized cost, as applicable), if the hedge is effective.

20. What is the accounting treatment of the hedging instrument and the hedged item under cash flow hedge accounting?

(a) The hedged item and hedging instrument are both measured at fair value with respect to the hedged risk, and changes in fair value are recognized in profit or loss.

(b) The hedged item and hedging instrument are both measured at fair value with respect to the hedged risk, and changes in fair value are recognized in other comprehensive income.

(c) The hedging instrument is measured at fair value, with changes in fair value recognized in other comprehensive income to the extent that the hedge is effective. The accounting for the hedged item is not adjusted.

(d) The hedging instrument is accounted for in accordance with the accounting requirements for the hedged item (i.e., at fair value, cost or amortized cost, as applicable), if the hedge is effective.

Chapter 25

EARNINGS PER SHARE (IAS 33)

BACKGROUND AND INTRODUCTION

Earnings per share (EPS) is simply a profit figure divided by a number of shares. The Standard concentrates on determining the number of shares to be used in the computation and gives limited guidance on the computation of the profit figure. The consistent use of the price/earnings ratio (P/E) by users of financial statements as an indicator of corporate performance led to the need for a Standard on earnings per share, which is a key component of the P/E ratio.

However, any inconsistency of accounting policies between entities will result in a lack of comparability of the earnings per share figure. IAS 33 enhances financial reporting by ensuring that there is at least consistency in the calculation of the denominator in the earnings per share statistic.

IAS 33 applies to

- Entities whose ordinary shares or potential ordinary shares are publicly traded or that are in the process of issuing shares in the public markets
- Entities that voluntarily choose to disclose

When both parent and group information are presented together, only the earnings per share for the group are required to be disclosed. If the parent discloses earnings per share information in its separate accounts, then this information should not be disclosed in the consolidated financial statements.

DEFINITIONS OF KEY TERMS
(in accordance with IAS 33)

Ordinary share. An equity instrument that is subordinate to all other classes of equity instrument.

Potential ordinary share. A financial instrument or other contract that may entitle its holder to ordinary shares. Examples are options, warrants, and financial liabilities, or equity instruments that are convertible into ordinary shares.

Basic earnings per share. Calculated by dividing the profit or loss attributable to the ordinary shareholders by the weighted-average number of ordinary shares outstanding during the accounting period.

Dilution. The reduction in earnings per share or increase in the loss per share resulting from the assumption that potential ordinary shares will materialize.

Antidilution. An increase in earnings per share or a reduction in loss per share resulting from the assumption that potential ordinary shares will materialize.

ORDINARY SHARES

An "ordinary share" participates in profit for the period only after other types of shares, such as preferred shares, have participated.

An entity may have more than one class of ordinary shares. For example, Entity A has two classes of "common" shares, Class X and Class Y. If Class X is entitled to a fixed dividend of $10 per share plus a dividend of 5%, and Class Y is entitled to a dividend of 5% only, then Class X shares are not ordinary shares, as the fixed dividend per share ($10) creates a preference over Class Y shares, and hence Class Y shares are subordinate to Class X shares.

PRESENTATION OF EARNINGS PER SHARE

An entity should present on the face of the statement of comprehensive income both basic and diluted earnings per share for profit or loss from continuing operations attributable to the ordinary equity holders of the parent and for profit or loss attributable to the ordinary equity holders of the parent for each class of ordinary shares with different rights.

Basic and diluted earnings per share must be presented with equal prominence for all periods presented, even if the amounts are negative. If a discontinued operation is reported, then basic and diluted amounts per share for the discontinued operation must be disclosed on the face of the statement of comprehensive income or in the notes.

BASIC EARNINGS PER SHARE

Basic earnings per share =

$$\frac{\text{Net profit or loss attributable to ordinary equity holder}}{\text{Weighted-average number of ordinary shares outstanding during the period}}$$

Earnings are calculated

- As amounts attributable to the ordinary equity holders in respect of profit or loss from continuing operations and net profit or loss
- After all expenses including taxes and minority interests
- After cumulative preference dividend *for period* whether declared or not
- After noncumulative preference dividend declared *for period*
- After other adjustments relating to preference shares

(Cumulative preference dividends for the prior periods are ignored.)

Basic earnings per share. The number of ordinary shares is the weighted-average number of ordinary shares outstanding during the period.

- The number of ordinary shares at the beginning of the period is added to the number of shares issued during the period less the number of shares bought back in the period.
- Shares issued and bought back are multiplied by a time weighting factor dependent on when the event took place.
- Shares are included from the date the consideration is receivable.
- Partly paid shares are included as fractional shares to the extent that they are entitled to participate in dividends during the period relative to a fully paid ordinary share. To the extent that partly paid shares are not entitled to participate in dividends during the period, they are treated as the equivalent of warrants or options.
- Contingently issuable shares are included when the conditions have been satisfied.
- Ordinary shares issued as part of a business combination are included from the acquisition date.

IAS 33 includes guidance on appropriate recognition dates for shares issued in various circumstances (IAS 33, paragraph 21).

An entity may increase or reduce its ordinary shares without a change in its resources. Examples of this are bonus issues, stock dividends, share splits (i.e., where shares are issued for no consideration), and reverse share splits (consolidation of shares). In these cases, the weighted-average number of shares is adjusted in line with the transaction as if the event had occurred at the beginning of the period. All periods presented should be adjusted for such events.

If the bonus issue, stock dividend, and other similar events occurred after the reporting period but before the financial statements are authorized, then the earnings per share calculations should reflect these changes. This applies also to prior periods and to diluted earnings per share.

Basic and diluted earnings per share are also adjusted for

- The effects of errors and adjustments resulting from changes in accounting policies, accounted for retrospectively but not adjusted for
- Changes in assumptions used in earnings per share calculations or for conversion of potential ordinary shares into ordinary shares (IAS 33, paragraphs 64–65)

CASE STUDY 1

Facts

Entity A has a profit after tax of $15 million for the year ended December 31, 20X9. These appropriations of profit have not been included in this amount:

		$m
(1)	Arrears of cumulative preference dividend for 2 years ended December 31, 20X9	4
(2)	Ordinary dividends	5
(3)	Preference share premium payable on redemption—appropriation of profit	1
(4)	Exceptional profit (net of tax)	4

These share transactions occurred during the year ended December 31, 20X9. The entity had 3 million ordinary shares of $1 outstanding at January 1, 20X9:

Date	Ordinary shares issued/purchased	
January 1	250,000	Issued at $5 per share–$1 paid to date: entitled to participate in dividends to the extent paid up
April 1	600,000	Full market price $3 per share issue
July 1	(400,000)	Purchase of own shares at $3.5 per share

Required

Calculate basic earnings per share.

Solution

	$m
Profit after tax	15
Plus: exceptional profit	4
Less: preference dividend (current year)	(2)
Preference share appropriation	(1)
Profit available for ordinary shareholders	16

Date	Number of shares ('000)	Weighting (months)	Weighted-average ('000)
1/1/X9	3,000	1	3,000
1/1/X9	(250 × 1/5)	1	50
4/1/X9	600	9/12	450
7/1/X9	(400)	6/12	(200)
			3,300

	('000)		
Basic earnings per share 16,000/3,300		=	$4.85

CASE STUDY 2

Facts

A had a two-for-one share split on December 31, 20X9, in which two shares were awarded for every share held, and in 20X8 there was a reported basic earnings per share of $3.30.

Required

Show the effect on the basic earnings per share calculated in Case Study 1 and the previous year's basic earnings per share. State the effect on your answer if the share split had occurred on February 1, 20X0, before the approval of the financial statements for the year ended December 31 20X9.

Solution

20X8:	Basic earnings per share	$3.30 \times 1/3$	= $1.10
20X9:	Basic earnings per share	$\dfrac{16,000}{(3,300 + 3,300 \times 2)}$ =	$1.62

If the share split had occurred on February 1, 20X0, then this would still have been taken into account in the calculation, as such events after the reporting period should be adjusted retrospectively (IAS 33, paragraph 64).

PRACTICAL INSIGHT
Clariant Ltd, a Swiss entity, adds a note to its financial statements that a proposal is to be made at the Annual General Meeting to increase its share capital by means of a rights issue. The disclosure follows the requirements in IAS 33 (paragraph 70d) to disclose potential ordinary share transactions that occur after the reporting period.

RIGHTS ISSUES

Enterprises may issue capital instruments that give existing shareholders the right to purchase ordinary shares at below-market price. These "rights issues" have the same effect as issuing shares at full market price and then immediately making a bonus issue to the shareholder. In order to reflect the bonus element, the number to be used in calculating basic earnings per share, for all periods prior to the rights issue, is the number of ordinary shares outstanding prior to the rights issue (time apportioned if necessary) and multiplied by this factor:

$$\frac{\text{Fair value per share immediately prior to the exercise of rights}}{\text{Theoretical ex-rights fair value per share}}$$

The *theoretical ex-rights fair value* is the sum of the market value of the shares outstanding prior to the exercise of rights and the proceeds of the rights issue, divided by the total shares in issue after the exercise of the rights.

After the exercise of rights issue, the number of shares in issue is weighted for the proportion of the year remaining, as would happen with an issue at full market price. Hence the bonus element of the rights issue is dealt with by applying the aforementioned factor prior to the issue, and the full market price element is dealt with by time apportionment/weighting after the issue.

CASE STUDY 3

Facts

Entity B

Net profit available for ordinary shareholders year:

December 31, 20X8	2,100
December 31, 20X9	3,500

The ordinary shares in issue on January 1, 20X9, were 800,000.

Entity B offered existing shareholders a rights issue of one for five shares at a price of $6 per share to be exercised on April 1, 20X9. The market value of Entity B's shares on that date was $10 per share.

Required

Calculate the basic earnings per share for the years 20X8 and 20X9.

Solution

Calculation of factor

Theoretical ex-rights value per share is $\dfrac{(800,000 \times \$10 + 160,000 \times \$6)}{960,000}$ = $9.33

Adjustment factor is $\dfrac{\$10.00}{9.33}$ = 1.07

Basic earnings per share 20X9 = $\dfrac{3,500}{[800 \times 3/12 \times 1.07 + (960 \times 9/12)]}$ = $3.75

Basic earnings per share 20X8 = $\dfrac{2,100}{800 \times 1.07}$ = $2.45

DILUTED EARNINGS PER SHARE

Diluted earnings per share is an important statistic for analysts and potential investors as it shows the effect on earnings per share of all dilutive potential ordinary shares that were outstanding during the year. Potential ordinary shares include preference shares convertible into ordinary shares, share warrants, and options, shares that may be issued to employees as part of their remuneration or as part of other share purchase plans, and contingently issuable shares, say on the purchase of an enterprise.

When calculating diluted earnings per share, there will be adjustments to both the "earnings" and to the "per share" part of the statistic. If the potential ordinary share has given rise to any income or expense in the period, then its effect on profit has to be reversed, as the assumption is that it has now been converted into ordinary shares that would not have given rise to that income or expense.

Thus the net profit attributable to ordinary shareholders is adjusted for the *after-tax* effects of

1. Preference dividends on convertible preference shares.
2. Interest on capital instruments such as convertible bonds.
3. Other changes in income or expense. For example, the changes in profit in points (a) and (b) above may mean that employees may receive an increase or decrease in their profits share due to an employee profit-sharing plan. This must be taken into account in calculating the net profits used in the diluted earnings per share calculation.

Dilutive potential shares are deemed to be converted at the beginning of the period or the date of issue, if a new potential share (dilutive) was issued during the period.

The conversion rate or exercise price should reflect the most favorable rate or price to the potential ordinary shareholder.

Potential ordinary shares that have lapsed or been cancelled are included for the time they were outstanding. Potential ordinary shares that were converted during the period are included in

1. Diluted earnings per share up to the date of conversion.
2. The weighted-average number of ordinary shares after the date of conversion. This latter figure will be then used in calculating both basic earnings per share and diluted earnings per share.

Contingently issuable ordinary shares are included in the calculation of diluted earnings per share from the beginning of the period or the date of the contingency agreement (if later) if the conditions have been met. In the basic earnings per share calculation, these shares are included from the date the conditions are met, not the beginning of the period/date for contingency agreement.

Potential ordinary shares issued by a subsidiary, associate, or joint venture of the enterprise can have a dilutive effect on the earnings per share of the reporting enterprise and must be reflected in the calculation. For example, a subsidiary may have share warrants that can be exercised to purchase shares in the subsidiary. Exercise of the share warrants may change the minority interest in the subsidiary and hence the profit attributable to the minority interest. Thus the consolidated profit attributable to the ordinary shareholders will change with the resultant effect on the diluted earnings per share calculation.

CASE STUDY 4

Facts

Entity A has made a net profit attributable to ordinary shareholders of $2 million for the year to December 31, 20X7.

Ten million ordinary shares were outstanding for the entire year. Since January 20X6 there has been $800,000 of 5% convertible loan stock in issue. The terms of conversion are for every $100 nominal value of stock.

On	June 30, 20X7	120 ordinary shares
	June 30, 20X8	150 ordinary shares
	June 30, 20X9	140 ordinary shares

Assume that interest on loan stock is allowable for tax relief at 30%.

Required

Calculate basic and diluted earnings per share. (Assume that no conversion takes place in the year.)

Solution

Basic earnings per share is

$$\frac{\$'000}{\frac{2,000}{10,000}} = 20c \text{ per share}$$

Diluted earnings per share

	$'000
Effect on earnings	
Profit for basic earnings per share	2,000
Add interest saved	40
Less tax relief	(12)
Adjusted earnings	2,028
Number of ordinary shares if loan stock was converted:	
Basic earnings per share—ordinary shares	10,000
On conversion, most favorable terms [800,000 × (150/100)]	1,200
	11,200

Diluted earnings per share

$$\frac{2,028}{11,200} = 18.1c$$

Share options and other share purchase arrangements are dilutive to the extent that they result in the issue of ordinary shares for less than fair value. IAS 33 wants to reflect this fact by requiring this treatment:

1. The options/share purchase arrangements are deemed to have been exercised at the exercise price.
2. The "deemed" proceeds are then converted into a number of shares at fair value.
3. The difference between the shares deemed to have been issued and the shares that would have been issued at full market price is the dilution and are shares issued for "no consideration."

This method is often called the treasury stock method.

CASE STUDY 5

Facts

Net profit for year 20X9	$ 3	million
Ordinary shares outstanding during 20X9	$10	million
Average fair value of one ordinary share: year 20X9	$ 8	
Shares under option during 20X9, convertible at $6 per share	2	million

Required

Calculate basic and diluted earnings per share.

Solution

Basic earnings per share

$$\frac{\$3 \text{ million}}{10 \text{ million}} = 30c$$

Diluted earnings per share

Shares under option	2 million
Number of shares that would have been issued at fair value if converted (2 million × $6 = $12 million): $12 million/$8	= (1.5 million)
Therefore shares for "no consideration" (2 million – 1.5 million)	(0.5 million)

Diluted earnings per share

$$\frac{\$3 \text{ million}}{10.5 \text{ million}} = 28.6c \text{ per shar}$$

Any potential ordinary shares that expired or were cancelled are included in the diluted earnings per share calculation for the period in which they were outstanding. Thus share options that lapsed during the period would be included in the calculation and weighted for the period they were outstanding.

Potential ordinary shares are dilutive if their deemed conversion to ordinary shares would decrease net profit per share from *continuing ordinary operations.* Thus the "control number" is the net profit from continuing operations. It is the effect of potential ordinary shares on this "number" that determines whether the issue of potential ordinary shares is dilutive or antidilutive.

The effects of all antidilutive potential ordinary shares are ignored in the calculation of diluted earnings per share. Each issue of potential ordinary shares is considered individually in the order most dilutive to least dilutive. Net profit from continuing operations is the net profit from ordinary activities after deducting preference dividends and after excluding items relating to discontinued operations.

CASE STUDY 6

Facts

Extracts from group financial statements of AB, a public limited company, year ended April 30, 20X7.

	$m
Profit from continuing operations	35,000
Loss on discontinued operations (tax relief $500 million)	(1,500)
Income tax	(7,500)
Minority interest (loss on discontinued activities $500 million)	(1,500)
Preference share appropriation—dividend (2 years)	(30)
Preference share appropriation—other	(5)
Share capital at April 30, 20X9	
Ordinary shares of $1	1,000
5% Convertible preference shares	300

Other Information

1. On January 1, 20X7, 48 million ordinary shares were issued on the acquisition of CD PLC at a valuation of $190 million. If CD earns cumulative profits in excess of $8,000 million up to April 30, 20X8, an additional 10 million shares are issuable to the vendors. If the profits do not reach that amount, then only 2 million shares are issuable on April 30, 20X8.
2. The profits for the three months to April 30, 20X7, are $1,200 million.
3. On May 11, 20X7, there was a bonus issue of one for four ordinary shares. The financial statements are made up to April 30, 20X7, and had not yet been published.
4. The company has a share option scheme. The directors exercised options relating to 18 million shares on February 28, 20X7, at a price of $3 per share. In addition, options were granted during the year on March 1, 20X7, to subscribe for 10 million shares at $2 each. The fair value of the shares on March 1, 20X7, was $4, and the average fair value for the year was $5.
5. The preference shares are convertible into ordinary shares on May 1, 20X8, on the basis of one ordinary share for every two preference shares or on May 1, 20X9, on the basis of one ordinary share for every four preference shares.
6. There is a profit share scheme in operation whereby employees receive a bonus of 5% of profits from continuing operations after tax and preference dividends.
7. XY PLC, a 100% owned subsidiary of AB, has in issue 9% convertible bonds of $200 million that can be converted into one ordinary share of AB for every $10 worth of bonds. Income tax is levied at 33%.

Required

Calculate basic and diluted earnings per share.

Solution

Earnings per share

Earnings: basic earnings per share

	$m
Profit after tax	26,000
Minority interest	(1,500)
Preference dividend (1 year)	(15)
Appropriation	(5)
Share capital	24,480

	Shares (m)	Weight	
May 1, 20X0 (1000 – 48 – 18)	934	1	934
January 1, 20X7	48	4/12	16
February 28, 20X7	18	2/12	3
			953
Bonus issue 1 for 4			238
			1,191

Basic earnings per share: 24,480 ÷ 1,191 = $20.6

Earnings: diluted earnings per share

Profit per basic earnings per share	24,480
Interest (18 – tax 6)	12
Preference shares (15 + 5)	20
Employee remuneration (5% of 32 previously)	(1.6)
	24,510.4
Ordinary shares (ahead)	1,370
Diluted earnings per share	$ 17.89

Dilutive/antidilutive computations

Net profit from continuing operations	35,000
Taxation	(8,000)
Minority interest	(2,000)
Preference dividend, etc.	
(5% × 300 = 15 plus appropriation 5)	(20)
	24,980

	Profit	Shares	EPS
Net profit from continuing activities	24,980	1,191	20.97
Options 18m × [(5 – 3) ÷ 5] × (10 ÷ 12)		6	
10m × [(5 – 2) ÷ 5] × (2 ÷ 12)		1	
	24,980	1,198	20.85
Contingently issuable		2	
	24,980	1,200	20.81
Preference shares	20	150	
	25,000	1,350	18.52
Bonds ($18m × .67)	12	20	
	25,012	1,370	18.25

Therefore, all issues are dilutive and are ranked from the most to the least dilutive.

Explanatory Notes

1. *Contingently issuable shares.* The target profit is $8,000 million and the total to date is only $1,200 million. Therefore, the number of shares to be included is the number issuable if the current year-end were the end of the contingency period. If this were the case, then the profits had not reached the target and only 2 million shares were issuable.
2. *Bonus issue.* Even though the bonus issue was after the period end, the financial statements have not yet been published. This fact is taken into account in calculating basic and diluted earnings per share.
3. *Share options.* The options exercised are included in basic earnings per share (and thus diluted earnings per share) from the date exercised. Up to the date exercised (February 28, 20X7), they are included in diluted earnings per share only. In calculating the shares issued for no consideration, the average fair value is used, not the current value of the share.
4. *Preference shares.* The most advantageous conversion rate is used, which is one ordinary share for every two preference shares.
5. The amount of the profit receivable by employees will change when the profit adjustments regarding the preference shares and the convertible bonds are used in the calculation of diluted earnings per share.

CASE STUDY 7

Facts

An entity issues 4 million convertible bonds at January 1, 20X9. The bonds mature in three years and are issued at their face value of $10. The bonds attract interest arrears. Each bond can be converted into two ordinary shares. The company can settle the principal amount of the bonds in ordinary shares or in cash.

When the bonds are issued, the interest rate for a similar debt without the conversion rights is 10%. At the issue date the market price of an ordinary share is $4. Ignore taxation. The company is likely to settle the contract by issuing shares.

Profit attributable to ordinary shareholders to December 31, 20X9	$33 million
Ordinary shares outstanding	10 million
Allocation of proceeds of bond	
Liability	$30 million
Equity	$10 million
Total	$40 million

Required

Calculate basic and diluted earnings per share for the year to December 31, 20X9.

Solution

Basic EPS
$$\frac{\$33 \text{ million}}{10 \text{ million}} = \$3.3 \text{ per share}$$

Diluted EPS
$$\frac{\$(33 + \text{interest } 10\% \text{ of } \$30 \text{ million})}{10 \text{ million} + 8 \text{ million}} = \frac{\$36 \text{ million}}{18 \text{ million}} = \$2$$

In June 2008, the IASB issued an Exposure Draft of proposed amendments to IAS 33, *Earnings Per Share*, as part of the short-term convergence project between the IASB and FASB. These amendments propose to simplify the calculation of earnings per share (EPS) and to eliminate differences between IFRS and US accounting standards. They provide a principle to determine which instruments should be included in the EPS calculation; clarify the EPS calculation for particular instruments, such as contracts to sell or repurchase an entity's own shares and participating instruments; and simplify the EPS calculation for instruments that are accounted for at fair value through profit or loss. In April 2009, the IASB considered comments on the Exposure Draft, however, it has paused the project with no current date for resumption.

PRESENTATION

An entity whose securities are traded on a securities exchange (or that is in process of public issuance) must present, on the face of the statement of comprehensive income, basic and diluted earnings per share for [IAS 33.66]:

- Profit or loss from continuing operations attributable to the ordinary equity holders of the parent entity.
- Profit or loss attributable to the ordinary equity holders of the parent entity, for the period, for each class of ordinary shares that has a different right to share in profit for the period.

Basic and diluted earnings per share must be presented with equal prominence for all periods presented [IAS 33.66].

Basic and diluted EPS must be presented even if the amounts are negative (that is, a loss per share) [IAS 33.69].

If an entity reports a discontinued operation, basic and diluted amounts per share must be disclosed for the discontinued operation either on the face of the statement of comprehensive income or in the notes to the financial statements [IAS 33.68].

DISCLOSURES

- Basic and diluted earnings per share should be presented on the face of the statement of comprehensive income for each class of ordinary shares.
- Basic and diluted earnings per share are presented with equal prominence.
- If an entity reports a discontinued operation, it should report the basic and diluted amounts per share for the discontinued operation.
- An entity should report basic and diluted earnings per share even if it is a loss per share.
- The amounts used as the numerators in calculating basic and diluted EPS, and reconciliation of those amounts to profit or loss attributable to the parent for the period.
- The weighted-average number of ordinary shares used as the denominator in calculating basic and diluted EPS, and a reconciliation of these denominators to each other.

- Instruments (including contingently issuable shares) that could potentially dilute basic earnings per share in the future, but were not included in the calculation of diluted EPS because they are antidilutive for the period(s) presented.
- A description of those ordinary share transactions or potential ordinary share transactions that occur after the reporting period and that would have changed significantly the number of ordinary shares or potential ordinary shares outstanding at the end of the period if those transactions had occurred before the end of the reporting period. Examples include issues and redemptions of ordinary shares, warrants, and options.

EXTRACTS FROM PUBLISHED FINANCIAL STATEMENTS

J. SAINSBURY PLC Financial Statements to March 21, 2009

Earnings per share

Basic earnings per share is calculated by dividing the earnings attributable to ordinary shareholders by the weighted-average number of ordinary shares in issue during the year, excluding those held by the Employee Share Ownership Plan trusts, which are treated as cancelled.

For diluted earnings per share, the weighted-average number of ordinary shares in issue is adjusted to assume conversion of all potential dilutive ordinary shares. These represent share options granted to employees where the exercise price is less than the average market price of the Company's ordinary shares during the year.

Underlying earnings per share is provided by excluding the effect of any gain or loss on the sale of properties, impairment of goodwill, investment property fair value movements, financing fair value movements, and one-off items that are material and infrequent in nature.

This alternative measure of earnings per share is presented to reflect the Group's underlying trading performance.

All operations are continuing for the periods presented.

	2009 million	2008 million
Weighted-average number of shares in issue	1,738.5	1,718.7
Weighted-average number of dilutive share options	24.7	48.5
Total number of shares for calculating diluted earnings per share	1,763.2	1,767.2

	£m	£m
Profit for the financial year	289	329
(Less)/add: profit on sale of properties, net of tax	(36)	(7)
Investment property fair value movements, net of tax	124	--
Financing fair value movements, net of tax	8	3
Costs relating to approach from Delta Two, net of tax	--	5
Fair value gain on other financial asset, net of tax	--	(20)
Costs associated with Office of Fair Trading dairy inquiry, net of tax	--	27
Underlying profit after tax	385	337

	pence per share	pence per share
Basic earnings	16.6	19.1
Diluted earnings	16.4	18.6
Underlying basic earnings	22.1	19.6
Underlying diluted earnings	21.8	19.1

UNILEVER GROUP, Annual Report, 2009

Notes to the consolidated financial statements Unilever Group

Combined earnings per share

Combined earnings per share	€ *2009*	€ *2008*	€ *2007*
From continuing operations			
Basic earnings per share	**1.21**	1.79	1.32
Diluted earnings per share	**1.17**	1.73	1.28
From discontinued operations			
Basic earnings per share	--	--	0.03
Diluted earnings per share	--	--	0.03
From total operations			
Basic earnings per share	**1.21**	1.79	1.35
Diluted earnings per share	**1.17**	1.73	1.31
From total operations before RDIs (see below)			
Basic earnings per share	**1.33**	1.43	1.42
Diluted earnings per share	**1.29**	1.38	1.37

Basis of calculation

The calculations of combined earnings per share are based on the net profit attributable to ordinary capital divided by the average number of share units representing the combined ordinary share capital of NV and PLC in issue during the year, after deducting shares held as treasury stock.

The calculations of diluted earnings per share are based on: (1) conversion into PLC ordinary shares of those shares in a group company which are convertible in the year 2038, as described in Corporate governance on page 58; and (2) the effect of share-based compensation plans, details of which are set out in note 29 on pages 126 to 127.

Calculation of average number of share units	*Millions of share units* *2009*	*2008*	*2007*
Average number of shares			
NV	**1,714.7**	1,714.7	1,714.7
PLC	**1,310.2**	1,310.2	1,310.2
Less shares held by employee share, trusts, and companies	**(228.6)**	(215.3)	(150.3)
Combined average number of share units for all bases except diluted earnings per share	**2,796.3**	2,809.6	2,874.6
Add shares issuable in 2038	**70.9**	70.9	70.9
Add dilutive effect of share-based compensation plans	**22.8**	25.4	30.6
Adjusted combined average number of share units for diluted earnings per share basis	**2,890.0**	2,905.9	2,976.1

Calculation of earnings	*€ million* *2009*	*€ million* *2008*	*€ million* *2007*
For earnings per share from total operations:			
Net profit attributable to ordinary capital for total operations	**3,370**	5,027	3,888
For earnings per share from continuing operations:			
Net profit from continuing operations	**3,659**	5,285	4,056
Minority interest in continuing operations	**(289)**	(258)	(248)
Net profit attributable to ordinary capital for continuing operations	**3,370**	5,027	3,808
For earnings per share before restructuring, business disposals, and other one-off items (RDIs)			
Net profit attributable to ordinary capital for total operations	**3,370**	5,027	3,888
RDIs included in operating profit	**868**	(1,269)	569
Tax impact of RDIs in operating profit	**(249)**	333	(242)
Other RDIs within income statement[a]	**(264)**	(82)	(141)
Net profit attributable to ordinary capital before RDIs	**3,725**	4,009	4,074

(a) In 2009 this included a gain of €327 million from the disposal of the majority of our equity interest in JohnsonDiversey.

The numbers of shares included in the calculation of earnings per share is an average for the period. These numbers are influenced by the share buy-back programs that we undertook during 2007 and 2008. During those periods the following movements in shares took place:

	Millions of share units		
	2009	*2008*	*2007*
Number of shares at January 1 (net of treasury stock)	**2,789.1**	2,853.1	2,889.9
Net movements in shares under incentive schemes	**15.1**	11.4	29.7
Share buy-back	--	(75.4)	(66.5)
Number of shares at December 31	**2,804.2**	2,789.1	2,853.1

MULTIPLE-CHOICE QUESTIONS

1. Entity A has an ordinary "A" class, non-voting share, which is entitled to a fixed dividend of 6% per annum. The "A" class ordinary share will
- (a) Be included in the "per share" calculation after adjustment for the fixed dividend.
- (b) Be included in the "per share" calculation for EPS without adjustment for the fixed dividend.
- (c) Not be included in the "per share" calculation for EPS.
- (d) Be included in the calculation of diluted EPS.

2. Earnings per share is calculated before accounting for which of the following items?
- (a) Preference dividend for the period.
- (b) Ordinary dividend.
- (c) Taxation.
- (d) Minority interest.

3. Ordinary shares issued as part of a business combination are included in the EPS calculation in the case of the "purchase" method from
- (a) The beginning of the accounting period.
- (b) The date of acquisition.
- (c) The end of the accounting period.
- (d) The midpoint of the accounting year.

4. When an enterprise makes a bonus issue/stock split/stock dividend or a rights issue, then
- (a) The previous year's EPS is not adjusted for the issue.
- (b) The previous year's EPS is adjusted for the issue.
- (c) Only a note of the effect on the previous year's EPS is made.
- (d) Only the diluted EPS for the previous year is adjusted.

5. If a stock option is converted on March 31, 20X9, then
- (a) The potential ordinary shares (stock option) are included in diluted EPS up to March 31, 20X9, and in basic EPS from the date converted to the year-end (both weighted accordingly).
- (b) The ordinary shares are not included in the diluted EPS calculation but are included in basic EPS.
- (c) The ordinary shares are not included in the basic EPS but are included in diluted EPS.
- (d) The effects of the stock option are included only in previous year's EPS calculation.

6. In calculating whether potential ordinary shares are dilutive, the profit figure used as the "control number" is
- (a) Net profit after taxation (including discontinued operations).
- (b) Net profit from continuing operations.
- (c) Net profit before tax (including discontinued operations).
- (d) Retained profit for the year after dividends.

7. Potential ordinary shares issued by a subsidiary should be included in the diluted EPS calculation as they could potentially have an impact on the net profit for the period and the number of shares to be included in the calculation.
- (a) True
- (b) False

8. An enterprise needs to disclose diluted EPS only if it differs from basic EPS by a material amount.
- (a) True
- (b) False

9. If a bonus issue occurs between the year-end and the date that the financial statements are authorized, then
- (a) EPS both for the current and the previous year are adjusted.
- (b) EPS for the current year only is adjusted.
- (c) No adjustment is made to EPS.
- (d) Diluted EPS only is adjusted.

10. If a new issue of shares for cash is made between the year-end and the date that the financial statements are authorized, then
- (a) EPS for both the current and the previous year are adjusted.
- (b) EPS for the current year only is adjusted.
- (c) No adjustment is made to EPS.
- (d) Diluted EPS only is adjusted.

11. The weighted-average number of shares outstanding during the period for all periods (other than the conversion of potential ordinary shares) shall be adjusted for
- (a) Any change in the number of ordinary shares without a change in resources.
- (b) Any prior-year adjustment.
- (c) Any new issue of shares for cash.
- (d) Any convertible instruments settled in cash.

12. Where ordinary shares are issued but not fully paid, then the ordinary shares are treated in the calculation of basic EPS
- (a) In the same way as fully paid ordinary shares.
- (b) As a fraction of an ordinary share to the extent that they are entitled to participate in dividends.

(c) In the same way as warrants or options and are included only in diluted EPS.

(d) Are ignored for the purposes of basic and diluted EPS.

13. When an entity issues both consolidated and separate financial statements, the EPS information disclosed under IAS 33 is required

(a) For both sets of financial statements.

(b) In neither set of statements.

(c) Only for the consolidated information.

(d) Only for the separate financial statements.

14. Dilution of EPS is defined in IAS 33 as

(a) A decrease in earnings per share when any financial instrument is converted to any form of share capital.

(b) A decrease in share capital.

(c) A decrease in earnings per share when convertible instruments are converted to ordinary shares.

(d) A decrease in earnings per share when share capital is converted to debt capital.

15. Which of the following is not an example of potential ordinary shares?

(a) Financial liabilities that are convertible into ordinary shares.

(b) Share options.

(c) Contingently issuable shares.

(d) Cancelled treasury shares.

16. Which figure for earnings does basic earnings per share use?

(a) Profit attributable to ordinary equity holders and preference shareholders of the parent.

(b) Profit before taxation.

(c) Profit from operations.

(d) Profit attributable to ordinary equity holders of the parent.

17. Shares which are issued to settle a liability are included in the EPS calculation from

(a) The date of the contract for services.

(b) Halfway through the rendering of services.

(c) The completion of the services.

(d) The settlement date.

18. Shares, which are to be issued upon the conversion of a mandatorily convertible instrument are included in the calculation of basic earnings per share from

(a) The date of the contract for the shares.

(b) Half way through the period.

(c) The date of conversion.

(d) The issue of the share certificate.

19. For the purpose of calculating diluted earnings per share, which of the following will not require an after-tax adjustment:

(a) Any dividends relating to dilutive potential shares, deducted in arriving at profit.

(b) Any interest recognized in the period, related to dilutive potential shares.

(c) Any dividends, which are proposed on existing shares after the period end.

(d) Any other changes in income (or expense) that would result from the conversion of the dilutive potential shares.

20. At what point are dilutive potential shares deemed to have been converted into ordinary shares?

(a) At the start of the period.

(b) At the end of the period.

(c) The date of the issue of the dilutive shares.

(d) At the start of the period or, if later, the date of the issue of the potential shares.

Chapter 26

INTERIM FINANCIAL REPORTING
(IAS 34)

OBJECTIVE

The purpose of IAS 34, *Interim Financial Reporting,* is to set out the minimum content of such a report and to describe the recognition and measurement principles in interim financial statements.

IAS 34 does not detail which entities should publish interim financial reports, how frequently they should be published, or how soon they should be published after the end of the interim period. The Standard applies where an entity is required or elects to publish an interim financial report. The International Accounting Standards Board (IASB) encourages publicly traded entities to provide such reports at least at the end of the half year, and such reports are to be made available not later than 60 days after the end of the interim period. An entity that does not prepare interim financial reports or provides ones that do not comply with IAS 34 does not compromise its compliance with International Financial Reporting Standards (IFRS) in its annual financial statements.

DEFINITIONS OF KEY TERMS
(in accordance with IAS 34)

Interim period. A financial reporting period shorter than a full financial year.

Interim financial report. A financial report that contains either a complete set of financial statements (as described in IAS 1, as revised in 2007) or a set of condensed financial statements (as described in IAS 34) for an interim period.

FORM AND CONTENT OF INTERIM REPORTS

IAS 34 defines the minimum content of an interim financial report as including condensed financial statements and selected explanatory notes. It does not detail the information that should be included in these condensed financial statements. An entity should determine the level of detail and ensure that the condensed financial statements can be compared with the previous annual financial statements. The interim financial report should provide an update on the latest financial statements.

The minimum elements specified for an interim financial report are a

- Condensed statement of financial position
- Condensed statement of comprehensive income, presented as either

  - A condensed single statement
  - A condensed separate income statement and a condensed statement of comprehensive income

- Condensed statement of changes in equity
- Condensed statement of cash flows
- Selected explanatory notes

If an entity issues a complete set of financial statements in the interim report, those financial statements should comply with IAS 1 (as revised in 2007).

If the entity publishes interim financial statements that are condensed, then they should include, as a minimum, the headings and subtotals included in the most recent annual financial statements and the explanatory notes as required by IAS 34. Additional line items or notes should be included if omitting them would make the interim financial statements misleading.

In the statement that presents the components of profit or loss for an interim period, an entity shall present basic and diluted earnings per share for the period when the entity falls within the scope of IAS 33, *Earning Per Share*. If an entity presents the components of profit or loss in a separate income statement as described in IAS 1 (as revised in 2007), it shall present basic and diluted earnings per share in that separate statement.

If the entity's most recent annual financial statements are prepared on a consolidated basis, the interim financial report should be prepared on the same basis.

SELECTED EXPLANATORY NOTES

The selected explanatory notes are designed to provide an explanation of significant events and transactions arising since the last annual financial statements. IAS 34 assumes that readers of an entity's interim report will also have access to its most recent annual report. As a result, IAS 34 prevents the repetition of annual disclosures in interim reports. IAS 34, paragraph 16, sets out a list of disclosures including

- Accounting policy changes
- Seasonality or cyclicality of operations
- Unusual items and changes in estimates
- Dividends paid and material events after the end of the interim period
- Changes in the structure of the entity including business combinations and restructurings
- Changes in contingent liabilities or assets since the last annual reporting period
- Issue, repurchase, and repayment of debt and equity

  - The effect of changes in the composition of the entity during the interim period, including business combinations, obtaining or losing control of subsidiaries and long-term investments, restructurings, and discontinued operations. (In case of business combinations, information required by IFRS 3 is required to be disclosed)
  - Segment information such as

    - Revenues from external customers and intersegment revenues (these disclosures are required if they are included in the measure of segment profit or loss reviewed by or regularly provided to the "chief operating decision maker")
    - A measure of segment profit or loss
    - Total assets for which there has been a material change from the amount disclosed in the last annual financial statements
    - A description of differences from the last annual financial statements in the basis of segmentation or in the basis of measurement of segment profit or loss
    - A reconciliation of the total of the reportable segments' measure of profit or loss to the entity's profit or loss before tax expense (tax income) and discontinued operations. If an entity allocates to reportable segments items such as tax expense or tax income, an entity may reconcile the total of the segments' measure of profit or loss to

the profit or loss of the entity after those items. Material reconciling items shall be separately identified and described in that reconciliation.

(Disclosure of segment information is required in an interim financial report only if IFRS 8 requires that entity to disclose segment information in its annual financial statements.)

DISCLOSURE OF COMPLIANCE WITH IFRS

If the entity's interim financial report is in compliance with IAS 34, that fact should be disclosed. An interim financial report should not claim compliance with IFRS generally unless it complies with all applicable International Financial Reporting Standards and interpretations of the International Financial Reporting Interpretations Committee (IFRIC).

PERIODS TO BE PRESENTED BY INTERIM FINANCIAL STATEMENTS

IAS 34 requires this information to be presented:

- Statement of financial position as of the end of the current interim period and a comparative statement of financial position as of the end of the preceding financial year.
- Statements of comprehensive income for the current interim period and for the current financial year to date, with comparative statements of comprehensive income for the comparable interim periods (current and year-to-date) of the preceding financial year. As permitted by IAS 1 (as revised in 2007), an interim report may present for each period **either** a single statement of comprehensive income, **or** a statement displaying components of profit or loss (separate income statement) and a second statement beginning with profit or loss and displaying components of other comprehensive income (statement of comprehensive income).
- Statement showing changes in equity for the current financial year to date, with a comparative statement for the comparable year-to-date period of the preceding financial year.
- Statement of cash flows for the current financial year to date, with a comparative statement for the comparable year-to-date period of the preceding financial year.

IAS 34 recognizes the usefulness of additional information if the business is seasonal by encouraging for those businesses the disclosure of financial information for the latest 12 months, and comparative information for the prior 12-month period, in addition to the interim period financial statements.

MEASUREMENT

Measurements for interim reporting purposes should be made on a "year-to-date" basis, so that the frequency of the entity's reporting should not affect the measurement of its annual results.

The same definitions and recognition criteria apply whether dealing with interim or annual financial reports.

IAS 34 requires the entity to consider these points:

- Revenues that are received seasonally, cyclically, or occasionally within a financial year should not be treated differently from in the annual financial statements.
- Costs and expenses are recognized as incurred and are not treated differently than from in the annual financial statements.
- Income tax expenses should be recognized based on the best estimate of the weighted-average annual income tax rate expected for the full financial year.
- It is recognized that the preparation of interim reports will often require the greater use of estimates.

SUNDRY POINTS

The materiality of items is to be assessed in relation to the interim period's financial data with the main aim being to include all information relevant to the entity's financial position and performance during that period.

The same accounting policies should be applied for interim reporting as are applied in the entity's annual financial statements.

An entity should use the same accounting policy throughout a single financial year. Where a new accounting policy is adopted in an interim period, that policy should be applied and previously reported interim data should be restated in accordance with IAS 8.

If an estimate of an amount reported in an interim period has changed significantly during the final interim period of the financial year but a separate financial report is not published for that period, the nature and amount of that change must be disclosed in the notes to the annual financial statements.

IFRIC 10 INTERIM FINANCIAL REPORTING AND IMPAIRMENT

At each reporting date an entity is required to assess the impairment of assets and, in certain cases, such impairment cannot be reversed at a subsequent reporting date. Such nonreversing impairments are addressed in the IFRS:

- Goodwill (IAS 36)
- Investments in equity instruments (IAS 39)
- Financial assets carried at cost (IAS 39)

IFRIC 10 clarifies that an entity shall not reverse impairment losses relating to the aforementioned assets, recognized in a previous interim period, at a subsequent balance sheet date even if the conditions might have changed at a subsequent reporting or balance sheet date.

IFRIC 10 is effective for annual periods beginning on or after November 1, 2006.

CASE STUDY

Facts

Joy, an entity publicly quoted on a stock exchange, owns 15% of the equity capital of Ash. This equity investment is classified as "available for sale" under IAS 39. The year-end of Joy is December 31, 20X9, and an interim report has been prepared at June 30, 20X9, using IAS 34. At January 1, 20X6, the fair value of the investment in Ash was $2 million. The investment in Ash was deemed to be impaired at June 30, 20X9, and an impairment loss of $500,000 was determined at that date. However, at December 31, 20X9, the fair value of the investment in Ash had risen to $2.3 million.

Required

Explain how the preceding transaction should be shown in the financial statements for the period to December 31, 20X9.

Solution

The financial asset should be reviewed for impairment at the date of the interim financial report, and therefore an impairment loss of $500,000 should be recognized in the statement of comprehensive income at that date. The increase in value of $800,000 from July 1, 20X9, to December 31, 20X9, should be taken to equity. If the entity had not prepared an interim report, then a gain of $300,000 would have been taken to other comprehensive income at December 31, 20X9. It is the frequency of the preparation of the statement of financial position that affects the annual results.

EXTRACTS FROM PUBLISHED FINANCIAL STATEMENTS

NESTLÉ, Half-Yearly Report January/June, 2009

Notes

Accounting policies

Basis of preparation

These financial statements are the unaudited interim consolidated financial statements for the six-month period ended June 30, 2009. They have been prepared in accordance with IAS 34, *Interim Financial Reporting,* and should be read in conjunction with the 2008 Consolidated Financial Statements.

The accounting conventions and accounting policies are the same as those applied in the 2008 Consolidated Financial Statements, except for the changes mentioned below.

Changes in accounting policies

The Group has applied the following International Financial Reporting Standards (IFRS) and Interpretations (IFRIC) as from January 1, 2009, onwards:

January–June

In millions of CHF	Notes		2009	
Sales	3		**52,267**	
Cost of goods sold			**(22,214)**	
Distribution expenses			**(4,215)**	
Marketing and administration expenses			**(17,484)**	
Research and development costs			**(917)**	
EBIT Earnings Before Interest, Taxes, restructuring and impairments	3		**7,383**	
Net other income/(expenses)	5			
Other income		**146**		132
Other expenses		**(348)**		(366)
			(202)	
Profit before interest and taxes			**7,181**	
Net financing cost				
Financial income		**73**		100
Financial expense		**(394)**		(637)
			(321)	
Profit before taxes and associates			**6,860**	
Taxes			**(1,646)**	
Share of results of associates	6		**521**	
Profit for the period			**5,735**	
of which attributable to noncontrolling interests			**664**	
of which attributable to shareholders of the parent (net profit)			**5,071**	
As % of Sales				
EBIT Earnings Before Interest, Taxes, restructuring and impairments			14.1%	
Profit for the period attributable to shareholders of the parent (net profit)			9.7%	
Earnings per share (in CHF)				
Basic earnings per share			1.41	

Modification of the scope of consolidation

There were no major acquisitions or disposals affecting the scope of consolidation for this interim period.

NESTLÉ, Half-Yearly Report January/June, 2009

Consolidated income statement for the period ended June 30, 2009

In millions of CHF	January–June 2009	January–June 2008
Profit for the period recognized in the income statement	**5,735**	**5,591**
Currency retranslations	1,605	(3,252)
Fair value adjustments on available-for-sale financial instruments		
Unrealized results	(84)	(228)
Recognition of realized results in the income statement	2	8
Fair value adjustments on cash flow hedges		
Recognized in hedging reserve	30	162
Removed from hedging reserve	142	(18)
Actuarial gains/(losses) on defined benefit schemes	(360)	(33)
Share of other comprehensive income of associates	(311)	(1,138)
Taxes	(121)	63
Other comprehensive income for the period	903	(4,436)
Total comprehensive income for the period	6,638	1,155
of which attributable to noncontrolling interest	731	238
of which attributable to shareholders of the parent	5,907	917

NESTLÉ, Half-Yearly Report January/June, 2009

Consolidated balance sheet at June 30, 2009

In millions of CHF	Notes	June 30, 2009	December 31, 2008	June 30, 2008
Assets				
Current assets				
Cash and cash equivalents		6,031	5,835	7,301
Short-term investments		1,560	1,296	2,671
Inventories		9,835	9,342	10,534
Trade and other receivables		14,013	13,442	14,494
Prepayments and accrued income		828	627	851
Derivative assets		1,479	1,609	1,008
Current income tax assets		590	889	533
Assets held for sale		23	8	74
Total current assets		**34,359**	**33,048**	**37,466**
Noncurrent assets				
Property, plant, and equipment		21,936	21,097	20,890
Goodwill		31,462	30,637	31,045
Intangible assets		6,912	6,867	7,014
Investments in associates		7,844	7,796	7,668
Financial assets		3,893	3,868	3,784
Employee benefits assets		80	60	1,294
Deferred tax assets		2,748	2,842	1,746
Total noncurrent assets		74,875	73,167	73,441
Total assets		**109,234**	**106,215**	**110,907**

NESTLÉ, Half-Yearly Report January/June 2009

Consolidated balance sheet at June 30, 2009

In millions of CHF	Notes	June 30, 2009	December 31, 2008	June 30, 2008
Liabilities and equity				
Current liabilities				
Financial liabilities		16,669	15,383	29,234
Trade and other payables		12,044	12,608	12,558
Accruals and deferred income		2,903	2,931	3,230
Derivative liabilities		1,611	1,477	543
Current income tax liabilities		813	824	869
Liabilities directly associated with assets held for sale		5	--	11
Total current liabilities		**34,045**	**33,223**	**46,445**
Noncurrent liabilities				
Financial liabilities		8,371	6,344	6,544
Employee benefits liabilities		5,761	5,464	4,439
Provisions		3,797	3,663	3,135
Deferred tax liabilities		1,401	1,341	1,039
Other payables		1,251	1,264	944
Total noncurrent liabilities		**20,581**	**18,076**	**16,101**
Total liabilities		**54,626**	**51,299**	**62,546**
Equity				
Share capital		365	383	383
Treasury shares		(2,494)	(9,652)	(5,147)
Translation reserve		(9,550)	(11,103)	(9,415)
Retained earnings and other reserves		62,040	71,146	60,412
Total equity attributable to shareholders of the parent		50,361	50,774	46,233
Noncontrolling interest		4,247	4,142	2,128
Total equity		**54,608**	**54,916**	**48,361**
Total liabilities and equity		**109,234**	**106,215**	**110,907**

NESTLÉ, Half-Yearly Report January/June, 2009

Consolidated cash flow statement for the period ended June 30, 2009

January–June

In millions of CHF	Notes	2009
Operating activities		
Profit for the period		5,735
Noncash items of income and expense	8	1,574
Decrease/(increase) in working capital		(1,356)
Variation of other operating assets and liabilities		478
Operating cash flow		**6,431**
Investing activities		
Capital expenditure		(1,521)
Expenditure on intangible assets		(182)
Sale of property, plant, and equipment		68
Acquisitions of businesses	9	(151)
Disposals of businesses	9	53
Cash flows with associates		344
Other investing cash flows		(70)
Cash flow from investing activities		**(1,459)**
Financing activities		
Dividend paid to shareholders of the parent	7	(5,047)
Purchase of treasury shares		(1,544)
Sale of treasury shares		157
Cash flows with noncontrolling interests		(650)
Bonds issued	10	2,997
Bonds repaid	10	(1,122)
Increase in other noncurrent financial liabilities		94
Decrease in other noncurrent financial liabilities		(47)
Increase/(decrease) in current financial liabilities		(448)
Decrease/(increase) in short-term investments		(204)
Cash flow from financing activities		**(4,918)**
Currency retranslations		142
Increase/(decrease) in cash and cash equivalents		**196**
Cash and cash equivalents at beginning of year		5,835
Cash and cash equivalents at end of period		**6,031**

NESTLÉ, Half-Yearly Report January/June 2009

Consolidated statement of changes in equity for the period ended June 30, 2009

In millions of CHF

	Share capital	Treasury shares	Translation reserve	Retained earnings and other reserves	Total equity attributable to shareholders of the parent company	Non-controlling interest	Total equity
Equity as at December 31, 2007	393	(8,013)	(6,302)	66,549	52,627	2,149	54,776
Total comprehensive income			(3,113)	4,030	917	238	1,155
Dividend paid to shareholders of the parent				(4,573)	(4,573)		(4,573)
Dividends paid to noncontrolling interests						(313)	(313)
Movement of treasury shares (net)		(2,622)		(266)	(2,888)		(2,888)
Changes in noncontrolling interests						41	41
Equity compensation plans		209		(59)	150	13	163
Reduction in share capital	(10)	5,279		(5,269)			
Equity as at June 30, 2008	383	(5,147)	(9,415)	60,412	46,233	2,128	48,361
Equity as at December 31, 2008	383	(9,652)	(11,103)	71,146	50,774	4,142	54,916
Total comprehensive income			1,553	4,354	5,907	731	6,638
Dividend paid to shareholders of the parent				(5,047)	(5,047)		(5,047)
Dividends paid to noncontrolling interest						(653)	(653)
Movement of treasury shares (net)		(1,366)		(21)	(1,387)		(1,387)
Changes in noncontrolling interest						5	5
Equity compensation plans		134		(20)	114	22	136
Reduction in share capital	(18)	8,390		(8,372)			
Equity as at June 30, 2009	365	(2,494)	(9,550)	62,040	50,361	4,247	54,608

MULTIPLE-CHOICE QUESTIONS

1. Under IAS 34, interim financial reports should be published
  (a) Once a year at any time in that year.
  (b) Within a month of the half-year-end.
  (c) On a quarterly basis.
  (d) Whenever the entity wishes.

2. The IASB encourages publicly traded entities to provide interim financial reports
  (a) At least at the end of the half-year and within 60 days of the end of the interim period.
  (b) Within a month of the half-year-end.
  (c) On a quarterly basis.
  (d) Whenever the entity wishes.

3. If an entity does not prepare interim financial reports, then
  (a) The year-end financial statements are deemed not to comply with IFRS.
  (b) The year-end financial statements' compliance with IFRS is not affected.
  (c) The year-end financial statements will not be acceptable under local legislation.
  (d) Interim financial reports should be included in the year-end financial statements.

4. Interim financial reports should include as a minimum
  (a) A complete set of financial statements complying with IAS 1.
  (b) A condensed set of financial statements and selected notes.
  (c) A balance sheet and income statement only.
  (d) A condensed balance sheet, income statement, and cash flow statement only.

5. IAS 34 states a presumption that anyone reading interim financial reports will
  (a) Understand all International Financial Reporting Standards.
  (b) Have access to the records of the entity.
  (c) Have access to the most recent annual report.
  (d) Not make decisions based on the report.

6. An entity owns a number of farms that harvest produce seasonally. Approximately 80% of the entity's sales are in the period August to October. Because the entity's business is seasonal, IAS 34 suggests
  (a) Additional notes be written in the interim reports about the seasonal nature of the business.
  (b) Disclosure of financial information for the latest and comparative 12-month period in addition to the interim report.
  (c) Additional disclosure in the accounting policy note.
  (d) No additional disclosure.

7. An entity is preparing half-yearly financial information in line with IAS 34. The period to be covered by the financial statements is the six months to June 30,20X9. A new IFRS has been published that is effective for periods beginning on or after January 1, 20X9. The entity must adopt the IFRS
  (a) In the financial statements for the year to December 31, 20X9, only.
  (b) In its interim financial statements to June 30, 20X9, only.
  (c) In its interim financial statements to June 30, 20X9, and its annual financial statements to December 31,20X9.
  (d) At its own discretion.

8. An entity operates in the travel industry and incurs costs unevenly through the financial year. Advertising costs of $2 million were incurred on March 1, 20X9, and staff bonuses are paid at year-end based on sales. Staff bonuses are expected to be around $20 million for the year; of that sum, $3 million would relate to the period ending March 31, 20X9. What costs should be included in the entity's quarterly financial report to March 31, 20X9?
  (a) Advertising costs $2 million; staff bonuses $5 million.
  (b) Advertising costs $0.5 million; staff bonuses $5 million.
  (c) Advertising costs $2 million; staff bonuses $3 million.
  (d) Advertising costs $0.5 million; staff bonuses $3 million.

9. An entity prepares quarterly interim financial reports in accordance with IAS 34. The entity sells electrical goods, and normally 5% of customers claim on their warranty. The provision in the first quarter was calculated as 5% of sales to date, which was $10 million. However, in the second quarter, a design fault was found and warranty claims were expected to be 10% for the whole of the year. Sales in the second quarter were $15 million. What would be the provision charged in the second quarter's interim financial statements?
  (a) $750,000.
  (b) $1.25 million.
  (c) $1.5 million.
  (d) $2 million.

Chapter 27

IMPAIRMENT OF ASSETS (IAS 36)

SCOPE

The purpose of the Standard is to ensure that assets are carried at no more than their recoverable amount. If an asset's carrying value exceeds the amount that could be received through use or through selling the asset, then the asset is impaired and IAS 36 requires an entity to make provision for the impairment loss. IAS 36 also sets out the situations where an entity can reverse an impairment loss. Certain assets are not covered by the Standard, including

- Inventories (IAS 2)
- Assets arising from construction contracts (IAS 11)
- Deferred tax assets (IAS 12)
- Assets arising from employee benefits (IAS 19)
- Financial assets dealt with under IAS 39 or IFRS 9
- Investment property carried at fair value under IAS 40
- Biological assets carried at fair value (IAS 41)
- Assets arising from insurance contracts (IFRS 4)
- Assets that are held for sale (IFRS 5)

The Standard does apply to

- Subsidiaries, associates, and joint ventures
- Property, plant, and equipment
- Investment property carried at cost
- Intangible assets and goodwill

DEFINITIONS OF KEY TERMS
(in accordance with IAS 36)

Recoverable amount of an asset or a cash-generating unit. The higher of its fair value less costs to sell and its value in use.

Value-in-use. The discounted present value of the future cash flows expected to arise from an asset or a cash-generating unit.

> **Cash-generating unit.** The smallest group of assets that can be identified that generates cash flows independently of the cash flows from other assets.
>
> **Fair value less costs to sell.** The amount obtainable from the sale of an asset or cash-generating unit in an arm's-length transaction between knowledgeable, willing parties, less the costs of disposal.
>
> **Impairment loss.** The amount by which the carrying amount of an asset or cash-generating unit exceeds its recoverable amount.

IDENTIFYING AN IMPAIRMENT LOSS

An entity has to assess at the end of each reporting period whether there is any indication that an asset is impaired.

Additionally, even if there is no indication of any impairment, these assets should be tested for impairment:

- An intangible asset that has an indefinite useful life
- An intangible asset that is not yet available for use
- Goodwill that has been acquired in a business combination

IAS 36 sets out the events that might indicate that an asset is impaired. These are

- External sources, such as a decline in market value, increases in market interest rates, the carrying amount of net assets being valued at more than the stock market value of the entity, and economic, legal, or technological changes that have had an adverse affect on the entity
- Internal sources of information, such as physical damage to an asset, or its obsolescence, or an asset becoming idle, or if the asset is part of a restructuring, or if the entity's performance has suffered during the period, or if there has been a significant decline or reduction in the cash flows generated or to be generated from the asset

If there is an indication that an asset is impaired, the asset's useful life, depreciation, or residual value may need adjusting.

CASE STUDY 1

Facts

An entity has purchased the whole of the share capital of another entity for a purchase consideration of $20 million. The goodwill arising on the transaction was $5 million. It was planned at the outset that the information systems would be merged in order to create significant savings. Additionally the entity was purchased because of its market share in a particular jurisdiction and because of its research projects. Subsequently the cost savings on the information systems were made. The government of the jurisdiction introduced a law that restricted the market share to below that anticipated by the entity, and some research projects were abandoned because of lack of funding.

Required

Explain any potential indicators of the impairment of goodwill.

Solution

The entity would have paid for the goodwill in anticipation of future benefits arising therefrom. The benefit in terms of the cost savings on the information systems has arisen, but the market share increase and the successful outcome of the research projects has not occurred. Therefore, these events may indicate the impairment of goodwill.

Goodwill has to be impairment tested at least annually under IFRS 3.

DETERMINATION OF A RECOVERABLE AMOUNT

The recoverable amount of an asset is the higher of the asset's fair value less costs to sell and its value in use. (The term "cash-generating unit" could be used as a substitute for the term "asset.")

If it is not possible to determine the fair value less costs to sell because there is no active market for the asset, the entity can use the asset's value in use as its recoverable amount. Similarly, if there is no reason for the asset's value in use to exceed its fair value less costs to sell, the latter amount may be used as its recoverable amount. An example of this is where an asset is being held for disposal, as the value of this asset is likely to be the net disposal proceeds, the future cash flows from this asset from its continuing use are likely to be negligible.

In the case of an intangible asset with an indefinite useful life, it is possible to use a calculation of the asset's recoverable amount that has been made in the preceding period as long as certain conditions are met. These conditions are that the intangible asset is part of a cash-generating unit whose value has not changed significantly since the most recent recoverable amount calculation. Also, the recent calculation must have resulted in an amount that was substantially in excess of the asset's carrying amount, and it would be unlikely that a current calculation of the recoverable amount would show a value less than the asset's carrying amount.

CASE STUDY 2

Facts

An entity is preparing its financial statements for the year ending November 30, 20X8. Certain items of plant and equipment were scrapped on January 1, 20X9. At November 30, 20X8, these assets were being used in production by the entity and had a carrying value of $5 million. The value-in-use of the asset at November 30, 20X8, was deemed to be $6 million, and its fair value less costs to sell was thought to be $50,000 (the scrap value).

Required

What is the recoverable amount of the plant and equipment at November 30, 20X8?

Solution

The recoverable amount is the higher of the assets' fair value less costs to sell and its value-in-use. In this case, even though the assets were scrapped on January 1, 20X9, the value-in-use at November 30, 20X8, was $6 million, which was higher than the fair value less costs to sell and their carrying value. Therefore, the assets are not impaired. The scrapping of the assets may be disclosed as a nonadjusting event after the reporting period if material.

FAIR VALUE LESS COSTS TO SELL

IAS 36 sets out how an entity should determine the fair value less costs to sell. The Standard sets out these examples:

- Where there is a buying and selling agreement, the price in that agreement less the costs to sell can be used.
- The price in an active market less the cost of disposal can be used.
- The fair value less costs to sell can be based on the best information available, which reflects the proceeds that could be obtained from the disposal of the asset in an arm's-length transaction.
- The Standard says that the best evidence is the price in a binding sale agreement in an arm's-length transaction adjusted for the costs of disposal.

VALUE-IN-USE

These elements should be used when calculating the value-in-use:

- Estimates of the future cash flows that the entity expects to get from the asset
- Any possible variations that may occur in the amount or timing of the future cash flows
- The time value of money represented by the current market risk-free rate of interest
- The uncertainty inherent in the asset
- Any other factors that should be borne in mind when determining the future cash flows from the asset

Typically an entity should estimate the future cash inflows and outflows from the asset and from its eventual sale, and then discount the future cash flows accordingly.

PRACTICAL INSIGHT

Interroll Holding AG, a Swiss entity, discloses in its accounts that it had revised the calculation of value-in-use as a result of a more realistic estimate of future cash flows. As a result, goodwill was impaired. Thus it can be seen that the estimates of future cash flows are critical to the impairment review.

FUTURE CASH FLOWS

It is important that any cash flow projections are based on reasonable and supportable assumptions. They should be based on the most recent financial budgets and forecasts. The cash flows should not include any cash flows that may arise from future restructuring or from improving or enhancing the asset's performance.

The Standard also says that any predictions incorporated into budgets and forecasts shall cover only a five-year period at maximum. Extrapolation should be used for periods beyond the five-year period. However, if management is confident that any projections beyond the five-year period are reliable, and management can demonstrate that, based on past experience, the cash flows that will be generated beyond this five-year period are likely to be accurate, then it is possible to use these forecasts.

Any future cash flows should not include inflows or outflows from financing activities or income tax receipts and payments. However, they should include the estimated disposal proceeds from the asset. If any future cash flows are in a foreign currency, they are estimated in that currency and discounted using a rate appropriate for that currency. The resultant figure will then be translated using the exchange rate at the date of the value-in-use computation.

CASE STUDY 3

Facts

An entity is reviewing one of its business segments for impairment. The carrying value of its net assets is $20 million. Management has produced two computations for the value-in-use of the business segment. The first value ($18 million) excludes the benefit to be derived from a future reorganization, but the second value ($22 million) includes the benefits to be derived from the future reorganization. There is no active market for the sale of the business segments.

Required

Explain whether the business segment is impaired.

Solution

The benefit of the future reorganization should not be taken into account in calculating value-in-use. Therefore, the net assets of the business segment will be impaired by $2 million because the value-in-use ($18 million) is lower than the carrying value ($20 million). The value-in-use can be used as the recoverable amount as there is no active market for the sale of the business segment.

PRACTICAL INSIGHT

Nokia discloses that it plans to reconstruct its business. In connection with this reconstruction, it has reviewed the carrying values of capitalized development costs. An impairment loss of €275 million was recognized. Nokia had discounted the cash flows expected to arise from the continuing use of the assets and from disposal at the end of their useful lives at discount rates of 15% and 12%.

DISCOUNT RATE

The discount rate to be used in measuring value-in-use should be a pretax rate that reflects current market assessments of the time value of money and the risks that relate to the asset for which the future cash flows have not yet been adjusted.

CASE STUDY 4

Facts

Management of an entity is carrying out an impairment test on an asset. The posttax market rate of return from the asset is 7% and profits are taxed at 30%. Management intends to use the posttax rate of return in discounting the posttax cash flows from the asset of $2 million, as management says it will make no difference to the calculation of value-in-use.

Required

Explain whether the use of the posttax rate is acceptable in the aforementioned circumstances.

Solution

In theory, discounting posttax cash flows at a posttax discount rate should give the same result as discounting pretax cash flows at a pretax discount rate. However, this depends upon future tax cash flows and deferred tax considerations. Therefore, the posttax calculation will not always give the same results as a pretax computation. Also, the pretax discount rate is not always the posttax discount rate grossed up by a standard rate of tax. Management should gross up the posttax discount rate based on an assessment of what the long-term effective tax rate might be.

PRACTICAL INSIGHT

Zentel NV, a Belgian entity, recognized an impairment of €1.2 million and discloses that it calculates the value-in-use of goodwill using discounted cash flows and a market-based discount rate, although there is no disclosure of the rate used in its accounts.

RECOGNITION AND MEASUREMENT OF AN IMPAIRMENT LOSS

Where the recoverable amount of an asset is less than its carrying amount, the carrying amount will be reduced to its recoverable amount. This reduction is the impairment loss.

The impairment loss should be recognized in profit or loss unless the asset is carried at a revalued amount, in which case the impairment loss is treated as a revaluation decrease in accordance with the respective Standard.

If the impairment loss is greater than the carrying amount of the asset to which it relates, the entity shall recognize a liability if it is the requirement of another Standard.

Where an impairment loss has been recognized, any depreciation charged for the asset will be adjusted to reflect the asset's revised carrying value.

CASH-GENERATING UNITS

If an asset appears to be impaired, the recoverable amount for that asset should be calculated. However, if it is not possible to calculate the recoverable amount of an individual asset, the recoverable amount of the cash-generating unit to which the asset belongs should be calculated.

A cash-generating unit is the smallest identifiable group of assets that can generate cash flows from continuing use and that are mainly independent of the cash flows from other assets or groups of assets.

CASE STUDY 5

Facts

A manufacturing entity owns several vehicles. The vehicles are several years old and could be sold only for scrap value. They do not generate cash independently from the entity.

Required

How will the recoverable value of the vehicles be determined?

Solution

The entity cannot estimate the recoverable amount of the vehicles because their value-in-use cannot be determined separately, and it will be different from the scrap value. Therefore, the entity would incorporate the vehicles into the cash-generating unit to which they belong and estimate the recoverable amount of that cash-generating unit.

Cash-generating units should be identified on a consistent basis, period to period, for the same asset or types of asset unless the entity can justify a change.

CASE STUDY 6

Facts

A railway entity has a contract with the government that requires service on each of ten different routes. The trains operating on each route and the income from each route can be identified easily. Two of the routes make substantially more profit than the others. The entity also operates a taxi service, a bus company, and a travel agency.

Required

What is the lowest level of cash-generating units that can be used by the entity?

Solution

The taxi service, bus company, and travel agency will each constitute cash-generating units. However, because the entity is required to operate on all ten rail routes, the lowest level of cash flows that are independent of cash flows from other groups of assets is the cash flows generated by the ten routes together.

Goodwill that has been acquired in a business combination should be allocated to cash-generating units. Normally internal management records will be used for the allocation of goodwill. The reported segments of the entity will be the minimum size of cash-generating units to which goodwill will be allocated.

CASE STUDY 7

Facts

An entity operates an oil platform in the sea. The entity has provided the amount of $10 million for the financial costs of the restoration of the seabed, which is the present value of such costs. The entity has received an offer to buy the oil platform for $16 million, and the disposal costs would be $2 million. The value-in-use of the oil platform is approximately $24 million before the restoration costs. The carrying value of the oil platform is $20 million.

Required

Is the value of the oil platform impaired?

Solution

The fair value less cost to sell of the oil platform is $14 million, which is the $16 million offered minus the disposal costs. The value-in-use of the platform will be $24 million minus $10 million, which is $14 million. The carrying amount of the platform is $20 million minus $10 million, which is $10 million. Therefore, the recoverable amount of the cash-generating unit exceeds its carrying amount, and it is not impaired.

If an entity disposes of an operation within the cash-generating unit, the goodwill associated with that operation will be included in the carrying amount of the operation when calculating the gain or loss on disposal. The amount included in the gain or loss on disposal will be based on the proportion of the cash-generating unit that is disposed of.

> **PRACTICAL INSIGHT**
>
> Fraport AG, a German entity, discloses in its accounts that evidence of its internal reporting suggested that the economic performance of an asset was going to be worse than expected. A review of the assets revealed that earnings performance had been lower than expected, and impairments of €38 million were recognized against property, plant, and equipment.

Sometimes an entity may reorganize its business so that changes will be made to the composition of the cash-generating units. If this is the case, goodwill will be reallocated to new cash-generating units based on their relative values.

CASE STUDY 8

Facts

An entity has an oil platform in the sea. The entity has to decommission the platform at the end of its useful life, and a provision was set up at the commencement of production. The carrying value of the provision is $8 million. The entity has received an offer of $20 million (selling costs $1 million) for the rights to the oil platform, which reflects the fact that the owners have to decommission it at the end of its useful life. The value-in-use of the oil platform is $26 million ignoring the decommissioning costs. The current carrying value of the oil platform is $28 million.

Required

Determine whether the value of the oil platform is impaired.

Solution

The fair value less costs to sell is $(20 – 1) million, or $19 million.

The value-in-use is $(26 – 8) million, or $18 million.

The carrying value is $(28 – 8) million, or $20 million.

Therefore, the recoverable amount ($19 million) is less than its carrying value ($20 million), and the asset is impaired.

A cash-generating unit to which goodwill has been allocated will be tested for impairment annually and also when there is an indication that the unit might be impaired.

GOODWILL

An entity has the option of measuring noncontrolling interest (NCI) at fair value or its proportionate share of the acquiree's identifiable net assets at the acquisition date. If the fair value method is chosen, the amount of goodwill recognized will increase. Thus the valuation method chosen will have ongoing consequences for the impairment testing of goodwill

For the purpose of impairment testing, if the proportionate method is used then the carrying amount of goodwill is grossed up to include the goodwill attributable to NCI. This notionally adjusted figure is then compared with the recoverable amount of the unit to decide whether the cash-generating unit is impaired.

CASE STUDY 9

Facts

An entity A acquires 60% of the ownership interest in another entity B. The goodwill arising on acquisition was $24 million, and the carrying value of entity B's net assets in the consolidated financial statements is $60 million at December 31, 20X9. The recoverable amount of the cash-generating unit B is $80 million at December 31, 20X9.

Required

Calculate any impairment loss arising at December 31, 20X9, for the cash-generating unit B.

Solution

	Goodwill	*Net assets*	*Total*
	$m	*$m*	*$m*
Carrying amount	24	60	84
Unrecognized minority interest	16	--	16
Notionally adjusted carrying amount	40	60	100
Recoverable amount			(80)
Impairment loss			20

This impairment loss will reduce goodwill on acquisition to $12 million [$24 – (60% of $20) million].

Goodwill that is recorded under the fair value method is subject to the ordinary impairment testing requirements of IAS 36. Any impairment loss is allocated to the controlling and NCI. Entities will need to track goodwill to determine whether it arose before or after IFRS 3 (Revised).

CASE STUDY 10

An entity has recorded goodwill of $8 million from 100% acquisitions arising before IFRS 3 (Revised). It subsequently records goodwill of $4 million on a 60% acquisition and uses the fair value method to value NCI. An impairment test is carried out at the period end and goodwill is impaired by $3 million.

Required

How is the impairment loss recorded in the entity's records?

Answer

As all existing goodwill was from 100% subsidiaries, goodwill gross-up is not required. The impairment loss is allocated first between the wholly owned portion of the group and the later acquisition by the relative carrying amounts. Thus $2 million is allocated to the wholly owned portion and $1 million to the recent acquisition. This latter amount is further allocated to the controlling and NCI on the same basis as profit or loss. Therefore the controlling interest is allocated $600,000 and NCI $400,000. The total amount allocated to the controlling interest is $2.6 million. The income statement is charged with the full impairment loss of $3 million.

TIMING OF IMPAIRMENT TEST

The annual impairment test for the cash-generating unit can be performed at any time during the financial year, provided the test is carried out at the same time every year.

Different cash-generating units can be tested for impairment at different times of the year. The exception to this is where the cash-generating unit was acquired in a business combination during the current period. In this case, the unit shall be tested for impairment before the end of the current financial year.

GROUP OR DIVISIONAL ASSETS (CORPORATE ASSETS)

Corporate assets should be allocated to cash-generating units. If the asset can be allocated on a reasonable and consistent basis, there is no problem.

However, if the asset cannot be allocated on such a basis, then three processes should occur:

1. An impairment test should be carried out on the cash-generating unit without the corporate asset.
2. The smallest group of cash-generating units should be identified that includes the cash-generating unit under review and to which part of the corporate assets can be reasonably allocated.
3. This group of cash-generating units should then be tested for impairment.

CASE STUDY 11

Facts

An entity has two cash-generating units, X and Y. There is no goodwill within the units' carrying values. The carrying values are X $10 million and Y $15 million. The entity has an office building that has not been included in the above values and can be allocated to the units on the basis of their carrying values. The office building has a carrying value of $5 million.

The recoverable amounts are based on value-in-use of $9 million for X and $19 million for Y.

Required

Determine whether the carrying values of X and Y are impaired.

Solution

	X	Y	Total
Carrying value	10	15	25
Office building (10:15)	2	3	5
	12	18	30
Recoverable amount	9	19	
Impairment loss	3	0	

The impairment loss will be allocated on the basis of 2/12 against the building ($0.5 million) and 10/12 against the other assets ($2.5 million).

ALLOCATION OF IMPAIRMENT LOSS

Any impairment loss calculated for a cash-generating unit should be allocated to reduce the carrying amount of the asset in this order:

1. The carrying amount of goodwill should be first reduced, then the carrying amount of other assets of the unit should be reduced on a pro rata basis determined by the relative carrying value of each asset.
2. Any reductions in the carrying amount of the individual assets should be treated as impairment losses. The carrying amount of any individual asset should not be reduced below the highest of its fair value less cost to sell, its value-in-use, and zero.

If this rule is applied, the impairment loss not allocated to the individual asset will be allocated on a pro rata basis to the other assets of the group.

CASE STUDY 12

Facts

A cash-generating unit has these net assets:

	$m
Goodwill	10
Property	20
Plant and equipment	30
	60

The recoverable amount has been determined as $45 million.

Required

Allocate the impairment loss to the net assets of the entity.

Solution

	Goodwill	Property	Plant	Total
	$m	$m	$m	$m
Carrying value	10	20	30	60
Impairment loss	(10)	(2)	(3)	(15)
Carrying value after impairment	–	18	27	45

REVERSAL OF AN IMPAIRMENT LOSS

At each reporting date, an entity should determine whether an impairment loss recognized in the previous period may have decreased. This does not apply to goodwill.

In determining whether an impairment loss has reversed, the entity should consider the same sources of information as for the original impairment loss.

An impairment loss may be reversed only if there has been a change in the estimates used to determine the asset's recoverable amount since the last impairment loss had been recognized. If this is the case, then the carrying amount of the asset shall be increased to its recoverable amount. The increase will effectively be the reversal of an impairment loss.

However, the increase in the carrying value of the asset can only be up to what the carrying amount would have been if the impairment had not occurred.

Any reversal of an impairment loss is recognized immediately in the profit or loss unless the asset is carried at a revalued amount; in this case, the reversal will be treated as a revaluation increase.

The reversal of an impairment loss may require an adjustment to the depreciation of the asset in future periods.

CASE STUDY 13

Facts

The calculation refers to an impairment loss suffered by subsidiary Zen at December 31, 20X8:

	Goodwill	Net assets	Total
	$m	$m	$m
December 31, 20X4—carrying value	300	900	1200
Impairment	(300)	(200)	(500)
	--	700	700

There has been a favorable change in the estimates of the recoverable amount of Zen's net assets since the impairment loss was recognized. The recoverable amount is now $800 million at December 31, 20X9. The net assets' carrying value would have been $720 million at December 31, 20X9. Assets are depreciated at 20% reducing balance.

Required

Show the accounting treatment for the reversal of the impairment loss as of December 31, 20X9.

Solution

The reversal of the impairment loss on goodwill cannot be accounted for under IAS 36. The carrying amount of Zen can be increased up to the lower of the recoverable amount ($800 million) and the carrying value ($720 million) of the net assets.

Carrying amount of Zen's net assets at December 31, 20X9:

	Goodwill $m	Net assets $m	Total $m
Carrying amount [700 – (20% of 700)]	--	560	560
Reversal of impairment loss	0	160	160
Carrying amount after reversal of impairment loss	--	720	720

PRACTICAL INSIGHT

Austrian Airlines disclosed in its accounts that it had recognized an impairment loss against its aircraft. The entity intended to dispose of its aircraft and had valued them at their disposal proceeds. Subsequently the entity decided not to dispose of all of the aircraft, and the recoverable amounts were measured at value-in-use. This resulted in a reversal of the impairment loss of €51 million.

A reversal of an impairment loss for a cash-generating unit shall be allocated to the assets of that unit on a pro rata basis. Any impairment loss that relates to goodwill will not be reversed.

IAS 36 has been amended to clarify a perceived inconsistency in determining the upper limit of a cash-generating unit. Formerly, IAS 36 stipulated that a cash-generating unit should not be larger than "an operating segment in accordance with IFRS 8." As IFRS 8 distinguishes between "operating" and "reportable" segments, uncertainty existed as to whether IAS 36 refers to the operating segment before or after aggregation permitted by IFRS 8. The amendment clarified that a cash-generating unit shall not be larger than an operating segment according to IFRS 8, that is, before aggregation of operating segments to reportable segments.

The amendment is effective for annual periods beginning on or after January 1, 2010, with earlier application permitted. The amendment is adopted prospectively; that means it has no effect on prior periods' impairment tests.

CASE STUDY 14

Facts

An entity, X, has five operating segments (A, B, C, D, E) for which operating results are regularly reviewed by the chief operating decision maker. Operating segments C and D are aggregated, as they meet all the aggregation criteria of IFRS 8. Segments B and E do not meet the quantitative threshold of IFRS 8, but are aggregated, because they meet the majority of the aggregation criteria of IFRS 8.

Required

Discuss the application of IAS 36 to the above scenario.

Solution

X has only three reportable segments (A, B/E, C/D). For goodwill impairment test purposes, however, the cash-generating units (or groups of cash-generating units) cannot be larger than the five operating segments. Goodwill can therefore not be tested on the aggregated level of C/D and B/E.

DISCLOSURE REQUIREMENTS

For each class of asset an entity shall disclose

1. Impairment losses recognized in profit or loss
2. Impairment losses reversed in profit or loss
3. The line item in profit or loss in which the impairment losses are included

Additionally, any impairment losses recognized in other comprehensive income should be disclosed, including reversals of impairment losses.

Each segment should disclose these items for each reportable segment: impairment losses recognized and reversed in the period both in profit or loss and in other comprehensive income.

If an individual impairment loss or reversal is material, then this information should be disclosed:

1. The events and circumstances leading to the impairment loss.
2. The amount of the loss.
3. If it relates to an individual asset, the nature of the asset and the segment to which it relates.
4. For a cash-generating unit, the description of the amount of the impairment loss or reversal, by class of asset and segment should be disclosed.
5. If the recoverable amount is fair value less costs to sell, the basis for determining fair value must be disclosed.
6. If the recoverable amount is the value-in-use, the discount rate should be disclosed.

If the impairment losses recognized or reversed are material in relation to the financial statements as a whole, the main classes of assets affected should be disclosed and the main events and circumstances that lead to the recognition of those losses should be disclosed.

Detailed information about the estimates used to measure the recoverable amounts of the cash-generating units that contain goodwill or intangible assets with an indefinite useful life should also be set out.

EXTRACTS FROM PUBLISHED FINANCIAL STATEMENTS

UNILEVER PLC, Annual Report, 2009

Goodwill and intangible assets

Indefinite-lived intangible assets principally comprise those trademarks for which there is no foreseeable limit to the period over which they are expected to generate net cash inflows. These are considered to have an indefinite life, given the strength and durability of our brands and the level of marketing support. Brands that are classified as indefinite have been in the market for many years, and the nature of the industry we operate in is such that brand obsolescence is not common, if appropriately supported by advertising and marketing spend. Finite-lived intangible assets, which primarily comprise patented and nonpatented technology, know-how, and software, are capitalized and amortized in operating profit on a straight-line basis over the period of their expected useful lives, none of which exceeds ten years. The level of amortization for finite-lived intangible assets is not expected to change materially over the next five years.

At cost less amortization and impairment	€ million 2009	€ million 2008
Goodwill	12,464	11,665
Intangible assets:	4,583	4,426
Indefinite-lived intangible assets	4,050	3,886
Finite-lived intangible assets	153	206
Software	380	334
	17,047	16,091

Movements during 2009	€ million Goodwill	€ million Indefinite-lived Intangible assets	€ million Finite-lived Intangible assets	€ million Software	€ million Total
Cost					
January 1, 2009	**12,617**	**4,107**	**598**	**580**	**17,902**
Acquisitions of group companies	350	105	1	--	456
Disposals of group companies	--	(1)	--	--	(1)
Additions	--	1	--	149	150
Disposals	--	--	--	(72)	(72)
Currency retranslation	441	57	12	30	540
December 31, 2009	13,408	4,269	611	687	18,975
Amortization and impairment					
January 1, 2009	(952)	(221)	(392)	(246)	(1,811)
Disposal of group companies	--	--	--	--	--
Amortization for the year	--	--	(58)	(110)	(168)
Disposals	--	--	--	62	62
Currency retranslation	8	2	(8)	(13)	(11)
December 31, 2009	(944)	(219)	(458)	(307)	(1,928)
Net book value December 31, 2009	**12,464**	**4,050**	**153**	**380**	**17,047**

Movements during 2008	€ million Goodwill	€ million Indefinite-lived Intangible assets	€ million Finite-lived Intangible assets	€ million Software	€ million Total
Cost					
January 1, 2008	13,182	4,134	621	501	18,438
Acquisitions of group companies	60	90	1	--	151
Disposals of group companies	(129)	--	--	--	(129)
Additions	--	1	--	146	147
Disposals	--	--	(3)	(33)	(36)
Currency retranslation	(496)	(81)	(20)	(34)	(631)
Reclassification as held for sale	--	(37)	(1)	--	(38)
December 31, 2008	12,617	4,107	598	580	17,902
Amortization and impairment					
January 1, 2008	(938)	(213)	(348)	(184)	(1,683)
Disposal of group companies	12	--	--	--	12
Amortization for the year	--	--	(59)	(109)	(168)
Impairment	--	(37)	(1)	--	(38)
Disposals	--	--	2	33	35
Currency retranslation	(26)	(8)	13	14	(7)
Reclassification as held for sale	--	37	1	--	38
December 31, 2008	(952)	(221)	(392)	(246)	(1,811)
Net book value December 31, 2008	11,665	3,886	206	334	16,091

There are no significant carrying amounts of goodwill and intangible assets that are allocated across multiple cash-generating units (CGUs).

Impairments charge in the year

There were no material impairments in 2009. The impairments charged in 2008 principally related to a noncore Savoury business in the Americas, which was subsequently classified as held for sale.

Significant CGUs

The goodwill and indefinite-lived intangible assets (predominantly Knorr and Hellmann's) held in the regional Savoury and Dressings CGUs are considered significant in comparison to the total carrying amounts of goodwill and indefinite-lived intangible assets at December 31, 2009. No other CGUs are considered significant in this respect.

The goodwill and indefinite-lived intangible assets held in the regional Savoury and Dressings CGUs are

	€ billion 2009	€ billion 2009 Indefinite-lived	€ billion 2008	€ billion 2008 Indefinite-lived
	Goodwill	intangibles	Goodwill	intangibles
Western Europe	**5.2**	**1.3**	5.1	1.3
The America's	**3.9**	**1.3**	3.6	1.3
AAC	**1.9**	**0.6**	1.9	0.5

During 2009, we conducted an impairment review of the carrying value of these assets. Value in use in the regional Savoury and Dressings CGUs has been calculated as the present value of projected future cash flows. A pretax discount rate of 10% was used.

The following key assumptions were used in the discounted cash flow projections for the regional Savoury and Dressings CGUs:

- A longer-term sustainable growth rate of 2% to 3% for Western Europe, 5% for the Americas and 9% to 10% for AAC.
- Average near-term nominal growth rates for the major product groups within the CGUs of 2% Western Europe, 4.5% The Americas, 9% for AAC.
- Average operating margins for the major product groups within the CGUs ranging from 16% to 20% Western Europe, 19% to 20% The Americas and 10% to 12% AAC.

The growth rates and margins used to estimate future performance are based on past performance and our experience of growth rates and margins achievable in our key markets as a guide. We believe that the assumptions used in estimating the future performance of the regional Savoury and Dressings CGUs are consistent with past performance.

The projections covered a period of ten years as we believe this to be a suitable timescale over which to review and consider annual performance before applying a fixed terminal value multiple to the final year cash flows of the detailed projection. Stopping the detailed projections after five years and applying a terminal value multiple thereafter would not result in a value-in-use that would cause impairment.

The growth rates used to estimate future performance beyond the periods covered by our annual planning and strategic planning processes do not exceed the long-term average rates of growth for similar products.

We have performed sensitivity analyses around the base case assumptions and have concluded that no reasonable possible changes in key assumptions would cause the recoverable amount of the regional Savoury and Dressings CGUs to be less than the carrying amount.

MULTIPLE-CHOICE QUESTIONS

1. IAS 36 applies to which of the following assets?
   (a) Inventories.
   (b) Financial assets.
   (c) Assets held for sale.
   (d) Property, plant, and equipment.

2. Value-in-use is
   (a) The market value.
   (b) The discounted present value of future cash flows arising from use of the asset and from its disposal.
   (c) The higher of an asset's fair value less cost to sell and its market value.
   (d) The amount at which the asset is recognized in the statement of financial position.

3. If the fair value less costs to sell cannot be determined
   (a) The asset is not impaired.
   (b) The recoverable amount is the value-in-use.
   (c) The net realizable value is used.
   (d) The carrying value of the asset remains the same.

4. If assets are to be disposed of
   (a) The recoverable amount is the fair value less costs to sell.
   (b) The recoverable amount is the value-in-use.
   (c) The asset is not impaired.
   (d) The recoverable amount is the carrying value.

5. Estimates of future cash flows normally would cover projections over a maximum of
   (a) Five years.
   (b) Ten years.
   (c) Fifteen years.
   (d) Twenty years.

6. An entity has a database that it purchased five years ago. At that date, the database had 15,000 customer addresses on it. Since the date of purchase, 1,000 addresses have been taken from the list and 2,000 addresses have been added to the list. It is anticipated that in two years' time, a further 4,000 addresses will have been added to the list. In determining the value-in-use of the customer lists, how many addresses should be taken into account at the current date?
   (a) 15,000
   (b) 16,000
   (c) 20,000
   (d) 21,000

7. Which of the following is the best evidence of an asset's fair value less costs to sell?
   (a) An asset that is trading in an active market.
   (b) The price in a binding sale agreement.
   (c) Information available that determines the disposal value of the asset in an arm's-length transaction.
   (d) The carrying value of the asset.

8. When calculating the estimates of future cash flows, which of the following cash flows should **not** be included?
   (a) Cash flows from disposal.
   (b) Income tax payments.
   (c) Cash flows from the sale of assets produced by the asset.
   (d) Cash outflows on the maintenance of the asset.

9. When deciding on the discount rate that should be used, which factors should **not** be taken into account?
   (a) The time value of money.
   (b) Risks that relate to the asset for which future cash flow estimates have not been adjusted.
   (c) Risks specific to the asset for which future cash flow estimates have been adjusted.
   (d) Pretax rates.

10. An impairment loss that relates to an asset that has been revalued should be recognized in
   (a) Profit or loss.
   (b) Revaluation reserve that relates to the revalued asset.
   (c) Opening retained profits.
   (d) Any reserve in equity.

11. A cash-generating unit is
   (a) The smallest business segment.
   (b) Any grouping of assets that generates cash flows.
   (c) Any group of assets that is reported separately to management.
   (d) The smallest group of assets that generates independent cash flows from continuing use.

12. Goodwill should be tested for impairment
   (a) If there is an indication of impairment.
   (b) Annually.
   (c) Every five years.
   (d) On the acquisition of a subsidiary.

13. Where part of the cash-generating unit is disposed of, the goodwill associated with the element disposed of
   (a) Shall be written off to the statement of comprehensive income entirely.
   (b) Shall not be included in the calculation of gain or loss on disposal.

(c) Shall be included in the calculation of gain or loss on disposal.

(d) Shall be written off against retained profits.

14. When impairment testing a cash-generating unit, any corporate assets, such as the head office business or computer equipment, should

(a) Be allocated on a reasonable and consistent basis.

(b) Be separately impairment tested.

(c) Be included in the head office assets or parent's assets and impairment tested along with that cash-generating unit.

(d) Not be allocated to cash-generating units.

15. When allocating an impairment loss, such a loss should reduce the carrying amount of which asset first?

(a) Property, plant, and equipment.

(b) Intangible assets.

(c) Goodwill.

(d) Current assets.

16. Which of the following impairment losses should never be reversed?

(a) Loss on property, plant, and equipment.

(b) Loss on goodwill.

(c) Loss on a business segment.

(d) Loss on inventory.

Chapter 28

PROVISIONS, CONTINGENT LIABILITIES, AND CONTINGENT ASSETS (IAS 37)

BACKGROUND AND INTRODUCTION

This Standard prescribes rules regarding the recognition and measurement of provisions, contingent liabilities, and contingent assets, and also mandates disclosures in footnotes that would enable users of financial statements to comprehend their nature, timing, and amount.

Prior to the promulgation of IAS 37, in the absence of clear-cut rules of recognition and measurement, entities could charge huge provisions to profit or loss (often referred to as big bath provisions) and thereby manipulate earnings or financial performance.

It is worth noting that previously the term "provisions" was used very loosely in financial reporting. With the enactment of IAS 37, rules with respect to recognition and measurement of provisions, contingent liabilities, and contingent assets have been codified. Since then, entities preparing financial statements in accordance with International Financial Reporting Standards (IFRS) used these terms strictly based on their prescribed definitions under IAS 37. Furthermore, IAS 37 also has clarified certain misconceptions about the term "provision." For instance, "provisions" that are envisioned by this Standard are now "liabilities" (of uncertain timing or amount). The "provision for depreciation" and the "provision for doubtful debts" are really not provisions according to this Standard but are contra accounts or adjustments to the carrying value of assets.

SCOPE

The requirements of IAS 37 are applicable to recognition and measurement of all provisions, contingent liabilities, and contingent assets *except*

1. Those resulting from executory contracts, other than onerous contracts
2. Those covered by other Standards

In other words, when provisions, contingent liabilities, and contingent assets are specifically addressed by other Standards, then they are not within the scope of this Standard. Standards that specifically deal with provisions that are not covered by IAS 37 are

- Construction contracts (IAS 11)
- Income taxes (IAS 12)
- Leases (IAS 17) (However, onerous leases are covered by IAS 37.)
- Employee benefits (IAS 19)
- Insurance contracts (IFRS 4) (However, IAS 37 still applies to provisions, contingent liabilities, and contingent assets of an insurer, other than those arising from its contractual obligations and rights under insurance contracts within the scope of IFRS 4.)

The Standard also does not apply to financial instruments (including guarantees) that are within the scope of IAS 39.

DEFINITIONS OF KEY TERMS
(in accordance with IAS 37)

Provision. A liability of uncertain timing or amount.

Liability. A present obligation of an entity arising from past events, the settlement of which is expected to result in an outflow of resources embodying economic benefits.

Contingent liability.

1. A possible obligation arising from past events whose existence will be confirmed only by the occurrence or nonoccurrence of one or more uncertain future events that are not completely within the control of the entity.
2. A present obligation that arises from past events but is not recognized because either it is not possible to measure the amount of the obligation with sufficient reliability or it is not probable that an outflow of resources will be required to settle the obligation.

Contingent asset. A possible asset arising from past events and whose existence will be confirmed only by the occurrence or nonoccurrence of one or more uncertain future events that are not completely within the control of the entity.

Executory contract. A contract under which neither party (to the contract) has performed its obligations or both the parties (to the contract) have performed their obligations partially to an equal extent.

Onerous contract. A contract in which the unavoidable costs of meeting the obligations under the contract exceed the economic benefits expected to be received under the contract.

Restructuring. A program that is planned and controlled by the management and materially changes either the scope of a business undertaking by an entity or the manner in which that business is conducted.

PROVISIONS

Recognition of Provisions

Those liabilities that are of uncertain timing or amount are "provisions," according to the Standard. Creditors (trade payables) and accrued expenses are therefore *not* considered "provisions" by this Standard because they do not meet the above criteria. Similarly, as explained, the term "provision" is used in some countries in the context of "depreciation" and "doubtful debts," but these are not the type of provisions that are envisaged by this Standard.

Provisions should be recognized if, and only if, *all* of these conditions are met:

1. An entity has a *present obligation* resulting from a past event.
2. It is *probable* that an outflow of resources embodying economic benefits would be required to settle the obligation.
3. A *reliable estimate* can be made of the amount of the obligation.

Not all obligations would make it incumbent upon an entity to recognize a provision. Only present obligations resulting from a *past obligating event* give rise to a provision.

An obligation could either be a legal obligation or a constructive obligation.

A *legal obligation* is an obligation that could

1. Be contractual
2. Arise due to a legislation
3. Result from other operation of law

A *constructive obligation,* however, is an obligation that results from an entity's actions where

1. By an established pattern of past practice, published policies, or a sufficiently specific current statement, the entity has indicated to other (third) parties that it will accept certain responsibilities
2. As a result, the entity has created a valid expectation in the minds of those parties that it will discharge those responsibilities

It should be "probable that the outflow of resources embodying economic benefits would occur." The term "probable" is interpreted, for the purposes of this Standard, as "more likely than not" (i.e., the chances of occurrence are more than 50%).

CASE STUDY 1

Facts

Excellent Inc. is an oil entity that is exploring oil off the shores of Excessoil Islands. It has employed oil exploration experts from around the globe. Despite all efforts, there is a major oil spill that has grabbed the attention of the media. Environmentalists are protesting and the entity has engaged lawyers to advise it about legal repercussions. In the past, other oil entities have had to settle with the environmentalists, paying huge amounts in out-of-court settlements. The legal counsel of Excellent Inc. has advised it that there is no law that would require it to pay anything for the oil spill; the parliament of Excessoil Islands is currently considering such legislation, but that legislation would probably take another year to be finalized as of the date of the oil spill. However, in its television advertisements and promotional brochures, Excellent Inc. often has clearly stated that it is very conscious of its responsibilities toward the environment and will make good any losses that may result from its exploration. This policy has been widely publicized, and the chief executive officer has acknowledged this policy in official meetings when members of the public raised questions to him on this issue.

Required

Does the above give rise to an obligating event that requires Excellent Inc. to make a provision for the cost of making good the oil spill?

Solution

1. Present obligation as a result of a past obligating event. The obligating event is the oil spill. Because there is no legislation in place yet that would make a clean up mandatory for any entity operating in Excessoil Islands, there is no legal obligation. However, the circumstances surrounding the issue clearly indicate that there is a constructive obligation since the company, with its advertised policy and public statements, has created an expectation in the minds of the public at large that it will honor its environmental obligations.
2. An outflow of resources embodying economic benefits in settlement. Probable.
3. Conclusion. A provision should be recognized for the best estimate of the cost to clean up the oil spill.

Measurement of Provisions

The amount to be recognized, as a provision is the *best estimate* of the expenditure required to settle the present obligation at the end of the reporting period. While a reliable estimate is usually possible, in rare circumstances, it may not be possible to obtain a reliable estimate. In such cases, the liability is to be disclosed as a contingent liability (and not recognized as a provision).

"Best estimate" is a matter of judgment and is usually based on past experience with similar transactions, evidence provided by technical or legal experts, or additional evidence provided by events after the reporting period.

Risks and uncertainties surrounding events and circumstances should be considered in arriving at the best estimate of a provision.

- If a group of items is being measured, it is the "expected value."
- If a single obligation is being measured, it is the "most likely outcome."

CASE STUDY 2

Facts

A car dealership also owns a workshop that it uses for servicing cars under warranty. In preparing its financial statements, the car dealership needs to ascertain the provision of warranty that it would be required to provide at year-end. The entity's past experience with warranty claims is

- 60% of cars sold in a year have zero defects.
- 25% of cars sold in a year have normal defects.
- 15% of cars sold in a year have significant defects.

The cost of rectifying a "normal defect" in a car is $10,000. The cost of rectifying a "significant defect" in a car is $30,000.

Required

Compute the amount of "provision for warranty" needed at year-end.

Solution

The expected value of the provision for warranty needed at year-end is:

$$(60\% \times 0) + (25\% \times \$10,000) + (15\% \times \$30,000) = \$7,000.$$

Where the effect of time value is material, the amount of provision is to be discounted to its present value using a pretax discount rate that reflects current market assessments of time value of money and the risks specific to the liability.

Future events that are expected to affect the measurement of the provision should be taken into account in arriving at the amount of the provision if there is sufficient objective evidence that the future events will occur. Gains from expected future disposals should not be considered in arriving at the amount of the provision to be recognized. However, if amounts are expected to be reimbursed by another party, these should be taken into consideration in arriving at the amount of the provision (only when it is virtually certain that the reimbursement will be received).

Changes in Provisions and Use of Provisions

Changes in provisions shall be reviewed at each balance sheet date, and the amount of the provision should be adjusted accordingly to reflect the current best estimate. When it is no longer probable that an outflow of resources would be required to settle the obligation, the provision should be reversed. A provision should be used only for the purpose for which it was originally recognized or set up.

PRACTICAL INSIGHT

In the past, entities used to rationalize a shortfall in a provision based on the premise that for the same time period, there were more than required amounts provided as provisions in other cases. In other words, a shortfall in one provision was justified (and not adjusted) because it was balanced by excess in another provision. This practice would not be possible now since IAS 37 categorically states that a provision should be used for the purpose for which it was initially created or recognized. Furthermore, IAS 37 also mandates that changes in provisions shall be reviewed at the end of each reporting period and provision amounts should be adjusted accordingly to reflect the current best estimate.

Based on these rules promulgated under IAS 37, if, after recognizing a provision, say, for bonus, it is believed that it is excessive, an entity cannot justify the excess under the plea that there is a shortfall in another provision, say, provision for warranty, and considering them together, on an overall basis, the total provisions at a given point in time are adequate. Instead, under IAS 37, the excess provision for the bonus should be written back or released to the income statement and the shortfall in the provision for warranty should be supplemented through an additional provision.

Future Operating Losses

It is *not* permissible to recognize a provision for future operating losses, because they do not meet the criteria for recognition of a provision. As future losses are not present obligations arising from past obligating events and could be avoided by a future action of the entity (say, by disposing of the business), they do not clearly meet the recognition criteria for "provisioning." Hence IAS 37 does not allow for them to be provided for at year-end. An expectation of future losses may, however, lead one to believe that certain assets of the operations may be impaired; in this case, an entity should test assets for impairment under IAS 36.

Onerous Contracts

Although executory contracts are outside the general purview of IAS 37, it is required to recognize a provision under an executory contract that is "onerous." An onerous contract that is covered under IAS 37 is an executory contract where the unavoidable costs exceed the benefits expected.

Example

An onerous contract is an agreement that an entity cannot get out of legally even though it has signed another parallel agreement under which it is able to undertake the same activities at a better price. As it is locked into the existing agreement, it would need to incur costs under both contracts but derive economic benefits from only one of them. The next example explains this better.

An entity is bound under the terms of a franchise agreement for a local brand that it has marketed for years. Based on market survey and a cost-benefit study, the entity decided to stop marketing the local brand and entered into a new agreement to market an international brand. Although the entity does not derive any economic benefit from the franchise agreement for the local brand, there is an obligation to pay a lump-sum amount to the franchiser under the noncancelable franchise agreement for a period of two more years. Thus the entity would need to make a provision for the commitment under the franchise agreement (since it is an onerous contract).

CASE STUDY 3

Facts

XYZ Inc. is getting ready to move its factory from its existing location to a new industrial free trade zone specially created by the government for manufacturers. To avail itself of the preferential licensing offered by the local governmental authorities as a reward for moving into the free trade zone and the savings in costs that would ensue (since there are no duties or taxes in the free trade zone), XYZ Inc. has to move into the new location before the end of the year. The lease on its present location is noncancelable and is for another two years from year-end. The obligation under the lease is the annual rent of $100,000.

Required

Advise XYZ Inc. what amount, if any, it needs to provide at year-end toward this lease obligation.

Solution

The lease agreement is an executory onerous contract because after moving to the new location, XYZ Inc. would derive no economic benefits from the existing factory building but would still need to pay rent under the agreement since the lease is noncancelable. Thus the unavoidable costs exceed the benefits expected under the lease contract.

Based on the annual lease obligation under the lease agreement, the total amount needed to be provided at year-end is the present value of the total commitment under the lease = PV of \$200,000 [\$100,000 × 2 (years)].

Restructuring

In the past, entities used to accrue lump-sum provisions for restructuring, because there were no Standards governing this important area. In some cases, this led to abusive practices of manipulation and creative accounting referred to as big bath provisions. In order to control the practice of dumping of all kinds of provisions under the banner of provision for restructuring, IAS 37 prescribed rules to regulate it. First and foremost, it defined the term, thereby restricting restructuring to a structured program that is planned and controlled by the management that materially changes *either* the scope of the business of an entity *or* the manner in which that business is conducted.

To provide guidance on this contentious issue, IAS 37 provides these examples of events that may qualify as restructuring:

- Sale or termination of a line of business
- Closure of business locations in a region or relocation of business activities from one location to another
- Changes in management structure, such as elimination of a layer of management
- Fundamental reorganization of the entity such that it has a material and a significant impact on its operations

Although many fundamental structural changes to an entity's operations would be significant enough to warrant disclosure in footnotes to the financial statements, not all of these changes qualify as restructuring that necessitates recognition (as opposed to disclosure), because they do not meet the criteria for recognizing a provision. Recognition of the provision is required because a constructive obligation may arise from the decision to restructure. In other words, a constructive obligation may not arise in all cases. A constructive obligation arises when, and only when, an entity

- Has a *detailed formal plan* for the restructuring, outlining *at least*
  - The business or the part of the business being restructured
  - The principal locations affected by the restructuring
  - The location, function, and approximate number of employees who will be compensated for terminating their employment
  - When the plan will be implemented
  - The expenditures that will be undertaken

- Has *raised valid expectations* in the minds of those affected that the entity will carry out restructuring by starting to implement that plan or announcing its main features to those affected by it.

PRACTICAL INSIGHT

A decision taken by the board of directors of an entity contemplating embarking on a restructuring program but not communicated to the parties affected by the decision (such that it creates a valid expectation in their minds that the restructuring decision will in reality be implemented) would not by itself give rise to a constructive obligation. Thus communication of the decision of the board of directors to parties affected is a prerequisite if an entity wants to make a provision for "restructuring" on the basis of a constructive obligation.

A restructuring provision should include only direct expenditures arising from the restructuring, which are those that are necessarily entailed by the restructuring and not associated with the ongoing activities of the entity.

The Standard has specifically excluded certain types of expenditures as expenditure arising from restructuring:

- Costs of retraining or relocating continuing staff
- Marketing
- Investment in new systems and distribution networks

CASE STUDY 4

Facts

The board of directors of ABC Inc. at their meeting held on December 15, 2009, decided to close down the entity's international branches and shift its international operations and consolidate them with its domestic operations. A detailed formal plan for winding up the international operations was also formalized and agreed to by the board of directors in that meeting. Letters were sent out to customers, suppliers, and workers soon thereafter. Meetings were called to discuss the features of the formal plan to wind up international operations, and representatives of all interested parties were present in those meetings.

Required

Do the actions of the board of directors create a constructive obligation that needs a provision for restructuring at the end of the reporting period, December 31, 2009?

Solution

The conditions prescribed by IAS 37 are

- There should be a detailed formal plan of restructuring.
- The formal plan should have raised valid expectations in the minds of those affected that the entity would carry out the restructuring by announcing the main features of its plans to restructure.

The board of directors did discuss and formalize a formal plan of winding up the international operations. This plan was communicated to the parties affected and created a valid expectation in their minds that ABC Inc. will go ahead with its plans to wind up international operations. Thus there is a constructive obligation that needs to be provided for at the end of the reporting period, December 31, 2009.

Disclosures

For each class of provision, an entity should disclose

- The carrying amount at the beginning and the end of the period
- Additional provisions made in the period, including increases to existing provisions
- Amounts utilized during the period
- Unused amounts reversed during the period
- The increase during the period in the discounted amount arising from the passage of time and the effect of any change in the discount rate

An entity should also disclose, for each class of provision

- A brief description of the nature of the obligation and the expected timing of any resulting outflows of economic benefits
- An indication about the uncertainties about the amount and timing of those outflows (and, where necessary, major assumptions made concerning future events)
- The amount of any expected reimbursement, stating the amount of any asset that has been recognized for that expected reimbursement

In extremely rare circumstances, when disclosure of any or all of this information is considered to be seriously prejudicial to the position of the entity in a dispute with other parties on the subject matter of the provision, an entity need not disclose the information but should disclose the general nature of the dispute, together with the fact that, and reason why, the information has not been disclosed.

CONTINGENT LIABILITIES

Possible Obligation

In order to recognize a provision (and record it on the books as opposed to only disclosing it in footnotes), certain conditions (as discussed earlier) need to be satisfied. However, when one of the prescribed conditions is not satisfied, then a provision cannot be recognized. It is then a contingent liability needs to be disclosed in footnotes, unless the probability of the outflow embodying economic benefits is remote (in which case it does not even have to be disclosed).

A contingent liability is a *possible obligation* arising from past events, the outcome of which will be confirmed only on the occurrence or nonoccurrence of one or more uncertain future events. A contingent liability is also a *present obligation that is not recognized,* either because it is not probable that an outflow of resources will be required to settle an obligation or the amount of the obligation cannot be measured with sufficient reliability.

Once recognized as a contingent liability, an entity should continually assess the probability of the outflow of the future economic benefits relating to that contingent liability. If the probability of the outflow of the future economic benefits changes to more likely than not, then the contingent liability may develop into an actual liability and would need to be recognized as a provision.

Disclosures

Unless the possibility of any outflow is remote, for each class of contingent liability an entity should disclose at the end of the reporting period a brief description of the nature of the contingent liability and, where practicable

- An estimate of its financial effect
- An indication of the uncertainties relating to the amount or timing of any outflow
- The possibility of any reimbursement

Where any of the required previously stated information is not disclosed because it is not practicable to do so that fact should be disclosed.

In extremely rare circumstances, when disclosure of any or all of the previous information is considered to be seriously prejudicial to the position of the entity in a dispute with other parties on the subject matter of the contingent liability, an entity need not disclose the information but should disclose the general nature of the dispute, together with the fact that, and reason why, the information has not been disclosed.

CASE STUDY 5

Facts

Amazon Inc. has been sued for the following three alleged infringements of law:

1. Unauthorized use of a trademark; the claim is for $100 million.
2. Nonpayment of end-of-service severance pay and gratuity to 5,000 employees who were terminated without Amazon Inc. giving any reason; the class action lawsuit is claiming $3 million.
3. Unlawful environmental damage for dumping waste in the river near its factory; environmentalists are claiming unspecified damages as cleanup costs.

Legal counsel is of the opinion that not all the legal cases are tenable in law and has communicated to Amazon Inc. this assessment of the three lawsuits:

Lawsuit 1: The chances of this lawsuit are remote.
Lawsuit 2: It is probable that Amazon Inc. would have to pay the displaced employees, but the best estimate of the amount that would be payable if the plaintiff succeeds against the entity is $2 million.
Lawsuit 3: There is no current law that would compel the entity to pay for such damages. There may be a case for constructive obligation, but the amount of damages cannot be estimated with any reliability.

Required

What should be the provision that Amazon Inc. should recognize or the contingent liability that it should disclose in each of the lawsuits, based on the assessments of its legal counsel?

Solution

Lawsuit 1: Because the probability of an outflow of economic benefits is remote, no provision or disclosure is required.

Lawsuit 2: Because it is probable ("more likely than not") that Amazon Inc. would ultimately have to pay the dues to the displaced employees and the best estimate of the settlement is $2 million (as against the claim of $3 million), Amazon Inc. would have to make a provision for $2 million.

Lawsuit 3: There is no legal obligation, but there is a constructive obligation. However, an estimate of the obligation with reasonable reliability is not possible. Hence this qualifies for disclosure as a contingent liability because it cannot be recognized as a provision (as it does not meet all the prescribed conditions for recognition of a provision).

CONTINGENT ASSETS (Possible Assets)

Contingent assets are *possible assets* that arise from a past event and whose existence is confirmed only by the occurrence or nonoccurrence of one or more uncertain future events not wholly within the control of the entity.

INTERPRETATION OF IAS 37 (IFRIC)

IFRIC Interpretation 1

IFRIC 1 is titled *Changes in Existing Decommissioning, Restoration, and Similar Liabilities*. IAS 37 contains requirements on how to measure decommissioning, restoration, and similar liabilities. IFRIC 1 provides guidance on how to account for the effect of changes in the measurement of existing decommissioning, restoration, and similar liabilities. This IFRIC interpretation addresses the issue of how the effect of a change in the current market-based discount rate (as defined in IAS 37) should be accounted for. According to the "consensus," the periodic unwinding of the discount shall be recognized in profit or loss as a finance cost as it occurs.

IFRIC Interpretation 5

This interpretation applies to accounting in the financial statements of a contributor for interests arising from decommissioning funds. As per the "consensus," the contributor shall recognize its obligation to pay decommissioning costs as a liability and recognize its interest in the fund separately unless the contributor is not liable to pay decommissioning costs even if the fund fails to pay.

Further, if the contributor does not have control, joint control, or significant influence over the fund, the contributor shall recognize the right to receive reimbursement from the fund as a reimbursement in accordance with IAS 37. This reimbursement should be measured at the lower of

1. The amount of decommissioning obligation recognized.
2. Contributor's share of fair value of the net costs of the fund attributable to contributors.

In case a contributor has an obligation to make additional contributions (e.g., in the event of the bankruptcy of another contributor), this obligation is a contingent liability that is within the scope of IAS 37, which shall be disclosed as per disclosure requirements of IAS 37.

IFRIC Interpretation 6

The European Union's Directive on Waste Electrical and Electronic Equipment (WE & EE) has given rise to questions about when the liability for the decommissioning of "WE & EE" shall be recognized. This Interpretation provides guidance on the recognition of liabilities for waste management under this EU Directive.

IFRIC was asked to determine in the context of the decommissioning of "WE & EE" as to what constitutes the "obligating event" in accordance with IAS 37. Whether (a) it is "manufacture or sale of the historical household equipment," or (b) it is "the participation in the market during the measurement period," or (c) it is the "incurrence of costs in the performance of waste management activities" and as per the "consensus" (b) triggers the "obligating event" under IAS 37 at which point a liability has to be recognized.

IFRIC Interpretation 17

IFRIC 17 deals with distributions of noncash assets to owners or when the owners are given the choice of taking cash in lieu of the noncash assets. It applies to entities making the distributions and not to the recipient of the distributions.

According to IFRIC 17 the dividend payable should be measured at the fair value of the net assets to be distributed and the entity recognizing the dividend payable should remeasure the liability at each reporting date and at settlement, with changes in values being recognized directly in equity. Further, the entity making the distributions should recognize the difference between the dividend paid and the carrying amount of the net assets distributed in profit or loss, or should disclose it separately.

If the assets being held for distribution to owners meet the definition of "discontinued operations" under IFRS 5, the entity distributing the assets to owners should make additional disclosures.

IFRIC 17 applies to pro rata distributions of noncash assets (and all owners are treated equally) but does not apply to "common control" transactions.

DISCLOSURES

Where inflow of economic benefits is probable, an entity should disclose a brief description of the nature of the contingent assets at the balance sheet date and, where practicable, an estimate of their financial estimate.

Where any of the information required previously is not disclosed because it is not practicable to do so, that fact should be disclosed.

In extremely rare circumstances, when disclosure of any or all of the previous information is considered to be seriously prejudicial to the position of the entity in a dispute with other parties on the subject matter of the contingent asset, an entity need not disclose the information but should disclose the general nature of the dispute, together with the fact that, and reason why, the information has not been disclosed.

CASE STUDY 6

Facts

A Singapore-based shipping company lost an entire shipload of cargo valued at $5 million on a voyage to Australia. It is, however, covered by an insurance policy. According to the report of the surveyor the amount is collectible, subject to the deductible clause (i.e., 10% of the claim) in the insurance policy. Before year-end, the shipping company received a letter from the insurance company that a check was in the mail for 90% of the claim.

The international freight forwarding company that entrusted the shipping company with the delivery of the cargo overseas has filed a lawsuit for $5 million, claiming the value of the cargo that was lost on high seas, and also consequential damages of $2 million resulting from the delay. According to the legal counsel of the shipping company, it is probable that the shipping company would have to pay the $5 million, but it is a remote possibility that it would have to pay the additional $2 million claimed by the international freight forwarding company, since this loss was specifically excluded in the freight-forwarding contract.

Required

What provision or disclosure would the shipping company need to make at the end of the reporting period?

Solution

The shipping company would need to recognize a contingent asset of $4.5 million (the amount that is virtually certain of collection). Also it would need to make a provision for $5 million toward the claim of the international freight forwarding company. Because the probability of the claim of $2 million is remote, no provision or disclosure would be needed for that at the end of the reporting period.

EXTRACTS FROM PUBLISHED FINANCIAL STATEMENTS

HOLCIM, Annual Report, 2009

Notes to the Financial Statements

Accounting Policies

Site restoration and other environmental provisions

The Group provides for the costs of restoring a site where a legal or constructive obligation exists. The cost of raising a provision before exploitation of the raw materials has commenced is included in property, plant, and equipment and depreciated over the life of the site. The effect of any adjustments to the provision due to further environmental damage is recorded through operating costs over the life of the site to reflect the best estimate of the expenditure required to settle the obligation at the end of the reporting period. Changes in the measurement of a provision that result from changes in the estimated timing, or amount of cash outflows, or a change in the discount rate, are added to, or deducted from, the cost of the related asset as appropriate in the current period. All provisions are discounted to their present value based on a long-term borrowing rate.

Emission rights

The initial allocation of emission rights granted is recognized at nominal amount (nil value). Where a Group company has emissions in excess of the emission rights granted, it will recognize a provision for the shortfall based on the market price at that date. The emission rights are held for compliance purposes only and therefore the Group does not intend to speculate with these in the open market.

Other provisions

A provision is recognized when there exists a legal or constructive obligation arising from past events and it is probable that an outflow of resources embodying economic benefits will be required to settle the obligation and a reliable estimate can be made of this amount.

Contingent liabilities

Contingent liabilities arise from conditions or situations where the outcome depends on future events. They are disclosed in the notes to the financial statements.

Provisions

Million CHF	Site restoration and other environmental liabilities	Specific business	Other provisions	Total 2009	Total 2008
January 1	**518**	**365**	**605**	**1,488**	**1,488**
Change in structure	8	4	(33)	(21)	(21)
Provisions recognized	75	129	139	343	343
Provisions used during the year	(35)	(20)	(91)	(146)	(146)
Provisions reversed during the year	(13)	(26)	(27)	(66)	(66)
Currency translation effects	(75)	(71)	(77)	(223)	(223)
Of which short-term provisions	29	29	143	201	201
Of which long-term provisions	449	352	373	1,174	1,174

Site restoration and other environmental liabilities represent the Group's legal or constructive obligations of restoring a site. The timing of cash outflows of this provision is dependent on the completion of raw material extraction and the commencement of site restoration.

Specific business risks comprise litigation and restructuring costs, which arise during the normal course of business. Provisions for litigations mainly relate to antitrust investigations, product liability, as well as tax claims and are set up to cover legal and administrative proceedings. It includes CHF 27 million (2008: 120) related to the German antitrust investigation set up in 2002. The total provisions for litigations amounted to CHF 210 million (2008: 309) at December 31. The timing of cash outflows of provisions for litigations is uncertain since it will largely depend upon the outcome of administrative and legal proceedings. Provisions for restructuring costs relate to various restructuring programs and amounted to CHF 72 million (2008: 72) at December 31. These provisions are expected to result in future cash outflows mainly within the next one to three years.

Other provisions relate mainly to provisions that have been set up to cover other contractual liabilities. The composition of this item is extremely manifold and comprises as at December 31, among other things: various severance payments to employees of CHF 101 million (2008: 71), provisions for sales and other taxes of CHF 104 million (2008: 70), and provisions for health insurance and pension scheme, which do not qualify as benefit obligations, of CHF 64 million (2008: 68). The expected timing of the future cash outflows is uncertain.

Contingencies, guarantees, and commitments

Contingencies

In the ordinary course of business, the Group is involved in lawsuits, claims, investigations, and proceedings, including product liability, commercial, environmental, health and safety matters, etc. There are no single matters pending that the Group expects to be material in relation to the Group's business, financial position, or results of operations.

At December 31, 2009, the Group's contingencies amounted to CHF 436 million (2008: 347). It is possible, but not probable, that the respective legal cases will result in future liabilities.

The Group operates in countries where political, economic, social, and legal developments could have an impact on the Group's operations. The effects of such risks, which arise in the normal course of business are not foreseeable and are therefore not included in the accompanying consolidated financial statements.

Guarantees

At December 31, 2009, guarantees issued to third parties in the ordinary course of business amounted to CHF 335 million (2008: 330).

MULTIPLE-CHOICE QUESTIONS

1. When can a "provision" be recognized in accordance with IAS 37?
   (a) When there is a legal obligation arising from a past (obligating) event, the probability of the outflow of resources is more than remote (but less than probable), and a reliable estimate can be made of the amount of the obligation.
   (b) When there is a constructive obligation as a result of a past (obligating) event, the outflow of resources is probable, and a reliable estimate can be made of the amount of the obligation.
   (c) When there is a possible obligation arising from a past event, the outflow of resources is probable, and an approximate amount can be set aside toward the obligation.
   (d) When management decides that it is essential that a provision be made for unforeseen circumstances and keeping in mind this year the profits were enough but next year there may be losses.

2. Amazon Inc. has been served a legal notice on December 15, 20X1, by the local environmental protection agency (EPA) to fit smoke detectors in its factory on or before June 30, 20X2 (before June 30 of the following year). The cost of fitting smoke detectors in its factory is estimated at $250,000. How should Amazon Inc. treat this in its financial statements for the year ended December 31, 20X1?
   (a) Recognize a provision for $250,000 in the financial statements for the year ended December 31, 20X1.
   (b) Recognize a provision for $125,000 in the financial statements for the year ended December 31, 20X1, because the other 50% of the estimated amount will be recognized next year in the financial statement for the year ended December 31, 20X2.
   (c) Because Amazon Inc. can avoid the future expenditure by changing the method of operations and thus there is no present obligation for the future expenditure, no provision is required at December 31, 20X1, but as there is a possible obligation, this warrants disclosure in the footnotes to the financial statements for the year ended December 31, 20X1.
   (d) Ignore this for the purposes of the financial statements for the year ended December 31, 20X1, and neither disclose nor provide the estimated amount of $250,000.

3. A competitor has sued an entity for unauthorized use of its patented technology. The amount that the entity may be required to pay to the competitor if the competitor succeeds in the lawsuit is determinable with reliability, and according to the legal counsel it is less than probable (but more than remote) that an outflow of the resources would be needed to meet the obligation. The entity that was sued should at year-end
   (a) Recognize a provision for this possible obligation.
   (b) Make a disclosure of the possible obligation in the footnotes to the financial statements.
   (c) Make no provision or disclosure and wait until the lawsuit is finally decided and then expense the amount paid on settlement, if any.
   (d) Set aside, as an appropriation, a contingency reserve, an amount based on the best estimate of the possible liability.

4. A factory owned by XYZ Inc. was destroyed by fire. XYZ Inc. lodged an insurance claim for the value of the factory building, plant, and an amount equal to one year's net profit. During the year there were a number of meetings with the representatives of the insurance company. Finally, before year-end, it was decided that XYZ Inc. would receive compensation for 90% of its claim. XYZ Inc. received a letter that the settlement check for that amount had been mailed, but it was not received before year-end. How should XYZ Inc. treat this in its financial statements?
   (a) Disclose the contingent asset in the footnotes.
   (b) Wait until next year when the settlement check is actually received and not recognize or disclose this receivable at all since at year-end it is a contingent asset.
   (c) Because the settlement of the claim was conveyed by a letter from the insurance company that also stated that the settlement check was in the mail for 90% of the claim, record 90% of the claim as a receivable as it is virtually certain that the contingent asset will be received.
   (d) Because the settlement of the claim was conveyed by a letter from the insurance company that also stated that the settlement check was in the mail for 90% of the claim, record 100% of the claim as a receivable at year-end as it is virtually certain that the contingent asset will be received, and adjust the 10% next year when the settlement check is actually received.

5. The board of directors of ABC Inc. decided on December 15, 20XX, to wind up international operations in the Far East and move them to Australia. The decision was based on a detailed formal plan of restructuring as required by IAS 37. This

decision was conveyed to all workers and management personnel at the headquarters in Europe. The cost of restructuring the operations in the Far East as per this detailed plan was $2 million. How should ABC Inc. treat this restructuring in its financial statements for the year-end December 31, 20XX?

  (a) Because ABC Inc. has not announced the restructuring to those affected by the decision and thus has not raised an expectation that ABC Inc. will actually carry out the restructuring (and as no constructive obligation has arisen), only disclose the restructuring decision and the cost of restructuring of $2 million in footnotes to the financial statements.

  (b) Recognize a provision for restructuring since the board of directors has approved it and it has been announced in the headquarters of ABC Inc. in Europe.

  (c) Mention the decision to restructure and the cost involved in the chairman's statement in the annual report since it a decision of the board of directors.

  (d) Because the restructuring has not commenced before year-end, based on prudence, wait until next year and do nothing in this year's financial statements.

Chapter 29

INTANGIBLE ASSETS (IAS 38)

INTRODUCTION AND BACKGROUND

The purpose of this Standard is to prescribe the recognition and measurement criteria for intangible assets that are not covered by other Standards. This Standard will enable users of financial statements to understand the extent of an entity's investment in such assets and the movements therein.

The principal issues involved relate to the nature and recognition of intangible assets, determining their costs, and assessing the amortization and impairment losses that need to be recognized.

SCOPE

The Standard is to be applied in accounting for all intangible assets except

- Those that are within the scope of another Standard
- Financial assets as defined in IAS 32, *Financial Instruments: Presentation*
- Mineral rights and expenditure on the exploration for, or development and extraction of, minerals, oil, natural gas, and similar nonregenerative resources

The Standard does *not* apply to those intangible assets covered by other Standards, such as

- Intangible assets held for sale in the ordinary course of business (IAS 2)
- Deferred tax assets (IAS 12)
- Leases within the scope of IAS 17
- Assets arising from employee benefit plans (IAS 19)
- Financial assets covered by IAS 32, IAS 27, IAS 28, or IAS 31
- Goodwill acquired in a business combination (IFRS 3)
- Deferred acquisition costs and intangible assets arising from insurance contracts (IFRS 4) (However, the disclosure requirements for such intangible assets are applicable)
- Noncurrent intangible assets classified as held for sale in accordance with IFRS 5

In some cases, an intangible asset may be contained on or in a tangible item. Obvious examples are computer software, films, and licensing agreements. In such situations, judgment is required to determine which is the more significant element. In the case of a machine incorporating software that cannot be operated without the software, the entire item would be treated as property, plant, and equipment under IAS 16. However, add-in software on a computer, such as some forms of report writing software or antivirus software, are not required for operating the tangible asset and therefore would be accounted for under IAS 38.

This Standard does apply to expenditure such as advertising, training, start-up costs, research and development, patents, licensing, motion picture film, software, technical knowledge, franchises, customer loyalty, market share, market knowledge, customer lists, and the like.

DEFINITIONS OF KEY TERMS
(in accordance with IAS 38)

Intangible asset. An identifiable, nonmonetary asset without physical substance.

Asset. A resource controlled by an entity as a result of past events and from which future economic benefits are expected to flow to the entity.

Research. Original and planned investigation undertaken with the prospect of gaining new scientific or technical knowledge and understanding.

Development. The application of research findings or other knowledge to a plan or design for the production of new or substantially improved materials, devices, products, processes, systems, or services before the start of commercial production or use.

Cost. The amount paid or fair value of other consideration given to acquire or construct an asset.

Useful life. The period over which an asset is expected to be utilized, or the number of production units expected to be obtained from the use of the asset.

Residual value of an asset. The estimated amount, less estimated disposal costs that could be currently realized from the asset's disposal if the asset were already of an age and condition expected at the end of its useful life.

Depreciable amount. The cost of an asset less its residual value.

Depreciation. The systematic allocation of the depreciable amount of an asset over its expected useful life.

Fair value. The amount for which an asset could be exchanged between knowledgeable, willing parties in an arm's-length transaction.

ELABORATION AND INTERPRETATION OF THE DEFINITIONS

Identifiability

In order to meet the definition of an intangible asset, expenditure on an item must be separately identifiable in order to distinguish it from goodwill. An asset meets the identifiability criterion when it

- Is capable of being separated from the entity and sold, transferred, licensed, or rented either individually or in combination with a related contract, asset, or liability
- Arises from contractual or other legal rights, regardless of whether those rights are transferable or separable from the entity or other rights or obligations

Control

An entity controls an asset if it has the power to obtain the future economic benefits flowing from the underlying resource and to restrict the access of others to those benefits. Usually this control would flow from legally enforceable rights. However, legal enforceability is not necessary if control can be enforced in some other way. For example, one method of control is keeping something secret through employee confidentiality.

Control needs to be looked at carefully. An entity may be able to identify skills in its workforce and to measure the costs of providing those skills to its staff (via training). However, the entity usually does not have control over the expected economic benefits arising from the skilled staff, as they can leave their employment. Even if the skills are protected in some way such that departing staff are not permitted to use them elsewhere, the entity has lost the future benefit of the skills imbued in the departing staff member.

Similarly, the purchase of customer lists or expenditure on advertising, while identifiable, does not provide control to an entity over the expected future benefits. Customers are not forced to buy from the entity and can go elsewhere.

Future Economic Benefit

Future economic benefit may include revenue from the sale of products, services, or processes, but also includes cost savings or other benefits from use of an asset. Use of intellectual property can reduce operating costs rather than produce revenue.

RECOGNITION AND MEASUREMENT

An item may be recognized as an intangible asset when it meets the definition of an intangible asset (see previous) and meets these recognition criteria

- It is probable that the expected future economic benefits that are attributable to the asset will flow to the entity.
- The cost of the asset can be measured reliably.

Initially, intangible assets shall be measured at cost. The cost of separately acquired intangible assets comprises

- Purchase price, including any import duties and nonrefundable purchase taxes, less discounts and rebates.
- Directly attributable costs of preparing the asset for use.

Directly attributable costs can include employee benefits, professional fees, and costs of testing.

Costs that *cannot* be included are

- Costs of introducing new products or services, such as advertising
- Costs of conducting new business
- Administration costs
- Costs incurred while an asset that is ready for use is awaiting deployment
- Costs of redeployment of an asset
- Initial operating losses incurred from operation

PRACTICAL INSIGHT

In the corporate world, it is often noticed that entities spend huge sums of money on advertising campaigns to launch new products. Some multinational entities even hire famous performing artists or movie stars to act as brand ambassadors of the new products. Because the amounts spent on these advertising campaigns are so huge, these entities sincerely believe that the benefits from this promotion would last longer than a year and thus they are inclined to defer the costs of introducing new products over a period of two to three years. When the financial statements of these entities have to be audited, this is usually a contentious issue. Auditors generally find it very difficult to convince the entity's management that the Standard categorically disallows deferring such costs.

If payment for an intangible asset is deferred beyond normal credit terms, then the cost is the cash price and the balance is treated as a finance charge over the period of the finance.

If intangible assets are acquired as part of a business combination, as defined in IFRS 3, their cost is their fair value at the acquisition date. The probability of future economic benefit is reflected in their fair value, and, therefore, the probability of future economic benefit required for recognition is presumed. In a business combination, such intangible assets are to be recognized separately from goodwill.

Assessing the fair value of an intangible asset in a business combination can be difficult; obvious techniques are the use of comparable market transactions or quoted prices. Sometimes there may be a range of values to which probabilities can be assigned. Such uncertainty enters into the measurement of the asset rather than demonstrating an inability to measure the value. If an intangible asset has a finite life, then it is presumed to have a reliably measurable fair value.

In some circumstances, it may not be possible to reliably measure the fair value of an intangible asset in a business combination because it is inseparable or there is no history or evidence of exchange transactions for the asset, and any fair value estimates would be based on immeasurable variables.

If an intangible asset is acquired in exchange for another asset, then the acquired asset is measured at its fair value unless the exchange lacks commercial substance or the fair value cannot be reliably measured, in which case the acquired asset should be measured at the carrying amount of the asset given up, where carrying amount is equal to cost less accumulated depreciation and impairment losses. For impairment losses, reference should be made to IAS 36. In this context, any compensation received for impairment or loss of an asset shall be included in the income statement.

CASE STUDY 1

Facts

Brilliant Inc. acquires copyrights to the original recordings of a famous singer. The agreement with the singer allows the company to record and rerecord the singer for a period of five years. During the initial six-month period of the agreement, the singer is very sick and consequently cannot record. The studio time that was blocked by the company had to be paid even during the period the singer could not sing. These costs were incurred by the company:

1. Legal cost of acquiring the copyrights: $10 million
2. Operational loss (studio time lost, etc.) during start-up period: $2 million
3. Massive advertising campaign to launch the artist: $1 million

Required

Which of the above items is a cost that is eligible for capitalization as an intangible asset?

Solution

1. The legal cost of acquiring the copyright can be capitalized.
2. "Operational costs" during the start-up period are not allowed to be capitalized.
3. A massive advertising campaign to launch the artist is not allowed to be capitalized.

INTERNALLY GENERATED INTANGIBLE ASSETS

With internally generated intangible assets, problems arise in identifying whether there is an identifiable asset that will generate future economic benefit and in reliably determining its cost.

Goodwill

The Standard proscribes the recognition of internally generated goodwill as an asset. The rationale behind this is that any expenditure incurred does not result in an asset that is an identifiable resource—it is not separable, nor does it arise from contractual or other legal rights—or that is controlled by the entity. In addition, any costs incurred are unlikely to be specifically identifiable as generating the goodwill. The position that the difference between a valuation of a business and the carrying amount of its individual assets and liabilities may be capitalized as goodwill falls down insofar as that difference cannot be categorized as the cost and therefore cannot be recognized as an asset.

Other Internally Generated Intangible Assets

The Standard sets out rules for the recognition of other internally generated intangible assets and broadly defines such expenditures as research and development. It proscribes the recognition of internally generated brands, mastheads, publishing titles, customer lists, and similar items, because expenditure thereon, like expenditure on internally generated goodwill, cannot be distinguished from the cost of developing the business as a whole and is therefore not separately identifiable.

In order to determine whether an internally generated intangible asset qualifies for recognition, its generation is divided into a research phase and a development phase. If the two phases cannot be distinguished, then the entire expenditure is classified as research.

Expenditure on research (or the research phase of an internal project) is to be written off as an expense as and when incurred, as it is not possible to demonstrate that an asset exists that will generate future economic benefit. Examples include

- Activities aimed at obtaining new knowledge
- The search for, evaluation, and selection of applications of research findings or knowledge
- The search for alternatives for materials, devices, products, systems, or processes
- The formulation, design, evaluation, and selection of possible alternatives for new or improved materials, devices, products, systems, or processes

Development expenditure may be recognized as an intangible asset when, and only when, *all* of the following can be demonstrated:

- The technical feasibility of completing the asset so that it will be available for use or sale
- The intention to complete the asset and use or sell it
- The ability to use or sell the asset
- How the asset will generate probable future economic benefit, including demonstrating a market for the asset's output, or for the asset itself, or the asset's usefulness
- The availability of sufficient technical, financial, and other resources to complete the development and to use or sell the asset
- The ability to reliably measure the expenditure attributable to the asset during its development

Examples of activities that may fail to be recognized as intangible assets include

- The design, construction, and testing of preuse prototypes or models
- The design of tools and jigs involving new technology
- The design, construction, and operation of a pilot plant that is not capable of commercial production
- The design, construction, and testing of a chosen alternative for new or improved materials, devices, products, systems, or processes

---

PRACTICAL INSIGHT

In order to implement the foregoing in practice, generally some form of business plan will be required to demonstrate the feasibility of a project, the availability of resources, and the future cash flows that can reasonably be expected to be derived therefrom.

PRACTICAL INSIGHT

Very often a project will commence with a research phase and after a time will evolve into the development phase. It will be necessary to determine at what point in time the project has so evolved, as expenditure up to that date will have to be recognized as an expense in the income statement and expenditure incurred after that date can be capitalized as an intangible asset. The use of hindsight and the resultant claim to capitalize the entire expenditure is not permissible, as research expenditure must be expensed *when incurred* and the Standard does allow the reinstatement of previously written-off costs. One is not permitted to accumulate costs in an account and then consider the nature of the entire project only when preparing the year-end financial statements.

CASE STUDY 2

Facts

Extreme Inc. is a newly established enterprise. It was set up by an entrepreneur who is generally interested in the business of providing engineering and operational support services to aircraft manufacturers. Extreme Inc., through the contacts of its owner, received a confirmed order from a well-known aircraft manufacturer to develop new designs for ducting the air conditioning of their aircraft. For this project, Extreme Inc. needed funds aggregating to $1 million. It was able to convince venture capitalists and was able to obtain funding of $1 million from two Silicon Valley venture capitalists.

The expenditures Extreme Inc. incurred in pursuance of its research and development project follow, in chronological order:

- January 15, 20X9: Paid $175,000 towards salaries of the technicians (engineers and consultants)
- March 31, 20X9: Incurred $250,000 towards the cost of developing the duct and producing the test model
- June 15, 20X9: Paid an additional $300,000 for revising the ducting process to ensure that product could be introduced in the market
- August 15, 20X9: Developed, at a cost of $80,000, the first model (prototype) and tested it with the air conditioners to ensure its compatibility
- October 30, 20X9: A focus group of other engineering providers was invited to a conference for the introduction of this new product. Cost of the conference aggregated to $50,000.
- December 15, 20X9: The development phase was completed and a cash flow budget was prepared. Net profit for the year 20X9 was estimated to equal $900,000

Required

What is the proper accounting treatment for the various costs incurred during 20X9?

Solution

Treatment of various costs incurred during 20X9 depends on whether these costs can be capitalized or have to be expensed as per IAS 38. Although IAS 38 is clear that costs incurred during the research phase should be expensed, it is important to note that not all development costs can be capitalized. In order to be able to capitalize costs, strict criteria established by IAS 38 should be met. Based on the criteria prescribed by IAS 38, these five conclusions can be drawn

1. It could be argued that the technical feasibility criterion was established at the end of August 20X9, when the first prototype was produced.
2. The intention to sell or use criterion was met at the end of August 20X9, when the sample was tested with the air-conditioning component to ensure it functions. But it was not until October 20X9 that the product's marketability was established. The reason is attributable to the fact that the entity had doubts about the new models being compatible with the air conditioners and that the sample would need further testing, had it not functioned.
3. In October 20X9, the existence of a market was clearly established.
4. The financial feasibility and funding criterion was also clearly met because Extreme Inc. has obtained a loan from venture capitalists and it had the necessary raw materials.
5. Extreme Inc. was able to measure its cost reliably, although this point was not addressed thoroughly in the question. Extreme Inc. can easily allocate labor, material, and overhead costs reliably.

Therefore, the costs that were incurred before October 20X9 should be expensed. The total costs that should be expensed = $175,000 + $250,000 + $300,000 + $80,000 = $805,000.

The costs eligible for capitalization are those incurred after October 20X9. However, conference costs of $50,000 would need to be expensed because they are independent from the development process.

Thus there are no total costs to be capitalized in terms of IAS 38.

RECOGNITION OF AN EXPENSE

The Standard requires that all expenditure on an intangible item be written off as an expense unless it meets the recognition criteria or it is acquired as part of a business combination and cannot be separately identified, in which case it is subsumed as part of goodwill and treated in accordance with IFRS 3. Examples include

- Expenditure on start-up activities (start-up costs) or on opening a new facility or business (preoperative expenses)
- Expenditure on training
- Expenditure on advertising and promotional activities (including mail order catalogues)
- Expenditure on relocating or reorganizing part or all of an entity

---

PRACTICAL INSIGHT

In the case where an entity paid in advance towards promotional material such as mail-order catalogues that have not yet been received by the entity at the end of reporting period (as they are not ready for distribution), then should such expenditure be treated as an expense in accordance with IAS 38 was a contentious issue needing clarification. The IASB through its "Improvements to IFRSs 2008" amended IAS 38 and clarified that IAS 38, paragraph 68, does not preclude an entity from recognizing a prepayment as an asset when payment for goods has been made in advance although the entity has obtained a "right to access" those goods (as opposed to "access to goods" themselves which is what the wording of the initial amendment was). With the current wording of the amendment, the IASB clearly set forth its views on this issue that an entity's "right to access" as against 'physical access' is what is envisaged by the revision to the standard in order to avail the treatment as per IAS 38.

CASE STUDY 3

Facts

Costs generally incurred by a newly established entity include

1. Preopening costs of a business facility
2. Recipes, secret formulas, models and designs, prototype
3. Training, customer loyalty, and market share
4. An in-house-generated accounting software
5. The design of a pilot plan
6. Licensing, royalty, and stand-still agreements
7. Operating and broadcast rights
8. Goodwill purchased in a business combination
9. A company-developed patented drug approved for medical use
10. A license to manufacture a steroid by means of a government grant
11. Cost of courses taken by management in quality engineering management
12. A television advertisement that will stimulate the sales in the technology industry

Required

Which of the previously mentioned costs are eligible for capitalization according to IAS 38, and which of them should be expensed when they are incurred?

Solution

Costs that are eligible for capitalization include items 2., 5., 6., 7., and 8.; for item 10., after initial recognition at cost, both the asset and the grant can be recognized at fair value.

These costs are eligible for capitalization under IAS 38 because

- They meet the criteria of "identifiability" (i.e., they are separable or they arise from contractual rights).

- It is probable that future economic benefits will flow to the entity.
- These costs can be measured reliably.

Costs that should be expensed because they do not meet the criteria under IAS 38 include items 1., 3., and 4. Item 9. is a case of an internally generated intangible asset that can be capitalized only provided it meets the development criterion. The main issue with item 11. is that the entity does not have "control" over its workforce. Despite the obvious benefit of item (l) to the business, such expenditure on advertisement does not meet the criterion of "control."

WEB SITE DEVELOPMENT COSTS

The advent of the Internet has created new ways of performing tasks that were unknown in the past. Most entities have their own Web site that serves as an introduction of the entity and its products and services to the world at large. A Web site has many of the characteristics of both tangible and intangible assets. With virtually every entity incurring costs on setting up its own Web site, there was a real need to examine this issue from an accounting perspective. An interpretation was issued that addressed Web site costs: SIC 32, *Intangible Assets—Web site Costs.*

SIC 32 lays down guidance on the treatment of Web site costs consistent with the criteria for capitalization of costs established by IAS 38. According to SIC 32, a Web site that has been developed for the purposes of promoting and advertising an entity's products and services does not meet the criteria for capitalization of costs under IAS 38. Thus costs incurred in setting up such a Web site should be expensed.

MEASUREMENT AFTER RECOGNITION

The Standard states that, after recognition, intangible assets may be measured using either a cost model or a revaluation model. However, if the revaluation model is used, then all assets in the same class are to be treated alike unless there is no active market for those assets.

"Classes of intangible assets" refers to groupings of similar items, such as patents and trademarks, concession rights, or brands. Assets in each class must be treated alike in order to avoid mixes of costs and values.

If the cost model is selected, then after initial recognition, an intangible asset shall be carried at cost less accumulated amortization and impairment losses.

If the revaluation model is selected, the intangible asset shall be carried at its fair value less subsequent accumulated amortization and impairment losses. Fair values are to be determined from an active market and are to be reassessed with regularity sufficient to ensure that, at the end of the reporting period, the carrying amount does not differ materially from its fair value.

PRACTICAL INSIGHT

Revaluations are to be determined *only* by reference to an active market. Use of valuation models and other techniques is *not* permitted. In this respect, an active market is one in which the items traded are homogeneous, willing buyers and sellers can be found at any time, *and prices* are available to the public. Therefore, in most instances, the revaluation model will not be a realistically usable model. Brands, trademarks, film titles, and the like are all individually unique and therefore fail on the homogeneity criterion.

If the revaluation model is used, at the date of the revaluation, accumulated amortization and impairment losses are either eliminated against the cost and then the net amount is uplifted to the revalued amount or are restated proportionately to the restatement of the gross carrying amount such that the net amount is equal to the fair value.

CASE STUDY 4

Facts

Active Asset Inc. owns a freely transferable taxi operator's license, which it acquired on January 1, 20X1, at an initial cost of $10,000. The useful life of the license is five years (based on the date it is valid for). The entity uses the straight-line method to amortize the intangible.

Such licenses are frequently traded either between existing operators or with aspiring operators. At the balance sheet date, on December 31, 20X2, due to a government-permitted increase in fixed taxi fares, the traded values of such a license was $12,000. The accumulated amortization on December 31, 20X2, amounted to $4,000.

Required

What journal entries are required at December 31, 20X2, to reflect the increase/decrease in carrying value (cost or revalued amount less accumulated depreciation) on the revaluation of the operating license based on the traded values of similar license? Also, what would be the resultant carrying value of the intangible asset after the revaluation?

Solution

The journal entries to be recorded in the books of account are

Intangible asset—accumulated amortization	$4,000	
Intangible asset—cost		$4,000

(Being elimination of accumulated depreciation against the cost of the asset)

Intangible asset—cost	$6,000	
Revaluation reserve		$6,000

(Being uplift of net book value to revalued amount)

The net result is that the asset has a *revised* carrying amount of $12,000 ($10,000 – $4,000 + $6,000).

A revaluation increase is to be recognized in other comprehensive income and accumulated in equity unless it reverses a previously recognized impairment loss, in which case it shall be recognized in profit or loss. If, in subsequent years, revaluation decreases *on the same asset* occur, such decreases are recognized in other comprehensive income to the extent of any credit balance in the revaluation surplus in respect of that asset. Otherwise the reduction is recognized in profit or loss.

Any revaluation reserve in respect of a particular intangible asset is transferred to retained earnings when it is realized. This could be on disposal, although it is permitted to treat the additional amortization resulting from the revaluation as a realization of that surplus and transfer this amount from revaluation reserve to retained earnings. Under *no circumstances* can the revaluation reserve, or part thereof, be credited to profit or loss.

USEFUL LIFE

The useful life of an intangible asset must be assessed on recognition as either indefinite or finite. If the assessment determines the life to be finite, then the length of life or number of units to be produced must be determined also. An indefinite useful life may be determined when there is no foreseeable limit to the period over which the entity will continue to receive economic benefit from the asset. All relevant factors must be considered in this assessment and may include

- Expected usage by the entity and whether it could be used by new management teams
- Product life cycles
- Rates of technical or commercial change
- Industry stability
- Likely actions by competitors
- Legal restrictions
- Whether the useful life is dependent on the useful lives of other assets

"Indefinite" does not mean "infinite." Additionally, assessments should not be made based on levels of future expenditure over and above that which would normally be required to maintain the asset at its initial standard of performance.

AMORTIZATION

The depreciable amount of an intangible asset with a finite useful life is to be allocated over its useful life. The depreciable amount is the cost of the asset (or other amount substituted for cost, e.g., in a revaluation model) less its residual value. Amortization shall commence when the asset is ready for use and shall cease when it is derecognized or is reclassified as held for sale under IFRS 5.

The residual value is to be assumed to be zero unless there is a commitment by a third party to acquire the asset at the end of its useful life or there is an active market for the asset and the residual value can be determined by reference to that market, and it is probable that an active market will continue to exist at the end of the asset's useful life.

Therefore, an asset with a residual value at anything other than zero assumes that the entity will dispose of the asset prior to the end of the asset's economic life.

The Standard requires that the residual value be reassessed at each balance sheet date. Any changes are to be treated as changes in accounting estimates. In practice, this is unlikely to have any impact in view of the basic presumption of a zero residual value.

Similarly, the useful life is to be reassessed annually. Any changes are also to be treated as changes in accounting estimates.

Intangible assets with indefinite useful lives are *not* to be amortized. However, the asset must be tested for impairment annually and whenever there is an indication that it may be impaired. IAS 36 provides guidance on impairment. Additionally, the determination of an indefinite useful life must be reassessed at each balance sheet date. If the assessment changes, it is to be treated as a change in accounting estimate.

IMPAIRMENT

Entities are to apply the provisions of IAS 36 in assessing the recoverable amount of an intangible asset and when and how to determine whether an asset is impaired.

RETIREMENTS AND DISPOSALS

Intangible assets shall be derecognized on disposal or when no future economic benefits are expected to be derived from their use or disposal.

Any gain or loss on derecognition amounts to the difference between the net disposal proceeds, if any, less the carrying amount of the asset. The gain or loss is to be recognized in profit or loss.

DISCLOSURES

The Standard requires these disclosures for each class of intangible asset, distinguishing between internally generated and other assets:

- Whether useful lives are indefinite or finite and, if finite, the useful lives or amortization rates used
- The amortization methods used
- The gross carrying amount and accumulated amortization and impairment losses at the beginning and end of the period
- The line items in the statement of comprehensive income in which amortization is included
- Additions, separately showing those internally generated, those acquired separately, and those acquired through business combinations
- Assets classified as held for sale under IFRS 5
- Increases or decreases during the period resulting from revaluations
- Impairment losses
- Reversals of impairment losses

- Amortization recognized during the period
- Net exchange differences on retranslation
- Other changes during the period
- For assets with indefinite useful lives, the carrying amount of the asset and the reasons supporting such an assessment
- Description, carrying amount, and remaining amortization period of any intangible assets that are material to the entity's financial statements
- The existence and carrying amounts of intangible assets whose title is restricted or pledged as security for liabilities
- Contractual commitments for the acquisition of intangible assets
- Intangible assets acquired by way of government grant and initially recognized at fair value, including their fair values, their carrying amounts, and whether subsequently carried under the cost or revaluation model
- The amount of research and development expenditure expensed during the period

If intangible assets are stated at revalued amounts, then these points are to be disclosed:

- For each class of asset

  - The effective date of revaluation
  - The carrying amount
  - The carrying amount that would have been recognized had the cost model been used
  - The revaluation surplus that relates to intangible assets at the beginning and end of the period, indicating changes during the period and any restrictions on distributions to shareholders

  - The methods and significant assumptions used in estimating fair values

In addition to the preceding disclosures, entities are encouraged to disclose the description of any fully amortized intangible assets that are still in use and of any significant intangible assets controlled by the entity not recognized as assets as they failed to meet the recognition criteria.

EXTRACTS FROM PUBLISHED FINANCIAL STATEMENTS

BASF, Annual Report, 2009

Notes to the Financial Statements

Accounting Policies

Intangible assets

Internally generated intangible assets are primarily comprised of internally developed software. Such software, as well as other internally generated assets for internal use, are valued at cost and amortized over their useful lives. Impairments are recorded if the carrying amount of an asset exceeds the recoverable amount.

Costs also include, in addition to those costs directly attributable to the asset, an appropriate allocation of overhead cost. Borrowing costs are capitalized to the extent that they are material and relate to the period over which the asset is generated.

The weighted-average useful lives of intangible assets amounted to

Average amortization in years

	2009	2008
Distribution, supply, and similar rights	14	16
Product rights, licenses, and trademarks	17	18
Know-how, patents, and production technologies	9	12
Internally generated intangible assets	6	6
Other rights and values	3	6

ADIDAS GROUP, Annual Report, 2009

Notes to the Financial Statements

Trademarks and Other Intangible Assets

Trademarks and other intangible assets consist of the following:

Trademarks and other intangible assets € in millions

	Dec. 31, 2009	Dec. 31, 2008
Trademarks, gross	1,342	1,390
Less: accumulated amortization	0	0
Trademarks, net	1,342	1,390
Software, patents, and concessions, gross	538	517
Less: accumulated amortization	378	313
Other intangible assets, net	160	204
Trademarks and other intangible assets, net	1,502	1,594

	Trademarks R'000	Goodwill R'000	Total R'000
2009			
Opening net book amount		287, 444	287, 444
Amortization charge			
Closing net book amount		287, 444	287, 444
At March 31, 2009			
Cost	50,500	287, 444	337,944
Accumulated amortization and impairment	(50,500)		(50,500)
Net book amount		287, 444	287, 444
2008			
Opening net book amount		287, 444	287, 444
Amortization charge			
Closing net book amount		287, 444	287, 444
At March 31, 2008			
Cost	50,500	287,444	337,944
Accumulated amortization and impairment	(50,500)		(50,500)
Net book amount		287,444	287,444

The Group determines whether trademarks with indefinite useful lives are impaired at least on an annual basis. This requires an estimation of the fair value less costs to sell of the cash-generating units to which the trademark is allocated. Estimating the fair value less costs to sell requires the Group to make an estimate of the expected future brand-specific sales and appropriate arm's-length royalty rates from the cash-generating unit and also to choose a suitable discount rate in order to calculate the present value of those cash flows. There was no impairment expense for the years ending December 31, 2009 and 2008.

Future changes in expected cash flows and discount rates may lead to impairment of the accounted trademarks in the future.

RAINBOW CHICKEN, Annual Report, 2009

Notes to Group Financial Statements

Trademarks

	2009 R'000	2008 R'000
Finite life/indefinite life	Finite life	Finite life
Amortization period	15 years	15 years
Method of amortization	Straight-line	Straight-line
Is intangible title restricted in any way	No	No
Net book amount pledged as security	Nil	Nil

Trademarks comprise Farmer Brown, Bonny Bird, FarmFare and Epol, all of which were acquired on acquisition of Bonny Bird Farms (Proprietary) Limited and Epol (Proprietary) Limited in 1991.

Goodwill

Goodwill relates to the acquisition of Vector Logistics (Proprietary) Limited in 2005. The recoverable amount of a cash-generating unit is determined based on value-in-use calculations. These calculations use cash flow projections based on financial budgets approved by management and future periods based on estimated growth rates. Cash flows beyond a five-year period are extrapolated using the estimated growth rates stated below.

Key assumptions used in the goodwill impairment test	*2009*	*2008*
Discount rate (%)	13.5	18.8
Perpetuity growth rate (%)	5.0	5.0
Period (years)	5	5

The perpetuity growth rate is consistent with long-term inflation forecasts. The discount rate reflects specific risks relating to the cash-generating unit.

No impairment was required in the current year or prior year.

Sensitivity analysis of assumptions used in the goodwill impairment test:

Assumption

	2009	*2008*
Discount rate (%)		
Movement	+5	+5
Impairment	Nil	Nil
Perpetuity growth rate (%)		
Movement	-5	-5
Impairment	Nil	Nil

MULTIPLE-CHOICE QUESTIONS

1. A newly set up dot-com entity has engaged you as its financial advisor. The entity has recently completed one of its highly publicized research and development projects and seeks your advice on the accuracy of the following statements made by one of its stakeholders. Which one is true?

(a) Costs incurred during the "research phase" can be capitalized.

(b) Costs incurred during the "development phase" can be capitalized if criteria such as technical feasibility of the project being established are met.

(c) Training costs of technicians used in research can be capitalized.

(d) Designing of jigs and tools qualify as research activities.

2. Which item listed below does **not** qualify as an intangible asset?

(a) Computer software.

(b) Registered patent.

(c) Copyrights that are protected.

(d) Notebook computer.

3. Which of the following items qualify as an intangible asset under IAS 38?

(a) Advertising and promotion on the launch of a huge product.

(b) College tuition fees paid to employees who decide to enroll in an executive M.B.A. program at Harvard University while working with the company.

(c) Operating losses during the initial stages of the project.

(d) Legal costs paid to intellectual property lawyers to register a patent.

4. Once recognized, intangible assets can be carried at

(a) Cost less accumulated depreciation.

(b) Cost less accumulated depreciation and less accumulated amortization.

(c) Revalued amount less accumulated depreciation.

(d) Cost plus a notional increase in fair value since the intangible asset is acquired.

5. Which of the following disclosures is **not** required by IAS 38?

(a) Useful lives of the intangible assets.

(b) Reconciliation of carrying amount at the beginning and the end of the year.

(c) Contractual commitments for the acquisition of intangible assets.

(d) Fair value of similar intangible assets used by its competitors.

Chapter 30

INVESTMENT PROPERTY (IAS 40)

BACKGROUND AND INTRODUCTION

This Standard prescribes criteria for the accounting treatment for, and disclosures relating to, investment property.

The Standard shall be applied in the recognition, measurement, and disclosure of investment property.

The Standard applies to the measurement in a lessee's financial statements of investment property held under a finance lease and to the measurement in the lessor's financial statements of investment property leased out under an operating lease. However, all other aspects relating to leases, their accounting, and their disclosure, are dealt with in IAS 17, *Leases*. Additionally, the Standard does not deal with biological assets related to agricultural activity (see IAS 41) or to mineral rights and mineral reserves such as oil, natural gas, and similar nonregenerative resources (see IFRS 6).

DEFINITIONS OF KEY TERMS
(In accordance with IAS 40)

Investment property. Land or building, or part of a building, or both, held by the owner or the lessee under a finance lease to earn rentals and/or for capital appreciation, rather than for use in production or supply of goods and services or for administrative purposes or for sale in the ordinary course of business.

Owner-occupied property. Property held by the owner or the lessee under a finance lease for use in production or supply of goods and services or for administrative purposes.

INVESTMENT PROPERTY

Property interests held by a lessee under an operating lease *may* (i.e., it is optional) be classified and recognized as an investment property *if and only if* the property would otherwise meet the definition of an investment property and the property is measured using the *fair value model* described later. This aspect of recognizing investment property is a comparatively recent addition and was included in response to the fact that in some countries, properties are held under long leases that provide, for all intents and purposes, rights that are similar to those of an outright buyer. The inclusion in the Standard of such interests permits the lessee to measure such assets at fair value.

407

One of the distinguishing characteristics of investment property (compared to owner-occupied property) is that it generates cash flows that are largely independent from other assets held by an entity. Owner-occupied property is accounted for under IAS 16, *Property, Plant, and Equipment.*

In some instances, an entity occupies part of a property and leases out the balance. If the two portions can be sold separately, each is accounted for appropriately. If the portions cannot be sold separately, then the entire property is treated as investment property *only if an insignificant proportion is owner-occupied.*

PRACTICAL INSIGHT

Precisely what is meant by "insignificant" is not defined and is left to judgment. However, in other Standards, indications are that 2% may be an applicable level.

Sometimes a property owner provides ancillary services, such as cleaning, maintenance, and security. Provided that such services are insignificant to the arrangement as whole, then the property is an investment property.

In other cases—for instance, a hotel—services can be significant, such as services provided to guests. Some hotel management arrangements render the owner merely a passive investor. Judgment must be used in determining whether the property satisfies the definition of an investment property.

An issue arises with groups of companies wherein one group company leases a property to another. At group, or consolidation level, the property is owner-occupied. However, at individual company level, the owning entity treats the building as investment property. Appropriate consolidation adjustments would need to be made in the group accounts.

CASE STUDY 1

Facts

XYZ Inc. and its subsidiaries have provided you, their International Financial Reporting Standards (IFRS) specialist, with a list of the properties they own:

1. Land held by XYZ Inc. for undetermined future use
2. A vacant building owned by XYZ Inc. and to be leased out under an operating lease
3. Property held by a subsidiary of XYZ Inc., a real estate firm, in the ordinary course of its business
4. Property held by XYZ Inc. for the use in production
5. A hotel owned by ABC Inc., a subsidiary of XYZ Inc., and for which ABC Inc. provides security services for its guests' belongings

Required

Advise XYZ Inc. and its subsidiaries as to which of the aforementioned properties would qualify under IAS 40 as investment properties. If they do not qualify thus, how should they be treated under IFRS?

Solution

Properties described under items 1., 2., and 5. would qualify as investment properties under IAS 40. With respect to item 5., it is to be noted that IAS 40 requires that when the ancillary services are provided by the entity and they are considered a relatively insignificant component of the arrangement, then the property is considered an investment property.

These properties qualify as investment properties because they are being held for rental or for capital appreciation as opposed to actively managed properties that are used in the production of goods.

Property described in item 3. is to be treated as "inventory" under IAS 2.

Property described in item 4. is treated as a long-lived asset under IAS 16.

RECOGNITION

Investment property shall be recognized as an asset *when and only when*

- It is probable that future economic benefits will flow to the entity.
- The cost of the investment property can be measured reliably.

Recognition principles are similar to those contained in IAS 16.

MEASUREMENT

Measurement at Recognition

An investment property shall be measured initially at cost, including transaction charges. Again, the principles for determining cost are similar to those contained in IAS 16, in particular for replacement and subsequent expenditure.

However, property held under an operating lease shall be measured initially using the principles contained in IAS 17, *Leases*—at the lower of the fair value and the present value of the minimum lease payments. A key matter here is that the item accounted for at fair value is *not the property itself* but the *lease interest.*

Measurement after Recognition

An entity shall select either the cost model or the fair value model for *all of its investment property.* There are, however, two exceptions. If an entity elects to classify property held under an operating lease as investment property, then it *must select the fair value model for all of its investment property.* The second exception is if the entity has investment property backing liabilities that pay a return linked to the fair value of the assets; if so, regardless of which model is selected for measuring such investment property, the entity continues to have a choice of models for its other investment property.

Fair Value Model

If the fair model value is selected, after initial recognition, investment property shall be measured at fair value. Fair value is the amount for which an asset could be exchanged between knowledgeable, willing parties in an arm's-length transaction.

Any gains or losses arising from changes in fair value shall be recognized in the income statement. This is quite a radical divergence from previous practices but is consistent with other Standards wherein assets are held in part for capital appreciation. The issue is that any gain on such remeasurement is unrealized, and, in many jurisdictions, the retained earnings of an entity are considered distributable (although some jurisdictions have legal definitions of distributable reserves). Consequently, many entities then transfer an amount from retained earnings to a capital reserve that may be treated as distributable only upon disposal of the related asset.

When applying the fair value model, the fair values should reflect the market conditions *at the end of the reporting period.* Valuations, therefore, carried out at dates too far removed from the end of the reporting period could reflect market conditions that are markedly different from those at the end of the reporting period and would be unacceptable. In addition, care needs to be taken as equipment, such as elevators, air conditioning, and the like, may be recognized as separate assets. Valuations usually include such assets, which should not be double counted.

If, on acquisition, it is not possible to determine fair value reliably on a continuing basis, then the asset shall be measured using the cost model under IAS 16 until disposal. Residual value shall be assumed to be zero. Therefore, it is possible for an entity to hold investment property, some of which is measured at fair value and some under the cost model.

If an entity measures investment property at fair value, it shall continue to do so until disposal, even if readily available market data become less frequent or less readily available.

Cost Model

An entity that selects the cost model shall measure all of its investment property in accordance with IAS 16's requirements for that model except those classified as held-for-sale in accordance with IFRS 5.

CASE STUDY 2

Facts

Investors Galore Inc., a listed company in Germany, ventured into the construction of a mega shopping mall in south Asia, which is rated as the largest shopping mall of Asia. The company's board of directors after market research decided that instead of selling the shopping mall to a local investor, who had approached them several times during the construction period with excellent offers, which he progressively increased during the year of construction, the company would hold this property for the purposes of earning rentals by renting out space in the shopping mall to tenants. For this purpose it used the services of a real estate company to find an anchor tenant (a major international retail chain) that then attracted other important retailers locally to rent space in the mega shopping mall, and within months of the completion of the construction the shopping mall was fully rented out.

The construction of the shopping mall was completed and the property was placed in service at the end of 20X1. According to the company's engineering department the computed total cost of the construction of the shopping mall was $100 million. An independent valuation expert was used by the company to fair value the shopping mall on an annual basis. According to the fair valuation expert the fair values of the shopping mall at the end of 20X1 and at each subsequent year-end thereafter were

20X1	$100 million
20X2	$120 million
20X3	$125 million
20X4	$115 million

The independent valuation expert was of the opinion that the useful life of the shopping mall was ten years and its residual value was $10 million.

Required

What would be the impact on the profit and loss account of the company if it decides to treat the shopping mall as an investment property under IAS 40

(a) Using the fair value model.
(b) Using the cost model.

(Since the rental income for the shopping mall would be the same under both the options, for the purposes of this exercise do not take into consideration the impact of the rental income from the shopping mall on the net profit or loss for the period.)

Solution

(a) Fair value model

If the company chooses to measure the investment property under the fair value model it will have to recognize in net profit or loss for each period **changes in fair value** from year to year. Thus the impact on profit or loss for the various years would be

Year	Cost ($millions)	Fair value ($millions)	Profit & Loss a/c ($millions)
20X1	100	100	0
20X2		120	20
20X3		125	5
20X4		115	(10)

(b) Cost model

If the company decided to measure the investment property under the cost model it would have to account for it under IAS 16 using the cost model prescribed under that Standard (which requires that the asset should be carried at its cost less accumulated depreciation and any accumulated impairment losses). Therefore, when investment property is measured under the cost model, the fluctuations in the fair value of the investment property from year to year would have no effect on profit or loss of the entity. Instead, the annual depreciation, which is computed based on the acquisition cost of the investment property will be the only charge to net profit or loss for each period (unless there is impairment which will also be a charge to net profit or loss for the year).

Based on the acquisition cost of $100 million (assuming there is no subsequent expenditure that would be capitalized), a residual value of $10 million, a useful life of ten years, and using the straight-line method of depreciation, the **annual impact** of **depreciation** on **net profit or loss** for each year would be

20X1	$ (100 – 10)/10 million = **9 million**
20X2	$ (100 – 10)/10 million = **9 million**
20X3	$ (100 – 10)/10 million = **9 million**
20X4	$ (100 – 10)/10 million = **9 million**

Transfers

Transfers to and from investment property shall be made *when and only when there is a change of use* evidenced by

- Commencement of owner occupation (transfer from investment property to property, plant, and equipment)
- Commencement of development with a view to sale (transfer from investment property to inventories)
- End of owner occupation (transfer from property, plant, and equipment to investment property)
- Commencement of an operating lease to another party (transfer from inventories or property, plant, and equipment to investment property)

In cases where the fair value model is *not* used, transfers between classifications are made at the carrying value: the lower of cost and net realizable value if inventories, or cost less accumulated depreciation and impairment losses if property, plant, and equipment.

If owner-occupied property is transferred to investment property that is to be carried at fair value, then, up to the change, IAS 16 is applied. That is to say, any revaluation in fair value is treated in accordance with IAS 16.

Transfers from investment property at fair value to property, plant, and equipment shall be at fair value, which becomes deemed cost.

For transfers from inventories to investment properties that are to be carried at fair value, the remeasurement to fair value is recognized in profit or loss.

When a property under construction is completed and transferred to investment property to be carried at fair value, the remeasurement to fair value is recognized in profit or loss.

DISPOSALS

An investment property shall be derecognized on disposal or at the time that no benefit is expected from future use or disposal. Any gain or loss is determined as the difference between the net disposal proceeds and the carrying amount and is recognized in profit or loss.

DISCLOSURES

Fair Value and Cost Model

An entity shall disclose

- Whether it applies the cost or fair value model
- If it applies the fair value model, whether and under what circumstances property interests held under operating leases are classified and accounted for as investment property
- When classification is difficult, the criteria used to distinguish investment property, owner-occupied property, and property held for disposal in the ordinary course of business
- The methods used and significant assumptions made in determining fair value

- The extent to which fair values are based on assessments by an independent and qualified valuer. If there are no such valuations, that fact shall be stated.
- The amounts recognized in profit or loss for

    - Rental income from investment property
    - Direct operating expenses that generated rental income
    - Direct operating expenses that did not generate rental income
    - Cumulative change in fair value recognized in profit or loss on sale of investment property from a pool of assets in which the cost model is used to a pool in which the fair value model is used

- Existence and amounts of restrictions on the realizability of investment property; or for the remittance of income and proceeds on disposal
- Contractual obligations to purchase, construct, or develop investment property or for repairs, maintenance, or enhancements

Fair Value Model

If an entity applies the fair value model, it shall also disclose a reconciliation of the opening and closing carrying values of investment property, showing

- Additions, showing separately, acquisitions, subsequent expenditure, and additions through business combinations
- Assets classified as held for sale under IFRS 5
- Net gains or losses from fair value adjustments
- Net exchange differences arising on translation of financial statements in a different reporting currency
- Transfers to and from inventories and owner-occupied property
- Other changes

When a valuation for an investment property is adjusted to avoid double counting of assets such as equipment that may be recognized separately, a reconciliation of the adjustments shall be disclosed.

When fair value cannot be measured reliably and the asset is stated in accordance with IAS 16, such assets shall be disclosed separately from those at fair value. In addition to the movement disclosures set out previously, disclosures shall be made of the

- Description of properties stated in accordance with IAS 16
- Explanation as to why fair value cannot be reliably measured
- Range of estimates, if possible, within which the fair value is highly likely to fall
- Disposals of investment property not carried at fair value

Cost Model

For investment properties measured under the cost model, an entity shall disclose

- Depreciation methods used
- Useful lives or depreciation rates used
- A reconciliation of the opening and closing gross carrying amounts and the accumulated depreciation and impairment losses, showing

    - Additions, showing separately, acquisitions, subsequent expenditure, and additions through business combinations

- Assets classified as held for sale under IFRS 5
- Impairment losses recognized and reversed
- Net exchange differences
- Transfers to and from inventories and owner-occupied property
- Other changes
- The fair value of investment property and, if fair value cannot be reliably measured

- Explanation as to why fair value cannot be reliably measured
- Range of estimates, if possible, within which the fair value is highly likely to fall
- Disposals of investment property not carried at fair value

PRACTICAL INSIGHT

Even if an entity measures an investment property under the cost model it is still required by IAS 40 to disclose the "fair value" of such an investment property measured at cost. (Such a disclosure is usually made in the notes to the financial statements). This may not appear to be an unusual requirement for disclosure of fair value in these days when fair value accounting seems to be the order of the day, but from the perspective of entities that are required to make such a disclosure such a requirement of IAS 40 is definitely being construed as an impractical and an expensive choice to implement. In other words, while IAS 40 is *apparently* giving an entity a free choice of measuring investment properties using either the cost model or the fair value model, this requirement to disclose fair value (despite allowing an entity to measure the invest-ment property under the cost model) compels it to undertake an exercise to fair value an in-vestment property that it is carrying at cost in its books of account. In practice, this **mandatory disclosure** under IAS 40 is seen by some as a really onerous requirement of the standard since it makes it incumbent upon an entity to undertake a fair valuation exercise even in a case when an entity is carrying an investment property at cost in its books of accounts (as allowed by the standard as a *free choice*) and only for the purposes of satisfying this disclosure requirement the entity has to undertake the same kind of a fair valuation exercise that it would otherwise have gone through had it chosen to measure this investment property under the fair value model.

Compare this to the **recommended disclosure** requirement under IAS 16, paragraph 79, in the case of property, plant, and equipment carried under the cost model wherein that standard *does not make it mandatory* but **"encourages"** the entity to disclose the fair value of such a property, plant, and equipment only in a situation when the fair value is materially different from the as-set's carrying value.

In practice, undertaking a fair valuation of an investment property on an **annual basis**, usually by an independent expert, is a very expensive exercise and thus entities are seen to prefer using the cost model over the fair value model. But if the standard makes it a compulsory requirement that an entity also disclose the fair value in a case wherein it measures the investment property using the cost model, such a disclosure requirement, in a way, amounts to taking away the free choice of allowing an entity to use either the cost model or the fair value model. In practice, therefore, such a mandatory disclosure requirement is construed by some as the proverbial case of the *fine print* taking away what the *large print* apparently allowed.

MULTIPLE-CHOICE QUESTIONS

1. A gain arising from a change in the fair value of an investment property for which an entity has opted to use the fair value model is recognized in
- (a) Net profit or loss for the year.
- (b) General reserve in the shareholders' equity.
- (c) Valuation reserve in the shareholders' equity.
- (d) None of the above.

2. An investment property should be measured initially at
- (a) Cost.
- (b) Cost less accumulated impairment losses.
- (c) Depreciable cost less accumulated impairment losses.
- (d) Fair value less accumulated impairment losses.

3. The applicable IFRS/IAS for a property being constructed or developed for future use as investment property is
- (a) IAS 2, *Inventories,* until construction is complete and then it is accounted for under IAS 40, *Investment Property.*
- (b) IAS 40, *Investment Property.*
- (c) IAS 11, *Construction Contracts,* until construction is complete and then it is accounted for under IAS 40, *Investment Property.*
- (d) IAS 16, *Property, Plant, and Equipment,* until construction is complete and then it is accounted for under IAS 40, *Investment Property.*

4. In the case of property held under an operating lease and classified as investment property
- (a) The entity has to account for the investment property under the cost model only.
- (b) The entity has to use the fair value model only.
- (c) The entity has the choice between the cost model and the fair value model.
- (d) The entity needs only to disclose the fair value and can use the cost model under IAS 38.

5. Transfers from investment property to property, plant, and equipment are appropriate
- (a) When there is change of use.
- (b) Based on the entity's discretion.
- (c) Only when the entity adopts the fair value model under IAS 38.
- (d) The entity can never transfer property into another classification on the balance sheet once it is classified as investment property.

6. An investment property is derecognized (eliminated from the balance sheet) when
- (a) It is disposed to a third party.
- (b) It is permanently withdrawn from use.
- (c) No future economic benefits are expected from its disposal.
- (d) In all of the above cases.

7. An entity has a factory that has been shut down for a year due to various reasons, including worker unrest and strike. The entity plans to sell this factory. It should
- (a) Classify the factory as investment property.
- (b) Classify the factory as property held for sale in the ordinary course of business under IAS 2.
- (c) Classify the factory as property, plant, and equipment under IAS 16.
- (d) Write off the net book value and disclose that fact in the footnotes to the financial statements.

Chapter 31

AGRICULTURE (IAS 41)

BACKGROUND AND INTRODUCTION

The main objective of IAS 41 is to establish accounting standards for agricultural activity. This Standard applies to biological assets, agricultural produce at the point of harvest, and government grants. The Standard does not apply to land related to agricultural activity, which is covered by IAS 16, *Property, Plant, and Equipment,* and IAS 40, *Investment Property,* or to intangible assets related to agricultural activity, which are covered by IAS 38, *Intangible Assets.*

DEFINITIONS OF KEY TERMS
(In accordance with IAS 41)

Agricultural produce. The harvested product of the entity's biological assets, for example, milk and coffee beans.

Agricultural activity. The management of the biological transformation and harvest of the biological assets for sale or for conversion into agricultural produce or into additional biological assets.

Biological assets. Living plants and animals.

Biological transformation. Relates to the processes of growth, degeneration, and production that can cause changes of a quantitative or qualitative nature in a biological asset.

Active market. One where these conditions exist: The items traded in the market are homogenous; willing buyers and sellers normally can be found at any time; and prices are available to the public.

Fair value. The amount for which an asset can be exchanged or a liability settled in an arm's-length transaction between knowledgeable and willing parties. The fair value of an asset is based on its present location and condition.

Government grants. Those as defined in IAS 20, *Accounting for Government Grants and Disclosure of Government Assistance.*

Harvest. The detachment of produce from a biological asset or the cessation of a biological asset's life process.

CASE STUDY 1

Facts

An entity on adoption of IAS 41 has reclassified certain assets as biological assets. The total value of the group's forest assets is $2,000 million comprising

	$m
Freestanding trees	1,700
Land under trees	200
Roads in forests	100
	2,000

Required

Show how the forests would be classified in the financial statements.

Solution

The forests would be classified as

	$m
Biological assets	1,700
Noncurrent assets—land	200
Noncurrent assets—other tangible assets	100
	2,000

RECOGNITION AND MEASUREMENT

An entity should recognize a biological asset or agricultural produce when the enterprise

- Controls the asset as a result of past events.
- It is probable that future economic benefits will flow to the entity.

Additionally, the fair value or cost of the asset should be able to be measured reliably. Any biological asset should be measured initially and at the end of each reporting period, at its fair value less estimated point-of-sale costs. The only exception to this is where the fair value cannot be measured reliably.

Agricultural produce should be measured at fair value less estimated point-of-sale costs at the point of the harvest. *Unlike a biological asset, there is no exception in cases in which fair value cannot be measured reliably.* According to IAS 41, agricultural produce can always be measured reliably. Point-of-sale costs include brokers' and dealers' commissions, any levies by regulatory authorities and commodity exchanges, and any transfer taxes and duties. They exclude transport and other costs necessary to get the assets to a market.

In deciding on the fair value for a biological asset or agricultural produce, it is possible to group together items in accordance with, for example, their age or quality. Determination of fair value, especially in the case of biological assets or agricultural produce, could be challenging and in some cases is not straightforward since there might be a tendency to use short cuts in the valuation process. IAS 41 cautions against this possibility and draws attention to situations where entities contract to sell their biological assets or produce at a future date. The Standard points out that these contract prices do not necessarily represent fair value. Therefore, the fair value of a biological asset or produce is not necessarily adjusted because of the existence of a contract. In many cases, these contracts may in fact be onerous contracts, as defined in IAS 37.

If an active market **exists** for the asset or produce, then the price in that market may be the best way of determining fair value.

If an entity has access to **different active markets**, then the entity will choose the most relevant and reliable price, that is, the one at which it is most likely to sell the asset.

If an active market **does not exist**, then these methods can be used to determine fair value:

- The most recent market transaction price
- Market prices for similar assets after adjustment to reflect any differences in the asset
- Any benchmarks within the sector, such as the value of cattle per kilogram

In some cases, market prices or values may not be available for an asset in its present condition. In these cases, the entity can use the present value of the expected net cash flow from the asset. The IASB through its Annual Improvements Project, *"Improvements to IFRS 2008,"* amended the requirements relating to the use of the discount rate. Prior to the amendment, IAS 41 required that the discount rate to be used should be the "pretax rate;" however, the Standard as amended requires a current market-determined rate and permits this to be either a "pretax" or "posttax" rate depending on the valuation methodology used in determining fair value.

In some circumstances, costs may be an indicator of fair value, especially where little biological transformation has taken place or the impact of biological transformation on the price is not expected to be significant.

GAINS AND LOSSES

Any gain on the initial recognition of biological assets at fair value less estimated point-of-sale costs and any changes in the fair value less estimated point-of-sale costs of biological assets during the reporting period are included in profit or loss for the period. Any gain on the initial recognition of agricultural produce at fair value less estimated point-of-sale costs will be included in profit or loss for the period to which it relates. All costs related to biological assets that are measured at fair value are recognized in profit or loss when incurred, except for costs to purchase biological assets.

The Standard does not explicitly prescribe how to account for subsequent expenditure related to biological assets. A gain or loss can, therefore, arise when an animal is born, plants and animals grow, plants are harvested, or animals generate agricultural produce. Losses can arise on the initial recognition of the purchase of animals, as their fair value less estimated point-of-sale costs are likely to be less than the purchase price plus any transaction and transportation costs.

CASE STUDY 2

Facts

An entity has these balances in its financial records:

	$m
Value of biological asset at cost 12/31/X8	600
Fair valuation surplus on initial recognition at fair value 12/31/X8	700
Change in fair value to 12/31/X9 due to growth and price fluctuations	100
Decrease in fair value due to harvest	90

Required

Show how these values would be incorporated into the financial statements at December 31, 20X9.

Solution

Extract from "Statement of Financial Position" at December 31, 20X9:

	$m
Biological assets	600
Fair valuation (included in profit or loss year ended 12/31/X8)	700
Carrying value 1/1/20X9	1,300
Change in fair value	100
Decrease due to harvest	(90)
Carrying value at December 31, 20X9	1,310

Extract from "Statement of Comprehensive Income" for year ended December 31, 20X9:

Biological assets change in fair value	100
Decrease due to harvest	(90)
Net gain	10

PRACTICAL INSIGHT

Stora Enso Oyj, a Finnish entity, applied IAS 41 in its financial statements for the year ended December 31, 2003. The entity is a producer of timber and timber products. It previously classified its forests as land within noncurrent assets and valued them at cost. Following the adoption of IAS 41, the entity reclassified the forests as biological assets and measured them at fair value. The effect was to increase the carrying value of the forests from €706 million to €1,562 million.

FAIR VALUE RELIABILITY

IAS 41 presumes that fair value can be measured reliably for a biological asset. However, it is possible that this presumption can be rebutted for a biological asset that, when it is first recognized, does not have a quoted market price in an active market and for which other valuation methods are clearly inappropriate or unworkable. In this case, the asset is measured at cost less accumulated depreciation and any impairment losses. All the other biological assets of the entity still must be measured at fair value. If circumstances do change and fair value becomes reliably measurable, then the entity must switch its valuation method to fair value less point-of-sale costs.

If a noncurrent biological asset meets the criteria to be classified as held for sale or is included in a disposal group in accordance with IFRS 5, then it is presumed that fair value can be measured reliably.

In determining cost, depreciation, and impairment losses, the entity should use IAS 2, IAS 16, and IAS 36.

GOVERNMENT GRANTS

A government grant that is related to a biological asset measured at fair value less estimated point-of-sale costs should be recognized as income when the government grant becomes receivable. If there are conditions attached to the government grant, then the government grant shall be recognized only when those conditions are met. IAS 20 is applied only to a government grant that is related to a biological asset, which has been measured at cost less accumulated depreciation and impairment losses.

IAS 41 does not deal with government grants that relate to agricultural produce. These grants may include subsidies. Subsidies are normally payable when the produce is sold and would therefore be recognized as income on the sale.

ISSUES IN IAS 41

The change in the fair value of biological assets is twofold: There can be physical change through growth, and there can be a price change. Separate disclosure of these two elements is encouraged but not required. Where biological assets are harvested, then fair value measurement stops at the time of the harvest, and IAS 2, *Inventories,* applies after that date.

Agricultural land is accounted for under IAS 16, but biological assets that are attached to the land are measured separately from the land.

CASE STUDY 3

Facts

A Colombian entity is considering the valuation of its harvested coffee beans. Industry practice is to value the coffee beans at market value. The national accounting body has always used this practice and uses as its source of reference "Accounting for Successful Farms," a local publication.

Required

The entity wishes to adopt IAS 41 but does not know what the impact will be on its inventory of coffee beans.

Solution

Fair value measurement stops at the time of harvest, and IAS 2, *Inventories*, applies after that date. Therefore, the inventory will be measured at the lower of cost and net realizable value.

CASE STUDY 4

Facts

A public limited company, Dairy, produces milk on its farms. It produces 30% of the country's milk that is consumed. Dairy owns 450 farms and has a stock of 210,000 cows and 105,000 heifers. The farms produce 8 million kilograms of milk a year, and the average inventory held is 150,000 kilograms of milk. However, the company is currently holding stocks of 500,000 kilograms of milk in powder form. At October 31, 20X9, the herds are

- 210,000 cows (3 years old), all purchased on or before November 1, 20X8
- 75,000 heifers, average age 1.5 years, purchased on April 1, 20X9
- 30,000 heifers, average age 2 years, purchased on November 1, 20X8. No animals were born or sold in the year.

The unit values less estimated point-of-sale costs were

1-year-old animal at October 31, 20X9	$32
2-year-old animal at October 31, 20X9	$45
1.5-year-old animal at October 31, 20X9	$36
3-year-old animal at October 31, 20X9	$50
1-year-old animal at November 1, 20X8 and April 1, 20X9	$30
2-year-old animal at November 1, 20X8	$40

The company has had problems during the year: Contaminated milk was sold to customers. As a result, milk consumption has gone down. The government has decided to compensate farmers for potential loss in revenue from the sale of milk. This fact was published in the national press on September 1, 20X9. Dairy received an official letter on October 10, 20X9, stating that $5 million would be paid to it on January 2, 2010.

The company's business is spread over different parts of the country. The only region affected by the contamination was Borthwick, where the government curtailed milk production in the region. The cattle were unaffected by the contamination and were healthy. The company estimates that the future discounted cash flow income from the cattle in the Borthwick region amounted to $4 million, after taking into account the government restriction order. The company feels that it cannot measure the fair value of the cows in the region because of the problems created by the contamination. There are 60,000 cows and 20,000 heifers in the region. All these animals had been purchased on November 1, 20X8. A rival company had offered Dairy $3 million for these animals after point-of-sale costs and further offered $6 million for the farms themselves in that region. Dairy has no intention of selling the farms at present. The company has been applying IAS 41 since November 1, 20X8.

Required

Advise the directors on how the biological assets and produce of Dairy should be accounted for under IAS 41, discussing the implications for the financial statements.

Solution

Biological assets should be measured at the end of each reporting period at fair value less estimated point-of-sale costs unless fair value cannot be measured reliably. The Standard encourages companies to separate the change in fair value less estimated point-of-sale costs between those changes due to physical reasons and those due to price.

Fair value of cattle excluding Borthwick region:

	$000	*$000*
Fair value at November 1, 20X8		
Cows (210,000 – 60,000) × $40		6,000
Heifers (30,000 – 20,000) × $30		300
Purchase 75,000 heifers × $30		2,250
		8,550

Increase due to price change

150,000 × $(45 – 40)	750	
10,000 × $(32 – 30)	20	
75,000 × $(32 – 30)	150	
		920

Increase due to physical change

150,000 × $(50 – 45)	750	
10,000 × $(45 – 32)	130	
75,000 × $(36 – 32)	300	
		1,180

Fair value less estimated point-of-sale costs at October 31, 20X9

150,000 × $50	7,500	
10,000 × $45	450	
75,000 × $36	2,700	
		10,650

Borthwick region—fair value of cattle:

This region has an inventory of cattle of 60,000 cows and 20,000 heifers. Fair value is difficult to ascertain because of the region's problems. However, according to IAS 41, if fair value was used on initial recognition, then it should be continued to be used. The cattle in this region would have been fair valued at November 1, 20X8, under the Standard. Therefore, the cattle must be valued at fair value less estimated point-of-sale costs as at October 31, 20X9. Although $3 million has been offered for these animals, this may be an onerous contract as rival companies are likely to wish to take advantage of the problems in this region. The future discounted income is again an inappropriate value as the cattle are healthy and could be moved to another region and sold.

The cattle in this region would therefore be valued at

	$000
60,000 cows × $50	3,000
20,000 heifers × $45	900
	3,900

Additional Points

- The powdered milk inventory will be valued using IAS 2, *Inventories,* and will be valued at the lower of cost and net realizable value. Because of the large amount of inventory, there may be an issue regarding obsolescence or possibly contamination, which might result in a reduction in the asset's value.
- Biological assets that meet the criteria to be classified as held for sale should be accounted for using IFRS 5. The offer for the farms and cattle would not meet the criteria under IFRS 5, as from Dairy's viewpoint, the carrying amount of the assets (disposal group) is unlikely to be recovered now principally through a sale transaction.
- Unconditional government grants should be recognized when the grants become receivable. The statement in the national press on September 1, 20X9, would not be sufficient to recognize the grant, but the official letter of October 10, 20X9, would be sufficient. Therefore, a receivable of $5 million would be shown in the financial statements to October 31, 20X9, and credited to income.

DISCLOSURES

- An entity shall disclose the aggregate gain or loss that arises on the initial recognition of biological assets and agricultural produce and from the change in value less estimated point-of-sale costs of the biological assets.
- A description of each group of biological assets is also required. If it is not disclosed anywhere else in the financial statements, then the entity shall also set out the nature of its activities and nonfinancial measures or estimates of the physical quantity of each group of the entity's biological assets at period end. It should supply the same information for the output for agricultural produce during the period.
- The methods and assumptions applied in determining fair value should also be disclosed.
- The fair value less estimated point-of-sale costs of agricultural produce harvested during the period shall be disclosed at the point of harvest.

- The existence and carrying amounts of biological assets whose title is restricted and any biological assets placed as security should be disclosed.
- The amount of any commitments for the development or acquisition of biological assets and management's financial risk strategies should also be disclosed.
- A reconciliation of the changes in the carrying amount of biological assets, showing separately, changes in value, purchases, sales, harvesting, business combinations, and exchange differences should be disclosed.
- Where fair value cannot be measured, then additional disclosure is required including the description of the asset, an explanation of the circumstances, if possible a range within which the fair value is likely to fall, any gain or loss recognized on disposal, the depreciation method, and useful lives or depreciation rates.
- The gross carrying amounts on the accumulated depreciation should also be shown.
- If the fair value of biological assets previously measured at cost less accumulated depreciation and impairment losses is now ascertainable, then additional disclosures are required, such as a description of the biological assets, an explanation as to why fair value is now reliably measurable, and the effect of the change.
- Regarding government grants, disclosures should be made as to the nature and extent of the grants, any conditions that have not been fulfilled, and any significant decreases in the expected level of the grants.

EXTRACTS FROM PUBLISHED FINANCIAL STATEMENTS

RAINBOW CHICKEN, Annual Report, 2009

Notes to Group Financial Statements
Accounting Policies

Biological Assets

Breeding stock includes the Cobb grandparent breeding and the parent rearing and laying operations. Broiler hatching eggs are included in breeding stock.

Biological assets are measured at fair value less estimated point-of-sale costs at reporting dates. Fair value is determined based on market prices or, where market prices are not available, by reference to sector benchmarks.

Gains and losses arising on the initial recognition of biological assets at fair value less estimated point-of-sale costs and from a change in fair value less estimated point-of-sale costs are charged to the income statement in the year in which they arise.

Biological Assets

	2009 R'000	2008 R'000
Breeding stock		
At the beginning of the year	212 315	159,822
Gain arising from cost inputs	728,982	575,560
Decrease due to harvest	(700,411)	(526,380)
Fair value adjustment	3,346	3,313
At the end of the year at fair value	**244,232**	**212,315**
Broiler stock		
At the beginning of the year	156 909	156 909
Gain arising from cost inputs	3,577,857	2,810,293
Decrease due to harvest	(3,558,795)	(2,774,593)
Fair value adjustment	9,350	11,753
At the end of the year at fair value	**109,456**	**98,885**
Total at the end of the year at fair value	**269,278**	**242,199**

MULTIPLE-CHOICE QUESTIONS

1. Which of the following is **not** dealt with by IAS 41?

    (a) The accounting for biological assets.

    (b) The initial measurement of agricultural produce harvested from the entity's biological assets.

    (c) The processing of agricultural produce after harvesting.

    (d) The accounting treatment of government grants received in respect of biological assets.

2. Where there is a long aging or maturation process after harvest, the accounting for such products should be dealt with by

    (a) IAS 41.

    (b) IAS 2, *Inventory.*

    (c) IAS 16, *Property, Plant, and Equipment.*

    (d) IAS 40, *Investment Property.*

3. Generally speaking, biological assets relating to agricultural activity should be measured using

    (a) Historical cost.

    (b) Historical cost less depreciation less impairment.

    (c) A fair value approach.

    (d) Net realizable value.

4. Entity A had a plantation forest that is likely to be harvested and sold in 30 years. The income should be accounted for in the following way

    (a) No income should be reported until first harvest and sale in 30 years.

    (b) Income should be measured annually and reported using a fair value approach that recognizes and measures biological growth.

    (c) The eventual sale proceeds should be estimated and matched to the profit and loss account over the 30-year period.

    (d) The plantation forest should be valued every five years and the increase in value should be shown in the statement of recognized gains and losses.

5. Regarding the choice of measurement basis used for valuing biological assets, IAS 41

    (a) Sets out several ways of measuring fair value.

    (b) Recommends the use of historical cost.

    (c) Recommends the use of current cost.

    (d) Recommends the use of present value.

6. Where the fair value of the biological asset cannot be determined reliably, the biological asset should be measured at

    (a) Cost.

    (b) Cost less accumulated depreciation.

    (c) Cost less accumulated depreciation and accumulated impairment losses.

    (d) Net realizable value.

7. Which of the following costs are **not** included in point-of-sale costs?

    (a) Commissions to brokers and dealers.

    (b) Levies by regulatory agencies.

    (c) Transfer taxes and duties.

    (d) Transport and other costs necessary to get the assets to a market.

8. Which of the following values is unlikely to be used in fair value measurement?

    (a) Quoted price in a market.

    (b) The most recent market transaction price.

    (c) The present value of the expected net cash flows from the assets.

    (d) External independent valuation.

9. A gain or loss arising on the initial recognition of a biological asset and from a change in the fair value less estimated point-of-sale costs of a biological asset should be included in

    (a) The net profit or loss for the period.

    (b) The statement of recognized gains and losses.

    (c) A separate revaluation reserve.

    (d) A capital reserve within equity.

10. When agricultural produce is harvested, the harvest should be accounted for by using IAS 2, *Inventories,* or another applicable International Accounting Standard. For the purposes of that Standard, cost at the date of harvest is deemed to be

    (a) Its fair value less estimated point-of-sale costs at point of harvest.

    (b) The historical cost of the harvest.

    (c) The historical cost less accumulated impairment losses.

    (d) Market value.

11. Contract prices are not necessarily relevant in determining fair value, and the fair value of a biological asset or agricultural produce is not adjusted because of the existence of a contract.

    (a) True.

    (b) False.

12. Land that is related to agricultural activity is valued

    (a) At fair value.

    (b) In accordance with IAS 16, *Property, Plant, and Equipment*, or IAS 40, *Investment Property.*

    (c) At fair value in combination with the biological asset that is being grown on the land.

    (d) At the resale value separate from the biological asset that has been grown on the land.

13. An unconditional government grant related to a biological asset that has been measured at fair value less point-of-sale costs should be recognized as

    (a) Income when the grant becomes receivable.

    (b) A deferred credit when the grant becomes receivable.

    (c) Income when the grant application has been submitted.

    (d) A deferred credit when the grant has been approved.

14. If a government grant is conditional on certain events, then the grant should be recognized as

    (a) Income when the conditions attached to the grant are met.

    (b) Income when the grant has been approved.

    (c) A deferred credit when the conditions attached to the government grant are met.

    (d) A deferred credit when the grant is approved.

15. Where there is a production cycle of more than one year, the Standard encourages separate disclosure of the

    (a) Physical change only.

    (b) Price change only.

    (c) Total change in value.

    (d) Physical change and price change.

16. Which of the following information should be disclosed under IAS 41?

    (a) Separate disclosure of the gain or loss relating to biological assets and agricultural produce.

    (b) The aggregate gain or loss arising on the initial recognition of biological assets and agricultural produce and the change in fair value less estimated point-of-sale costs of biological assets.

    (c) The total gain or loss from biological assets, agricultural produce, and from changes in fair value less estimated point-of-sale costs of biological assets.

    (d) There is no requirement in the Standard to disclose separately any gains or losses.

Chapter 32

FIRST-TIME ADOPTION OF INTERNATIONAL FINANCIAL REPORTING STANDARDS (IFRS 1)

BACKGROUND

When an entity that reports under an accounting framework other than the International Financial Reporting Standards (IFRS)—say, its own set of national accounting standards—decides to change to IFRS, it has to comply with certain requirements (prescribed by IFRS) on conversion to IFRS; these requirements are outlined in IFRS 1, *First-Time Adoption of IFRS*. This IASB standard has gained considerable importance in recent years due to the phenomenal popularity of IFRS globally. Since the IFRS regime makes it incumbent upon all new adherents to IFRS to compulsorily pass the "IFRS 1 test" on conversion to IFRS, this standard is becoming more important by the day as more and more countries of the world are adopting IFRS as their national accounting standards.

Michel Prada, former chairman of the Technical committee of IOSCO, in his keynote address at a round table on global accounting convergence sponsored by the Financial Stability Forum and held in Paris in February 2006, had made the following interesting observations about the global acceptance of IFRS vis-à-vis other recognized international standards such as US GAAP (generally accepted accounting principles):

1. Out of a worldwide market capitalization totaling over 36 trillion US dollars at the end of 2005, 11 trillion US dollars correspond to markets where IFRS are either required or permitted, and 17 trillion US dollars to markets where US GAAP is the rule; out of the balance, 4 trillion US dollars correspond to Japanese GAAP
2. However, in terms of the largest companies included in the coveted "Fortune 500" listing for that year, 176 prepared their accounts under US GAAP, 81 entities prepared their financial statements under Japanese GAAP but 200 conglomerates used IFRS.

Such insightful statistics on global acceptance of IFRS are thought-provoking and lend support to the fact that the IASB is taking giant strides forward as far more countries are adopting IFRS as their national accounting standards as opposed to other recognized accounting frameworks.

The year 2007 proved to be an exceptional year of groundbreaking achievements for the IASB. A leading international accounting journal described it as a "watershed year" for the IASB due to the following significant milestones achieved by it during 2007:

1. Firstly, the November 15, 2007 announcement by the US SEC (securities and exchange commission), *a year sooner than expected*, to allow foreign private issuers to enter the US capital market using IFRS-compliant financial statements (without reconciling to US GAAP), which came as a surprise to many in the international financial circles and was considered a historic move on the part of the US SEC; some even believe that this favorable nod by the US SEC to the IASB standards undoubtedly paved the way for further acceptance of IFRS globally.
2. Secondly, the year "2007 also saw the 108th country sign up to international financial reporting standards" (*Accountancy*, January 2008)

With such extraordinary achievements to its credit the IASB feels confident that more and more global players will sooner or later convert to IFRS. In fact, major economic players such as Canada and India have already announced their plans to go the "IFRS route" by 2011. Commenting on how many more countries are expected to adopt IFRS by 2011, Sir David Tweedie, chairman of the IASB, remarked, "We reckon by about 2011 there'll be 150—all the major economies" (*Accountancy*, January 2008).

IFRS 1 had assumed great practical significance for many countries when they first adopted IFRS. In fact, in 2005, when more than 8,000 listed entities in all countries within the European Union (EU) adopted IFRS for the first time in their consolidated financial statements, this standard was extensively applied by these first-time adopters of IFRS. Many global players outside Europe have also adopted IFRS as their national standards since then. In fact, Australia, Hong Kong, New Zealand, Philippines, and Singapore have adopted national standards that mirror IFRS. In all cases, when entities are preparing to adopt IFRS for the first time, they need to understand and apply the requirements of IFRS 1.

This subject was earlier dealt with by an interpretation of IAS 1, namely, SIC 8 that was issued by the erstwhile Standing Interpretations Committee (SIC) of the International Accounting Standards Committee (IASC), the predecessor standard-setting body of the International Accounting Standards Board (IASB), and addressed matters arising from an entity's first-time application of IAS. For this reason it was called SIC 8, *First-Time Application of IAS as the Primary Basis of Accounting*. Being an interpretation of a Standard (as opposed to a Standard itself), the guidance in SIC 8 was rather limited and not as detailed as IFRS 1, covering various aspects of first-time adoption of IFRS as contained in IFRS 1. Due to the practical importance of this matter, the IASB issued it as a separate Standard.

In 2008, IFRS 1 was substantially rewritten (without altering the technical content) with the objective of making the Standard clearer and easier to follow by reorganizing and moving the exceptions and exemptions into appendices. The improved structure is also intended to better accommodate ongoing changes to the Standard.

The revised Standard is effective for periods beginning on or after July 1, 2009, with earlier application permitted. In January 2009, an additional exemption was introduced as a consequential amendment of IFRIC 18, *Transfers of Assets from Customers*; and in July 2009, additional exemptions were introduced relating to oil and gas assets, and arrangements involving leases.

IFRS 9 prohibits retrospective application and instead says that the assessment as to whether the financial asset meets the criteria for amortized cost classification is made on the basis of facts and circumstances at the date of transition.

SCOPE

IFRS 1 applies to an entity that presents its first IFRS financial statements and sets out ground rules that an entity needs to follow when it adopts IFRS for the first time as the basis for preparing its general-purpose financial statements. In other words, it applies to all those entities that present for the first time their financial statements under IFRS. The Standard refers to such entities as "First-Time Adopters of IFRS."

Furthermore, according to IFRS 1, an entity shall apply this Standard not only in its *first IFRS financial statements* but also in *each interim financial report* it presents, under IAS 34, for the part of the period covered by its first IFRS financial statements. An entity's first IFRS financial statements are those that are the *first annual financial statements* in which the entity adopts IFRS by an *explicit and unreserved statement* (in those financial statements) *of compliance with IFRS.*

Financial statements presented by an entity in the current year would qualify as "first IFRS financial statements," as explained in the Standard, if an entity presented its most recent previous financial statements:

1. Under national generally accepted accounting principles or Standards that were inconsistent with IFRS in all respects
2. In conformity with IFRS in all respects, however, these financial statements did not contain an explicit and unreserved statement that they complied with IFRS
3. Categorically stating that the financial statements comply with certain IFRS but not all
4. Under national GAAP or Standards that differ from IFRS but using some individual IFRS to account for items that are not addressed by its national GAAP or Standards
5. Under national GAAP or Standards with a reconciliation of some items to amounts determined under IFRS

Other examples of situations when an entity's current year's financial statements would qualify as "first IFRS financial statements" are when

6. The entity prepared financial statements in the previous period under IFRS but the financial statements were meant for "internal use only" and were not made available to the entity's owners or any other external users
7. The entity prepared a reporting package in the previous period under IFRS for consolidation purposes without preparing a complete set of financial statements as mandated by IAS 1
8. The entity did not present financial statements for the previous periods

**DEFINITIONS OF KEY TERMS
(in accordance with IFRS 1)**

Date of transition to IFRS. A critical date for first-time adopters of IFRS. Refers to the beginning of the earliest period for which an entity presents full comparative information under IFRS in its "first IFRS financial statements."

Deemed cost. An amount substituted for "cost" or "depreciated cost" at a given date. In the subsequent period, depreciation or amortization is based on such deemed cost on the premise that the entity had initially recognized the asset or liability at the given date and that its cost was equal to the deemed cost.

Fair value. The amount for which an asset could be exchanged, or a liability settled, between knowledgeable, willing parties in an arm's-length transaction.

First IFRS financial statements. The first annual financial statements in which an entity adopts IFRS by an *explicit and unreserved* statement of compliance with IFRS.

First-time adopter (of IFRS). Term used for an entity that presents its "first IFRS financial statements" in the period in which it does so.

International Financial Reporting Standards (IFRS). Collective name for the Standards issued by the International Accounting Standards Board (IASB) and the interpretations issued by the International Financial Reporting Standards Interpretations Committee (IFRSIC). They also include all previous standards (IAS) issued by the International Accounting Standards Committee (IASC), the IASB's predecessor standard-setting body, and the interpretations issued by the erstwhile Standards Interpretations Committee (SIC) and adopted by the IASB.

Opening IFRS statement of financial position. The statement of financial position prepared in accordance with the requirements of IFRS 1 as of the "date of transition to IFRS." (Since IFRS 1 only requires that a first-time adopter *prepare* an opening statement of financial position, as opposed to *present* an opening statement of financial position, whether this statement of financial position is *published* along with the "first IFRS financial statements" or not, it would still be considered an opening IFRS statement of financial position.)

Previous GAAP. Refers to the basis of accounting (say, national standards) that a first-time adopter used immediately prior to IFRS adoption.

Reporting date. The end of the latest period covered by financial statements or by an interim financial report. (For IFRS 1, this is another critical date since, based on this date, a first-time adopter determines accounting policies to be applied in the preparation of the opening IFRS statement of financial position; these policies have to be compliant with IFRS effective on that date.)

DEEMED EXCEPTIONS TO THE "FIRST-TIME ADOPTER" RULE

In a case where an entity's financial statements in the previous year contained an explicit and unreserved statement of compliance with IFRS but in fact did not fully comply with all aspects of IFRS, such an entity would *not* be considered a first-time adopter for the purposes of IFRS 1. In other words, disclosed or undisclosed departures from IFRS in the previous year's financial statements of an entity that has made an explicit and unreserved statement of IFRS compliance would be treated by IFRS 1 as "errors" that warrant correction under IAS 8.

IFRS 1 identifies three instances, including the one described above, and categorically states that in such cases, this Standard does not apply. These *deemed exceptions* are

- When an entity presented its financial statements in the previous year that contained an explicit and unreserved statement of compliance with IFRS and auditors qualified their report on those financial statements
- When an entity in the previous year presented its financial statements under national requirements (i.e., its national GAAP) along with another set of financial statements that contained an explicit or unreserved statement of compliance with IFRS and in the current year it discontinues this practice of presenting under its national GAAP and presents only under IFRS
- When an entity in the previous year presented its financial statements under national requirements (its national GAAP) and those financial statements contained an explicit and unreserved statement of IFRS compliance

OPENING IFRS STATEMENT OF FINANCIAL POSITION

An entity adopting IFRS for the first time is obliged, under this Standard, to prepare an opening statement of financial position on the *date of transition to IFRS*. This opening IFRS statement of financial position serves as the starting point for the entity's accounting under IFRS. Although the requirement under IFRS 1 is to "prepare" an opening statement of financial position, this does not imply that the opening IFRS statement of financial position should also be *presented* in the entity's first IFRS financial statements.

According to the definition of the expression "date of transition to IFRS" contained in Appendix A to IFRS 1, this date refers to *the beginning of the earliest period for which an entity presents full comparative information under IFRS in its first IFRS financial statements*. Therefore, the date of transition to IFRS depends on two factors: the date of adoption of IFRS and the number of years of comparative information that the entity decides to present along with the financial information of the year of adoption.

CASE STUDY 1

Facts

Fickle Inc. presented its financial statements under its previous GAAP annually as at December 31 each year. The most recent financial statements it presented under its previous GAAP were as of December 31, 20X8. Fickle Inc. decided to adopt IFRS as of December 31, 20X9, and to present one-year comparative information for the year 20X8.

Required

When should Fickle Inc. prepare its opening IFRS statement of financial position?

Solution

The beginning of the earliest period for which Fickle Inc. should present full comparative information would be January 1, 20X8. In this case, the opening IFRS statement of financial position that the entity would need to prepare under IFRS 1 would be as of January 1, 20X8.

Alternatively, if Fickle Inc. decided to present two-year comparative information (i.e., for 20X8 and 20X7), then the beginning of the earliest period for which the entity should present full comparative information would be January 1, 20X7. In this case, the opening IFRS statement of financial position that Fickle Inc. would need to prepare under IFRS 1 would be as of January 1, 20X7.

ADJUSTMENTS REQUIRED IN PREPARING THE OPENING IFRS STATEMENT OF FINANCIAL POSITION (OR IN TRANSITION FROM PREVIOUS GAAP TO IFRS AT THE TIME OF FIRST-TIME ADOPTION)

In preparing the opening IFRS statement of financial position, an entity should apply these four rules, except in cases where IFRS 1 grants targeted exemptions and prohibits retrospective application:

1. *Recognize* all assets and liabilities whose recognition is required under IFRS.
2. *Derecognize* items as assets or liabilities if IFRS do not permit such recognition.
3. *Reclassify* items that it recognized under previous GAAP as one type of asset, liability, or component of equity, but are a different type of asset, liability, or component of equity under IFRS.
4. *Measure* all recognized assets and liabilities according to principles enshrined in IFRS.

CASE STUDY 2

Facts

Exuberance Corp. presented its financial statements under the national GAAP of "Strangeland" (country) until 20X8. It adopted IFRS from 20X9 and is required to prepare an opening IFRS statement of financial position as at January 1, 20X8. In preparing the IFRS opening statement of financial position Exuberance Corp. noted

- Under its previous GAAP, Exuberance Corp. had deferred advertising costs of $1,000,000 and had classified proposed dividends of $500,000 as a current liability.
- It had not made a provision for warranty of $200,000 in the financial statements presented under previous GAAP since the concept of "constructive obligation" was not recognized under its previous GAAP.
- In arriving at the amount to be capitalized as part of costs necessary to bring an asset to its working condition, Exuberance Corp. had not included professional fees of $300,000 paid to architects at the time when the building it currently occupies as its head office was being constructed.

Required

Advise Exuberance Corp. on the treatment of all the above items under IFRS 1.

Solution

In order to prepare the opening IFRS statement of financial position at January 1, 20X8, Exuberance Corp. would need to make these adjustments to its statement of financial position at December 31, 20X7, presented under its previous GAAP:

1. IAS 38 does not allow advertising costs to be deferred whereas Exuberance Corp.'s previous GAAP allowed this treatment. Thus, $1,000,000 of such deferred costs should be derecognized (expensed) under IFRS.
2. IAS 37 requires recognition of a provision for warranty but Exuberance Corp.'s previous GAAP did not allow a similar treatment. Thus, a provision for warranty of $200,000 should be recognized under IFRS.

3. IAS 10 does not allow proposed dividends to be recognized as a liability; instead, under the latest revision to IAS 10, they should be disclosed in footnotes. Exuberance Corp.'s previous GAAP allowed proposed dividends to be treated as a current liability. Therefore, proposed dividends of $500,000 should be disclosed in footnotes.

4. IAS 16 requires all directly attributable costs of bringing an asset to its working condition for its intended use to be capitalized as part of the carrying cost of property, plant, and equipment. Thus $300,000 of architects' fees should be capitalized as part of (i.e., used in the measurement of) property, plant, and equipment under IFRS.

ACCOUNTING POLICIES

IFRS 1 requires that in preparing an "opening IFRS statement of financial position," the "first-time adopter" shall use the same accounting policies as it has used throughout all periods presented in its first IFRS financial statements. Furthermore, the Standard stipulates that those accounting policies shall comply with each IFRS effective at the "reporting date" (explained ahead) for its first IFRS financial statements, except under certain circumstances wherein the entity claims targeted *exemptions* from retrospective application of IFRS or is *prohibited* by IFRS to apply IFRS retrospectively *(both concepts discussed later)*. In other words, a "first-time adopter" should consistently apply the same accounting policies throughout the periods presented in its first IFRS financial statements, and these accounting policies should be based on "latest version of the IFRS" (rationale for this discussed later) effective at the reporting date. In case a new IFRS has been issued on the reporting date but it is not yet mandatory to apply it, but entities are encouraged to apply it before the effective date, then the "first-time adopter" is permitted but not required to apply it.

REPORTING PERIOD

The "reporting date" for an entity's first IFRS financial statements refers to the end of the latest period covered by the annual financial statements or interim financial statements, if any, that the entity presents under IAS 34 for the period covered by its first IFRS financial statements.

Example 1

Brilliant Corp. presents its first annual financial statements under IFRS for the calendar year 20X9. The statements include an explicit and unreserved statement of compliance with IFRS in the footnotes. Brilliant Corp. also presents full comparative financial information for the calendar year 20X8. In this case, the latest period covered by these annual financial statements would end on December 31, 20X9, and the "reporting date" for the purposes of IFRS 1 is December 31, 20X9 (presuming the entity does not present interim financial statements under IAS 34 for the calendar year 20X9).

Example 2

Alternatively, if Brilliant Corp. decides to present its first IFRS interim financial statements for the six months ended June 30, 20X9, in addition to the first IFRS annual financial statements for the year ended December 31, 20X9, the "reporting date" may no longer be December 31, 20X9; it is dependent on how the interim financial statements are prepared. If the interim financial statements for the six months ended June 30, 20X9, were prepared in accordance with IAS 34, then the "reporting period" would be June 30, 20X9 (instead of December 31, 20X9). If, however, the interim financial statements for the six months ended June 30, 20X9, were not prepared in accordance with IAS 34, then the reporting date would continue to be December 31, 20X9 (and not June 30, 20X9).

RATIONALE BEHIND USING THE "CURRENT VERSION OF IFRS"

Over time, International Accounting Standards have been revised or amended several times. In some instances, the current version of IFRS (IAS) is vastly different from the earlier versions, which have either been superseded or amended. IFRS 1 requires a first-time adopter to use the current version of IFRS, without considering the superseded or amended versions.

By contrast, under Exposure Draft (ED) 1, which gave the first-time adopter an option to elect application of IFRS *as if it had always applied IFRS (i.e., from inception)*, the first-time adopter would have had to consider different versions of IAS promulgated over a period of time until the date of adoption of IFRS.

To comprehend the practical significance of this change in the requirements, let us examine an illustration.

Example 3

According to a previous version of the Standard relating to property, plant, and equipment (IAS 16), under the allowed alternative treatment, when property was revalued, the "fair value" was its market value "for existing use." Later this aspect of IAS 16 was revised in order to conform to the guidance in IAS 22. Now the Standard stipulates that when property, plant, and equipment is revalued, the market value should be fair value, which is the amount for which it can be exchanged between knowledgeable, willing parties in an arm's-length transaction, without restricting the definition of fair value to market value for "existing use."

In some cases, this difference in terminology could have a significant impact on the valuation of the property if different versions of the IAS are applied for different time periods during which the requirement changed. Consider the case of land and building that is currently being used as a factory building by an entity that is contemplating switching from national GAAP to IFRS. According to the earlier version of IAS 16, the fair value would be based on its market value for "existing use;" under the revised version of IAS 16, where that restriction has been removed, the market value would be its fair value (i.e., "the amount for which it can be exchanged between knowledgeable, willing parties in an arm's-length transaction"). Thus, if the intention of the entity is to convert the factory building at a later date into a shopping mall, then its market value would be quite different (compared to a case where there is no such plan of change in "existing use") because it would be a valuation driven by the market value of the property based on its "intended use" (as opposed to its "existing use").

TRANSITIONAL PROVISIONS IN OTHER IFRS

Certain IAS have transitional provisions that are included at the end of those Standards, just before the paragraph(s) relating to the "effective date" of the IFRS, and are meant to facilitate transition to the new Standard. In other words, transitional provisions allow entities adopting a new Standard to deviate from the provisions of other existing Standards, to an extent; usually this takes place in cases when retrospective application of those Standards would make it cumbersome to apply the new Standard.

IFRS 1 recognizes that the transitional provisions in other IFRS apply to changes in accounting policies made by an entity that already uses IFRS, and thus it provides that the transitional provisions in other IFRS do not apply to first-time adopters. If IFRS 1 had not provided this clarification, then there would be confusion as to whether first-time adopters, would need to apply the transitional provisions in certain International Accounting Standards (IAS)

TARGETED EXEMPTIONS FROM OTHER IFRS

IFRS 1 allows a first-time adopter to elect to use one or more targeted exemptions.

Under IFRS 1, paragraph 13, a first-time adopter of IFRS may elect to use exemptions from the general measurement and restatement principles in one or more of these instances:

1. Business combinations
2. Share-based payment transactions
3. Insurance contracts and oil and gas assets
4. Deemed cost
5. Leases
6. Employee benefits
7. Cumulative translation differences
8. Investments in subsidiaries, jointly controlled entities, and associates
9. Assets and liabilities of subsidiaries, associates, and joint ventures
10. Financial instruments
11. Decommissioning liabilities included in the cost of property, plant, and equipment
12. Financial assets or intangible assets accounted for in accordance with IFRIC 12, *Service Concession Arrangements*
13. Borrowing costs
14. Transfers of assets from customers

BUSINESS COMBINATIONS

IFRS 3 was revised in January 2008. The new Standard is applicable to business combinations for which the acquisition date occurs during the first annual reporting period beginning on or after July 1, 2009. Earlier application is permitted, subject to transitional provisions–but not for accounting periods beginning before June 30, 2007. For first-time adopters

- If the first IFRS reporting period begins between July 1, 2007 and June 30, 2009, IFRS 3 (2008) may be applied in advance of its effective date, subject to the general transitional provisions.
- If the first IFRS reporting period begins on or after July 1, 2009, IFRS 3 (2008) must be applied.

It is important to note that if retrospective application of IFRS 3 (2008) is selected, IFRS 1 requires consistent application of IFRS 3 (2008)—that is, IFRS 3 (2004) should not be applied to any of the entity's previous business combinations.

One of the most complex areas that first-time adopters will need to address is the accounting for business combinations. Entities will need to consider whether to apply IFRS 3, *Business Combinations,* retrospectively to all past business combinations, or to avail of the IFRS 1 exemption in this regard. Even where the exemption is applied, significant issues can arise. Entities are permitted to apply IFRS 3 retrospectively to all past business combinations.

Full retrospective application could be very onerous and, in many cases, will be impracticable. Any entity intending to follow this path will need to ensure that it has the information needed to apply the acquisition method retrospectively in accordance with IFRS 3, which in particular includes

- Calculation of the cost of the business combination.
- Identification of assets acquired (including any intangible assets), and liabilities, and contingent liabilities assumed.
- Measurement of fair value at the date of acquisition of assets acquired and liabilities and contingent liabilities assumed.
- Impairment test of goodwill each year subsequent to the date of acquisition.

As an alternative to applying IFRS 3 retrospectively, IFRS 1 includes an optional exemption for business combinations. The most significant features of the accounting under IFRS 1, are that

- The classification of former business combinations (acquisition or uniting of interests) under previous GAAP is maintained.
- There is no remeasurement of original "fair values" determined at the time of the business combination (date of acquisition).
- The carrying amount of goodwill recognized under previous GAAP is not adjusted, other than in specific instances.

Example 4

For instance, if Merger Inc., a first-time adopter, did not seek this exemption but instead opted to apply IFRS 3 retrospectively and restated a major business combination that took place two years ago, then under this requirement of IFRS 3, Merger Inc. is required to restate all business combinations that took place subsequent to the date of this major business combination to which it applied IFRS 3 retrospectively.

CASE STUDY 3

Facts

An entity A adopts IFRS in 20X9 with a date of transition of January 1, 20X8. The entity acquired an 80% interest in another entity on June 30, 20X6 and has decided not to restate the business combination on adoption of IFRS. Under previous GAAP, A measured identifiable assets and liabilities acquired in a business combination at the acquirer's interest obtained in the exchange transaction plus the (noncontrolling interest) NCI's portion of the preacquisition carrying amounts. This treatment is not permitted under IFRS 3.

Required

Discuss the way the previous item should be treated under IFRS 1.

Solution

IFRS 3 requires that assets and liabilities acquired in a business combination be measured at their values at the date of acquisition. Under IFRS 3 (2008), there is a choice between measuring the NCI at either fair value or the NCI's proportionate share of the fair value of the net identifiable assets acquired. Although the manner in which NCI was calculated under previous GAAP is not supportable under IFRS, A is not required to adjust the amount attributed to NCI at the date of transition. A has chosen not to restate business combinations that occurred before the date of transition to IFRS; therefore, it need not adjust NCI to conform to the measurement basis under IFRS 3.

However, the requirements of IFRS 1 may require some assets acquired, or liabilities assumed, in a business combination to be measured at amounts different from the carrying amounts immediately used after the business combination under previous GAAP. In such circumstances, because the measurement of NCI follows the measurement of the other assets and liabilities, NCI will be adjusted for the effects of the differences.

SHARE-BASED PAYMENT TRANSACTIONS

Equity-Settled Transactions

IFRS 1 includes two exemptions for equity-settled transactions:

* First-time adopters are not required to apply IFRS 2 for equity-settled share-based payments granted on or before November 7, 2002.
* First-time adopters are not required to apply IFRS 2 to share-based payments granted after November 7, 2002, that vested before the date of transition to IFRS.

Cash-Settled Transactions

A first-time adopter is encouraged, but not required, to apply IFRS 2 to liabilities arising from share-based payment transactions that were settled before the later of

* The date of transition to IFRS
* January 1, 2005

This exemption is of limited relevance as the date of transition will be later than January 1, 2005.

INSURANCE CONTRACTS AND OIL AND GAS ASSETS

IFRS 4 was issued in 2004 and is seen as an interim Standard pending completion of the IASB's project on insurance contracts. IFRS 4 allows entities to continue to use their existing accounting policies for liabilities arising from insurance contracts as long as the existing policies meet certain minimum requirements as set out in IFRS 4. IFRS 4 also requires disclosures that identify and explain the amounts in an insurer's financial statements arising from insurance contracts. The IASB recognized that it could be quite onerous for entities to apply the requirements of IFRS 4 retrospectively. Therefore, IFRS 1 provides an optional exemption whereby an entity issuing insurance contracts (an insurer) may elect upon first-time adoption to apply the transitional provisions of IFRS 4, *Insurance Contracts*. These transitional provisions require an insurer to apply IFRS 4 prospectively for reporting periods beginning on or after January 1, 2005, with earlier application permitted. While this may have represented significant relief for entities that adopted IFRS in 2005, its benefit for the "second wave" of adopters is primarily in restricting the amount of retrospective application required (i.e., from 2005 to date of transition).

On July 23, 2009, the IASB amended IFRS 1 to exempt entities using the full cost method from retrospective application of IFRS for oil and gas assets.

FAIR VALUE OR REVALUATION AS DEEMED COST

An entity may elect to measure an item of property, plant, and equipment at fair value at the date of its transition to IFRS and use the fair value as its deemed cost at that date. A first-time adopter may elect to use a previous GAAP revaluation of an item of property, plant, and equipment at or before the date of transition to IFRS as deemed cost at the date of revaluation if the revaluation amount, at the date of revaluation, was broadly comparable to either its fair value or cost (or depreciated cost under IFRS adjusted for changes in general or specific price index).

These elections are equally available for investment property measured under the cost model and intangible assets that meet the recognition criteria and the criteria for revaluation (including existence of an active market).

If a first-time adopter has established a deemed cost under the previous GAAP for any of its assets or liabilities by measuring them at their fair values at a particular date because of an event such as privatization or an initial public offering (IPO), it is allowed to use such an event-driven fair value as deemed cost for IFRS at the date of that measurement.

CASE STUDY 4

Facts

An entity acquires a factory building for $6 million on January 1, 20X7, with an expected remaining useful life of 40 years at that date. The building is revalued on January 1, 20X8, to $6.5 million and the resulting adjustment is recognized in equity. The building has a depreciated carrying amount of $5.85 million on January 1, 20X8, and $6.3 million on January 1, 20X9. The depreciation method under previous GAAP is acceptable under IAS 16 and the revaluation is equivalent to fair value at the date of revaluation.

The entity selects the cost model as its accounting policy for measurement after recognition of buildings in accordance with IAS 16 and has a date of transition of January 1, 20X9. At January 1, 20X9, the building has a market value of $6.92 million.

Required

Discuss the options available to the entity at the date of transition regarding the valuation of the building.

Solution

Under IFRS 1, the entity has an option to measure the building at

1. Fair value at the date of transition
2. The previous GAAP revaluation
3. An amount where it applies IAS 16 retrospectively

The following journal entries are required in each case:

1. Fair value at January 1, 20X9

Factory building (6.92–6.3)	$0.62 million	
Retained earnings		$0.62 million
Adjustment of carrying amount to fair value as deemed cost		

Revaluation surplus (6.5–5.85)	$0.65 million	
Retained earnings		$0.65 million
Reversal of original revaluation at January 1, 2008		

2. No journal entry is required as the carrying amount under previous GAAP is acceptable under IAS 16.
3. Retrospective application of IAS 16

Revaluation surplus	$0.65 million	
Factory building (6.5–6)		$0.5 million
Accumulated depreciation		$0.15 million
Reversal of original revaluation at January 1, 20X8		

Accumulated depreciation (6.5 × 1/39)	$0.17 million	
Retained earnings		$0.17 million
Reversal of additional depreciation on revaluation at January 1, 20X9		

LEASES

There are no explicit exemptions or exceptions in IFRS 1 from retrospective application of IAS 17, *Leases*. A first-time adopter is therefore required to recognize all assets held under finance lease at the date of transition. If not previously recognized, this involves determining the fair value of the asset at inception of the lease (or the present value of the minimum lease payments, if lower) depreciated to the date of transition and calculating the finance lease liability based on the net present value of the minimum lease payments, amortized using the rate implicit in the lease (or, in certain circumstances, the lessees' incremental borrowing rate). It may be difficult and even impracticable to determine the fair value of the asset acquired in the lease; however, the entity may elect to measure the asset capitalized under a finance lease at fair value at the date of transition in accordance with the optional exemption in IFRS 1. In July 2009, the IASB amended IFRS 1 to exempt entities with existing leasing contracts from reassessing the classification of those contracts in accordance with IFRIC 4, *Determining Whether an Arrangement Contains a Lease,* when the application of their national accounting requirements produced the same result.

EMPLOYEE BENEFITS

Under IAS 19, an entity may have unrecognized actuarial gains or losses in case it uses the corridor approach. Retrospective application of this approach would necessitate splitting the cumulative gains and losses, from inception of the plan until the date of transition to IFRS, into a recognized and an unrecognized portion.

IFRS 1 allows a first-time adopter to elect to recognize all cumulative actuarial gains and losses at the date of transition to IFRS, even if it uses the corridor approach for subsequent actuarial gains or losses. IFRS 1 does, however, mandate that if an election is made for one employee benefit plan, it should apply to all other employee plans.

CUMULATIVE TRANSLATION DIFFERENCES

IAS 21 requires an entity to recognize some translation differences in other comprehensive income and accumulate these in a separate component of equity and on disposal of the foreign operation to reclassify the cumulative translation difference (CTA) relating to the foreign operation to profit or loss as part of the gain or loss on disposal.

A first-time adopter is exempted from this transfer of the CTA that existed on the date of transition to IFRS. If it uses this exemption, the CTD for all foreign operations would be deemed to be zero at the date of transition to IFRS, and the gain or loss on subsequent disposal of any foreign operation should exclude translation differences that arose before the date of transition to IFRS but should include all subsequent translation adjustments.

INVESTMENTS IN SUBSIDIARIES, JOINTLY CONTROLLED ENTITIES, AND ASSOCIATES

The option to use deemed cost to measure investments in subsidiaries, jointly controlled entities, and associates was added to IFRS 1 in 2008 and is effective for annual periods beginning on or after July 1, 2009, with earlier application permitted. The amendment addressed concerns that it may be difficult, or even impossible, and costly to determine cost in accordance with IAS 27.

The alternative of accounting for such investments at fair value in accordance with IAS 39 will often be unattractive because of the cost of obtaining annual valuations on an ongoing basis.

First-time adopters are permitted to choose which measurement basis to use for each investment on an individual basis. Some may be measured at cost in accordance with IAS 27 and others at deemed cost. For those measured at deemed cost, the choice between fair value and previous GAAP carrying amount may also be made on an individual investment basis. If an entity uses the deemed cost exemption for measurement of investments in subsidiaries, jointly controlled entities, and associates, it must make certain specific disclosures in its first IFRS financial statements.

FINANCIAL INSTRUMENTS

If an entity has issued a compound financial instrument, say, a convertible debenture, IAS 32 requires that at inception, it should split and separate the liability component of the compound financial instrument from equity. If the liability portion is no longer outstanding, retrospective application of IAS 32 would produce this result with respect to the equity portion still outstanding: The part representing cumulative interest accreted to the liability component is in retained earnings and the other portion represents the original equity component.

IFRS 1 exempts a first-time adopter from this split accounting if the liability component is no longer outstanding at the date of transition to IFRS.

An entity is permitted to designate any financial asset, other than an asset that meets the definition of "held for trading," as an "available-for-sale" financial asset at the date of transition to IFRS.

A first-time adopter of IFRS must de-designate financial assets and financial liabilities that under previous GAAP were designated as "at fair value through profit or loss" if they do not qualify for such designation under IAS 39. An entity that presents its first IFRS financial statements for an annual period beginning on or after September 1, 2006, is permitted to designate, at the date of transition to IFRS, any financial asset or financial liability as at fair value through profit or loss, provided that the asset or liability meets the criteria for such classification at that date. The criteria are detailed in IAS 39.

This designation is made at the date of transition as if the entity had never made a choice under a previous GAAP, and this is so even when that previous GAAP was identical to IAS 39.

On January 28, 2010, the IASB amended IFRS 1 to exempt first-time adopters of IFRS from providing the additional disclosures introduced in March 2009 by Improving Disclosures about Financial Instruments (Amendments to IFRS 7). The amendment gives first-time adopters the same transition provisions that Amendments to IFRS 7 provides to current IFRS preparers. The amendment is effective on July 1, 2010, with earlier application permitted.

IFRIC 1, *CHANGES IN EXISTING DECOMMISSIONING, RESTORATION, AND SIMILAR LIABILITIES*

Under IFRIC 1, specified changes in a decommissioning, restoration, or similar liability are added to or deducted from the cost of the asset to which it relates, and the adjusted depreciable amount of the asset is then depreciated prospectively over its remaining useful life. Retrospective application of the requirements of IFRIC 1 at the date of transition would require an entity to construct a historical record of all such adjustments that would have been made in the past.

The IASB felt that in many cases this would not be practicable and provided an exemption for first-time adopters. Under the exemption, a first-time adopter may elect not to comply with requirements of IFRIC 1 for changes in such liabilities that occurred before the date of transition to IFRS.

BORROWING COSTS

The IASB noted that it would be too onerous for first-time adopters who may have previously expensed all borrowing costs to be required to gather the necessary information for the retrospective capitalization of borrowing costs. In addition, the IASB acknowledged that the requirements for application of mandatory capitalization should be the same for entities that already apply IFRS and for first-time adopters. Therefore, IFRS 1 was amended to add a new exemption from full retrospective application of IAS 23.

IFRIC 18, *TRANSFERS OF ASSETS FROM CUSTOMERS*

IFRIC 18 was issued in January 2009 to address divergent practice, in the accounting by recipients, for transfers of property, plant, and equipment from customers. The Interpretation does not apply to government grants or service concession arrangements. IFRIC 18 concludes that when the item of property, plant, and equipment transferred meets the definition of an asset from the perspective of the recipient, the recipient should recognize the asset at its fair value on the date of the transfer, with the credit recognized as revenue in accordance with IAS 18, *Revenue*.

In finalizing IFRIC 18, the IFRIC noted that applying the change in accounting policy retrospectively would require entities to establish a carrying amount for assets that had been transferred in the past. That carrying amount would be based on historical fair values, which may or may not be based on an observable price or observable inputs. Therefore, the IFRIC concluded that retrospective application could be impracticable and that the Interpretation should require prospective application to transfers received after its effective date.

To provide first-time adopters with the same relief, an exemption was also added to IFRS 1 under which first-time adopters may also apply the transitional provisions set out in paragraph 22 of IFRIC 18, *Transfers of Assets from Customers*. IFRS 1 notes that reference to the effective date within the transitional provisions of IFRIC 18 should be interpreted as July 1, 2009, or the date of transition to IFRS, whichever is later. Earlier application is permitted provided that the valuations and other information needed to apply IFRIC 18 to past transfers were obtained at the time those transfers occurred. An entity must disclose the date from which IFRIC 18 is applied.

ASSETS AND LIABILITIES OF SUBSIDIARIES, ASSOCIATES, AND JOINT VENTURES

IFRS 1 discusses exemptions under two circumstances.

1. If a subsidiary becomes a first-time adopter later than its parent, the subsidiary shall, in its separate ("stand-alone") financial statements, measure its assets and liabilities at either: (a) the carrying amounts that would be included in its parent's consolidated financial statements, based on its parent's date of transition to IFRS (if no adjustments were made for consolidation procedures and for the effect of the business combination in which the parent acquired the subsidiary), or (b) the carrying amounts required by the rest of this IFRS, based on the subsidiary's date of transition to IFRS.
2. If an entity becomes a first-time adopter later than its subsidiary (or associate or joint venture), the entity shall, in its consolidated financial statements, measure the assets and liabilities of the subsidiary (or associate or joint venture) at the same carrying amounts as in the separate ("stand-alone") financial statements of the subsidiary (or associate or joint venture), after adjusting for consolidation and equity accounting adjustments and for the effects of the business combination in which an entity acquired the subsidiary. In a similar manner, if a parent becomes a first-time adopter for its separate financial statements earlier or later than for its consolidated financial statements, it shall measure its assets and liabilities at the same amounts in both financial statements, except for consolidation adjustments.

EXCEPTIONS TO RETROSPECTIVE APPLICATION OF OTHER IFRS

IFRS 1 *prohibits* retrospective application of some aspects of other IFRS relating to

1. *Derecognition of financial assets and financial liabilities.* If a first-time adopter derecognized financial assets or financial liabilities under its previous GAAP in a financial year prior to January 1, 2001, it should not recognize those assets and liabilities under IFRS.

   However, a first-time adopter should recognize all derivatives and other interests retained after derecognition, still existing, and consolidate all special-purpose entities (SPEs) that it controls at the date of transition to IFRS (even if SPEs existed before the date of transition to IFRS or hold financial assets or financial liabilities that were derecognized under previous GAAP).
2. *Hedge accounting.* A first-time adopter is required, at the date of transition to IFRS, to measure all derivatives at fair value and eliminate all deferred losses and gains on derivatives that were reported under its previous GAAP.

   However, a first-time adopter shall not reflect a hedging relationship in its opening IFRS statement of financial position if it does not qualify for hedge accounting under IAS

39. But if an entity designated a net position as a hedged item under its previous GAAP, it may designate an individual item within that net position as a hedged item under IFRS, provided it does so prior to the date of transition to IFRS. Transitional provisions of IAS 39 apply to hedging relationships of a first-time adopter at the date of transition to IFRS.

3. *Estimates.* An entity's estimates under IFRS at the date of transition to IFRS should be consistent with estimates made for the same date under its previous GAAP, unless there is objective evidence that those estimates were in "error."

   Any information an entity receives after the date of transition to IFRS about estimates it made under previous GAAP should be treated by it as a "nonadjusting" event after the reporting period and accorded the treatment prescribed by IAS 10 (i.e., "disclosure" in footnotes as opposed to "adjustment" of items in the financial statements).

4. *Noncontrolling interests.* This exception applies for entities that have adopted the 2008 amendments to IFRS 3, *Business Combinations,* and IAS 27, *Consolidated and Separate Financial Statements.* These amendments introduced new measurement requirements for noncontrolling interests (previously described as "minority" interests) and a new mandatory exception to IFRS 1. The exception stipulates that a first-time adopter should apply the following requirements of IAS 27 (2008) prospectively from the date of transition to IFRS:

- The requirement that total comprehensive income be attributed to the owners of the parent and to the noncontrolling interests even if this results in the noncontrolling interests having a deficit balance.
- The requirements regarding the accounting for changes in the parent's ownership interest in a subsidiary that do not result in a loss of control.
- The requirements regarding the accounting for a loss of control over a subsidiary, and the related requirements in paragraph 8A of IFRS 5, *Noncurrent Assets Held for Sale and Discontinued Operations.*

   This exception is effective for annual periods beginning on or after July 1, 2009. However, if a first-time adopter elects to apply IFRS 3 (2008) and IAS 27 (2008) for an earlier period, the amendments to IFRS 1 should also be applied for that earlier period.

PRESENTATION AND DISCLOSURE

IFRS 1 requires disclosures that explain how the transition from previous GAAP to IFRS affected the entity's reported financial position, financial performance, and cash flows.

This includes reconciliations of equity reported under previous GAAP to equity under IFRS both (1) at the date of the opening IFRS statement of financial position and (2) the end of the last annual period reported under the previous GAAP. [IFRS 1.24(a)] (For an entity adopting IFRS for the first time in its December 31, 2009 financial statements, the reconciliations would be as of January 1, 2008 and December 31, 2008.)

It also includes reconciliations of total comprehensive income for the last annual period reported under the previous GAAP to total comprehensive income under IFRS for the same period and an explanation of material adjustments that were made, in adopting IFRS for the first time, to the statement of financial position, statement of comprehensive income, and cash flow statement.

If errors in previous GAAP financial statements were discovered in the course of transition to IFRS, those must be separately disclosed, and also if the entity recognized or reversed any impairment losses in preparing its opening IFRS statement of financial position, these must be disclosed.

COMPREHENSIVE CASE STUDY

Facts

This information relates to Van Products, a private limited entity, which is a paper and packaging company and paper machinery supplier.

Statement of financial position at May 31, 20X9

Assets	$m
Property, plant, and equipment	45
Goodwill	10
	55
Inventories	12
Trade receivables	8
Cash	4
	24
Total assets	79

Equity and liabilities	$m
Share capital	20
Other reserves	10
Retained earnings	31
Total equity	61
Total liabilities	18
Total equity and liabilities	79

Year ended May 31	Profit before tax $m	Tax $m	Profit for period $m
20X8	14	4	10
20X9	11	3	8

The shares of the entity are owned equally by two directors who have decided to sell their shareholdings. At present the financial statements are drawn up using generally accepted accounting practices.

The directors wish to ascertain whether it would be advantageous to move to International Financial Reporting Standards as a basis for the preparation of the financial statements for the purpose of valuing their shares.

The directors have ascertained this information:

1. Certain property has been valued on an existing use basis at $10 million at March 31, 20X9. If the land were sold for building purposes, the entity would expect to receive $15 million when planning permission was received. At present, planning approval has not been obtained. Without planning permission, the land could be sold for $12 million.
2. The entity acquired another entity on November 30, 20X7. Goodwill of $16 million arose on the acquisition. No impairment of goodwill had occurred since that date, and the entity was amortizing the goodwill over a four-year period.

   During 20X9, an error was discovered whereby $4 million of plant and equipment had been omitted from the schedule of assets acquired. The plant and equipment had a remaining useful life at acquisition of four years with a residual value of zero. A charge is made for amortization of goodwill, and depreciation of plant and equipment is on a time apportionment basis.

3. The entity has developed a new product. During 20X8 the expenditure incurred on the development of the product was $5 million. The entity could demonstrate that the development expenditure met the recognition criteria as an intangible asset on November 30, 20X7, at which point $3 million had been spent on the development. The recoverable amount of the intangible asset was estimated at $2 million at May 31, 20X8, in terms of the "know-how" gained to date. During 20X9, the entity incurred further costs of $3 million and estimated the recoverable amount of the total expenditure to be $25 million at May 31, 20X9. The entity currently writes off all development expenditure under local GAAP. If IFRS were to be utilized, the entity would opt for the cost model with amortization over four years on a time apportionment basis.
4. The entity currently has classified its forests as land within property, plant, and equipment, at $6 million. It wishes to reclassify the forests as biological assets under IFRS. The fair value of the forests was

May 31	$m
20X8	10
20X9	11

5. When paper machines sold by the entity are returned for repair, the entity provides a substitute unit until the machine is repaired. The value of the returned machines is included in inventory and in turnover. When the machine is repaired, the value of the machine is taken out of the financial records and the costs of the repair charged to the customer. This practice is known as pass-

through business and has been accepted by the local auditors. At May 31, 20X8, and May 31, 20X9, there were $1.5 million and $2.5 million of pass-through business included in the financial statements. Machines are normally returned repaired within a month of receipt.

6. The net realizable value of the inventory excluding pass-through business at May 31, 20X9, was $9 million, and trade receivables are expected to realize their full amount.

The price/earnings ratio of quoted entities in the same industrial sector as Van Products is approximately 8. Assume there would be no effects of a change to IFRS other than those just set out and that the book values of assets and liabilities reflect their fair values unless otherwise stated. Any taxation effects can be ignored.

Required

Advise the company's directors on the value of their shares, setting out the impact that a move to IFRS may have on the share valuation.

Solution

In valuing the shares of Van Products, two main methods could be used:

1. Assets basis
2. Price/earnings ratio basis

The assets basis would normally measure the maximum amount that a purchaser would pay for the shares. A major element of the business's value will be goodwill. A move to IFRS should not really affect this basis of valuation, as a purchaser would not normally use carrying value as a basis for pricing the shares. In valuing the net assets, all the items have been valued at their fair value or recoverable amount. Including goodwill and intangibles, the value of the shares is placed at $72 million.

On a price/earnings ratio basis, it may be best to use an average of the last two years' earnings, as there is an element of fluctuation in the profit levels. IFRS will affect this valuation, as the basis of computing profits after tax will be different from GAAP. Thus the average of the last two years' profits is ($15.25 million + $10.75 million)/2, or $13 million. The P/E ratio of a similar quoted company is 8; thus a lower ratio would be applicable to the company, say 6. The value of the shares would be 6 × $13 million, or $78 million. When compared to the purchase price on an assets basis ($72 million), there is not a significant difference. Therefore, this calculation would give the parameters for any negotiations with potential purchasers. If GAAP were used to value the shares on a P/E ratio basis, the value would be 10 + 8/2, or $9 million × 6, or $54 million, which is significantly different from the preceding calculations.

Assets Valuation

	May 31, 20X9	*Adjustment*	*Value*
	$m	*$m*	*$m*
Property, plant, and equipment:	45		
Increase in value of land		2	
Plant and machinery omitted (Workings [1]*)		2.5	
Forests (Workings [3])	—	5	
	45	9.5	54.5
Inventory			9
Trade receivables			8
Cash			4
Total liabilities			(18)
Value of tangible net assets			57.5
Intangible assets			
Goodwill (Workings [1])			12
Intangible assets (Workings [2])			2.5
Value of total assets			72

Price/Earnings Ratio Valuation

	20X8	*20X9*
	$m	*$m*
Profit after tax	10	8
Amortization of goodwill (Workings [1])	12	4
Depreciation of plant and equipment	(0.5)	(1)
	11.5	11
Intangibles: development costs (Workings [2])	2	3
Amortization	(0.75)	(0.75)

	20X8 $m	20X9 $m
Impairment (Workings [2])		(1)
Biological assets	4	1
Pass-through business (Workings [4])	(1.5)	(2.5)
Revised profit after tax	15.25	(10.75)
Price/earnings ratio value—Local GAAP:		
Profit after tax above	11.5	11
Less amortization of goodwill	(1.5)	(3)
	10	8

* Workings numbers refer to the workings section that follows.

Workings

1. Goodwill and Plant and Equipment

	$m
Value of goodwill	16
Less plant and equipment	(4)
Goodwill	12

    As goodwill is capitalized and not amortized under IFRS, the amortization of $6 million will be added back to profit in 20X8 and 20X9.

    In addition, plant and equipment will be included in the statement of financial position at $4 million less depreciation of [$0.5 million (20X8) + $1 million (20X9)], or $2.5 million.

2. At May 31, 20X8, $2 million will be recognized as an intangible asset less amortization of $0.25 million ($2 million/4 years/ ½), or $1.75 million. The recoverable amount is $2 million, and, therefore, no impairment has occurred.

    At May 31, 20X9, the intangible asset would be stated at

Year	Intangible asset $m	Amortization $m	Carrying value $m
20X8	2	(0.75)	1.25
20X9	3	(0.75)	2.25
			3.5

    The recoverable amount is $2.5 million; therefore, an impairment loss of $1 million is recognized in 20X9.

3. A gain or loss on the initial recognition of a biological asset at fair value and from a change in fair value under IAS 41 is included in profit or loss for the period. Thus a gain of $4 million will be included in the 20X8 statement of comprehensive income and a further $1 million will be included in the 20X9 statement of comprehensive income.

4. The pass-through business should be eliminated, as it does not comply with IAS 18, *Revenue,* which states that revenue should include only economic benefits received and receivable by the company on its own account. Therefore, turnover should be reduced by $1.5 million + $2.5 million in 20X8 and 20X9, respectively, and inventory by the same amount in both years.

PRACTICAL INSIGHT

This optional exemption for employee benefits may result in a significant adjustment to total equity at the date of transition, but as a result the first-time adopter avoids amortizing the accumulated losses in profit or loss after transition. Only those actuarial gains and losses arising subsequent to the date of transition will be recognized in profit or loss. It is likely that most first-time adopters applying the corridor approach will make use of the election to recognize all cumulative actuarial gains and losses at the date of transition; this means that the full amount of the surplus or deficit is recognized at the date of transition to IFRS. If this exemption is not used, it would be necessary to go back to the start of the pension scheme (or, if later, the date on which the scheme was acquired in a business combination) and obtain actuarial valuations at the end of each subsequent reporting period to apply the corridor approach with retrospective effect.

For a pension scheme that has been established for more than a few years, this is likely to involve significant cost and may be impracticable.

EXTRACTS FROM PUBLISHED FINANCIAL STATEMENTS

UNILEVER

Restatement of financial information for the year ended December 31, 2004, under International Financial Reporting Standards (IFRS).

Summary

The adoption of IFRS has been a major change project affecting the measurement and classification of a number of items in our income statement and balance sheet. For Unilever the impact of the transition to IFRS is less significant than for many other European companies because

- Unilever was an early adopter (in 2003) of FRS 17, the UK accounting standard for pensions. FRS 17 has many similarities with IAS 19, the IFRS accounting standard for pensions. Therefore the impact on the restated balance sheet and income statement is limited.
- The introduction of IFRS 2, *Share-Based Payments,* will not have a significant impact on Unilever's results because from 2003 we began recognizing a charge in respect of the fair value of all unvested share options (calculated on a basis consistent with IFRS 2).
- Under IFRS, goodwill and most of Unilever's acquired intangible assets are not amortized. Unilever's headline performance measures have, since 2000, been expressed on a "before amortization" basis (BEIA).

The most significant impacts of the transition to IFRS on Unilever's restated consolidated financial statements are a matter of the timing of the recognition of income and expenses in the income statement. Reported net assets are impacted as a result of these timing changes, but there is no impact on the underlying cash generation of the business.

MULTIPLE-CHOICE QUESTIONS

1. Under which one of the following circumstances would an entity's current year's financial statements **not** qualify as first IFRS financial statements?

    (a) The entity prepared its financial statements under IFRS in the previous year and these were meant for internal purposes only.

    (b) The entity prepared the previous year's financial statements under its national GAAP.

    (c) The entity prepared its previous year's financial statements in conformity with all requirements of IFRS, but these statements did not contain an explicit and unreserved statement that they complied with IFRS.

    (d) The entity prepared its previous year's financial statements in conformity with all requirements of IFRS, and these statements did contain an explicit and unreserved statement that they complied with IFRS.

2. XYZ Inc. is a first-time adopter under IFRS 1. The most recent financial statements it presented under its previous GAAP were as of December 31, 2005. It has adopted IFRS for the first time and intends to present the first IFRS financial statements as of December 31, 2006. It plans to present two-year comparative information for the years 2005 and 2004. The opening IFRS statement of financial position should be prepared as of

    (a) January 1, 2005.

    (b) January 1, 2003.

    (c) January 1, 2004.

    (d) January 1, 2006.

3. Which one of the following is **not** a required adjustment in preparing an opening IFRS statement of financial position?

    (a) Recognize all assets and liabilities whose recognition is required under IFRS.

    (b) Derecognize items as assets or liabilities if IFRS do not permit such recognition.

    (c) Disclose as comparative information all figures under previous GAAP alongside figures for the current year presented under IFRS.

    (d) Measure all recognized assets and liabilities according to principles contained in IFRS.

4. Which one of the following does **not** qualify for an exemption allowed by IFRS 1?

    (a) Business combinations that occurred before or prior to the date of transition to IFRS.

    (b) Financial instruments (other than compound financial instruments).

    (c) Cumulative translation differences.

    (d) Cumulative unrecognized actuarial gains and losses under IAS 19.

5. Which one of the following does **not** qualify for exemption under IFRS 1 for the purposes of retrospective application?

    (a) Hedge accounting.

    (b) Financial assets and financial liabilities derecognized prior to January 1, 2001.

    (c) Estimates made under previous GAAP.

    (d) Fair value accounting for investment property.

6. A local standard on employee benefits became effective for annual financial periods beginning on or after January 1, 20X8. The local GAAP is similar to IAS 19. An entity chose to adopt this standard early in its previous GAAP financial statements and applied it from January 1, 20X7, using the "corridor" approach.

    Under the local standard, the entity recognized the net defined benefit liability at January 1, 20X7. The entity will be a first-time adopter in 20X9 and has made an accounting policy choice to apply IAS 19's corridor approach. Under IFRS 1, a first-time adopter has only two choices regarding defined benefit liabilities: (1) either reset the corridor at the date of transition (2) retrospective application of IAS 19.

    Therefore, if the entity wishes to maintain the carrying amount of the defined benefit liability determined under previous GAAP

    (a) The entity's date of transition must be January 1, 20X7. If January 1, 20X8 is the date of transition, the net liability will have to be recalculated once again.

    (b) The entity's date of transition must be January 1, 20X8. If January 1, 20X8 is the date of transition, the net liability will not have to be recalculated once again.

    (c) The entity's date of transition must be January 1, 20X7. If January 1, 20X7 is the date of transition, the net liability will have to be recalculated once again.

    (d) The entity's date of transition must be January 1, 20X8. If January 1, 20X7 is the date of transition, the net liability will have to be recalculated once again.

7. The option to use deemed cost to measure investments in subsidiaries, jointly controlled entities, and associates was added to IFRS 1 in 2008 and is effective for annual periods beginning on or after July 1, 2009. The amendment addressed concerns that it may be difficult and costly to determine cost in accordance with IAS 27. The alternative of accounting for such investments at fair value in accordance with IAS 39 will often be unattractive because

(a) Of the complexity of IAS 39.
(b) Of the cost of obtaining annual valuations on an ongoing basis.
(c) Of the potential changes to IAS 39.
(d) Of the impact on OCI.

8. Under previous GAAP, an entity measured impairment of financial assets carried at cost on an undiscounted basis. The entity is a first-time adopter of IFRS. IAS 39 requires impairment losses to be measured in a different way. Therefore, at the date of transition to IFRS, the entity makes an adjustment to the carrying amount of those financial assets that are measured at amortized cost under IAS 39

(a) To reflect the effect of discounting expected future cash flows.
(b) To reflect net realizable value.
(c) To reflect cost.
(d) To reflect amortized cost.

9. An entity acquired a foreign currency receivable. Company V reports in dollars and the receivable is denominated in pounds sterling. Under previous GAAP, foreign currency receivables are measured at the spot rate on the date of the transaction and are not retranslated subsequently. The foreign currency receivable recognized is $1 million. At the same date, the entity entered into a derivative contract that it designated as a hedge against the foreign exchange risk inherent in the receivable. Derivatives were not recognized in the statement of financial position under previous GAAP.

At the date of transition, the fair value of the derivative is $100,000 and the receivable retranslated at the spot rate at the date of transition is $950,000. Under IFRS 1, the entity will recognize

(a) A derivative asset of $1 million and adjust the carrying amount of the hedged item downwards by $50,000.
(b) A derivative asset of $100,000 and adjust the carrying amount of the hedged item downwards by $950,000.
(c) A derivative asset of $100,000 and adjust the carrying amount of the hedged item downwards by $50,000.
(d) A derivative asset of $1 million and adjust the carrying amount of the hedged item downwards by $950,000.

10. A acquired a subsidiary B on January 1, 20X8. B had incurred development costs up to the date of acquisition amounting to $7 million. The development costs satisfied the recognition criteria in IAS 38 at the date of acquisition. The asset was not recognized under previous GAAP. The development costs relate to a project with a useful life of seven years starting from January 1, 20X8. No active market exists where such costs are traded. A has selected as its accounting policy to measure

intangible assets after recognition under the cost model. A has a date of transition of January 1, 20X9. The following journal entries are required

(a)

Development costs	$7 million
Goodwill	$7 million

(b)

Development costs	$7 million
Accumulated amortization	$1 million
Goodwill	$6 million

(c)

Development costs	$6 million
Goodwill	$6 million

(d)

Development costs	$7 million
Accumulated amortization	$2 million
Goodwill	$5 million

Chapter 33

SHARE-BASED PAYMENTS (IFRS 2)

BACKGROUND AND INTRODUCTION

This Standard applies to situations where an entity acquires or receives goods and services for equity-based payment. These goods can include inventories; property, plant, and equipment; intangible assets; and other nonfinancial assets. However, there are two exemptions to the general scope of the Standard. The first is, the issue of shares to acquire the net assets in a business combination is accounted for under IFRS 3, *Business Combinations*. The IFRS does not apply to share-based payment transactions that are covered by the scope of paragraphs 8 to 10 of IAS 32, *Financial Instruments, Disclosure, and Presentation*, or paragraphs 5 to 7 of IAS 39, *Financial Instruments, Recognition, and Measurement*. Thus contracts for the purchase of goods that are within the scope of IAS 32 and IAS 39 are excluded from this Standard.

Similarly, IFRS 2 does not apply to those transactions that are carried out with employees in their capacity as holders of equity shares of the entity. Thus, if the entity purchases its own shares from employees at the fair value of those shares, this transaction would be dealt with as a purchase of treasury shares and would not fall within the scope of IFRS 2 unless the price paid was in excess of the fair value, in which case that excess would be considered to be remuneration.

Another exempt situation would be where the entity makes a rights issue of shares to all shareholders, and these include some of the entity's employees. Examples of some of the share arrangements that would be accounted for under IFRS 2 are call options, share appreciation rights, share ownership schemes, and payments for services made to external consultants that are based on the entity's equity capital.

DEFINITION OF KEY TERM
(in accordance with IFRS 2)

Share-based payment. One in which the entity receives or acquires goods and services for equity instruments of the entity or incurs a liability for amounts that are based on the prices of the entity's shares or other equity instruments of the entity.

The accounting for the payment depends on how the transaction is settled. The main ways of settling the transaction will be through issuing equity shares or paying cash or where the third party has a choice of receiving either equity or cash.

RECOGNITION OF SHARE-BASED PAYMENT

IFRS 2 requires an expense to be recognized for the goods or services received by the entity. The corresponding entry in the accounting records will be either a liability or an increase in the equity of the entity, depending on whether the transaction is to be settled in cash or equity shares. If the payment for the goods and services qualifies for recognition as an asset, then the expense will be charged to the statement of comprehensive income only once the asset is sold or impaired.

An example of this would be the purchase of inventory where the purchase cost is to be settled by the issuing of equity shares or rights to equity shares. In this instance the expense would only be recognized once the inventory is sold or written down.

Goods or services acquired in a share-based payment transaction should be recognized when they are received. In the case of goods, this will be obviously when this occurs. However, sometimes it is more difficult to determine when services are received. In the case of goods, the vesting date is not really relevant; however, it is highly relevant for employee services. If shares are issued that vest immediately, there is a presumption that these are a consideration of past employee services. In this case, there should be immediate recognition of the expense for the employee services, as they are deemed to have been received in full on the date on which the shares or share options are granted.

Alternatively, if the share options do not vest for a period of time then it is considered that the equity instruments relate to services, which are to be provided over this period which is called the vesting period.

EQUITY-SETTLED TRANSACTIONS

Equity-settled transactions with employees and directors would normally be expensed on the basis of their fair value at the grant date. Fair value should be based on market prices wherever possible. Many shares and share options will not be traded on an active market. In this case, valuation techniques, such as the option pricing model, would be used. The purpose of the technique is to arrive at an estimate of the price of the equity instrument at the measurement date that would be paid in an arm's-length transaction between knowledgeable parties. IFRS 2 does not set out which pricing model should be used but describes the factors that should be taken into account.

IFRS 2's objective for equity-based transactions with employees is to determine and recognize compensation costs over the period in which the services are rendered. For example, if an entity grants to employees share options that vest in three years' time on the condition that they remain in the entity's employ for that period, these steps will be taken:

- The fair value of the options will be determined at the date on which they were granted.
- This fair value will be charged to the statement of comprehensive income equally over the three-year vesting period with adjustments made at each accounting date to reflect the best estimate of the number of options that eventually will vest.
- Shareholders' equity will be increased by an amount equal to the statement of comprehensive income charge. The charge in the statement of comprehensive income reflects the number of options that are vested, not the number of options granted or the number of options that are exercised. If employees decide not to exercise their options because the share price is lower than the exercise price, then no adjustment is made to the statement of comprehensive income.

Many employee share option schemes contain conditions that must be met before the employee becomes entitled to the shares or options. These are called vesting conditions and could require, for example, an increase in profit or growth in the entity's share price before the shares are invested in the employees.

The treatment of such performance conditions is determined by whether they are market conditions, that is, whether the conditions are specifically related to the market price of the entity's shares. Such conditions are ignored for the purposes of estimating the number of equity shares that will vest, as IFRS 2 feels that these conditions are taken into account when determining the fair value of the equity instruments granted.

CASE STUDY 1

Facts

An entity grants an employee a share option on the condition that the employee remains in employment for four years and that the share price at the end of that four-year period exceeds $10.

Required

How will these conditions affect the accounting for the share-based payment?

Solution

IFRS 2 says that the share price condition will be effectively reflected in the initial valuation of the option and that if the employee remains in employment for four years, the options will be considered to have vested irrespective of what the share price actually is. The employee will have to be still employed for the shares to vest.

If the performance condition is not based on the market and is based on, for example, the growth in profit or earnings per share, it is not deemed to have been taken into account in estimating the fair value of the option at the grant date. Thus the condition is taken into account at each accounting date, when assessing the number of share options or shares that will vest.

CASE STUDY 2

Facts

An employee has been granted share options to buy shares on the condition that the employee remains in employment for two years and that the entity's earnings per share increases by at least 30% over that period. The share option will vest only if both those conditions are satisfied.

Required

How will these conditions affect the accounting for the share-based payment?

Solution

The performance conditions will both have to be met for the shares to vest. However, the expense for share options is still recognized over the vesting period irrespective of whether those share options are exercised or not. No adjustments other than perhaps a reclassification of the equity are made after the vesting date. In the case of share options, for example, no adjustments are made even if those share options are not exercised.

Modifications to equity instruments are to be treated as additional instruments in their own right. IFRS 2 effectively requires an entity to ignore any modification if it does not increase the total fair value of the share-based payments or if it is not otherwise beneficial to the employee. This means that even if the total fair value of the equity instruments granted is reduced as a result of changes to its terms and conditions, the expense relating to the original option is still recognized as if the modification had not happened. Any modification that increases the total fair value of the share-based payment is recognized as an expense over the period from the date that the modification occurred until the date on which the shares vest.

If a modification occurs after the vesting period, the increase in fair value should be recognized immediately over any revised vesting period. If the modification provides some additional benefit to the employees—for example, a performance condition might be eliminated—this should be taken into account in determining the number of equity instruments that are expected to vest.

If the equity instrument is canceled or settled during the vesting period, it is treated as if the vesting date had been brought forward, and the balance of the fair value not yet expensed is charged to income immediately. If compensation is paid for the cancelation or settlement, any cash paid up to the fair value of the options at the date of the cancelation is deducted from equity and any amount paid in excess of the fair value is treated as an expense. If an entity cancels an equity instrument and issues replacement instruments, the transaction is treated as a modification. The incremental fair value is the difference between the fair value of the replacement instrument and the fair value of the original instrument.

PRACTICAL INSIGHT

Zurich Financial Services used Exposure Draft (ED) 2, *Share-Based Payment,* in its financial statements for the year ended December 31, 2003. The result was an increase in the opening balance of reserves of $135 million to reflect as additional paid-in capital the fair value of share-based payments made.

CASH-SETTLED TRANSACTIONS

Cash-settled share-based payment transactions occur where goods or services are paid for at amounts that are based on the price of the entity's shares or other equity instruments. The expense for cash-settled transactions—for example, share appreciation rights—is basically the cash paid by the entity. Share appreciation rights entitle employees to cash payments equal to the increase in the share price of a given number of the entity's shares over a given period. A cash-settled transaction creates a liability. The cost that is recognized for this liability is based on the fair value of the instrument at the reporting date. The fair value of the liability is remeasured at each reporting until it is finally settled.

Thus the cumulative expense recognized at the reporting date is the fair value on the reporting date times the amount of the vesting period that has lapsed. Any change in the fair value between the vesting date and the settlement date is recognized immediately.

CASE STUDY 3

Facts

An entity issues share appreciation rights on July 1, 20X5, and the entity's year-end is June 30, 20X6. The rights vest on June 30, 20X9. The value of the share appreciation rights was $1 million at the beginning of the year. The fair value on June 30, 20X6, had increased by $600,000.

Required

What is the expense for share appreciation rights for the year ended June 30, 20X6?

Solution

The expense for the year would increase to $400,000 from $250,000 per year (250 + 600/4), leaving the remaining balance of $1.2 million to be recognized over the remaining three-year period. If the share appreciation rights were to be settled in 2X11, any change in the fair value between 20X9 and 2X11 would be shown in the financial statements immediately.

Unlike equity-settled transactions, any reduction in the value of the award is recognized immediately, even if the award is not exercised. The payment of a cash-settled share-based transaction can occur after the services are rendered.

TRANSACTIONS THAT CAN BE SETTLED FOR SHARES OR CASH

Some share-based payment transactions allow the entity or the employee the choice as to whether to settle the transaction in cash or by issuing equity instruments. An employee may have the right to choose between a payment equal to the market price of the shares or be given shares subject to certain conditions—for example, not being able to sell them for a period of time. The accounting for this type of instrument depends on which party has the choice of settlement method and the extent to which the entity has incurred a liability.

If the employee has the right to choose the settlement method, the entity is deemed to have issued a compound financial instrument (i.e., it has issued an instrument with a debt element—the cash component—and an equity element—where the employee has the right to receive equity instruments).

If the fair value of the goods or services received can be measured directly and easily, the equity element is determined by taking the fair value of the goods or services less the fair value of the debt element of this instrument. The debt element is essentially the cash payment that will occur. If the fair value of the goods or services is measured by reference to the fair value of the equity instruments given, the whole of the compound instrument should be fair valued. The equity element becomes the difference between the fair value of the equity instruments granted less the fair value of the debt component.

CASE STUDY 4

Facts

An entity has purchased property, plant, and equipment for $10 million. The supplier can choose how the purchase price can be settled. The choices are the receipt of one million shares of the entity in one year's time or the receipt of a cash payment in six months' time equivalent to the market value of 800,000 of the entity's shares. It is estimated that the fair value of the first alternative would be $11 million and the fair value of the second alternative would be $9 million.

Required

Explain how this transaction is accounted for.

Solution

When the entity receives the property, plant, and equipment, it should record a liability of $9 million and an increase in equity of $1 million (the difference between the value of the property, plant, and equipment and the fair value of the liability).

CASE STUDY 5

Facts

An entity grants one of its employees the right to choose either one million shares or to receive a cash payment equal to 750,000 shares. At the grant date, the value of the market price of the share is $6. The entity estimates that the fair value of the share alternative is $5 per share.

Required

Explain how this transaction is accounted for.

Solution

The fair value of the equity alternative will be one million multiplied by $5, or $5 million. The value of the cash alternative will be $6 multiplied by 750,000 shares, or $4.5 million. Therefore, the fair value of the equity component of the compound financial instrument is deemed to be the difference between these two values, or $500,000. At the settlement date, the liability element of the debt component should be measured at fair value. The method of settlement chosen by the employee will then determine the final accounting.

Where the right to equity settlements is more valuable than the right to a cash settlement, the incremental fair value is accounted for as an equity-settled transaction.

Where the entity chooses the method of settlement, it should decide whether an obligation to settle in cash has been created or not. Normally the transaction will be treated as a cash-settled transaction if the entity has a past practice or a stated policy of settling in cash or if the choice of settlement in equity instruments has no commercial substance or if the equity instruments to be issued are redeemable. If none of the other conditions is apparent, the entity accounts for the transaction as an equity-settled transaction. If the transaction is accounted for as an equity-settled transaction, the accounting when the settlement occurs depends on which alternative has the greater value.

PRACTICAL INSIGHT

Unilever adopted the US Standard on share-based payment in its financial statements ending December 31, 2003. The effect is to reduce the operating profit for the year by €116 million and the prior year by €99 million. Unilever intends to use IFRS 2 in the future.

IFRIC 11, *IFRS 2—Group and Treasury Share Transactions*

IFRIC 11, which was issued in November 2006 and was made effective for annual periods beginning on or after March 1, 2007, deals with the following two issues:

1. Whether the following transactions should be accounted for as equity-settled or as cash-settled under the requirements of IFRS 2:

   a. An entity grants to its employees rights to equity instruments of the entity, and either chooses or is required to buy equity instruments from another party, to satisfy its obligations to its employees.

   b. An entity's employees are granted rights to equity instruments of the entity, either by the entity itself or by its shareholders, and the shareholders of the entity provide the equity instruments needed.

2. Share-based payment arrangements that involve two or more entities within the same group. For instance, when employees of a subsidiary are granted rights to equity instruments of the parent as consideration for the services provided to the subsidiary.

According to the consensus in IFRIC 11:

   a. Share-based payment transactions in which an entity receives services as consideration for its own equity instruments shall be accounted for as "equity-settled." This will apply regardless of whether the entity chooses or is required to buy those equity instruments from another party to satisfy its obligations to its employees under the share-based payment arrangement whether the instrument is granted or settled by the entity itself or by its shareholders(s).

   b. In case of share-based payment arrangements involving equity instruments of the parents:

   • When the parent grants rights to the employees of the subsidiary and the arrangement is accounted as "equity-settled," the subsidiary shall measure the services received by its employees in accordance with the requirements applicable to equity-settled share-based payments transactions, with a corresponding increase recognized in equity as a contribution from the parent. In case the grant of rights is conditional upon completion of service, the subsidiary shall measure the services received from the employee by reference to the fair value of the equity instruments at the date of original grant of the right.

   • When the subsidiary grants rights to equity instruments of its parents to its employees, the subsidiary shall account for the transaction with its employees as "cash-settled."

IFRIC 11 has now been withdrawn; see ahead.

DEFERRED TAX IMPLICATIONS

In some jurisdictions, a tax allowance is available for share-based transactions. It is unlikely that the amount of the tax deduction will equal the amount charged to the statement of comprehensive income under the Standard.

Quite often, the tax deduction is based on the option's intrinsic value, which is the difference between the market price and exercise price of the share option. It is likely that a deferred tax asset will arise that represents the difference between a tax base of the employee's services received to date and the carrying amount, which will effectively normally be zero.

A deferred tax asset will be recognized if the entity has sufficient future taxable profits against which it can be offset. The anticipated future tax benefit should be allocated between the statement of comprehensive income and equity.

The recognition of the deferred tax asset should be dealt with on this basis:

- If the estimated or actual tax deduction is less than or equal to the cumulative recognized expense, the associated tax benefits are recognized in the statement of comprehensive income.
- If the estimated or actual tax deduction exceeds the cumulative recognized compensation expense, the excess tax benefits are recognized directly in a separate component of equity.

CASE STUDY 6

Facts

An entity operates in a tax jurisdiction that receives a tax deduction equal to the intrinsic value of the share options at the date that they are exercised. The entity grants share options to its employees with a fair value of $1.6 million at the grant date. The tax jurisdiction gives a tax allowance for the intrinsic value of the options, which is $2 million. The tax rate applicable to the entity is 30%, and the share options vest in two years' time.

Required

Explain how this transaction is accounted for.

Solution

A deferred tax asset would be recognized of $2 million multiplied by the 30% tax rate multiplied by one year divided by two years, which equals $300,000. The statement of comprehensive income would be credited with $1.6 million multiplied by 30% multiplied by 1/2, which is $240,000, and equity would be credited with $0.4 million multiplied by 30% multiplied by 1/2, which is $60,000. Because the intrinsic value of $2 million exceeds the expense that will be charged of $1.6 million, part of the deferred tax asset is recorded in equity. If in the future the expense exceeds the intrinsic value, the amount recorded in equity will be taken to income. Obviously the deferred tax will be recognized only if there are sufficient taxable profits predicted for the future against which it can be offset.

For cash-settled share-based payment transactions, the Standard requires the estimated tax deduction to be based on the current share price. As a result, all tax benefits received or expected to be received are recognized in the statement of comprehensive income.

DISCLOSURE

IFRS 2 requires extensive disclosure requirements under three main headings:

1. Information that enables users of financial statements to understand the nature and extent of the share-based payment transactions that existed during the period
2. Information that allows users to understand how the fair value of the goods or services received or the fair value of the equity instruments that have been granted during the period was determined

3. Information that allows users of financial statements to understand the effect of expenses that have arisen from share-based payment transactions on the entity's statement of comprehensive income in the period

A key date for the Standard's transitional provisions is November 7, 2002, the publication date of the Exposure Draft on share-based payments. The Standard is applicable to equity instruments granted after November 7, 2002, but not yet vested on the effective date of the Standard, which is January 1, 2005. IFRS 2 applies to liabilities arising from cash-settled transactions that exist at January 1, 2005.

CASE STUDY 7

Facts

Placebo, a public limited company, purchased all of the shares of Medicine, a public limited company, by issuing ordinary shares of Placebo. The business combination was accounted for as an acquisition. Medicine had been the subject of a management buyout where all of the shares were currently owned by the management of the company. As part of the purchase consideration, Placebo had agreed to pay a further amount to the management team if the company's earnings per share increased by 50% over the next year and if the management team was still employed by Placebo at the end of this period. The contingent consideration was one ordinary share in Placebo for every ten shares held by the management team.

Placebo has also issued share options to certain employees of Medicine as a goodwill gesture on the acquisition of the company.

Placebo is a company that has the dollar as its functional currency. The company is registered on several stock exchanges and currently has a quotation on the German stock exchange. The market price of the quotation is currently €25 per share. Share options issued to the employees of Medicine were those that were currently quoted on the German stock exchange. The share options have a vesting period of three years.

Required

Discuss the implications of the above events.

Solution

The shares issued to the management team for the purchase of the company, Medicine, would not be within the scope of IFRS 2. They would be dealt with under IFRS 3, *Business Combinations,* as the acquisition was essentially a business combination. However, the shares issued as contingent consideration may or may not be accounted for under IFRS 2. The nature of the issue of shares will need to be examined. The question is whether the additional shares that are going to be issued are compensation or whether they are part of the purchase price. There is a need to understand why the acquisition agreement includes a provision for a contingent payment. It is possible that the price paid initially by Placebo was quite low and, therefore, this represents further purchase consideration. However, in this instance, the additional payment is linked to continuing employment. Therefore, it could be argued that because of the link between the contingent consideration and continuing employment, it represents a compensation arrangement, which should be included within the scope of IFRS 2.

Medicine has received the benefit of the services provided by its employees. As a result, it should record the expense that relates to this share-based payment even though the share options have been granted by Placebo.

There is no embedded derivative in this share-based payment to employees that would be accounted for under IAS 39. It may seem that there is an embedded derivative because the shares are quoted in another currency. However, equity-settled share-based payments should always be denominated in the entity's functional currency. Therefore, the total fair value of the options at the date of the grant will be determined in dollars and not in euros. The value of the grant would not change over the life of the options even if the exchange rate or market price fluctuates.

Note, however, that if the share options were to be cash settled, the liability would be recorded as a euro-denominated liability that would have to be remeasured at the end of each reporting period. Any changes in the fair value of this liability would be recognized in profit and loss.

CASE STUDY 8

Facts

Playful has ordered an amount of inventory from a supplier on July 1, 20X5. The supplier has said that the goods will be shipped and delivered on September 1, 20X5. The goods were actually received on September 30, 20X5. The supplier has agreed to accept 2,000 shares in Playful as payment for the inventory. Playful has received an invoice for $50,000. This invoice is only for accounting purposes as the fair value of the goods is difficult to determine because of the highly specialized nature of the inventory. The shares vest immediately in the supplier as soon as they are received.

The directors of the entity are unsure as to the effect that a movement in the entity's share price will have on equity-settled share-based payments.

Prior to the applicable date in IFRS 2, Playful had granted share options to each of its directors. On January 1, 20X6, Playful decided to reprice the options at a new exercise price.

Playful has also granted share appreciation rights to the members of a middle management committee. The share appreciation rights provide these employees with the right to receive cash equal to the appreciation in the entity's share price since the grant date, which was January 1, 20X6. All of the rights vest on December 31, 20X7, and they can be exercised during 20X8. It is anticipated that 5% of the middle management personnel will leave during the period to December 31, 20X7.

Required

The entity wishes to know what the implications of the above issuance of shares and share options are for the financial statements of Playful and its subsidiary. Ignore the deferred taxation effects.

Solution

Under IFRS 2, the date at which the value of the shares is measured will be the date at which Playful obtains the goods; therefore, this date will be September 30, 20X5. Because the fair value of the goods cannot be determined reliably and the invoice value of $50,000 is purely cosmetic, the fair value of the shares should be used for accounting purposes. The market price of the shares on September 30 multiplied by the shares issued will give the amount that should be expensed and treated as the assets' value.

A change in the entity's share price has no effect on the valuation of equity-settled share-based payments. Obviously, in the case of the inventory, its value will be determined by the market price of the share in this instance. Normally the amount recognized as the remuneration expense will be determined at the grant date and is based on the number of shares that will eventually vest. However, for cash-settled share-based payment, these liabilities are remeasured at the end of each reporting period. Therefore, a change in the price of the share of an entity can affect the liability that is recognized.

Playful is not required to apply IFRS 2 to the original grant of share options as the instruments were granted prior to the applicable date for IFRS 2. However, it is required to apply IFRS 2 to the modification as the repricing occurred after January 1, 20X5. The total compensation expense will be calculated by initially calculating the incremental value of the repriced award. This is the difference between the fair value of the re-priced award and the fair value of the original award. This incremental value of each share option will be multiplied by the number of share options that are expected to vest and would give a total compensation expense. This expense will be spread over the vesting period and will also take into account any revised estimates of directors who may be expected to leave.

At the grant date, Playful will need to estimate the fair value of each share appreciation right. A calculation of the expense and the liability will be carried out as of December 31, 20X6. This will be the number of employees who will be eligible for the share appreciation rights multiplied by the number of share appreciation rights that they would each receive multiplied by the fair value multiplied by one year divided by two years, as the share appreciation rights vest over the two-year period. A similar calculation would be carried out in the year to December 31, 20X7, where the expense for 20X7 is calculated as the difference between the fair value of the liability at December 31, 20X6, and December 31, 20X7. If one assumes that all of the share appreciation rights will be exercised on December 31, 20X8, then the value of the cash payment to the employees will be recalculated using the fair value of the share appreciation rights at the date on which they are exercised, that is, December 31, 20X8. Any increase in the anticipated liability at December 31, 20X7, will be expensed also.

CASE STUDY 9

Facts

Mack, a public limited company, grants 5,000 share options each to its 20 executives on June 1, 20X5, on these vesting conditions:

- The executives must remain in the company's employment during the vesting period.
- The share price must reach $10 a share before the share options vest.
- The company's earnings must increase cumulatively by more than 5% in the first year, 10% in second year, and 16% in the third year after the grant date for the options to vest in that year.

The company has calculated that the fair value of each option at the grant date is $5. The exercise price of the option is $3, and the exercise date is August 1, 20X8. The shares will vest as soon as all of the above conditions are met.

The company's earnings increased by 4% in the year to May 31, 20X6. At that date, it expects that the earnings will increase by 7% in 20X7 and 6% in 20X8. Additionally, it is anticipated that one director will leave every year.

At May 31, 20X6, no directors had left, but it is anticipated that two directors will leave in the next year (they did) and two in the year to May 31, 20X8. The cumulative increase in earnings by the end of May 31, 20X7, is 10%. The performance target will be met in 20X8, and only one director will leave in that year.

The shares of the entity are ordinary shares of $1, and the tax rate applicable in the jurisdiction is 30%. Tax allowances are based on the intrinsic value of the share. The share price of Mack was

	$ per share
June 1, 20X5	5
May 31, 20X6	7
May 31, 20X7	10
May 31, 20X8	13
August 1, 20X8	14

Required

Show the accounting entries, including deferred taxation, for the above share-based payment transactions.

Solution

IFRS 2, paragraph 21, states that the grant date fair value of the share-based payment with a market-based condition that has met all the other vesting conditions should be recognized irrespective of whether the market condition is achieved. Thus the market condition can be ignored for the purpose of accounting for the share-based transaction.

Calculation of Charge

Fair value of award expected to vest is 5000 × (20 – 2) × $5 = $450,000.

May 31, 20X6

The earnings have not met the target, but it is expected that by May 31, 20X7, the earnings target will have been met. Therefore, the vesting period is taken as two years as of the date. Also, it has been anticipated that two directors will have left by this date.

	$
Compensation charge is therefore $450,000/2 = $225,000	
Employee benefits expense—statement of comprehensive income	225,000
Equity (separate account)	225,000

May 31, 20X7

It is estimated that by this date, four directors will leave. The shares do not vest because the earnings have cumulatively increased only by 10%, and not more than 10%. Therefore the vesting period is taken as three years.

Compensation charge is, therefore, (cumulative)
$5,000 \times (20 - 4) \times \$5 \times 2/3$ 266,667

Employee benefits expense – statement of comprehensive income
$(266,667 - 225,000)$ 41,667
Equity (separate component)   41,667

May 31, 20X8

Compensation charge $[5,000 \times (20 - 3) \times 5]$ 425,000
Employee benefits expense $(425,000 - 266,667)$ 158,333
Equity (separate component)   158,333

Recording shares issued
Dr   Equity accumulation account   425,000
Cr   Equity share capital   85,000
      Share premium   340,000

August 1, 20X8

Cash received $5,000 \times 17 \times \$3$ 255,000
Share premium   255,000

Tax Consequences

	May 31, 20X6	May 31, 20X7	May 31, 20X8 (vesting date)	August 1, 20X8 (exercise date)
Intrinsic value				
(Share price – Exercise price)	$ 4	$ 7	$ 10	$ 11
Options expected to vest	90,000	80,000	85,000	85,000
	_$_	_$_	_$_	_$_
Tax benefit (intrinsic value)	180,000[1]	373,333[2]	850,000	945,000
Compensation expense (cumulative)	225,000	266,667	425,000	425,000
Deferred tax asset @ 30% of tax benefit	54,000	112,000	255,000	--
Tax receivable				283,500[3]
Movement in deferred tax asset	54,000	58,000	143,000	(255,000)
Recognized in profit/loss	54,000	26,000[4]	47,500[5]	(127,500)
Recognized in equity		32,000 (balance)	95,500 (balance)	(127,500)

[1] $(90,000 \times 4 \times 1/2)$
[2] $(80,000 \times 7 \times 2/3)$
[3] (945×0.3)
[4] $(266,667 \times 30\% - 54,000)$
[5] $(425,000 \times 30\% - 54,000 - 26,000)$

AMENDMENTS TO IFRS 2

The IASB has issued amendments to IFRS 2. These revisions primarily seek to clarify the definition of "vesting conditions" and also the accounting treatment of cancelations by the counterparty to a share-based payment agreement. These revisions to the Standard are effective for annual periods beginning on or after January 1, 2009, with earlier application permitted. The main amendments to IFRS 2 are briefly explained ahead.

Vesting Conditions

Vesting conditions are terms attached to a share-based payment arrangement that must be met by the counterparty to the agreement (say, an employee) before they are entitled to receive cash, other assets, or equity instruments of the entity. According to the existing requirements of IFRS 2 vesting conditions include

1. *Service conditions,* that is, stipulations in a share-based payment arrangement that the counterparty (say, an employee) should work for the entity for a period of time (say, five years of continuous service) before qualifying for the share-based payment.
2. *Performance conditions,* that is, requirement in a share-based agreement that requires a counterparty (say, the newly appointed "chief executive officer") to achieve a predetermined "performance" target over a period of time (say, increase of net margin from 5% to 15% in three years from the date of share-based payment arrangement).

The existing IFRS 2 did not specify other features of "vesting conditions." In other words, the Standard, as it exists currently, is silent on this aspect of vesting conditions. The recent amendment to IFRS 2 clarifies this beyond a doubt by restricting the definition of "vesting conditions" to service conditions and performance conditions and by amending the definition of "performance conditions" to require the completion of a service period in addition to specified performance targets. Therefore, under the revised IFRS 2, all features of a share-based payment arrangement other than service conditions and performance conditions will be considered to be **nonvesting conditions**.

Furthermore, the revised IFRS 2 also clarifies that in determining "fair value" of equity instruments granted (under a share-based payment arrangement), an entity shall take into account:

1. All nonvesting conditions (i.e. all conditions other than service and performance conditions).
2. Vesting conditions that are market conditions (for instance, a stipulation that is related to a counterparty achieving a certain predetermined level of market price of the entity's equity instruments).

Failure to Meet a Nonvesting Condition and Cancelations

Once again, this revision is more a clarification as opposed to a change in the requirements of IFRS 2. While the present IFRS 2 describes the treatment of a failure to meet a vesting condition, it does not categorically set out the accounting treatment for a failure to meet a condition other than a vesting condition.

While the existing IFRS 2 describes scenarios wherein an entity canceled share-based payment arrangements resulting from a failure to meet nonvesting conditions, it does not provide guidance on accounting treatment that is needed in the following situations:

1. Wherein the cancelation results from an act(s) of the counterparty (say, discontinuance of payment by an employee of contributions to an employee-saving scheme that was a precondition for qualifying for vesting).
2. Circumstances beyond the control of either the entity or the counterparty leading to nonfulfillment of a nonvesting condition (say, loss of 10,000 points on a single day within a certain month on a specified index of an internationally recognized stock market).

The revised IFRS 2 specifically addresses both of the aforementioned scenarios and prescribes the following accounting treatment:

1. If the entity or the counterparty have the option to choose as to whether to meet a nonvesting condition, a failure by the entity or the counterparty to meet the nonvesting condition will be treated as a cancelation.
2. If neither the entity nor the counterparty has the choice as to whether to meet a nonvesting condition, a failure to meet this nonvesting condition does not have any accounting effect, similar to the treatment of market conditions.

If a grant of equity instruments (under a share-based arrangement) is canceled or settled by the entity or the counterparty, the entity recognizes immediately the amount of expense that would otherwise have been recognized over the remainder of the vesting period (i.e., the share-based payment expensed is accelerated and recognized immediately). If the share-based payment contains a liability component, the liability should be fair valued at the date of cancelation or settlement. Any payment made to settle the liability component should be accounted for as an extinguishment of the liability.

IFRS 2 has been amended to state that business combinations as defined in IFRS 3 (2008) are outside the scope of IFRS 2, notwithstanding that they may be outside the scope of IFRS 3. Therefore business combinations among entities under common control and the contribution of a business upon the formation of a joint venture will not be accounted for under IFRS 2.

The IASB has issued amendments to IFRS 2, *Share-Based Payment,* that clarify the accounting for group cash-settled share-based payment transactions. The amendments clarify how an individual subsidiary in a group should account for some share-based payment arrangements in its own financial statements. In these arrangements, the subsidiary receives goods or services from employees or suppliers but its parent or another entity in the group must pay those suppliers. The amendments make clear that

- An entity that receives goods or services in a share-based payment arrangement must account for those goods or services no matter which entity in the group settles the transaction, and no matter whether the transaction is settled in shares or cash.
- In IFRS 2 a "group" has the same meaning as in IAS 27, *Consolidated and Separate Financial Statements*, that is, it includes only a parent and its subsidiaries.

The amendments to IFRS 2 also incorporate guidance previously included in IFRIC 8, *Scope of IFRS 2,* and IFRIC 11, *IFRS 2—Group and Treasury Share Transactions.* As a result, the IASB has withdrawn IFRIC 8 and IFRIC 11. The amendments are effective for annual periods beginning on or after January 1, 2010, and must be applied retrospectively. Earlier application is permitted.

CASE STUDY 10

An entity had three different employee share purchase plans (ESPP). Under plans 1 and 3, all employees were invited to participate in a savings plan whereby a certain amount was withdrawn from their net monthly salaries during a year and transferred into a separate account. The balance of this account was used to purchase shares after a one-year service period at a 15% discount to the fair value at the start of the plan or the fair value at the end of the plan. Under plan 2, eligible employees were invited to participate in a savings plan whereby they could contribute a limited amount of cash up-front into a separate account, which was used to purchase shares after a one-year service period at a 30% discount to the fair value at the start of the plan or the fair value at the end of the plan. The entity was of the opinion that the ESPP plans were share-based payments within the scope of IFRS 2, and that, in principle, they should be measured at fair value in accordance with IFRS 2, paragraph 11. However, as the entity was of the opinion that the fair value of the ESPP programs could not be reliably measured, the entity had therefore accounted for the plans using the intrinsic value method in accordance with IFRS 2, paragraph 24. The entity argued that it had no basis on which to estimate a reliable fair value at the inception of the plan, as there was uncertainty about how many shares the employees would be entitled to buy and what the future market price of those shares would be.

Required

Should the plans be valued at fair value?

Solution

The ESPP plans could be reliably measured, and the plans, therefore, should have been measured at fair value in accordance with IFRS 2, paragraph 11.

According to IFRS 2, paragraph 24, an entity may, in rare cases, be unable to estimate reliably the fair value of the equity instruments granted at the measurement date. In these rare cases only, the entity is required to measure the option to employees at intrinsic value. IFRS 2 gives unlisted or newly listed companies as examples of entities that might not be able to estimate reliably the fair value of share options at the grant date. The issuer's ESPP plans are similar to those described in US GAAP and as there are valuation methods that can be used to reliably measure the issuer's ESPP plans, it can be concluded that they should have been measured at fair value in accordance with IFRS 2.

EXTRACTS FROM PUBLISHED FINANCIAL STATEMENTS

UNILEVER PLC Annual Report, 2009

Share-based compensation plans

As at December 31, 2009, the Group had share-based compensation plans in the form of performance shares, share options, and other share awards. Starting in 2007, performance share awards and restricted stock awards were made under the Global Share Incentive Plan (GSIP), except in North America where awards were made under the Unilever North America 2002 Omnibus Equity Compensation Plan.

The numbers in this note include those for Executive Directors shown in the Directors' Remuneration Report on pages 67 to 73 and those for key management personnel shown in note 4 on page 90. No awards were made to Executive Directors in 2007, 2008, or 2009 under the Unilever North America 2002 Omnibus Equity Compensation Plan. Non-Executive Directors do not participate in any of the share-based compensation plans.

The economic fair value of the awards is calculated using option pricing models and the resulting cost is recognized as remuneration cost amortized over the vesting period of the grant.

Unilever will not grant share options in total in respect of share-based compensation plans for more than 5% of its issued ordinary capital, and for all plans together, for more than 10% of its issued ordinary capital. The Board does not apportion these limits to each plan separately.

The actual remuneration cost charged in each period is shown below, and relates almost wholly to equity-settled plans:

	€ million 2009	*€ million 2008*	*2007*
Income statement charge			
Performance share plans	(166)	(97)	(103)
Other plans[a]	(29)	(28)	(49)
	(195)	(125)	(152)

[a]   *The Group also provides a Share Matching Plan, an All-Employee Share Option Plan, a TSR Long-Term Incentive Plan (no awards after 2006), and an Executive Option Plan (no awards after 2005).*

Performance Share Plans

In 2007 we introduced the Global Share Incentive Plan (GSIP). The provisions of this plan are comparable with the GPSP (Global Performance Share Plan), with the same performance conditions of underlying sales growth and ungeared free cash flow for middle management, and the additional target based on TSR ranking for senior executives. Starting in 2008, awards made to GSIP participants normally vest at a level between 0% and 200%. Monte Carlo simulation is used to value the TSR component of the awards.

North America managers participate in the North America Performance Share Program, introduced in 2001, that awards Unilever shares if North America company performance targets are met over a three-year period. The amount to be paid to the company by participants to obtain the shares at vesting is zero.

The GPSP was introduced in 2005. Under this plan, managers were awarded conditional shares, which vest three years later at a level between 0% and 150% (for middle management) or 200% (for senior executives). The GPSP performance conditions for middle management were achievement of underlying sales growth and ungeared free cash flow targets over a three-year period. For senior executives, in addition to these two conditions, there was an additional target based on TSR ranking in comparison with a peer group over the three-year period.

A summary of the status of the Performance Share Plans as at December 31, 2009, 2008, and 2007 and changes during the years ended on these dates is presented below:

	2009 **Number of shares**	*2008* *Number of shares*	*2007* *Number of Shares*
Outstanding at January 1	**16,353,251**	16,843,769	15,270,180
Awarded	**8,867,844**	6,887,890	6,209,781
Vested	**(6,278,634)**	(6,415,295)	(3,465,990)
Forfeited	**(1,406,313)**	(963,113)	(1,170,202)
Outstanding at December 31	**17,536,148**	16,353,251	16,843,769

	2009 **Number of shares**	2008 *Number of shares*	2007 *Number of Shares*
Exercisable at December 31	--	--	--
Share award value information			
Fair value per share award during the year	€ **13.02**	€ 19.11	€ 19.06

Additional information

At December 31, 2009, there were options outstanding to purchase 41,786,145 (2008: 53,373,170) ordinary shares in NV or PLC in respect of share-based compensation plans of NV and its subsidiaries and the North American plans, and 14,260,636 (2008: 16,807,546) ordinary shares in NV or PLC in respect of share-based compensation plans of PLC and its subsidiaries.

To satisfy the options granted, certain NV group companies hold 45,317,466 (2008: 58,100,378) ordinary shares of NV or PLC, and trusts in Jersey and the United Kingdom hold 7,150,549 (2008: 9,450,493) PLC shares. The trustees of these trusts have agreed, until further notice, to waive dividends on these shares, save for the nominal sum of 0.01p per $3\frac{1}{9}$p ordinary share. Shares acquired for this purpose during 2009 represented less than 0.1% of the Group's called up capital. The balance of shares held in connection with share plans at December 31, 2009, represented 1.7% (2008: 2.2%) of the Group's called up capital.

The book value of €965 million (2008: €1,191 million) of all shares held in respect of share-based compensation plans for both NV and PLC is eliminated on consolidation by deduction from other reserves. Their market value at December 31, 2009 was €1,187 million (2008: €1,134 million).

At December 31, 2009, there were no options for which the exercise price was above market price. At December 31, 2008, the exercise price of 27,102,133 NV and PLC options were above the market price of the shares.

Shares held to satisfy options are accounted for in accordance with IAS 32 and SIC 12. All differences between the purchase price of the shares held to satisfy options granted and the proceeds received for the shares, whether on exercise or lapse, are charged to reserves. In 2008 this included € 6 million for shares held to meet options expiring in the short term which were priced above market value. The basis of the charge to operating profit for the economic value of options granted is discussed on page 126.

Between December 31, 2009, and March 1, 2010, no grants were made and 144,276 shares were forfeited related to the performance share plans.

MULTIPLE-CHOICE QUESTIONS

1. Which of the following transactions involving the issuance of shares does **not** come within the definition of a "share-based" payment under IFRS 2?

    (a) Employee share purchase plans.

    (b) Employee share option plans.

    (c) Share-based payment relating to an acquisition of a subsidiary.

    (d) Share appreciation rights.

2. Which of the following is true regarding the requirements of IFRS 2?

    (a) Private companies are exempt.

    (b) "Small" companies are exempt.

    (c) Subsidiaries using their parent entity's shares as consideration for goods and services are exempt.

    (d) There are no exemptions from IFRS 2.

3. An entity issues shares as consideration for the purchase of inventory. The shares were issued on January 1, 20X4. The inventory is eventually sold on December 31, 20X5. The value of the inventory on January 1, 20X4, was $3 million. This value was unchanged up to the date of sale. The sale proceeds were $5 million. The shares issued have a market value of $3.2 million. Which of the following statements correctly describes the accounting treatment of this share-based payment transaction?

    (a) Equity is increased by $3 million, inventory is increased by $3 million; the inventory value is expensed on sale on December 31, 20X5.

    (b) Equity is increased by $3.2 million, inventory is increased by $3.2 million; the inventory value is expensed on sale on December 31, 20X5.

    (c) Equity is increased by $3 million, inventory is increased by $3 million; the inventory value is expensed over the two years to December 31, 20X5.

    (d) Equity is increased by $3.2 million, inventory is increased by $3.2 million; the inventory value is expensed over the two years to December 31, 20X5.

4. An entity issues fully paid shares to 200 employees on December 31, 20X4. Normally shares issued to employees vest over a two-year period, but these shares have been given as a bonus to the employees because of their exceptional performance during the year. The shares have a market value of $500,000 on December 31, 20X4, and an average fair value for the year of $600,000. What amount would be expensed in the statement of comprehensive income for the above share-based payment transaction?

    (a) $600,000

    (b) $500,000

    (c) $300,000

    (d) $250,000

5. An entity grants 1,000 share options to each of its five directors on July 1, 20X4. The options vest on June 30, 20X8. The fair value of each option on July 1, 2004, is $5, and it is anticipated that all of the share options will vest on June 30, 20X8. What will be the accounting entry in the financial statements for the year ended June 30, 20X5?

    (a) Increase equity $25,000, increase in expense statement of comprehensive income $25,000.

    (b) Increase equity $5,000, increase in expense statement of comprehensive income $5,000.

    (c) Increase equity $6,250, increase in expense statement of comprehensive income $6,250.

    (d) Increase equity zero, increase in expense statement of comprehensive income zero.

6. Entity A is an unlisted entity, and its shares are owned by two directors. The directors have decided to issue 100 share options to an employee in lieu of many years of service. However, the fair value of the share options cannot be reliably measured as the entity operates in a highly specialized market where there are no comparable companies. The exercise price is $10 per share, and the options were granted on January 1, 20X4, when the value of the shares was also estimated at $10 per share. At the end of the financial year, December 31, 20X4, the value of the shares was estimated at $15 per share and the options vested on that date. What value should be placed on the share options issued to the employee for the year ended December 31, 20X4?

    (a) $1,000

    (b) $1,500

    (c) $ 500

    (d) $ 250

7. On June 1, 20X4, an entity offered its employees share options subject to the award being ratified in a general meeting of the shareholders. The award was approved by a meeting on September 5, 20X4. The entity's year-end is June 30. The employees were to receive the share options on June 30, 20X6. At which date should the fair value of the share options be valued for the purposes of IFRS 2?

    (a) June 1, 20X4.

    (b) June 30, 20X4.

    (c) September 5, 20X4.

    (d) June 30, 20X6.

8. Many shares and most share options are not traded in an active market. Therefore, it is often difficult to arrive at a fair value of the equity instruments being issued. Which of the following option valuation techniques should **not** be used as a measure of fair value in the first instance?

    (a) Black-Scholes model.
    (b) Binomial model.
    (c) Monte Carlo model.
    (d) Intrinsic value.

Items 9 through 11 are based on the following information:

Ashleigh, a public limited company, has granted share options to its employees with a fair value of $6 million. The options vest in three years' time. The Monte Carlo model was used to value the options, and these estimates had been made:

- Grant date (January 1, 20X4): estimate of employees leaving the entity during the vesting period—5%
- January 1, 20X5: revision of estimate of employees leaving to 6% before vesting date
- December 31, 20X6: actual employees leaving 5%

  9. What would be the expense charged in the statement of comprehensive income in year to December 31, 20X4?

    (a) $6 million.
    (b) $2 million.
    (c) $1.90 million.
    (d) $5.70 million.

  10. Year to December 31, 20X5?

    (a) $1.90 million.
    (b) $1.88 million.
    (c) $2 million.
    (d) $3.78 million.

  11. Year to December 31, 20X6?

    (a) $1.90 million.
    (b) $1.88 million.
    (c) $2 million.
    (d) $1.92 million.

  12. Joice, a public limited company, has granted share options to its employees prior to the date from which IFRS 2 became applicable (November 7, 2002). The company decided after the issuance of IFRS 2 to reprice the options. The original exercise price of $20 was repriced at $15 per option. IFRS 2 would require the company to

    (a) Apply the Standard to the share options from the original grant date and ignore the repricing.
    (b) Apply the Standard to the share options from the original grant date, taking into account the repriced award.
    (c) Apply the Standard to the repriced award only.
    (d) Ignore the Standard for the whole award of share options.

  13. An entity has granted share options to its employees. The total expense to the vesting date of December 31, 20X6, has been calculated as $8 million. The entity has decided to settle the award early, on December 31, 20X5. The expense charged in the statement of comprehensive income since the grant date of January 1, 20X3, had been year to December 31, 20X3, $2 million, and year to December 31, 20X4, $2.1 million. The expense that would have been charged in the year to December 31, 20X5, was $2.2 million. What would be the expense charged in the statement of comprehensive income for the year to December 31, 20X6?

    (a) $2.2 million.
    (b) $8 million.
    (c) $3.9 million.
    (d) $2 million.

  14. Elizabeth, a public limited company, has granted 100 share appreciation rights to each of its 1,000 employees in January 20X4. The management feels that as of December 31, 20X4, 90% of the awards will vest on December 31, 20X6. The fair value of each share appreciation right on December 31, 20X4, is $10. What is the fair value of the liability to be recorded in the financial statements for the year ended December 31, 20X4?

    (a) $300,000
    (b) $10 million
    (c) $100,000
    (d) $90,000

Items 15 and 16 are based on the following information:

Jay, a public limited company, has granted 20 share appreciation rights to each of its 500 employees on January 1, 20X4. The rights are due to vest on December 31, 20X7, with payment being made on December 31, 20X8. Assume that 80% of the awards vest. Share prices are

	$
January 1, 20X4	15
December 31, 20X4	18
December 31, 20X7	21
December 31, 20X8	19

  15. What liability will be recorded on December 31, 20X7, for the share appreciation rights?

    (a) $ 60,000
    (b) $210,000
    (c) $ 48,000
    (d) $150,000

  16. How should the settlement of the transaction be accounted for on December 31, 20X8?

    (a) Payment to employees of $32,000, no gain recorded.
    (b) Payment to employees of $16,000, gain of $32,000 is recorded.
    (c) Payment to employees of $48,000, no gain recorded.

(d) Payment to employees of $32,000, gain of $16,000 is recorded.

17. Doc, a public limited company, has purchased inventory of $100,000. The company has offered the supplier a choice of settlement alternatives. The alternatives are either receiving 1,000 shares of Doc six months after the purchase date (valued at $110,000 at the date of purchase) or receiving a cash payment equal to the fair value of 800 shares as of December 31, 20X4 (estimated value $90,000 at the date of purchase). What should be the accounting entry at the date of purchase of the inventory?

(a) Inventory $90,000, liability $90,000.
(b) Inventory $100,000, liability $100,000.
(c) Inventory $100,000, liability $110,000, intangible asset $10,000.
(d) Inventory $100,000, liability $90,000, equity $10,000.

18. In the tax jurisdiction of Mack, a public limited company, a tax deduction is allowed for the intrinsic value of the share options issued to employees. The company issued options on January 1, 20X4, worth $15 million to employees. They vest in three years. The share options' intrinsic value at December 31, 20X4, was $12 million. The tax rate in the jurisdiction is 30%. What is the tax effect of the above issue of share options at December 31, 20X4?

(a) $1.5 million benefit to statement of comprehensive income.
(b) $1.2 million benefit to statement of comprehensive income.
(c) $1.5 million benefit recognized in equity.
(d) $1.2 million benefit recognized in equity.

19. In the previous question, what would be the tax effect if the intrinsic value at December 31, 20X4, was $21 million?

(a) $2.1 million tax benefit to income.
(b) $2.1 million recognized in equity.
(c) $1.5 million tax benefit to income, $0.6 million recognized in equity.
(d) $1.5 million recognized in equity, $0.6 million tax benefit to income.

Chapter 34

BUSINESS COMBINATIONS (IFRS 3)

BACKGROUND AND INTRODUCTION

IFRS 3 (2008) replaced IFRS 3 (2004). IFRS 3 (2008) resulted from a joint project with the US Financial Accounting Standards Board. FASB issued a similar standard in December 2007 (SFAS 141[R]). The revisions will result in a high degree of convergence between IFRS and US GAAP in these areas, although some potentially significant differences remain. The International Financial Reporting Standards (IFRS) assume that an acquirer can be determined and identified in nearly all business combinations. IFRS 3 applies to all business combinations except combinations of entities under common control, combinations of mutual entities, combinations by contract without exchange of any ownership interest, and any joint venture operations.

DEFINITIONS OF KEY TERMS

Business combination. Occurs where several entities are brought together to form a single reporting entity.

Acquisition method. Looks at the business combination from the perspective of the acquiring company. It measures the cost of the acquisition and allocates the cost of the acquisition to the net assets acquired.

Control. The power to govern the financial and operating policies of an entity so as to obtain benefits from its activities.

Business Combination

If a business combination involves the purchase of net assets, including goodwill of another entity, rather than the purchase of the equity of the other entity, this does not result in a parent/subsidiary relationship. All business combinations within the scope of IFRS 3 have to be accounted for, by using the acquisition method. The pooling method of accounting for business combinations is no longer acceptable, and an acquirer must be identified for all business combinations.

Acquisition Method

Net assets acquired and contingent liabilities assumed are measured from the viewpoint of the acquirer. The measurement of the acquirer's net assets is not affected by the acquisition nor are any additional assets or liabilities of the acquirer recognized because of it. The reason for this is that these net assets have not been the subject of a transaction. An acquirer must be identified for all business combinations. The acquirer is the entity that obtains control of the other combining entities and businesses.

Four steps in applying the acquisition method are [IFRS 3.5]

1. Identification of the "acquirer"–the combining entity that obtains control of the acquiree [IFRS 3.7]
2. Determination of the "acquisition date"–the date on which the acquirer obtains control of the acquiree [IFRS 3.8]
3. Recognition and measurement of the identifiable assets acquired, the liabilities assumed and any noncontrolling interest (NCI, formerly called noncontrolling interest) in the acquiree
4. Recognition and measurement of goodwill or a gain from a bargain purchase

Control

There is a presumption that control is obtained when an entity acquires more than half of the other entity's voting rights unless it can be shown otherwise. It is possible not to hold more than half of the voting rights of the other entity and still obtain control of that entity where

- An entity has power over more than half of the voting rights because of an agreement with other investors.
- It has power to control the financial and operating policies of another entity because of a law or an agreement.
- It has the power to appoint or remove the majority of the board of directors.
- It has the power to cast the majority of votes at board meetings or equivalent bodies within the entity.

CASE STUDY 1

Facts

A, a public limited company, owns 50% of B and 49% of C. There is an agreement with the shareholders of C that the group will control the board of directors.

Required

Should C be consolidated as a subsidiary in the group accounts?

Solution

C will be consolidated on the basis of actual dominant influence and control exercised by the group because of the control contract.

IDENTIFYING AN ACQUIRER

Occasionally it may be difficult to identify an acquirer, but normally there will be indications that one exists; for example, when entities combine, the fair value of one of the entities is likely to be significantly greater than that of the other entity, or one entity may provide the bulk of the management expertise. In this case, the entity with the greater fair value and that provides the management expertise is probably the acquirer. Similarly, if the combination results in the management of one of the entities being able to dominate the composition of the management team of the combined entity, then the entity whose management is dominating the composition of the management team is likely to be the acquirer.

CASE STUDY 2

Facts

X, a public limited company, is to merge its operations with Z, a public limited company. The terms of the merger will be that Z will offer two of its shares for every one share of X. There will be no cash consideration. Z's market capitalization is $500 million and X's is $250 million. After the issue of shares, the board of directors will be comprised of only directors from Z. The group is to be named Z Group. Three months after the acquisition, 20% of X is sold.

Required

Is it possible to identify an acquirer?

Solution

It seems obvious that Z is the acquirer of X and not vice versa. Z is a much larger company and will dominate the business combination because of its control of the board of directors. Also the group is to be named the Z Group, which really confirms that Z is the acquirer. Additionally, part of X is sold after the acquisition, which again seems to indicate that Z acquired X.

Generally speaking, the entity that issues the equity shares in exchange for the net assets of the other entity normally can be designated the acquirer. However, in some business combinations that are referred to as reverse acquisitions, the acquirer could be the entity whose equity interests are acquired and the issuing entity is the acquiree. This can be the case where a private entity decides to have itself "acquired" by a smaller public entity in order to obtain a stock exchange listing. The entity issuing the shares will be regarded as the parent, and the private entity will be regarded as the subsidiary. The legal subsidiary will be deemed to be the acquirer if it has the power to govern the financial and operating policies of the legal parent.

PRACTICAL INSIGHT

Alliance Pharma, plc, a UK company, was "acquired" by Peerless Technology. Peerless became the legal parent of Alliance but due to the relative values of the companies, the former shareholders of Alliance became the majority shareholder with 67% of the combined company. The management of the new group was that of Alliance, and Peerless changed its name to Alliance Pharma. This was a reverse acquisition.

As a result of this reverse acquisition, the financial statements would comprise those of Alliance plus those of Peerless from the date of acquisition, and the comparative results of Alliance.

COST OF ACQUISITION

The cost of the acquisition has to be measured. It is the sum of the fair values of the assets given or liabilities incurred at the date of the acquisition plus the equity shares issued by the acquirer in exchange for control of the acquiree plus any costs that are directly related to the business combination. Equity shares issued as consideration for the acquisition of the other entity will be valued at their market price. If a market price is not in existence or cannot be reliably determined, then other valuation methods can be used.

Future losses or other costs that are expected to be incurred as a result of the business combination are not deemed to be liabilities incurred by the acquirer and are, therefore, not included as part of the cost of the acquisition.

Thus consideration for an acquisition, including any contingent consideration arrangements, is recognized and measured at fair value at the acquisition date. Subsequent changes in those fair values can only affect the measurement of goodwill where they occur during the "measurement period" and are as a result of additional information becoming available about facts and circumstances that existed at the acquisition date. All other changes (e.g., due to the acquiree meeting an earnings target, reaching a specific share price, or meeting a milestone on a research and development project) are dealt with in accordance with relevant IFRS. This will usually mean that changes in the fair value of consideration are recognized in profit or loss (e.g., where the contingent consideration is classified as debt under IAS 32, *Financial Instruments: Presentation*). This change is a further application of the Board's move to focus on what is given to the vendor as consideration in the business combination. The consequence is separation of, and separate accounting for, aspects of the transaction that are not part of the business combination.

IFRS 3 has a 12-month time limit for recognizing adjustments to the acquisition accounting. IFRS 3 states that an acquirer can only make adjustments to the provisional accounting when it obtains new information about facts and circumstances that existed at acquisition date. The measurement period ends as soon as the acquirer receives the information it was seeking or learns that the information cannot be obtained. The measurement period is limited to a maximum of one year from the acquisition date.

There is a requirement to expense transaction costs associated with a business combination, rather than capitalize them to the cost of acquisition. These costs could include legal and accounting fees for due diligence performed before the acquisition occurs.

IAS 32, *Financial Instruments: Presentation,* applies to costs related to the issue of debt or equity securities.

Acquisition, related costs are not part of the fair value exchange between the buyer and seller of a business. They are separate transactions in which the buyer pays for the fair value of the services received. These costs generally do not represent assets of the acquirer at the acquisition date because the acquirer receives the benefits as the services are given.

The requirement to expense transaction costs differs from the treatment of similar costs when an entity acquires an individual asset. In the latter case, transaction costs are generally included in the cost of the asset.

If the amount of contingent consideration changes as a result of a postacquisition event (such as meeting an earnings target), accounting for the change in consideration depends on whether the additional consideration is an equity instrument or cash or other assets paid or owed. If it is equity, the original amount is not remeasured. If the additional consideration is cash or other assets paid or owed, the changed amount is recognized in profit or loss. If the amount of consideration changes because of new information about the fair value of the amount of consideration at acquisition date rather than because of a postacquisition event, then retrospective restatement is required.

CASE STUDY 3

Facts

James has acquired 100% of the equity of Bang on December 31, 20X9. There are three elements to the purchase consideration. An immediate payment of $10 million and two further payments of $2 million if the return on capital employed (ROCE) exceeds 10% in each of the subsequent financial years ending December 31. James uses a discount rate of 7% in any present value calculations.

Required

Value the total consideration at the acquisition date.

Solution

The two payments that are conditional upon reaching the target ROCE are contingent consideration and their fair value of $(1/1.07 +1/1.07/1.07), that is, $3.62 million will be added to the immediate cash payment of $10 million to give a total consideration of $13.62 million.

PRACTICAL INSIGHT

Newmark Security plc acquired a subsidiary. The company paid an initial amount with a further sum, not exceeding $3.5 million, being due over the next four years. The deferred consideration is payable subject to the subsidiary achieving an agreed level of average profit over the period. Newmark felt that it would be payable in full and, therefore, included the additional amount in the initial cost of acquisition.

NET ASSETS ACQUIRED

The acquirer must recognize separately at the date of acquisition the acquiree's identifiable assets, liabilities, and contingent liabilities that satisfy the recognition criteria at that date set out in the IFRS. These net assets must be recognized irrespective of whether they have previously been recognized in the acquiree's financial statements. To qualify for recognition as part of applying the acquisition method, an item should

- Meet the definition of an asset or liability in the *Framework for the Preparation and Presentation of Financial Statements* at the acquisition date (IFRS 3.11).
- Be part of the business acquired (the acquiree) rather than the result of a separate transaction (IFRS 3.12).

Costs that the acquirer expects but is not obliged to incur in the future to effect its plan to exit an activity of an acquiree or to terminate the employment of or relocate an acquiree's employees are not liabilities at the acquisition date. (IFRS 3.11).Thus any agreed restructuring provisions would generally not be recognized unless the acquiree has at the acquisition date an existing liability for restructuring that has been recognized in accordance with IAS 37. Identifiable assets, liabilities, and contingent liabilities must be measured initially at full fair value, which includes any noncontrolling interest share of those items. The acquirer should not recognize any liabilities for future losses or other costs expected to be incurred as a result of the acquisition. If the acquiree's restructuring plan is conditional on it being acquired, then just before the acquisition, the provision does not represent a present obligation, nor is it a contingent liability.

The acquirer may recognize some assets and liabilities that the acquiree had not previously recognized in its financial statements. For example, intangible assets acquired must be recognized as assets separately from goodwill. These intangible assets must meet the definition of an asset in that they should be controlled and there should be an unconditional right or obligation.

Thus, such items as trademarks, trade names, customer lists, order or production backlogs, customer contracts, artistic-related intangible assets, and contract-based intangible assets such as licensing and royalty agreements and lease agreements may meet the definition of an intangible asset for the purpose of IFRS 3.

Similarly, in applying the acquisition method, all contingent liabilities assumed must be recognized if their fair value can be measured reliably. After their initial recognition, the contingent liabilities must be remeasured at the higher of the amount that will be recognized in accordance with IAS 37 and the amount initially recognized less cumulative amortization (where appropriately recognized in accordance with IAS 18). Any contingent liability recognized under IFRS 3 continues to be recognized subsequently, even though it may not qualify for recognition under IAS 37.

IFRS 3 requires that, at the acquisition date, the identifiable assets acquired and liabilities assumed should be classified or designated as necessary to apply other IFRS subsequently.

The acquirer makes those classifications or designations on the basis of contractual terms, economic conditions, its operating or accounting policies, and other pertinent conditions as they exist at the acquisition date. (IFRS 3.15)

Examples of classifications or designations made at the acquisition date include classification of financial assets and designation of a derivative as a hedging instrument.

The Standard provides two exceptions to the principle that classifications or designations are based on the terms of instruments and conditions at the acquisition date. The two exceptions relate to

1. The classification of a lease contract as either an operating lease or a finance lease in accordance with IAS 17, *Leases.*
2. The classification of a contract as an insurance contract in accordance with IFRS 4, *Insurance Contracts.*

Identifiable assets acquired and liabilities assumed are measured at their acquisition-date fair values.

For each business combination, any noncontrolling interest in the acquiree is measured either (IFRS 3.19):

- At fair value
- At the noncontrolling interest's proportionate share of the acquiree's identifiable net assets.

This choice is available for each business combination, so an entity may use fair value for one business combination and the proportionate share of the acquiree's identifiable net assets for another. For the purpose of measuring noncontrolling interests at fair value, it may be possible to determine the acquisition-date fair value on the basis of active market prices for the equity shares not held by the acquirer. When a market price for the equity shares is not available because the shares are not publicly traded, the acquirer should measure the fair value of the noncontrolling interests using other valuation techniques.

If the acquirer and acquiree were parties to a preexisting relationship (for instance, the acquirer had granted the acquiree a right to use its intellectual property), this must be accounted for separately from the business combination. In most cases, this will lead to the recognition of a gain or loss for the amount of the consideration transferred to the vendor, which effectively represents a "settlement" of the preexisting relationship. The amount of the gain or loss is measured as follows:

1. For preexisting noncontractual relationships (for example, a lawsuit): by reference to fair value.
2. For preexisting contractual relationships: at the lesser of (a) the favorable/unfavorable contract position and (b) any stated settlement provisions in the contract available to the counterparty to whom the contract is unfavorable.

However, where the transaction effectively represents a reacquired right, an intangible asset is recognized and measured on the basis of the remaining contractual term of the related contract excluding any renewals. The asset is then subsequently amortized over the remaining contractual term, again excluding any renewals.

CASE STUDY 4

Facts

X PLC	$m
Cost of acquisition	700
Less fair value of net assets	300
Less restructuring provision	(70)
Goodwill	470
Statement of comprehensive income at year-end	
Profit before amortization	140
Amortization of goodwill	(47)
	93
Interest	(13)
Profit before tax	80

This information relates to the acquisition of X, a public limited company, by Z, a public limited company. At the date of acquisition, the fair value of the intangible assets and the contingent liabilities of X were $100 million and $30 million respectively. At the date of the preparation of the financial statements, the value of the net assets of X had increased significantly. The intangible assets have a life of ten years.

Required

How would the acquisition be accounted for under IFRS 3?

Solution

	$m
Cost of acquisition	700
Less fair value of net assets	(300)
Less fair value of intangibles	(100)
Contingent liabilities	30
Goodwill	330

Statement of comprehensive income at year-end	*$m*
Profit before amortization	140
Amortization of intangibles	(10)
Goodwill impairment	0
	130
Interest	(13)
Profit before tax	117

The restructuring provision is not allowed under IFRS. The intangibles will have to be accounted for and amortized over ten years. The contingent liabilities will need recording also. The net assets of X have increased significantly, and, therefore, it is unlikely that goodwill will be impaired at the financial year-end.

GOODWILL

As mentioned previously, noncontrolling interests can be measured on two bases—by reference to their share of the identifiable net assets of the acquiree or the fair value of the noncontrolling interests. The former measure results in goodwill being recognized at the acquisition date as an asset and is initially measured at its cost, being the excess of the cost of the acquisition over the acquirer's interest in the net fair value of the identifiable assets, liabilities, and contingent liabilities. The latter measure results in the recognition of the noncontrolling interest's share of goodwill. Because noncontrolling interests can be measured by alternative methods, it is necessary to include the noncontrolling interests within the calculation of goodwill, and also to deduct the entire identifiable acquiree net assets (rather than only the acquirer's share of those net assets).

The acquirer therefore accounts for goodwill at the date of acquisition measured as a difference between

1. The aggregate of the following three:

   a. The fair value on the acquisition date of the consideration transferred
   b. The amount of any noncontrolling interest (NCI) in the acquiree
   c. In case of a "business combination achieved in stages," the acquisition-date fair value of the acquiree's previously held equity interest in the acquiree

2. The net of the acquisition-date amounts of the identifiable assets acquired and the acquired liabilities assumed, both measured in accordance with the provisions of IFRS 3 (revised)

Goodwill should be measured after initial recognition at cost less any accumulated impairment charge.

Goodwill should not be amortized but tested at least annually for impairment in accordance with IAS 36.

A bargain purchase is a business combination in which the net fair value of the identifiable assets acquired and liabilities assumed exceeds the aggregate of the consideration transferred, the noncontrolling interests, and the fair value of any previously held equity interest in the acquiree.

A bargain purchase might happen, for example, in a business combination that is a forced sale in which the seller is acting under compulsion. However, the recognition and measurement exceptions for particular items might also lead to the recognition of a gain (or a change in the amount of a recognized gain) on a bargain purchase (IFRS 3.35).

If, after applying the requirements ahead it is determined that the acquisition is a bargain purchase, the acquirer recognizes the resulting gain in profit or loss on the acquisition date.

Before recognizing any gain, the Standard requires that the acquirer should reassess whether it has correctly identified all of the assets acquired and all of the liabilities assumed. The acquirer should recognize any additional assets or liabilities that are identified in that review. The acquirer is then required to review the procedures used to measure the amounts that IFRS 3 requires to be recognized at the acquisition date for all of the following:

1. The identifiable assets acquired and liabilities assumed.
2. The noncontrolling interest in the acquiree, if any.

3. For a business combination achieved in stages, the acquirer's previously-held equity interest in the acquiree.
4. The consideration transferred.

The objective of the review is to ensure that the measurements appropriately reflect consideration of all available information as of the acquisition date.

CASE STUDY 5

Facts

Mark has acquired a subsidiary on January 1, 20X9. The fair value of the net assets of the subsidiary was $434 million. Mark acquired 70% of the shares of the subsidiary for $429 million. The noncontrolling interest was fair valued at $136 million.

Required

Calculate goodwill using both methods allowed in IFRS 3.

Solution

Goodwill based on the two goodwill methods under IFRS 3 would be

Method 1	
Purchase consideration	429
Noncontrolling interest (30% × 434)	130.2
	559.2
Identifiable net assets-fair value	(434)
Goodwill	125.2
Method 2	
Purchase consideration	429
Noncontrolling interest	136
	565
Identifiable net assets—fair value	(434)
Goodwill	131

It can be seen that goodwill is effectively adjusted for the change in the value of the noncontrolling interest, which represents the goodwill attributable to the NCI.

This choice of method of accounting for NCI only makes a difference in an acquisition where less than 100% of the acquired business is purchased. Method 2 will increase reported net assets on the statement of financial position, which means that any future impairment of goodwill will be greater. Although measuring noncontrolling interest at fair value may prove difficult, goodwill impairment testing may be easier under method 2, as there is no need to gross-up goodwill for partially owned subsidiaries.

CASE STUDY 6

Facts

On January 1, 2009, an entity, Y, acquires 85% of the equity interests of X, a private entity, in exchange for cash of $45 million. The owners of X wish to sell the entity quickly. Y measures the separately recognizable identifiable assets acquired and the liabilities assumed as of the acquisition date in accordance with the requirements of IFRS 3. The identifiable assets are measured at $75 million and the liabilities are measured at $15 million. The fair value of the 15% noncontrolling interest in X is $12 million.

Required

Calculate the gain on the bargain purchase.

Solution

The amount of X's identifiable net assets $60 million exceeds the fair value of the consideration transferred $45 million plus the fair value of the noncontrolling interest $12 million in X. Therefore, Y reviews the procedures it used to identify and measure the assets acquired and liabilities and to measure the fair value of both the noncontrolling interest in X and the consideration transferred. After that review, Y decides that the procedures and resulting measures were appropriate then $3 million is recognized in profit or loss.

STEP ACQUISITION

Business combination requiring acquisition accounting is triggered only at the point of attaining control in the acquiree. It has different implications depending upon whether the acquirer has a preexisting equity interest in the acquiree (in which case, prior to attaining control in the acquiree, the equity interest in the acquiree may be accounted for either as a financial asset in accordance with IAS 39, or as an associate under IAS 28, or as a joint venture under IAS 31, as appropriate), subsequently, upon further increase in equity interest in the acquiree *in stages*, once the equity ownership in the acquiree reaches the (trigger) point when control is achieved, the acquirer must remeasure its previously held equity interest in the acquiree at fair value on the acquisition date and recognize the resulting gain or loss, if any, in profit or loss. Once control is attained in the acquiree, all further increases and decreases in equity interests are treated as transactions among equity holders and reported within equity (neither goodwill arises on any increase in equity interest, nor is any gain or loss recognized on any decrease in equity interest).

Thus prior to control being obtained, the investment is accounted for under the relevant standard. On the date that control is obtained, the fair values of the acquired entity's assets and liabilities, including goodwill, are measured, with the option to measure full goodwill or only the acquirer's percentage of goodwill. Any resulting adjustments to previously recognized assets and liabilities are recognized in profit or loss. Attaining control triggers remeasurement.

Example

Step acquisition

On January 1, 20X9, Angel acquired a 50% interest in Gabriel for $120 million. Angel already held a 20% interest which had been acquired for $40 million but which was valued at $48 million at January 1, 20X9. The fair value of the noncontrolling interest at January 1, 20X9 was $80 million and the fair value of the identifiable net assets of Gabriel was $220 million. The goodwill calculation would be as follows using the fair value of NCI:

	$m	$m
January 1, 20X9 consideration	120	
Fair value of interest held	48	
		168
Noncontrolling interest		80
		248
Fair value of identifiable net assets		(220)
Goodwill		28

A gain of $8 million would be recorded on the increase in the value of the previous holding in Gabriel.

The accounting for a business combination initially involves the identification of the fair values to be given to the acquiree's net assets, contingent liabilities, and the cost of the acquisition.

Sometimes the initial accounting can be determined only provisionally by the time the first accounts are drawn up after the acquisition. If this is the case, then the acquiring entity should use those provisional values. However, any adjustments to those provisional values should be made within 12 months of the acquisition and from the date of the acquisition. Any further adjustments to the values given to the net assets and contingent liabilities and cost of the combination after the initial accounting has been completed should be made only to correct an error, as set out in IAS 8.

The requirements of IFRS 3 have resulted in amendments to IAS 12, *Income Taxes*. In addition to consequential changes in terminology, a more significant change is made in respect of the postcombination recognition of deferred tax assets acquired in a business combination as follows:

- Acquired deferred tax benefits recognized within the measurement period that result from new information about facts and circumstances that existed at the acquisition date reduce the carrying amount of any goodwill related to that acquisition. If the carrying amount of that goodwill is zero, any remaining deferred tax benefits are recognized in profit or loss.

- All other acquired deferred tax benefits realized are recognized in profit or loss or outside profit or loss if otherwise required by IAS 12.

CASE STUDY 7

Facts

JCE, a public limited company, acquired LZE, a public limited company, on December 31, 20X7. LZE has among its net assets customer lists of information in the form of a database. LZE has two such databases: one where the nature of the information is subject to national laws regarding confidentiality and another where the information can be sold or leased. LZE also has contracts for the supply of maintenance services for computer systems. These contracts have another five years left to run. The company insures computer systems against potential disasters, and these contracts are renewable every year.

Additionally, JCE requested an official valuation of the computer equipment of LZE. By the time of the 20X7 annual financial statements, the valuation had not been completed and a provisional value for the assets was included in the financial statements. The final valuation was received on June 30, 20X8. On March 1, 20X9, the auditors discover an error in the valuation of property, plant, and equipment as at December 31, 20X7. A piece of equipment had been omitted from the valuation listing.

Required

Describe the implications of the preceding information for accounting for the acquisition of LZE.

Solution

The customer lists meet the definition of an intangible asset and should be accounted for separately. However, the customer list that is subject to national laws regarding confidentiality would not meet the criteria for an intangible asset, as the laws would prevent the entity from disseminating the information about its customers. The contract-based intangibles—the contracts for the supply of maintenance services—would meet the definition of an intangible asset. These intangibles will be recognized separately from goodwill, provided that the fair value can be measured reliably. In deciding on the fair value of a customer relationship, for example, JCE will consider assumptions such as the expected renewal of the supply agreement. The insurance contracts that it already has with its customers meet the contractual legal criterion for identification as an intangible asset and will be recognized separately from goodwill, providing the fair value can be measured reliably.

In determining the fair value of the liability relating to these insurance contracts, the holding company will bear in mind potential estimates of cancelations by policyholders. Currently IFRS 4, *Insurance Contracts*, deals with the accounting for such contracts. Also, the number of policyholders that are expected to renew their contracts each year must be borne in mind when assessing the accounting for these contracts.

Regarding the computer equipment that has been acquired, at year-end the entity has not determined the value of this equipment. Therefore, a provisional value will be placed on the computer equipment. Any adjustment to this provisional value will be made from the acquisition date and has to be made within 12 months of that acquisition date. The valuation was received on June 30; as a result, goodwill at December 31, 20X7, will be recalculated. In the 20X8 accounts, an adjustment will be made to the opening carrying value of the computer equipment less any depreciation for the period. The carrying value of goodwill will be adjusted for the reduction in value at the acquisition date, and the 20X7 comparative information will be restated to reflect the adjustment. In the 20X7 accounts, the financial statements should disclose that the initial accounting for the business combination has been determined only provisionally and explain why this is so. In the 20X8 accounts, there should be an explanation of what adjustments have been made to the provisional values during the period.

The error in 20X9, regarding the omission of a piece of plant and equipment, should be accounted for under IAS 8. IAS 8 requires the correction of an error to be accounted for retrospectively and for the financial statements to be presented as if the error had never occurred by correcting the prior period's information. In the 20X9 financial statements, an adjustment will be made to the opening value of property, plant, and equipment. The adjustment will be the fair value of the equipment at December 31, 20X7, less any amounts that should have been recognized for the depreciation of that equipment. The carrying value of goodwill is also adjusted for the reduction in value. Also, the comparative information for the year to December 31, 20X8, will be restated, and any additional depreciation relating to that period will be charged.

CASE STUDY 8

Facts

Complex groups

Joanne purchased its shareholding in Graham on January 1, 20X8, and Brian purchased its shareholding in David on December 31, 20X8. Control was achieved on these acquisition dates.

The following financial statements relate to the J group as at December 31, 20X9:

	Joanne $m	Graham $m	David $m
Cost of investment in Graham (80% holding)	640		
Cost of investment in David (60% holding)		440	
Other net assets	520	264	600
	1160	704	600
Equity shares	800	480	400
Retained earnings	360	224	200
	1160	704	600

The retained earnings were:

	Brian $m	David $m
January 1, 20X8	80	20
December 31, 20X8	260	64

The fair value of the NCI based on effective shareholdings were:

	Brian $m	David $m
January 1, 20X8	160	378
December 31, 20X8	196	400

The goodwill of Brian is impaired as at December 31, 20X9, by $4 million following poor trading results for the year. There was no impairment prior to this date.

Required

For both methods, of accounting for goodwill, show the statement of financial position at December 31, 20X9.

Solution

Under both scenarios the group's effective share of David will be 80% of 60% that is 48%.

Joanne (J)

    80%

Graham (G)

    60%

David (D)

Joanne controls Graham from January 1, 20X8, and David from December 31, 20X8, therefore the relevant acquisition date retained earnings are $4 million and $3.2 million respectively. By the same token the fair values of the NCI at acquisition are $8 million and $20 million respectively.

Full method

a) Goodwill

The goodwill relating to G is the same as it would be under a simple group scenario.

The fair value of the consideration held in D represents the 60% shareholding purchased by G. The 20% element that belongs to the NCI of G needs to be deducted thereby giving the net balance representing the effective 48% shareholding from the group viewpoint.

In adding the fair value of NCI in D (based on 52% shareholding) we arrive at the total fair value of 100% of D including the element attributable to goodwill. Finally by deducting the fair value of the identifiable net assets the balance represents goodwill attributable to both group and NCI.

	G $m	D $m
Fair value of consideration	640	440
Indirect holding in D belonging to NCI (20% × $22m)		(88)
Fair value of NCI	160	400
	800	752
Fair value of identifiable net assets at acquisition		
(480m + 80m) and (400m + 64m)	(560)	(464)
Goodwill	240	288

As at December 31, the total goodwill is $528m ($240m + $288m) less impairment $80m, that is, $448m

b) Noncontrolling interest

As with simple groups the NCI calculation takes

- The fair value as at the acquisition date
- Includes the share of post-acquisition retained earnings based on effective shareholdings
- Includes any goodwill impairment/credit attributable to the NCI based on effective shareholding

The only additional element is to reflect the fact that NCI obtain their share of B's investment in D. This needs to be deducted in the NCI calculation as shown below.

	G $m	D $m
At acquisition: January 1, 20X8	160	
December 31, 20X8		400
Indirect holding in D belonging to NCI (20% × $440m)		(88)
Post-acquisition profit		
20% × (224m – 80m) and 52% × (200m – 64m)	28	70
Goodwill impairment (20% × 80m)	(16)	
Total NCI	172	382

This makes a total NCI of $554m.

c) Retained earnings

The retained earnings calculation does not differ significantly as compared to the previous version of IFRS 3. It is important to realize that effective shareholdings are always used within this calculation.

	D $m
J retained earnings	360
Share of postacquisition G, 80% × (224m – 80m)	116
Share of postacquisition D, 48% × (200m – 64m)	66
Less goodwill impaired, (80% × 80m)	(64)
	478

Joanne Group Statement of Financial Position as at December 20X9

	$m
Net assets (520m + 264m + 600m)	1,384
Goodwill (working a)	448
Total net assets	1,832
Equity shares	800
Retained earnings (working c)	478
NCI (working b)	554
	1,832

Partial method

The approach under the partial method will need to change as compared to previous version of IFRS 3 on grounds of comparability being maintained between the two methods according to IFRS 3 (Revised).

This revised approach in many respects is simpler than that according to the previous version of the standard. This revised method follows exactly the same approach as the full method with the exception that the measurement of NCI is not at fair value and hence within the goodwill calculation only a proportion of the identifiable net assets are included.

a) Goodwill

The goodwill relating to G is the same as it would be under a simple group scenario.

The fair value of the consideration held in D represents the 60% shareholding purchased by G and therefore the 20% element that belongs to the NCI of G still needs to be deducted thus giving the net balance representing the effective 48% shareholding.

Fair value of identifiable net assets at acquisition will be based on the proportion acquired based on effective shareholdings. The balance resulting is goodwill attributable to the group's effective shareholdings.

	G $m	D $m
Fair value of consideration	640	440
Indirect holding in D to NCI (20% of $22m)		(88)
Fair value of identifiable net assets at acquisition		
80% × 28m and 48% × 23.2m	(448)	(222)
Goodwill	192	130

Assuming that the impairment of goodwill relates only to the effective shareholding then total goodwill as at December 31, is $322m ($192m + $130m) less impairment $80m, that is, $242m.

The difference in the goodwill under the partial method as compared to full method is the goodwill that is attributable to NCI valued at fair value.

b) Noncontrolling interest

As with the full method the NCI calculation needs to include the cost of investment that G has in D. As NCI is not at fair value, the goodwill calculated previously only relates to the effective shareholding the group has and hence is not part of this calculation.

	B $m	D $m
At acquisition		
20% × 560m and 52% × 464m	112	242
Indirect holding		(88)
Postacquisition profit		
20% × (224m – 80m) and 52% × (200m – 64m)	28	70
Total NCI	140	224

This makes a total NCI of $364m. Note that NCI is not charged with their share of the goodwill impairment.

The difference in the goodwill amounts of ($448m – $242m), that is, $206m, under the two methods, can be seen to be the difference in the NCI figures of ($454m – $364m), that is, $190m plus the impairment of goodwill charged against the NCI of $16m.

c) Retained earnings

The rule within the retained earnings calculation is to always use the effective shareholding. It should be noted that the assumption was that the goodwill impairment related to the proportion of G held by J.

	$m
J retained earnings	360
Share of postacquisition G, 80% × (224m – 80m)	116
Share of postacquisition D, 48% × (200m – 64m)	66
Less goodwill impaired	(80)
	462

Joanne Group Statement of Financial Position as at December 20X9

	$m
Net assets (520m + 264m + 600m)	1,384
Goodwill (working a)	242
Total net assets	1,626
Equity shares	800
Retained earnings (working c)	462
NCI (working b)	364
	1,626

It is important to consider how the exercise would differ if the shareholding in the indirect subsidiary D had been acquired by G prior to J purchasing its shareholding in G.

DISCLOSURES

The acquirer shall disclose information that enables users of its financial statements to evaluate the nature and financial effect of a business combination that occurs either during the current reporting period or after the end of the period but before the financial statements are authorized for issue. [IFRS 3.59]

Among the disclosures required to meet the foregoing objective are the seventeen following: [IFRS 3.B64-66]

1. Name and a description of the acquiree
2. Acquisition date
3. Percentage of voting equity interests acquired
4. Primary reasons for the business combination and a description of how the acquirer obtained control of the acquiree. Description of the factors that make up the goodwill recognized.
5. Qualitative description of the factors that make up the goodwill recognized, such as expected synergies from combining operations and intangible assets that do not qualify for separate recognition
6. Acquisition-date fair value of the total consideration transferred and the acquisition-date fair value of each major class of consideration
7. Details of contingent consideration arrangements and indemnification assets
8. Details of acquired receivables
9. The amounts recognized as of the acquisition date for each major class of assets acquired and liabilities assumed
10. Details of contingent liabilities recognized
11. Total amount of goodwill that is expected to be deductible for tax purposes
12. Details of any transactions that are recognized separately from the acquisition of assets and assumption of liabilities in the business combination
13. Information about a bargain purchase ("negative goodwill")
14. For each business combination in which the acquirer holds less than 100% of the equity interests in the acquiree at the acquisition date, various disclosures are required
15. Details about a business combination achieved in stages
16. Information about the acquiree's revenue and profit or loss
17. Information about a business combination whose acquisition date is after the end of the reporting period but before the financial statements are authorized for issue

Disclosure of Information about Adjustments of Past Business Combinations

The acquirer shall disclose information that enables users of its financial statements to evaluate the financial effects of adjustments recognized in the current reporting period that relate to business combinations that occurred in the period or previous reporting periods [IFRS 3.61].

Among the disclosures required to meet the foregoing objective are the five following [IFRS 3.B67]:

1. Details when the initial accounting for a business combination is incomplete for particular assets, liabilities, noncontrolling interests, or items of consideration (and the fact that the amounts recognized in the financial statements for the business combination thus have been determined only provisionally)
2. Follow-up information on contingent consideration
3. Follow-up information about contingent liabilities recognized in a business combination
4. A reconciliation of the carrying amount of goodwill at the beginning and end of the reporting period, with various details shown separately
5. The amount and an explanation of any gain or loss recognized in the current reporting period that both

a. Relates to the identifiable assets acquired or liabilities assumed in a business combination that was effected in the current or previous reporting period

b. Is of such a size, nature, or incidence that disclosure is relevant to understanding the combined entity's financial statements

EXTRACTS FROM PUBLISHED FINANCIAL STATEMENTS

J SAINSBURY PLC, 2009

Notes to financial statements

Consolidation

The Group's financial statements include the results of the Company and all of its subsidiaries, together with the Group's share of the posttax results of its joint ventures.

Subsidiaries

Subsidiaries are all entities over which the Group has the power to govern the financial and operating policies generally accompanying a shareholding of more than one half of the voting rights. The results of subsidiaries are included in the Group statement of comprehensive income from the date of acquisition, or in the case of disposals, up to the effective date of disposal. Intercompany transactions and balances between Group companies are eliminated upon consolidation.

The purchase method of accounting is used to account for the acquisition of subsidiaries by the Group. The cost of acquisition is measured as the fair value of the assets given, equity instruments issued, and liabilities incurred or assumed at the date of exchange, plus costs directly attributable to the acquisition. Identifiable assets and liabilities acquired are measured at fair value at the acquisition date. The excess of cost over the fair value of the Group's share of identifiable assets and liabilities acquired is recorded as goodwill.

Joint ventures

Joint ventures are jointly controlled entities in which the Group has an interest. The Group's share of the results of its joint ventures is included in the Group statement of comprehensive income using the equity method of accounting. Where the Group transacts with a joint venture, profits and losses are eliminated to the extent of the Group's interest in the joint venture. Losses may provide evidence of an impairment of the assets transferred in which case appropriate provision is made for impairment.

Investments in joint ventures are carried in the Group statement of financial position at cost plus post-acquisition changes in the Group's share of net assets of the entity, less any impairment in value.

Investments in subsidiaries and joint ventures are carried at cost less any impairment loss in the financial statements of the Company.

BARLOWORLD

Consolidated Financial Statements 2009

Interest in subsidiaries

The consolidated financial statements incorporate the assets, liabilities, income, expenses, and cash flows of the Company and all entities controlled by the Company as if they are a single economic entity. Control is achieved where the Company has the power to govern the financial and operating policies of an entity so as to obtain benefits from its activities.

The results of subsidiaries acquired or disposed of during the period are included in the consolidated statement of comprehensive income from the date of acquisition or up to the date of disposal.

Intercompany transactions and the resulting unrealized profits and balances between group entities are eliminated on consolidation.

Minority interests in the net assets of consolidated subsidiaries are shown separately from the group equity therein. It consists of the amount of those interests at acquisition plus the minorities' subsequent share of changes in equity of the subsidiary. On acquisition date, the minorities' interest is measured at the proportion of the fair values of the identifiable assets and liabilities acquired. Losses applicable to minorities in excess of its interest in the subsidiaries' equity are allocated against the group's interest except to the extent that the minorities have a binding obligation and the financial ability to cover losses.

Minorities are considered to be equity participants and all transactions with minorities are recorded directly within equity.

BP Annual Report, 2009

Acquisitions

Acquisitions in 2009

BP made no significant acquisitions in 2009.

Acquisitions in 2008

BP made a number of acquisitions in 2008 for a total consideration of $403 million. These business combinations were in the Exploration and Production segment and Other businesses and corporate and the most significant was the acquisition of Whiting Clean Energy, a cogeneration powerplant. Fair value adjustments were made to the acquired assets and liabilities.

Acquisitions in 2007

BP made a number of acquisitions in 2007 for a total consideration of $1,200 million. These business combinations were predominantly in the Refining and Marketing segment, the most significant of which was the acquisition of Chevron's Netherlands manufacturing company, Texaco Raffiniderij Pernis B.V. The acquisition included Chevron's 31% minority shareholding in Nerefco, its 31% shareholding in the 22.5M wind farm colocated at their refinery as well as a 22.8% shareholding in the TEAM joint venture terminal and shareholdings in two local pipelines linking the TEAM terminal to their refinery. Fair value adjustments were made to the acquired assets and liabilities. Goodwill of $270 million arose on these acquisitions.

Goodwill

Business combinations are accounted for using the purchase method of accounting. The cost of an acquisition is measured as the cash paid and the fair value of other assets given, equity instruments issued, and liabilities incurred or assumed at the date of exchange, plus costs directly attributable to the acquisition. The acquired identifiable assets, liabilities, and contingent liabilities are measured at their fair values at the date of acquisition. Any excess of the cost of acquisition over the net fair value of the identifiable assets, liabilities, and contingent liabilities acquired, is recognized as goodwill. Where the group does not acquire 100% ownership of the acquired company, the interest of minority shareholders is stated at the minority's proportion of the fair values of the assets and liabilities recognized. At the acquisition date, any goodwill acquired is allocated to each of the cash-generating units expected to benefit from the combination's synergies. For this purpose, cash-generating units are set at one level below a business segment. Following initial recognition, goodwill is measured at cost less any accumulated impairment losses. Goodwill is reviewed for impairment annually or more frequently if events or changes in circumstances indicate that the carrying value may be impaired. Impairment is determined by assessing the recoverable amount of the cash-generating unit to which the goodwill relates. Where the recoverable amount of the cash-generating unit is less than the carrying amount, an impairment loss is recognized. The cost of goodwill arising on business combinations prior to January 1, 2003 is stated at the previous carrying amount under UK generally accepted accounting practice. Goodwill may also arise upon investments in jointly controlled entities and associates, being the surplus of the cost of investment over the group's share of the net fair value of the identifiable assets. Such goodwill is recorded within investments in jointly controlled entities and associates, and any impairment of the investment is included within the earnings from jointly controlled entities and associates.

Not yet adopted

The following pronouncements from the IASB will become effective for future financial reporting periods and have not yet been adopted by the group. In January 2008, the IASB issued a revised version of IFRS 3, *Business Combinations.* The revised standard still requires the purchase method of accounting to be applied to business combinations but will introduce some changes to the existing accounting treatment. For example, contingent consideration is measured at fair value at the date of acquisition and subsequently remeasured to fair value with changes recognized in profit or loss. Goodwill may be calculated based on the parent's share of net assets or it may include goodwill related to the minority interest. All transaction costs are expensed. The standard is applicable to business combinations occurring in accounting periods beginning on or after July 1, 2009 and BP will adopt it with effect from January 1, 2010. Assets and liabilities arising from business combinations that occurred before the date of adoption by the group will not be restated and thus there will be no effect on the group's reported income or net assets on adoption. The revised standard has been adopted by the EU. Also in January 2008, the IASB issued an amended version of IAS 27, *Consolidated and Separate Financial Statements.* This requires the effects of all transactions with noncontrolling interests to be recorded in equity if there is no change in control. When control is lost, any remaining interest in the entity is remeasured to fair value and a gain or loss recognized in profit or loss. The amendment is effective for annual periods beginning on or after July 1, 2009, and is to be applied retrospectively, with certain exceptions. BP will adopt the amendment with effect from January 1, 2010, and there will be no effect on the group's reported income or net assets on adoption. The revised standard has been adopted by the EU. In November 2009, the IASB issued IFRS 9, *Financial Instruments,* which deals with the classification and measurement of financial assets. This new standard represents the first phase of the IASB's project to replace IAS 39, *Financial Instruments: Recognition and Measurement.* The new standard is effective for annual periods beginning on or after January 1, 2013, with transitional arrangements depending upon the date of initial application. BP has not yet decided the date of initial application for the group and has not yet completed its evaluation of the effect of adoption. The new standard has not yet been adopted by the EU. There are no other standards and interpretations in issue but not yet adopted that the directors anticipate will have a material effect on the reported income or net assets of the group.

MULTIPLE-CHOICE QUESTIONS

1. Which of the following accounting methods must be applied to all business combinations under IFRS 3, *Business Combinations*?
   (a) Pooling of interests method.
   (b) Equity method.
   (c) Proportionate consolidation.
   (d) Acquisition method.

2. Purchase accounting requires an acquirer and an acquiree to be identified for every business combination. Where a new entity (H) is created to acquire two preexisting entities, S and A, which of these entities will be designated as the acquirer?
   (a) H.
   (b) S.
   (c) A.
   (d) A or S.

3. IFRS 3 requires all identifiable intangible assets of the acquired business to be recorded at their fair values. Many intangible assets that may have been subsumed within goodwill must be now separately valued and identified. Under IFRS 3, when would an intangible asset be "identifiable"?
   (a) When it meets the definition of an asset in the *Framework* document only.
   (b) When it meets the definition of an intangible asset in IAS 38, *Intangible Assets,* and its fair value can be measured reliably.
   (c) If it has been recognized under local generally accepted accounting principles even though it does not meet the definition in IAS 38.
   (d) Where it has been acquired in a business combination.

4. Which of the following examples is unlikely to meet the definition of an intangible asset for the purpose of IFRS 3?
   (a) Marketing related, such as trademarks and Internet domain names.
   (b) Customer related, such as customer lists and contracts.
   (c) Technology based, such as computer software and databases.
   (d) Pure research based, such as general expenditure on research.

5. An intangible asset with an indefinite life is one where
   (a) There is no foreseeable limit on the period over which the asset will generate cash flows.
   (b) The length of life is over 20 years.
   (c) The directors feel that the intangible asset will not lose value in the foreseeable future.

   (d) There is a contractual or legal arrangement that lasts for a period in excess of five years.

6. An intangible asset with an indefinite life is accounted for as follows
   (a) No amortization but annual impairment test.
   (b) Amortized and impairment tests annually.
   (c) Amortized and impairment tested if there is a "trigger event."
   (d) Amortized and no impairment test.

7. An acquirer should at the acquisition date recognize goodwill acquired in a business combination as an asset. Goodwill should be accounted for as follows
   (a) Recognize as an intangible asset and amortize over its useful life.
   (b) Write off against retained earnings.
   (c) Recognize as an intangible asset and impairment test when a trigger event occurs.
   (d) Recognize as an intangible asset and annually impairment test (or more frequently if impairment is indicated).

8. If the impairment of the value of goodwill is seen to have reversed, then the company may
   (a) Reverse the impairment charge and credit income for the period.
   (b) Reverse the impairment charge and credit retained earnings.
   (c) Not reverse the impairment charge.
   (d) Reverse the impairment charge only if the original circumstances that led to the impairment no longer exist and credit retained earnings.

9. On acquisition, all identifiable assets and liabilities, including goodwill, will be allocated to cash-generating units within the business combination. Goodwill impairment is assessed within the cash-generating units. If the combined organization has cash-generating units significantly below the level of an operating segment, then the risk of an impairment charge against goodwill as a result of IFRS 3 is
   (a) Significantly decreased because goodwill will be spread across many cash-generating units.
   (b) Significantly increased because poorly performing units can no longer be supported by those that are performing well.
   (c) Likely to be unchanged from previous accounting practice.
   (d) Likely to be decreased because goodwill will be a smaller amount due to the greater recognition of other intangible assets.

10. Goodwill must not be amortized under IFRS 3. The transitional rules do not require restatement of previous balances written off. If an entity is adopting IFRS for the first time, and it wishes to restate all prior acquisitions in accordance with IFRS 3, then it must apply the IFRS to

    (a) Those acquisitions selected by the entity.

    (b) All acquisitions from the date of the earliest.

    (c) Only those acquisitions since the issue of the IFRS 3 and IAS 22, *Business Combinations,* to the earlier ones.

    (d) Only past and present acquisitions of entities that have previously and currently prepared their financial statements using IFRS.

11. The "excess of the acquirer's interest in the net fair value of acquiree's identifiable assets, liabilities, and contingent liabilities over cost" (formerly known as negative goodwill) should be

    (a) Amortized over the life of the assets acquired.

    (b) Reassessed as to the accuracy of its measurement and then recognized immediately in profit or loss.

    (c) Reassessed as to the accuracy of its measurement and then recognized in retained earnings.

    (d) Carried as a capital reserve indefinitely.

12. Which one of the following reasons would **not** contribute to the creation of negative goodwill?

    (a) Errors in measuring the fair value of the acquiree's net identifiable assets or the cost of the business combination.

    (b) A bargain purchase.

    (c) A requirement in an IFRS to measure net assets acquired at a value other than fair value.

    (d) Making acquisitions at the top of a "bull" market for shares.

13. The management of an entity is unsure how to treat a restructuring provision that they wish to set up on the acquisition of another entity. Under IFRS 3, the treatment of this provision will be

    (a) A charge in the statement of comprehensive income in the post-acquisition period.

    (b) To include the provision in the allocated cost of acquisition.

    (c) To provide for the amount and, if the provision is overstated, to release the excess to the statement of comprehensive income in the postacquisition period.

    (d) To include the provision in the allocated cost of acquisition if the acquired entity commits itself to a restructuring within a year of acquisition.

14. IFRS 3 requires that the contingent liabilities of the acquired entity should be recognized in the statement of financial position at fair value. The existence of contingent liabilities is often reflected in a lower purchase price. Recognition of such contingent liabilities will

    (a) Decrease the value attributed to goodwill, thus decreasing the risk of impairment of goodwill.

    (b) Decrease the value attributed to goodwill, thus increasing the risk of impairment of goodwill.

    (c) Increase the value attributed to goodwill, thus decreasing the risk of impairment of goodwill.

    (d) Increase the value attributed to goodwill, thus increasing the risk of impairment of goodwill.

15. How is goodwill measured under IFRS 3 (2008)?

    (a) Partial goodwill.

    (b) Full goodwill.

    (c) Parent company method.

    (d) Choice of partial or full goodwill on individual transaction basis.

16. On January 1, 20X9, A acquired a 60% interest in B for $80 million. A already held a 10% interest which had been acquired for $12 million but which was fair valued at $15 million at January 1, 20X9. The fair value of the noncontrolling interest at January 1, 20X9, was $47 million and the fair value of the identifiable net assets of B was $130 million. The goodwill would be as follows using the full goodwill method:

    (a) $1 million.

    (b) $12 million.

    (c) $35 million.

    (d) $38 million.

17. Corin, a private limited company, has acquired 100% of Coal, a private limited company, on January 1, 2005. The fair value of the purchase consideration was $10 million ordinary shares of $1 of Corin, and the fair value of the net assets acquired was $7 million. At the time of the acquisition, the value of the ordinary shares of Corin and the net assets of Coal were only provisionally determined. The value of the shares of Corin ($11 million) and the net assets of Coal ($7.5 million) on January 1, 2005, were finally determined on November 30, 2005. However, the directors of Corin have seen the value of the company decline since January 1, 2005, and as of February 1, 2006, wish to change the value of the purchase consideration to $9 million. What value should be placed on the purchase consideration and net assets of Coal as at the date of acquisition?

    (a) Purchase consideration $10 million, net asset value $7 million.

(b) Purchase consideration $11 million, net asset value $7.5 million.

(c) Purchase consideration $9 million, net asset value $7.5 million.

(d) Purchase consideration $11 million, net asset value $7 million.

18. Mask, a private limited company, has arranged for Man, a public limited company, to acquire it as a means of obtaining a stock exchange listing. Man issues 15 million shares to acquire the whole of the share capital of Mask (6 million shares). The fair value of the net assets of Mask and Man are $30 million and $18 million respectively. The fair value of each of the shares of Mask is $6 and the quoted market price of Man's shares is $2. The share capital of Man is 25 million shares after the acquisition. Calculate the value of goodwill in the above acquisition.

(a) $16 million.
(b) $12 million.
(c) $10 million.
(d) $6 million.

19. What is meant by "full goodwill" method?

(a) The recognition of the goodwill, which relates to the parent companies interest.

(b) The recognition of the goodwill, which relates to the noncontrolling interest and the controlling interest.

(c) The recognition of the goodwill, which relates to the noncontrolling interest.

(d). A bargain purchase.

20. A has acquired a subsidiary on January 1, 20X9. The fair value of the net assets of the subsidiary acquired was $16 million. A acquired 60% of the shares of the subsidiary, for $11 million. The noncontrolling interest was fair valued at $8 million. Goodwill based on the partial goodwill method under IFRS 3 (revised) would be

(a) $3 million.
(b) $1.4 million.
(c) $5 million.
(d) $8 million.

21. A has acquired a subsidiary on January 1, 20X9. The fair value of the net assets of the subsidiary acquired was $16 million. A acquired 60% of the shares of the subsidiary for $11 million. The noncontrolling interest was fair valued at $8 million. Goodwill based on the full goodwill method under IFRS 3 (revised) would be

(a) $3 million.
(b) $1.4 million.
(c) $5 million.
(d) $8 million.

22. Partial sale of an investment in a subsidiary, which does not result in a change of control, is treated as follows:

(a) It is recorded directly in income.
(b) It is recorded directly in equity.
(c) It results in the adjustment of the goodwill.
(d) It results in the revaluation of the whole of the equity interest.

23. Partial sale of a subsidiary, which results in the retention of significant influence so that the remaining investment constitutes an associate, is dealt with as follows:

(a) It is recorded directly in income.
(b) It is recorded directly in equity.
(c) It results in the retained interest being measured at fair value and a gain or loss being calculated on the disposal of the subsidiary.
(d) It results in the revaluation of the whole of the equity interest.

24. A company has finalized the deferred tax calculation on 01/10/X9 in relation to its acquisition of a subsidiary on 01/01/X9. The adjustment required will

(a) Be adjusted through income.
(b) Be ignored as it is too long since the acquisition.
(c) Be adjusted through equity.
(d) Affect the calculation of goodwill.

25. On January 1, 2008, A acquired a 60% interest in B for $80 million. A already held a 10% interest which had been acquired for $12 million but which was fair valued at $15 million at January 1, 2008. The fair value of the noncontrolling interest at January 1, 2008, was $47 million and the fair value of the identifiable net assets of B was $130 million. A gain relating to the revaluation of the original equity interest would be recorded as follows

(a) $3 million.
(b) $12 million.
(c) $35 million.
(d) $38 million.

Chapter 35

INSURANCE CONTRACTS (IFRS 4)

BACKGROUND AND INTRODUCTION

IFRS 4 is the first Standard from the International Accounting Standards Board (IASB) on insurance contracts. The extent of guidance in IFRS 4 is quite modest in comparison with the more comprehensive overhaul of insurance accounting that is envisaged by the IASB in the future. IFRS 4 was introduced in time for insurance companies to comply with the adoption of International Financial Reporting Standards (IFRS) in Europe and elsewhere in 2005. The Standard is designed to make limited improvements to accounting practices and to provide users with an insight into the key areas that relate to accounting for insurance contracts.

All entities that issue policies that meet the definition of an insurance contract in IFRS 4 have to apply the Standard. Additionally, the Standard applies to financial instruments with so-called discretionary participation features. The Standard does not apply to other assets and liabilities of the insurance companies, such as financial assets and financial liabilities, which fall within the scope of IAS 39. Similarly, it does not address the accounting required by policyholders. Additionally, IFRS 4 sets out new disclosure requirements for contracts that qualify as insurance, including details about future cash flows.

DEFINITION OF KEY TERM
(in accordance with IFRS 4)

Insurance contract. A contract under which one party (the insurer) accepts significant insurance risk from another party (the policyholder) by agreeing to compensate the policyholder if a specified uncertain future event (the insured event) adversely affects the policyholder.

IFRS 4 covers most motor, travel, life, and property insurance contracts as well as most reinsurance contracts. However, some policies that transfer no significant insurance risk, such as savings and pension plans, are covered by IAS 39 and accounted for as financial instruments irrespective of their legal form.

IAS 39 also applies to those contracts that principally transfer financial risk, such as credit derivatives and some financial reinsurance contracts. IFRS 4 does not apply to: product warranties, which are covered by IAS 18 and IAS 37; employers' assets and liabilities under employee benefits plans, which are covered by IAS 19 and IFRS 2; and contingent consideration payable or receivable in a business combination, which is covered by IFRS 3, *Business Combinations*.

Financial guarantee contracts are outside the scope of IFRS 4 unless the issuer elects to apply IFRS 4 to such contracts. An issuer may make such an election only if it has previously asserted explicitly that it regards such contracts as insurance contracts and has used accounting applicable to insurance contracts.

FIRST PHASE

Insurance contracts continue to be covered by existing accounting practices during this first phase of the development of a comprehensive set of standards on insurance. The IFRS actually exempts an insurer temporarily from some requirements of other Standards, including the requirement to consider the IASB's *Framework* in determining accounting policies.

IFRS 4 makes limited improvements to accounting policies for insurance contracts in order to bring them more into line with IFRS. The Standard

1. Prohibits provisions for possible claims under contracts that are not in existence at the end of the reporting period date. This includes catastrophe provisions and equalization provisions.
2. Sets out a minimum liability adequacy test that requires insurers to compare their recognized insurance liabilities against estimates of future cash flows. Additionally, there is a requirement to carry out an impairment test for reinsurance assets.

There is a requirement for an insurer to keep insurance liabilities in its statement of financial position until they are discharged. The IFRS also prohibits offsetting insurance liabilities against related reinsurance assets.

CHANGES IN ACCOUNTING POLICIES

Insurers are permitted to modify their existing accounting policies for insurance contracts as long as any changes meet the IASB's criteria for improving the relevance of their financial statements without making them less reliable. An insurer cannot introduce any of these practices, although it can continue using accounting policies that involve any of them:

- Measuring insurance liabilities on a nondiscounted basis
- Measuring contractual rights to future investment management fees at an amount that exceeds their fair value
- Using nonuniform accounting policies for the insurance liabilities of a subsidiary

Insurers can use current market interest rates to value liabilities, thus bringing them more into line with movements in associated assets that are interest-sensitive. This measure does not need to be applied consistently across all insurance liabilities. However, insurers will need to designate the liabilities that will be measured using market rates.

An insurer does not need to change its accounting policies on insurance contracts in order to eliminate excessive prudence. However, an insurer that already measures its insurance contracts with sufficient prudence should not introduce additional prudence.

An insurer need not change its accounting policies for insurance contracts to eliminate future investment margins. However, entities cannot change to an accounting policy that adjusts their liabilities to reflect future investment margins unless, for example, this is part of a wider switch to a comprehensive investor-based accounting system.

The IASB would require proof that this switch improves the relevance and reliability of the financial statements to such an extent that it outweighs the disadvantage caused by the inclusion of future investment margins.

CONCESSIONS IN IFRS 4

There is a concession to insurers regarding the accounting on a business combination. Insurers can recognize an intangible asset that is the difference between the fair value and book value of the insurance liabilities taken on board. Such an asset is excluded from the scope of IAS 36, *Impairment of Assets,* and IAS 38, *Intangible Assets.*

Entities can continue to value insurance and investment contracts that have discretionary participation in profit features using their existing accounting policies. Any fixed guaranteed amount should be regarded as the minimum liability, with the rest of the contract classified as an additional liability, or included in equity, or evenly split between equity and liabilities. If the contract is not split in this way, the issuer of the contract should classify the whole contract as a liability. These requirements also apply to any financial instruments that contain a discretionary participation future.

ACCOUNTING UNDER IFRS 4

Certain derivative features in a contract, such as an index-linked option, may need to be separated at fair value. IAS 39 applies to derivatives that are embedded in an insurance contract unless the embedded derivative is itself an insurance contract. An insurer need not account for an embedded derivative separately at fair value if the embedded derivative meets the definition of an insurance contract.

IFRS 4 requires an insurer to account separately for the deposit components of some insurance contracts in order to avoid the omission of assets and liabilities from the statement of financial position. An insurance contract can contain both deposit and insurance components.

An example might be a profit-sharing reinsurance contract where the cedent is given a guarantee as to the minimum repayment of the premium. As with embedded derivatives, insurers need to identify any policies that may require unbundling. Generally speaking, any deposit component is subject to IAS 39 and any insurance feature is subject to existing accounting policies.

PRACTICAL INSIGHT

An entity is required or permitted to unbundle the insurance and deposit components of insurance contracts that contain both. For a contract that is unbundled, the entity is required to apply IAS 39 to the deposit component.

IFRS 4 also clarifies the applicability of a practice that is often called shadow accounting. This practice allows insurers to adjust their liabilities for any changes that have arisen if any unrealized gains and losses on assets have been realized. An insurer is permitted to change its accounting policies such that recognized, but unrealized gains or losses, also adjust their liabilities. Any movements in the liability may be recognized in equity only if unrealized gains or losses are recognized directly in equity.

RECENT PRONOUNCEMENTS

The IASB has issued an Exposure Draft in July 2010 that will fundamentally change the accounting by insurers and other entities that issue contracts with insurance risk. The proposals are the output of the IASB and FASB's joint efforts to develop a single converged insurance standard. The proposed standard would replace IFRS 4, which currently permits a variety of practices in accounting for insurance contracts. The proposed standard would apply to all entities that issue contracts that contain insurance risk. The Exposure Draft retains the IFRS 4 definition of an insurance contract. However, unlike IFRS 4, fixed-fee service contracts where the level of service depends on an uncertain future event will not be within the scope of the proposed standard. Insurance contracts often contain other elements such as financial or service components. These are required to be unbundled and accounted for separately if they are not closely related to the insurance coverage.

The proposals require that all insurance contracts will use a current measurement model of the present value of expected cash flows to fulfill the obligation, where estimates are remeasured at each reporting period. Except for certain short duration contracts, this measurement model is based on the building blocks of discounted probability-weighted cash flows, a risk adjustment, and a residual margin to eliminate any initial profit.

CASE STUDY 1

Facts

Entity A has a reinsurance contract that has these elements to it: A policyholder under a reinsurance contract pays premiums of $200 every year for ten years. The entity sets up an experience account equal to 80% of the cumulative premiums less 80% of the cumulative claims under the policy. If the balance in the experience account ever becomes negative, the policyholder has to pay an additional premium based on the balance on the experience account divided by the number of years the policy has left to run. At the end of the contract, if the balance on the experience account is positive, it is refunded to the policyholder. If the balance is negative, the policyholder has to pay the amount as an additional premium. The policy cannot be cancelled before the end of the contract, and the maximum loss that the policyholder is required to pay in any year is $300.

Required

Discuss how the reinsurance contract should be accounted for in the financial statements of the insurer.

Solution

The contract is an insurance contract because it transfers a significant insurance risk to the reinsurer. Where there are no claims on the contract, the policyholder will receive $1,600 at the end of year ten, which is 80% of the cumulative premiums of $2,000. IFRS 4 basically says that the policyholder has made a loan that the reinsurer will repay in one installment in year ten. If current policies of the reinsurer are that it should recognize a liability under the contract, then unbundling is permitted but not required. However, if the reinsurer does not have such policies, then IFRS 4 would require the reinsurer to unbundle the contract. If the contract is unbundled, each payment by the policyholder has two components: a loan advance payment and a payment for insurance cover. IAS 39 will be used to value the deposit element—the loan—and it will be measured initially at fair value. The fair value of the deposit element would be calculated by discounting back the future loan repayment in year ten using an annuity method. If the policyholder makes a claim, then this in itself will be unbundled into a claim of $X and a loan of $Y, which will be repaid in installments over the life of the policy.

DISCLOSURES

IFRS 4 adopts the so-called principles-based approach to disclosure. Information should be disclosed that helps the user to understand the amounts in the insurer's financial statements that arise from insurance contracts.

Insurers also need to give details about the insurance risk to which they are exposed, including any concentration of risk and the impact of changes in variables on the key assumptions that are used.

Information that helps users understand the amount, timing, and uncertainty of future cash flows is required. The terms and conditions of insurance contracts that have a material affect on the amount, timing, and uncertainty of the insurer's future cash flows also have to be disclosed.

Information about the actual claims as compared with previous estimates needs disclosure, and information about interest rate risk and credit rate risk that IAS 32 would require should be shown.

Information about exposures to interest rate risk or market risk under embedded derivatives contained in a host insurance contract should be shown if the insurer does not show the embedded derivatives at fair value. However, insurers do not need to disclose the fair value of their insurance contracts at present but need to disclose the gains and losses from purchasing reinsurance contracts.

PRACTICAL INSIGHT

A typical insurer's statement of financial position might comprise these assets and liabilities and be covered by the following IFRS:

Assets	*IAS/IFRS*
Investments	IAS 39
Property	IAS 16/40
Investments contracts	IAS 18
Insurance contracts	IFRS 4
Other assets	Various
Liabilities	
Equity	IAS 32/39
Insurance liabilities	IFRS 4
Investment contract liabilities	IAS 39
Other liabilities	Various

CASE STUDY 2

Facts

Entity A writes a single policy for a $1,000 premium and expects claims to be made of $600 in year 4. At the time of writing the policy, there are commission costs paid of $200. Assume a discount rate of 3% risk-free. The entity says that if a provision for risk and uncertainty were to be made, it would amount to $250, and that this risk would expire evenly over years 2, 3, and 4. Under existing policies, the entity would spread the net premiums, the claims expense, and the commissioning costs over the first two years of the policy. Investment returns in years 1 and 2 are $20 and $40 respectively.

Required

Show the treatment of this policy using a deferral and matching approach in years 1 and 2 that would be acceptable under IFRS 4.

How would the treatment differ if a "fair value" approach were used?

Solution

Deferral and Matching (IFRS 4):

	Year 1	*Year 2*
Premium earned	500	500
Claims expense	(300)	(300)
Commission costs	(100)	(100)
Underwriting profit	100	100
Investment return	20	40
Profit	120	140

If a fair value approach were used, the whole of the premium earned would be credited in year 1. The expected claims would be provided for on a discounted basis and then unwound over the period to year 4. The provision for risk and uncertainty would be made in year 1 and unwound over the following three years. Commission costs would all be charged in year 1 also. The investment returns would be treated in the same way as in the deferral approach.

EXTRACTS FROM PUBLISHED FINANCIAL STATEMENTS

BARLOWORLD Annual Report

Year Ended September 30, 2009

Insurance contracts

An insurance contract is a contract under which one party (the insurer) accepts significant insurance risk from another party (the policyholder) by agreeing to compensate the policyholder if a specified uncertain future event (the insured event) adversely affects the policyholder. Certain transactions are entered into by the group as insurer, which fall within this definition. Significant items included are maintenance contracts, guaranteed residual values on sold equipment/vehicles, as well as credit life and warranty products sold.

Maintenance contracts

Revenue on maintenance contracts is recognized on the percentage-of-completion method based on the anticipated cost of repairs over the life cycle of the equipment.

Guaranteed residual values

Guaranteed residual values are periodically given on repurchase commitments with customers. The likelihood of the repurchase commitments being exercised is assessed at the inception of the contract to determine whether significant risks and rewards have been transferred to the customer and if revenue should be recognized. If significant risks and rewards have not been transferred, revenue is not recognized and the transaction is accounted for as a prepaid operating lease. Where the initial assessment was made that significant risks and rewards were transferred and revenue was recognized, but subsequent market conditions are considered to change the likelihood of the exercise of the buyback to become probable, the present value of the net expected future outflow is provided for, after taking into consideration any proceeds on subsequent disposal of the equipment. All repurchase commitments as well as the related asset's expected values are disclosed under contingent liabilities.

Credit life and warranty products

Premiums are recognized as revenue proportionally over the period of coverage. The portion of premium received on in-force contracts that relates to unexpired risks at the statement of financial position date is recognized as an unearned premium liability. Premiums are reflected before deduction of commission and are gross of any taxes or duties levied on premiums.

Claims and loss adjustment expenses are charged to profit and loss as incurred based on the estimated liability for compensation owed to contract holders or third parties damaged by the contract holders. These include direct and indirect claims settlement costs and arise from events that have occurred up to the statement of financial position date even if it has not yet been reported to the company. Liabilities for unpaid claims are not discounted and are estimated using the input of assessments for individual cases reported to the group and statistical analyses for claims incurred but not reported as well as the expected ultimate cost of more complex claims that may be affected by an external factor (such as court decisions).

Acquisition costs, which include commission and other related expenses, are recognized in the period in which they are incurred.

FUTURE DEVELOPMENTS—AN INSIGHT

The IASB and FASB are undertaking a comprehensive project on the accounting for insurance contracts. The Boards' objective is to develop a common, high-quality standard that will address recognition, measurement, presentation, and disclosure requirements for insurance contracts.

On July 31, 2010, the IASB issued ED/2010/08, *Insurance Contracts,* with a comment period ending November 30, 2010. The boards tentatively decided to improve the definition of an insurance contract that is currently in IFRS 4, *Insurance Contracts,* to clarify the role of timing in insurance risk and specifying that insurance risk would exist if there is at least one scenario in which the present value of net cash flows due under the insured event could exceed the present value of premiums.

The Boards will slightly adjust the scope of the current IFRS 4. The insurer would recognize the rights and obligations arising from an insurance contract on the earlier of the insurer being obligated to provide coverage to the policyholder for insured events and the signing of the insurance contract. The core of the proposed insurance model is a direct measurement of the insurance contract supplemented with an allocation over time of any accounting day one gain. The measurement of an insurance contract should include the probability weighted present value of all incremental cash flows arising from the insurer's estimate of its fulfillment of the contract. The discount rate should reflect the characteristics of the cash flows from the insurance contract. For recognition and measurement, a component of an insurance contract should be unbundled if it functions independently from other components of that contract. The recognition and measurement criteria for reinsurance assets would be based on the building blocks approach, except that measurement of reinsurance assets should include an adjustment for reinsurer's expected credit losses.   The presentation of insurance contracts in the statement of comprehensive income will be driven by the measurement model.

MULTIPLE-CHOICE QUESTIONS

1. IFRS 4 was introduced principally for what reason?
- (a) To make limited improvements to the accounting for insurance accounting.
- (b) To completely overhaul insurance accounting.
- (c) As a response to recent scandals within the insurance industry.
- (d) Because of pressure from the financial services authorities in several countries.

2. Which of the following types of insurance contracts would probably **not** be covered by IFRS 4?
- (a) Motor insurance.
- (b) Life insurance.
- (c) Medical insurance.
- (d) Pension plan.

3. Which International Financial Reporting Standard would apply to those contracts that principally transfer financial risk, such as a credit derivative?
- (a) IAS 23.
- (b) IAS 18.
- (c) IAS 39.
- (d) IFRS 4.

4. If an entity gives a product warranty that has been issued directly by a manufacturer, dealer, or retailer, which International Financial Reporting Standard is likely to cover this warranty?
- (a) IFRS 4.
- (b) IAS 39.
- (c) IAS 18 and IAS 37.
- (d) IAS 32.

5. IFRS 4 says that insurance contracts should
- (a) Generally continue to be subject to existing accounting policies during phase one.
- (b) Comply with the IFRS *Framework* document.
- (c) Comply with all existing IFRS.
- (d) Be covered by IAS 32 and IAS 39 only.

6. Insurers can recognize an intangible asset that is the difference between the fair value and book value of insurance liabilities taken on in a business combination. This asset should be accounted for using
- (a) IAS 38, *Intangible Assets.*
- (b) IFRS 4, *Insurance Contracts,* only.
- (c) IAS 16, *Property, Plant, and Equipment.*
- (d) Such an asset should not be accounted for until phase two of the insurance contract.

7. Which of the following accounting practices is prohibited by IFRS 4?
- (a) Shadow accounting.
- (b) Catastrophe provisions.
- (c) A test for the adequacy of recognized insurance liabilities.
- (d) An impairment test for reinsurance assets.

8. An insurance contract can contain both deposit and insurance elements. An example might be a reinsurance contract where the cedent receives a repayment of the premiums at a future time if there are no claims under the contract. Effectively this constitutes a loan by the cedent that will be repaid in the future. IFRS 4 requires that
- (a) Each payment by the cedent is accounted for as a loan advance and as a payment for insurance cover.
- (b) The insurance premium is accounted for as a revenue item in the statement of comprehensive income.
- (c) The premium is accounted for under IAS 18.
- (d) The premium paid is treated purely as a loan, and it is accounted for under IAS 39.

Chapter 36

NONCURRENT ASSETS HELD FOR SALE AND DISCONTINUED OPERATIONS (IFRS 5)

BACKGROUND AND SCOPE

The purpose of IFRS 5 is to specify the accounting for assets held for sale and the presentation and disclosure of discontinued operations.

IFRS 5 was issued by the IASB in 2004 and replaced IAS 35, *Discontinued Operations*, which was issued by the International Accounting Standards Committee (IASC), the IASB's predecessor.

IFRS 5 and its accompanying documents have been amended by the following IFRS:

IFRS 8 (issued November 2006), IAS 1 (as revised in 2007), IFRS 3 (as revised in 2008), IAS 27 (as amended in 2008), "Improvements to IFRS 2008" (issued in 2008), IFRIC 17 (issued in 2008), "Improvements to IFRS 2009"(issued in 2009), and IFRS 9 (issued in 2009).

The measurement provisions of this International Financial Reporting Standard (IFRS) do not apply to deferred tax assets, assets arising from employee benefits, financial assets within the scope of IAS 39, noncurrent assets accounted for in accordance with the fair value model in IAS 40, noncurrent assets that are measured at fair value less estimated point-of-sale costs under IAS 41, and contractual rights under insurance contracts as defined in IFRS 4.

The IASB's Annual Improvements Project, "Improvements to IFRS 2009," added paragraphs 5B and 44E to IFRS 5. These amendments to IFRS 5 clarify that IFRS 5 prescribes disclosure requirements in respect of noncurrent assets (or disposal groups) classified as held for sale or discontinued operations and disclosures in other IFRS do not apply to such assets (or disposal groups) **unless** those IFRS require specific disclosures in respect of noncurrent assets (or disposal groups) classified as held for sale or discontinued operations or disclosures about the measurement of assets and liabilities within the disposal group that are not within the scope of the measurement requirements of IFRS 5 and such disclosures are not already provided in other notes to the financial statements. These amendments are to be applied prospectively for annual periods beginning on or after January 1, 2010 (earlier application is permitted with disclosure).

> **DEFINITIONS OF KEY TERMS**
> **(in accordance with IFRS 5)**
>
> **Held for sale.** The carrying amount of a noncurrent asset will be recovered mainly through selling the asset rather than through usage.
> **Disposal group.** A group of assets and possibly some liabilities that an entity intends to dispose of in a single transaction.

For a noncurrent asset or disposal group to be classified as held for sale, the asset must be available for immediate sale in its present condition and its sale must be highly probable. In addition, the asset must be currently being marketed actively at a price that is reasonable in relation to its current fair value.

The sale should be completed, or expected to be so, within a year from the date of the classification.

The actions required to complete the planned sale will have been made, and it is unlikely that the plan will be significantly changed or withdrawn.

For the sale to be highly probable, management must be committed to selling the asset and must be actively looking for a buyer.

It is possible that the sale may not be completed within one year.

In this case, the asset could still be classified as held for sale if the delay is caused by events beyond the entity's control and the entity is still committed to selling the asset.

CASE STUDY 1

Facts

An entity is committed to a plan to sell a building and has started looking for a buyer for that building. The entity will continue to use the building until another building is completed to house the office staff located in the building. There is no intention to relocate the office staff until the new building is completed.

Required

Would the building be classified as held for sale?

Solution

The building will not be classified as held for sale as it is not available for immediate sale.

> **PRACTICAL INSIGHT**
>
> Aare-Jessin AG, a Swiss entity, discloses in its financial statements of December 31, 2003, that it intends to sell a subsidiary. The subsidiary was deconsolidated and classified as a current asset using the criteria set out in IAS 1. However, if the subsidiary was to be classified as a "disposal group" under IFRS 5, then the net assets should be broken down and shown separately from other assets in the balance sheet in separate categories. (See Case Study 6.)

EXTENSION OF PERIOD BEYOND ONE YEAR

Situations where an extension of the period required to complete the sale are allowable include these:

1. The entity has committed itself to sell a noncurrent asset, and it expects that others may impose conditions on the transfer of the asset and where the conditions could not be completed until after a firm purchase commitment has been made and a firm purchase commitment is highly probable within a year.

2. A firm purchase commitment is made but a buyer unexpectedly imposes conditions on the transfer of the noncurrent asset held for sale. Timely actions should be taken to respond to the conditions, and a favorable resolution is anticipated.
3. During the one-year period, unforeseen circumstances arise that were considered unlikely, and the noncurrent asset is not sold. Necessary action to respond to the change in circumstances should be taken. The noncurrent asset should be being actively marketed at a reasonable price and the criteria set out for the asset to be classified as held-for-sale should have been met.

CASE STUDY 2

Facts

An entity is planning to sell part of its business that is deemed to be a disposal group. The entity is in a business environment that is heavily regulated, and any sale requires government approval. This means that the sale time is difficult to determine. Government approval cannot be obtained until a buyer is found and known for the disposal group and a firm purchase contract has been signed. However, it is likely that the entity will be able to sell the disposal group within one year.

Required

Would the disposal group be classified as held for sale?

Solution

The disposal group would be classified as held for sale because the delay is caused by events or circumstances beyond the entity's control and there is evidence that the entity is committed to selling the disposal group.

CASE STUDY 3

Facts

An entity has an asset that has been designated as held for sale in the financial year to December 31, 2008. During the financial year to December 31, 2009, the asset still remains unsold, but the market conditions for the asset have deteriorated significantly. The entity believes that market conditions will improve and has not reduced the price of the asset, which continues to be classified as held for sale. The fair value of the asset is $5 million, and the asset is being marketed at $7 million.

Required

Should the asset be classified as held for sale in the financial statements for the year ending December 31, 2009?

Solution

Because the price is in excess of the current fair value, the asset is not available for immediate sale and should not be classified as held for sale.

SUNDRY POINTS

Exchanges of noncurrent assets between companies can be treated as held for sale when such an exchange has a commercial substance in accordance with IAS 16.

Occasionally companies acquire noncurrent assets exclusively with a view to disposal. In these cases, the noncurrent asset will be classified as held for sale at the date of the acquisition only if it is anticipated that it will be sold within the one-year period and it is highly probable that the held-for-sale criteria will be met within a short period of the acquisition date. This period normally will be no more than three months.

If the criteria for classifying a noncurrent asset as held for sale occur after the end of the reporting period, the noncurrent asset should not be shown as held for sale. However, certain information should be disclosed about the noncurrent assets.

Operations that are expected to be wound down or abandoned do not meet the definition of held for sale. However, a disposal group that is to be abandoned may meet the definition of a discontinued activity.

"Abandonment" means that the noncurrent asset (disposal group) will be used to the end of its economic life, or the noncurrent asset (disposal group) will be closed rather than sold. The reasoning behind this is because the carrying amount of the noncurrent asset will be recovered principally through continued usage.

A noncurrent asset that has been temporarily taken out of use or service cannot be classified as being abandoned.

CASE STUDY 4

Facts

An entity is reorganizing its business activities. In one location, it is stopping the usage of certain equipment because the demand for the product produced by that equipment has reduced significantly. The equipment is to be maintained in good working order, and it is expected that it will be brought back into use if the demand increases. Additionally, the entity intends to close three out of five manufacturing units. The manufacturing units constitute a major activity of the entity. All the work within the three units will end during the current year, and as of the year-end all work will have ceased.

Required

How will the piece of equipment and the closure of the manufacturing units be treated in the financial statements for the current year?

Solution

The equipment will not be treated as abandoned, as it will subsequently be brought back into usage. The manufacturing units will be treated as discontinued operations.

MEASUREMENT OF NONCURRENT ASSETS THAT ARE HELD FOR SALE

Just before an asset is initially classified as held for sale, it should be measured in accordance with the applicable IFRS.

When noncurrent assets or disposal groups are classified as held for sale, they are measured at the lower of the carrying amount and fair value less costs to sell.

When the sale is expected to occur in over a year's time, the entity should measure the cost to sell at its present value. Any increase in the present value of the cost to sell that arises should be shown in profit and loss as a finance cost.

Any impairment loss is recognized in profit or loss on any initial or subsequent write-down of the asset or disposal group to fair value less cost to sell.

Any subsequent increases in fair value less cost to sell of an asset can be recognized in profit or loss to the extent that it is not in excess of the cumulative impairment loss that has been recognized in accordance with IFRS 5 or previously in accordance with IAS 36.

Any impairment loss recognized for a disposal group should be applied in the order set out in IAS 36.

Noncurrent assets or disposal groups classified as held for sale should not be depreciated.

Any interest or expenses of a disposal group should continue to be provided for.

The IASB issued IFRIC 17 in 2008. This interpretation clarified that an entity shall measure a noncurrent asset (or disposal group) classified as held for distribution to owners at the lower of its carrying amount and fair value less costs to distribute. This amendment to IFRS 5 is to be applied prospectively in annual periods beginning on or after July 1, 2009.

CHANGE OF PLANS

If criteria for an asset to be classified as held for sale are no longer met, then the asset or disposal group ceases to be held for sale.

In this case, the asset or disposal group should be valued at the lower of the carrying amount before the asset or disposal group was classified as held for sale (as adjusted for any subsequent depreciation, amortization, or revaluation) and its recoverable amount at the date of the decision not to sell.

Any adjustment to the value should be shown in income from continuing operations for the period.

If an asset is removed from a disposal group, the disposal group will continue to be classified as such only if it still meets the criteria set out in the Standard.

If the criteria are not met, then the individual noncurrent assets of the group will be reviewed to see if they meet the criteria to be classified as held for sale.

DISCLOSURE: NONCURRENT ASSETS

Noncurrent assets held for sale and assets of disposal groups must be disclosed separately from other assets in the balance sheet. The liabilities must also be disclosed separately in the balance sheet.

Several other disclosures are required, including a description of the noncurrent assets of a disposal group, a description of the facts and circumstances of the sale, and the expected manner and timing of that disposal.

Any gain or loss recognized for impairment or any subsequent increase in the fair value less costs to sell should also be shown in the applicable segment in which the noncurrent assets or disposal group is presented in accordance with IFRS 8.

CASE STUDY 5

Facts

Lynch, a parent entity, approved on June 30, 2008, a plan to sell its subsidiary, Pin. The sale is expected to be completed on September 1, 2008. The year-end of Lynch is July 31, 2008, and the financial statements were approved on August 16, 2008. The subsidiary had net assets of $15 million (including goodwill of $2 million) at carrying value at year-end. Pin made a loss of $3 million from August 1 to August 16, 2008, and is expected to make a further loss of $2 million up to the date of sale. At the date of approval of the financial statements, Lynch was in negotiation for the sale of Pin, but no contract had been signed. Lynch expects to sell Pin for $9 million and to incur costs of selling of $1 million. The value in use of Pin at August 16, 2008, was estimated at $8 million.

Lynch had approved the relocation of the administrative headquarters of the group. Lynch does not intend to sell the property until it has renovated it. The renovations were completed on June 30, 2008. However, on July 30, 2008, environmental contamination was found within the headquarters that necessitated the transfer of the staff to temporary premises. The hazard was removed at a cost of $50,000 and the building declared safe on November 1, 2008. At July 31, 2008, the carrying value of the building was $3 million and its market value (assuming no contamination) was $4 million before estimated selling costs of $500,000.

The administrative headquarters were moved on December 1, 2008, and the property was offered for sale at a price of $4 million. The market for such property was in decline, and a buyer had not been found by July 31, 2009. The market price at that date was around $3.5 million, but the entity refused to reduce the sale price of the property. On September 1, 2009, a bid of $3.3 million was accepted for the property and costs of $600,000 were incurred in its sale. The carrying value of the property at cost was $2.8 million as of July 31, 2009.

Lynch also has equipment that it recently had leased to third parties. At July 31, 2008, there was $5 million (carrying value) of this equipment, and at July 31, 2009, there was an additional $8 million (carrying value) of this equipment. The leases had expired at the respective dates but no decision had been made as to whether to refurbish and sell the equipment or to abandon it. The entity subsequently refurbished both sets of equipment and sold them on December 1, 2008, for $10 million and on December 15, 2009, for $16 million. The refurbishment costs were $2 million and $3 million respectively for the two sets of assets.

Required

Discuss the treatment of the above elements in the financial statements as of July 31, 2008, and July 31, 2009.

Solution

Under IFRS 5, an entity should classify a disposal group, which Pin is, as held for sale if its carrying amount will be recovered principally through a sales transaction rather than through continuing use. The basic criteria to be met are that: there must be a commitment to a plan to sell the asset, an active program to locate a buyer and complete the plan must have been initiated, the asset must be actively marketed at a reasonable price in relation to its fair value, the sale should be expected to occur within one year, and it would appear that significant changes to the plan are unlikely. In this situation, the entity has approved the plan prior to the year-end and the sale is expected to be completed within 12 months, on September 1, 2008. By the time the financial statements were approved, the entity was in negotiation for the sale of Pin, so it would appear that the entity is actively trying to find a buyer and that the sale is highly probable. Additionally, if the entity is in negotiation for the sale, then the asset would appear to be actively marketed. Finally, there does not appear to be any intention to change the plan of sale significantly; therefore, the disposal group would appear as if it is held for sale.

Before classification of the item as held for sale, an impairment review will have to be undertaken. In this case, there is indication of possible impairment in any event because the subsidiary is making a loss in the postacquisition period. Any loss arising on the impairment review will be charged to profit or loss. An item that is held for sale should be reported at the lower of carrying value and fair value less costs to sell. An impairment calculation will have to be carried out as of July 31, 2008, before Pin can be measured in the balance sheet. The value in use of Pin at August 16, 2008, is estimated at $8 million. The loss up to that date is $3 million. Therefore, the value in use at July 31 will be $8 million plus $3 million, or $11 million. The net realizable value of Pin will be $9 million less the costs of selling it of $1 million, or $8 million. The recoverable amount is the higher of the net realizable value and the value in use. Therefore, in any impairment test at year-end, the value in use of $11 million would be used.

However, because the disposal group has been classified as held for sale, any impairment loss will be calculated by reference to different criteria. That is, any disposal group that is classified as held for sale should be measured at the lower of carrying amount and fair value less costs to sell. In this case, the fair value less cost to sell will be $8 million. Therefore, an impairment loss of $7 million will be recognized in profit or loss.

Regarding the administrative headquarters, the noncurrent assets will qualify as held for sale if they are available for immediate sale in their present condition subject to the usual selling terms. However, as of July 31, 2008, the administrative building could not be sold because of the environmental contamination. Therefore, it would simply be shown at carrying value within the financial statements. The entity has the intent and the ability to sell the asset, but it would be unlikely to find a buyer while this contamination was present. It does not appear there is any impairment of the carrying value of the building due to the contamination; the building's carrying value is $3 million and the market value was $4 million before estimated selling costs of $500,000. In rectifying the environmental contamination, the cost was only $50,000, and therefore it does not seem that the value of the building is impaired.

In the year to July 31, 2009, the property has been offered for sale at a price of $4 million. The market is in decline, and by year-end a buyer had not been found. The market price at that date was much less than the offer price, and the entity has refused to reduce the selling price of the property. The property has been vacated; therefore, it is available for sale, but because the price is not reasonable in relation to its current fair value—$4 million as opposed to $3.5 million—then the entity's intention to sell the asset might appear be questionable. The property fails the test in IFRS 5 regarding the reasonableness of price and, therefore, should not be classified as held for sale. If the property had been classified as held for sale at July 31, 2009, then it would have had to be carried at the lower of the carrying value and fair value less costs to sell. This would have meant that the carrying value of $2.8 million would have been compared with the fair value of $3.3 million less the costs of $600,000, or $2.7 million, and there would have been the need to write down the value of the asset by $100,000. To qualify for classification as held for sale, the sale of a noncurrent asset must be highly probable and the sale of the asset must be expected to qualify for recognition as a completed sale within one year.

In the case of the equipment that had recently been leased, at July 31, 2008, and July 31, 2009, there was a significant amount of this equipment in the balance sheet. The leases had expired but no decision had been made as to whether to refurbish and sell the equipment or to abandon it. Therefore, these assets will not qualify as held-for-sale assets at either date. They should be shown as noncurrent assets and depreciated. Held-for-sale assets are not depreciated. It would appear also that the fair value less costs to sell is significantly higher than the carrying value.

The selling prices of the two sets of assets are $10 million and $16 million respectively, and the refurbishment costs are $2 million and $3 million respectively. Therefore, even taking into account the refurbishment costs, the expectation is that they will recover significantly more revenue than the carrying value. Thus, the assets are not impaired at July 31, 2008, or July 31, 2009.

DISCONTINUED OPERATIONS: PRESENTATION AND DISCLOSURE

Any cumulative income or expense recognized directly in equity relating to a noncurrent asset or disposal group classified as held for sale must be disclosed.

A discontinued operation is a part of an entity that has either been disposed of or is classified as held for sale and

1. Represents a separate major line of business or geographical area of operations.
2. Is part of a single coordinated plan to dispose of a separate major line of business or geographical area of operations.
3. Is a subsidiary acquired exclusively with a view to resale.

In the statement of comprehensive income, the total of the after-tax profit or loss of the discontinued operation and the after-tax gain or loss recognized on the measurement to fair value less cost to sell (or on the disposal) should be presented as a single figure.

IFRS 5 requires detailed disclosure of revenue, expenses, pretax profit or loss, and the related income tax expense, either in the notes or on the face of the statement of comprehensive income. If this information is presented on the face of the statement of comprehensive income, the information should be separately disclosed from information relating to continuing operations.

Regarding the presentation in the statement of cash flows, the net cash flows attributable to the operating, investing, and financing activities of the discontinued operation should be shown separately on the face of the statement or disclosed in the notes. Any disclosures should cover both the current and all prior periods that have been shown in the financial statements. Retrospective classification as a discontinued operation where the criteria are met after the reporting date is prohibited by IFRS 5.

In addition, adjustments made in the current accounting period to amounts that have previously been disclosed as discontinued operations from prior periods must be separately disclosed. If an entity ceases to classify a component as held for sale, the results of that element must be reclassified and included in income from continuing operations.

FUTURE DEVELOPMENTS

The IASB plans to issue an Exposure Draft to amend IFRS 5 proposing that the definition of a discontinued operation be revised. The main proposed change to the definition would require that a discontinued operation be part of a single coordinated plan to dispose of a major geographical area of operations. The current definition does not explicitly require that the geographical area of operations is major. The board expects to issue the Exposure Draft in 2011.

CASE STUDY 6

Facts

Z plans to dispose of a group of net assets that form a disposal group. The net assets at December 31, 20X5, are

	Carrying value at December 31, 20X5 $m
Goodwill	6
Property, plant, and equipment	18
Inventory	10
Financial assets (profit of $2 million recognized in equity)	7
Financial liabilities	(4)
	37

On moving to accounting under IFRS, some of the assets had been transferred at deemed cost and had not been remeasured under IFRS. These assets were property, plant, and equipment, and inventory. Under IFRS, property, plant, and equipment (PPE) would be stated at $16 million and inventory stated at $9 million. The fair value less costs to sell of the disposal group is $25 million. Assume that the disposal group qualifies as held for sale. Therefore, under IAS 36, any impairment loss will be allocated to goodwill and PPE.

Required

Describe how the disposal group would be shown in the financial statements for the year ended December 31, 20X5.

Solution

	Carrying value $m	Remeasured $m	Impairment $m	Carrying amount after impairment $m
Goodwill	6	6	(6)	--
Property, plant, and equipment	18	16	(3)	13
Inventory	10	9		9
Financial assets	7	7		7
Financial liabilities	(4)	(4)	—	(4)
	37	34	(9)	25

IFRS 5 requires that, immediately before the initial classification of the disposal group as held for sale, the carrying amounts of the disposal group be measured in accordance with applicable IFRS and any profit or loss dealt with under those IFRS. The reduction in the carrying amount of property, plant, and equipment will be dealt with in accordance with IAS 16; the inventory will be dealt with in accordance with IAS 2.

After the remeasurement, the entity will recognize an impairment loss of $9 million. This loss is allocated in accordance with IAS 36. Thus goodwill will be reduced to zero and property, plant, and equipment to $13 million. The loss will be charged against profit or loss. If not separately presented on the face of the income statement, the caption in the income statement that includes the loss should be disclosed.

The major classes of assets and liabilities classified as held for sale should be separately disclosed on the face of the statement of financial position or in the notes. In this case there would be separate disclosure of the disposal group:

	$m
Assets	
Noncurrent assets	
Current assets	
Noncurrent and current assets classified as held for sale	29
Total assets	
Equity and liabilities	
Equity attributable to parent	
Amounts recognized directly in equity relating to	
noncurrent assets held for sale (18-16)	2
Noncontrolling interest	
Total equity	

> *Noncurrent liabilities*
> Current liabilities
> Liabilities directly associated with noncurrent assets
>   classified as held for sale   <u>4</u>
> Total liabilities
>
> Total equity and liabilities

Assets classified as held for sale at the reporting date are not reported retrospectively; therefore, comparative statements of financial position are not restated.

EXTRACTS FROM PUBLISHED FINANCIAL STATEMENTS

DEUTSCHE TELEKOM AG, Annual Report, 2009

Noncurrent assets and disposal groups held for sale

As of December 31, 2009, current assets recognized in the consolidated statement of financial position included EUR 6.5 billion in noncurrent assets and disposal groups held for sale as well as directly associated liabilities of EUR 1.4 billion. The following table sets out the major classes of assets and liabilities classified as held for sale.

The assets and liabilities shown here that are classified as held for sale, and the assets and liabilities associated with disposal groups, are not included in the further explanations in the notes to the consolidated financial statements or presented as reconciliation.

T-Mobile UK

On November 5, 2009, Deutsche Telekom AG and France Télécom S.A. signed an agreement on the combination of T-Mobile UK and Orange UK in a joint venture in which the two companies will hold 50% each. After completion of the transaction, Deutsche Telekom AG will account for its share in the joint venture using the equity method.

The entire transaction is subject to approval by the relevant competition authorities. In addition to the assets and liabilities shown in the table, EUR–2.2 billion (translation of foreign operations) of the total other comprehensive income reported as of December 31, 2009, is attributable to T-Mobile UK. In addition, T-Mobile UK received funds totaling EUR 1.3 billion from Deutsche Telekom as of the reporting date. This amount is not included in the liabilities shown, since funding was provided from within the Group. Obligations from operating leases totaling EUR 1.1 billion that existed at T-Mobile UK at the reporting date were not included in future obligations from operating leases. In addition, T-Mobile UK had commitments for the acquisition of property, plant, and equipment in the amount of EUR 0.3 billion.

Real estate portfolio

Real estate was shown as held for sale in the consolidated statement of financial position at the reporting date as a result of measures to make the use of floor space more efficient, especially in technical facilities (December 31, 2008: EUR 0.4 billion). This primarily relates to real estate owned by Deutsche Telekom AG. Impairment losses of EUR 0.2 billion were expensed in 2009 in connection with the reclassification of real estate. Given the current difficult market environment for real estate, Deutsche Telekom does not anticipate disposal of certain land and buildings intended for sale in the near future. According to the relevant accounting regulations (IFRS 5), this real estate at Group Headquarters & Shared Services was no longer permitted to be recognized in the consolidated statement of financial position as held for sale and had to be reclassified as noncurrent assets and measured at the lower of amortized cost and recoverable amount. The resulting measurement differences of EUR 0.1 billion have been recognized under "Other operating income" in the income statement.

Millions of EUR	T-Mobile UK Europe operating segment	Real estate portfolio Group Headquarters & Shared Services	Other	Dec. 31, 2009
Current assets	547	--	--	547
Trade and other receivables	314	--	--	314
Other current assets	233	--	--	233
Noncurrent assets	5,870	55	55	5,980
Intangible assets	3,821	--	26	3,847
Property, plant, and equipment	1,608	55	29	1,692
Other noncurrent assets	441	--	--	441
Noncurrent assets and disposal groups held for sale	6,417	55	55	6,527
Current liabilities	761	--	--	761
Trade and other payables	503	--	--	503
Other current liabilities	258	--	--	258
Noncurrent liabilities	662	--	--	662
Liabilities directly associated with noncurrent assets and disposal groups held for sale	1,423	--	--	1,423

MULTIPLE-CHOICE QUESTIONS

1. How should the income from discontinued operations be presented in the income statement?

    (a) The entity should disclose a single amount on the face of the income statement with analysis in the notes or a section of the income statement separate from continuing operations.

    (b) The amounts from discontinued operations should be broken down over each category of revenue and expense.

    (c) Discontinued operations should be shown as a movement on retained earnings.

    (d) Discontinued operations should be shown as a line item after gross profit with the taxation being shown as part of income tax expense.

2. How should the assets and liabilities of a disposal group classified as held for sale be shown in the balance sheet?

    (a) The assets and liabilities should be offset and presented as a single amount.

    (b) The assets of the disposal group should be shown separately from other assets in the balance sheet, and the liabilities of the disposal group should be shown separately from other liabilities in the balance sheet.

    (c) The assets and liabilities should be presented as a single amount and as a deduction from equity.

    (d) There should be no separate disclosure of assets and liabilities that form part of a disposal group.

3. An entity is planning to dispose of a collection of assets. The entity designates these assets as a disposal group. The carrying amount of these assets immediately before classification as held for sale was $20 million. Upon being classified as held for sale, the assets were revalued to $18 million. The entity feels that it would cost $1 million to sell the disposal group. What would be the carrying amount of the disposal group in the entity's accounts after its classification as held for sale?

    (a) $20 million.

    (b) $18 million.

    (c) $17 million.

    (d) $19 million.

4. An entity is planning to dispose of a collection of assets. The entity designates these assets as a disposal group, and the carrying amount of these assets immediately before classification as held for sale was $20 million. Upon being classified as held for sale, the assets were revalued to $18 million. The entity feels that the fair value less cost to sell would be $17 million. How would the reduction in the value of the assets on classification as held for sale be treated in the financial statements?

    (a) The entity recognizes a loss of $2 million immediately before classification as held for sale and then recognizes an impairment loss of $1 million.

    (b) The entity recognizes an impairment loss of $3 million.

    (c) The entity recognizes an impairment loss of $2 million.

    (d) The entity recognizes a loss of $3 million immediately before classifying the disposal group as held for sale.

5. In order for a noncurrent asset to be classified as held for sale, the sale must be highly probable. "Highly probable" means that

    (a) The future sale is likely to occur.

    (b) The future sale is more likely than not to occur.

    (c) The sale is certain.

    (d) The probability is higher than more likely than not.

6. An entity acquires a subsidiary exclusively with a view to selling it. The subsidiary meets the criteria to be classified as held for sale. At the balance sheet date, the subsidiary has not yet been sold, and six months have passed since its acquisition. How will the subsidiary be valued in the balance sheet at the date of the first financial statements after acquisition?

    (a) At fair value.

    (b) At the lower of its cost and fair value less cost to sell.

    (c) At carrying value.

    (d) In accordance with applicable IFRS.

7. Any gain on a subsequent increase in the fair value less cost to sell of a noncurrent asset classified as held for sale should be treated as follows

    (a) The gain should be recognized in full.

    (b) The gain should not be recognized.

    (c) The gain should be recognized but not in excess of the cumulative impairment loss.

    (d) The gain should be recognized but only in retained earnings.

8. An entity has an asset that was classified as held for sale. However, the criteria for it to remain as held for sale no longer apply. The entity should therefore

    (a) Leave the noncurrent asset in the financial statements at its current carrying value.

    (b) Remeasure the noncurrent asset at fair value.

    (c) Measure the noncurrent asset at the lower of its carrying amount before the asset was classified as held for sale (as adjusted for subsequent depreciation, amortization, or revaluations) and its recoverable amount at the date of the decision not to sell.

    (d) Recognize the noncurrent asset at its carrying amount prior to its classification as held for sale as adjusted for subsequent depreciation, amortization, or revaluations.

9.   Which of the following criteria do **not** have to be met in order for an operation to be classified as discontinued?

    (a) The operation should represent a separate line of business or geographical area.

    (b) The operation is part of a single plan to dispose of a separate major line of business or geographical area.

    (c) The operation is a subsidiary acquired exclusively with a view to resale.

    (d) The operation must be sold within three months of the year-end.

10. IFRS 5 states that a noncurrent asset that is to be abandoned should not be classified as held for sale. The reason for this is because

    (a) Its carrying amount will be recovered principally through continuing use.

    (b) It is difficult to value.

    (c) It is unlikely that the noncurrent asset will be sold within 12 months.

    (d) It is unlikely that there will be an active market for the noncurrent asset.

Chapter 37

EXPLORATION FOR AND EVALUATION OF MINERAL RESOURCES (IFRS 6)

INTRODUCTION

IFRS 6 addresses the financial reporting for the exploration for and evaluation of mineral resources, including minerals, oil, natural gas, and similar nonregenerative resources. The Standard is intended to provide some limited, initial guidance about the accounting for such activities until the International Accounting Standards Board (IASB) has made a more comprehensive review of the accounting for extractive industries. In particular, the Standard modifies the requirements of other Standards so as to minimize disruption to entities in the extractive industries applying International Financial Reporting Standards (IFRS) for the first time.

More specifically, IFRS 6

- Identifies expenditures to be included in and excluded from exploration and evaluation assets
- Provides an exemption for exploration and evaluation assets from part of the hierarchy in IAS 8, *Accounting Policies, Changes in Accounting Estimates, and Errors,* of criteria that an entity should use to develop an accounting policy if no IFRS applies specifically to an item
- Requires an entity that recognizes exploration and evaluation assets to assess such assets for impairment in accordance with IFRS 6 and to measure such impairment in accordance with IAS 36, *Impairment of Assets*
- Requires disclosures that identify and explain financial statement amounts that arise from evaluation for and exploration of mineral resources, including

  - The entity's accounting policies for exploration and evaluation expenditures
  - The amounts of assets, liabilities, income, and expense, and operating and investing cash flows arising from the exploration for and evaluation of mineral resources

IFRS 6 is effective for annual periods beginning on or after January 1, 2006. Earlier application is encouraged.

SCOPE

IFRS 6 applies to expenditures incurred in the exploration and evaluation of mineral resources. It does not apply to expenditures incurred

1. Before an entity has obtained the legal rights to explore a specific area (i.e., preacquisition or preexploration expenditures).
2. After the technical feasibility and commercial viability of extracting a mineral resource are demonstrable (i.e., development expenditure).

DEFINITIONS OF KEY TERMS
(In accordance with IFRS 6)

Exploration and evaluation expenditures. Expenditures incurred by an entity in connection with the exploration for and evaluation of mineral resources before the technical feasibility and commercial viability of extracting a mineral resource are demonstrated. Mineral resources include minerals, oil, natural gas, and similar nonregenerative resources.

Exploration for and evaluation of mineral resources. The search for mineral resources after the entity has obtained legal rights to explore in a specific area as well as the determination of the technical feasibility and commercial viability of extracting the mineral resources.

Exploration and evaluation assets. Exploration and evaluation expenditures that are recognized as assets in accordance with the entity's accounting policy under IFRS 6. Such assets are scoped out of IAS 16, *Property, Plant, and Equipment,* and IAS 38, *Intangible Assets.*

RECOGNITION

Development of Accounting Policies

IFRS 6 does not contain recognition requirements for exploration and evaluation assets, so an entity needs to develop its own accounting policies for recognition of such assets.

PRACTICAL INSIGHT

Entities follow a wide variety of accounting practices for exploration and evaluation expenditures. At one end of the spectrum, some entities defer nearly all exploration and evaluation expenditure as assets on the statement of financial position. At the other end of the spectrum, some entities recognize all such expenditure in profit or loss as incurred. An entity is permitted to continue to apply its previous accounting policies upon adoption of IFRS 6 provided that the resulting information is relevant and reliable.

IAS 8 specifies a hierarchy of criteria that an entity ordinarily should use to develop an accounting policy if no IFRS applies specifically to an item. When developing accounting policies for exploration and evaluation assets, however, IFRS 6 exempts an entity from part of the hierarchy in IAS 8. In the absence of such an exemption, the hierarchy in IAS 8 would have required an entity to refer to, and consider the applicability of, these sources of authoritative requirements and guidance in developing and applying an accounting policy for exploration and evaluation assets:

1. The requirements and guidance in Standards and Interpretations dealing with similar and related issues.
2. The definitions, recognition criteria, and measurement concepts for assets, liabilities, income, and expenses in the *Framework*.

The reason for the exemption is that the IASB wanted to minimize disruption on first-time adoption of IFRS both for users (e.g., due to lack of continuity of trend data) and for preparers (e.g., due to the need to do costly system changes) until the IASB has made a comprehensive review of accounting for extractive industries.

The requirement in IAS 8 for management to use its judgment in developing and applying an accounting policy that results in information that is relevant and reliable applies to exploration and evaluation assets. This means, for instance, that information that results from the entity's accounting policy needs to be complete in all material respects, reflect economic substance (not merely legal form), and be neutral.

PRACTICAL INSIGHT

Two common accounting methods in the oil and gas industry are the "full-cost" method and the "successful efforts" method.

Under the full-cost method, all costs incurred in acquiring, exploring, and developing within a broadly defined cost center (e.g., a country or group of countries) are capitalized and amortized. Under this method, costs are capitalized even if a specific project in the cost center was a failure.

Under the successful efforts method, many costs are capitalized and amortized. Unlike the full-cost method, however, costs of unsuccessful acquisition and exploration activities are charged to expense. Costs whose outcome is unknown are either expensed or capitalized.

Changes in Accounting Policies

Once an entity has established accounting policies for exploration and evaluation expenditures, it is permitted to change those policies only if the change makes the financial statements more relevant to the economic decision-making needs of users and no less reliable, or more reliable and no less relevant to those needs. The concepts of relevance and reliability are found in IAS 8.

MEASUREMENT

Initial Measurement

If an entity's accounting policy results in the recognition of an exploration and evaluation asset, IFRS 6 requires the entity to measure the asset initially at cost.

An entity is required to determine a policy that specifies which expenditures are recognized as part of the cost of exploration and evaluation assets. That policy should consider the degree to which the expenditure can be associated with finding specific mineral resources.

Examples

Expenditures that according to an entity's policy might be recognized as exploration and evaluation assets include expenditures for

- Acquisition of rights to explore
- Topographical, geological, geochemical, and geophysical studies
- Exploratory drilling
- Trenching
- Sampling
- Activities in relation to evaluating the technical feasibility and commercial viability of extracting a mineral resource

In some cases, general and administrative and overhead costs directly attributable to exploration and evaluation activities might also qualify for recognition as exploration and evaluation assets.

Expenditures related to the development of mineral resources (i.e., preparations for commercial production, such as building roads and tunnels) cannot be recognized as an exploration and evaluation asset. Property, plant, and equipment used to develop or maintain exploration or evaluation assets also cannot be recognized as exploration and evaluation assets.

Classification

An entity classifies an exploration or evaluation asset as either a tangible asset or an intangible asset according to the nature of the asset.

Examples

Vehicles and drilling rigs would be classified as tangible assets. Drilling rights would be classified as intangible assets.

Subsequent Measurement

After initial recognition, an entity applies one of two measurement models to exploration and evaluation assets:

1. The cost model
2. The revaluation model

Exploration and evaluation assets that are classified as tangible assets are measured in accordance with IAS 16. Those that are classified as intangible assets are measured in accordance with IAS 38.

IMPAIRMENT

Because of the difficulties in obtaining the information necessary to estimate future cash flows of exploration and evaluation assets, IFRS 6 modifies the requirements of IAS 36 regarding the circumstances in which exploration and evaluation assets are required to be assessed for impairment.

IFRS 6 requires exploration and evaluation assets to be assessed for impairment when facts and circumstances suggest that the carrying amount of an exploration and evaluation asset may exceed its recoverable amount. Facts or circumstances that may indicate that impairment testing is required include

- The period for which the entity has the right to explore in the specific area has expired or is expected to expire in the near future, unless the right is expected to be renewed.
- Substantive expenditure on further exploration and evaluation activities in the specific area is neither budgeted nor planned.
- Exploration and evaluation activities in the specific area have not led to the discovery of commercially viable quantities of mineral resources, and the entity has decided to discontinue such activities in the specific area.
- Although a development in the specific area is likely to proceed, there is sufficient data to indicate that the carrying amount of the exploration and evaluation asset is unlikely to be recovered in full from successful development or by sale.

If such facts or circumstances exist, the entity is required to perform an impairment test in accordance with IAS 36, subject to special requirements with respect to the level at which impairment is assessed: In assessing evaluation and exploration assets for impairment, an entity allocates the assets either to cash-generating units or to groups of cash-generating units. Cash-generating units are the smallest identifiable group of assets that generate cash inflows that are largely independent of the cash inflows from other assets or groups of assets (e.g., an oilfield). IFRS 6 requires an entity to determine an accounting policy for its allocations. In no case would an entity assess impairment at a level larger than a segment.

DISCLOSURE

IFRS 6 requires an entity to disclose information that identifies and explains the amounts recognized in its financial statements arising from the exploration for and evaluation of mineral resources. Such disclosures include

- Accounting policies for exploration and evaluation expenditures, including the recognition of exploration and evaluation assets

- The amounts of assets, liabilities, income, and expense, and operating and investing cash flows arising from the exploration for and evaluation of mineral resources

In addition, an entity is required to make the disclosures required by IAS 16 or IAS 38 consistent with an asset's classification as either tangible or intangible.

In August 2010, the IFRIC published a draft interpretation on stripping costs that may have a significant impact for IFRS mining companies. Some entities expense stripping costs and some entities capitalize some or all of these costs. The Interpretation will apply to all stripping campaigns in progress and require existing stripping cost balances to be reclassified and associated with specific ore quantities. Balances that cannot be associated with specific ore bodies will be written off to profit and loss on adoption. The Interpretation will apply only to stripping costs that are incurred in surface mining activity during the production phase of the mine.

EXTRACTS FROM PUBLISHED FINANCIAL STATEMENTS

BP PLC Annual Report, 2009

Oil and natural gas exploration, appraisal, and development expenditure is accounted for using the principles of the successful efforts method of accounting.

License and property acquisition costs. Exploration license and leasehold property acquisition costs are capitalized within intangible assets and are reviewed at each reporting date to confirm that there is no indication that the carrying amount exceeds the recoverable amount. This review includes confirming that exploration drilling is still under way or firmly planned or that it has been determined, or work is under way to determine, that the discovery is economically viable based on a range of technical and commercial considerations and sufficient progress is being made on establishing development plans and timing. If no future activity is planned, the remaining balance of the license and property acquisition costs is written off. Lower value licenses are pooled and amortized on a straight-line basis over the estimated period of exploration. Upon recognition of proved reserves and internal approval for development, the relevant expenditure is transferred to property, plant, and equipment.

Exploration and appraisal expenditure

Geological and geophysical exploration costs are charged against income as incurred. Costs directly associated with an exploration well are initially capitalized as an intangible asset until the drilling of the well is complete and the results have been evaluated. These costs include employee remuneration, materials and fuel used, rig costs, delay rentals, and payments made to contractors. If potentially commercial quantities of hydrocarbons are not found, the exploration expenditure is written off as a dry hole. If hydrocarbons are found and, subject to further appraisal activity, are likely to be capable of commercial development, the costs continue to be carried as an asset. Costs directly associated with appraisal activity, undertaken to determine the size, characteristics and commercial potential of a reservoir following the initial discovery of hydrocarbons, including the costs of appraisal wells where hydrocarbons were not found, are initially capitalized as an intangible asset. All such carried costs are subject to technical, commercial, and management review at least once a year to confirm the continued intent to develop or otherwise extract value from the discovery. When this is no longer the case, the costs are written off. When proved reserves of oil and natural gas are determined and development is approved by management, the relevant expenditure is transferred to property, plant, and equipment.

Development expenditure

Expenditure on the construction, installation, or completion of infrastructure facilities such as platforms, pipelines, and the drilling of development wells, including service and unsuccessful development or delineation wells, is capitalized within property, plant, and equipment and is depreciated from the commencement of production as described in the section that deals with the accounting policy for property, plant, and equipment.

Exploration for and evaluation of oil and natural gas resources

The following financial information represents the amounts included within the group totals relating to activity associated with the exploration for and evaluation of oil and natural gas resources. All such activity is recorded within the Exploration and Production segment.

		$million	
	2009	*2008*	*2007*
Exploration and evaluation costs			
Exploration expenditure written off	593	385	347
Other exploration costs	523	497	409
Exploration expense for the year	1,116	882	756
Intangible assets	10,338	9,031	5,252
Net assets	10,338	9,031	5,252
Capital expenditure	2,715	4,780	2,000
Net cash used in operating activities	523	497	409
Net cash used in investing activities	3,306	4,163	2,000

MULTIPLE-CHOICE QUESTIONS

1. IFRS 6 applies to expenditures incurred
    (a) When searching for an area that may warrant detailed exploration, even though the entity has not yet obtained the legal rights to explore a specific area.
    (b) When the legal rights to explore a specific area have been obtained, but the technical feasibility and commercial viability of extracting a mineral resource are not yet demonstrable.
    (c) When a specific area is being developed and preparations for commercial extraction are being made.
    (d) In extracting mineral resources and processing the resource to make it marketable or transportable.

2. Does IFRS 6 require an entity to recognize exploration and evaluation expenditure as assets?
    (a) Yes, but only to the extent such expenditure is recoverable in future periods.
    (b) Yes, but only to the extent the technical feasibility and commercial viability of extracting the associated mineral resource have been demonstrated.
    (c) Yes, but only to the extent required by the entity's accounting policy for recognizing exploration and evaluation assets.
    (d) No, such expenditure is always expensed in profit or loss as incurred.

3. What is an entity required to consider in developing accounting policies for exploration and evaluation activities?
    (a) The requirements and guidance in Standards and Interpretations dealing with similar and related issues.
    (b) The definitions, recognition criteria, and measurement concepts for assets, liabilities, income, and expenses in the *Framework.*
    (c) Recent pronouncements of standard-setting bodies, accounting literature, and accepted industry practices.
    (d) Whether the accounting policy results in information that is relevant and reliable.

4. Is an entity ever required or permitted to change its accounting policy for exploration and evaluation expenditures?
    (a) Yes, entities are required to change their accounting policy for these expenditures if the change would result in more useful information for users of financial statements.
    (b) Yes, entities are free to change accounting policy for these expenditures as long as the selected policy results in information that is relevant and reliable.

(c) Yes, but only if the change makes the financial statements more relevant to the economic decision-making needs of users and no less reliable, or more reliable and no less relevant to those needs.
(d) No, entities would be permitted to change accounting policy only on adoption of a new or revised Standard that replaces the existing requirements in IFRS 6.

5. Which of the following expenditures would never qualify as an exploration and evaluation asset?
    (a) Expenditure for acquisition of rights to explore.
    (b) Expenditure for exploratory drilling.
    (c) Expenditures related to the development of mineral resources.
    (d) Expenditure for activities in relation to evaluating the technical feasibility and commercial viability of extracting a mineral resource.

6. Which measurement model applies to exploration and evaluation assets subsequent to initial recognition?
    (a) The cost model.
    (b) The revaluation model.
    (c) Either the cost model or the revaluation model.
    (d) The recoverable amount model.

7. Which of the following facts or circumstances would not trigger a need to test an evaluation and exploration asset for impairment?
    (a) The expiration—or expected expiration in the near future—of the period for which the entity has the right to explore in the specific area, unless the right is expected to be renewed.
    (b) The absence of budgeted or planned substantive expenditure on further exploration and evaluation activities in the specific area.
    (c) A decision to discontinue exploration and evaluation activities in the specific area when those activities have not led to the discovery of commercially viable quantities of mineral resources.
    (d) Lack of sufficient data to determine whether the carrying amount of the exploration and evaluation asset is likely to be recovered in full from successful development or by sale.

8. Which of the following is not a disclosure required by IFRS 6?
    (a) Information about commercial reserve quantities.
    (b) Accounting policies for exploration and evaluation expenditures, including the rec-

ognition of exploration and evaluation assets.

(c) The amounts of assets, liabilities, income and expense, and operating and investing cash flows arising from the exploration for and evaluation of mineral resources.

(d) Information that identifies and explains the amounts recognized in the financial statements arising from the exploration for and evaluation of mineral resources.

Chapter 38

FINANCIAL INSTRUMENTS: DISCLOSURES (IFRS 7)

INTRODUCTION

This Standard includes disclosure requirements about financial instruments and their associated risks, including

- The significance of financial instruments for the entity's financial position and performance, including certain specified information about

  - Statement of financial position items
  - Statement of comprehensive income items
  - Accounting policies
  - Hedge accounting
  - Fair value

- The nature and extent of risks arising from financial instruments to which the entity is exposed, including

  - Qualitative disclosures
  - Quantitative disclosures (credit risk, liquidity risk, market risk)

The purpose of IFRS 7 is to require entities to provide disclosures in their financial statements that enable users to evaluate, first, the significance of financial instruments for the entity's financial position and performance, and, second, the nature and extent of risks arising from financial instruments to which the entity is exposed, and how the entity manages those risks.

The disclosure requirements in IFRS 7 complement the recognition, measurement, and presentation requirements for financial instruments in IAS 32, *Financial Instruments: Presentation,* IAS 39, *Financial Instruments: Recognition and Measurement,* and IFRS 9, *Financial Instruments.*

IFRS 7 is effective for annual periods beginning on or after January 1, 2007. The International Accounting Standards Board (IASB) encourages entities to apply the Standard early. IFRS 7 includes some of the disclosure requirements that were previously in IAS 30, *Disclosures in the Financial Statements of Banks and Similar Financial Institutions,* and IAS 32, *Financial Instruments: Disclosure and Presentation.* The remaining disclosure requirements that were in IAS 30 and IAS

32 are replaced by those in IFRS 7. Therefore, IAS 30 was withdrawn when IFRS 7 became effective. Additionally, IASB shortened the initial title of IAS 32 to *Financial Instruments: Presentation* to reflect the relocation of its disclosure requirements to IFRS 7.

PRACTICAL INSIGHT

As part of its project to develop IFRS 7, *Financial Instruments: Disclosures,* the IASB also amended IAS 1 to add requirements for disclosures of

- The entity's objectives, policies, and processes for managing "capital."
- Quantitative data about what the entity regards as "capital."
- Whether the entity has complied with any capital requirements and if it has not complied, the consequences of such noncompliance.

These disclosure requirements apply to all entities, effective for annual periods beginning on or after January 1, 2007.

It was not apparently evident to some as to why such disclosure requirements (developed during the project on IFRS 7) could not be part of IFRS 7 itself and why was it necessary for the IASB to add disclosure requirements developed during the project on IFRS 7 (regarding an entity's "capital") to IAS 1, *Presentation of Financial Statements.* Logical reasoning for this approach of the IASB could be that because an entity's "capital" would not be covered by the definition of the term "financial instruments" (refer to IAS 32), such disclosure requirements on "capital" adequacy could not be included within a standard on "financial instruments" and were therefore added to another IASB standard. For that purpose an appropriate standard for this kind of an addition would be a general standard such as IAS 1.

SCOPE

IFRS 7 applies to financial instruments. Refer to the chapter on IAS 32 for a more detailed discussion of the definition of a financial instrument.

In addition, IFRS 7, like IAS 32 and IAS 39, also applies to some contracts that do not meet the definition of a financial instrument but have characteristics similar to derivative financial instruments. This expands the scope of IFRS 7, IAS 32, and IAS 39 to contracts to purchase or sell nonfinancial items (e.g., gold, electricity, or gas) at a future date when, and only when, a contract has both of these two characteristics: (1) it can be settled net in cash or some other financial instrument, and (2) it is not for receipt or delivery of the nonfinancial item in accordance with the entity's expected purchase, sale, or usage requirements. Chapter on IAS 39 provides a more detailed discussion of this scope expansion.

The scope of IFRS 7 is similar to that of IAS 32. Like IAS 32, IFRS 7 has scope exceptions for some items that meet the definition of a financial instrument. Such scope exceptions are listed in the table.

Scope Exception	*Applicable Standard*
Interests in subsidiaries	IAS 27, *Consolidated and Separate Financial Statements*
Interests in associates	IAS 28, *Investments in Associates*
Interests in joint ventures	IAS 31, *Interests in Joint Ventures*
Employee benefit plans	IAS 19, *Employee Benefits*
Share-based payment transactions	IFRS 2, *Share-Based Payment*
Contracts for contingent consideration in business combinations	IFRS 3, *Business Combinations*
Insurance contracts	IFRS 4, *Insurance Contracts*

In developing IFRS 7, IASB considered whether to make scope exceptions for insurers, small and medium-size entities, and the separate financial statements of subsidiaries, but decided not to do so.

SIGNIFICANCE OF FINANCIAL INSTRUMENTS FOR FINANCIAL POSITION AND PERFORMANCE

One of the two principal objectives of IFRS 7 is to require entities to disclose information that enables users of financial statements to evaluate the significance of financial instruments for the entities' financial position and performance. To help achieve this objective, IFRS 7 requires disclosure about balance sheet items, income statement and equity items, accounting policies, hedge accounting, and fair value.

Statement of Financial Position

Carrying amounts. IFRS 7 requires disclosures about the carrying amounts of each of the categories of financial assets and financial liabilities defined in IAS 39. These disclosures are to be provided either on the face of the statement of financial position or in the notes. The disclosure of carrying amounts by category helps users of financial statements understand the extent to which accounting policies for each category affect the amounts at which financial assets and financial liabilities are measured.

Example

The carrying amounts of each of these categories defined in IAS 39 are required to be disclosed:

- Financial assets at fair value through profit or loss, showing separately

  - Those designated as such upon initial recognition
  - Those classified as held for trading in accordance with IAS 39

- Held-to-maturity investments
- Loans and receivables
- Available-for-sale financial assets
- Financial liabilities at fair value through profit or loss, showing separately

  - Those designated as such upon initial recognition
  - Those classified as held for trading in accordance with IAS 39

- Financial liabilities measured at amortized cost

Items at fair value through profit or loss. Under IAS 39, entities are permitted to designate financial assets and financial liabilities at fair value through profit or loss if specified conditions are met. For some assets and liabilities so designated, IFRS 7 requires special disclosures. These disclosure requirements apply to those loans and receivables (i.e., where the entity is lending cash) and financial liabilities (i.e., where the entity is borrowing cash) that are designated as at fair value through profit or loss.

The required disclosures include information about the amount of change in the fair value of the asset or liability that is attributable to changes in the credit risk of that asset or liability (i.e., the risk that the borrower will cause a financial loss for the lender by failing to discharge the obligation). Such information shall be provided both about the change during the period and the cumulative change since the asset or liability was designated as at fair value through profit or loss.

Without such information, there is a concern that users of financial statements may misinterpret the profit or loss effects of changes in credit risk. For instance, if the credit risk of a financial liability increases because of an entity's financial difficulties, the fair value of the financial liability will decrease, resulting in a gain for the entity. Some view this as counterintuitive, since the reason for the gain is the entity's financial problems.

PRACTICAL INSIGHT

To provide this disclosure about the change in fair value attributable to credit risk, an entity needs to determine what portion of the total change in the fair value of the asset or liability is attributable to credit risk. One way to do this is to estimate the amount of the change in fair value that is attributable to risks other than credit risk (i.e., changes in the fair value of the asset or liability attributable to changes in the benchmark interest rate, foreign exchange rates, and other market conditions), and compare it with the total change in fair value. The difference is the change that is attributable to credit risk. An entity is required to disclose the methods it uses to compute this amount.

In addition, for loans and receivables designated as at fair value through profit or loss, an entity is required to disclose information about

1. The maximum exposure to credit risk at the reporting date
2. The amount of credit risk mitigation achieved using credit derivatives or similar instruments
3. The amount of the change in the fair value of those related credit derivatives or similar instruments during the period and cumulatively

Moreover, for financial liabilities designated as at fair value through profit or loss, an entity is required to disclose information about the difference between the carrying amount and the amount the entity would be contractually required to repay at maturity to the holder of the obligation (i.e., the principal or settlement amount).

Example

Entity A incurs a financial liability by issuing a bond obligation at par (i.e., the proceeds received by Entity A equal the principal or settlement amount). Later, Entity A encounters financial difficulties such that its creditworthiness deteriorates. As a result, the fair value of the liability may decline and be significantly less than the principal or settlement amount in that subsequent period. In this case, disclosure about the difference between the carrying amount and the settlement amount suggests that the carrying amount is less than the amount that Entity A is contractually required to pay to settle the obligation.

Reclassifications. If an entity reclassifies a financial asset such that the reclassification changes the measurement of the asset from one that is measured at cost or amortized cost to one that is measured at fair value, or vice versa (from fair value to cost or amortized cost), the entity is required to disclose the amount reclassified and the reason for the reclassification. Such information is useful because reclassifications affect how the financial asset is measured.

IAS 39 severely restricts the ability to reclassify a financial asset from one category to another. Please refer to Chapter 26 for a discussion of when reclassifications may occur.

Derecognition. As discussed in an earlier chapter on financial instruments, in some circumstances, sales or other transfers of financial assets do not qualify for derecognition (i.e., the entity that transferred the financial asset is not allowed to remove the financial asset [or part of it] from its financial statements). For instance, the entity may have sold a financial asset but retained substantially all of the risks and rewards of ownership, such that derecognition is not permitted.

For each class of financial assets transferred that do not qualify for derecognition, an entity is required to disclose information about

1. The nature of the assets
2. The nature of the risks and rewards of ownership to which the entity remains exposed
3. The total carrying amount of the original assets, the amount of the assets that the entity continues to recognize (if different from the total carrying amount of the original assets), and the carrying amount of the associated liabilities

This information is intended to assist users of financial statements in evaluating the significance of the risks retained in transfers that do not qualify for derecognition.

Collateral. If an entity has pledged its own financial assets as collateral for liabilities or contingent liabilities that it has, it is required to disclose the carrying amount of those financial assets and the terms and conditions related to its pledge. Such information helps users of financial statements evaluate the extent to which the entity's financial assets would be unavailable to the general creditors of the entity in case of bankruptcy.

If an entity holds collateral (whether financial or nonfinancial) and is permitted to sell or repledge the collateral in the absence of default by the owner of the collateral, it is required to disclose the fair value of the collateral held, the fair value of any such collateral sold or repledged, whether the entity has an obligation to return it, and the terms and conditions associated with its use of the collateral. For example, an entity may hold collateral that it can sell or repledge in sale and repurchase transactions or securities lending transactions.

Allowance account for credit losses. When an entity uses a separate account to record impairment of a financial asset (i.e., an allowance account) rather than directly reducing the carrying amount of the asset, IFRS 7 requires disclosure of a reconciliation of changes in that account during the period for each class of financial assets.

PRACTICAL INSIGHT

Typically, entities use an allowance account to record impairment losses on a group basis under IAS 39, because such losses cannot yet be identified with individual assets. Analysts and other users of financial statements use information about the amount of impairment allowances and changes therein to assess the adequacy of an entity's allowance for impairment losses, for example, by comparing it to industry benchmarks or through time.

Compound financial instruments with multiple embedded derivatives. If an entity has issued an instrument that contains both a liability and an equity component (as determined in accordance with IAS 32) and the instrument has multiple embedded derivatives whose values are interdependent, it shall disclose the existence of those features.

Example

One example of an instrument with multiple embedded derivatives is an issued callable convertible bond that gives the issuer a right to call the instrument back from the holder (i.e., an embedded call option feature) and the holder a right to convert the instrument into equity of the issuer (i.e., an embedded equity conversion option feature). For such a financial instrument, the embedded features are interdependent because if one is exercised, the other one is extinguished. This means that the sum of the separately determined fair values of the components of the financial instrument will not necessarily equal the fair value of the financial instrument as a whole.

Defaults and breaches. Under IFRS 7, an entity is required to provide disclosures about defaults and breaches of loans payable and other loan agreements, such as details of any defaults during the period of principal or interest of those loans payable. Such disclosures provide information about the entity's creditworthiness and its prospects of obtaining future loans.

Statement of Comprehensive Income and Equity Items

IFRS 7 requires an entity to disclose certain specified items of income, expense, gains, or losses, either on the face of the **statement of comprehensive income** or in the notes. These disclosures help users assess the performance of an entity's financial instruments and activities. The required disclosures include

- Net gains or net losses for each of the categories of financial assets and financial liabilities in IAS 39 (This requirement contained in paragraph 20 of IFRS 7 has been amended as a consequential amendment to IFRS 9 by deletion of references to classifications of financial instruments that do not exist under IFRS 9, for example, "available for sale" or "held to maturity." However, as entities are not required to apply IFRS 9 until January 2013, though earlier application is permitted, the chapters on "financial instruments," other than the chapter on IFRS 9, have been retained as they are based on requirements of IASB's financial instruments' standards that are applicable currently, namely IAS 32, IAS 39, and IFRS 7.)
- Total interest income and total interest expense (calculated using the effective interest method) for financial assets or financial liabilities that are not at fair value through profit or loss
- Fee income and expense (other than amounts included in determining the effective interest rate) arising from financial assets or financial liabilities that are not at fair value through

profit or loss; and trust and other fiduciary activities that result in the holding or investing of assets on behalf of individuals, trusts, retirement benefit plans, and other institutions

- Interest income on impaired financial assets accrued in accordance with IAS 39
- The amount of any impairment loss for each class of financial asset

Example

The required disclosures of income statement gains and losses include amounts for

- Financial assets or financial liabilities at fair value through profit or loss, showing separately those on financial assets or financial liabilities designated as such upon initial recognition, and those on financial assets or financial liabilities that are classified as held for trading in accordance with IAS 39
- Available-for-sale financial assets, showing separately the amount of gain or loss recognized directly in equity during the period and the amount removed from equity and recognized in profit or loss for the period
- Held-to-maturity investments
- Loans and receivables
- Financial liabilities measured at amortized cost

Other Disclosures

Accounting policies. IFRS 7 includes a reference to IAS 1, which requires an entity to disclose, in the summary of significant accounting policies, the measurement basis (or bases) used in preparing the financial statements and the other accounting policies used that are relevant to an understanding of the financial statements.

Hedge accounting. Because hedge accounting is elective and subject to restrictive conditions under IAS 39, it is important that entities provide information about the extent to which they have applied hedge accounting and its effects on the financial statements in order to enable users to compare financial statements of different entities. IFRS 7 contains detailed disclosure requirements in this respect. An entity shall disclose separately for designated fair value hedges, cash flow hedges, and hedges of a net investment in a foreign operation

- A description of each type of hedge
- A description of the financial instruments designated as hedging instruments and their fair values at the reporting date
- The nature of the risks being hedged

For cash flow hedges, an entity shall also disclose the periods in which the cash flows are expected to occur, when they are expected to enter into the determination of profit or loss, and a description of any forecast transaction for which hedge accounting had previously been used but which is no longer expected to occur.

When a gain or loss on a hedging instrument in a cash flow hedge has been recognized directly in equity, through the statement of changes in equity, an entity shall disclose

- The amount that was so recognized in equity during the period
- The amount that was removed from equity and included in profit or loss for the period
- The amount that was removed from equity during the period and included in the initial measurement of the acquisition cost or other carrying amount of a nonfinancial asset or nonfinancial liability in a hedged highly probable forecast transaction

An entity is also required to disclose

- In fair value hedges, gains or losses on

  - The hedging instrument
  - The hedged item attributable to the hedged risk

- The ineffectiveness recognized in profit or loss that arises from cash flow hedges
- The ineffectiveness recognized in profit or loss that arises from hedges of net investments in foreign operations

Fair value. IFRS 7 requires an entity to disclose, for each class of financial assets and financial liabilities, the fair value of that class of assets and liabilities. Disclosure of fair value shall be made in a way that permits the information to be compared with the corresponding carrying amount in the balance sheet. Many users of financial statements consider fair value information useful, because it provides a market-based assessment of the value of financial instruments that does not depend on the cost of the instruments when they were recognized initially by the entity or the category in which they were classified by the entity.

Fair value information is not required when the carrying amount is a reasonable approximation to fair value. In addition, when investments in unquoted equity instruments or derivatives linked to such equity instruments are measured at cost under IAS 39 because their fair value cannot be measured reliably, that fact shall be disclosed together with a description of the financial instruments, their carrying amount, an explanation of why fair value cannot be measured reliably, and, if possible, the range of estimates within which fair value is highly likely to lie. Disclosure of fair value is not required for such an instrument. Additionally, fair value information is not required for contracts containing a discretionary participation feature (as described in IFRS 4) if the fair value of that feature cannot be measured reliably.

To complement the fair value information provided, an entity shall also disclose

1. The methods and assumptions applied in determining fair values (e.g., the assumptions relating to prepayment rates, rates of estimated credit losses, and interest rates, or discount rates)
2. Whether fair values are determined directly, in full or in part, by reference to published price quotations in an active market or are estimated using a valuation technique
3. Whether its financial statements include financial instruments measured at fair values that are determined in full or in part using a valuation technique based on assumptions that are not supported by observable current market transactions in the same instrument and not based on available observable market data, including information about the sensitivity of the fair value estimates to changes in assumptions
4. The total amount of the change in fair value estimated using a valuation technique that was recognized in profit or loss during the period

If there is a difference between the transaction price fair value at initial recognition and the amount that would be determined at that date using a valuation technique, an entity also discloses its accounting policy for recognizing that difference in profit or loss and the aggregate difference yet to be recognized in profit or loss. Such differences may arise, for instance, for dealers in financial instruments.

NATURE AND EXTENT OF RISKS ARISING FROM FINANCIAL INSTRUMENTS

The second of the two principal objectives of IFRS 7 is to require entities to disclose information that enables users of its financial statements to evaluate the nature and extent of risks arising from financial instruments to which the entity is exposed at the reporting date. These disclosure requirements focus on the risks that arise from financial instruments (including credit risk, liquidity risk, and market risk) and how they have been managed by an entity. The extent of disclosure depends on the extent of the entity's exposure to risks arising from financial instruments.

Qualitative Disclosures

For each type of risk arising from financial instruments, IFRS 7 requires an entity to disclose qualitative information about

- The exposures to risk and how they arise
- The entity's objectives, policies, and processes for managing the risk, and its methods to measure the risk
- Any changes from the previous period in the exposures or its objectives, policies, processes, and methods

Quantitative Disclosures

For each type of risk arising from financial instruments, IFRS 7 requires an entity to disclose

- Summary quantitative data about its exposure to that risk at the reporting date
- Concentrations of risk

IFRS 7 requires the disclosure about an entity's exposure to risks to be based on how the entity views and manages its risks (i.e., the information that it uses internally to assess risks).

If the quantitative data disclosed as of the reporting date are unrepresentative of an entity's exposure to risk during the period, an entity shall provide further information that is representative.

Credit risk. IFRS 7 defines "credit risk" as the risk that one party to a financial instrument will cause a financial loss for the other party by failing to discharge an obligation.

IFRS 7 requires these credit risk–related disclosures by class of financial instrument:

- The amount that best represents its maximum exposure to credit risk at the reporting date without taking account of any collateral held or other credit enhancements (i.e., in many cases, the carrying amount)
- A description of collateral held as security and other credit enhancements
- Information about the credit quality of financial assets that are neither past due nor impaired
- The carrying amount of financial assets that would otherwise be past due or impaired whose terms have been renegotiated

To complement the above information, IFRS 7 also requires disclosure of

- An analysis of the age of financial assets that are past due as of the reporting date but not impaired
- An analysis of financial assets that are individually determined to be impaired as of the reporting date
- A description of collateral held by the entity as security and other credit enhancements associated with past due or impaired assets
- The nature and carrying amount of financial or nonfinancial assets obtained during the period by taking possession of collateral or through guarantees or other credit enhancements as well as policies for disposing of or using such assets that are not readily convertible to cash

Credit risk information helps users of financial statements assess the credit quality of the entity's financial assets and level and sources of impairment losses.

Liquidity risk. IFRS 7 defines "liquidity risk" as the risk that an entity will encounter difficulty in meeting obligations associated with financial liabilities.

IFRS 7 requires an entity to disclose both

- A maturity analysis for financial liabilities that shows the remaining contractual maturities
- A description of how it manages the liquidity risk inherent in those liabilities

Market risk. IFRS 7 defines "market risk" as the risk that the fair value or future cash flows of a financial instrument will fluctuate because of changes in market prices. Market risk comprises three types of risk: currency risk, interest rate risk, and other price risk.

IFRS 7 requires an entity to disclose a sensitivity analysis to market risk. Sensitivity analyses help users of financial statements evaluate what are reasonably possible changes in the entity's financial position and financial performance due to changes in market risk factors.

Unless the entity uses a sensitivity analysis that reflects interdependencies between risk variables to manage financial risks, the sensitivity analysis should be broken down by type of market risk to which the entity is exposed at the reporting date, showing how profit or loss and equity would have been affected by changes in the relevant risk variable that were reasonably possible at that date. The entity is also required to disclose the methods and assumptions used in preparing the sensitivity analysis. When the sensitivity analyses disclosed are unrepresentative (e.g., because the year-end exposure does not reflect the exposure during the year), the entity shall disclose that fact and the reason it believes the sensitivity analyses are unrepresentative.

PRACTICAL INSIGHT

In managing financial risks (in particular market risks), banks and securities firms often use value at risk (VAR) as a measure of risk. VAR is a statistical measure of downside risk that reflects interdependencies between risk variables. The VAR of a portfolio of financial instruments is the maximum loss that the portfolio is expected to suffer over a specified holding period horizon (such as one or ten days) with a given level of confidence (such as 95% or 99%). For example, if the 1-day VAR of an entity's trading portfolio is $10,000,000 at the 99% confidence level, this suggests that the entity will lose more than $10,000,000 in only one out of 100 days.

AMENDMENT TO IFRS 7, *IMPROVING DISCLOSURES ABOUT FINANCIAL INSTRUMENTS,* ISSUED MARCH 2009, EFFECTIVE FOR ANNUAL PERIODS BEGINNING ON OR AFTER JANUARY 1, 2009.

On March 5, 2009, the IASB amended IFRS 7 in response to calls from the global financial leadership (such as finance ministers representing the G20 nations) and several constituents, for enhanced disclosures about fair value measurements and liquidity risk. The recent financial crisis that rocked the financial world and several economies around the world created the need for such additional disclosures.

The amendments expand the disclosures required in respect of fair value measurements recognized in the statement of financial position. Following the precedent from the disclosures requirements in US GAAP (specifically SFAS 157 on fair value measurement) a three-level hierarchy has been introduced in IFRS 7.

PRACTICAL INSIGHT

The "three-level hierarchy" in IFRS 7 has relevance only to disclosures and not to measurement of financial instruments. According to the IASB (as per the "Basis of Conclusions") there is no connection between the fair value measurement hierarchy in IAS 39 and the expanded disclosure requirements of the "three-level hierarchy" in IFRS 7.

Three-Level Hierarchy for fair value disclosures—a Guide:

Level 1

Fair values are determined based on **"quoted prices."** (These are unadjusted in active markets for identical assets or liabilities).

Level 2

Fair values are determined based on inputs other than quoted prices included within Level 1, which are **observable** for the asset or liability. These inputs are observable either: directly (i.e., as prices) or indirectly (i.e., derived from prices).

Level 3

Fair values are determined based on **"unobservable inputs."** (In other words, inputs for the asset or liability that are not based on observable market data).

Expanded Disclosure Regarding Fair Value Measurements—Highlights

When financial instruments are carried in the statement of financial position at fair values, an entity shall disclose the following for **each class** of financial instruments with respect to their measurement:

1. The level (in the fair value hierarchy) into which the fair value measurements are categorized in their entirety. For this purpose an entity should follow guidance that is provided in

the standard, which is summarized previously in a schematic titled "Three-Level Hierarchy for Fair Value Disclosures–a Guide."

2. When there are transfers between Levels there should be disclosure of "significant" transfers between Level 1 and Level 2 of the fair value hierarchy and the reasons for those transfers ("significance" being assessed based on profit or loss, and total assets or total liabilities). Separate disclosures are required for "transfers into each level" and "transfers out of each level."

3. In the case of fair value measurements with respect to Level 3 hierarchy, a reconciliation is required between the beginning balances and the ending balances, disclosing separately changes during the period on account of the following four:

   a. Total gains or losses for the period recognized in profit or loss (and a description of where they are presented in the statement of comprehensive income or the separate income statement, if presented).
   b. Total gains or losses recognized in "other comprehensive income."
   c. Purchases, sales, issues, and settlements.
   d. Transfers into or out of Level 3 (e.g., transfers attributable to changes in the observability of market data) and the reasons for those transfers. For significant transfers, transfers into Level 3 shall be disclosed and discussed separately from transfers out of Level 3.

4. The amount of total gains or losses for the period in 3.a. above included in profit or loss that are attributable to gains or losses relating to those assets and liabilities held at the end of the reporting period.

5. In case of fair value measurements in Level 3, if changing one or more inputs to reasonable alternative assumptions would modify fair value significantly, that should be disclosed with the effect ("significance" to be assessed based on profit or loss, and total assets or total liabilities).

Practical Considerations

The following practical considerations are to be borne in mind in applying the requirements of the expanded disclosure amendments to IFRS 7:

- Financial instruments measured at fair value in the statement of financial position are the only financial instruments that these expanded IFRS 7 disclosure requirements apply to. (In other words, in case of financial instruments *not measured at fair value*, there is no change in the requirements regarding disclosure of their fair values).
- A financial instrument is always categorized as Level 1, 2, or 3 *in its entirety*.
- All quantitative disclosures are required to be presented in tabular format unless another format is more appropriate.
- In the three-level hierarchy of disclosures as required by these amendments, the level for an instrument is determined on the basis of the *lowest level* input that is "significant" to the fair value measurement.

Example

If the fair value measurement uses "observable inputs" that require "significant adjustment" based on "unobservable inputs," then such a financial instrument is required to be classified as Level 3. This is so even if Level 1 and Level 2 inputs may also have been used.

(It is to be noted that in assessing "significance," judgment is required which would warrant consideration of factors specific to the financial asset or financial liability.)

Liquidity risk disclosures—Clarification of scope of liquidity risk disclosures. The amendments have amended the definition of "liquidity risk" to state that liquidity risk only includes financial liabilities that are settled by delivering cash or another financial asset. (This would imply that financial liabilities that are settled by the entity delivering its own equity instruments or nonfinancial assets are excluded). The amendments also clarify the following:

- The scope of items to be included in the "maturity analyses" required under IFRS 7
- That a hybrid contract (i.e., a contract that contains one or more embedded derivatives) that is a financial liability is not separated for the purpose of providing the maturity analysis and is treated as a nonderivative financial liability

Maturity analysis expanded. This amendment to IFRS 7 has expanded the disclosures of maturity analyses by prescribing different liquidity risk disclosures for "derivatives" and "non-derivative financial liabilities. In case of the former, the remaining contractual maturities where these are essential for an understanding of the timing of the cash flows, whereas in case of the latter, it is the remaining contractual maturities that are required to be disclosed.

Relationship between qualitative and quantitative disclosures. In order to enhance the relationship between the two kinds of disclosures for liquidity risk required by the standard, the amendments require that an entity should explain how data is determined.

EXTRACTS FROM FINANCIAL STATEMENTS

LPKF, Annual Report, 2009

Notes on financial statements

3. Details pursuant to IFRS 7

Carrying amount, amounts recognized, and fair values by measurement category

			Amounts recognized in balance sheet according			
T€	*Category in accordance with IAS 39**	*Carrying amount 12/31/2009*	*Amortized cost*	*Fair value recognized in equity*	*Fair value recognized in profit or loss*	*Fair value 12/31/2009*
Assets						
Other loans	LaR	20	20			20
Cash and cash equivalents	LaR	10,772	10,772			10,772
Trade receivables	LaR	10,929	10,929			10,929
Other receivables	LaR	1,627	1,627			1,627
Securities	AfS	236		236		236
Derivative financial assets						
Derivatives	FAHfT	14			14	14
Liabilities						
Trade payables	FLAC	2,162	2,162			2,162
Liabilities to banks	FLAC	4,076	4,076			3,658
Other interest-bearing liabilities	FLAC	205	205			205
Other noninterest-bearing liabilities	FLAC	6,120	6,120			6,120
Derivate finanzielle Verbindlichkeiten						
Derivatives	FAHfT	0			0	0
Thereof accumulated by measurement categories acc. IAS 39						
Loans and receivables	LaR	23,348	23,348			23,348
Available for sale	AfS	236		236		236
Financial assets held for trading	FAHfT	14			14	14
Financial liabilities measured at amortized cost	FLAC	12,563	12,563			12,145
Financial liabilities held for trading	FLHfT	0			0	0

* *LaR = Loans and Receivables*
AfS = Available for Sale

HtM = Held-to-Maturity Investment
FAHfT = Financial Assets Held for Trading

FLAC = Financial Liabilities Measured at Amortized Cost
FLHfT = Financial Liabilities Held for Trading

The fair value of payment instruments and payment instrument equivalents, current assets, trade payables and current financial assets and liabilities corresponds closely to the carrying amounts because of the short maturities. The AfS securities are listed on the stock exchange and are measured on the basis of the stock exchange price on the reporting date. The carrying amount of derivative financial instruments corresponds to the fair value.

The securities assigned to the category "financial assets available for sale" reported under "other original financial assets" and totaling T€ 236 are listed on the stock exchange and measured on the basis of the stock exchange price on the reporting date (Step 1 of the fair value hierarchy). The financial instruments in the category "financial assets held for trading" totaling T€ 14 (previous year: T€ 4) and the category "financial liabilities held for trading" totaling T€ 0 (previous year: T€ 71) have been assigned by the Company to Step 2 of the fair value hierarchy. The condition for Step 2 is the availability of a stock exchange price or a market price for a similar financial instrument, or that the calculation parameters are based on data from observable markets. There are no financial instruments for which measurement methods have been applied using significant input parameters which are not based on data from observable markets (Step 3 of the fair value hierarchy).

		Amounts recognized in balance sheet according to IAS 39			
Category in accordance with IAS 39	*Carrying amount 12/31/2008*	*Amortized cost*	*Fair value recognized in equity*	*Fair value recognized in profit or loss*	*Fair value 12/31/2008*
LaR	0	0			0
LaR	6,005	6,005			6,005
LaR	10,164	10,164			10,164
LaR	658	658			658
AfS	214		214		214
FAHfT	4			4	4
FLAC	1,640	1,640			1,640
FLAC	6,642	6,642			6,392
FLAC	234	234			234
FLAC	4,514	4,514			4,514
FLHfT	71			71	71
LaR	16,827	16,827			16,827
AfS	214		214		214
FAHfT	4			4	4
FLAC	13,030	13,030			12,780
FLHfT	71			71	71

The net profits/losses from financial instruments are as follows:

T€		*2009*	*2008*
Loans and receivables	LaR	7	267
Financial assets and liabilities held for trading	FAHft + FLHft	0	(67)
Financial liabilities measured at amortized cost	FLAC	313	372
		320	**572**

The total interest expenditure calculated using the effective interest method is T€ 4.

The net profits/losses from loans and claims include changes to value adjustments, profits and losses from disposals, incoming payments, revaluations of originally value-adjusted loans and claims, and currency translations.

BP PLC, Annual Report, 2009

Notes on Financial Statements

31. Derivative financial instruments

An outline of the group's financial risks and the objectives and policies pursued in relation to those risks is set out in Note 24.

In the normal course of business the group enters into derivative financial instruments (derivatives) to manage its normal business exposures in relation to commodity prices, foreign currency exchange rates and interest rates, including management of the balance between floating-rate and fixed-rate debt, consistent with risk management policies and objectives. Additionally, the group has a well-established entrepreneurial trading operation that is undertaken in conjunction with these activities using a similar range of contracts.

IAS 39 prescribes strict criteria for hedge accounting, whether as a cash flow or fair value hedge or a hedge of a net investment in a foreign operation, and requires that any derivative that does not meet these criteria should be classified as held for trading and fair valued, with gains and losses recognized in the income statement.

The fair values of derivative financial instruments at December 31 are set out below

$ million	2009 Fair value asset	Fair value liability	2008 Fair value asset	Fair value liability
Derivative held for trading				
Currency derivatives	318	(226)	278	(273)
Oil price derivatives	1,140	(1,191)	3,813	(3,523)
Natural gas price derivative	5,636	(3,960)	6,945	(6,113)
Power price derivative	682	(497)	978	(904)
Other derivatives	47	(47)	90	(96)
	7,823	(5,921)	12,104	(10,909)
Embedded derivative commodity contracts	137	(1,468)	397	(2,264)
Cash flow hedges				
Currency forwards, futures and cylinders	182	(114)	120	(1,175)
Cross-currency interest rate swaps	44	(298)	109	(558)
	226	(412)	229	(1,733)
Fair value hedges				
Currency forwards, futures and swaps	490	(232)	465	(342)
Interest rate swaps	256	(122)	367	--
	746	(354)	832	(342)
Hedges of net investments in foreign operations	--	--	2	--
	8,932	(8,155)	13,564	(15,248)
Of which –current	4,967	(4,681)	8,510	(8,977)
–noncurrent	3,965	(3,474)	5,054	(6,271)

Derivatives held for trading

The group maintains active trading positions in a variety of derivatives. The contracts may be entered into for risk management purposes, to satisfy supply requirements or for entrepreneurial trading. Certain contracts are classified as held for trading, regardless of their original business objective, and are recognized at fair value with changes in fair value recognized in the income statement. Trading activities are undertaken by using a range of contract types in combination to create incremental gains by arbitraging prices between markets, locations and time periods. The net of these exposures is monitored using market value-at-risk techniques as described in Note 24.

The following tables show further information on the fair value of derivatives and other financial instruments held for trading purposes.

Derivative assets held for trading have the following fair values and maturities.

$ million 2009	Less than 1 year	1-2 years	2-3 years	3-4 years	4-5 years	Over 5 years	Total
Currency derivatives	162	83	33	22	16	2	318
Oil price derivative	814	136	69	59	44	18	1,140
Natural gas price derivatives	2,958	1,059	582	354	186	497	5,636
Power price derivatives	496	139	32	12	3	--	682
Other derivatives	47	--	--	--	--	--	47
	4,477	1,417	716	447	249	517	7,823

$ million 2008	Less than 1 year	1-2 years	2-3 years	3-4 years	4-5 years	Over 5 years	Total
Currency derivatives	53	90	67	37	20	11	278
Oil price derivative	3,368	353	61	11	11	9	3,813
Natural gas price derivatives	3,940	1,090	545	436	271	663	6,945
Power price derivatives	688	256	31	1	2	--	978
Other derivatives	90	--	--	--	--	--	90
	8,139	1,789	704	485	304	683	12,104

Derivative liabilities held for trading have the following fair values and maturities.

$ million 2009	Less than 1 year	1-2 years	2-3 years	3-4 years	4-5 years	Over 5 years	Total
Currency derivatives	(110)	(58)	(20)	(32)	(4)	(2)	(226)
Oil price derivative	(1,083)	(67)	(29)	(11)	(1)	--	(1,191)
Natural gas price derivatives	(2,381)	(607)	(248)	(222)	(78)	(424)	(3,960)
Power price derivatives	(335)	(109)	(39)	(11)	(3)	--	(497)
Other derivatives	(47)	--	--	--	--	--	(47)
	(3,956)	(841)	(336)	(276)	(86)	(426)	(5,921)
Currency derivatives	(257)	--	(2)	(1)	(13)	--	(273)
Oil price derivative	(3,001)	(458)	(36)	(18)	(9)	(1)	(3,523)
Natural gas price derivatives	(3,484)	(987)	(438)	(310)	(238)	(611)	(6,113)
Power price derivatives	(722)	(159)	(18)	(4)	(1)	--	(904)
Other derivatives	(95)	(1)	--	--	--	--	(96)
	(7,559)	(1,605)	(494)	(333)	(306)	(612)	(10,909)

If at inception of a contract the valuation cannot be supported by observable market data, any gain or loss determined by the valuation methodology is not recognized in the income statement but is deferred on the balance sheet and is commonly known as "day-one profit or loss." This deferred gain or loss is recognized in the income statement over the life of the contract until substantially all of the remaining contract term can be valued using observable market data at which point any remaining deferred gain or loss is recognized in the income statement. Changes in valuation from this initial valuation are recognized immediately through the income statement.

The following table shows the changes in the day-one profits and losses deferred on the balance sheet.

	2009		2008	
	Oil	Natural	Oil	Natural
$ million	price	gas price	price	gas price
Fair value of contracts not recognized through the income statement at January 1	32	83	--	36
Fair value of new contracts at inception not recognized in the income statement	--	(14)	66	49
Fair value recognized in the income statement	(11)	(36)	(34)	(2)
Fair value of contracts not recognized through the income statement at December 31	21	33	32	83

The table shows the fair value of derivative assets and derivative liabilities held for trading, analyzed by maturity period and by methodology of fair value estimation.

IFRS 7, *Financial Instruments: Disclosures*, sets out a fair value hierarchy which consists of three levels that describe the methodology of estimation as follows:

- Level 1—using quoted prices in active markets for identical assets or liabilities.
- Level 2—using inputs for the asset or liability, other than quoted prices, that are observable either directly (i.e., as prices) or indirectly (i.e., derived from prices).
- Level 3—using inputs for the asset or liability that are not based on observable market data such as prices based on internal models or other valuation methods.

This information is presented on a gross basis, that is, before netting by counterparty.

$million 2009	Less than 1 year	1-2 years	2-3 years	3-4 years	4-5 years	Over 5 years	Total
Fair value of derivative assets							
Level 1	163	76	23	17	10	1	290
Level 2	9,544	2,182	915	357	146	--	13,144
Level 3	264	188	162	148	128	527	1,417
	9,971	2,446	1,100	522	284	528	14,851
Less: netting by counterparty	(5,494)	(1,029)	(384)	(75)	(35)	(11)	(7,028)
	4,477	1,417	716	447	249	517	7,823

$million 2009	Less than 1 year	1-2 years	2-3 years	3-4 years	4-5 years	Over 5 years	Total
Fair value of derivative liabilities							
Level 1	(95)	(39)	14	(24)	--	(1)	(173)
Level 2	(9,086)	(1,681)	(597)	(234)	(47)	--	(11,645)
Level 3	(269)	(150)	(109)	(93)	(74)	(436)	(1,131)
	(9,450)	(1,870)	(720)	(351)	(121)	(437)	(12,949)
Less: netting by counterparty	5,494	1,029	384	75	35	11	7,028
	(3,956)	(841)	(336)	(276)	(86)	(426)	(5,921)
Net fair value	521	576	380	171	163	91	1,902
Fair value of derivative assets							
Level 1	40	43	30	7	6	2	128
Level 2	19,737	3,477	871	508	225	56	24,874
Level 3	687	196	148	140	137	672	1,980
	20,464	3,716	1,049	655	368	730	26,982
Less: netting by counterparty	(12,325)	(1,927)	(345)	(170)	(64)	(47)	(14,878)
	8,139	1,789	704	485	304	683	12,104
Fair value of derivative liabilities							
Level 1	(227)	--	(2)	--	(13)	--	(242)
Level 2	19,106	(3,345)	(683)	(356)	(217)	(27)	(23,734)
Level 3	(551)	(187)	(154)	(147)	(140)	(632)	(1,811)
	(19,884)	(3,532)	(839)	(503)	(370)	(659)	(25,787)
Less: netting by counterparty	12,325	1,927	345	170	64	47	14,878
	(7,559)	(1,605)	(494)	(333)	(306)	(612)	(10,909)
Net fair value	580	184	210	152	(2)	71	1,195

The following table shows the changes during the year in the net fair value of derivatives held for trading purposes within Level 3 of the fair value hierarchy.

$ million	Currency	Oil price	Natural gas price	Power price	Other	Total
Net fair value of contracts at January 1, 2009	3	149	17	--	--	169
Gains (losses) recognized in the income statement	(1)	205	91	--	(1)	294
Settlements	--	(91)	(5)	--	--	(96)
Purchases	--	--	--	1	--	1
Sales	--	--	--	(2)	1	(1)
Transfers out of Level 3	(2)	(50)	(4)	--	--	(56)
Transfers in to Level 3	--	2	(25)	--	--	(23)
Exchange adjustments	--	--	(2)	--	--	(2)
Net fair value of contracts at December 31, 2009	--	215	72	(1)	--	286
Net fair value of contracts at January 1, 2008	(17)	1	(67)	(1)	--	(84)
Gains (losses) recognized in the income statement	8	148	160	--	--	316
Settlements	--	18	3	1	--	22
Transfers out of Level 3	12	(25)	(79)	--	--	(92)
Transfers in to Level 3	--	7	3	--	--	10
Exchange adjustments	--	--	(3)	--	--	(3)
Net fair value of contracts at December 31, 2008	3	149	17	--	--	169

The amount recognized in the income statement for the year relating to Level 3 derivatives still held at December 31, 2009, was a $278 million gain (2008: $199 million gain relating to derivatives still held at December 31, 2008).

Gains and losses relating to derivative contracts are included either within sales and other operating revenues or within purchases in the income statement depending upon the nature of the activity and type of contract involved. The contract types treated in this way include futures options, swaps and certain forward sales and forward purchases contracts. Gains or losses arise on contracts entered into for risk management purposes, optimization activity and entrepreneurial trading. They also arise on certain contracts that are for normal procurement or sales activity for the group but that are required to be fair valued under accounting standards. Also included within sales and other operating revenues are gains and losses on inventory held for trading purposes. The total amount relating to all of these items was a net gain of $3,735 million (2008: $6,721 million net gain and 2007: $376 million net gain).

Embedded derivatives

Prior to the development of an active gas trading market, UK gas contracts were priced using a basket of available price indices, primarily relating to oil products, power and inflation. After the development of an active UK gas market, certain contracts were entered into or renegotiated using pricing formulae not directly related to gas prices, for example, oil product and power prices. In these circumstances, pricing formulae have been determined to be derivatives, embedded within the overall contractual arrangements that are not clearly and closely related to the underlying commodity. The resulting fair value relating to these contracts is recognized on the balance sheet with gains or losses recognized in the income statement.

All the embedded derivatives are valued using inputs that include price curves for each of the different products that are built up from active market pricing data. Where necessary, these are extrapolated to the expiry of the contracts (the last of which is in 2018) using all available external pricing information. Additionally, where limited data exists for certain products, prices are interpolated using historic and long-term pricing relationships.

Embedded derivative assets have the following fair values and maturities.

$ million 2009	Less than 1 year	1-2 years	2-3 years	3-4 years	4-5 years	Over 5 years	Total
Commodity price embedded derivatives	134	--	--	--	--	3	137

$ million 2008	Less than 1 year	1-2 years	2-3 years	3-4 years	4-5 years	Over 5 years	Total
Commodity price embedded derivatives	50	116	75	45	36	75	397

Embedded derivative liabilities have the following fair values and maturities.

$ million 2009	Less than 1 year	1-2 years	2-3 years	3-4 years	4-5 years	Over 5 years	Total
Commodity price embedded derivatives	(154)	(236)	(231)	(227)	(232)	(388)	(1,468)

$ million 2008	Less than 1 year	1-2 years	2-3 years	3-4 years	4-5 years	Over 5 years	Total
Commodity price embedded derivatives	(404)	(322)	(365)	(303)	(271)	(599)	(2,264)

The following table shows the fair value of embedded derivative assets and liabilities analyzed by maturity period and by methodology for fair value estimation.

$ million 2009	Less than 1 year	1-2 years	2-3 years	3-4 years	4-5 years	Over 5 years	Total
Fair value of embedded derivative assets							
Level 1	--	--	--	--	--	--	--
Level 2	--	--	--	--	--	--	--
Level 3	134	--	--	--	--	3	137
	134	--	--	--	--	3	137
Fair value of embedded derivative liabilities							
Level 1	--	--	--	--	--	--	--
Level 2	--	--	--	--	--	--	--
Level 3	(154)	(236)	(213)	(227)	(232)	(388)	(1,468)
	(154)	(236)	(213)	(227)	(232)	(388)	(1,468)
Net fair value	(20)	(236)	(213)	(227)	(232)	(385)	(1,331)

$ million 2008	Less than 1 year	1-2 years	2-3 years	3-4 years	4-5 years	Over 5 years	Total
Fair value of embedded derivative assets							
Level 1	--	--	--	--	--	--	--
Level 2	35	--	--	--	--	--	35
Level 3	15	116	75	45	36	75	362
	50	116	75	45	36	75	397
Fair value of embedded derivative liabilities							
Level 1	--	--	--	--	--	--	--
Level 2	(10)	--	--	--	--	--	(10)
Level 3	(394)	(322)	(365)	(303)	(271)	(599)	(2,254)
	(404)	(322)	(365)	(303)	(271)	(599)	(2,264)
Net fair value	(354)	(206)	(290)	(258)	(235)	(524)	(1,867)

The following table shows the changes during the year in the net fair value of embedded derivatives within Level 3 of the fair value hierarchy.

	2009			2008
$ million	Commodity price	Commodity price	Interest rate	Total
Net fair value of contracts at January 1	(1,892)	(2,146)	(33)	(2,179)
Settlements	221	414	38	452
Gains (losses) recognized in the income statement[a]	535	(1,011)	(5)	(1,016)
Exchange adjustments	(195)	851	--	851
Net fair value of contracts at December 31	(1,331)	(1,892)	--	(1,892)

[a] The amount for gains (losses) recognized in the income statement for 2009 includes a loss of $224 million arising as a result of refinements in the modeling and valuation methods used for these contracts.

The amount recognized in the income statement for the year relating to Level 3 embedded derivatives still held at December 31, 2009, was a $347 million gain (2008: $985 million loss relating to embedded derivatives still held at December 31, 2008).

The fair value gain (loss) on embedded derivatives is shown below.

$ million	2009	2008	2007
Commodity price embedded derivatives	607	(106)	--
Interest rate embedded derivatives	--	(5)	(7)
Fair value gain (loss)	607	(111)	(7)

Cash flow hedges

At December 31, 2009, the group held currency forwards and futures contracts and cylinders that were being used to hedge the foreign currency risk of highly probable forecast transactions, as well as cross-currency interest rate swaps to fix the US dollar interest rate and US dollar redemption value, with matching critical terms on the currency leg of the swap with the underlying non-US dollar debt issuance. Note 24 outlines the management of risk aspects for currency and interest rate risk. For cash flow hedges the group only claims hedge accounting for the intrinsic value on the currency with any fair value attributable to time value taken immediately to the income statement. There were no highly probable transactions for which hedge accounting has been claimed that have not occurred and no significant element of hedge ineffectiveness requiring recognition in the income statement. For cash flow hedges the pretax amount removed from equity during the period and included in the income statement is a loss of $366 million (2008: loss of $45 million and 2007: gain of $74 million). Of this, a loss of $332 million is included in production and manufacturing expenses (2008: $1 million loss and 2007: $143 million gain) and a loss of $34 million is included in finance costs (2008: $44 million loss and 2007: $69 million loss). The amount removed from equity during the period and included in the carrying amount of nonfinancial assets was a loss of $136 million (2008: $38 million gain and 2007: $40 million gain).

The amounts retained in equity at December 31, 2009, are expected to mature and affect the income statement by a $146 million gain in 2010, a loss of $26 million in 2011, and a loss of $65 million in 2012 and beyond.

Fair value hedges

At December 31, 2009, the group held interest rate and cross-currency interest rate swap contracts as fair value hedges of the interest rate risk on fixed rate debt issued by the group. The effectiveness of each hedge relationship is quantitatively assessed and demonstrated to continue to be highly effective. The loss on the hedging derivative instruments taken to the income statement in 2009 was $98 million (2008: $2 million gain and 2007: $334 million gain) offset by a gain on the fair value of the finance debt of $117 million (2008: $20 million loss and 2007: $327 million loss).

The interest rate and cross-currency interest rate swaps have an average maturity of four to five years, (2008: three to four years) and are used to convert sterling, euro, Swiss Franc, Australian dollar, Japanese yen and Hong Kong dollar denominated borrowings into US dollar floating rate debt. Note 24 outlines the group's approach to interest rate risk management.

Hedges of net investments in foreign operations

The group held currency swap contacts as a hedge of a long-term investment in a UK subsidiary that expired in 2009. At December 31, 2008, the hedge had a fair value of $2 million and the loss on the hedge recognized in equity in 2008 was $38 million (2007: $67 million loss). US dollars had been sold forward for sterling purchased and matched the underlying liability with no significant ineffectiveness reflected in the income statement.

MULTIPLE-CHOICE QUESTIONS

1.   What are the principal objectives of IFRS 7?
     (a)   To provide presentation and disclosure requirements for financial instruments.
     (b)   To require disclosures about the significance of financial instruments for an entity's financial position and financial performance and qualitative and quantitative information about exposure to risks arising from financial instruments.
     (c)   To set out specified balance sheet and income statement formats for financial entities.
     (d)   To require disclosures about an entity's exposure to off–balance sheet instruments and other complex transactions.

2.   Which of the following types of information does IFRS 7 **not** require to be disclosed about the significance of financial instruments?
     (a)   Carrying amounts of categories of financial instruments.
     (b)   Fair values of financial instruments.
     (c)   Information about the use of hedge accounting.
     (d)   Information about financial instruments, contracts, and obligations under share-based payment transactions.

3.   Which of the following types of information does IFRS 7 **not** require to be disclosed about exposure to risks arising from financial instruments?
     (a)   Qualitative and quantitative information about market risk.
     (b)   Qualitative and quantitative information about credit risk.
     (c)   Qualitative and quantitative information about operational risk.
     (d)   Qualitative and quantitative information about liquidity risk.

4.   How does IFRS 7 define "liquidity risk"?
     (a)   The risk that an entity will encounter difficulty in meeting obligations associated with financial liabilities.
     (b)   The risk that an entity will encounter difficulty in disposing a financial asset due to lack of market liquidity.
     (c)   The risk that an entity will encounter difficulty in meeting cash flow needs due to cash flow problems.
     (d)   The risk that an entity's cash inflows will not be sufficient to meet the entity's cash outflows.

5.   When is an entity required to apply IFRS 7 for the first time?
     (a)   For annual periods beginning on or after January 1, 2005.
     (b)   For annual periods beginning on or after January 1, 2006.
     (c)   For annual periods beginning on or after January 1, 2007.
     (d)   For annual periods beginning on or after January 1, 2010.

Chapter 39

OPERATING SEGMENTS (IFRS 8)

INTRODUCTION

The IASB issued IFRS 8, *Operating Segments,* in November 2006, effective for annual periods beginning on or after January 1, 2009. IAS 14, *Segment Reporting,* was the previous standard on segment reporting that was issued by the International Accounting Standards Committee (IASC), the IASB's predecessor.

Since its issuance in 2006, IFRS 8 has already been amended by the following three IFRS:

- IAS 1 (as revised in 2007), effective date January 1, 2009.
- IASB's annual improvements standard, "Improvements to IFRS 2009," effective date January 1, 2010.
- IAS 24, (as revised in 2009), effective date January 1, 2011 (with earlier application permitted).

As a result of the IASB's joint short-term convergence project with the US Financial Accounting Standards Board (FASB), which project was launched with the primary objective of reducing differences between IFRS and US GAAP, and based on research carried on by both standard setters, the IASB adopted the approach of the US Standard on segmental reporting, namely, SFAS 131, *Disclosures about Segments of an Enterprise and Related Information*, and revised its previous Standard on segment reporting.

The IASB believes that requiring entities to report segmental information using the approach prescribed by IFRS 8 (i.e., a "management approach") allows the financial statement user to review segmental information from the "eyes of the management" as opposed to a "risks and rewards" approach under its erstwhile standard on segment reporting.

Furthermore, with the issuance of this standard on segment reporting, the emphasis has shifted to disclosing segmental information for external reporting purposes based on internal reporting within the entity to its "chief operating decision maker." Therefore the cost and time needed to produce such segmental information is greatly reduced since most if not all of this information is already available with the entity, which in the case of public companies that are required to report on a quarterly basis is a distinct advantage.

SCOPE

IFRS 8 applies to both the separate or individual financial statements of an entity and to consolidated financial statements of a group within which the entity is the parent:

- Whose debt or equity instruments are publicly listed.
- That files, or is in the process of filing, its financial statements with a securities commission or other regulatory authority for the purpose of issuing any class of instruments in a public market.

The Standard clarifies that when both the parent's separate (stand-alone) financial statements and its consolidated financial statements are presented in the same financial report, segment information as required by IFRS 8 needs to be presented only for the consolidated financial statements.

Upon first adoption of IFRS 8, "comparatives," as reported under IAS 14, are required to be restated.

DEFINITIONS OF KEY TERMS

Operating segment. It is a component of the entity that engages in business activities from which it may or may not earn revenues and incur expenses and whose results are regularly reviewed by the chief operating decision maker to make decisions about resource allocations to segments and assess their performance and for which discrete financial information is available.

Reportable segment. Under IFRS 8 a publicly listed entity is required to report segmental information for an operating segment that has been identified by IFRS 8 and which has exceeded the quantitative thresholds (such as 10% of its reported revenue).

Chief operating decision maker (CODM). The term "CODM" identifies a function as opposed to a person and that function is allocating the entity's resources and assessing the performance of the entity.

CORE PRINCIPLE

According to the "core principle" of IFRS 8, an entity should disclose information to enable users of its financial statements to evaluate the *nature and financial effects* of the types of *business activities* in which it engages and the *economic environments* in which it operates.

CHIEF OPERATING DECISION MAKER

In some cases, the highest ranking individual in any organization may qualify as the Chief Operating Decision Maker (CODM). However, since the term CODM does not always refer to an individual, but to a function, in the case of a complex organizational and reporting setup (where decision-making responsibilities are split amongst the top management personnel), it could make the assessment of who the CODM is, difficult. In such a case, where it is difficult to determine the CODM, other factors, such as, who decides the management bonuses or who approves the financial information presented to the Board of Directors, may need to be considered as well.

The CODM could be the chief executive officer (CEO), the chief operating officer (COO), or the Board of Directors (Board), depending on who within the organization is responsible for the allocation of resources and assessing the performance of the entity's operating segments.

CASE STUDY 1

Facts

Goodwill Inc. is a company listed on an international stock exchange. It has four major lines of business, namely, manufacturing, retail, real estate, and telecommunications. Each major line of business has a chief operating officer ("COO") who is responsible for the business component's profitability. The company has a chief executive officer ("CEO") who is overall in charge of the entire business of the entity and reports to the Board of Directors ("Board") on the results of operations of Goodwill Inc. The CEO has the authority from the Board to decide on the performance bonus of each COO, for which the CEO has set key performance indications (KPIs) against which they are evaluated each year by the CEO. Discrete financial information for each of the major lines of business of Goodwill Inc. is available. The CEO has been entrusted by the Board to allocate funds for the day-to-day operations of the four lines of business, which he does based on criteria such as their comparative profitability, size of business generated, and cash flows from operations.

Required

Based on the previously mentioned details about the functioning of Goodwill Inc. and other relevant information provided, who is the CODM for the purposes of IFRS 8? Is it the Board, the CEO, or each COO for the line of business he or she is responsible for?

Solution

Firstly, a COO of any line of business of Goodwill Inc. is only responsible for the results of the line of business he or she is responsible for, but is certainly not responsible for the overall business of the entity and thus cannot qualify as the CODM. Secondly, while the Board is the highest authority in the hierarchy, the CEO has been given the required powers by the Board, that is, the power of allocation of resources and the power to assess the performance of the four major lines of business of the company. In accordance with the requirements of IFRS 8 the CODM is not the Board, but is the CEO.

OPERATING SEGMENTS

An "operating segment" is a component of an entity

- That engages in business activities from which it may earn revenues and incur expenses (including revenues and expenses relating to transactions with other components of the same entity).
- Whose operating results are reviewed regularly by the entity's chief operating decision maker to make decisions about resources to be allocated to the segment and assess its performance.
- For which discrete financial information is available.

CASE STUDY 2

Facts

Excellent Inc. is a publicly listed computer hardware dealership company. Based on the decision of the Board of Directors the entity is managed and controlled through three divisions, namely, the "spare parts division," the "workshop division," and the "sales division." Both the sales division and the workshop division deal with external customers and handle orders of both walk-in customers as well as long-term customers who have purchased computers through earlier sales through this dealership. The entity's spare parts division, however, only supplies spare parts to its workshop division and does not cater to the demands of any outside customers. In other words, if outside customers desire to purchase spare parts directly from the spare parts division of Excellent Inc. they cannot do so unless their computers are serviced by the workshop division of Excellent Inc. and the workshop division (of Excellent Inc.) purchases spare parts from its spare parts division for the purposes of undertaking repairs of computers they have been contracted to undertake repair work for.

The CODM, in this case the Board of Directors of Excellent Inc., allocates resources and assesses performance based on the results of the three components, namely, the spare parts division, the workshop division, and the sales division, for which Excellent Inc.'s financial controller maintains separate and discrete financial information.

Required

For the purposes of IFRS 8, how many operating segments should Excellent Inc. report segmental disclosures for?

Solution

IFRS 8 clearly specifies that some operating segments may derive their revenue solely or primarily from other segments of the same entity and, if they meet other requirements to qualify as operating segments, these segments cannot be precluded from qualifying as operating segments for the purposes of IFRS 8 reporting on the grounds that they do not derive their revenues from external sources. In other words, for the purposes of IFRS 8 a segment is not required to have external customers or revenues in order to be classified as an operating segment for financial reporting purposes. Therefore, all three divisions of Excellent Inc. qualify as "operating segments" for the purposes of IFRS 8.

REPORTABLE SEGMENTS

According to IFRS 8 an entity should report financial and descriptive information about its "reportable segments." Not all operating segments would automatically qualify as reportable segments. The Standard prescribes criteria for an operating segment to qualify as a reportable segment, and these alternative quantitative thresholds are set out below:

1. Its reported revenue, from both external customers and intersegment sales or transfers, is 10% or more of the combined revenue, internal and external, of all operating segments.
2. The absolute measure of its reported profit or loss is 10% or more of the greater, in absolute amount, of (1) the combined reported profit of all operating segments that did not report a loss and (2) the combined reported loss of all operating segments that reported a loss.
3. Its assets are 10% or more of the combined assets of all operating segments.

Furthermore, if the total revenue attributable to all operating segments (as identified by applying the "alternative quantitative thresholds criteria" aforementioned) constitutes less than 75% of the entity's total revenue as per its financial statements, the entity should look for additional operating segments until it is satisfied that at least 75% of the entity's revenue is captured through such a segmental reporting. In identifying the additional operating segments as reportable segments (i.e., for the purposes of meeting the 75% threshold) the Standard has relaxed its requirements of meeting the "alternative quantitative thresholds" criteria. In other words, an entity has to keep identifying more segments even if they do not meet the "alternative quantitative thresholds" test (set out previously) until at least 75% of the entity's revenue is included in reportable segments.

CASE STUDY 3

Revenue Test

Facts

Brilliant Inc. has five operating segments: electronics, restaurants, recreational clubs, travel agencies, car rental. Their revenues, both from external and internal sources, are as follows:

Revenue (in millions of $)

Segments	External	Internal	Total
Electronics	100	50	150
Restaurants	20	10	30
Recreational clubs	40	10	50
Travel agencies	75	25	100
Car rentals	60	40	100
Combined	295	135	430
Reconciling items & eliminations	(100)	(50)	(150)
Consolidated	195	85	280

Required

Based on the "revenue test" which of the following segments would qualify as "reportable segments"?

Solution

Based on the revenue test the following segments would qualify as reportable segments:

Electronics	$150 million vs $43 million = Yes
Restaurants	$ 30 million vs $43 million = No
Recreational clubs	$ 50 million vs $43 million = Yes
Travel agencies	$100 million vs $43 million = Yes
Car rentals	$100 million vs $43 million = Yes

DISCLOSURE REQUIREMENTS OF IFRS 8

IFRS 8 prescribes **extensive** segmental reporting disclosures. These include

1. *General information* about how the entity identified its operating segments and the types of products and services from which each operating segment derives its revenues.
2. Information about the *reported segment* profit or loss, including certain specified revenues and expenses included in segment profit or loss, segment assets, and segment liabilities, and the basis of measurement.
3. *Reconciliations* of the totals of segment revenues, reported segment profit or loss, segment assets, segment liabilities, and other material items to corresponding items in the entity's financial statements.

The Standard clarifies that certain **entity-wide disclosures** are required even when an entity has **only one reportable segment**. These disclosures include information about each product and service or groups of products and services.

The standard mandates **additional disclosures,** which are set out here:

1. Analyses of revenues and certain noncurrent assets by geographical area, with an expanded requirement to disclose revenues/assets by individual foreign country (if material), irrespective of identification of the operating segments.
2. Information about transactions with "major customers" (i.e., those customers that individually account for revenues of 10% or more of the entity's revenues).

Interim Reporting

Compared to its predecessor standard (IAS 14) the present IASB's segmental reporting standard *expands considerably* the disclosure of segment information at **interim reporting dates**.

Disclosure of the following segment information at interim reporting dates is prescribed by IAS 34:

- Revenues from external customers and intersegment revenues (these disclosures are required if they are included in the measure of segment profit or loss reviewed by or regularly provided to the "chief operating decision maker").
- A measure of segment profit or loss.
- Total assets for which there has been a material change from the amount disclosed in the last annual financial statements.
- A description of differences from the last annual financial statements in the basis of segmentation or in the basis of measurement of segment profit or loss.
- A reconciliation of the total of the reportable segments' measure of profit or loss to the entity's profit or loss before tax expense (tax income) and discontinued operations. If an entity allocates to reportable segments items such as tax expense or tax income, an entity may reconcile the total of the segments' measure of profit or loss to the profit or loss of the entity after those items. Material reconciling items shall be separately identified and described in that reconciliation.

Disclosure of segment information is required in an interim financial report of an entity only if that entity is required under IFRS 8 to disclose segment information in its annual financial statements.

MULTIPLE CHOICE QUESTIONS

1. Which one of the following disclosures is not required under IFRS 8?

   (a) The total amount of revenues from a major external customer (with revenues from that external customer exceeding 50% of the entity's revenues).

   (b) The identity (say, the name) of a major customer that accounts for 20% of the entity's revenues.

   (c) Revenue from external customers attributed to the entity's country of domicile and attributed to all foreign countries in total from which the entity derives revenues (assuming that necessary information is available and the cost to develop it is not excessive).

   (d) Revenues from external customers for each product and service, or each group of similar products and services, unless the necessary information is not available and the cost to develop it would be excessive.

2. IFRS 8 requires that an entity should provide reconciliations of segment information to the entity's financial information. One of the following reconciliations is not required by IFRS 8. Which one is it?

   (a) The total of the reporting segments' revenues to the entity's revenues.

   (b) The total of the reportable segments' measures of profit or loss to the entity's profit or loss before tax expense (tax income) and discontinued operations, and if the entity allocates to reportable segments items such as tax expense (tax income), the entity may reconcile the total of the segments' measures of profit or loss to the entity's profit or loss after those items.

   (c) The total number of major customers of all segments to the total number of major customers of the entity.

   (d) The total of the reportable segments' assets to the entity's assets.

3. Which one of the following statements is **not** true in the context of IFRS 8?

   (a) The present IASB standard on segmental reporting requires entities to report segmental information using a "management approach" that allows the financial statement user to review segmental information from the "eyes of the management."

   (b) The "core principle" of IFRS 8 requires that an entity should disclose information to enable users of its financial statements to evaluate the nature and fi-

nancial effects of the types of business activities in which it engages and the economic environments in which it operates.

   (c) If an entity that is not required to apply IFRS 8 (such as an entity whose equity or debt is not traded in a public market) but still chooses to disclose information about segments in its financial statements, it shall not describe the information as segment information.

   (d) The present IASB standard on segmental reporting requires entities to report segmental information using a "risks and rewards" approach.

4. Not all operating segments would automatically qualify as reportable segments. IFRS 8 prescribes criteria for an operating segment to qualify as a reportable segment; these are alternative quantitative thresholds. One of the quantitative thresholds listed below is not a requirement of IFRS 8. Which one is it?

   (a) Its reported revenue, from both external customers and intersegment sales or transfers, is 10% or more of the combined revenue, internal and external, of all operating segments.

   (b) The absolute measure of its reported profit or loss is 10% or more of the greater, in absolute amount, of (1) the combined reported profit of all operating segments that did not report a loss and (2) the combined reported loss of all operating segments that reported a loss.

   (c) Its assets are 10% or more of the combined assets of all operating segments.

   (d) Its assets are 20% or more of the combined assets of all operating segments.

5. Which statement is **not** true with respect to a "chief operating decision maker" as envisaged by IFRS 8?

   (a) The term "chief operating decision maker" identifies a function and not necessarily a manager with a specific title.

   (b) In some cases the "chief operating decision maker" could be its chief operating officer.

   (c) The Board of directors (Board), acting collectively, could qualify as the "chief operating decision maker."

   (d) The chief internal auditor who reports to (and takes directions from) the Board usually plays a very important role in any organization and would generally qualify as a "chief operating decision maker."

Chapter 40

FINANCIAL INSTRUMENTS (IFRS 9)

INTRODUCTION AND PURPOSE

The International Accounting Standards Board (IASB) issued IFRS 9 Financial Instruments in November 2009. This is the first installment of a phased replacement of the existing standard IAS 39, *Financial Instruments: Recognition and Measurement*. This Standard introduces new requirements for the classification and measurement of financial assets and is effective from January 1, 2013, with early adoption permitted.

New requirements for classification and measurement of financial liabilities, derecognition of financial instruments, impairment, and hedge accounting are to be added to IFRS 9 in 2011.

Early adoption of the standard is a major step for any entity as an early adopter of IFRS 9 continues to apply IAS 39 for other accounting requirements for financial instruments that are not covered by IFRS 9, that is, classification and measurement of financial liabilities, recognition and derecognition of financial assets and financial liabilities, impairment of financial assets, and hedge accounting.

In some jurisdictions, the new standards will have to be adopted before they can be applied and in others there will be some restrictions on early adoption. It would seem wise to wait until the whole of the new standard has been finalized.

The aim of the revision of IAS 39 is to remove inconsistencies between US GAAP and IFRS and to improve IFRS in accounting for financial instruments.

This will enable comparisons to be made more easily between entities applying IFRS and those using US GAAP.

IFRS 9 was a first step in this direction. In order to work towards convergence of their requirements, both the IASB and the US Financial Accounting Standards Board (FASB) are reconsidering the financial instruments standards.

Scope of IFRS 9: Phase 1 of IFRS 9 is applicable to all financial assets within the scope of IAS 39.

CLASSIFICATION

The standard retains a mixed measurement model with some assets measured at amortized cost and others at fair value. The distinction between the two models is based on the business model of each entity and a requirement to assess whether the cash flows of the instrument are only principal and interest.

At initial recognition, all financial assets (including hybrid contracts with a financial asset host) are measured at fair value.

For subsequent measurement, financial assets that are debt instruments are classified at amortized cost or fair value on the basis of both

1. The entity's business model for managing the financial assets.
2. The contractual cash flow characteristics of the financial asset.

Debt instruments may be subsequently measured at amortized cost if

1. The asset is held within a business model whose objective is to hold the asset to collect the contractual cash flows.
2. The contractual terms of the financial asset give rise, on specified dates, to cash flows that are solely payments of principal and interest on the principal outstanding.

All other debt instruments are subsequently measured at fair value.

Equity Investments

All financial assets that are equity investments are measured at fair value either through Other Comprehensive Income (OCI) or profit or loss.

This is an irrevocable choice the entity makes instrument by instrument unless the equity investments are held for trading, in which case, they must be measured at fair value through profit or loss.

THE BUSINESS MODEL TEST

The business model approach is fundamental to the standard and is an attempt to align the accounting with the way in which management uses its assets in its business while also looking at the characteristics of the business. A debt instrument generally must be measured at amortized cost if both the "business model test" and the "contractual cash flow characteristics test" are to be satisfied.

If the financial asset does not meet both of these conditions, then it is measured at fair value.

The business model test is whether the objective of the entity's business model is to hold the financial asset to collect the contractual cash flows rather than have the objective to sell the instrument prior to its contractual maturity to realize its fair value changes.

The assessment of a "business model" is not made at an individual financial instrument level. In addition, the assessment is based on how key management personnel actually manage the business, rather than management's intent for specific financial assets.

An entity may have more than one business model for managing its financial assets, and the classification need not be determined at the reporting entity level. As such, an entity needs to use judgment to determine the level at which this condition should be applied.

The application guidance in the IFRS gives examples to help explain the concept of "business model."

Example 1

An entity holds investments to collect their contractual cash flows, but would sell the investment in particular circumstances. For example, an investment may be sold if

1. The instrument no longer meets the entity's investment policy (e.g., the credit rating of the instrument falls below that required by the entity's investment policy).
2. The entity is an insurer and adjusts its portfolio to reflect a change in expected duration (i.e., the expected timing of payouts).
3. An entity needs to fund capital expenditures.

Discussion

Although an entity may consider, among other information, the financial assets' fair values from a liquidity perspective (i.e., the cash amount that would be realized if the entity needs to sell assets), the entity's objective is to hold the financial assets and collect the contractual cash flows. Some sales would not contradict that objective.

However, if more than an infrequent number of sales are made out of a portfolio, the entity needs to assess whether and how such sales are consistent with an objective of collecting contractual cash flows.

Example 2

An entity's business model is to purchase portfolios of financial assets, such as loans. Those portfolios may or may not include financial assets with incurred credit losses. If payment on the loans is not made on a timely basis, the entity attempts to extract the contractual cash flows through various means—for example, by contacting the debtor through mail, telephone, etc.

In some cases, the entity enters into interest rate swaps to change the interest rate on particular financial assets in a portfolio from a floating interest rate to a fixed interest rate.

Discussion

The objective of the entity's business model is to hold the financial assets and collect the contractual cash flows. The entity does not purchase the portfolio to make a profit by selling them. The same analysis would apply even if the entity does not anticipate collecting all of the contractual cash flows (e.g., some of the assets have incurred credit losses). Moreover, as long as the entity holds the assets in the portfolio to collect their contractual cash flows, the fact that the entity entered into interest rate swaps does not in itself change the entity's business model. If the portfolio is not managed on a fair value basis, the objective of the business model could be to collect the contractual cash flows.

Example 3

An entity has a business model with the objective of originating loans to subsequently sell those loans to a securitization vehicle. The vehicle issues instruments to investors.

The originating entity controls the vehicle and thus consolidates it. The consolidated entity collects the contractual cash flows from the loans and passes them on to the investors in the vehicle.

It is assumed, for the purposes of this example, that the loans continue to be recognized in the consolidated entity's statement of financial position, as they are not derecognized by the securitization vehicle.

Discussion

The consolidated entity originates the loans with the objective of holding them to collect contractual cash flows. However, the originating entity has an objective of realizing cash flows on the loan portfolio by selling the loans to the securitization vehicle, so for the purposes of its separate financial statements, it would not be considered to be managing this portfolio in order to collect the contractual cash flows.

Example 4

An entity actively manages a portfolio of assets in order to realize fair value changes arising from changes in credit spreads and yield curves.

Discussion

The entity's objective results in active buying and selling, and the entity is managing the instruments to realize fair value gains rather than collect cash flows.

All recognized financial assets that are currently in the scope of IAS 39 will be measured at either amortized cost or fair value. The standard contains only the two primary measurement categories for financial assets, unlike IAS 39 where there were multiple measurement categories.

Thus the existing IAS 39 categories of held to maturity, loans and receivables, and available for sale are eliminated along with the tainting provisions of the standard.

A debt instrument (e.g., loan receivable) that is held within a business model whose objective is to collect the contractual cash flows and has contractual cash flows that are solely payments of principal and interest generally must be measured at amortized cost. All other debt instruments must be measured at fair value through profit or loss (FVTPL).

An investment in a convertible loan note would not qualify for measurement at amortized cost because of the inclusion of the conversion option, which is not deemed to represent payments of principal and interest.

This criterion will permit amortized cost measurement when the cash flows on a loan are entirely fixed, such as a fixed interest rate loan or where interest is floating or a combination of fixed and floating interest rates.

While the approach used in IFRS 9 eliminates the "tainting rules" relating to disposal of held-to-maturity investments under IAS 39, there will be a need for judgment in determining whether a portfolio is held for the collection of contractual cash flows or for realizing fair value changes.

CONTRACTUAL TERMS OF FINANCIAL ASSET TEST

Once an entity determines that the business model is to hold the assets to collect the contractual cash flows, it must assess whether the contractual terms of the financial asset give rise, on specified dates, to cash flows that are solely payments of principal and interest on the principal outstanding.

Interest is defined as the consideration for the time value of money and the credit risk associated with the principal amount outstanding during a particular period of time. Leverage is a contractual cash flow characteristic that amplifies the variability of contractual cash flows, which would not have the economic characteristics of interest.

Derivatives, such as options, forward and swap contracts, include leverage and therefore cannot be carried at amortized cost.

An instrument that is subordinated to other instruments that is ranked relative to general creditors may still have contractual cash flows of principal and interest. For example, trade receivables would generally qualify for amortized cost classification even if the debtor issued loans that are collateralized.

An important change from IAS 39 is that "whether or not the instrument is quoted in an active market" is not relevant for the measurement basis under IFRS 9.

However, unlike leverage, certain contractual provisions will not cause the "solely payments of principal and interest" test to be failed. For example, contractual provisions that permit the issuer to prepay a debt instrument or permit the holder to put a debt instrument back to the issuer before maturity result in contractual cash flows that are solely payments of principal and interest as long as the following certain conditions are met:

- The prepayment amount substantially represents unpaid amounts of principal and interest on the principal amount outstanding (which may include reasonable additional compensation for the early termination of the contract).
- The prepayment amount is not contingent on future events other than to protect the holder against the issuer's credit deterioration, or a change of control of the issuer or against changes in tax or law. Contractual provisions that permit the issuer or holder to extend the contractual term of a debt instrument are also regarded as being solely payments of principal and interest, provided that, during the term of the extension, the contractual cash flows are solely payments of principal and interest as well and the provision is not contingent on future events. For example, the interest rate does not step up to some leveraged multiple of LIBOR.

Examples of instruments that qualify for amortized cost accounting are as follows:

Example 5

A bond with a stated maturity date and payments of principal and interest are linked to an unleveraged inflation index of the currency in which the instrument is issued. The contractual cash flows are only payments of principal and interest. This linkage resets the time value of money to the current level. In other words, the interest rate on the instrument reflects "real" interest. Thus, the interest amounts are consideration for the time value of money on the principal amount outstanding.

Example 6

An instrument with a variable interest rate and a stated maturity date for which the borrower can choose a market interest rate on an ongoing basis. For example, at each interest rate reset date, the borrower can choose to pay three-month LIBOR for a three-month term or one-month LIBOR for a one-month term. The contractual cash flows are only payments of principal and interest as long as the interest paid over the life of the instrument reflects consideration for the time value of money and the credit risk associated with the instrument. The fact that the interest rate is reset during the life of the instrument does not in itself disqualify the instrument from amortized cost treatment.

Example 7

A bond with a stated maturity date. The bond pays a variable market interest rate, which is capped. As long as the interest reflects consideration for the time value of money and the credit risk associated with the instrument, amortized cost can be used. The instrument is similar to a combination of a fixed and floating-rate bond, as the cap reduces the variability of the cash flows.

Example 8

A full recourse loan secured by collateral. The fact that a full recourse loan is collateralized does not in itself affect the analysis of whether the contractual cash flows are only payments of principal and interest.

Examples of instruments that will **not** qualify for amortized cost accounting:

Example 9

The instrument is a bond convertible into equity instruments of the issuer. The contractual cash flows are not payments of principal and interest because the interest rate does not reflect only consideration for the time value of money and the credit risk, and the return is also linked to the value of the equity of the issuer.

Example 10

An inverse floating interest rate loan. The criterion is not met because interest has an inverse relationship to market rates and so does not represent consideration for the time value of money and credit risk.

Example 11

A perpetual instrument that is callable at any time by the issuer at par plus accrued interest but for which interest is only payable if the issuer remains solvent after payment and any deferred interest does not accrue additional interest. The criterion is not met as the issuer may defer payments and additional interest does not accrue on the amounts deferred. As a result, the holder is not entitled to the consideration for the time value of money and credit risk.

Any contractual term that is not genuine does not affect the classification of the financial asset.

The standard says that an entity should assess whether contractual cash flows are solely payments of principal and interest on the principal outstanding for the currency in which the financial asset is denominated. Thus a dual currency bond is likely to fail the criteria for utilizing amortized cost.

PRACTICAL INSIGHT

IFRS 9 states that interest is compensation for the time value of money and credit risk and may be fixed on recognition. The standard seems to indicate that credit risk may not be initially fixed but can change according to the creditworthiness of the borrower. If this causes variations in the contractual cash flows, then consideration should be given as to whether amortized cost can be used.

Entities may have to exercise judgment in order to determine whether cash flows from an instrument are leveraged and whether they increase the variability of contractual cash flows in a manner inconsistent with the amortized cost criteria.

MEASUREMENT

IFRS 9 retains a fair value option and at initial recognition, entities can elect to measure financial assets and financial liabilities that would otherwise qualify for amortized cost measurement, at fair value through profit or loss, provided the use of fair value eliminates or significantly reduces a measurement or recognition inconsistency, that is, an accounting mismatch.

An example of this may be where an entity holds a fixed-rate loan receivable that it hedges with an interest rate swap that swaps the fixed rates for floating rates. Measuring the loan asset at amortized cost would create a measurement mismatch, as the interest rate swap would be held at FVTPL. In this case the loan receivable could be designated at FVTPL under the fair value option to reduce the accounting mismatch that arises from measuring the loan at amortized cost.

The other criteria for the use of FVTPL currently contained in IAS 39 will no longer be needed. If an entity's business model is to manage financial assets on a fair value basis, the assets concerned cannot qualify for classification at amortized cost, and embedded derivatives are no longer separated (see ahead).

All equity investments within the scope of IFRS 9 are to be measured in the statement of financial position at fair value with the default recognition of gains and losses in profit or loss.

Only if the equity investment is not held for trading can an irrevocable election be made at initial recognition to measure it at fair value through other comprehensive income (FVTOCI) with only dividend income recognized in profit or loss.

The amounts recognized in OCI are not recycled to profit or loss on disposal of the investment although they may be reclassified in equity.

The standard eliminates the exemption allowing some unquoted equity instruments and related derivative assets to be measured at cost. As a limited concession, IFRS 9 states that cost may be the best estimate of fair value, if there is no, or insufficient, information available. It also provides guidance as to when cost is not appropriate and on the rare circumstances where the cost of such an instrument may be an appropriate estimate of fair value.

The following are indicators of when cost might not be representative of fair value for unquoted equity instruments:

1. A significant change in the performance of the investee company compared with the budget plan or milestone
2. Changes in expectation that technical milestones will be achieved
3. A significant change in the market for the investee company or its products or potential products

CASE STUDY 1

Facts

Amber is a start-up company and Light holds all of the share capital of the entity. Light wishes to value the financial asset at cost as there is very little information about value of the investment.

Required

Can the investment in Amber be valued at cost?

Solution

As Amber is a start-up company, performance even in accordance with original plans may lead to a significant increase in value as uncertainty over the future is removed. This means that even if there are no significant changes in performance over plan, cost may not be an appropriate estimate of fair value.

RECLASSIFICATION

The classification of an instrument is determined on initial recognition, and reclassifications are only permitted on the change of an entity's business model and are expected to occur only infrequently.

If an instrument is reclassified from amortized cost to fair value, it should be measured at fair value on that date with any difference between the carrying amount and fair value recognized in a separate line in the income statement. If an instrument is reclassified from fair value to amortized cost, the fair value of the instrument on the date of reclassification becomes its new carrying amount.

An example of where reclassification from amortized cost to fair value might be required would be when an entity decides to close its mortgage business, is no longer accepting new business, and is actively marketing its mortgage portfolio for sale.

When a reclassification is required it is applied from the first day of the first reporting period following the change in business model.

Example of change in business model allowing reclassification

An entity has a portfolio of commercial loans that it holds to sell in the short term. The entity acquires a company that manages commercial loans and has a business model that holds the loans to collect the contractual cash flows. The portfolio of commercial loans is no longer for sale, and the portfolio is now managed together with the acquired commercial loans and all are held to collect the contractual cash flows.

Examples of change in business model not allowing reclassification

1. A change in intention related to specific financial assets even in circumstances of significant changes in market conditions
2. A temporary disappearance of a particular market for financial assets
3. A transfer of financial assets between existing business models

If the entity reclassifies financial assets in accordance with IFRS 9, the entity is required to disclose the date of reclassification and the amount reclassified into or out of each category. In addition, a detailed explanation of the change in business model and a qualitative description has to be shown.

CASE STUDY 2

Facts

Garby wishes to reclassify its financial assets and does not understand the implications of IFRS 9. The entity wishes to reclassify and immediately use the new classifications in its financial statements.

Required

Advise Garby on the procedures for reclassification.

Solution

The date at which reclassification comes into effect is the beginning of the next reporting period. This may lead to a gap period during which financial assets continue to be accounted for as if the business model had not changed, even though this no longer reflects the business model in operation. The reason behind this is to prevent entities choosing a reclassification date, which affects the profit or loss.

EMBEDDED DERIVATIVES

IFRS 9 removes the requirement to separate derivatives embedded in financial host instruments.

Instead, the asset in its entirety is measured at amortized cost, or fair value, depending on the business model and the instrument's cash flow characteristics.

IFRS 9 does not retain IAS 39's approach to accounting for embedded derivatives.

Consequently, embedded derivatives that would have been separately accounted for at FVTPL under IAS 39 because they were not closely related to the financial asset host will no longer be separated. Instead, the contractual cash flows of the financial asset are assessed as a whole and are measured at FVTPL if any of its cash flows do not represent payments of principal and interest.

As a consequence, some embedded derivatives that were not separated under IAS 39 will result in the entire hybrid contract not being eligible for the amortized cost category, for example debt instruments with leveraged indexation on interest rate variables.

If the host contract is not within the scope of IFRS 9, the existing requirements for the separation of embedded derivatives will continue to apply. However, these requirements are expected to be revisited when the Board reviews the scope of IFRS 9.

CASE STUDY 3

Facts

Edel owns convertible bonds, which can be converted into a fixed number of equity shares of the issuer. Under IAS 39 the bond is held for trading and has been bifurcated into the conversion option and host debt instrument.

Required

How will this be treated under IFRS 9?

Solution

Under IFRS 9, the bond is analyzed for classification in its entirety and the presence of the conversion option means it cannot be measured using amortized cost. Thus the bond would be accounted for at FVTPL. IFRS 9 does not change the accounting for embedded derivatives with host contracts that are not financial assets.

LOANS AND RECEIVABLES, AND HELD TO MATURITY

The existing categories in IAS 39 of held-to-maturity, loans and receivables are eliminated.

Many loans and receivables and held-to-maturity investments will continue to be measured at amortized cost, but some will have to be measured instead at FVTPL.

For example some instruments, such as cash-collateralized debt obligations, that may under IAS 39 have been measured entirely at amortized cost or as available-for-sale, will more likely be measured at FVTPL.

Some financial assets that are currently disaggregated into host financial assets that are not at FVTPL will instead by measured at FVTPL in their entirety.

Assets that are currently classified as held-to-maturity are likely to continue to be measured at amortized cost as they are held to collect the contractual cash flows and often give rise to only payments of principal and interest.

IMPAIRMENT AND AVAILABLE FOR SALE

IFRS 9 does not address impairment.

However as IFRS 9 eliminates the available-for-sale (AFS) category, it also eliminates the AFS impairment rules.

Under IAS 39, measuring impairment losses on debt securities in illiquid markets based on fair value often led to reporting an impairment loss that exceeded the credit loss that management expected.

Additionally, impairment losses on AFS equity investments cannot be reversed under IAS 39 if the fair value of the investment increases.

Under IFRS 9, debt securities that qualify for the amortized cost model are measured under that model and declines in equity investments measured at FVTPL are recognized in profit or loss and reversed through profit or loss if the fair value increases.

PRACTICAL INSIGHT

One of the most frequent questions is whether IFRS 9 will result in more financial assets being measured at fair value. It will depend on the circumstances of each entity in terms of the way it manages the instruments it holds, the nature of those instruments, and the classification elections it makes. One of the most significant changes will be the ability to measure some debt instruments, for example investments in government and corporate bonds, at amortized cost. Many available-for-sale debt instruments currently measured at fair value will qualify for amortized cost accounting.

OTHER ISSUES

Two particular types of instrument are likely to pose difficulties: nonrecourse loans and securitized debt. The Standard indicates that some financial assets may have cash flows, which are described as principal and interest but do not in fact represent payment of such.

The example is given of nonrecourse debt where the creditor's claim is limited to certain assets or cash flows and where the contractual cash flows arising from the debt may not exclusively represent the payment of principal and interest—for example, they may include the time value of money and the credit risk involved.

However, the fact that a debt is nonrecourse does not necessarily mean that it cannot be classified at amortized cost. A holder of a nonrecourse instrument, in which the lender is entitled only to repayment from specific assets or cash flows, must look through to the ring-fenced assets or cash flows to determine whether payments arising from the contract meet the "contractual cash flow characteristics" test.

If the terms of the debt give rise to any other cash flows or limit the cash flows in a manner inconsistent with payments of principal and interest, it does not meet the test. Thus, for example, a nonrecourse property loan in which the return earned by the lender is significantly dependent upon the performance of the secured property may not meet the test.

IFRS 9 gives guidance in circumstances where an entity prioritizes payments to holders of multiple contractually linked instruments. Although an important objective of the Standard was to simplify financial instrument accounting, it was not possible to find a simple way to classify contractually linked instruments that create concentrations of credit risk, that is, the tranches of securitized debt.

The complexity arises because the junior tranches provide credit protection to the more senior tranches and the characteristics of the tranches depend on the underlying instruments held.

The right to payments on more junior tranches depends on the issuer's generation of sufficient cash flows to pay more senior tranches.

IFRS 9 takes a "look-through" approach to determine whether measurement at amortized cost is available.

A tranche meets the criterion if the following three conditions are met:

1. The contractual terms of the tranche being assessed have cash flow characteristics that are solely payments of principal and interest.
2. The underlying pool contains one or more instruments that have contractual cash flows that are solely payments of principal and interest, and any other instruments either

   a. Reduce the cash flow variability of other such instruments and result in cash flows that are solely payments of principal and interest (e.g., interest rate caps and floors, credit protection) or
   b. Align the cash flows of the tranches with the cash flows of the underlying pool of instruments to address differences in whether the interest rate is fixed or floating or the currency or timing of cash flows.

3. The exposure to credit risk in the tranche is equal to, or lower than, the exposure to credit risk of the underlying pool of instruments.

IFRS 9 states that this latter condition would be met if, in all circumstances in which the underlying pool of instruments loses 50% as a result of credit losses, the tranche would lose 50% or less.

If any instrument in the underlying pool does not meet the above conditions or if the pool can change in a way that would not meet these conditions, then the tranche cannot use amortized cost.

CASE STUDY 4

Facts

Exel is a special-purpose entity, which has issued two tranches of debt which are linked by contract. The first tranche has a value of $8 million and the second tranche is valued at $4 million. The second tranche is subordinated to the first tranche and receives distributions after payments to the first tranche. Exel has loans of $12 million, which are carried at amortized cost. The contractual terms of the first tranche only give rise to payments of principal and interest.

Required

Discuss how an investor in the two tranches should account for them in their financial statements.

Solution

An investor will have to look through to the investments of Excel, which are measured at amortized cost. The pool has at least one instrument with cash flows of principal and interest and Exel has no other instruments. Therefore the instruments held by Exel do not have any prohibitive features. The exposure to credit risk must be analyzed.

If the pool of loans were to lose 50%, then a loss of $6 million would arise. Of that loss $4 million would be absorbed by the second tranche, leaving $2 million to be absorbed by the first tranche. This means that the ratio of loss of tranche one would be $2 million/$8 million, that is, 25%. This is obviously less than 50%, which means the credit risk is lower than the credit risk of the underlying pool of assets. Therefore the first tranche can use amortized cost.

Tranche two does not meet the criterion because investors in this tranche lose 100% and therefore an investor should value the investment at fair value.

CASE STUDY 5

Facts

Bage has a financial asset that was accounted for as a loan and receivable under IAS 39 but under IFRS 9 it needs to be reclassified as FVTPL. Bage manages the asset together with an existing liability, which is accounted for at amortized cost.

Required

Bage wonders whether designating the liability at amortized cost under IFRS 9 would produce an accounting mismatch.

Solution

If at the date of the initial recognition, Bage feels that by designating the liability at FVTPL would reduce an accounting mismatch compared to measuring the liability at amortized cost and the financial asset at FVTPL, then Bage could designate the liability at FVTPL.

EQUITY INVESTMENTS AT FAIR VALUE THROUGH OTHER COMPREHENSIVE INCOME

IFRS 9 allows an option to designate nontrading equity investments at fair value through OCI upon initial recognition. Such a designation is irrevocable. However IFRS 9 requires that dividends received from these investments be recognized in profit or loss, unless they represent a recovery of part of the cost of investment.

Fair value changes in these investments will be recognized in OCI, without recycling of gains and losses between profit or loss and OCI, even on impairment or on sale or disposal of the investment.

For equity investments designated at fair value through OCI, an entity needs to make several additional disclosures, including the reasons for using this presentation alternative, the fair value of each such investment at the end of the reporting period, and dividends recognized.

EFFECTIVE DATE AND TRANSITION

The mandatory effective date for IFRS 9 will be January 1, 2013, with early adoption of Phase 1 permitted for reporting periods ending on or after December 31, 2009.

In some jurisdictions, the local authority is required to endorse the Standard before it becomes available for adoption in that jurisdiction.

IFRS 9 is required to be applied retrospectively. However, the assessment of whether instruments are to be measured at amortized cost or fair value will need to be made for instruments on the entity's statement of financial position, based on facts and circumstances existing as at the initial application date.

The determination of whether an instrument is "held for trading" is also made as at the initial application date. It is also possible to redesignate financial assets at fair value through profit or loss using the fair value as at the date of initial application and to apply the new designation retrospectively.

Entities will be allowed to redesignate financial liabilities at fair value through profit or loss, even though they are not otherwise within the scope of the Standard, to avoid measurement mismatches when there is a required change in the treatment of financial assets under IFRS 9.

Comparative figures are required to be restated. However, some transitional relief is available for early adopters.

CASE STUDY 6

Facts

Hant has an equity investment, which was measured at cost under IAS 39. The fair value of the investment is $6 million and the carrying value is $4 million. Hant has decided that the date of initial accounting for IFRS 9 is December 1, 20X9, and its period end is December 31, 20X9.

Required

How would the investment be treated on transition to IFRS 9?

Solution

The difference between the carrying amount and the fair value is recognized in opening retained earnings ($2 million) of the period of initial recognition which would be January 1, 20X0. Any fair value changes between December 1 and December 31, 20X9, are recognized in profit or loss unless Hant designates the investment as FVOCI.

MULTIPLE-CHOICE QUESTIONS

1. IFRS 9, *Financial Instruments,* deals with the measurement and classification of which of the following items?
- (a) Financial assets.
- (b) Impairment of assets.
- (c) Financial liabilities.
- (d) Hedge accounting.

2. Early adoption of IFRS 9 is permitted under the Standard. However there are obstacles to early adoption. Which of the following issues should not be an obstacle to early adoption?
- (a) In some jurisdictions early adoption may not be permitted.
- (b) In some jurisdictions IFRS 9 will not be adopted quickly.
- (c) Early adoption is a major step for an entity, as IAS 39 has to be used where there is no new standard.
- (d) Lack of training of staff.

3. IFRS 9 uses a mixed-model approach to measurement. Which of the following measurement methods are acceptable under IFRS 9?
- (a) Amortized cost, fair value, and replacement cost.
- (b) Amortized cost, fair value, and net realizable value.
- (c) Amortized cost and fair value.
- (d) Amortized cost, fair value, and depreciated replacement cost.

4. How does IFRS 9 distinguish between the measurement methods to be used in the standard?
- (a) By reviewing the business model of each entity and the risks and rewards of the transaction.
- (b) By reviewing the business model of each entity and the contractual cash flow characteristics of the instrument.
- (c) By reviewing the realizability and the contractual cash flow characteristics of the instrument.
- (d) By reviewing the realizability of the instrument and risks and rewards of ownership.

5. Under what circumstances can the profit or loss on an equity instrument carried at fair value be dealt with in Other Comprehensive Income?
- (a) When the equity investment is not held for trading.
- (b) When the profit or loss is capable of recycling.
- (c) When the equity investment is available for sale.
- (d) When the equity investment is held for trading.

6. Under what circumstances under IFRS 9 can an entity classify financial assets that meet the amortized cost criteria as at FVTPL?
- (a) Where the instrument is held to maturity.
- (b) Where the business model approach is adopted.
- (c) Where the financial asset passes the contractual cash flow characteristics test.
- (d) If doing so eliminates or reduces an accounting mismatch.

7. When can the classification of an instrument which has been determined on initial recognition, be changed?
- (a) Reclassifications are only permitted on the change of the contractual cash flows.
- (b) Reclassifications are only permitted on the change of an entity's business model and are expected to occur only infrequently.
- (c) Reclassifications are only permitted where a category becomes tainted.
- (d) Reclassifications are not permitted.

8. In what way does IFRS 9 require embedded derivatives to be accounted for?
- (a) Embedded derivatives that would have been separately accounted for at FVTPL under IAS 39 because they were not closely related to the financial asset host will have to be separated.
- (b) Embedded derivatives that would have been separately accounted for at FVTPL under IAS 39 because they were not closely related to the financial asset host will no longer be separated.
- (c) Embedded derivatives are accounted for at amortized cost.
- (d) Embedded derivatives are accounted for at fair value with gains and losses going to OCI.

9. Which of the following events will not necessarily be a consequence of IFRS 9?
- (a) Some instruments that may under IAS 39 have been measured entirely at amortized cost or as available for sale, will more likely be measured at FVTPL.
- (b) Some financial assets that are currently disaggregated into host financial assets that are not at FVTPL will instead be measured at FVTPL in their entirety.
- (c) Assets that are currently classified as held to maturity are likely to continue to be measured at amortized cost, as they are held to collect the contractual cash flows and often give rise to only payments of principal and interest.
- (d) More assets will be tested for impairment and the loss will be in excess of the expected credit loss.

10. What was the primary aim of the revision of IAS 39?

   (a) It was a response to the credit crisis.
   (b) IAS 39 was out of date.
   (c) To remove inconsistencies between US GAAP and to improve IFRS in accounting for financial instruments.
   (d) To stop management of earnings.

11. An entity has the following four financial instruments and wishes to know whether they will be valued at fair value or valued at amortized cost.

   1. Bond with stated maturity and payments of principal and interest linked to unleveraged inflation index of the currency in which the instrument is issued.
   2. Bond convertible into equity of the issuer.
   3. An inverse floating interest rate loan.
   4. Bond with a variable interest rate and an interest cap.

   (a) 1 and 2 at amortized cost, 3 and 4 at fair value.
   (b) 1 and 4 at amortized cost, 2 and 3 at fair value.
   (c) 2 and 3 at amortized cost, 1 and 4 at fair value.
   (d) 3 and 4 at amortized cost, 1 and 2 at fair value.

Chapter 41

IFRS FOR SMEs

INTRODUCTION

The principal aim when developing accounting standards for small to medium-sized enterprises (SMEs) is to provide a framework that generates relevant, reliable, and useful information which should provide a high-quality and understandable accounting standard suitable for SMEs.

In July 2009, the International Accounting Standards Board (IASB) issued the *IFRS for Small and Medium-Sized Entities* (*IFRS for SMEs*). This Standard provides an alternative framework that can be applied by eligible entities in place of the full set of International Financial Reporting Standards (IFRS).

The *IFRS for SMEs* is a self-contained Standard, incorporating accounting principles based on extant IFRS, which have been simplified to suit the entities that fall within its scope. There are a number of accounting practices and disclosures that may not provide useful information for the users of SME financial statements. There are a number of accounting standards and disclosures that may not be relevant for the users of SME financial statements.

DEFINITION OF SME

There is no universally agreed definition of an SME. No single definition can capture all the dimensions of a small or medium-sized business, or can be expected to reflect the differences between firms, sectors, or countries at different levels of development. Most definitions based on size use measures such as number of employees, balance sheet total, or annual turnover. However, none of these measures apply well across national borders.

The *IFRS for SMEs* is intended for use by entities that have no public accountability. Ultimately, the decision regarding which entities should use the *IFRS for SMEs* stays with national regulatory authorities and standard setters. These bodies will often specify more detailed eligibility criteria.

If an entity opts to use the *IFRS for SMEs*, it must follow the standard in its entirety—it cannot cherry-pick between the requirements of the *IFRS for SMEs* and those of full IFRS.

CASE STUDY 1

Facts

A is a subsidiary that is part of a consolidated group which uses full IFRS. A wishes to use the *IFRS for SMEs* to draw up its financial statements but wishes to capitalize its borrowing costs, which is allowed under IAS 23, *Borrowing Costs*.

Required

Discuss whether A can use the above accounting principles in its financial statements.

Solution

A is not prohibited from using the *IFRS for SMEs* in its individual financial statements, provided that the subsidiary itself does not have public accountability. If the subsidiary opts to use the *IFRS for SMEs*, it must follow that Standard in its entirety. It cannot pick and choose between the requirements of the *IFRS for SMEs* and those of full IFRS.

RATIONALE

The main argument for a separate SME accounting standard is the undue cost burden of reporting, which is proportionately heavier for smaller firms. The cost burden of applying the full set of IFRS may not be justified on the basis of user needs. Further, much of the current reporting framework is based on the needs of large business, so SMEs perceive that the full statutory financial statements are less relevant to the users of SME accounts.

SMEs also use financial statements for a narrower range of decisions, as they have less complex transactions and therefore less need for a sophisticated analysis of financial statements. Thus the disclosure requirements in the *IFRS for SMEs* are also substantially reduced when compared with those in full IFRS partly because they are not considered appropriate for users' needs and for cost-benefit considerations. Many disclosures in full IFRS are more relevant to investment decisions in capital markets than to the transactions undertaken by SMEs.

The Standard for SMEs is naturally a modified version of the full standards, and not an independently developed set of standards. It is based on recognized concepts and principles and it will allow easier transition to full IFRS if the SME decides to become a publicly listed entity.

In deciding on the modifications to make to IFRS, the needs of the users have been taken into account, as well as the costs and other burdens imposed upon SMEs by the IFRS. Relaxation of some of the measurement and recognition criteria in IFRS had to be made in order to achieve the reduction in these costs and burdens.

Some disclosure requirements are intended to meet the needs of listed entities, or to assist users in making forecasts of the future. Users of financial statements of SMEs often do not make such kinds of forecasts. Small companies pursue different strategies, and their goals are more likely to be survival and stability rather than growth and profit maximization. The stewardship function can be absent in small companies, with the accounts playing an agency role between the owner-manager and the bank.

TOPICS OMITTED FROM IFRS FOR SMEs

The Standard does not address the following five topics that are dealt with in full IFRS because these topics are not generally relevant to SMEs:

1. Earnings per share
2. Interim financial reporting
3. Segment reporting
4. Insurance (because entities that issue insurance contracts are not eligible to use the standard)
5. Assets held for sale

KEY PRINCIPLES

The International Accounting Standards Board (IASB) makes it clear that the prime users of International Financial Reporting Standards (IFRS) are the capital markets. This means that IFRS are primarily designed for quoted companies and not SMEs.

The vast majority of the world's companies are small and privately owned, and it could be argued that IFRS are not relevant to their needs or to their users. It is often thought that small business managers perceive the cost of compliance with accounting standards to be greater than their benefit. To this end, the *IFRS for SMEs* makes numerous simplifications to the recognition, measurement, and disclosure requirements in full IFRS.

The Standard is organized by topic to make it more user-friendly for SME preparers and users of SME financial statements.

The *IFRS for SMEs* and full IFRS are separate and distinct frameworks.

Entities that are eligible to apply the *IFRS for SMEs*, and that choose to do so, must apply that Standard in full.

The *IFRS for SMEs* includes requirements for the development and application of accounting policies in the absence of specific guidance on a particular subject. In particular, an entity may, but is not required to, consider the requirements and guidance in full IFRS dealing with similar and related issues.

TYPES OF SIMPLIFICATIONS

The *IFRS for SMEs* contains five types of simplifications of full IFRS:

1. Some topics in IFRS are omitted because they are not relevant to typical SMEs
2. Some accounting policy options in full IFRS are not allowed because a more simplified method is available to SMEs
3. Simplification of many of the recognition and measurement principles that are in full IFRS
4. Substantially fewer disclosures
5. Simplified redrafting

Examples of these simplifications are

1. Goodwill and other indefinite-life intangibles are amortized over their useful lives, but if useful life cannot be reliably estimated, then they are amortized over ten years
2. A simplified calculation is allowed if measurement of defined benefit pension plan obligations (under the projected unit credit method) involves undue cost or effort
3. The cost model is permitted for investments in associates and joint ventures

ACCOUNTING TREATMENTS DISALLOWED UNDER IFRS FOR SMEs

In addition there are certain accounting treatments which are not allowable under the Standard, because a simpler method is available to SMEs. Examples of these disallowable treatments are the revaluation model for property, plant, and equipment, and intangible assets, and proportionate consolidation for investments in jointly controlled entities. Generally there are simpler methods of accounting available to SMEs than those accounting practices which have been disallowed.

Additionally the Standard eliminates the "available-for-sale" and "held-to-maturity" classifications of IAS 39, *Financial Instruments: Recognition and Measurement*. All financial instruments are measured at amortized cost using the effective interest method except that investments in nonconvertible and nonputtable ordinary and preference shares that are publicly traded or whose fair value can otherwise be measured reliably are measured at fair value through profit or loss.

All amortized cost instruments must be tested for impairment. At the same time the Standard simplifies the hedge accounting and derecognition requirements. However, SMEs can choose to apply IAS 39 in full if they so wish.

Other accounting requirements or options disallowed include

- Investment property: Measurement is driven by circumstances rather than allowing an accounting policy choice between the cost and fair value models. Under the *IFRS for SMEs*, if an entity can measure the fair value of an item of investment property reliably without undue cost or effort, it must use fair value.

- Government grants: The various options permitted by IAS 20, *Accounting for Government Grants and Disclosure of Government Assistance,* are disallowed.
- Capitalization of borrowing costs
- Capitalization of development costs
- Deferral of actuarial gains and losses of defined benefit pension plans

SPECIFIC RECOGNITION AND MEASUREMENT SIMPLIFICATIONS

The main simplifications to the recognition and measurement principles in full IFRS include

Financial Instruments

Financial instruments meeting specified criteria are measured at cost or amortized cost. All others are measured at fair value through profit or loss. Thus the inherent complexities of classifying financial instruments into four categories, such as assessing management's intentions and dealing with "tainting provisions" are avoided. The IFRS establishes a simple principle for derecognition. The "pass-through" and "continuing involvement" tests in full IFRS are dropped. Hedge accounting requirements, including the detailed calculations, are simplified and tailored for SMEs.

Property, plant, and equipment, and intangible assets. The residual value, useful life, and depreciation method for items of property, plant, and equipment, and amortization period/method for intangible assets, need to be reviewed only if there is an indication they may have changed since the most recent annual reporting date. Full IFRS require an annual review.

Defined Benefit Plans

All past service cost must be recognized immediately in profit or loss. All actuarial gains and losses must be recognized immediately either in profit or loss or other comprehensive income. An entity is required to use the projected unit credit method to measure its defined benefit obligation and the related expense only if it is possible to do so without undue cost or effort.

Income tax—Requirements follow the approach set out in the Board's ED, *Income Tax*, published in March 2009, which proposes a simplified replacement for IAS 12, *Income Taxes*.

IFRS 5—There is no separate held-for-sale classification. It is deemed that holding an asset (or group of assets) for sale is an impairment indicator.

Biological Assets

The fair value through profit or loss model is required for biological assets only when fair value is readily determinable without undue cost or effort. Otherwise, SMEs follow the cost-depreciation-impairment model.

Equity–Settled Share–Based Payment

The directors' best estimate of the fair value of the equity-settled share-based payment is used to measure the expense if observable market prices are not available.

Sundry Points

Goodwill and other indefinite-life intangible assets are always amortized over their estimated useful lives (over ten years if useful life cannot be estimated reliably).

Investments in associates and joint ventures can be measured at cost unless there is a published price quotation (when fair value must be used).

Research and development costs must be recognized as expenses.

Borrowing costs must be recognized as expenses.

SUMMARY OF THE IFRS FOR SMEs

The *IFRS for Small and Medium-Sized Entities* is organized by topic, with each topic presented in a separate section. All of the paragraphs in the standard have equal authority. The standard is appropriate for general-purpose financial statements and other financial reporting of all profit-oriented entities.

Small and Medium-Sized Entities

SMEs are defined as entities that

1. Do not have public accountability
2. Publish general-purpose financial statements for external users

The standard does not contain a limit on the size of an entity that may use the *IFRS for SMEs* provided that it does not have public accountability. There is no restriction on its use by a public utility, not-for-profit entity, or public-sector entity. A subsidiary whose parent or group uses full IFRS may use the *IFRS for SMEs* if the subsidiary itself does not have public accountability. The standard does not require any special approval by the owners of an SME for it to be eligible to use the *IFRS for SMEs*. Listed companies, no matter how small, may not use the *IFRS for SMEs*.

Concepts and Pervasive Principles

This section sets out the objective of SMEs' financial statements and certain definitions, for example assets, liabilities, recognition, and total comprehensive income. There are only three items of other comprehensive income (OCI) in the *IFRS for SMEs*:

1. Some foreign exchange gains and losses relating to a net investment in a foreign operation.
2. Some changes in fair values of hedging instruments—in a hedge of variable interest rate risk of a recognized financial instrument, foreign exchange risk, or commodity price risk in a firm commitment or highly probable forecast transaction, or a net investment in a foreign operation. Hedge accounting is optional.
3. Some actuarial gains and losses. Reporting actuarial gains and losses in OCI is optional.

Financial Statement Presentation

Fair presentation is presumed to result if the *IFRS for SMEs* is followed. The entity states compliance with *IFRS for SMEs* only if the financial statements comply in full. This section does include "true and fair override" but this should be "extremely rare."

The SME can either show a single statement of comprehensive income, or two statements: an income statement and a statement of comprehensive income. If the only changes to equity arise from profit or loss, payment of dividends, corrections of errors, and changes in accounting policy, an entity may present a single (combined) statement of income and retained earnings instead of the separate statements of comprehensive income and of changes in equity. Further, an entity may present only an income statement (no statement of comprehensive income) if it has no items of other comprehensive income (OCI).

Statement of Financial Position

This may still be called "balance sheet" and the current/noncurrent split is not required if the entity concludes that a liquidity approach produces more relevant information. There are some minimum line items required. Sequencing, format, and titles are not mandated.

Statement of Comprehensive Income and Income Statement

An SME can adopt a one-statement or two-statement approach—either a single statement of comprehensive income, or two statements: an income statement and a statement of comprehensive income. The statements must segregate discontinued operations and no item may be labeled "extraordinary." However, unusual items can be separately presented.

Expenses may be presented by nature (depreciation, purchases of materials, transport costs, employee benefits, etc.) or by function (cost of sales, distribution costs, administrative costs, etc.) either on the face of the statement of comprehensive income (or income statement) or in the notes.

Statement of Changes in Equity and Statement of Comprehensive Income and Retained Earnings

The SME must show all changes to equity including total comprehensive income, owners' investments, dividends, owners' withdrawals of capital, and treasury share transactions but can omit the statement of changes in equity if the entity has no owner investments or withdrawals other than dividends and elects to present a combined statement of comprehensive income and retained earnings.

Statement of Cash Flows

SMEs have the option to use the indirect method or the direct method to present operating cash flows. Income tax cash flows are operating unless specifically identified with investing or financing activities. Separate disclosure is required of some noncash investing and financing transactions (for example, acquisition of assets by issue of debt).

Notes to the Financial Statements

Notes are normally in this sequence:

1. Basis of preparation (i.e., *IFRS for SMEs*)
2. Summary of significant accounting policies, including

   - Information about judgments
   - Information about key sources of estimation uncertainty

3. Supporting information for items in financial statements
4. Other disclosures

Consolidated and Separate Financial Statements

Consolidated financial statements are required when a parent company controls another entity, which is the power to govern financial and operating policies to obtain benefits.

A subsidiary is not excluded from consolidation because

1. The investor is a venture capital organization
2. The subsidiary's business activities are dissimilar to those of parent or other subsidiaries
3. The subsidiary operates in a jurisdiction that imposes restrictions on transferring cash or other assets out of the jurisdiction

However, consolidated financial statements are not required, even if a parent-subsidiary relationship exists in certain circumstances. For example the subsidiary was acquired with intent to dispose within one year or the parent itself is a subsidiary and its parent or ultimate parent uses IFRS or *IFRS for SMEs*. This section sets out the normal consolidation procedures.

Accounting Policies, Estimates, and Errors

If the *IFRS for SMEs* addresses an issue, then the entity must follow the *IFRS for SMEs*. However, if the *IFRS for SMEs* does not address an issue, an *SME* can

1. Choose policy that results in the most relevant and reliable information
2. Try to use principles from standards in the *IFRS for SMEs*
3. Use the concepts and pervasive principles in Section 2

An entity may look to guidance in full IFRS.

Basic Financial Instruments

The *IFRS for SMEs* has two sections on financial instruments:

1. Section 11 on basic financial instruments
2. Section 12 on other transactions

However, SMEs have the option to follow IAS 39 instead of Sections 11 and 12.

Even if IAS 39 is followed, SMEs make Section 11 and 12 disclosures and not IFRS 7 disclosures. Section 11 is an amortized historical cost model except for equity investments with quoted price or readily determinable fair value. These are measured at fair value through profit or loss.

Basic financial assets and financial liabilities are initially measured at the transaction price including transaction costs except in the initial measurement of financial assets and liabilities that are measured at fair value through profit or loss unless the arrangement constitutes, in effect, a financing transaction.

Subsequent to initial recognition, debt instruments are measured at amortized cost using the effective interest method, and debt instruments that are classified as current assets or current liabilities are measured at the undiscounted amount of the cash or other consideration expected to be paid or received (i.e., net of impairment) unless the arrangement constitutes, in effect, a financing transaction.

If the arrangement constitutes a financing transaction, the entity shall measure the debt instrument at the present value of the future payments discounted at a market rate of interest for a similar debt instrument.

SMEs must test all amortized cost instruments for impairment or uncollectibility.

The derecognition of financial assets and liabilities follows IAS 39 principles.

Additional Financial Instruments Issues

Financial instruments not covered by Section 11 (and, therefore, are within Section 12) are measured at fair value through profit or loss.

Hedge accounting is allowed only for the following kinds of risks:

1. Interest rate risk of a debt instrument measured at amortized cost
2. Foreign exchange or interest rate risk in a firm commitment or a highly probable forecast transaction
3. Price risk of a commodity that it holds, or in a firm commitment or highly probable forecast transaction to purchase or sell a commodity
4. Foreign exchange risk in a net investment in a foreign operation

The type of hedging instrument required for hedge accounting is defined in Section 12.

Hedges must be documented up front to qualify for hedge accounting and Section 12 provides guidance for measuring and assessing effectiveness.

Inventories

This section follows the principles of IFRS.

Investments in Associates

Associates are investments where significant influence exists. There is the option to use

1. The cost-impairment model except if there is a published quotation, then entities must use fair value through profit or loss.
2. The equity method (investor recognizes its share of profit or loss of the associate—detailed guidance is provided).
3. The fair value through profit or loss.

Investments in Joint Ventures

For investments in jointly controlled entities, there is an option for the venturer to use

1. The cost model except if there is a published quotation—then the venturer must use fair value through profit or loss.
2. The equity method (using the guidance in Section 14).
3. Fair value through profit or loss.

However, proportionate consolidation is prohibited.

For jointly controlled operations, the venturer should recognize assets that it controls and liabilities it incurs as well as its share of income earned and expenses that are incurred.

For jointly controlled assets, the venturer should recognize its share of the assets and liabilities it incurs as well as income it earns and expenses that are incurred.

Investment Property

Property interests that are held under an operating lease may be classified as an investment property, provided the property would otherwise have met the definition of an investment property. However, mixed-use property must be separated between investment and operating property.

If fair value can be measured reliably without undue cost or effort, the entity should use the fair value through profit or loss model. Otherwise, an entity must treat investment property as property, plant, and equipment (PPE).

Property, Plant, and Equipment

Entities must use the historical cost model only as the revaluation model is not permitted. This section will apply to most investment property (see previous section). This section applies to property held for sale as there is no special section on assets held for sale. Holding for sale is an indicator of possible impairment.

Component depreciation is used only if major parts of an item of PPE have significantly different patterns of consumption of economic benefits.

A review of the useful life, residual value, and depreciation rate is only required if there is a significant change in the asset or how it is used. Any adjustment is prospective.

Intangible Assets other than Goodwill

There is no recognition of internally generated intangible assets and therefore all research and development costs are expensed.

The amortization model is used for intangibles that are purchased separately or acquired. If the entity is unable to estimate useful life, then it must use a ten-year period. A review of the useful life, residual value, and depreciation rate is required only if there is a significant change in the asset or how it is used. Revaluation of intangible assets is prohibited.

Business Combinations and Goodwill

This section does not apply to combinations of entities under common control and follows the principles of IFRS 3.

Leases

The scope includes arrangements that contain a lease [IFRIC 4] and follows the principles of IAS 17.

Provisions and Contingencies

Provisions are recognized only when (1) there is a present obligation as a result of a past event, (2) it is probable that the entity will be required to transfer economic benefits, and (3) the amount can be estimated reliably. Provisions are to be reviewed at each reporting date and adjusted to meet the best current estimate. Entities may not accrue provisions for

1. Future operating losses, no matter how probable
2. A possible future restructuring plan which is not yet a legal or constructive obligation

Liabilities and Equity

This section gives guidance on classifying an instrument as liability or equity. An instrument is a liability if the issuer could be required to pay cash.

This section covers some material not covered by full IFRS, including original issuance of shares and other equity instruments. Shares are only recognized as equity when another party is obliged to provide cash or other resources in exchange for the instruments. The instruments are measured at the fair value of cash or resources received, net of direct costs of issuing the equity instruments, unless the time value of money is significant, in which case initial measurement is at the present value amount. When shares are issued before the cash or other resources are received, the amount receivable is presented as an offset to equity in the statement of financial position and not as an asset. Any shares subscribed for which no cash is received are not recognized as equity before the shares are issued.

The proceeds on issue of convertible and other compound financial instruments are split between liability component and equity component. The liability is measured at its fair value, and the residual amount is the equity component. The liability is subsequently measured using the effective interest rate, with the original issue discount amortized as added interest expense.

Dividends paid in the form of distribution of assets other than cash are recognized when the entity has an obligation to distribute the noncash assets. The dividend liability is measured at the fair value of the assets to be distributed.

Revenue

Revenue results from the sale of goods, services being rendered, construction contracts income by the contractor, and the use by others of the entity's assets. Some types of revenue are excluded from this section and dealt with elsewhere. There is an appendix of examples of revenue recognition under the principles in this section.

Government Grants

All grants are measured at the fair value of the asset received or receivable.

Grants without future performance conditions are recognized in profit or loss when proceeds are receivable. However, if there are performance conditions, the grant is recognized in profit or loss only when the conditions are met.

Borrowing Costs

All borrowing costs are charged to expense when incurred and none are capitalized.

Share-Based Payment

All share-based payment must be recognized under the following principles:

Equity-settled

1. Transactions with other than employees are recorded at the fair value of the goods and services received, if these can be estimated reliably
2. Transactions with employees or where the fair value of goods and services received cannot be reliably measured are measured with reference to the fair value of the equity instruments granted

Cash-settled

1. Liability is measured at fair value on the grant date and at each reporting date and settlement date, with each adjustment through profit or loss
2. For employees where shares only vest after a specific period of service has been completed, recognize the expense as the service is rendered

Share-based payment with cash alternatives

1. Account for all such transactions as cash settled, unless the entity has a past practice of settling by issuing equity instruments, or the option has no commercial substance because the cash settlement amount bears no relationship to, and is likely to be lower in value than, the fair value of the equity instrument.

Impairment of Assets

This section follows the basic principles of impairment set out in IFRS, together with simplified guidance on computing impairment of goodwill when goodwill cannot be allocated to cash-generating units

Employee Benefits

The measurement of short-term benefits is as follows:

1. Measured at an undiscounted rate and recognized as the services are rendered.
2. Other costs such as annual leave are recognized as a liability as services are rendered and expensed when the leave is taken or used.
3. Bonus payments are only recognized when an obligation exists and the amount can be reliably estimated.

The measurement of post employment benefits is as follows:

Defined contribution plans

1. Contributions are recognized as a liability or an expense when the contributions are made or due.

Defined benefit plans

1. Recognize a liability based on the net of present value of defined benefit obligations less the fair value of any plan assets at the reporting date.
2. The projected unit credit method is only used when it could be applied without undue cost or effort. An entity can simplify its calculation.

For group plans, the consolidated amount may be allocated to parent and subsidiaries on a reasonable basis.

The actuarial gains and losses may be recognized in profit or loss or as an item of other comprehensive income. However, there is no deferral of actuarial gains or losses, including no corridor approach.

All past service cost is recognized immediately in profit or loss and termination benefits are recognized in profit and loss immediately as there are no future economic benefits to the entity.

Income Tax

This section requires a temporary difference approach on a similar basis to IAS 12. A temporary difference arises if the tax basis of such assets or liabilities is different from the carrying amount. The tax basis assumes recovery by sale with one exception, which is, no deferred tax is recognized on unremitted earnings of foreign subsidiaries and jointly controlled entities. Entities should recognize deferred tax assets in full using the criterion that realization is probable.

The recognition of changes in current or deferred tax must be allocated to the related components of profit or loss, other comprehensive income, and equity.

Foreign Currency Translation

This section uses the functional currency approach, which is similar to that in IAS 21. Exchange differences arising from a monetary item that forms part of the net investment in a foreign operation are recognized in equity and are not "recycled" through profit or loss on disposal of the investment.

All exchange differences are recognized in other comprehensive income.

Hyperinflation

An entity must prepare general price-level adjusted financial statements when its functional currency is hyperinflationary and follow the principles of IAS 29. *IFRS for SMEs* provides indicators of hyperinflation but not an absolute rate. One indicator is where cumulative inflation approaches or exceeds 100% over a three-year period.

Events after the End of the Reporting Period

An entity must adjust financial statements to reflect adjusting events that provide further evidence of conditions that existed at the end of the reporting period.

Similarly, the entity does not adjust for nonadjusting events that arose after the end of the reporting period. In this case, the entity must disclose the nature of the event and an estimate of its financial effect.

If an entity declares dividends after the reporting period, the entity should not recognize those dividends as a liability at the end of the reporting period as it is a nonadjusting event.

Related-Party Disclosures

This section follows the principles of full IFRS.

Specialized Activities

Agriculture. If the fair value of a class of biological assets is readily determinable without undue cost or effort, use the fair value through profit or loss model. If the fair value is not readily determinable, or is determinable only with undue cost or effort, measure the biological assets at cost less any accumulated depreciation and impairment.

At harvest, agricultural produce is measured at fair value less estimated costs to sell. Thereafter it is accounted for as inventory.

Extractive industries. An entity is not required to charge exploration costs to expense and must test the capitalized costs for impairment. Any expenditure on tangible or intangible assets used in extractive activities is accounted as property, plant, and equipment or intangible assets other than goodwill.

Transition to the *IFRS for SMEs*

First-time adoption is the first set of financial statements in which the entity makes an explicit and unreserved statement of compliance with the *IFRS for SMEs*. The entity selects accounting policies based on *IFRS for SMEs* at the end of the reporting period of first-time adoption. Many accounting policy decisions depend on circumstances but the IFRS does allow some choice. The entity has to prepare the current year and one prior year's financial statements using the *IFRS for SMEs,* but there are optional and mandatory exceptions from restating specific items. There is a general exemption for impracticability. All of the special exemptions in IFRS 1 are included in the *IFRS for SMEs.*

The *IFRS for SMEs* gives some relief from the IFRS 1 requirement that in the entity's first IFRS financial statements, there must be at least one year's comparative information. The relief has been created by including the "impracticability" exemption. Similarly, it provides an impracticability exemption with respect to restating the opening statement of financial position.

Where financial statements are prepared using the Standard, the basis of presentation note and the auditor's report will refer to compliance with the *IFRS for SMEs*. This reference may improve SMEs' access to capital. The Standard also contains simplified language and explanations of the standard.

The IASB Has Produced Full Implementation Guidance for SMEs

The *IFRS for SMEs* is a response to international demand from developed and emerging economies for a rigorous and common set of accounting standards for small and medium-sized businesses that is much simpler than full IFRS. The *IFRS for SMEs* should provide improved comparability for users of accounts while enhancing the overall confidence in the accounts of SMEs, and reducing the significant costs involved of maintaining standards on a national basis. As a result of the above, the IFRS require SMEs to comply with less than 10% of the volume of accounting requirements applicable to listed companies complying with the full set of IFRS.

CASE STUDY 2

Facts

An SME faces a fine for operating without regard to the law. The entity expects to lose the case but does not expect the fine to be payable for 5 years. The fine will be $50,000. Market rate of interest is 5%.

Required

How would the SME account for this under the *IFRS for SMEs*?

Solution

The present value of the fine will be $50,000 discounted at 5% for 5 years, which is $39,177. Therefore in the current year this amount is recorded as an expense and provision. In subsequent years, the discount will unwind, thus increasing the provision and resulting in a charge to profit or loss. In the first year, the interest which will unwind will be $39,177 \times 5\%$, that is, $1,959.

CASE STUDY 3

Facts

Angel is a small company whose only asset is a loan received from the sole shareholder. According to IAS 24 it appears that the shareholder is a related party and on that basis the loan is material to the accounts; this loan is therefore required to be disclosed as a related-party transaction.

Required

Should the related-party note appear in the accounts of Angel under *IFRS for SMEs*?

Solution

Section 33 on related parties follows the principles of full IFRS, and therefore the loan should be disclosed as a related-party transaction.

CASE STUDY 4

Facts

Some small companies may choose not to apply the *IFRS for SMEs* on the basis that its provisions would not have made a significant difference to the costs they incur in producing financial statements. The IFRS provides significant disclosure exemptions, but exemptions from actual accounting entries are limited. For those preparers who are entitled to use the IFRS, this is no longer the case.

Required

Discuss how significant costs can be saved in adopting the *IFRS for SMEs*.

Solution

Cost savings will be made in three areas:

1. Not having to value PPE with the cost savings related to a professional valuer.
2. Not having to apply certain complicated accounting rules.
3. Potentially saving further costs in having these items audited.

CASE STUDY 5

Facts

Handy is adopting *IFRS for SMEs* in its financial statements for the year ended December 31, 20X9. The directors of the company are worried about the effect of the move to IFRS on their financial performance. The directors have highlighted some differences between *IFRS for SMEs* and their current local equivalent standards.

Plant and equipment

Local GAAP does not require the residual value of a noncurrent asset to be determined at the date of acquisition or latest valuation. The residual value of much of the plant and equipment is deemed to be negligible. However, a certain plant has a high residual value. Handy wishes to use the revaluation model for PPE.

Investment properties

Local GAAP requires investment property to be measured at cost. The company owns a hotel, which consists of land and building, and it has been designated as an investment property. The company could sell the land for redevelopment for $5 million, although it has no intention of doing so at the present time. This is the best price available for the land, and the hotel can easily be valued at market value.

Required

Discuss the impact on the financial statements of Handy.

Solution

Plant and equipment

Local GAAP does not require the residual value of a noncurrent asset to be determined at the date of acquisition or latest valuation. *IFRS for SMEs* requires residual values to be taken into account. The IFRS requires an asset's residual value to be reflected in the depreciation charge, thus reducing the expense in profit or loss. If the residual value exceeds or equals the asset's carrying value, then the depreciation charge is reduced to zero. Thus, under local GAAP, residual values are reflected in disposal profits rather than in lower depreciation. The effect on the financial statements will be that the depreciation charge for the year will decrease. The residual value of the asset should be based on the current price for an identical piece of plant already of the age and in the condition expected at the end of its useful life. *IFRS for SMEs* does not allow the use of the revaluation model for PPE.

Investment properties

IFRS for SMEs requires an entity to use fair value as an accounting policy for measuring investment property. Where fair value is used, gains and losses are normally recognized in profit or loss. Fair value generally means "market value" and is the price at which the property can be exchanged between knowledgeable and willing parties in an arm's-length transaction. The market value is the best price reasonably obtainable by the buyer. Therefore in the case of the hotel, the highest and the best price should be used for the land and none of the value allocated to the building. Therefore the land should be valued at $5 million and the building at zero. Any gain is recognized in equity on transition to *IFRS for SMEs*.

PRACTICAL EXAMPLES OF DISCLOSURE

The following two examples illustrate the nature of disclosures that could be appropriate to an SME.

There has been a significant reduction in requests for estimates for new decorating work and the directors expect sales to reduce significantly next year. However, costs are expected to reduce accordingly and the company should be able to operate within its overdraft. The directors are not aware of any reason why the overdraft facility should not be extended. As a result they have adopted the going concern basis of accounting.

The company has a contract for all of its available consulting capacity for the next six months and negotiations are at an advanced stage for a three-month extension. The director believes that the company will be able to maintain positive cash flows for the foreseeable future. As a result, the company has adopted the going concern basis of accounting.

MULTIPLE-CHOICE QUESTIONS

1. There are a number of accounting standards and disclosures that may not provide useful information to the users of SMEs financial statements. Which of the following topics does the Standard for SMEs not address?
  (a) Earnings per share.
  (b) Provisions and contingencies.
  (c) Liabilities and equity.
  (d) Revenue.
  (e) Transitional arrangements.

2. There are certain accounting treatments which are not allowable under the Standard for SMEs. Which of the following accounting treatments are not allowable under the Standard?
  (a) Weighted-average method for inventory.
  (b) Equity method for associates.
  (c) Revaluation model for property, plant, and equipment.
  (d) Temporary difference approach for deferred taxation.

3. If SMEs choose to follow the Standard, there are certain classifications of financial instruments which are not required by the Standard. Which of the following statements is a key requirement of the Standard, if SMEs choose to follow it?
  (a) Loans and receivables are accounted for at amortized cost.
  (b) Available-for-sale assets are accounted for at fair value.
  (c) Held to maturity investments must be held-to-maturity.
  (d) All financial instruments are measured at amortized cost with some exceptions.

4. Which of the following statements reflects the accounting for financial instruments under the standard?
  (a) All financial instruments should be measured at fair value.
  (b) Reversal of an impairment loss is not allowed.
  (c) All amortized cost instruments must be tested for impairment.
  (d) The hedge accounting requirements of IAS 39 must be followed in full.

5. The Standard contains a section on transition, which allows all of the exemptions in IFRS 1, *First-Time Adoption of International Financial Reporting Standards.* It also contains certain exemptions for comparative information and the restatement of the opening statement of financial position. What is the basis for the latter exemptions to IFRS 1?
  (a) Cost.
  (b) Impracticability.
  (c) Materiality.
  (d) Relevance.

6. The *IFRS for SMEs* is intended for use by certain types of entities. Which of the following descriptions accurately describes the definition of a SME used by the IASB?
  (a) Entities that have no public accountability.
  (b) Entities that have a specified number of employees.
  (c) Entities that have a certain balance sheet total.
  (d) Entities that have a certain annual turnover.

7. The *IFRS for SMEs* makes numerous simplifications to the recognition, measurement, and disclosure requirements in full IFRS. Which of the following is not a simplification of an accounting practice allowed by the Standard?
  (a) Goodwill and other indefinite-life intangibles are amortized over their useful lives.
  (b) SMEs do not have to derecognize a financial asset when the entity transfers to another party substantially all of the risks and rewards of the asset.
  (c) A simplified calculation is allowed if measurement of defined benefit pension plan obligations involves undue cost or effort.
  (d) The cost model is permitted for investments in associates and joint ventures.

8. Which of the following approaches has the IASB taken in developing a standard for SMEs?
  (a) The exemptions given to smaller entities are prescribed in the mainstream accounting standards.
  (b) GAAP for SMEs is to be developed on a national basis.
  (c) The standard is an independently developed set of standards.
  (d) The standard is a simplified self-contained set of accounting principles that are based on full IFRS.

9. Where financial statements are prepared using the Standard, the basis of presentation note and the auditor's report will refer to compliance with the *IFRS for SMEs*. Which of the following statements suitably describes the nature of the compliance with the Standard?
  (a) The accounting practices used are a mix of full IFRS and the Standard for SMEs.
  (b) The accounting practices used are a mix of local GAAP and the Standard for SMEs.
  (c) The accounting practices used are a mix of full IFRS and local GAAP.
  (d) The SME has followed the standard in its entirety.

10. The IASB sets effective dates for standards, which are sometimes prospective, and sometimes the standards become almost immediately effective. What is the effective date for the Standard for SMEs?

- (a) The IASB has not set an effective date for the Standard because the decision as to whether to adopt the *IFRS for SMEs* is a matter for each jurisdiction.
- (b) The IASB will set the date when the Standard has been in existence for a while in order to gauge the acceptance of the Standard.
- (c) The date will be set by the IASB as soon as possible.
- (d) The effective date was the date of the release of the Standard.

ANSWERS FOR MULTIPLE-CHOICE QUESTIONS

Chapter 2

1. c   2. a   3. c   4. a   5. a
6. d

Chapter 3

1. c   2. b   3. b   4. d   5. c

Chapter 4

1. b   2. c   3. g   4. g   5. c*

* The net realizable value is the subsequent sale price, $40, less any cost incurred to bring the good to its salable condition, $15. Thus, NRV = $40 – $15 = $25 per pack. The loss (inventory write-down) per pack is the difference between cost and net realizable value: $50 – $25 = $25 per pack.

Chapter 5

1. c   2. b   3. c   4. d   5. a

Chapter 6

1. c   2. a   3. b   4. a   5. c
6. c   7. d   8. a   9. d   10. a

Chapter 7

1. d   2. c   3. b   4. d   5. c

Chapter 8

1. b   2. a   3. a   4. c   5. a

Chapter 9

1. a   2. c*   3. b   4. b   5. a
6. c   7. d   8. b   9. a   10. b
11. d   12. a

* ($4m – $3m) × 30%

Chapter 10

1. b   2. c   3. b   4. b   5. d

Chapter 11

1. b   2. a   3. d   4. c   5. a
6. a   7. b   8. a   9. b   10. c
11. b   12. b   13. d   14. b   15. a
16. c

Chapter 12

1. d   2. c   3. d   4. b   5. a
6. d   7. d   8. c   9. b   10. d

Chapter 13

1. a   2. e   3. b   4. a   5. b
6. d   7. b   8. c   9. a   10. a
11. d   12. d   13. a   14. d

Chapter 14

1. c   2. b   3. b   4. c   5. d

Chapter 15

1. d   2. b   3. d   4. a   5. c
6. c   7. d   8. c*   9. c   10. a**
11. d***

　* [€(2.1–1.2) million @ €2 = $1, or $450,000]
　** (€1.2 million/2)
*** (52/1.3 = $40m – $34m = $6m + $8m = $14 million)

Chapter 16

1. a   2. b   3. c   4. d   5. c

Chapter 17

1. c   2. d   3. b   4. c   5. c

Chapter 18

1. b   2. a   3. b

Chapter 19

1. d   2. b   3. c   4. c   5. a
6. c   7. d   8. d   9. b   10. c
11. d   12. b   13. a   14. d

Chapter 20

1. b 2. b 3. d 4. b 5. a
6. b 7. c 8. b 9. c 10. d
11. b 12. b 13. c

Chapter 21

1. d 2. b 3. b 4. c 5. a
6. b

Chapter 22

1. d 2. b 3. d 4. a 5. b
6. d 7. c 8. a 9. b 10. b

Chapter 23

1. c 2. d 3. d 4. a 5. c
6. b 7. a 8. c 9. b

Chapter 24

1. c 2. c 3. b 4. d 5. d
6. d 7. c 8. a 9. d 10. c
11. a 12. c 13. d 14. c 15. b
16. a 17. d 18. d 19. a 20. c

Chapter 25

1. c 2. b 3. b 4. b 5. a
6. b 7. a 8. b 9. a 10. c
11. a 12. b 13. c 14. c 15. d
16. d 17. d 18. a 19. c 20. d

Chapter 26

1. d 2. a 3. b 4. b 5. c
6. b 7. c 8. c 9. d*

* [10% of ($10 + $15) – (5% of $10)], that is, $2 million

Chapter 27

1. d 2. b 3. b 4. a 5. a
6. b 7. b 8. b 9. c 10. b
11. d 12. b 13. c 14. a 15. c
16. b

Chapter 28

1. b 2. c 3. b 4. c 5. a

Chapter 29

1. b 2. d 3. d 4. b 5. d

Chapter 30

1. a 2. a 3. b 4. b 5. a
6. d 7. b

Chapter 31

1. c 2. b 3. c 4. b 5. a
6. c 7. d 8. d 9. a 10. a
11. a 12. b 13. a 14. a 15. d
16. b

Chapter 32

1. d 2. c 3. c 4. b 5. d
6. a 7. b 8. a 9. c 10. b

Chapter 33

1. c 2. d 3. a 4. b 5. c
6. c 7. c 8. d 9. c① 10. b②
11. d③ 12. c 13. c 14. a④ 15. c⑤
16. d⑥ 17. d 18. b⑦ 19. c⑧

① ($6 million × 95% × 1/3)
② ($6 million × 94% × 2/3 – $1.90 million)
③ ($6 million × 95% – $3.78 million)
④ (100 × 1,000 × 90% × $10 × 1/3)
⑤ [20 × 500 × 80% × ($21 – $15)]
⑥ [20 × 500 × 80% × ($19 – $15)] that is, $32,000
⑦ At December 31, 20X4, 30% of $12 million divided by three years = $1.2 million to statement of comprehensive income as the tax effect of the cumulative remuneration expense exceeds the tax benefit ($5 million @ 30% compared with $4 million @ 30%).
⑧ A portion of the tax benefit is recognized in equity as the tax benefit of $21 million × 1/3 × 30% ($2.1 million), exceeds the tax effect of the accumulated remuneration expense $15 million × 1/3 × 30% ($1.5 million).

Chapter 34

1. d 2. d 3. a 4. d 5. a
6. a 7. d 8. c 9. b 10. b
11. b 12. d 13. a 14. d 15. d
16. b 17. b 18. d* 19. b 20. b
21. a 22. b 23. c 24. d 25. a

* Cost of acquisition (Mask's shareholders own 60% of equity of Man)
In order for 40% of Mask's shares to be owned by shareholders of Man, Mask needs to issue 4 million shares. Therefore, cost of acquisition is

4 million × $6 each	$24 million
Fair value of assets of Man	($18 million)
Goodwill	$ 6 million

Chapter 35

1. a 2. d 3. c 4. c 5. a
6. b 7. b 8. a

Chapter 36

1. a 2. b 3. c 4. a 5. d
6. b 7. c 8. c 9. d 10. a

Chapter 37

1. b 2. c 3. d 4. c 5. c
6. c 7. d 8. a

Chapter 38

1. b 2. d 3. c 4. a 5. c

Chapter 39

1. b 2. c 3. d 4. d 5. d

Chapter 40

1. a 2. d 3. c 4. b 5. a
6. d 7. b 8. b 9. d 10. c
11. b

Chapter 41

1. a 2. c 3. d 4. c 5. b
6. a 7. b 8. d 9. d 10. a

INDEX